Listening to Music

Allan Schindler

Eastman School of Music

Holt, Rinehart and Winston

New York Chicago San Francisco Dallas
Montreal Toronto London Sydney

Senior Acquisitions Editor **Roth Wilkofsky**
Senior Development Editor **Thomas Hitchings**
Production Manager **Nancy Myers**
Art Director **Lou Scardino**
Text Design and Cover **Caliber**
Photo Researcher **Anita Duncan**

Library of Congress Cataloging in Publication Data

Schindler, Allan.
Listening to music.

Includes index.
1. Music—Analysis, appreciation. I. Title.
MT6.S293L6 780'.15 79-23653

ISBN 0-03-039906-8

Printed in the United States of America
0 1 2 3 4 032 9 8 7 6 5 4 3 2 1

All permissions and credits are on page 424

Preface

Listening to Music is designed for use in a one-term introductory music survey course at the undergraduate level. The primary aims of the book are to explore the nature of musical expression and to present this discussion in a manner that encourages perceptive and involved listening. Only by active participation in the process of musical communication, with both composer and performers, can the listener experience the unique insight and joy of musical understanding; this understanding is ultimately a journey into oneself, but it is also one that can be shared.

The principal focus of this book is on the music itself rather than its context. The first questions most people are likely to ask when confronted with an unfamiliar piece of music are not, "When and where was it written? What influence does it reflect?" but rather more elemental ones, such as, "What kind of statement does it make? How is it put together? How do I respond to the music, and why?" Historical information can immeasurably enrich our appreciation of the unique qualities of a musical work, but it becomes vital only after we have gained an initial feel for those qualities.

Whatever their historical period or style, the compositions examined in this book are viewed as living works, not as museum pieces. Ample historical and biographical information is introduced within this broader perspective, but it remains subordinate to the development of effective, individual listening skills. This is not meant to minimize the importance of historical scholarship. Without it we would have few objective criteria for evaluating a work, and would be left merely with subjective attitudes or allegorical description ("the cellos sing a mellifluous theme"). Basic historical and biographical information is necessary even at the introductory level, or else the music remains faceless. But once the listener has been seized by the strength or beauty of a musical statement, his or her own desire to understand it better and experience it more fully will encourage further exploration of its background. Without this initial involvement, the listener will be impervious to exhortations to study the music, because the listener's most basic question, "What's it to me?", has not been answered.

This book is organized into four basic units, which respectively examine: *1. The Language of Music.* What is it made of? *2. Forms.* How is it put together? *3. Styles.* What does a composition have in common with other works written at the same time, and in what ways is it unique? *4. Genres.* How is the music specifically tailored to its performing medium? The final unit examines the innovations in sounds and compositional media, and the profusion of musical styles, that have marked the last 30 years.

This text attempts to present a concise introduction to these essential facets of musical expression as we experience them in specific works. It also, however, endeavors to approach the compositions on their own terms, and to understand them *as a whole*, because that is how we hear and perceive music. Basic to this approach is the often neglected question of the listener's own intuitive responses to a piece of music. Many listeners are hesitant or mistrustful of these responses ("I really don't know much about music, so my opinions are not very . . ."). Such diffidence may be preferable to arrogance, but it can cut the listener off from a vital dimension of musical expression—him- or herself.

The rudimentary features of musical notation are laid out in the first two chapters, and notated musical excerpts are included throughout the book. Some students feel at a disadvantage in the face of musical notation, particularly when they discover that the student sitting next to them has studied piano for ten years as a child. Unfortunately, sounds cannot be presented in a book. The notated excerpts are meant to serve as visual representations of important passages. They are graphic aids, to be used *while listening* and in class discussion; the student is not expected to be able to pick up the book and whistle these excerpts. Other types of pictorial representations have been included to facilitate comprehension, including diagrams, pictures, graphs, and visual and dramatic analogies. They have been used sparingly, however. If overused, such secondary aids run the risk of reducing music to graphic depiction, taking it out of the realm of pure sound. Music does not sound "as though it were . . ."—it *is* the way it sounds.

The repetoire of concert music, particulary that of the 18th, 19th, and 20th centuries, forms the core of this book, but works drawn from other idioms and cultures are also introduced to broaden its scope. For those instructors who include more extensive coverage of jazz, examples "For Further Listening," drawn from jazz and jazz-related styles, are included at the end of selected chapters. In some one-term or one-quarter formats, it may not be possible to cover every composition included in the text. This abundance is by design. My intent was to provide the instructor with a sufficient breadth and choice of examples to meet the requirements of his or her own syllabus, whether its primary emphasis be the development of perceptive listening skills, a historical survey, an understanding of the principle elements and genres of music, or a balanced mix. The instructor's manual presents a variety of possible lesson plans and teaching suggestions.

A few other features should be mentioned. A record set is available to supplement the text. It includes individual demonstrations of the major musical instruments. The musical selections have been chosen with particular regard for performance quality and, wherever possible, historical appropriateness. The selections are whole works or whole movements, and the most frequently used selections are placed where they are most easily accessible. The records serve a dual purpose: they include most of the music for in-depth analysis, but they also provide a well-balanced introduction to the varieties of music that can serve as the core of a growing record library. A booklet provided with the record set discusses the individual performances as examples of musical interpretation, and offers further information on how to use these records and find and choose new ones. (A complete listing of the recorded selections is provided in the instructor's manual.)

To reinforce the historical context, there is a pull-out time-line of "Major Composers and Stylistic Developments" at the back of the book, designed to serve as a permanent reference for the student.

I am deeply grateful to the many people who assisted in the development of this text; to Roth Wilkofsky, Senior Acquisitions Editor, for initiating the project; to Tom Hitchings, Senior Editor, who has provided numerous suggestions for improvement and supervised the preparation of the record set; to Steven Moll, copy editor, for holding my feet to the coals on questions of content and organization as well as presentation. Reviewers of the manuscript also contributed valuable suggestions for clarification and strengthening of major points; my heartfelt thanks are extended to James Anthony, Towson State University; Robert Briggs, University of Houston; Kenneth Bruggers, University of Arkansas; Kathryn Bumpass, University of Illinois; Kenneth Cuthbert, North Texas State University; Richard von Grabow, Iowa State University; Harold Haughton, Jackson State University; Gene Hemmle, Texas Tech; Marie Henderson, University of Florida; Larry Jarvis, California State University, Northridge; Ingeborg Johnson, Ricks College; Rudolph Kremer, University of North Carolina; Louise Pinkow, University of Georgia; Elliott Schwartz, Bowdoin College; George Steiner, George Washington University; Dennis Wakeling, Northern Arizona University; Christopher Wilkinson, West Virginia University; Allen Winold, Indiana University; and Robert Winter, University of California, Los Angeles. To my wife Verna, who took part at every stage of the book's development, providing sensitive and objective appraisal and unflagging encouragement, I am particularly indebted.

Allan Schindler

Contents

Preface iii

Introduction: Musical Communication 1

The Process of Musical Communication 4
- The Composer 4
- The Performer 7
- The Listener 9

Why Study Music? 9

Recordings and Live Performances 12

How to Listen 12

Unit 1

The Language of Music 15

Chapter 1 Musical Time 17

Rhythmic Patterns 17
- Pulse 17
- Tempo 19
- Meter 20
- Phrases and Cadences 25

Rhythmic Notation 27
- Time Signatures 29
- Rhythmic Motives 30
- Syncopation 31
- Pacing: The Overall Rhythm of a Piece 32

Chapter 2 Tonal Organization 36

Pitch Notation 36
- Clefs 37
- Grand Staff 38
- The Octave 38
- Turning Systems 39
- Accidentals 39

Scales 39
The Chromatic Scale 40
Five- and Seven-Tone Scales 40
Transposition 42
The Major Scale 42
The Minor Scale 44
The Basic Principle of Tonality 45
Diatonic and Chromatic Styles 47
Modulation: A Shift of the Tonal Center 47
Tonal Organization in the 20th Century 51

Chapter 3 Melody 53

Melodic Countour 56
Melodic Continuity 57
Melodic Themes 62

Chapter 4 Harmony 66

The Origins of Harmony 66
Intervals: The Basis of Chords 69
Consonance and Dissonance 70
Triads 71
Major and Minor Triads 72
Tonic and Dominant Triads 73
Cadences 73
Simple Chord Progressions 74
Functional and Non-Functional Chords 75
Seventh Chords 75
Complex Styles of Tonal Harmony 78
Tonality and Dissonance in the 20th Century 80

Chapter 5 Instruments and Voices 86

Properties of Instruments 86
Pitch Range 86
Dynamic Range 87
Timbre 87
Idiomatic Characteristics 88
The Human Voice 88
Instruments 89
Strings 89
Woodwinds 92

Brass 95
Percussion 97
Other Major Instruments 99
The Symphony Orchestra 101

Unit 2

Musical Forms 105

Chapter 6 Sectional Forms 107

"Becoming" Music and "Being" Music 107
Themes: The Melodic Basis of Form 109
Form in Tonal Music 109
Connecting Passages 110
Sectional Construction 110
Two-Part Forms 111
The Baroque Suite 113
Three-Part Forms 115
Through-Composed Forms 120
Minuet and Trio Form 123
The Scherzo 125

Chapter 7 Rondo and Variation Forms 127

Refrain Forms 127
Rondo Forms 128
Variation Forms 132
Theme and Variation 133
Continuous Variation Forms 136
Continuous Variation in the Music of India 140

Chapter 8 Sonata Form 146

Structure of Multi-Movement Works 146
Sonata Form Procedures 147
Exposition 149
Development 149
Recapitulation 150
Sonata Form in the 19th Century 156
Sonata Form in the 20th Century 158

Chapter 9 Contrapuntal Forms 163

Contrapuntal Procedures 163
Independence of Voices 164
Imitation 165
Strict Imitation: Canon and Rounds 167
Freer Imitative Forms 168
The Fugue 171
Characteristics of Fugal Writing 171
Counterpoint in Later Music 175

Unit 3

Musical Styles 179

Chapter 10 Medieval, Renaissance, and Baroque Styles 182

The Medieval Period, 900–1450 183
Secular Music 185
Polyphony 185
Medieval and Renaissance Performance Practice 186
The Mass 188
The Renaissance, 1450–1600 191
Polyphonic and Homophonic Textures 191
Sacred and Secular Styles of Vocal Polyphony 192
Instrumental Music 193
Major Renaissance Composers 195
Baroque Music, 1600–1750 196
Stylistic Characteristics 197
The Culmination of Baroque Practice: Johann Sebastian Bach 200
Principal Composers of the Baroque Era 202

Chapter 11 Classical and Romantic Music 204

Classical Style, 1770–1830 205
Elements of Classical Style 206
Principal Composers: Haydn, Mozart, Beethoven 207
Romantic Style, 1830–1900 215
Musical Developments 217
Virtuosity and Lyricism 224
Growing Diversity in Idiom 226

Nationalism 227
End of an Age 228
Principal Composers of the Romantic Period 231

Chapter 12 An Age of Stylistic Diversity, 1900–1945 233

Impressionism: Claude Debussy 234
Maurice Ravel 237
Free Atonality: Arnold Schönberg 238
Schönberg's Esthetic 239
Perspective on Atonality 242
Serialism 243
Perspective on Serialism 246
The Emancipation of Rhythm: Igor Stravinsky 246
Neoclassicism 252
Stylistic Characteristics 253
National Influences and Idioms 256
Principal Composers of the Early 20th Century 258

Unit 4

Musical Genres 261

Chapter 13 Vocal Music 263

Vocal Genres 263
Text and Music 265
Idiomatic Characteristics of the Voice 265
The Renaissance: Mass and Madrigal 267
The Baroque Period: Handel and Bach 271
The Oratorio: Handel 271
Bach's Vocal Music 275
Solo Song: The German Lied 278
The Lieder of Schubert 279
Vocal Music in the 20th Century 283

Chapter 14 Piano Music 287

The Sonata 288
Character Pieces 290
Frédéric Chopin 290
Robert Schumann 292
Claude Debussy 294

Piano Idioms in the 20th Century 296
Sergei Prokofiev 297

Chapter 15 Chamber Music 301

Early Instrumental Music 303
The Classical String Quartet 304
Expansion of the Classical Genres 307
Johannes Brahms 307
Texture and Form 311
20th-Century Chamber Idioms 311
New Combinations of Instruments 313
Edgard Varèse 313

Chapter 16 Orchestral Music 318

Origins of the Symphony 319
The Classical Symphony 319
Beethoven's Symphonies 322
Romantic Orchestral Music 328
The German Symphonic Tradition 328
National Currents 329
Freer Symphonic Forms 332
Alternative Genres 332
Orchestral Music in the 20th Century 336
Charles Ives 337
Anton Webern 340

Chapter 17 The Concerto 342

The Baroque Concerto 342
The Classical Concerto 346
Expansion in the 19th Century 349
20th-Century Practices 352

Chapter 18 Introduction to Opera 356

The Libretto 357
Staging 359
Singers 360
Conductor, Orchestra, and Chorus 361
The Formal Structure of Opera 361
Serious and Comic Opera 362

Chapter 19 Opera 363

The Origins of Opera 363
Claudio Monteverdi 363
Later Baroque Opera 366
Opera in the Classical Period: Mozart 368
Romantic Opera: Wagner and Verdi 374
Richard Wagner 375
Giuseppe Verdi 379
Opera in the 20th Century 383
Expressionist Opera: Alban Berg 384
American Folk Opera: George Gershwin 388

Unit 5

The Music of Today 395

Chapter 20 New Materials, Forms, and Genres 396

New Coloristic Resources 397
"Getting Into Sound": Harry Partch and Others 398
Electronic Music 400
New Sounds from Traditional Instruments 406
Music Without Structure 408
Movements Toward Musical Synthesis 410

Appendix: Italian Tempo Markings 418
Glossary 419
Credits 424
Index 425

Introduction: Musical Communication

An old adage states that architecture is the one unavoidable art. We can refuse to have anything to do with paintings, poems, concerts, or plays, the argument runs, but we hardly can avoid all contact with buildings.

In our present electronic age, music has become nearly as unavoidable. Wherever we go, it is there. Retailers have decided that the time we spend buying a broom will be enriched if accompanied by canned music. Advertisers believe that their message is more persuasive if delivered by attractive young people singing, laughing, and having fun. Much of this "music we can't avoid" is slickly packaged to arrest our attention, create a common bond, tranquilize us, or provide the general impression that something is happening.

Often, the product being retailed is music itself. In promotion as a leisure time activity, music may be pitched as pure entertainment, an instant high, or a sauna for the ears. Such music usually is designed not for concentrated listening but as a *release* from mental concentration. The music is casual—something we slip into, like worn jeans and sandals, to escape mental pressures and hassles. It is there, but makes no demands. It soothes or energizes us but leaves us free to do something else as well. We often forget that we are hearing it. Much of this music is brewed to be *heard,* or even over-heard, rather than *listened to.*

There is nothing "wrong" with utilitarian music, unless it is relentlessly imposed upon us. Music always has fulfilled a wide variety of needs and functions in our society, many of which are utilitarian. Background scores heighten the emotional impact of dramas and films. As an integral part of most religious worship and public ceremony, music is an important element in shared experience. Music can lend festivity to an occasion, complement our moods and activities, heighten the expression of elemental feelings.

Music can be all of these things, but much more. Many musical compositions make *awful* background music. Such works are not designed to enhance whatever else we might be doing; they are meant to be a totally absorbing experience in their own right. If we listen casually to such music, it will make no sense; it will only annoy us, like a buzzing fly that won't go away.

We automatically adjust our listening to various kinds of music and do not accord a commercial jingle the same attention we give to our favorite performers. We are so surrounded by incidental music, however, that casual listening can become habitual, to the point where we begin applying it to virtually every musical experience. This casual approach is not necessarily "natural." One need only watch a group of young children singing to appreciate the sense of complete involvement in music that is an inherent human gift.

A work of art, be it a painting, a novel, or a symphony, will hold little meaning for an individual until he or she feels a personal involvement in what it is saying and begins asking, "How do *I* understand this work? What responses does it arouse in *me*?" If we look casually at Renoir's *Dance at Bougival,* reproduced on the color plate, we might say, "Oh—a guy with a yellow hat is dancing with a woman with a red hat." Nothing of much significance has been communicated.

If we look more closely, however, it becomes apparent that the man's straw hat serves to obscure his identity (we'll never know who he is), and so directs our attention back to the woman. She is the center of the painting. Renoir has set off the dancing couple in relief from the hazy background and, further, has shrouded the man in anonymity. The girl is the only sharply drawn figure. The motion of the dance is suggested in the play of her dress, while the man appears almost immobile, completely absorbed in her. She glances down, but the character of her face reveals that she is very much enjoying the moment, taking pleasure in herself and his attention. As our eyes run over the picture, they are likely to be drawn increasingly to her face. What, exactly, is she thinking? What is she feeling?

In observing these features we become personally involved in the painting. It begins to strike us in a very particular way. We understand the woman—and the moment—in the light of our own experience. The "little moment" depicted in the painting has become important. Something is being expressed, not only by Renoir, but from within us as well.

In similar fashion, to listen *actively* to a piece of music is to open ourselves to its special qualities and means of expression. Active listening is a process of discovery. As a piece of music stimulates personal responses, it enables us to recognize and voice feelings that are already within us, to experience and understand them more deeply, and so to know ourselves better. The ability to listen actively to music is not a special aptitude known only to a select few, nor is it a step-by-step routine for putting our ears in gear. It is a capacity we already possess, which will develop naturally as we put it to use.

Serious music—"serious" not in the sense of grim or humorless, but as an important means of human expression—demands this kind of involvement by the listener. A jazz improvisation, a symphony, or a lyrical song is more than a momentary diversion. It is a vital form of statement and communication between composer, performer, and listener. A serious piece of music—whether "classical," jazz, rock, or whatever—speaks to the listener in several ways. It engages our intellects ("minds") by the quality of its construction, our senses ("ears") by the force or beauty of its sounds, and our emotions ("hearts") by the manner in which it touches personal feelings. Whatever its tone (impassioned, detached, bright, dark, and so forth) or its "message" ("joy runs deeper than sorrow," "let the good times roll," or simply "listen to how I put these notes together"), a piece of music is serious—worthy of active listening—if it has something to say, and says it in such a manner that the music still sounds vital and fresh after many hearings.

Music is in many ways the most abstract of the arts. It cannot by itself, without words, tell a story or describe explicit situations. It operates on a more elemental level of expression. A composition has no single meaning. Rather, precisely because music *is* an abstract language without immediate concrete associations, its meaning occurs on several levels, some of which may be obvious and others only dimly perceived. We may not even be consciously aware of some of the most significant ways in which a piece of music moves or appeals to us, but we respond intuitively.

Listening

Gymnopédie No. 1 *by Erik Satie, orchestrated by Claude Debussy*

Record Set Side 1, Band 1

Listen to Erik Satie's Gymnopédie No. 1, a short piece written for piano in 1888 and later arranged for orchestra by Claude Debussy:

What is the nature of musical expression in this work?

How do you respond to this expression?

Do you find it difficult to put these responses into words?

Do you feel that other listeners would respond in roughly similar fashion, or would they likely "feel" the music in different ways?

If you heard the piece again—now or in a few days—would you listen and respond to it in the same way?

What are the most prominent features of the music? One listener might naturally focus on the melody; another might become immersed in the overall quality of sound. Is the essence of the piece a purely musical one—a pattern of notes—or is it a mood or emotional state which takes the outward form of notes?

How does the music fill time? Did you feel the *passage* of time, marked off by a series of musical events, or did time seem suspended, as though the clock had stopped on a fleeting moment of eternity and crystalized that moment?

Did you feel a sense of movement in the music, and of completion at its end, or did the music seem to linger on a single thought? Does the piece express one thought or many?

How would you characterize the tone of this piece? Introspective? Warm? Hollow? Rich? Haunting? Resolute? Plaintive? Distant? Very close?

Did you feel that the music was being directed toward you, that it created a private world that you could enter, or that in some way its expression was coming from within you?

Were you most aware of the composition itself, of the way in which it was performed, or of your own responses?

Was this a good performance? Was it a good listening?

These are highly subjective questions. They are intended not as an inquisition, but as representative of the kinds of questions we intuitively ask—and answer to our own satisfaction—when we actively listen to a musical performance. In active listening, musical expression is not a "thing" over *there,* but a process that is *happening,* here and now.

The Process of Musical Communication

Music consists of organized sounds that express thoughts and feelings. It exists not simply as notes on the printed page, but as a form of communication involving the composer, the performer(s), and the listener. The printed music, or **score,** is a blueprint for this communication, conveying the composer's intentions to the performer. Musical expression can only be shared, however, when the performer translates these notations into sounds that become significant to the listener.

The Composer

Musical composition is a process of beginning with isolated sounds and building something meaningful with them. For the composer one skill is necessary above all others: the ability to think directly in sound, as a writer thinks in words.

Although it might appear that the composer begins each piece from scratch, grabbing sounds from thin air, this is rarely the case. In the process of composing previous works, he or she has developed a special sensitivity to certain kinds of sounds, and has perfected techniques for fashioning them into a coherent musical statement. These distinguishing traits comprise the composer's *style*—the framework within which he or she works. A composer's style is not fixed, but will normally evolve over the years. It is something to build upon—an individual voice with which to express ideas, and a starting point for further creation.

A composition begins with new musical ideas—a fragmentary but memorable scrap of melody, a few chords or, perhaps, a particular quality of sound. The composer works with these initial ideas the way a sculptor works with clay, shaping, refining and combining them, seeking out their possibilities and implications. Sometimes this is a laborious process. Beethoven habitually carried sketchbooks with him, continuously jotting down and revising his musical ideas in them. He described his method of composing as follows: "I carry my thoughts about with me for a long time, often for a very long time, before writing them down . . . I change many things, discard others, and try again and again until I am satisfied." Beethoven's original ideas often underwent several stages of transformation, and the final version of one of his melodies may bear only superficial resemblance to the original. For Mozart, on the other hand, much of this effort seems to have taken place

The Process of Musical Communication

Beethoven's sketches for the last movement of his Ninth Symphony

in his head on a more instinctive level. When he actually sat down to write out a piece, he usually had already formed a clear impression of its structural outline, and was able to realize his conception with much greater facility and apparent ease.

Composers differ greatly in how they approach their art. Almost all, however, derive immense satisfaction from a process that begins with doodles on a blank sheet of paper and ends—days, months, or even years later—with a full-blown creation that reflects their own experience, beliefs, and craft. Robert Schumann noted that, "People compose for many reasons: to become immortal; because the pianoforte is open; to become a millionaire; because of the praise of friends; because they have looked into a pair of beautiful eyes; or for no reason whatsoever." Whatever the immediate motivation that sets a composer to work, the underlying spark is the desire for personal expression. No single work can encompass *all* of a composer's thoughts and creative skill. Each piece is a link in an ongoing process of self-discovery. "Genius is always prolific," Beethoven observed.

The Performer

Musical notation conveys many—but by no means all—of the composer's intentions to the performer. Some elements of music, such as pitch ("the notes") and duration (the relative length of each note) can be indicated precisely in the score. The notational symbols for other elements, such as dynamic level (loudness), are less exact and require interpretation. Some of the most important aspects of the composer's conception—for example, its unifying principles and emotional tone—cannot be notated at all. Only by studying the piece and living with it for a sufficient period will the performer come to understand these essential but implicit features of the music.

The performer's preparation of a work entails physical, intellectual, and emotional demands. He or she must, of course, be skilled enough to realize the pitch and rhythmic patterns accurately and fluently; no one wants to hear an "inspired" interpretation if it is also pimpled with many wrong notes. But beyond mere technical skill, a knowledge of performance practices is needed to determine matters of musical style not explicit in the notation: such questions as whether the tempo (speed) should be strict or flexible, and how much contrast between loud and soft passages is appropriate. In the light of their own musical experience, performers must develop a view of the composition as a whole so that they can project the continuity of the work. And finally, if the performers are to interpret the piece in a con-

vincing rather than a mechanical manner, they must give something of themselves to the performance, and communicate their own vision of its special character. Performers can convey the unity of the work, the way in which its structure inevitably grows out of fragmentary original ideas, only when they themselves are persuaded of it and have made the piece their own.

Listening

Two Performances of Scott Joplin's* Gladiolus Rag: *(1) by Joshua Rifkin, (2) by Dick Hyman

Record Set Side 1, Bands 2 and 3

As listeners, we hear a piece of music *through* the performer. What we are hearing is not "the score," but rather a performer's realization and interpretation of it. Our perceptions of the character and most prominent features of the music will depend in large measure on which aspects of the music the performer chooses to emphasize.

In the performances of *Gladiolus Rag* by Rifkin and Hyman we are hearing the same notes and durational patterns, but very different interpretations of the shape of the music. Rifkin adopts a slower tempo and maintains it with a rock-steady beat from beginning to end. Hyman begins at a more rapid tempo but frequently varies it, speeding up and slowing down to project individual details. If we heard only Rifkin's performance, we might assume that a strong, steady beat is an important feature of this piece; in Hyman's playing, the beat is more fluid, less easy to feel, and therefore a less prominent feature of the music.

Rifkin shapes the piece as a continuous accumulation of energy. In his interpretation, the music grows ever fuller and louder, from a restrained opening to a strong feeling of arrival on the final chord. The overall shape is cumulative, like a single long inhalation. The individual ideas of the rag are welded into a seamless chain.

Hyman lays greater stress on individual nuances, often bringing out short groups of notes so that the separate ideas of the work stand out in greater relief. We are less aware of an overall pattern of growth than of the moment-by-moment interplay of ideas. Hyman tapers the ending, so that it becomes an afterthought rounding off the rag, rather than the climax of the piece.

Hearing different interpretations of a composition can help us understand it better by spotlighting different features of the music. We don't listen to a new performance of a familiar work to see whether the performer plays it "correctly"; we listen to discover more about it, and to experience it in new ways.

The Listener

The listener is not a passive receiver at the end of the chain. The way we respond to a piece of music, and to a performer's interpretation of it, will be influenced by our own musical experience and perspective. Although the members of an audience may have similar reactions to a performance, it is unlikely that any two will hear the music in exactly the same way.

Listening—actively—is what music is all about. It is the fundamental skill, which makes expression and communication in music possible. The composer and performer are first of all *listeners;* they must "hear" the music mentally before they can bring it to life.

Recall for a moment how you listened to *Gymnopédie No. 1* and *Gladiolus Rag.* As we listen to a piece for the first time, our attention tends to focus initially on its most immediate and striking features: particular melodic ideas, rhythms, or qualities of sound. These individual ideas arouse our interest in the piece and enable us to "get a handle" on it. (If this doesn't happen—if we hear only "nice" sounds rather than specific musical ideas and gestures—we are apt to drift off into dreamland, and the performance becomes background music.) Gradually, however, we also become aware not only of individual ideas, but also of *structural patterns:* how those ideas are being combined into a larger statement. We also assimilate the *style* of the piece: the character of its musical language. And we appreciate the *craft* of both composer and performer, their ability to *convince* us of what they are saying so that the music strikes sparks within our own imagination. All of these many levels of appreciation may occur almost instantly during a performance, but most likely they will occur in stages over several hearings.

The "meaning" of a piece of music is, simply, the many ways in which it appeals to us. Study of the piece can sharpen and broaden our understanding of its intrinsic qualities and increase our enjoyment of them. But musical meaning is not confined to the substance and interpretation of a composition. Music is also capable of evoking powerful emotional responses from the listener. It touches, in some way, upon many aspects of our consciousness—thoughts, beliefs, feelings, images, memories, and much more. These subjective responses significantly color the way in which we listen. They are a vitally important part of what the piece means to *us.* Such responses vary among listeners, precisely because they are the unique way in which each of us participates in musical communication—by understanding the music in the light of our own experience.

Why Study Music?

"Why study music?" we might ask. Isn't a piece of music one of those things we either like or don't, and about which "no amount of argument is going to change our mind"? Shouldn't we trust our instincts, listen to music that makes us "feel good," and leave the study to other people?

Many listeners have the vague impression that music should not require study. Such misgivings often reflect a forbidding view of what is meant by the "study" of music: namely, "the opposite of fun." This attitude frequently is accompanied by suspicions that such study will rob us of our instincts, drain the joy out of music, reduce it to abstract concepts and diagrams, or—worse—that someone will try to inflict his or her opinions on us.

A meaningful study of music, however, is not a matter of "memorizing boring facts," but of thinking about what we already do: how we listen, what we respond to. It is a way of *understanding* our instincts, building upon them, stretching them, coming back to them, and enjoying them more deeply than before, through a fuller involvement in music. "Facts," whether intriguing or yawn-provoking in themselves, are merely aids to such understanding; if they don't lead to insight, they are dead bones. The real issue, once again, is the distinction between casual and active listening. Music is either something that simply washes over us or a means of expression we actively participate in with heart, mind, and soul.

The intellectual, sensuous, and emotional aspects of music are interrelated. Even the most "expressive" piece becomes more meaningful to us—and therefore more "expressive"—when we understand how it is put together, and how the performer elucidates this structure. Some music, such as songs that depict the joys and disappointments of love, demand our strong emotional involvement. Other pieces—Bach's fugues, for example—are more objective in quality; their expression lies primarily in the eloquence and perfection of the musical langauge itself; we can admire them as we would an exquisitely crafted jewel or precision instrument. In still other pieces, such as the *Gymnopédie No. 1,* the most enduring musical quality is the beauty or distinctive character of the sounds themselves.

Whatever the emphasis of a piece, the better we comprehend the ideas and techniques with which the composer and performer are working, the more sensitively we will be able to listen and respond to the music. Often, a second or third hearing will produce fresh insights, or even a quite different perspective, on the character of the music. Points of structure and quality of expression are easier to feel once we have gone beyond initial aural impressions. Conversely, only after we have grasped the overall design of the music can we fully appreciate its details and the ways in which individual ideas create this design. Repeated hearings are particularly important for works in unfamiliar styles; it may take more than one hearing to acclimate ourselves to the musical language of a piece—to the composer's choice and treatment of sounds—before we can discover the kind of statement he or she is making within that language.

Listening

Sound Patterns *by Pauline Oliveros*

Record Set Side 1, Band 4

Sound Patterns (1961) is a work for unaccompanied chorus. Singing, however, constitutes only a small part of the sounds produced by the vocalists. If the style of this piece is unfamiliar to us, we at first may be struck most by what is *missing* in the music: melodies, definite rhythms, chords, and so forth. We might feel adrift in a sea of curious sounds. We could respond in a number of ways:

1. Shrug our shoulders, observe that, "It all sounds kind of goofy to me," and wait impatiently for the piece to end.
2. Denounce everyone involved for wasting our time: "You call *that* music? I didn't ask for this. Harrumph!"
3. Take a "tolerant" view, and try to make the piece fit our expectations. "I think there's probably a melody in there somewhere but it's . . . um . . . different."
4. Listen for what *is* present in the music.

This work, as its title implies, is concerned *directly with sounds.* If we wait for some good tunes, we are apt to be late for dinner. Specifically, Oliveros is exploring the extensive range of sounds the human voice can project. The very absence of traditional musical elements forces us—if we listen actively—to concentrate on the emotive qualities of the individual sounds themselves (somewhat as Renoir directed our attention to the girl by means of the man's straw hat). Many of the sounds are of the "everyday" variety: whispers, tongue-clicks, lip-pops, etc. Individual sounds are defined by articulation (sharp or smooth), high or low pitch, loudness, and gesture (urgent, relaxed, and so forth). But most of all, sounds are defined by their unique colors—by how they "feel."

These sounds constitute the ideas of the piece. But do we hear *more* than random sounds? Can such sounds sustain our interest? Does the piece *communicate* something?

The title, again, provides a clue. Oliveros does not shape the various sounds into an obvious formal design. (There is no single climax to the work, for example.) If she had, our attention would be less riveted on the sounds themselves. But as there is a "shape" or "color" to each individual sound, so *patterns* begin to emerge as the sounds are combined into points of greater and lesser energy, of accumulation, accent, and relaxation. At the beginning of the piece, for example, a series of increasingly emphatic gestures grows out of an initial whispering sound. The sounds become increasingly percussive, as though made by rattles, cymbals, and drums. As Oliveros superimposes highly colored sounds, the result often seems less like choral music than like sound colors produced by instruments or electronic means.

Oliveros treats these sounds sensuously rather than in rigorous fashion. They are not arranged into a "logical argument"; rather, they come in impulsive thrusts. They are at times tightly controlled, and at other times simply allowed to speak and express *themselves.* Interpretive freedom is central to the *overall* gesture of the music; we are asked to follow sounds as they rumble like waves through the chorus, to be sensitive to them, savor them, smile at them. No more—but no less.

As we become accustomed to the particular aural environment this piece creates, its sounds are likely to seem less strange to us. They are, after all, actually familiar sounds, made by human voices, which any of us could easily produce (and without practicing scales first!). Oliveros is attempting to have some fun with them.

Recordings and Live Performances

In listening to the music discussed in this book, you will have to rely principally on recorded performances. The development of high-fidelity records, tapes, and reproduction equipment since 1950 has had an enormous impact on the musical world. A vast body of music from all periods and styles, in performances by the greatest artists, is now quickly and relatively inexpensively available. Recordings enable new composers and performers to receive a widespread hearing, and allow the listener to absorb and study a work at his or her own pace.

As valuable as recordings are, however, they cannot capture every aspect of a live performance. Some performing media, such as the organ or large symphony orchestra, are difficult to record; concert-goers familiar only with recorded versions of a composition often are electrified by the sheer power of sound in a live performance. And, since music is a form of communication, a live performance frequently generates a more exciting reading of a work, as the players sense and respond to the immediate presence of their audience. The feeling of sharing in this communication—of participating fully with the performers and other members of an audience—can heighten the individual listeners' enjoyment. Recordings and study should increase our desire to hear concert performances of a work.

How to Listen

For some people the vastness of the concert music repertoire can be initially overwhelming. Our study certainly will not turn you into an expert on all types of music. For almost everyone, an appreciation of the variety and types of musical expression begins with the enjoyment of a few select works, and with performances that speak with particular force to the listener. These works can serve as stepping stones to further exploration, arousing our curiosity in other pieces by the same composer or performer, or in other works in the same style or medium.

It is unlikely that you will respond to all different musical styles and genres in the same way. The purpose of this book is not to make you "like" symphonic music, opera, jazz, and the song repertoire equally. It is, rather, to acquaint the listener with the musical styles, forms, and genres that people of many periods and cultures have found consistently rewarding, and to attempt some perspective on the richness and variety of musical expression.

Nearly everyone has had the experience of initially responding in a bewildered or negative way to an unfamiliar work, then finding himself intrigued by some aspects of the music upon rehearing, and eventually becoming absorbed in the music. This is not always the case, and, alas, some pieces that are attractive on first hearing pall quickly. But the listener who adopts a cheerleading attitude, who is content with first impressions and who begins mentally applauding or booing after a few seconds, ultimately will live in a very small musical world. As the American composer Charles Ives observed, with some irony, "Beauty in music is too often confused with something that lets the ears lie back in an easy chair." Throughout this book the reader will be encouraged to approach each new work on its own terms, without preconceptions. To study a composition is to enter into the special world that the composer and performer create. Countless generations of listeners have found that this participation in musical communication richly repays the effort and is its own greatest reward.

Unit 1

The Language of Music

As a form of communication, music can be considered a language. Like any language, it consists of vocabulary, a syntax, and styles and forms of expression. Just as a literature is built of words arranged into meaningful patterns on a number of levels, so music is built of groups of sounds. We might pursue the parallels between music and English, for example, in the following table.

	English	*Music*
Vocabulary (basic elements)	Words	Sounds (pitches, rhythms, tone colors)
Syntax (how elements are combined)	Grammatical structure, sentences, paragraphs	Musical forms (rondo, theme and variations, scherzo)
Style (the manner and tone of expression)	Elizabethan verse, journalistic prose, informal conversation	Musical styles (Baroque, Romantic, ragtime, "hard" and "soft" rock)
Genre (the medium of expression)	Novel, short story, poem, play	Song, symphony, jazz improvisation, opera

The first four units of this book treat each of these aspects in turn. Thus, the five chapters of this unit examine the basic materials of music, the individual elements from which music is made.

Ultimately, however, there are only two elements to music: sounds *and* time; *a third element necessary to musical expression,* meaning, *comes largely from within each listener. In this study, music will be approached not as a foreign language, but as a native tongue, one we have heard and begun to comprehend since infancy. Throughout, the emphasis will be on the individual elements of which we are aware, and the patterns they form to which we respond.*

Chapter 1
Musical Time

Music is a performing art and therefore exists in time. Much as a play or film creates its own illusion of the passage of time, so a piece of music organizes the time it fills and gives this time a particular quality. The **rhythm** of a piece of music is the way it moves through time.

Rhythmic Patterns

There is a natural rhythm to our lives. The passage of time is measured, and made meaningful, by periodic change. Day alternates with night; weekly and monthly cycles recur. With the passing seasons and years we progress from youth to maturity to old age. Our daily routines become part of the larger patterns of a life cycle.

Music is similarly organized into many levels of patterns. Most of these patterns are based upon movement and change. Music is rarely static for very long. Rather, it alternately accumulates and releases energy, in much the same manner we breathe in and out. Patterns that grow in intensity produce a sense of direction, a feeling of heading toward some point of arrival. Other patterns perform an opposite function, dissipating tension or restoring balance.

Musical time is less a matter of how long a piece lasts, in minutes and seconds, than of *how* it fills and shapes this time. Musical time may seem compressed and highly charged, or it may create a distant, dreamlike quality in which time seems to stand still. The emotional tone of a work depends largely on how we feel and respond to its quality of motion—whether it seems urgent, deliberate, or relaxed.

Pulse

When we think of rhythm, the first thing likely to come to mind is **pulse,** or beat. Pulse is the basic unit of motion in a composition. Like the ticking of a clock, pulse marks off divisions of time. It is a musical form of pure energy, the heartbeat of most works.

A rhythmic pulse may be strong, like the pounding of a hammer, or weak. When strong, as in marches and most rock music, a pulse is easily felt. In other music rhythmic pulsation is less marked and obvious. Pieces of a lyrical or reflective nature, such as *Gymnopédie No. 1,* generally have a flowing pulse; it is there, but "in the background."

Whether fast or slow, strong or weak, a musical pulse is said to be **regular** if it remains constant. In many pieces, however, the pulse is not steady, but frequently speeds up and slows down. Such variations in pulse may be specified by the composer, or they may be added by the performer. *Rubato* is a common style of performance that features almost continuous variations in the pulse. Dick Hyman employs a rubato rhythmic style in his playing of *Gladiolus Rag.*

Strong, regular pulse

● ● ● ● ● ● ● ●

Strong, irregular pulse

● ● ●●●●●●●● ● ●●●●●

faster original pulse faster

Weak, regular pulse

• • • • • • • •

Weak, irregular pulse

• • ••••••••• • •••••

One of the most important decisions a performer makes is how to project the pulse of a work—exactly how fast it should be, how much to emphasize it, and whether to play "strictly in time" or freely vary the speed of the beat.

Listening

Two-Part Invention in F Major *by Johann Sebastian Bach*

Record Set Side 2, Band 1

In this brief composition the pulse is *strong and regular.* It is firmly established in the opening notes and remains constant until the very end of the piece. Insistent pulsation produces a vigorous rhythmic drive and a perpetual-motion quality that are among the most vital features of the music.

Listening

Prelude No. 4 in E Minor *by Frédéric Chopin*

Record Set Side 2, Band 2

The pulse in this piano piece is anchored in the left-hand chords, under a slower-moving melody. Although the pulse remains *strong* throughout the prelude, it is constantly *changing,* becoming faster and slower to underscore the expressive character of the music. If we were to liken the pulsation in Bach's Invention to a single, unbroken wave, which develops a cumulative momentum as it pushes forward at a constant speed, the pulse in this prelude would be more like a series of smaller waves that ebb and flow. These rubato variations comprise part

Jean Renoir,
Bal à Bougival
Courtesy of
Museum of Fine Arts, Boston

of the performer's interpretation of the work, and are not notated in the score. But without them the piece might sound stiff, like a "sing-song" recitation of a memorized poem.

Listening

Prelude to the Afternoon of a Faun *by Claude Debussy*

Record Set Side 11, Band 1

Listen to the first thirty seconds or so of this celebrated orchestral work. Here the pulse is *weak.* Occasionally it comes into focus briefly, but then it fades again. The pulse in this piece might be likened to the background figures in Renoir's *Dance at Bougival;* we are dimly aware of it, but we are *more* aware of the *quality* of musical motion—serene and unhurried—which Debussy creates through changes in volume, color, and density of sound.

Tempo

The speed of the pulse establishes the **tempo** of a piece of music. For many centuries composers relied upon accepted conventions and on the musical intelligence of performers to determine how fast to play a piece. In the 18th century, however, composers began to specify the approximate speed they intended by adding **tempo markings,** brief descriptions in Italian (the prevailing musical language of the time) at the beginning of a score. These traditional tempo indications are still in widespread use. They suggest not only the general speed of the music but also something of its character. The most common tempo markings are the following:

Tempo Marking	*Speed*	*Literal Meaning*
adagio	very slow	"at ease"
andante	slow but moving	"walking"
moderato	moderate	"moderate"
allegro	fast	"happy"
presto	very fast	"at once"

Deviations from the basic tempo are indicated by the following terms:

accelerando	gradually become faster
ritardando (or *rallentando*)	gradually slow down
a tempo	return to the original tempo

Over the last 150 years, composers increasingly have tended to substitute tempo indications in their own language for these Italian terms. They also have taken greater pains to notate subtle changes in tempo. A more complete list of common tempo and interpretive markings is given in the Appendix.

Tempo markings indicate a relative, rather than an absolute, speed. In deciding the exact speed at which to play a piece the performer takes into account not ony its tempo marking but also the character of the music, the complexity of the rhythms, and the nature of the melodies. Two performers or conductors will choose different tempos for the same work, because they find different clues in the music as to its appropriate character and speed.

Composers wary of too much interpretive leeway can indicate tempo more precisely by means of metronome markings. The **metronome** is a clocklike instrument perfected in the early 1800s. It produces regular audible clicks at a rate that can be varied between about 40 and 200 pulses per minute. Metronome markings (for example, ♩ = 80) indicate the exact number of beats per minute.

Meter

Music never consists of an unbroken series of exactly equal, undifferentiated beats. This would sound literally like a ticking clock, lacking any sense of direction, and would likely put the listener to sleep. Rather, musical pulses are grouped into patterns by **accents**—greater emphasis given to certain beats.

There are several types of musical accents. The most basic is the **metric** accent. In a metrical pattern, an accented beat is followed by one or more weaker, unaccented beats. Each group of accented and unaccented beats is called a **measure.** The following are examples of simple musical meters:

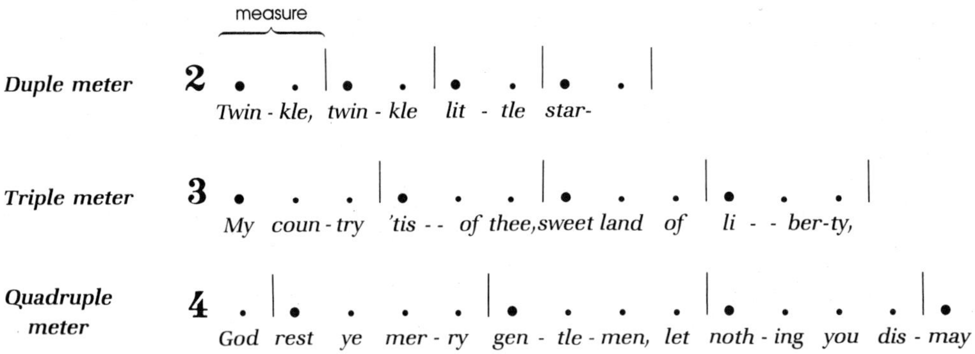

Metric accents are commonly called **downbeats,** because conductors indicate them with a downward motion of the arm. Many works, such as the first two examples above, begin with a metric accent. Others, like the third example, start on an **upbeat,** a preparatory unaccented pulse.

Like pulse, meter can be strong or weak. When strong, it is easily felt. *Gladiolus Rag* is unmistakably in duple meter (ONE–two, ONE–two); there is a clear distinction between accented and unaccented beats. When the downbeats are emphasized only slightly, meter is less prominent. In most lyrical works, metric accentuation is weak. Strong accents would sound clumsy, for example, in "America the Beautiful."

Listening

Papillons No. 3 *by Robert Schumann, contrasted with Satie's* Gymnopédie No. 1

Record Set Side 2, Band 3 (and Side 1, Band 1)

Schumann's energetic little waltz is in triple meter. Meter and pulse are both strong; they are, in fact, the primary sources of musical energy which propel the music forward. The piece is in three sections. The triple meter is particularly transparent in the middle section: here the left hand generally plays only on the downbeat of each measure, while the right hand maintains the pulse.

Gymnopédie No. 1 is also in triple meter, but the downbeats are much less emphatic. The meter is weaker, and we are less aware of it. Rhythmic interest is concentrated instead on larger patterns within the melody. The melody alternately presses forward in shorter notes, then comes briefly to rest on longer tones, in cyclical fashion:

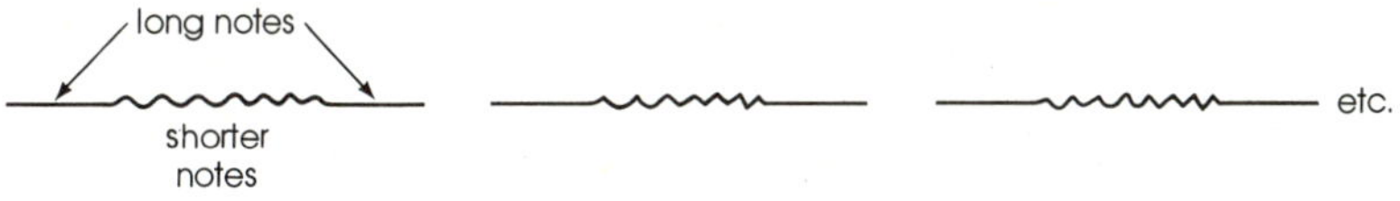

Pulse and meter are the backdrop against which we feel this patterned motion.

Many other metrical patterns are possible in addition to simple two-, three-, and four-beat groupings. Meters of six beats are also common. In a six-beat meter the pulse is patterned into two groups of three beats each within each measure. The primary metric stress occurs on the downbeat, and there is a less pronounced secondary accent on the fourth beat:

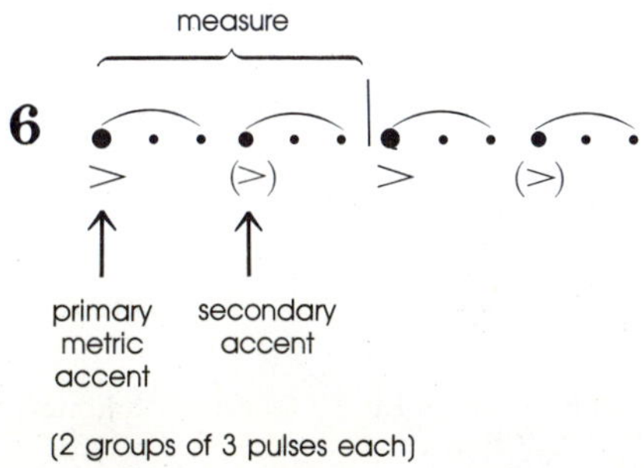

Asymmetric Meters. Most of the music we are familiar with is written in one of these basic metrical patterns. However, many different types of rhythms are possible within each, which accounts for their continued vitality after centuries of use. In the 20th century, many composers (and a growing number of jazz performers) have been attracted to more complex and freer types of metrical organization. Asymmetric meters of five and seven beats, which are common in eastern European folk music and the classical traditions of Asia, have become increasingly prevalent in Western music. Composers and performers also have explored uneven metrical groupings of eight, nine, or more pulses.

Suggested Listening

1. Take Five *by Paul Desmond;* 2. Blue Rondo a la Turk *by Dave Brubeck.* [1]

The Dave Brubeck Quartet pioneered in the use of asymmetric meters within a jazz idiom during the 1960s. *Take Five,* by the late saxophonist Paul Desmond, is a well-known piece in quintuple meter. The pulse is grouped into uneven units of 3 + 2 beats:

Brubeck's own *Blue Rondo a la Turk* features a metrical pattern of nine beats, divided into groupings of 2 + 2 + 2 + 3:

Listening

Baris, *performed by a Balinese gamelan ensemble*

Record Set Side 1, Band 4

Asymmetric metrical patterns are part of the musical heritage of many cultures and have been used for centuries. Such meters are often the "glue" that holds complex musical fabrics together.

Gamelan is a term used to describe Indonesian instrumental ensembles. The gamelan in this piece is fairly typical of the "orchestras"

[1] Both selections, performed by the Dave Brubeck Quartet, can be found on Columbia Record JCS-8645.

A Balinese gamelan ensemble

of Bali and Java. It consists mostly of percussive instruments: drums and cymbals, large and small gongs, and xylophone-like instruments with bronze bars. Bamboo flutes round out the ensemble, which contains between 20 and 30 players.

Baris is a war dance. As we listen to it we are apt to be struck most by the strong pulsation and frequent contrasts between loud and soft passages. There may seem to be no metrical framework—merely throbbing rhythms, with periodic outbursts in the drums.

Actually, a strict, but asymmetric, metrical pattern is maintained throughout the piece. The rhythmic motion, which might sound at first "free" (or even improvisatory), is tightly organized. The instruments are divided into four choirs. Each group provides a separate layer of sound and performs a specific rhythmic function. The bottom layer consists of two gongs, which play a three-note pattern over and over. The three-note pattern lasts eight beats, with a 3 + 5 grouping of the pulse:

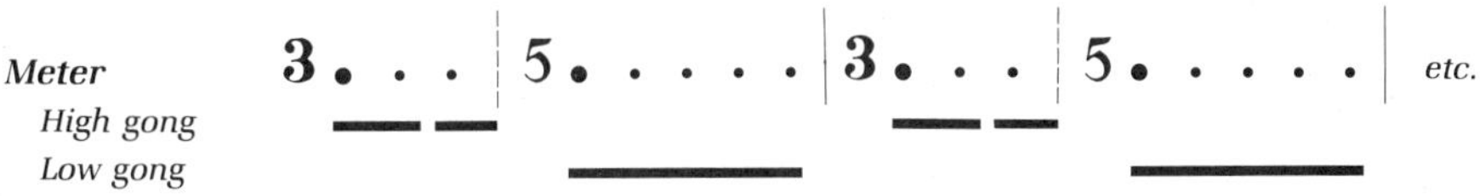

The second layer is played by the xylophone-like instruments, which beat out the pulse. The third group is the flutes, playing in more rapid, ornamental rhythms. The final layer is the drums and cymbals, which enter explosively in rapid rhythms at periodic intervals:

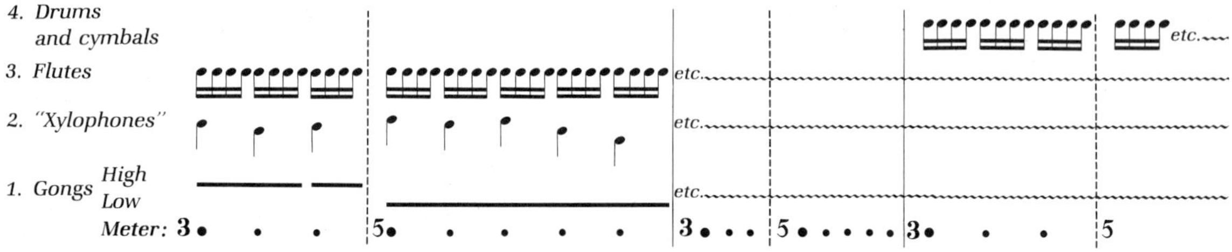

The larger rhythm in the music is the cyclical alternation of soft and loud passages. The soft passages are played by the first three layers, and the loud passages are played by everybody but dominated by the drums. In the soft passages we hear specific tones, such as the high and low notes of the gongs. When the drums enter, individual notes and instruments fuse together into a single wall of sound, pulsating with rhythmic fire. When we feel the metrical framework of *Baris* we can appreciate more fully how the instruments "fit together", and how each contributes a different kind of rhythmic energy to the piece.

Mixed Meter. In all the examples so far, the metrical pattern, whether simple or complex, has remained constant throughout a work. Many 20th-century composers employ shifting metric accents. The meter changes frequently, and accents come at irregular intervals. Mixing of meters is occasionally used in rock music to add rhythmic vitality by playing with the listener's expectations.

Stravinsky, "Cercles mystérieux des adolescents" from *Le Sacre du printemps*.

The Beatles, "All You Need is Love"

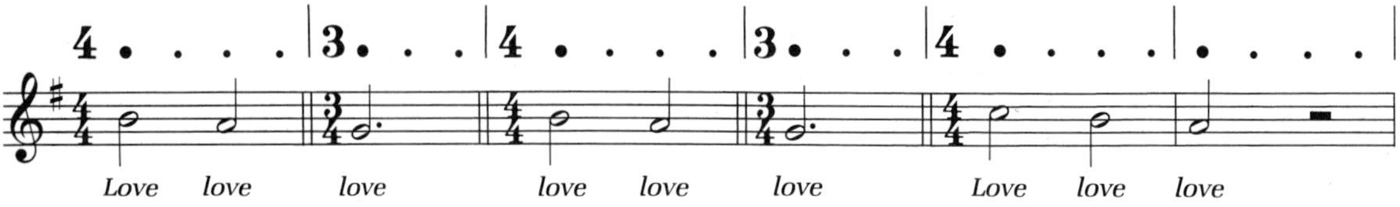

Music Without Meter. Not all music is metered. Most vocal music written before 1600, for example, consists of a smooth flow of pulses without metric accents. Stressed beats result from natural speech inflections and from the contour of the melodies. Such music often seems to "float" in long, continuous arcs, rather than to "bounce" from downbeat to downbeat. Rhythmic interest is centered in the flow of pulses and in durational rhythms within the melodies. (Suggested listening examples: the Gregorian chant *Salve Regina,* or the Kyrie from Palestrina's *Pope Marcellus Mass.*)

Some contemporary composers also have dispensed with meter, organizing rhythms instead in terms of "events" whose timing is indicated in seconds or left to the discretion of the performers. Oliveros' *Sound Patterns* is a representative example. The music has no pulse or meter. It is not without *rhythm,* however. Rapid and sustained sounds are combined, sometimes gliding smoothly into one another, at other times hurled at the listener like a slew of darts. The motion is by turn fluid and abrupt. There is a greater level of activity in the middle of the piece, and a tapering at the end. Rhythmic motion crests and recedes many times within this larger design. In short, sounds still are being grouped into patterns, but these patterns are longer and highly asymmetric. By organizing without a metrical framework, Oliveros directs our attention to the "inner rhythms" within each sound, and to the "larger rhythms" that result as the individual sounds are played off against each other.

Phrases and Cadences

As meter organizes pulse in most music, groups of measures are in turn combined into longer patterns called **phrases.** Phrases are the basis of the "larger rhythms" we have referred to vaguely until now. They are generally several seconds in length, often consisting of four or eight measures, and they usually end with a relaxation in the forward motion of the piece. This relaxation is called a **cadence.** It is normally a longer note, which serves as the musical goal of the phrase and a breathing spot in the piece. (Singers and wind players usually take a breath after each cadence.) Cadences serve to interrelate the musical ideas within a phrase as one thought, and to separate them from the ideas that follow.

"America" contains two phrases and cadences. The phrases are of unequal length.

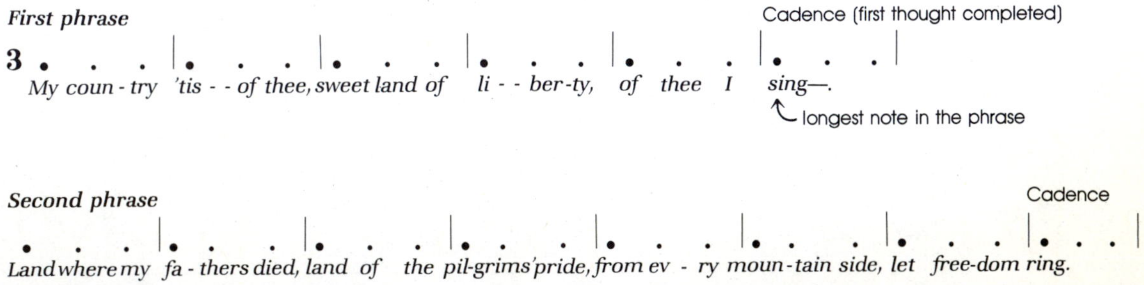

Gymnopédie No. 1 has six phrases. The phrase structure of this work—its "seams"—can be heard easily, because the six cadences not only fall on long notes but are followed by brief pauses in the melody. These "windows" in the melody space the phrases apart, and contribute to the introspective quality of the work. Each phrase of the melody enters only after what seems like a moment of hesitation or reflection, then expresses its thought in as few notes as possible.

Cadences, too, can be strong or weak. Each level of rhythmic organization is based on proportions—on how we hear notes and events in relation to one another. Such proportions not only govern the "smaller" rhythms of a work (long and short notes, accented and unaccented beats), but they also create larger rhythms that shape the music around points of particular emphasis. The rhythmic structure of music might be likened to the turning of "wheels within wheels"; we have been following it from the center outward and are approaching the largest ring.

A strong cadence, or **full stop,** fully resolves accumulated musical tension. It completes a musical thought and produces a point of rest and balance. The cadential note normally will be long, and will fall on a downbeat, thus receiving double emphasis. A full stop functions like a period at the end of a sentence. Almost all compositions end with a full stop. Weak cadences, called **half stops,** are momentary pauses. Like commas, they are inconclusive; the musical thought is not completed, and the piece must continue.

Listening

"Now is the Month of Maying" by Thomas Morley

Record Set Side 2, Band 4

The larger rhythm of this song from Shakespeare's time follows a single three-phrase pattern throughout. The first two phrases of each line end with half stops, and the third, with a full stop.

short phrase	short phrase	longer phrase
Half Stop	Half Stop	FULL STOP
Now is the month of may-ing,	*when merry lads are play-ing,*	*fa la la .... la.*
Each with his bonny lass,	*upon the greeny grass,*	*fa la la .... la.*
The spring clad all in glad-ness,	*doth laugh at winter's sad-ness,*	*fa la la .... la.*
	etc.	

To summarize, the three levels of rhythmic organization—pulse, meter, and phrases—can be diagramed as follows:

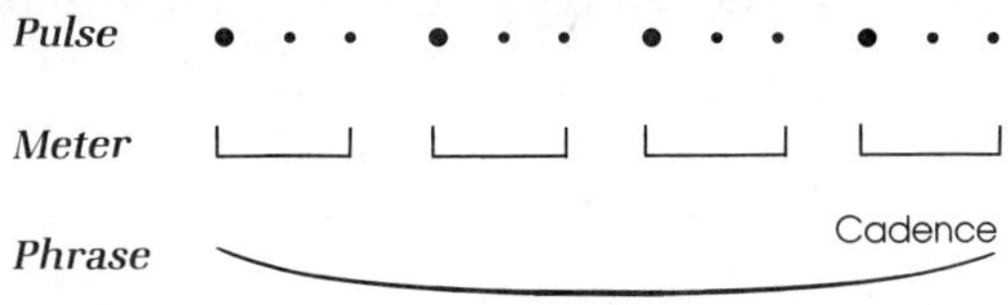

Rhythmic Notation

Our discussion so far has been confined largely to the framework of rhythm. Before we can examine the specific rhythms of a work—exactly how long its notes are in relation to one another, and how these durational patterns are fitted into a framework—it is necessary to lay out the elementary features of rhythmic notation. Notated examples will appear throughout this text. Musical notation can appear intimidating to the layman, as alien as something written in Russian or a computer language or some other unfamiliar alphabet. But it is not necessary to "read" music the way a musician does to make use of these notations. The musical examples in this text should be thought of as visual aids to understanding. They enable us to grasp at a glance the shape of a rhythm, melody, or musical texture and to see how it is put together. The musical examples are not meant to take the place of listening; rather they are a way of "taking a photograph" of the sounds we are hearing, of holding them still for a moment so we can consider what they are doing.

Musical notation indicates the relative duration (length) of each **note**, or sound, and each **rest**, or silence. This notation is proportional; that is, note symbols do not indicate absoulte timings (such as two seconds) but rather show how long a note is in relation to other notes and rests in the same passage. The basic durational symbols are:

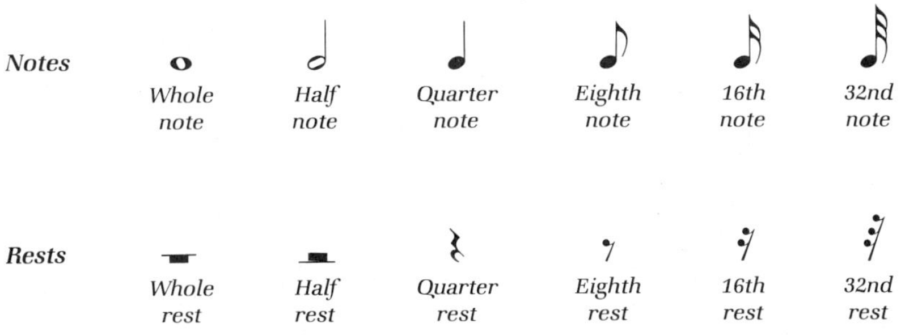

Reading from left to right, each note or rest symbol receives half the value of the preceding symbol. A quarter note is half as long as a half note, twice as long as an eighth note, four times as long as a 16th note, and so on. The name of each symbol indicates how many notes or rests of that duration are equal to a whole note; one whole note equals two half notes, equals four quarter notes, and so on. These relationships can be more easily seen in the following figure. Note that when two or more durations shorter than a quarter note occur in succession, they are beamed together:

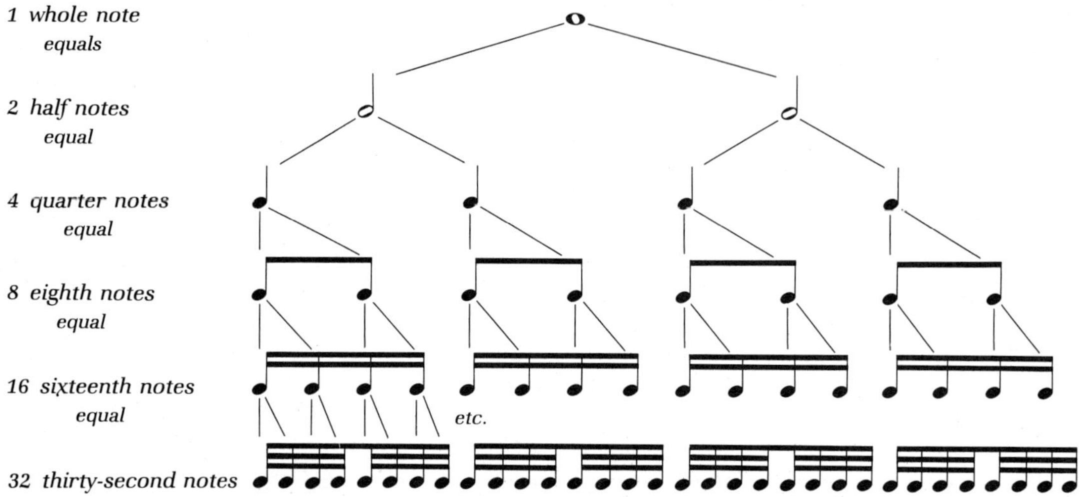

Sometimes a duration will be divided into three equal divisions rather than two. These rhythms are called **triplets.** This example begins with two triplet groups that each receive the value of a quarter-note.

Triplet division of quarter note

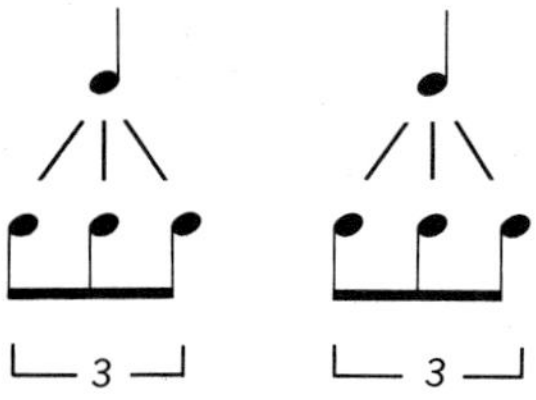

Piano motive of Schubert's "The Erlking"

A dot after a note or rest increases its length by one half:

Finally, to indicate a single long or complex duration, two or more note values are connected by a **tie.** These tied notes are played as a single note of the indicated duration:

Time Signatures

Pulse and meter are indicated at the beginning of a composition by a **time signature,** which contains two numbers. The upper number denotes the meter, that is, the number of beats per measure. The lower number specifies how the beat is notated—whether in quarter notes, eighth notes, or some other unit. (The symbol > indicates a stress on the first beat of the measure.)

Meter ⟶
Pulse (what duration ⟶
receives one beat)

Papillons No. 3, Gymnopédie No. 1 | *Gladiolus Rag* | *Prelude to the Afternoon of a Faun*

Listening

Papillons No. 3 ***by Robert Schumann***

Record Set Side 2, Band 3

Return to this short piano piece by Schumann. This time, while listening, follow it in the rhythmic score below, which indicates the durations and upward and downward pitch motion of the left- and right-hand parts:

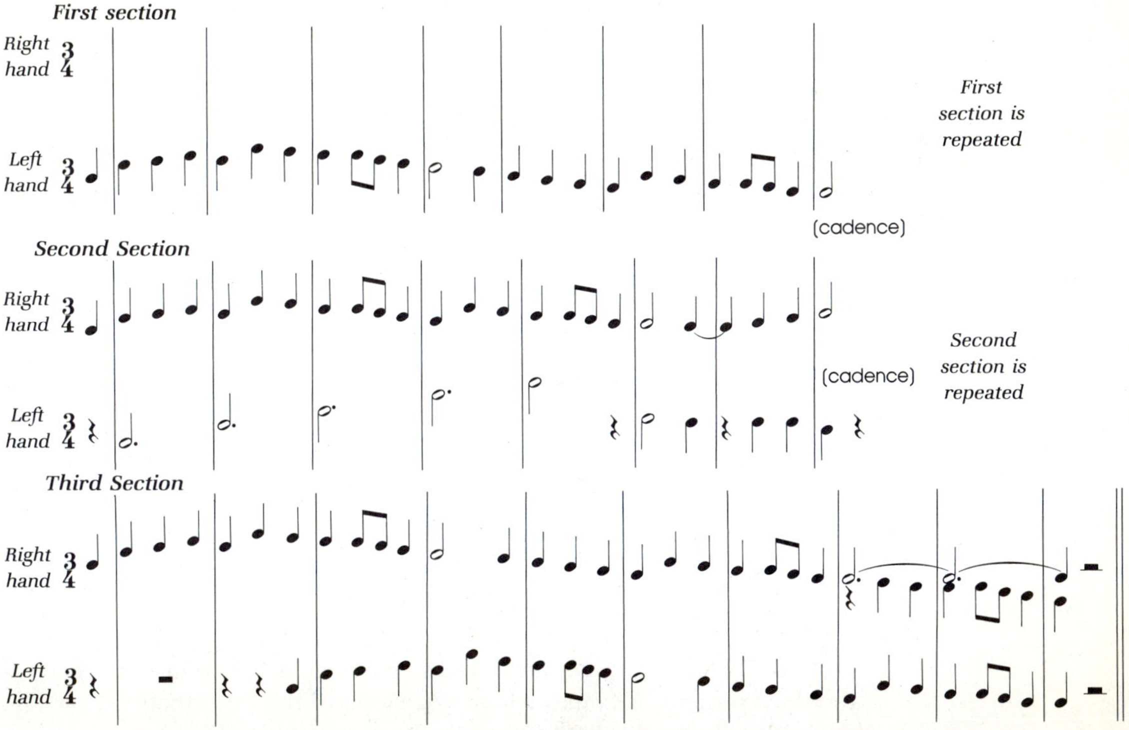

Rhythmic Motives

Pulse and meter provide a frame of reference against which we hear the specific rhythmic ideas of a work. A rhythmic **motive** is a fragmentary but memorable pattern of durations. Usually about a measure in length, a motive is the seed of a larger idea. It is repeated several times, either in exact or varied form, and may be combined or contrasted with other motives.

Some compositions feature continuous repetition of a motive. The three-note gong motive in the gamelan performance of *Baris* is repeated from the beginning to the end of the piece. Beethoven's uncompromising reiteration of a four-note motive in the first movement of his *Fifth Symphony* creates an insistent rhythmic drive and concentrated energy that largely define the tone of the movement. By contrast, Chopin's restrained use of a single, slow-moving two-note motive until the climax of his *Prelude in E Minor* is heard as a deliberate *lack* of forward motion. The melody remains poised on an isolated rhythmic fragment, which blossoms into a complete thought only near the end of the piece.

Beethoven, **Symphony No. 5**

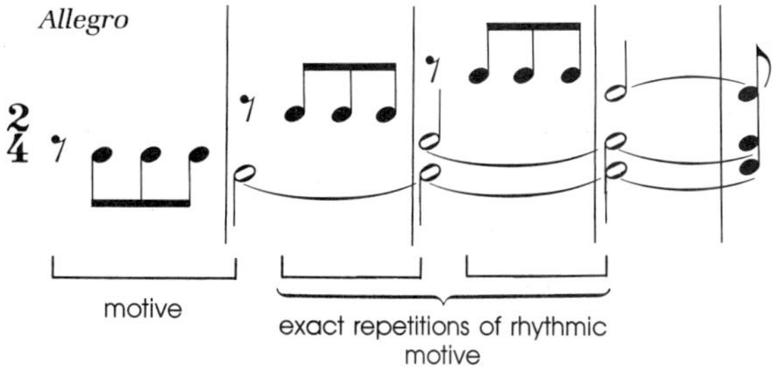

Chopin, **Prelude in E Minor**

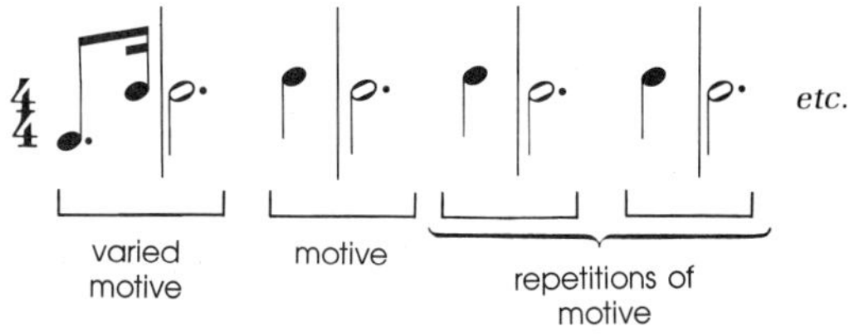

Bach's *Two-Part Invention in F* features an interplay of two motives, the second moving twice as fast as the first. The two motives are tossed back and forth between the right- and left-hand voices. In Debussy's *Prelude to the Afternoon of a Faun,* the serene flute motive alternates with a continuous series of new motives throughout the piece, causing periodic changes in mood and tone.

Bach, **Two-Part Invention in F Major**

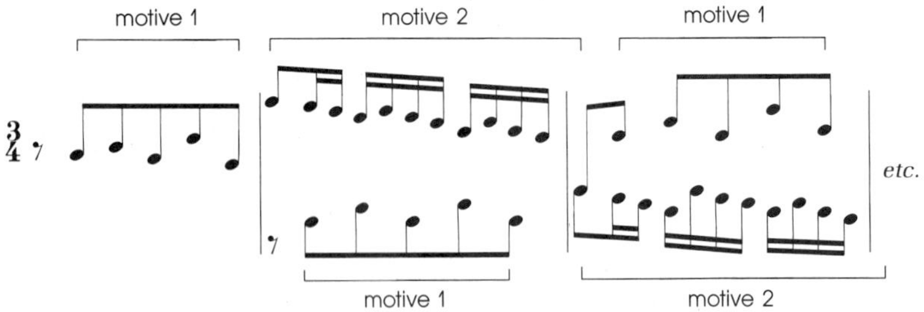

Debussy, **Prelude to the Afternoon of a Faun**

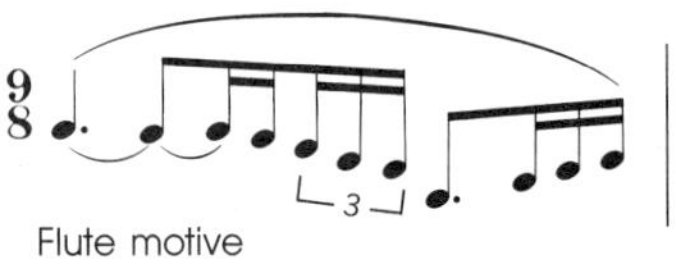

In *Gladiolus Rag,* Joplin introduces a succession of motives. Each is developed briefly, becomes a stepping stone to the next, then is heard no more. The "larger rhythm" of the piece is a progression of ideas, rather than the concentrated development of one or two intial motives.

Syncopation.

Motives and other durational patterns ride on top of the pulse and meter of a work. Durational patterns may fit neatly into the metrical framework, or they may cut against the grain of the meter.

There is a natural tendency for performers to emphasize slightly the longer durations in a phrase. When long durations occur on metrically stressed beats, they reinforce the meter:

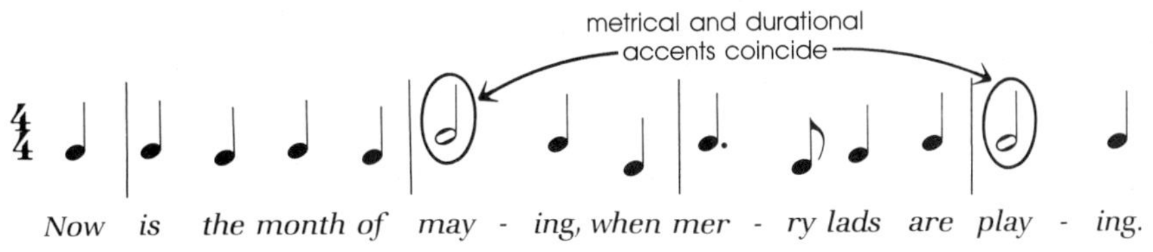

When longer durations fall on weak beats, or between beats, they create an effect called **syncopation.** Syncopated rhythms run counter to the metric grouping of the pulse. They produce "extra" accents, somewhat like kicking one's feet while walking; by injecting a temporary imbalance within the metrical flow, they impel the rhythm forward.

Listening

Gladiolus Rag ***by Scott Joplin***

Record Set Side 1, Band 2

Scott Joplin

Ragtime was the earliest form of black American music to achieve widespread hearing throughout the world, cresting in popularity shortly before World War I. Most rags were solo piano pieces, but arrangements for groups of instruments and for voice with piano accompaniment also were common. The "ragged time" rhythms consisted of syncopated melodies played in the right hand over a rigid metrical foundation in the left-hand bass.

Gladiolus Rag (1907), one of the most enchanting and, in its way, profound pieces by the "ragtime king" Scott Joplin (1868–1917), demonstrates how syncopation can form the basis of a rhythmic style. The strong pulse and duple meter are anchored in the bass in simple, marchlike rhythms; against this framework, Joplin superimposes more complex, syncopated rhythms in the melody. The result is **cross accents:** accents in the melody that do not coincide with those in the harmony. These cross accents are responsible for much of the rhythmic vitality, subtlety and expression of the music. The opening phrase of the second section, for example, contains a continuous series of syncopated accents in the melody, marked (*) in the example below. Only at the cadence (the last measure) do the two hands land together on a metric stress, producing a structural point of arrival that brings the musical thought of the phrase to completion:

Opening phrase of the second section of "Gladiolus Rag." The right-hand part has been reduced to a single line.

As in many of his other rags, Joplin included a note to the performer that cautioned, "Do not play this piece fast. It is never right to play 'Ragtime' fast."

Pacing: The Overall Rhythm of a Piece

To summarize briefly our survey of rhythmic structure: Rhythm organizes musical time by dividing it into patterns. Tempo, pulse, and meter establish a basic rate and quality of motion (regular or asymmetric). Motives and larger durational patterns—the *actual* rhythms we hear—determine the expressive character of this motion: tranquil, fiery, solemn, or whatever. As motives are developed into more complete thoughts, they form phrases. The length and complexity of these phrases further defines the quality of rhythmic movement. As the music unfolds in time, we grasp ever larger patterns and, finally, its overall design.

This overall quality of motion—what comes of the initial motives during the piece, and how broader patterns of tension and release result from changing levels of activity—is called musical direction, or **pacing.** Some pieces, like Satie's *Gymnopédie,* create little sense of direction. Although they may incorporate many musical ideas, they sustain one mood or quality throughout. That quality is the essence of the music, and it is what we respond to most strongly. When the rhythmic pacing of a piece is relatively static, we tend to be most aware of the primary rhythmic elements, because no obvious, larger design develops.

In other works, the level of rhythmic energy see-saws between high and low points. Larger patterns of tension and release, which may last a few seconds or several minutes, become the most distinctive feature of the rhythmic structure; they determine how we feel the shape of the music, and these patterns of tension and release become more important than individual rhythms.

In Bach's *Invention,* overall rhythmic motion is continuous and uniform. The most important rhythmic element is the driving pulsation created as the two motives are combined and contrasted. Chopin's *E Minor Prelude* begins with static pacing. But about two-thirds of the way through, the melody comes alive, moving in shorter notes. Rhythmic interest shifts from the primary level (the recurrent motive and rubato pulsation) to the broader shape of the melody. Increasingly rapid rhythmic attacks lead to a climactic point, followed by a gradual resolution of tension. The overall pacing of the Chopin piece might be represented graphically:

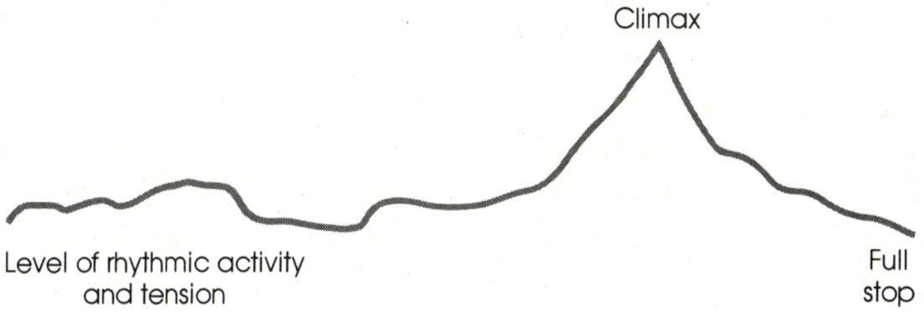

Pacing must be distinguished clearly from pulse and tempo. A rapid piece may generate little sense of direction if its level of activity remains the same; conversely, a slow piece can develop a powerful sense of momentum. Musical direction is not solely a function of rhythm; melody, harmony, and variations in density or loudness are important factors also. In Maurice Ravel's familiar *Bolero,* for instance, a single melody is repeated over and over, with no increase in rhythmic activity. But as more instruments are added and the piece becomes ever louder, the music relentlessly builds to a single forceful climax.

Our enjoyment of a piece of music is enhanced geatly when we can feel and understand how it moves through time. There is much more to the rhythmic structure of a work whether or not it has a strong beat—we don't feel rhythm merely from the ankle down. The way a piece is paced will determine where its rhythmic interest is concentrated—whether on impulse or on broader design.

For Further Listening[1]

Sundance, ***performed by a sextet led by Keith Jarrett***

Rhythmic energy, propulsive yet subtle in nuance, is a vital feature of all styles of jazz. Jazz rhythms can only be approximated in notation, because they are less a matter of metrical "accuracy" than of how the

[1] The selections "for further listening" at the ends of Chapters 1, 4, 14, and 15 extend the discussions of these chapters to include the important repertoire of jazz and jazz-influenced music. *Sundance* is available on Columbia recording PG-31580.

members of an ensemble jointly feel, place, and play with the beat. Duke Ellington put this in simpler terms with his famous aphorism, "It don't mean a thing if it ain't got the swing."

Most jazz idioms feature several layers of rhythmic patterns, which we hear as simultaneous (group) variations on a common framework. The framework itself is usually simple—strong, regular pulse and meter grouped into short phrases of equal length. On top of this foundation, the performers counterpose much freer patterns, playing a shade ahead of or behind the beat, lengthening and shortening the phrases in their individual melodic lines, and interjecting cross-accents. Cross-accents are successive punctuations, mostly off the beat, played by different performers. Like syncopation, they disturb or "loosen up" the metrical framework, as the performers emphasize and "land at" different points within a phrase.

Jazz rhythms have undergone periodic stylistic evolution. The foursquare pulsation and syncopated rhythms characteristic of ragtime, dixieland (1900–1930), and swing (1930s) were replaced by more relaxed pulsation and greater emphasis on individual interpretive freedom in later styles: bop (1940s), "cool" (1950s), and "funky" (1960s).[1] During the 1970s, many performers fused the free phrasing and cross-accents of the jazz tradition with the powerful beat of rock, creating the jazz-rock idiom we hear in *Sundance.*

Sundance is in quadruple meter, but this meter is merely a background framework around which the performers weave a complex web of asymmetric individual patterns. The piece begins with a repeated motive in the piano bass (left hand). On top of this syncopated motive, pianist Jarrett overlays a stream of jabbing rhythmic figures that cut against the grain of both pulse and meter. The figures frequently pull well ahead of the bass pulse. This is more than rubato; the figures often approximate the rhythms of speech, coming in impulsive thrusts and waves. Similar rhythms are incorporated later in solos by the guitarist and saxophonist. The rhythm section (bass player and two drummers) transcends its traditional function in earlier jazz styles of "holding things together"; here the bassist and drummers overlay their own cross-rhythms and explosive bursts.

The thread that unites all this stratified rhythmic energy is the driving pulsation. The music surges forward in an unbroken rush, without marked cadence points or sectional divisions. With considerable interpretive freedom the performers branch out in different directions from the metrical framework and meet again "downstream." There is no central focus of rhythmic and melodic interest; instead there is a group exploration in which each player develops his own patterns and rhythmic momentum, while maintaining a link to the common thread.

[1] Listen, for example, to *Hackensack,* performed by the Thelonius Monk Quartet (Columbia JCS-8838). The harmonic and melodic aspects of this number will be examined at the end of Chapter 4.

This music is not to be heard with a tapping foot, but to be experienced by "picking up one's feet" and being swept along with the tide. It is physical, earthy music, complex in organization but primal in utterance.

Terms and Concepts for Review

pulse
tempo
meter
accent
phrase
cadence
  full stop
  half stop
duration
motive
syncopation
pacing

Chapter 2
Tonal Organization

When we say that a sound is "high" or "low," we are referring to its **pitch.** The pitch of a musical tone—exactly how high or low it is—is one of its most obvious and important characteristics. Melodies are made up of successions of pitches in rhythm:

Chords, the basis of harmony, are combinations of pitches sounded together:

In this and the next two chapters, we will examine the ways in which pitches are organized and combined in musical language.

Pitch Notation

Our system of musical notation has evolved over many centuries to enable a composer to indicate the precise pitch and duration of each note of a piece. The basic symbols were devised during the Middle Ages. These symbols have been modified and supplemented with additional notations by each succeeding age. Musical notation is not a scientific system, but it has proven adaptable to continuous changes in musical style.

Modern notation consists of **note-heads** (half notes, quarter notes, and so on), which specify duration, placed on a five line **staff,** which indicates pitch level. Individual notes can be placed on any line or space of the staff. Each line and space denotes a different pitch; the higher a note is placed on the staff, the higher its intended pitch.

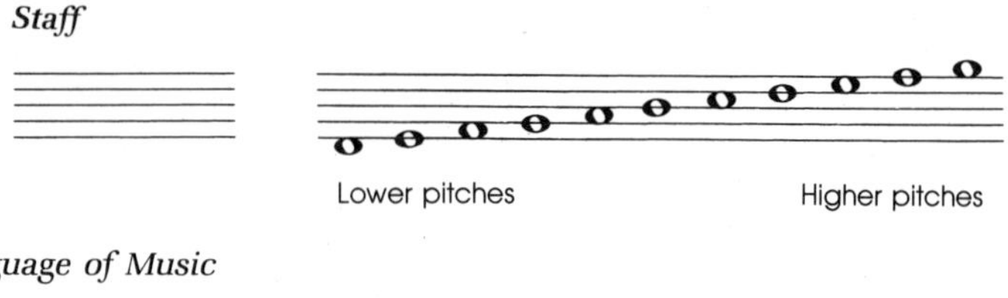

Clefs

By itself the staff does not signify exact pitches, but only the general high–low relationship of different tones. A **clef sign,** placed at the left edge of the staff, is used to clarify the notation. The clef indicates not only the general range of the tones (high or low), but also the exact pitch relationships between them. The two most common clef signs in modern notation are the **treble clef,** used for high pitches (such as women's voices):

and the **bass clef,** indicating a lower range (such as men's voices):

Specific pitches are designated by letters of the alphabet. During the Middle Ages, when our pitch symbols were created, most melodies contained seven basic tones. Thus the first seven letters of the alphabet—A through G—are used to label these tones, with A the lowest pitch and G the highest. After G, the scale pattern is then repeated in a higher range:

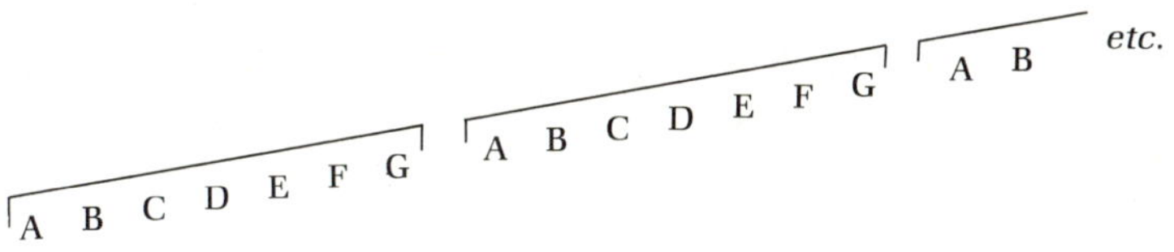

The modern treble clef evolved from the letter G and denotes this pitch by encircling it on the second line of the staff. Other pitches are positioned on the lines and spaces of the staff with respect to this reference pitch G. **Ledger lines,** additional lines running through, above, or below the noteheads, are used to notate pitches that exceed the upper and lower limits of the staff.

Treble clef

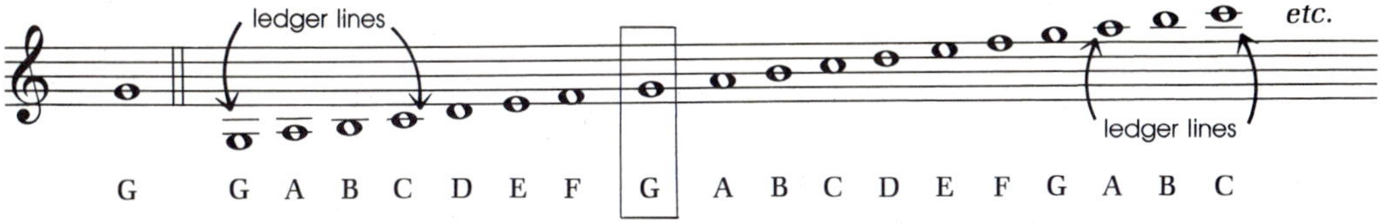

The bass clef evolved from the letter F. The pitch F occurs on the fourth line up, surrounded by two dots:

Bass clef

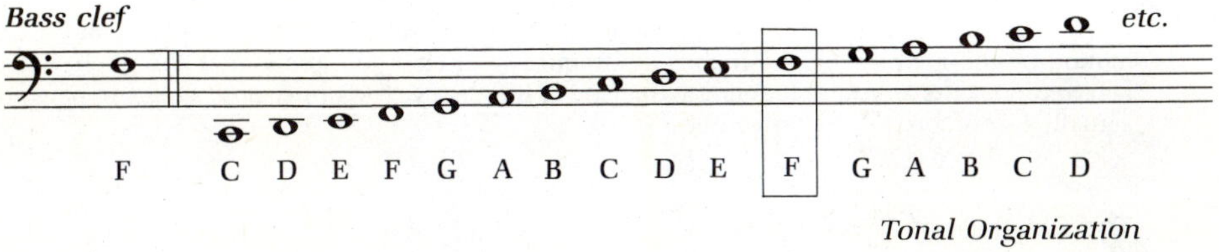

Grand Staff

Music for instruments that produce a very wide range of pitches, such as the piano, is written on a **grand staff.** The grand staff consists of a staff in treble clef over a staff in bass clef. The pitch "middle C" (the C closest to the center of the piano keyboard) has one ledger line in each clef.

Grand staff

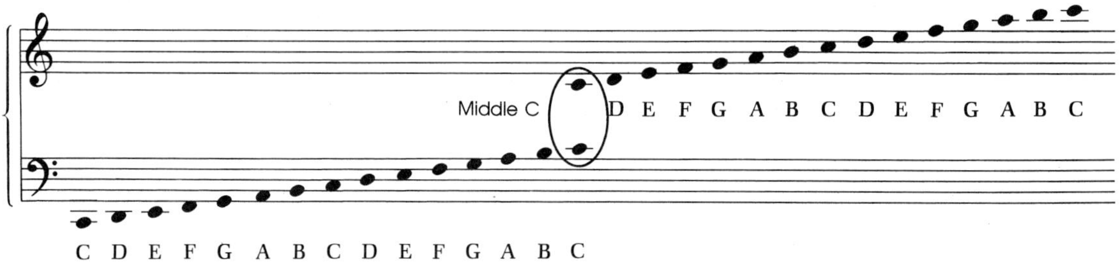

The Octave

If we begin on the pitch A and count up or down from it on the white keys of a piano, the eighth tone we come to is also called A. The musical interval, or distance, between any tone and the next highest or lowest tone with the same letter name is called an **octave.**

The octave is acoustically the simplest musical interval. When the two pitches are played simultaneously, they sound almost like a single tone.[1] We perceive an octave not so much as two distinct pitches, but as one pitch reproduced in a higher or lower range. For this reason any two pitches an octave apart are called by the same letter name.

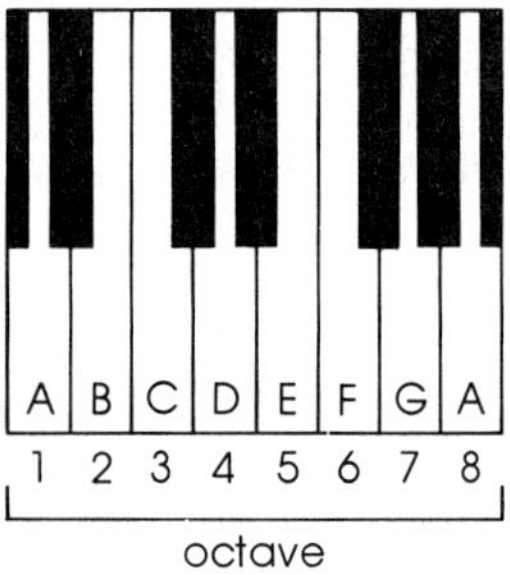

Octave

High women's voices (sopranos) have a range of pitches about one octave above that of high men's voices (tenors). Similarly, lower-pitched female voices (altos) are approximately one octave higher than lower-pitched male voices (basses). When women and men sing the same melody, each in a comfortable range, they will sing in octaves rather than at exactly the same pitch level.

[1] The pitch of a musical tone is determined by the rapidity of the air vibrations set in motion by the instrument; the higher the frequency of vibration, the higher the pitch. Each octave represents an exact doubling or halving of frequency. The upper note seems to be, and actually is, reinforcing the lower one.

Tuning Systems

The number of pitches available within a musical culture and the exact distances between these pitches are determined by a **tuning system.** While most Medieval music employed only seven tones within an octave, later Western styles made increasing use of five additional pitches that lie between some of these original notes. The tuning system that has governed Western music since the 18th century divides the octave into twelve pitches an equal distance apart. The distance between any two adjacent pitches is the interval of a **half step.**

Other musical cultures employ quite different tuning systems. Much of the music of India, Bali, and Java, for example, is based on tunings that divide the octave into five, six, or seven steps of unequal distance. Other Asian tunings involve more than twelve pitches. Such music cannot be performed on most Western instruments. The gamelan instruments in *Baris,* for example, employ a tuning that can only be approximated in Western notation. When we hear such music, it may at first sound "out of tune," because it does not conform to the particular tuning system to which we are accustomed. Usually, however, our ears quickly adjust.

Accidentals

Western tuning divides the octave into twelve tones, but our notational system contains only seven letter names. Thus, additional symbols are needed to notate some pitches. These added symbols, called **accidentals,** modify a notated pitch by raising or lowering it by one half step. The black keys of the piano are notated by means of accidentals.

Accidental	*Name*	*Meaning*
♯	sharp	raises the pitch by one half step
♭	flat	lowers the pitch by one half step
♮	natural	cancels a previous accidental

In music written before the 20th century, an accidental carries through the entire measure, and need not be rewritten every time it occurs:

In contemporary scores accidentals usually alter only the note they immediately precede.

Scales

A **scale** is a catalogue of the pitches most commonly used in a piece of music. These pitches are arranged in ascending or descending order within one octave. The characteristic sound of any scale is determined by the number of pitches it contains and by the intervals between these pitches.

The Chromatic Scale

The **chromatic scale** includes all twelve pitches, each a half step apart. This scale is a "full house" in terms of our tuning system, including all of the tones Western instruments are designed to play.

Ascending chromatic scale *Descending chromatic scale*

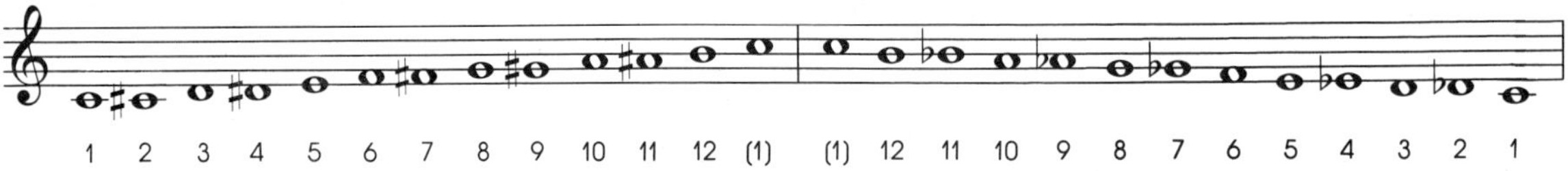

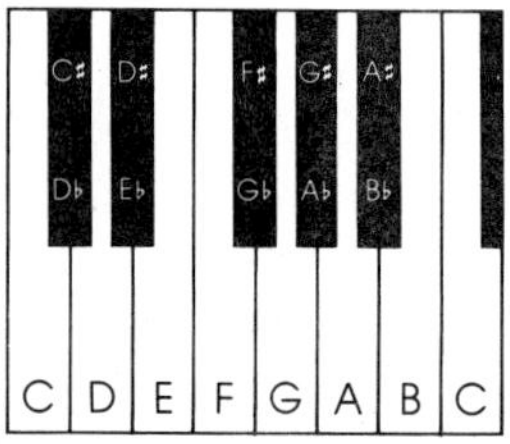

Notice in both the keyboard diagram and the written scale that there is no sharped or flatted note between the pitches E and F, and between B and C. In both cases the tones are a half step apart. The interval between any other adjacent white keys, such as C and D, is a **whole step** (two half steps).

Five- and Seven-Tone Scales

Most of the music we are familiar with makes regular use of only some of the twelve possible tones. The other tones are used only occasionally or not at all. This limitation in the number of tones employed in a given piece results in a specific scale, which determines the general pitch quality of a piece of music. Many folk songs are based on five-tone scales; the most common of these can be produced by playing only the black keys on a piano. (Examples include "Wayfaring Stranger," "Five Hundred Miles," and "Silver Dagger.") The use of only five pitches often lends a simple, unaffected quality to these tunes. *Baris* also employs only five tones, played in various octaves by the different instruments.

Five-tone scales

Black keys of the piano *Scale used in* Baris *(approximated in Western tuning)*

In most music, one scale tone receives particular emphasis, serving as the "home base" around which all the other tones of melodies and chords revolve. A melody will return frequently to this *central tone,* and will end on it, producing a feeling of completion.

The vast majority of compositions written before 1900, as well as many 20th century works and most popular music, are based on seven-tone scales. The scale tones form a pattern of five whole steps and two half steps. The central tone is written as the bottom and top note of the scale. The characteristic sound of any scale is determined by its unique pattern of intervals, rather than by the note on which the scale is begun.

In Medieval and Renaissance music, several different seven-tone scale patterns, called **modes,** were in common use. Note how the half-tone intervals appear between different notes in the following scales:

Common modes

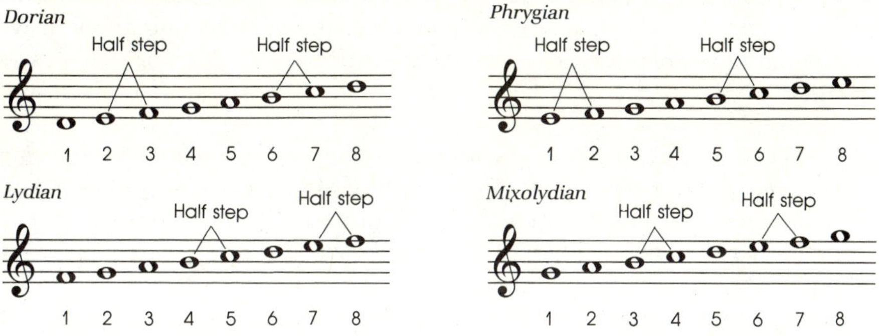

Many folk songs and some 20th-century works also employ these ancient modal scales. As a result of its unique arrangement of whole steps and half steps, each mode has a distinct tonal quality.

Listening

The Gregorian chant Salve Regina

Record Set Side 5, Band 1

Gregorian chant was the music of the Medieval Roman Catholic Church. Chant melodies were sung by male voices without instrumental accompaniment. *Salve Regina,* a hymn to the Virgin Mary, is a particularly moving example. It has been sung in monasteries at the end of the final service of the day for over 800 years.

The melody is in the Dorian mode, the first mode pictured above. It cadences frequently on the central tone D and uses only the seven tones of the Dorian scale pattern. Important words and syllables are stressed by a lengthening of certain notes, and by groups of tones sung on a single syllable (as in "Re-*gi*----na"). Gregorian melodies enhance but never overshadow the text. They are like a heightened form of speech, perfectly expressing the quality of the words. The style of chant is austere but moving in its simplicity and directness of expression.

***First four phrases of* Salve Regina**

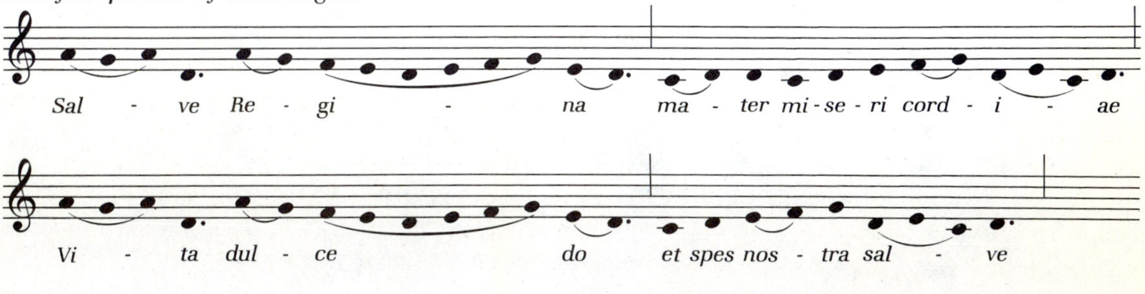

Transposition

We may choose to begin a scale, and any melody based upon that scale, on any starting note. Shifting a melody up or down in this manner, while maintaining the original intervals between scale tones is called **transposition.** When we sing a song without instrumental accompaniment we automatically transpose it to a comfortable pitch level. Transposition always results in a difference of at least one accidental between the original and transposed versions.

In the example below, the scale pattern and first phrase of *Salve Regina* have been transposed up one whole step. Since the scale pattern and melodic intervals remain constant, the melody sounds the same—except, of course, that it sounds *higher* in the transposed version.

Original pitch level

Transposed up a whole step

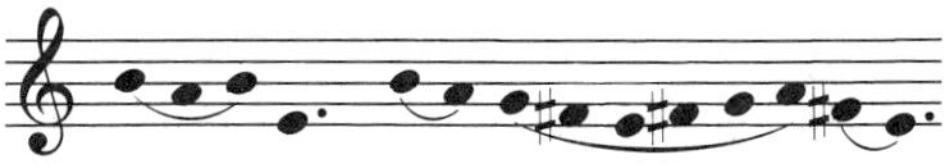

Scale

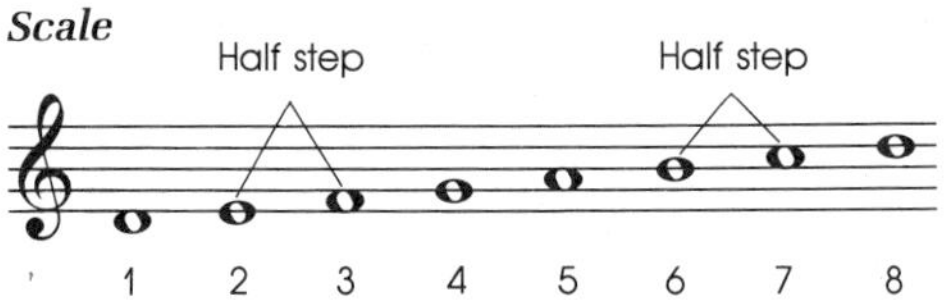

Scale

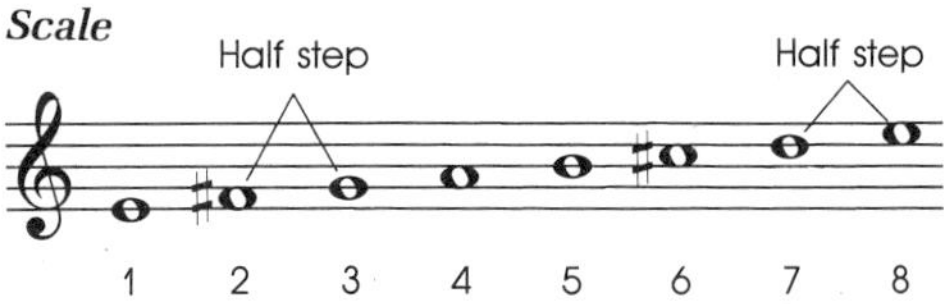

The Major Scale

During the 17th century, modal scales were replaced by a new system of pitch relationships called **tonality.** Tonal music makes use of only two seven-tone scales, termed *major* and *minor*. The central tone of a major scale is called the **tonic,** or key note.

The **major scale** contains half steps between scale steps 3 and 4, and between 7 and 8.

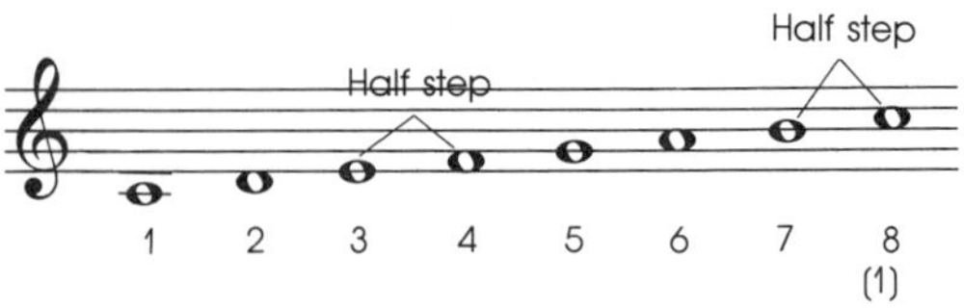

To hear a descending major scale, sing the opening of "Joy to the World":

8 7 6 5 4 3 2 1
Joy to the world, the Lord is born . . .

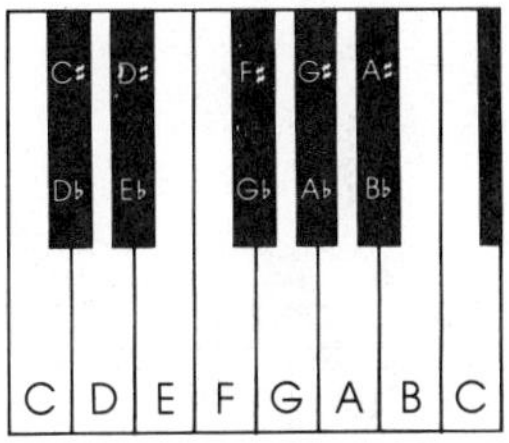

A major scale can be built on any note. Each different starting pitch requires a different set of accidentals, which preserve the characteristic pattern of whole steps and half steps. Three major scales are notated below. The C major scale contains no sharps or flats; it uses only the white keys of the piano. An E♭ major scale contains three flats, and an A major scale has three sharps:

C Major scale ***E♭ Major scale*** ***A Major scale***

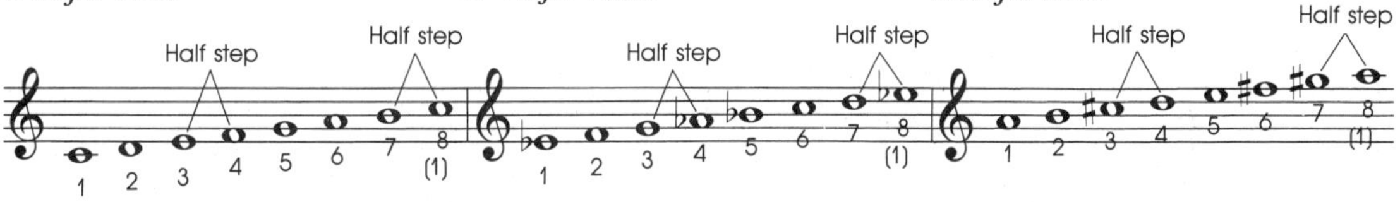

Rather than writing in the accidentals continuously throughout a piece, composers of tonal music use **key signatures,** which indicate all the sharps or flats of a given scale at the beginning of the staff:

C Major ***E♭ Major*** ***A Major***

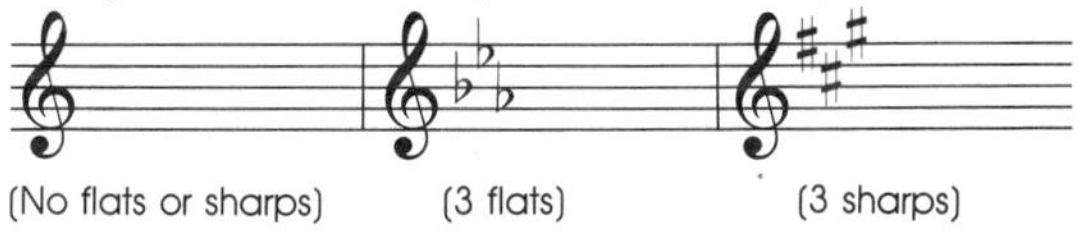

"America" is an example of a tonal melody built on the major scale. The first phrase of the melody is notated below in the keys of C major, E♭ major and A major:

Key of C major

Key of E♭ major

Key of A major

The Minor Scale

The **minor scale** is also a seven-note pattern of whole steps and half steps, but the half steps now occur between scale steps 2 and 3 and between 5 and 6. The following are three minor scales and key signatures. As with the major scales, the signature indicates the notes that are sharped or flatted to preserve the proper sequence of intervals:

Key of A minor

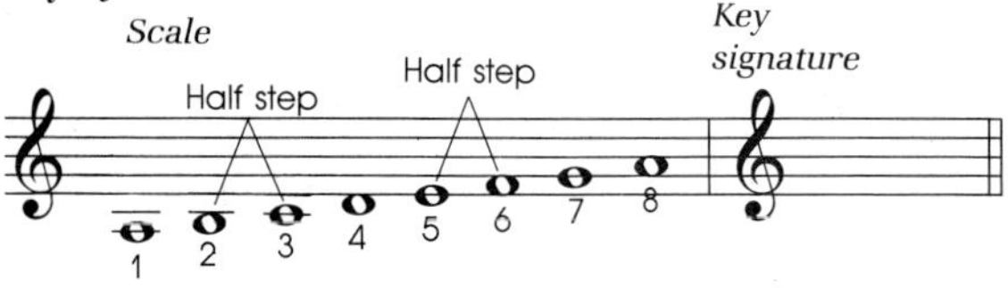

Key of C minor

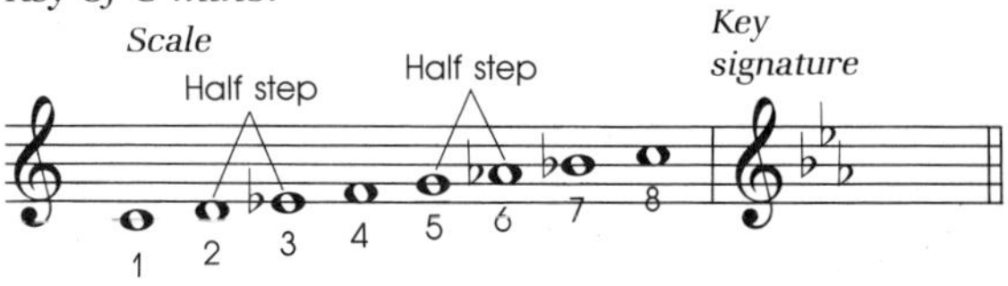

Key of F♯ minor

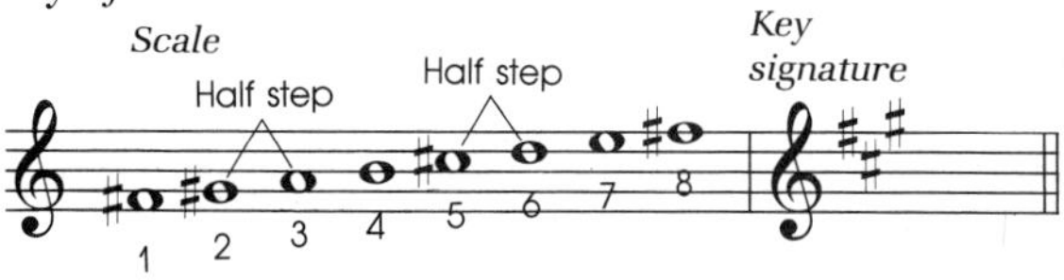

Notice that the key signature of A minor (no flats or sharps) is the same as the signature of C major. These two scales use the same seven pitches. However, they have different tonic notes and different interval patterns. As a result, pieces in A minor will have a very different quality from those in C major, because the pitches are heard in relation to a different center note. In the same way, a key signature of three flats indicates that a composition is written in either E♭ major or C minor. Three sharps indicates either A major or F# minor. Such pairs of major and minor keys, sharing the same scale tones and key signatures, are called **relative** keys. (C minor is the relative minor of E♭ major, and so forth.)

To Western ears, the minor scale often seems to have a more somber quality than the major. The minor mode is not inherently "sad"; the joyous carol "God Rest Ye Merry Gentlemen," for example, is in minor. The minor key is, however, the more likely choice for pieces of a reflective or pensive character.

Listening

Papillons No. 3 *by Robert Schumann*

Record Set Side 2, Band 3

The distinct tonal qualities of major and minor can be heard clearly in this piano piece which we studied in the last chapter. The same seven tones are used throughout the work (with a single "foreign" tone in the second section). The first and third sections are in minor, however, revolving around the tonic note F#, while the middle section is in the relative major, with the pitch A as tonic.

Listen to the piece twice. The first time, follow the music in the score below; the second time, listen *without* the score, and concentrate instead on the aural change in quality as the piece shifts into major and then back into minor.[1] Both hands play in octaves throughout the piece; the notation has been simplified here by eliminating the octave doublings of the melodies.

First Section: Minor

Second Section: Major

Third Section: Minor

The Basic Principle of Tonality

All tonal music, from a simple song like "America" to the longest symphony, is based on a fundamental pattern of tension and resolution. At the beginning of a tonal composition the tonic will be established as the most important tone. It will be heard as the point of departure to which the piece must ultimately return. As the piece continues, tonal motion is directed *away* from the tonic and toward other tones, which are heard as temporary points of arrival. Motion away from the tonic builds tonal tension. This tension will be resolved—either quickly or after an extended period—when the piece

[1] A double listening, once with and once without the printed score, is suggested for many of the notated excerpts in this book. The important thing is not to become a whiz at reading musical notation, but to be able to *hear* what is happening in the music.

returns to and cadences on the original key note. The basic pattern of tonal music is:

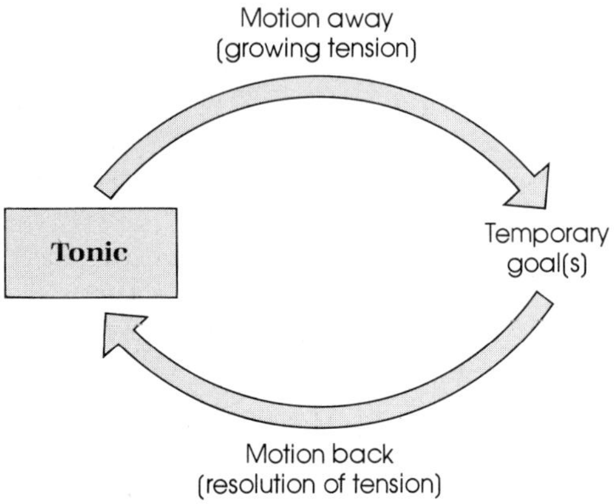

Short compositions may move away from and back to the tonic only once or twice, and this tonal motion will be comparatively rapid. In longer works, the pattern will recur many times.

In tonal music, each note is heard as part of a larger pattern which either pulls away from the tonic, prolongs tension by staying away, or returns to the tonic. The other notes of the scale are heard *in relation* to the stable tonic pitch. Some of the scale tones have a consistent function. The seventh degree of the major scale, which is a half step below the tonic is called the **leading tone,** because it customarily "leads" directly back to the tonic. The melody of "America" is a simple illustration of how each scale tone is heard in relation to the tonic:

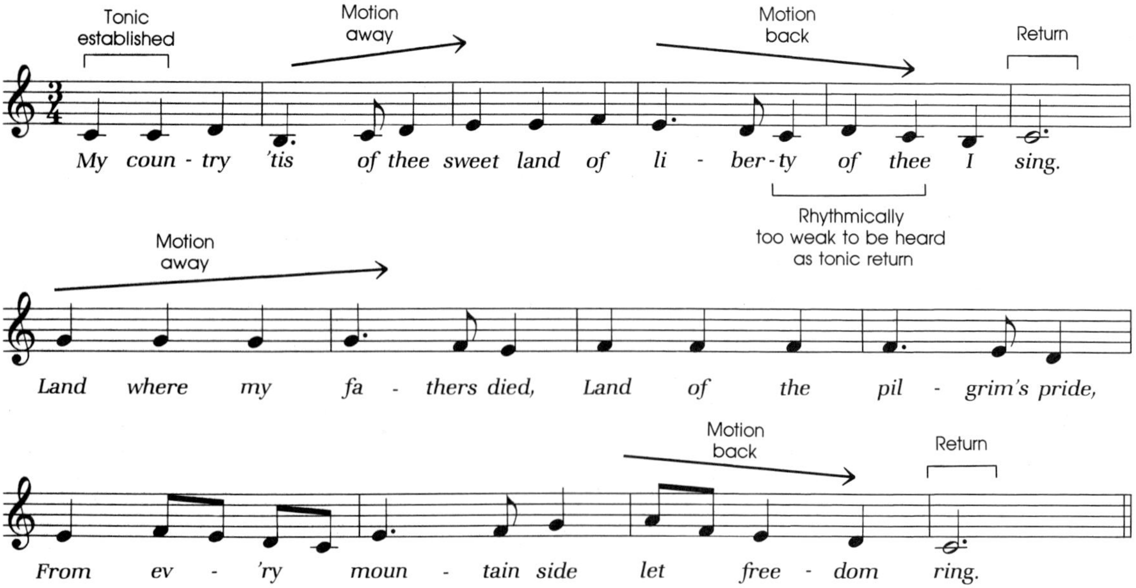

Diatonic and Chromatic Styles

A composer is not strictly limited to the seven tones of a major or minor scale. Any of the other five pitches of the chromatic scale may be introduced, but must be preceded by an accidental (♯, ♭, or ♮).

Tonal compositions that introduce few or no chromatic pitches are said to be **diatonic** in style, since they adhere closely to the diatonic (seven-note) major or minor scale. Tonally **chromatic** pieces, by contrast, include many notes foreign to the key. In general, early tonal music (of the 17th and 18th centuries) is diatonic, while music of the 19th century is more chromatic.

Modulation: A Shift of the Tonal Center

Even in an essentially diatonic piece, chromatic notes are often used to strengthen tonal motion away from the tonic toward temporary new tonal goals. When one or more chromatic tones are consistently used in a passage in place of original scale tones, they can lead to the temporary establishment of a new scale and tonic. Sometimes a single strong chromatic note (usually the leading tone of the new key) can produce a shift in the tonal center. The process by which chromaticism can lead to the establishment of a new key is called **modulation.** Modulation to the fifth degree of the original scale (called the **dominant** note) is particularly common, requiring only one chromatic alteration.

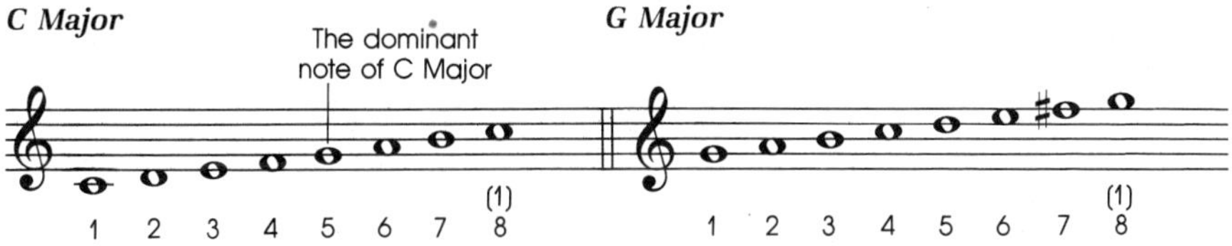

Martin Luther's hymn "A Mighty Fortress Is Our God" contains a modulation to the dominant, a prolongation of this new key, and a return to the original tonic. The first two phrases are in the tonic key of C major. The first phrase cadences inconclusively on the dominant note G, the second with more finality on the tonic. Taken together, the two phrases firmly establish the key of C major, using every scale tone.

The third phrase, however, introduces the foreign note F♯, the leading tone of a G major scale:

Notice that this phrase encircles the tone G and approaches this cadential note through its own leading tone, effecting a modulation to the key of G major. The fourth and fifth phrases are also heard with respect to the temporary new key note G:

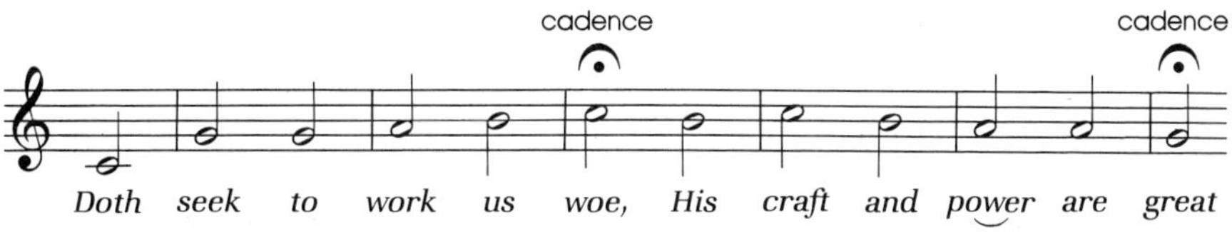

If the piece ended here it would sound incomplete, because we still remember the original key of C major. Tonal motion back to this original tonic has not been completed. The next phrase modulates back to the original key by reintroducing F♮ instead of F♯. The final phrase, based on a descending C major scale, concludes the tonal motion with a strong cadence on the tonic.

Many pieces, like "A Mighty Fortress," modulate to a single new key and back to the original tonic. Tonally more complex works may modulate through several new key areas. No matter how far away from the original tonic the tonal motion wanders, however, the listener's feeling for this pitch center is never fully obliterated. Modulation generates tonal tension by enabling the composer to establish temporary new pitch centers, delaying the return of the original tonic. A modulation may be smooth, almost imperceptible. It also may be abrupt and obvious, as in the unprepared "jump-shifts" between minor and major in *Papillons No. 3.*

"A Mighty Fortress"

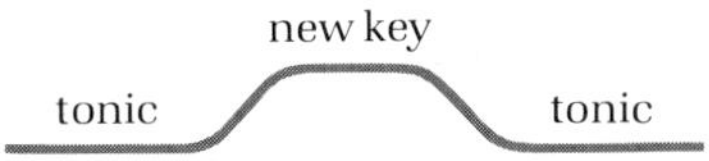

Papillons No. 3

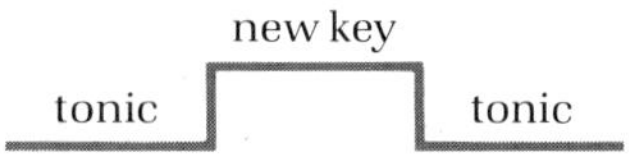

Listening

Two-Part Invention in F Major ***by J. S. Bach;*** **Prelude in E Minor** ***by Fréderic Chopin***

Record Set Side 2, Bands 1 and 2

These two works contrast not only in rhythmic emphasis, as we saw in the last chapter, but also in tonal style. The Bach Invention is diatonic. Although it contains shifts in tonal center, it adheres closely to the scale tones of the various keys it passes through. The first few measures firmly establish the tonic F. Motive 2 is essentially a descending F major scale:

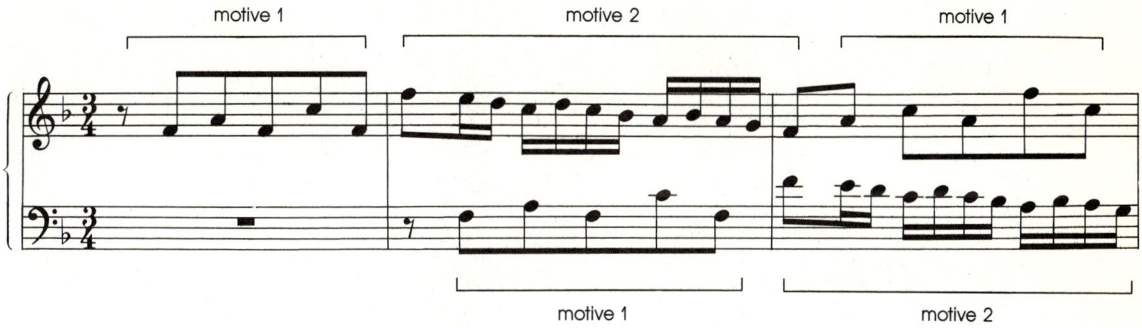

The main body of the work contains a series of brief excursions through several tonal areas: C major, G minor, D minor, B$^{\flat}$ major. Tonal motion through these areas is rapid and unbroken by cadences; thus, we are less aware of specific new key centers than of the continuous tonal instability. Our recognition that the tonic has been lost is heightened by recurrences of the original motives in different key areas. Notice particularly the change in quality when the motives are heard in minor:

Original motives heard in new keys

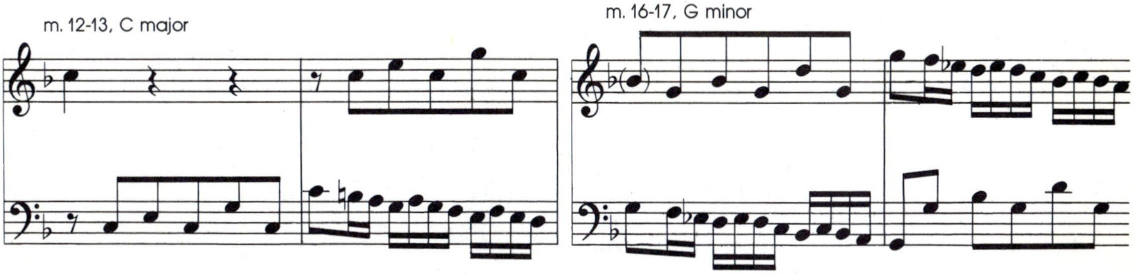

Near the end of the work the original tonic key of F major is reestablished, preparing the final cadence, which conclusively resolves tonal tension. The tonal plan of the piece may be graphed:

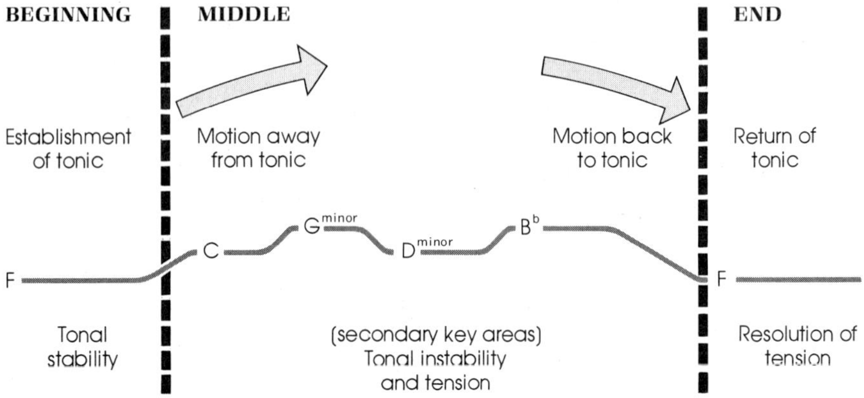

Chopin's *E Minor Prelude* remains essentially in the tonic key throughout, but in a highly chromatic context. The chords in the left hand continuously introduce notes foreign to the key (those indicated by accidentals):

We might expect a piece that remains in one key to sound simpler and more stable than the Bach Invention, but this is not the case, because the tonal center is much weaker in the Chopin work. The melody avoids the tonic note until near the end of the piece; the tonal center is established rather dimly at the outset and only occasionally reaffirmed by the chord progression. The chromatic tones are variable (and therefore do not produce specific modulation), but their unpredictability and sheer number cast shadows over the tonality. The pensive character of the piece stems largely from these coloristic chromatic inflections, and from the way the harmony hovers uneasily between tonal definition and uncertainty throughout most of the work. The tonality becomes clearer near the end, but Chopin delays its ultimate affirmation until the final chord. Only there do the melody and harmony come together on the tonic note.

These two pieces illustrate that tonality is not a single style of music, but rather a broad *method* of pitch organization that has made possible a wide variety of styles. A tonic may be affirmed unequivocally, or it may merely be suggested until brought to focus at the end of a work. Composers of the late 19th century often weakened the tonic still further, sometimes beginning and ending a piece in different keys. Such music contains no single tonic reference pitch, but rather a continuous series of tonal shifts, as well as "floating" chromatic passages not heard in any specific key. It was a relatively small but historically very important step from such "twilight" tonal works to the ultimate abandonment of tonality by many early 20th-century composers. A rubber band may be stretched very far and still snap back. If we stretch it far enough, however, it will break. The same is true of tonality, and of any other method of musical organization.

Tonal Organization in the 20th Century

The major–minor tonal system dominated Western music for over 250 years, and it remains the basis of most popular as well as much concert music. The vast repertoire of brilliant and expressive works composed according to tonal principles has made tonality seem a natural and inevitable system to many people. Several theorists have attempted to prove that tonality is in some way based upon inherent physical laws of nature, and that other methods of pitch organization are an "incomplete" or "transitional" forerunner of the "more perfect" tonal system.

To most present-day composers, performers, and listeners, however, such speculations are unconvincing. It seems unlikely that music—or any other art form—must follow a single predetermined course of evolution. It seems even less likely as we become more aware of the diversity of musical styles that exist in different cultures throughout the world. Particular styles and principes of pitch organization develop gradually from musical practice; they become—for a time—common elements, because they provide an effective framework through which composers and performers can communicate their unique musical ideas. These principles seem "inevitable" only when we hear them used in a convincing way in individual works.

The early years of the 20th century marked a watershed in the tonal organization of music, and the end of a common musical practice. Many composers attempted to build upon the tonal tradition, employing familiar scales, the concept of a central tone, and patterns of tension and resolution, but in new and freer ways. Others, however, felt that their musical ideas no longer could be contained within this system, and that new types of pitch organization were necessary to free their imaginations.

The 20th century has been an age of musical pluralism. Composers have pursued several alternative types of pitch organization. Probably the most basic distinction that can be made in contemporary concert music and jazz is between those works still based on specific scales with a central tone, and those that make equal use of all the chromatic pitches. Works of enduring quality have been created in both ways, and neither is necessarily the "musical mainstream" or "path of the future."

Depending upon one's personal viewpoint, the lack of a common practice and the coexistence of many disparate pitch styles may seem a symptom of confusion, or a sign of vitality. The major new types of pitch treatment, which we will examine in later chapters, represent serious new alternatives to traditional types of musical structure. Music—like all art forms—has always been a dynamic activity, its language and outward forms continuously changing. The rate of change has accelerated in the present century, leaving many people wondering what happened.

An original, compelling work of art can result only when the artist finds the materials of his or her craft fresh and stimulating. The joy of discovery is an integral part of music and one of its greatest satisfactions. For some composers, this joy occurs through *rediscovery:* finding new possibilities and avenues of exploration in traditional scales and pitch systems. For others, discovery means the creation of original new ways of organizing sounds which result, almost as a byproduct, as they work out the internal tonal logic and structure of specific works.

Debussy once observed, "Music is a very young art, from the point of view of technique as well as knowledge." This feeling holds true for the best composers and musicians of all periods. There are many musical avenues awaiting exploration, discovery, and rediscovery. For those involved in this exploration, whether as composers, performers, or listeners, music is as young an art today as it was for Bach or Debussy.

Terms and Concepts for Review

- pitch
- scale
  - chromatic scale
  - major scale
  - minor scale
- tonality
- tonic
- key
- leading tone
- diatonic and chromatic styles
- modulation
- notation
  - staff
  - treble clef
  - bass clef
  - interval
  - octave
  - half step
  - whole step
  - accidentals
  - key signature

Chapter 3
Melody

Melody is the element of music we comprehend most instinctively. It is generally what arrests our attention in a piece and what we remember when a performance is over. If rhythm is the lifeblood of music, melody is its voice.

It is curious that although melody is common to every musical period and culture, relatively little of substance has been written about it. A glance through the stacks of any well-stocked music library will reveal truckloads of books on harmony, instruments, singing, and music history, but only a few slender, moldering volumes on melody. Perhaps because our perception of melody is largely intuitive, it is a subject that resists study. Listeners may agree that a particular melody is "powerful" or "beautiful" but are hard-pressed to say precisely how or why it evokes this response. Few would dispute cellist Pablo Casals' assertion that, "The heart of a melody can never be put down on paper." Composers face a similar paradox. Igor Stravinsky noted that, "Of all the elements of music, melody is the most accessible, and for the composer, the least capable of acquisition." Richard Strauss expressed the same sentiment in more euphoric terms, finding melodic ideas "the greatest of divine gifts, not to be compared with any other."

The standard definition of melody is "a succession of tones in rhythm." This seems a dreary description of so rich and varied a phenomenon. One problem with it is that we rarely are aware of pitches and rhythms as distinct elements in a melody. They are not merely combined, but are inseparable features of a single design. When a melody comes to rest, for example, the quality of this cadence is affected equally by its rhythmic emphasis, by the particular pitch of the cadence tone, and by the way this pitch is approached. Melody shapes pitch and rhythm into an expressive whole.

A melody is made up of several phrases, each of which ends with a cadence. These phrases present melodic ideas, expand upon them, and bring them to conclusion. Individual tones are related to one another by means of a tonal framework. Most often, the tones revolve around a center pitch. In tonal music, a cadence on any note other than the tonic will sound inconclusive. In many 20th-century melodies, patterned *groups* of pitches or intervals, rather than a single reference tone, unify the pitch motion. But the special quality of a melody—what we respond to when we hear it—depends less on its particular pitch framework than on the unique design and continuity it creates within that framework. In this chapter we will survey different styles and types of melodies, and seek a fuller understanding of the particular ways in which they speak to us.

Gymnopédie No. 1 ***by Erik Satie, orchestrated by Claude Debussy***

Record Set Side 1, Band 1

The most winning quality of Satie's melody is its simplicity of expression. The tune employs only the seven tones of the minor scale. There is no embellishment or complication of ideas. Each phrase presents a particular shading of one musical thought.

The first three phrases are linked into a unit. Each is fragmentary in itself; but together, they comprise the starting point, continuation, and fulfillment of a single melodic design. The opening phrase begins on the tonic, descends four steps down the scale to the pitch D, circles around this temporary tonal goal, and comes to rest on it:

First phrase

Second phrase

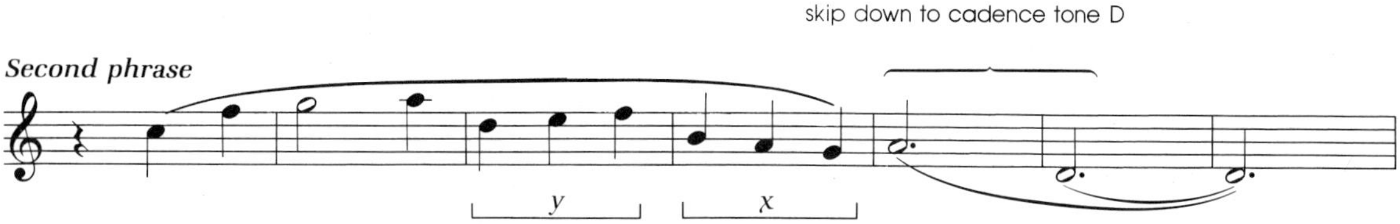

Third phrase

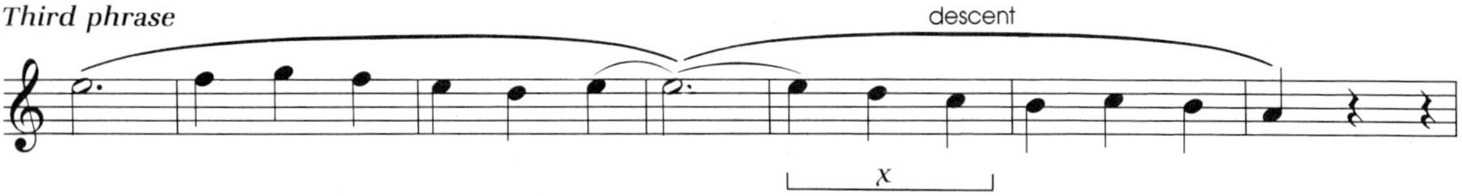

Prominent features of the pitch motion include three-note descending and ascending figures (labeled *x* and *y*), and a skip (a large interval) down to the cadential note.

The second phrase incorporates each of these features and ends on the same scale tone (D), one octave lower. It is related to the first phrase, carrying the thought further but maintaining its original quality. The third phrase rounds out the design. At the end of this phrase, the melody completes the descent down the scale with which it began. This leads to a more conclusive cadence on the tonic note. In the second half of the melody, these three phrases are repeated with minor alterations.

"When the Bells Justle" from Time Cycle by Lukas Foss

Record Set Side 2, Band 5

This song was written in 1960 to a text by A. E. Housman:

> When the bells justle in the tower
> The hollow night amid
> Then on my tongue the taste is sour
> of all I ever did.

The phrases of the vocal melody are separated by orchestral interludes. The melody employs no fixed scale and has no center tone. Instead, specific patterns of intervals are repeated and joined into associated phrases. A group of four tones provides a unifying point of departure and return. This melodic pattern is stated, amplified with additional tones, and shortened rhythmically during four opening phrases:

First phrase

Second phrase

The melody moves in large skips, rather than in scale steps, as it evokes the quality of bells. The pitches are related only to the pattern they form, rather than to a reference pitch. The melodic pattern gains structural significance, and becomes memorable, through varied repetition. It undergoes changes but remains recognizable. As yet the melody has little sense of direction, but it is imprinting its principal idea. This pitch pattern will return twice in altered form later in the song:

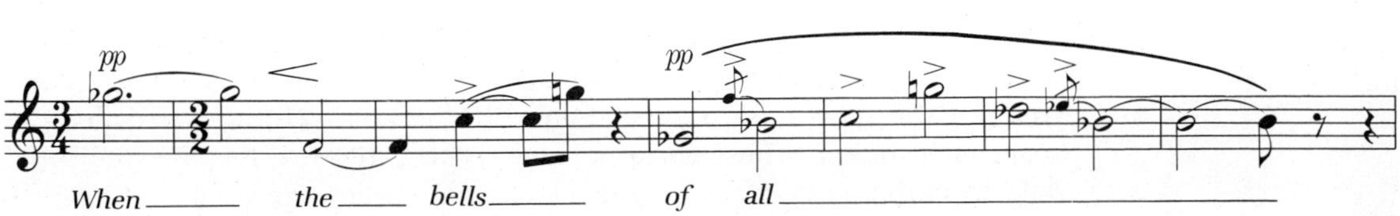

It also occurs in more rapid rhythms in an instrumental figure at the very beginning and end of the piece.

Between these recurrences, a series of new melodic figures is introduced, repeated, and varied in the vocal line. The figures grow out of the poetic imagery, and occur on the words "justle," "hollow night," "on my tongue," and "sour" (a nasty little figure that drives home the bitterness of the verse).

Rather than the unfolding of a single idea as in the *Gymnopédie,* this song projects a series of melodic ideas welded into a chain. There are frequent changes in pacing and mood. The vocal line grows more intense, culminating in a forceful climax ("of *all*"), as it mirrors the increasing anguish of the text; the "innocent" sound of ringing bells provokes a stabbing feeling of emptiness; a life's dreams have not been fulfilled. Through all of this, a melodic thread hangs together. Coherence results from immediate repetition of each new figure and the periodic return of the original vocal pattern.

Melodic Contour

The term *line* is often used as a synonym for melody. As the tones of a melody move up and down, they create a musical line with a particular shape, overall direction, and quality of motion. The **contour** of a melody is the curve, or profile, of this line.

First phrase

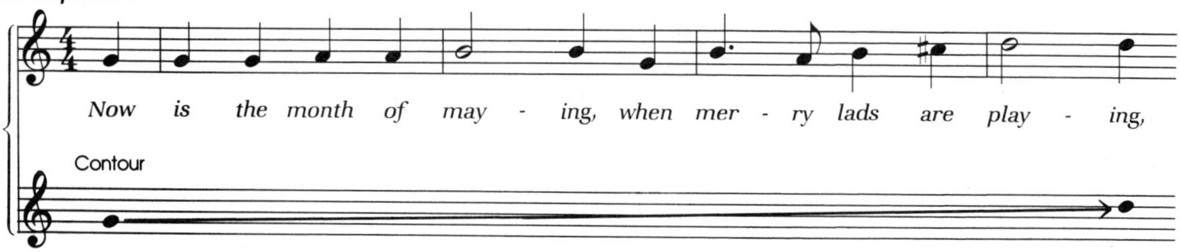

Answering phrase

At the beginning of Morley's song, the melody ascends in two short phrases. In a longer answering phrase, the contour descends twice, overshooting the tonic in skips the first time, then mirroring (in reverse order) the scalewise motion of the earlier phrases. The contour reinforces the tonal pattern of the melody, producing a balanced design typical of many songs:

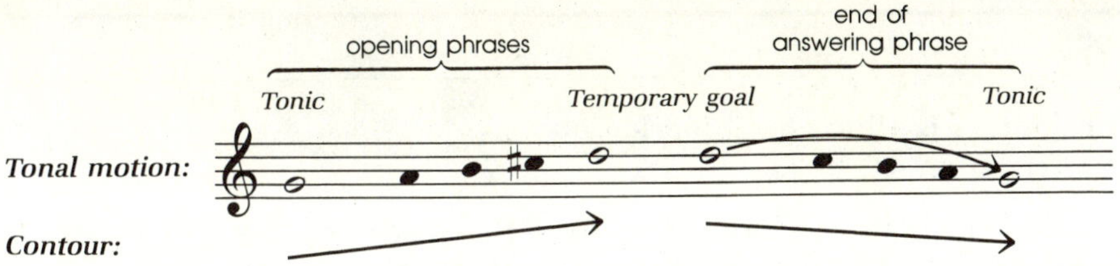

Some melodies have a more complex curve. The flute theme from Debussy's *Prelude to the Afternoon of a Faun,* for example, contains many small "waves." There is no strong direction to specific tones, but a series of subtle nuances:

The piece is in E major, but this tonal center is not asserted unequivocally until the very end. Throughout most of the piece, the melody hovers *around* the major scale, but the tonal framework frequently is obscured by many chromatic notes. The undulating nature of the melodic contour, which bobs up and down in ripples rather than moving in a sharply etched line, mirrors the unsettled tonal quality of the piece.

Melodic Continuity

Continuity is the unity of a melody—the way it develops a single idea, or links ideas together into a coherent design. A common means of continuity is motivic construction. A melodic **motive** is a short figure, with a characteristic pitch pattern and rhythm, that is repeated many times. Motivic melodies grow from one or two such "seeds" into a larger design. The two motives in Bach's *F Major Invention* contrast not only in rhythm (the second moving twice as fast as the first), but in pitch motion as well; motive 1 ascends in skips, while motive 2 descends in scale steps:

Frequent changes in direction, which result from the ping-pong alternation of these motives, give the melodies an animated momentum.

Prelude in E Minor *by Frédéric Chopin*

Record Set Side 2, Band 2

The essentially diatonic melody of this piece unfolds in two long, related phrases. The subdued quality of the first phrase results from its hesitant melodic motion. Reiteration of a two-note falling motive produces a concentration of mood, with little sense of direction. The melody encompasses a very small range of pitches, exceeded only in two brief ornamental flurries (measures 9 and 12). The underlying contour is a very slow descent through four scale steps (the circled notes), decorated and prolonged by motivic repetition:

Melody

Underlying contour

The second phrase begins like a replay of the first, then undergoes a critical change in character:

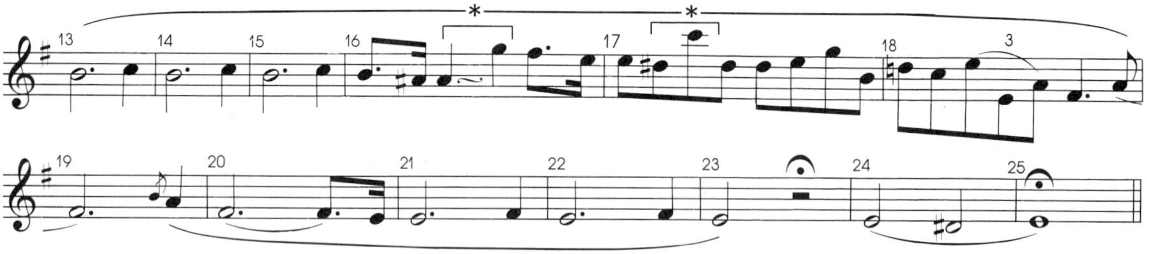

At measure 16, the melody finally bursts the narrow pitch and rhythmic confines of the two-note motive, moving in large leaps (*) to a climactic high note, followed by a gradual descent to the tonic note E. The motive reappears, and the tonic note is repeated several times, as the tension of the climactic outburst is slowly resolved. The two-note motive is the pivotal idea of the melody, its source of unity and basic character. The design of the melody, however, centers around the sudden accumulation and gradual dissipation of energy in the second phrase. What began as a reverie turns into a forceful personal statement.

Listening

Prelude to Tristan and Isolde *by Richard Wagner*

Record Set Side 10, Band 2

Wagner's prelude to the opera *Tristan and Isolde* is an expressive chromatic work that builds gradually but inevitably to a powerful climax. The principal melodic line has a continuous, unbroken quality—a sort of "endless melody" seldom interrupted by cadences. The melody grows like a snowball around an opening motive. This idea spawns a series of related new motives, which are similar in rhythm and contour:

Principal motives in the Prelude to Tristan and Isolde. *Dotted lines indicate similarities between motives.*

The new motives are introduced gradually. Each returns from time to time, echoing and re-echoing the same melodic patterns. The several motives function like variations of the original idea, which grows ever richer as it takes new forms. Something is always being added, but nothing is ever lost.

The contour of the melody creates the impression of an almost continuous ascent, rising to new heights, falling back briefly, then surging higher again:

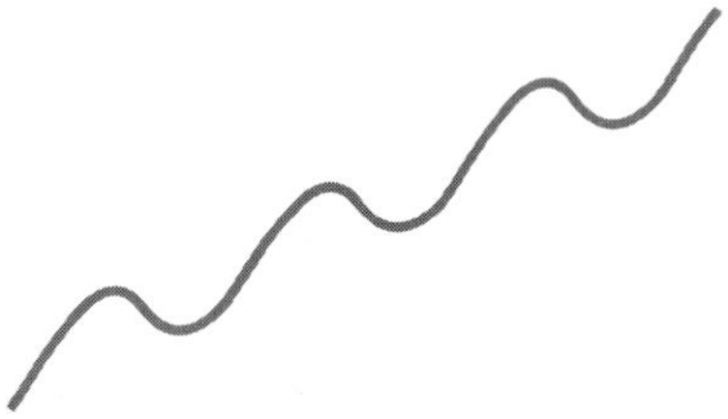

The sense of perpetual upward motion gives the melody an impassioned, searching quality. It never seems to arrive at a clear tonal goal or point of rest. This enables Wagner to sustain emotional tension throughout the piece. It is a skillful illusion; if the melody actually did ascend continuously, it soon would soar out of the range of the instruments. Wagner achieves this illusion by means of melodic **sequences**—repetitions of a motive at different pitch levels. In this piece, repetition of motives almost always occurs at a higher pitch level. It is the pattern of notes, rather than each individual note, which climbs ever higher:

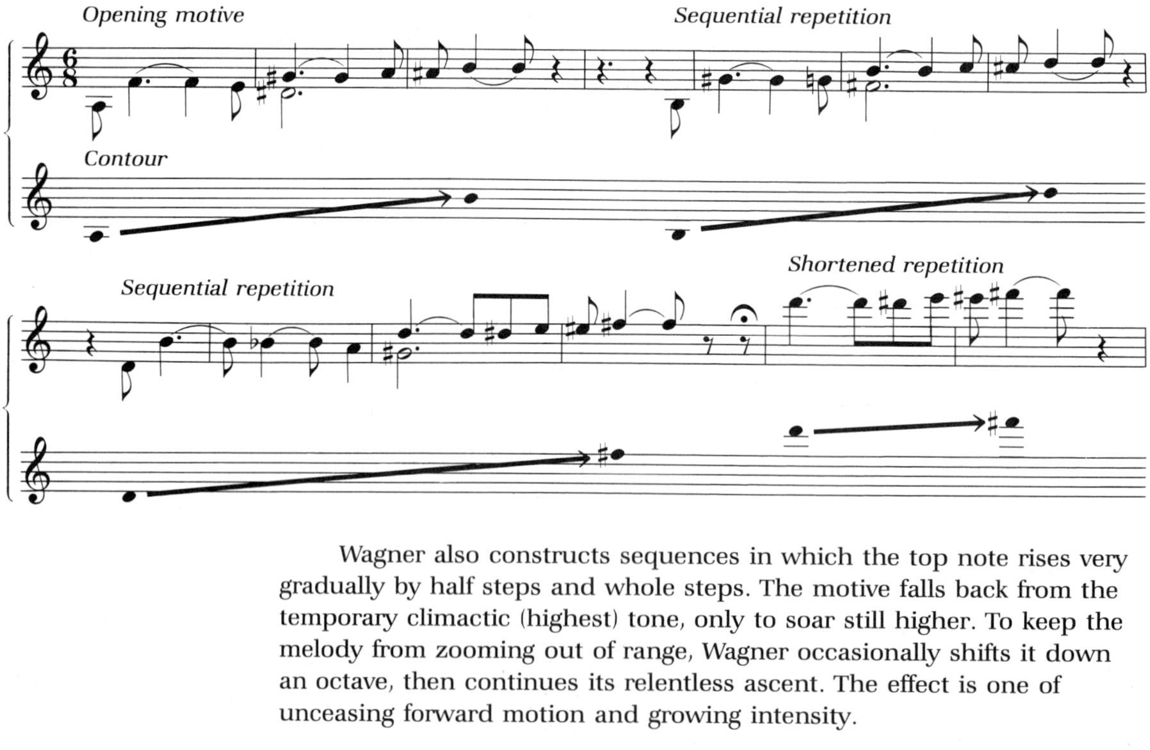

Wagner also constructs sequences in which the top note rises very gradually by half steps and whole steps. The motive falls back from the temporary climactic (highest) tone, only to soar still higher. To keep the melody from zooming out of range, Wagner occasionally shifts it down an octave, then continues its relentless ascent. The effect is one of unceasing forward motion and growing intensity.

There are many techniques other than motivic construction by which a composer can achieve melodic unity. In "When the Bells Justle," for example, several melodic ideas of quite different character are associated to form a larger design. In "Scarborough Fair," the individual phrases of the melody share common features and create a simple, balanced design.

Listening

"Scarborough Fair/Canticles" transcribed by Simon and Garfunkel

Record Set Side 2, Band 7

The traditional English folk song "Scarborough Fair" is best known today through the transcription (arrangement) of Paul Simon and Art Garfunkel. In their performance, a second traditional tune, "Canticles," is interwoven in the second vocal part.

The principal melody, which is based upon the same modal scale as *Salve Regina,* consists of four related phrases. While there are no repeated motives, melodic motion between the first and fifth scale steps (marked *) occurs in each phrase, a unifying tonal feature. Melodic skips at the beginnings of phrases are followed by smoother, stepwise motion at the ends. The phrases are similar in contour, beginning with a brief ascent, followed by a longer descent.

The opening phrase establishes E as the center tone, beginning and ending on this note. A melodic leap into the second measure stresses the key word of the phrase, "going." In the second phrase, the melody moves into a higher range, initiating melodic motion away from the center tone. The tune encircles the fifth scale step (B), and sounds as though it had "stepped up" temporarily to a higher level.

The third phrase presents the pivotal line of the text, and contains the greatest melodic motion. The upper octave E—the highest note in the piece— is repeated on the key word "remember," followed by a continuously descending contour, as the thought seems to trail off. The final phrase is similar to the first. The melody returns to the original lower pitch range. The key word "once" (implying "no longer") is stressed by a melodic leap.

The wistful quality of this song results partly from the prevailing descending contour within each phrase, and from the balanced arc-like sweep of the melody as a whole:

This quality is enhanced by the simple, flowing rhythmic pattern, the modal scale (similar to the quality of minor), and the nature of the text, which begins with "small talk" before expressing its central statement—that the singer's former love is still very much in his thoughts.

Melodic Themes

Longer compositions usually feature one, two, or more complete melodies which are developed and recalled later in the work. Melodies that serve as the basis for longer works are called **themes.** Themes may be short, like the four-measure flute melody that opens Debussy's *Prelude to the Afternoon of a Faun.* More often they contain several phrases, and incorporate a series of melodic ideas that can be quoted and expanded separately or in new combinations. In general, themes mark the stable beginning and ending points of a composition, presenting melodic ideas in their simplest, most balanced form. They contrast with other passages in which the tonal center shifts rapidly and the melody becomes fragmented.

Listening

Theme from the second movement of the* Piano Concerto No. 21 in C Major *by Wolfgang Amadeus Mozart

Record Set Side 3, Band 1

Listen only up to the entrance of the piano. This slow movement begins with an evocative theme, presented in its entirety by the violins. The theme recurs in varied form throughout the movement. It consists of four ideas (labeled A, B, C and D) of contrasting length and character, but with a continuity of expression. Each new idea seems to grow out of the preceding one, providing an added dimension and particular coloring to the poignant quality of the melody. This quality is all the more effective because it is understated.

Idea A unfolds in two phrases. In the first (measures 2–4), rhythmic motion is jagged, featuring an alternation of long and short durations. The second phrase "answers" this motion with a more even and relaxed rhythmic flow. The phrases are related by their similar contours—up in skips, then down in steps. They form the "head" (the beginning) of the theme, establishing the F major tonality and the basic structural character (restrained, balanced) that will serve as a point of departure and return for the rest of the melody.

Idea B is a brief but arresting fragment, notable for its large skips, which open up a wide new range and give the melody a sense of breadth. Idea C introduces further complication: chromatic tones that briefly nudge the melody into minor. A two-note motive is sequentially repeated, one step lower in each measure. This motive is derived from the first two notes of the melody.

The two phrases of idea D restore melodic balance and stability. The melody sinks back into F major, and the contour descends in simple scale steps. Original figures are recalled (measures 17 and 20, for example, are derived from measure 3). A full stop on the tonic, the first and only strong melodic cadence, brings the theme to completion.

The most basic characteristic of a melody is its sense of line. Melodies are memorable because of their shape and particular quality of motion. We may or may not be able to remember and whistle the exact notes of a melody: this depends upon the complexity of its pitch and rhythmic motion, and on whether it presents simple or highly embellished patterns. What we do respond to and remember is the essence of a melody—its unique design and character.

Contemporary composers are exploring new ways of defining musical line. Although their melodies at first may seem complex, this is often due to rapid surface motion, new types of pitch structure, and vivid tone colors. The underlying design of these melodies is sometimes surprisingly transparent, and may be similar in essence to that of the most ancient music we know. Stripped of metrical rhythms, broader patterns of tension and release, and developmental expansion of ideas, some contemporary melodies present an elemental expression, appealing to our "collective subconscious" memory of the roots of all music.

Listening

"Vocalise (. . . for the end of time)" from **Vox Balaenae** *by George Crumb*

Record Set Side 2, Band 6

George Crumb (b. 1929) often writes melodic lines that are non-developmental. These melodies have no clear overall design, but are based instead on an almost ritualistic reiteration of internal patterns. Crumb treats sound color as a principal element of musical interest. The particular color with which a line is played or sung may be as important to its emotional quality as the pitches and rhythms.

The opening movement of *Vox Balaenae* (1971) features a rhapsodic solo flute line, employing the unusual technique of *vocalise.* The performer sings (rather than blows) into the flute while playing, producing an eerie, emotionally-charged tone color. The long, chantlike phrases of the melody contain much internal repetition and several related motives. They have an incantation-like quality, and sound like improvisational variations on a scale pattern.

The opening two thirds of the movement (up until the piano entrance) is based entirely on a six-tone scale characterized by half steps:

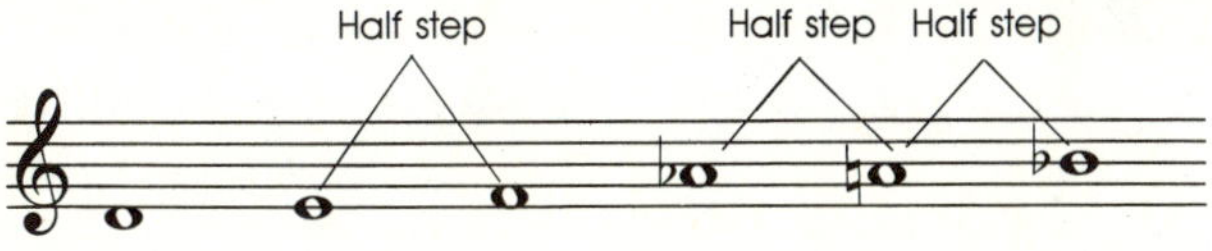

The melody uses only these six tones, always in the same octave. As a result, the melody has a very limited range and continuously repeats the same small intervals. The phrases are similar in construction; most begin on the pitch D, rise, encircle, and frequently reattack the pitch A♭ throughout the middle of the phrase, then fall and cadence on the pitch E.

Contour of most phrases

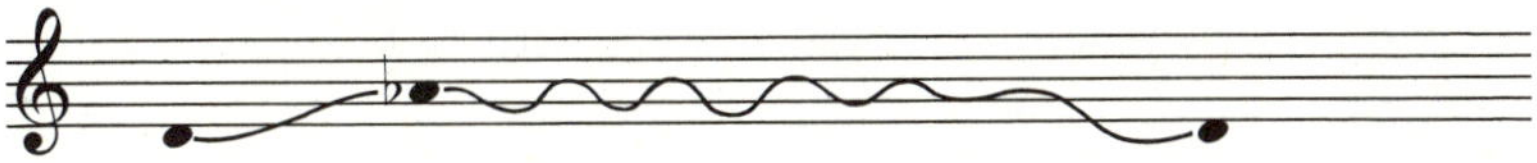

There is a primeval, ceremonial quality to the resulting line, which seems to exist outside of time. The melody is imbued with an emotional intensity just below the surface of the music. This tension remains constant, rather than coming to a climax and resolution. The melody is not "going anywhere"; its fundamental shape is established immediately and recurs cyclically. Each phrase seems to begin the melody again, rather than growing out of the preceding phrase. The melody is structured not around a progression of contrasting or related motives, but through focus on a single design, which grows more insistent and haunting through repetition.

Near the end of the movement, the flute introduces a new six-tone motive rapidly repeated in a high register. Through sequential repetition this gust-like figure gradually descends to the original low pitch level. A shortened final variation of the principal idea returns, rounding off the movement.

Terms and Concepts for Review

melodic line
contour
melodic continuity
motive
sequence
theme

Chapter 4
Harmony

When different pitches are sung or played at the same time, they form harmony. The basis of harmony is the **chord,** a group of three or more tones sounded together. When we hear a chord we are less aware of its separate tones than of the composite sound they form; we hear a chord as a single sound with a particular harmonic quality, which is determined by its construction.

Harmony is so much a part of our musical heritage that many people are surprised to learn it is a comparatively recent resource, and one rarely found in other musical cultures. Harmony is a distinguishing feature of Western music. It is not present, for example, in the gamelan performance *Baris,* which achieves richness of sound through other means, primarily rhythmic. The origins of harmony can be traced back about a thousand years. However, the systematic exploration of harmonic resources did not begin until the later 1600s, as the principles of tonality were becoming standardized.

In tonal music, it is most often harmony, rather than melody, that creates the formal design of a work. As we listen to a melody we generally are most aware of its shape (line), and only secondarily of its tonal framework. Harmony makes this tonal framework explicit; it makes complete a tonal progression that is merely outlined in the melody. Melody and harmony are closely related in Western music. Harmony has grown out of melody, and, as we shall see, it is permeated by melody.

The Origins of Harmony

Musical **texture** is a broad concept that refers to the particular way in which the various elements of music (rhythms, melodies, harmonies, tone colors) are combined and given focus in a work. The texture of a composition determines where the musical interest is concentrated: on melody, chords, or some other feature of the music. In most works, one or another of these elements is most prominent. In the *Gymnopédie* it is the melody, in *Baris* it is rhythm, and in Oliveros' *Sound Patterns* it is color. During a first hearing of a work, our attention tends to focus on this primary textural element. On subsequent hearings, we become increasingly conscious of the secondary elements, which add richness and depth to the musical fabric.

The simplest and oldest type of texture is unaccompanied melody, or **monophonic** texture. The term monophonic is derived from the Greek words for "single tone"—that is, one tone at a time. Both *Salve Regina* and the flute "Vocalise" from *Vox Balaenae* are examples of monophonic music. Unaccompanied melody was common to almost every ancient society, and some musical cultures have remained monophonic. Many of these cultures—particularly in Africa and Asia—have developed highly sophisticated rhythmic and melodic practices, far more complex than those to which we are accustomed.

Western music has developed along a different course. Composers have generally been less interested in exploring intricate melodic and rhythmic patterns than in creating expressive combinations of simultaneous tones. We do not know exactly when or where this practice began, but it marked an important turning point in musical style. The earliest known examples of rudimentary harmony were improvisational, that is, added in performance rather than composed. Were we to hear them today, they would sound disarmingly simple. Sometime around or before the year 900, singers began to reinforce certain Gregorian melodies with one or more added lines. The added part(s) generally duplicated the given melody at a fixed pitch interval:

Lacking independent contours and rhythms of their own, these added lines were not separate melodies but copies of the original. As this practice evolved over the next three centuries, however, the added voices became increasingly distinct from the chant melody. They began to assume an independent contour and rhythmic shape. The musical result was the simultaneous presentation of separate melodies.

When two or more independent melodies are performed at the same time, the musical texture is termed **polyphonic** (meaning "many tones"). Music of the later Middle Ages and the Renaissance is polyphonic; so, too, is much later music. In polyphonic music each line is a complete melody in its own right. As the lines are sounded together, however, they also form harmonies. The separate melodies and the harmonies they form comprise, respectively, the linear and vertical dimensions of a musical texture:

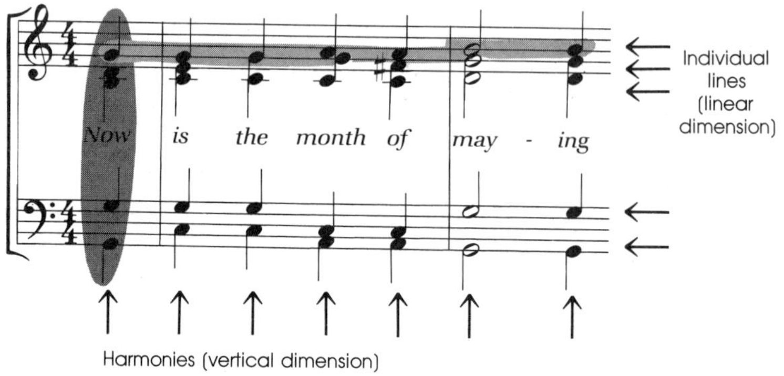

In polyphonic music, harmonies result from the interaction of simultaneous melodic lines. Harmonic considerations, however, influence a composer's choice of tones within each line. If the texture is to make sense, the harmonies cannot be random; they must form a coherent sequence.

With the evolution of tonality during the 17th century, the harmonic dimension of texture gained new importance. **Harmony**—the systematic organization of chords into logical progressions—developed out of polyphonic practice. In tonal music, harmonies are carefully controlled, so that each chord is heard in relation to the tonic pitch. Like polyphony, harmony consists of simultaneous melodic lines. In harmonic textures, however, we are more aware of the chords these lines create than of their separate melodic shapes.

In harmonic music, melodic interest generally is concentrated in one line (usually the top part), which we hear as the melody. The other lines move more or less together, usually in slower rhythms. Textures in which a principal melody is supported by chords are called **homophonic.** A song accompanied by piano or guitar is a familiar example. Many of the works we have listened to so far, including *Gladiolus Rag,* "Scarborough Fair," and *Gymnopédie No. 1,* are homophonic.

Gymnopédie No. 1

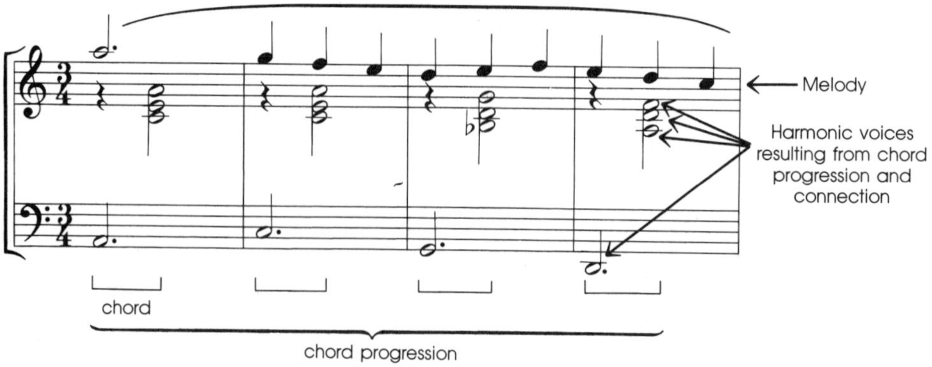

Even in simple homophonic textures, the harmonic voices, no matter how subordinate, must make sense as independent lines. Otherwise the harmony will sound amateurish.

Polyphony and harmony are not opposing principles, because they are based on the same musical concern: a striving for expressive lines and harmonies. They differ only in emphasis. In this sense they form a continuum of musical practice. The texture of many works features both strong independence of lines and vigorous harmonic motion, but usually one of these elements will be more prominent.

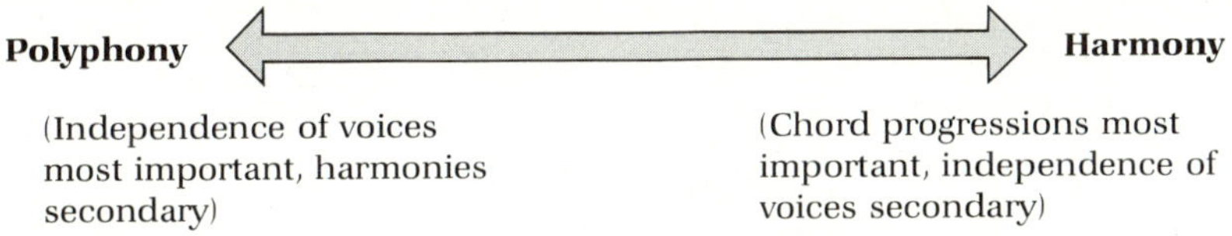

In Bach's *Two-Part Invention in F Major* we are most aware of the melodic independence of the two lines, as they imitate and exchange ideas and chase each other through the work. The texture is polyphonic. Neither part ever sounds like an accompaniment to the other. Each voice maintains a distinct melodic shape and a quality of individual freedom. At the same time, however, the two melodies are so constructed that, together, they create an implied chord progression that clarifies the cadences, modulations, and ultimate tonal unity of the work.

The texture of Chopin's *Prelude in E Minor* is homophonic. Under the principal melodic line, three lower voices form a progression of chords. These chords support the melody, but they also color our perception of it. The opening phrase of the melody would be dull and rather threadbare by itself—try imagining the melody as a solo line, without harmonic accompaniment. Only as it grinds against the harmony does this melody develop a cutting edge and sense of direction.

In Morley's "Now is the Month of Maying" the separate vocal lines and the chords they form are more or less equally prominent at the beginning of the piece. The texture becomes more polyphonic, however, during the "Fa-la-la" flourishes.

Intervals: The Basis of Chords

An **interval** is the distance between two pitches. A chord is defined by the intervals it contains. Intervals are labeled by counting the number of letter names between two notes, counting the bottom tone as "one":

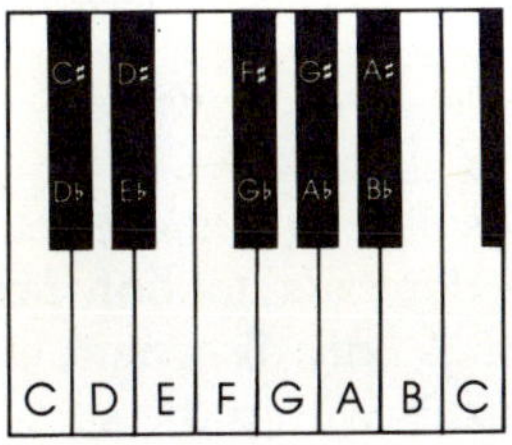

Intervals

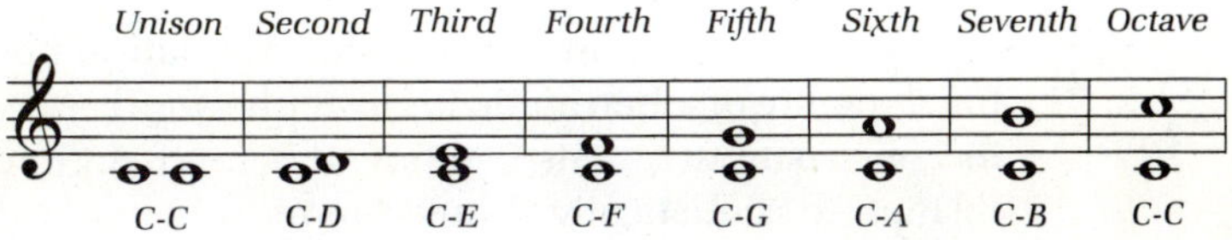

As we saw in the construction of scales, some intervals have two common forms. A second, for example, may be either a half step or a whole step. Seconds, thirds, sixths, and sevenths each have two common forms. The larger form is called a **major** interval, the smaller a **minor** interval. A major interval is always a half step larger than its corresponding minor interval. Major and minor thirds are particularly important in the construction of chords.

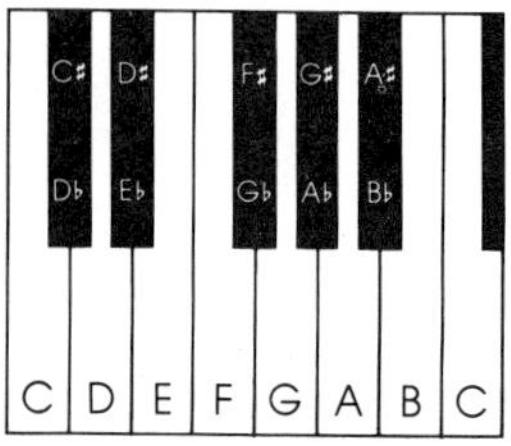

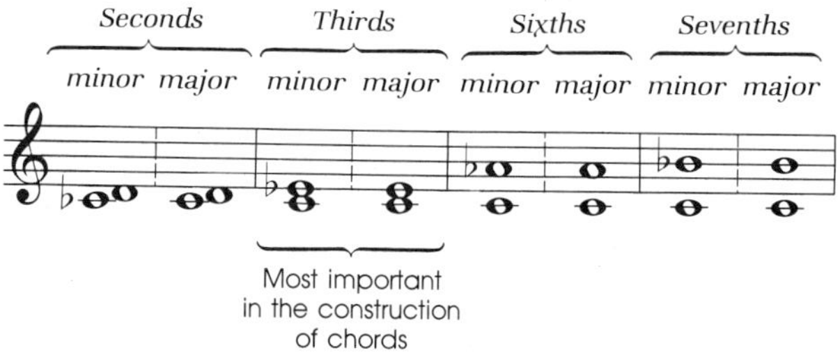

Consonance and Dissonance

Harmonic intervals can be divided into two groups. Some sound acoustically simple and at rest. These are termed **consonant** intervals. Others produce a denser, unstable harmonic quality; we hear an inner tension between the two notes. These are called **dissonant** intervals.

In tonal music, certain intervals are generally consonant. These include unisons, octaves, thirds, fifths and sixths, and often fourths. All other intervals are heard as dissonant.

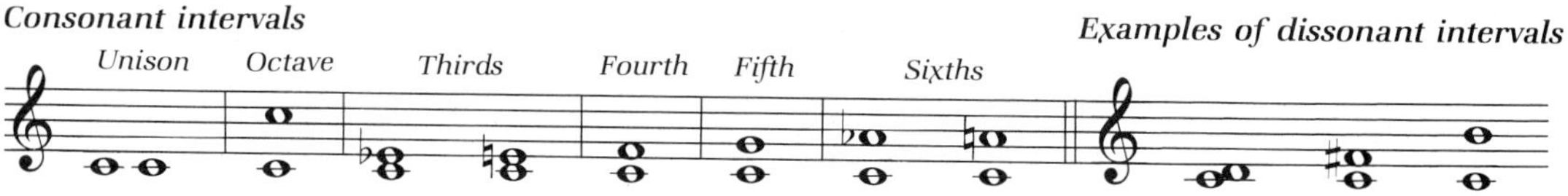

A dissonant interval **resolves** when one or both of the notes move to a new tone to create a consonant interval:

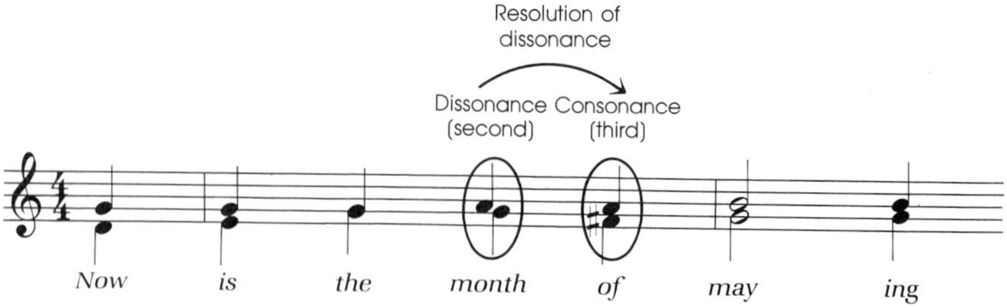

Consonance and dissonance are relative, not absolute, qualities. The tonal quality of a harmonic interval (the way it "feels") depends not only on its construction, but also on how it is used. An interval is only dissonant in relation to acoustically simpler, more consonant intervals within the same progression. Chords that are heard as dissonances in 17th-century music often function as consonances in the more complex styles of the 19th century. The way in which dissonance is defined and used is an important aspect of a musical style.

Triads

In tonal music, chords are built from the bottom up in intervals of thirds. The simplest and most common chord is the **triad.** A triad contains three tones: a bottom note, called the **root;** a tone a third higher, called the **third;** and a top note, another third higher, called the **fifth** because it forms the interval of a fifth with the root.

C Major triad

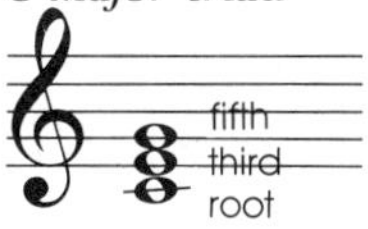

A triad can be constructed on any note of a major or minor scale, and is designated, in Roman numerals, by the scale step of its root:

Triads in the key of C Major

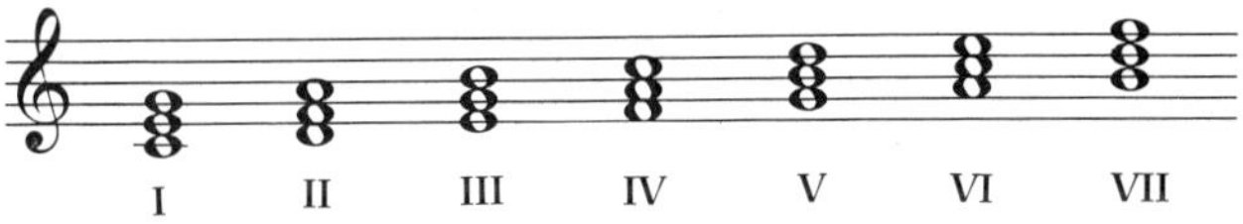

The three tones of a triad can be arranged in any order. The third or the fifth may appear in the bass (lowest) voice. Any or all of the tones may be **doubled** (sounded simultaneously) in various octaves. Doublings do not alter the identity or characteristic harmonic quality of a chord. Here are several possible arrangements of a C–E–G triad:

Doublings

Orchestral textures often double all the notes of a triad in several octaves, producing a rich, full sonority from a simple triad.

Triads frequently are incorporated into melodies. The root, third, and fifth of a chord are sounded in succession, sometimes many times each, producing a series of melodic skips. When the notes of a chord are played in melodic succession rather than together, they are called an **arpeggio.**

Brief arpeggios

Bach Invention in F

Longer arpeggio

Mozart Piano Concerto in C, *K. 467, Second movement*

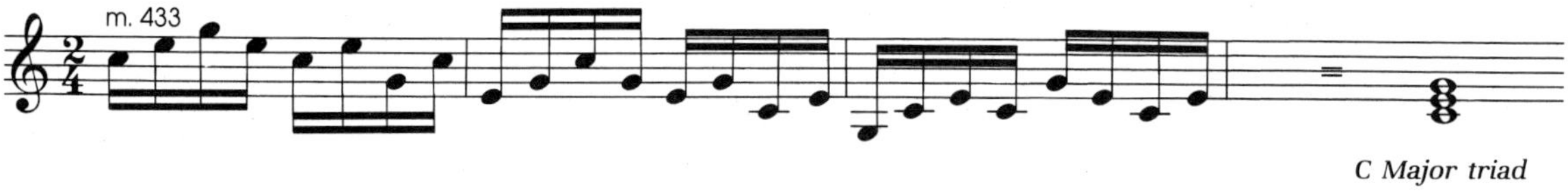

Major and Minor Triads

The harmonic quality of a chord is determined not only by the scale step in which the chord is built, but also by the intervals it contains. These intervals comprise the sonority, or characteristic sound, of the chord. In major keys, for example, the triads on I, IV, and V contain identical intervals. In each, the distance between the root and the third is a major third, while the distance between the third and the fifth is a minor third. Such chords are called **major triads** because in each case the third is major.

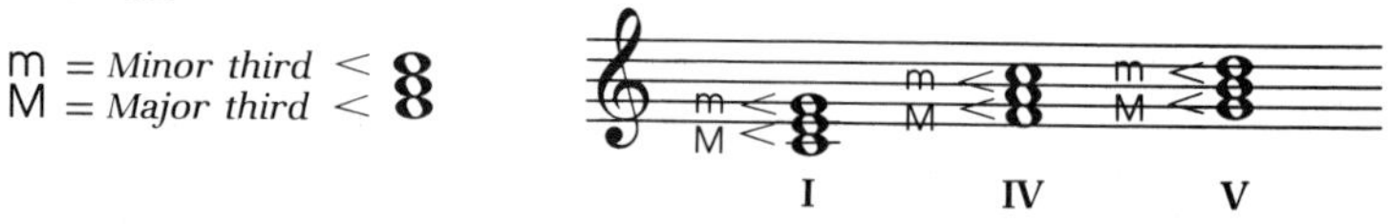

In the II, III, and VI triads, by contrast, the intervals are reversed, and the third is minor. This is the sonority of a **minor triad.**

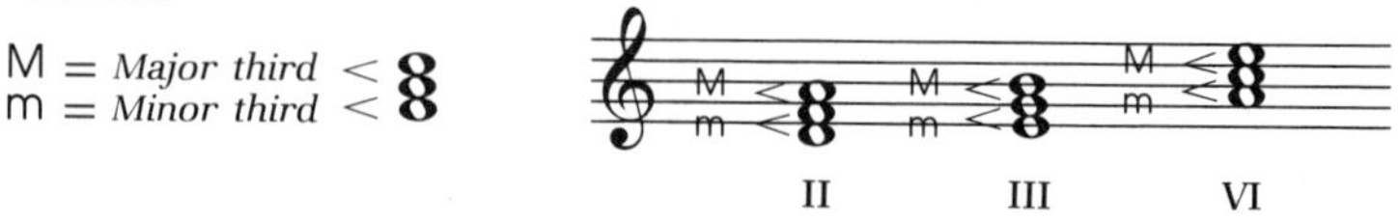

In minor keys, the tonic (I) chord is a minor triad.

Major and minor triads are consonant because they contain only consonant intervals (thirds and fifths). Other types of triads are also possible, but major and minor chords are by far the most common.

Tonic and Dominant Triads

In tonal harmony, the **tonic** triad is a stable reference chord. It is usually the first chord in a piece, and almost always is the final chord. The other chords *function* (are heard) with respect to the stable tonic. Chord progressions alternately pull away from the tonic, building tonal tension, and return, creating tonal completion and relaxation. Most triads have a consistent function. The II, IV, and VI chords, for example, generally direct the harmony away from the tonic.

The second most important triad in both major and minor keys is the **dominant** (V) chord. The dominant triad contains the leading tone and provides the strongest root motion back to the tonic. It is normally the chord that immediately precedes, and prepares, the return of the tonic triad.

Cadences

A **cadence** is a common melodic or harmonic pattern found at the end of most phrases. Cadences bring the music to a point of rest. In tonal music, the strength of a cadence—whether it sounds temporary or final—is influenced by melodic and rhythmic factors but is determined primarily by chord motion. A full stop, or conclusive cadence, results from the progression V–I at the end of a phrase. A half stop occurs when the cadential chord is some triad other than the tonic. The dominant triad is the most common cadential chord in half-stop cadences. By cadencing on the dominant, a composer initiates tonal motion back towards the tonic but stops short of full resolution.

Occasionally a chord progression will lead the listener to anticipate a full stop (V–I) cadence that never comes. The harmony moves to a dominant chord just before the end of a phrase. Instead of resolving to a tonic triad, however, the dominant chord moves unexpectedly ("deceptively") to some other chord. Such **deceptive cadences** actually heighten tonal tension rather than resolving it; the harmony circles around the tonic, then "jumps" somewhere else.

Mozart Piano Concerto No. 21 in C, Second movement

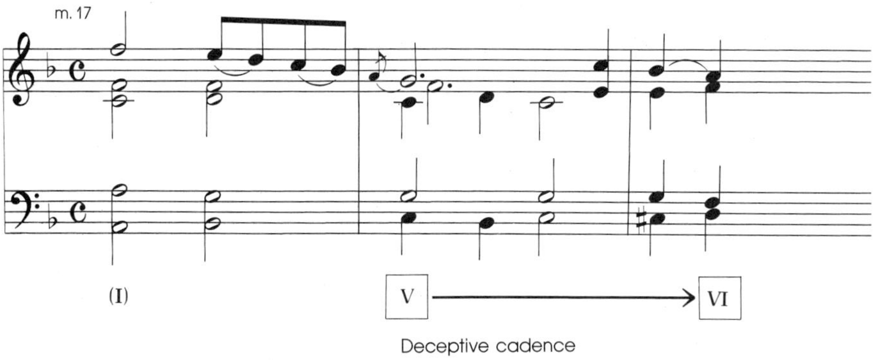

Simple Chord Progressions

Many folk tunes and familiar melodies are supported by simple chord progressions consisting of the alternation of only two or three chords. The harmonization of "Silent Night," for example, employs only the I, IV, and V chords of the major key. The only harmonic tension in the song results from a mild dissonance at "*hea*-venly":

"Silent Night"

Functional and Non-Functional Chords

In most music, the chords are not all equally important to the harmonic structure. Phrases are structured around **functional chords**—the tonic and those which produce a sense of motion (change) with respect to the tonic. Harmonic progressions pivot around these functional chords. Other chords are used to prolong and connect the functional harmonies. Connecting chords do not, by themselves, create any change with respect to the tonic, and are thus **non-functional.** They enrich the harmonic motion and give it a particular quality.

In simple tonal styles, most chords are functional. As a result, cadences are frequent. In more complex styles, only a few of the chords are functional.

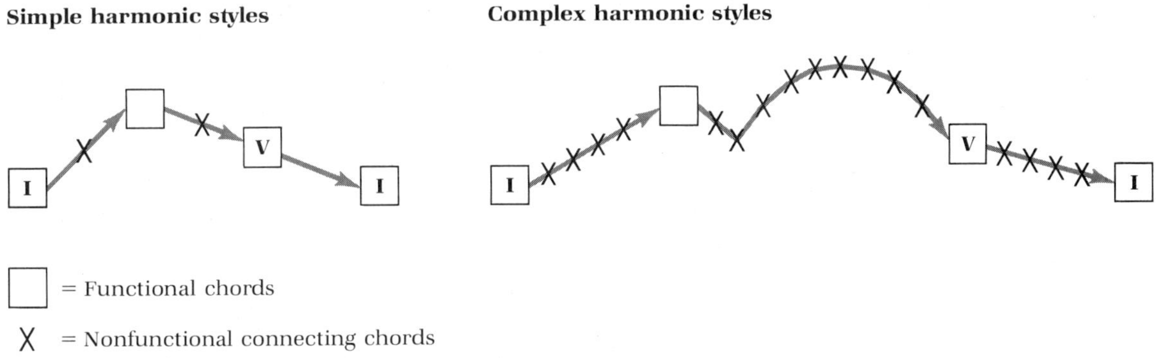

Seventh chords

All but the simplest harmonies include other types of chords in addition to triads. These more complex chords always contain at least one dissonant interval. (Major and minor triads are the only consonant chords.) The most common of these other sonorities is the **seventh chord.** Seventh chords are triads with an added note. The added note forms the interval of a seventh with the root:

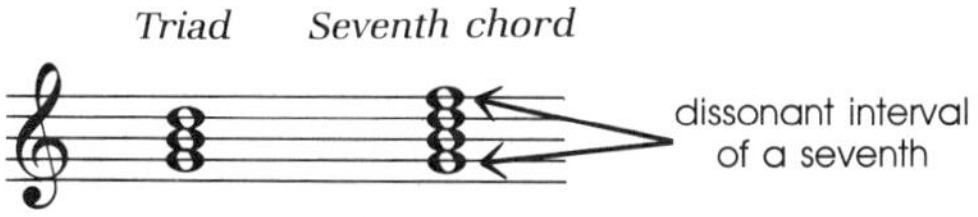

Sevenths can be added to any triad (though only rarely to the tonic) but are most common on the dominant:

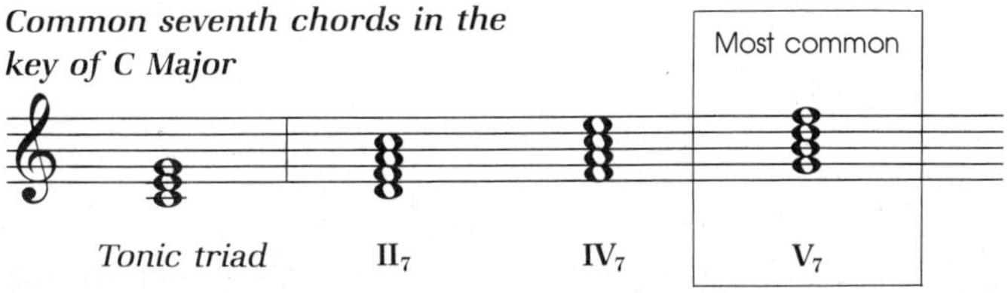

Addition of a seventh does not alter the function of a chord, but it does turn a consonant major or minor triad into a dissonant sonority. The dissonant interval produces harmonic tension and propels the harmony forward by requiring resolution to a consonant interval.

Theme from the second movement of the* Piano Concerto No. 21 in C Major *by Wolfgang Amadeus Mozart

Record Set Side 3, Band 1

Listen, once again, only up to the entrance of the piano. The texture of this theme is homophonic. The melody in the violins is supported by a chord progression in the lower strings. Wind instruments double the chord tones in a higher octave. The concerto as a whole is said to be in C major because that is the key of both outer movements. This contrasting slow movement, however, is in F major. F is the "home key" in which it begins and around which tonal motion is centered.

The theme divides into three harmonic units. The first, consisting of two phrases, is harmonically very simple; only two chords are used:

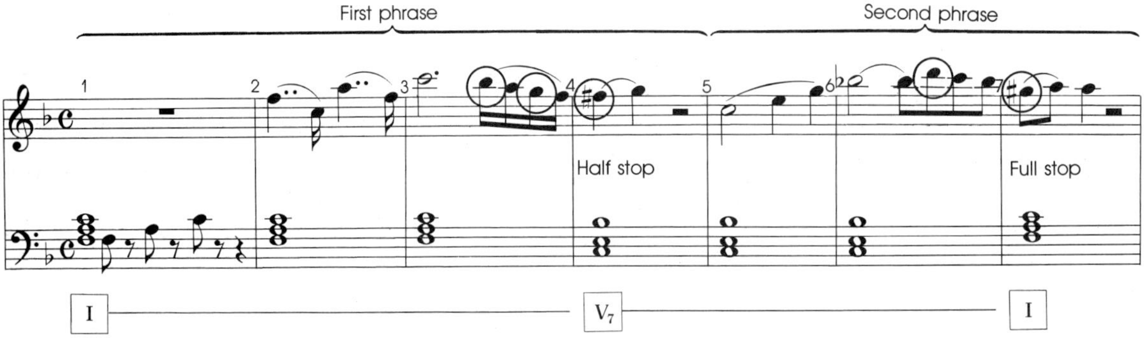

A tonic triad is prolonged for three measures. The harmony then moves directly to a V_7 chord in measure 4, creating a half stop. The V_7 chord, containing the dissonant note B♭, is also sustained for three measures. It resolves to a tonic triad, producing a stronger cadence. The two phrases firmly establish the F major tonality, pivoting between the two most important functional harmonies of this key.

Most of the notes in the melody duplicate the pitches of the harmony in a higher octave. The melody outlines a tonal progression (I–V_7–I) that is realized fully in the harmonic voices. The melody also incorporates occasional tones that are not part of the harmony; these notes are circled above. Called **non-harmonic** tones, they give the melody a more distinct and expressive contour. They also form momentary dissonances against the harmony, but resolve immediately by a step into chord tones. The circled F♯ in measure 4, for example, resolves up to G, the fifth of the V_7 chord.

The middle of the theme introduces tonal complication and tension. Mozart moves away from the tonic and delays its return. The harmony becomes more dissonant and chromatic. Dissonant non-harmonic tones are now sprinkled throughout the harmonic lines as well as the melody. (Nonfunctional connecting chords are marked X.)

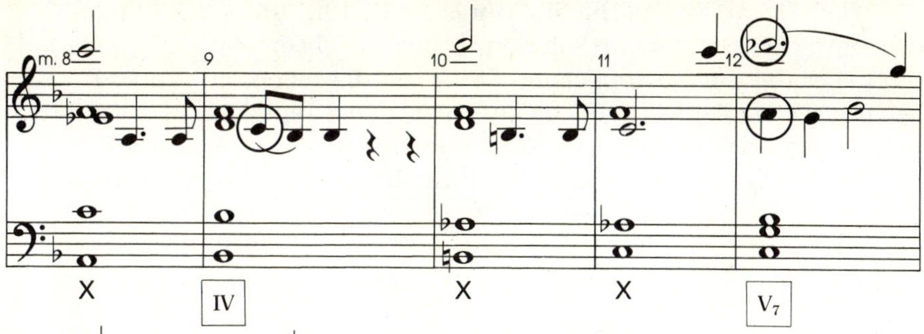

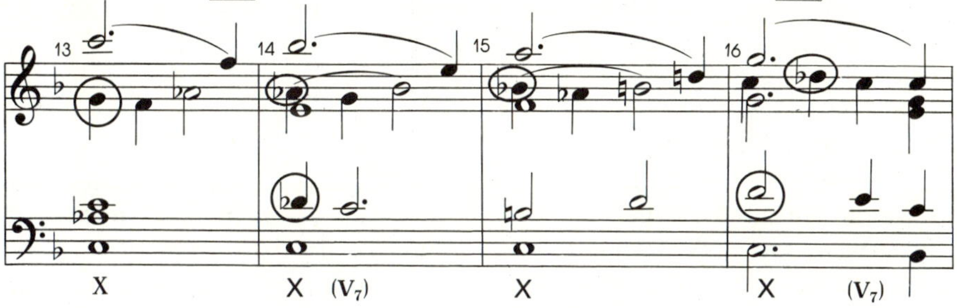

Although there are many more chords than in the opening phrases, only two of these chords are functional (IV . . V_7 . . . .). The other chords connect and prolong these two harmonies. From measure 11 on, the bass remains anchored on the dominant note C, while a series of chromatic tones in the upper voices hints at a possible modulation into minor. The clear tonality with which the theme began has been clouded.

The end of the theme serves to dispel these harmonic clouds. The level of chromaticism and dissonance subsides. Functional chord change is rapid, reaffirming the F major tonality.

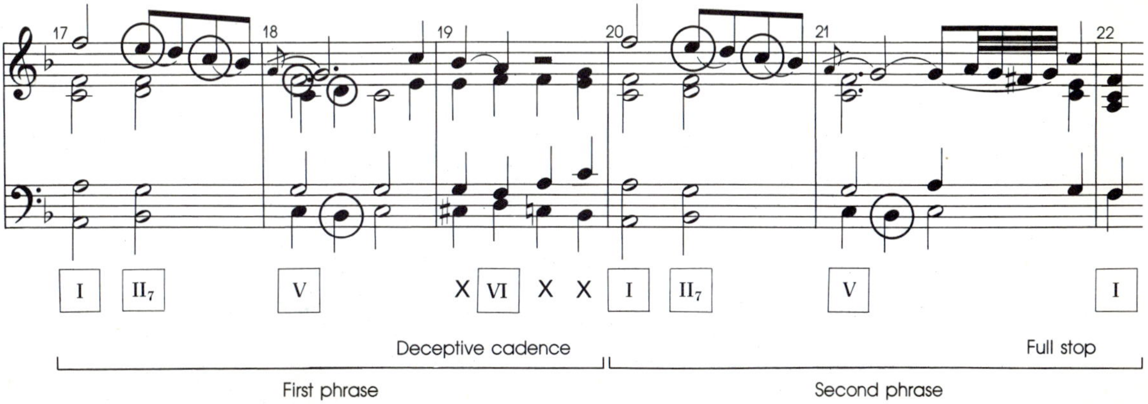

The two closing phrases are based on the same harmonic progression. Only the cadences are different:

I–II_7–V–VI (*deceptive cadence*)
I–II_7–V–I (*full stop*)

Had Mozart ended the first phrase with a full stop rather than a deceptive cadence, tonal resolution would have been abrupt, coming too soon after the tonal complication of the middle section to restore balance. The deceptive cadence and subsequent repetition of the chord progression enable Mozart to space out the tonal resolution more gradually. Full resolution comes with the long-delayed cadence on the tonic triad, bringing the theme to completion.

The three portions of this theme form a single harmonic pattern that gives both breadth and unity to the chord changes:

Stability—Tension—Resolution

Complex Styles of Tonal Harmony

During the 19th century composers explored the rich expressive and emotional potential of tonal harmony. Dissonance was an essential feature of this striving for personal expression. Works of the late tonal period are characterized by a concentrated, often continuous use of dissonant harmonies. Seventh chords replace triads as the most common sonority in many of these works. More complex chords are also introduced. The harmonic lines include many dissonant non-chord tones. Frequently, notes foreign to the harmony are accented rhythmically, while the tones to which they resolve are rhythmically weak. A resolution may be delayed, or may occur in an unexpected manner. Sometimes there is no resolution and a dissonance is left "hanging."

In these and other ways, 19th-century music reflects a shift in harmonic emphasis from systematic resolution of dissonance to intensification of the dissonance itself. Much of the emotional intensity in the Prelude to Wagner's *Tristan and Isolde,* for example, results from the continual churning of non-chord tones against the underlying harmonies. Sometimes the underlying chord progressions are virtually obscured by the abundance of non-harmonic tones. The dense texture frequently sounds more polyphonic than homophonic. Chords often seem to be byproducts of the linear motion of the voices. They appear as momentary consonances (marked └─┘), which quickly dissolve back into strings of dissonant intervals (marked with wavy lines):

Wagner Prelude to Tristan and Isolde

Non-harmonic tones are circled

Underlying chord progression:

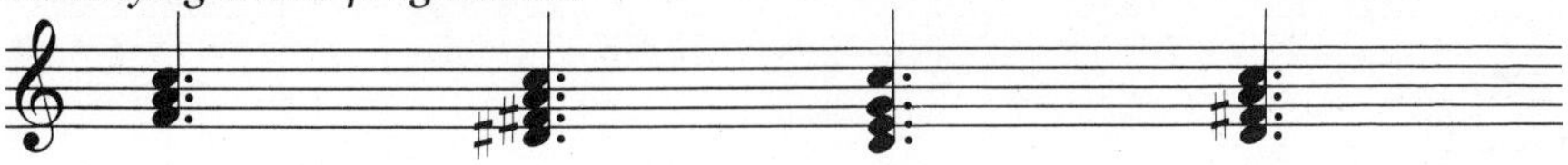

Highly chromatic chord motion also contributes to the sustained harmonic tension of many later tonal works. Chromatic inflections are so numerous in the *Tristan* prelude that several passages, like the one above, lack a well-defined key center or scale. Chromatic chords are rarely functional. When several occur in succession, functional harmonic motion stops, and the harmony is set adrift from a secure tonal framework. Functional chord motion, which lets us know where we are at any moment in relation to the tonic, is an essential feature of tonal harmony. As functional chords were spaced ever further apart by 19th-century composers, this important feature of tonality was weakened.

Listening

Prelude in E Minor *by Frédéric Chopin*

Record Set Side 2, Band 2

Chopin's prelude illustrates the more complex harmonic language of later tonal music. Most of the harmonies are seventh chords. The level of dissonance remains high and fairly constant until the final cadence. Three harmonic voices descend chromatically, creating many chords that lie outside the key of E minor.

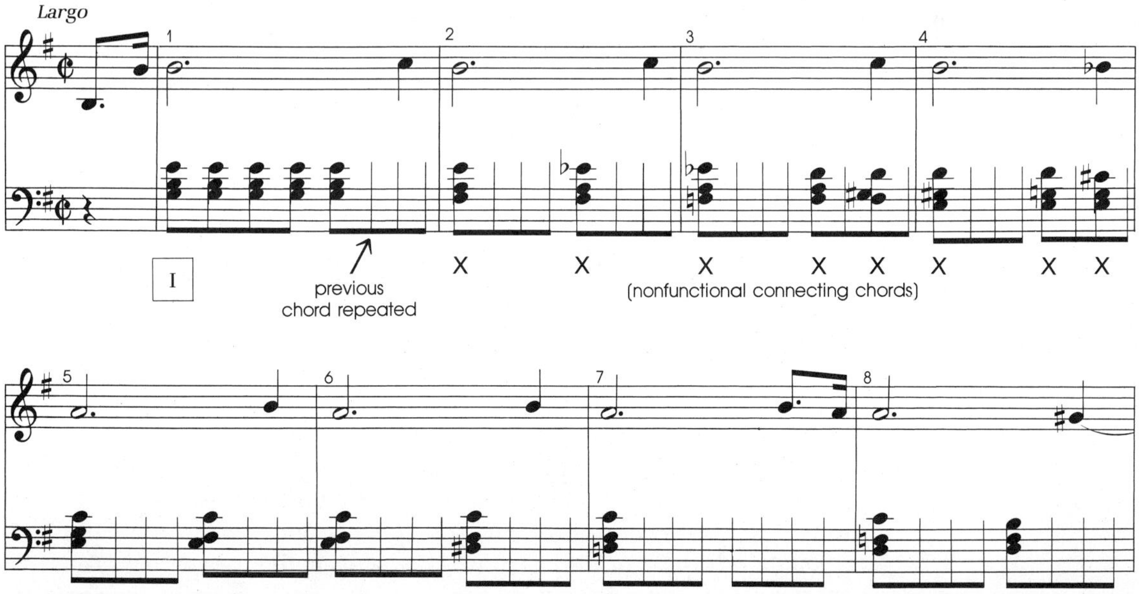

(continued)

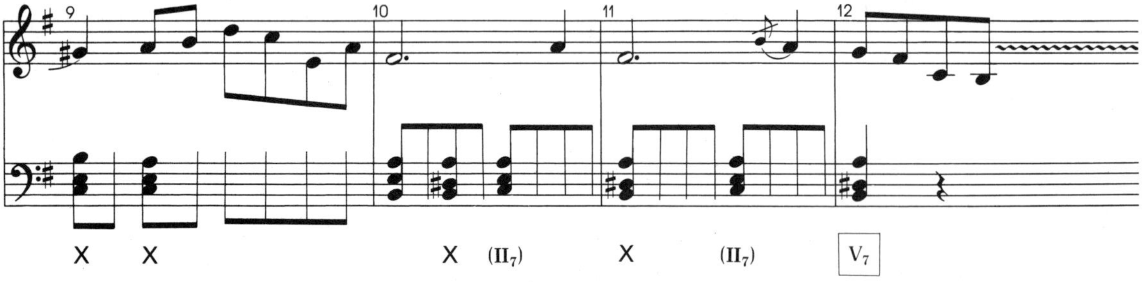

There are only three widely separated functional chords in the first phrase:

Functional chord progression:

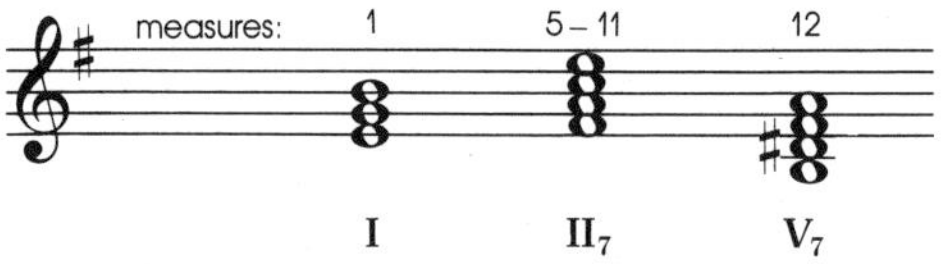

This underlying progression is very simple. It is the same sequence of chords that reaffirmed the tonic key at the end of the Mozart theme. In Chopin's piece, however, the progression is only dimly apparent to the ear because of the many chromatic connecting chords which intervene. The widely separated functional chords provide only a skeletal framework for the harmony. The musical interest of the chord progression is concentrated instead on harmonic color. Expressive sonorities, shaded with different amounts of dissonance, melt into one another in kaleidoscopic fashion. The E minor tonal center is weakened by all these features, but is never completely lost; we still feel its underlying, if remote, presence, and we wait for its eventual affirmation.

At the climax midway through the second phrase, Chopin introduces the most dissonant chord of the piece. The tension of this chord is dissipated gradually in the concluding measures. The only strong tonic triad in the entire prelude is the very last chord.

Tonality and Dissonance in the 20th Century

The tonal harmonic system evolved gradually from a diatonic, triadic style into the rich, complex vocabulary of 19th-century concert music. A similar (though more rapid) evolution has occurred within jazz idioms during the present century. Despite their vast differences in surface detail, the harmonies of "Silent Night," and of Bach, Mozart, Chopin, and Wagner, are based on the same fundamental tonal and harmonic principles. These principles are simple in theory, and they allowed for great (but not *limitless*) expansion in the use of dissonance, chromaticism, and harmonic color. Concentrated exploitation of these resources during the 19th century began to weaken the centrality of the tonic, paving the way for freer types of harmonic practice in the 20th century.

As the expressive harmonic resources of early tonal music became increasingly familiar, later tonal composers sought bolder means of harmonic tension. Their harmonies often seem to be directed continuously outward, toward ever new and more distant tonal goals, instead of making a balanced, circular pattern around the tonic. Composers came to rely less and less on harmonic formulas and conventions, and searched instead for novel, highly personal kinds of harmonic syntax.

These stylistic developments came to a head shortly after 1900. The tonal harmonic system exploded into a variety of new types of harmonic practice. Many composers abandoned the traditional concept of the necessary resolution of dissonance to consonance. Instead, they began to treat dissonance solely as an aspect of musical color, useful in creating striking sonorities that define the harmonic flavor of a work. Dissonance was often employed continuously, and for its own sake. Some composers took a greater step, organizing harmonies entirely by means of their intervallic construction, without the use of scales, functional progressions or a center tone. They saw no reason why compositions could not begin and end on any combination of pitches. The unity and expressive quality of such works depend not upon traditional tonal models and conventions, but upon the unique harmonic patterns and framework established within an individual work. Other composers, while seeking an expanded or freer harmonic framework, were reluctant to make what seemed like so large a break with tradition. Instead, they incorporated triads and tonal principles within their harmonies, but only as points of reference that could be twisted to new purpose.

The upheaval in tonal and harmonic practice that occurred around 1900 has had a profound impact on the music of this century. The problems caused by the lack of a common musical language, the "emancipation of dissonance" from necessary resolution, and the abandonment of tonal centers are issues still vital to today's composers. What Stravinsky called the "abyss of freedom"—the belief that there are no *inevitable* pre-set rules or conventions, that no series of tones or sonorities is necessarily musically "right" or "wrong"—can be a two-edged sword. It frees composers from habit, forcing them to seek out new methods of pitch organization. But it can also be paralyzing, offering an unlimited range of possibilities without providing a shared musical language between composer and listener.

Some composers have been troubled by this situation, but most have found it an added spur to their imagination and technical skill. In an important sense, music is a discipline more like philosophy than, say, medicine or physics: it does not "get better" with time, but it *does* change. To make a meaningful musical statement, composers must come to grips with the musical materials and concerns of their own time and make them vital and compelling to the listener. The basic compositional questions (how to organize pitch? how to organize rhythm? how to express meaning through sound?) do not change, but the approach to these questions is constantly changing.

To a degree rarely known to their predecessors, contemporary composers are compelled to forge their own stylistic frameworks and conventions. Composers who accept gladly this "abyss of freedom" must create their own musical world, logic, and meaning from the raw materials of pitch, rhythm, and color. By doing so, they discover their own creative voice and values. When we enter into these newer worlds, freely and without preconceptions, we can share in the joy of creative discovery, and we can more fully appreciate the diversity and vitality of musical expression.

For Further Listening

Hackensack,[1] ***performed by the Thelonius Monk Quartet;*** **Sundance,**[2] ***performed by a sextet led by Keith Jarrett***

Most jazz numbers are based on simple functional harmonic progressions employing only a few chords. The standard blues "changes," for example, comprise a twelve-measure pattern in which tonic harmonies alternate with IV and V chords:

Blues pattern

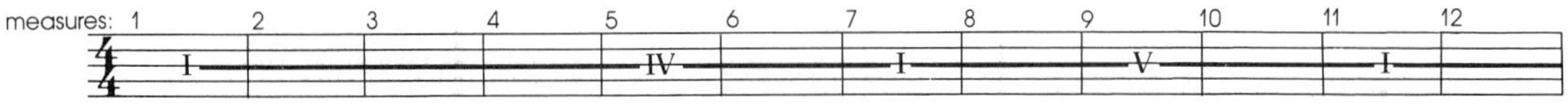

Such harmonic patterns provide the performers with a structural outline around which they are free to add as much embellishment as their creative imaginations suggest. Between the functional chords, the performers (and the arranger, if any) may interject any number of connecting chords. In jazz idioms, however, harmonic enrichment extends far beyond chord connection. Most of the functional chords are never heard in "pure" form. Instead, performers color these harmonies, chromatically altering some of the chord tones and introducing added dissonant notes. Chord substitutions, in which a chord with a different root and construction takes the place of a functional harmony, are also common:

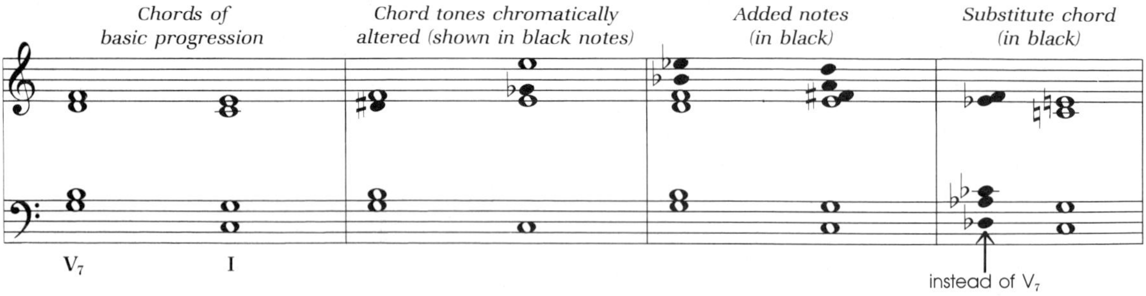

As the players improvise around a harmonic framework, the melodic direction taken by a soloist will influence a keyboard player's

[1] Available on Columbia Recording JCS-8838.
[2] Available on Columbia Recording PG-31580.

choice of chord shadings. As a result, a rudimentary progression can serve as the source of ever new harmonic possibilities. The same tune, played night after night by the same group, can assume a different complexion in each performance.

Hackensack, a theme by Thelonious Monk (b. 1920), features a simple variation on blues changes, arranged into four eight-measure phrases. As in so many jazz, rock, and pop tunes, three of the phrases are identical, producing an A–A–B–A structure to the theme:

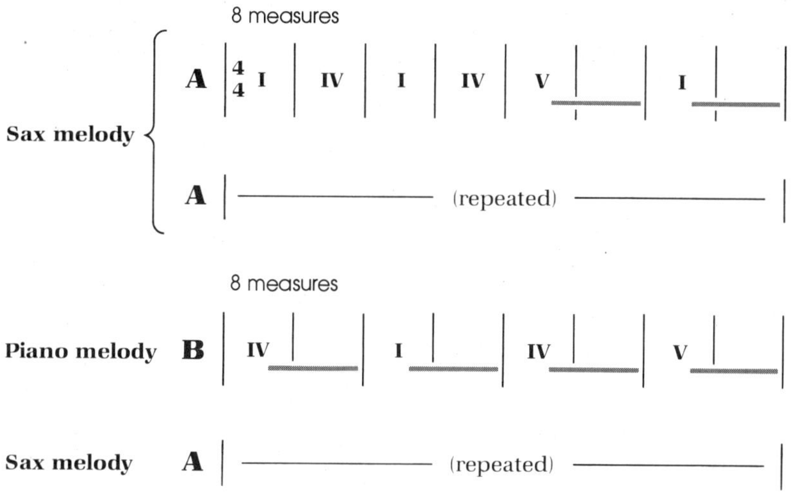

Few of these chords are played as simple triads. Added notes, alterations and chord substitutions are superimposed in both the melodic and harmonic (keyboard) voices to season and fortify these harmonies.

After the theme has been played, the 32-measure harmonic framework serves as the basis for improvisational solos. Each complete repetition of the A–A–B–A harmonic pattern is called a "chorus." In this performance, tenor saxophonist Charlie Rouse and pianist Monk each solo for two choruses. The entire number features six repetitions of the harmonic pattern:

(Piano introduction)
Theme
Sax solo: 2 choruses
Piano solo: 2 choruses
Theme repeated

After a harmonic framework has been established by a theme, it can be subjected to more extensive embellishment or maintained by a few chordal punctuations. In this performance, the players adhere rather closely to the original harmonic pattern. The harmonies with which Monk supports the solo lines are fragmentary, opening up large blocks of musical space for the exposition of melodic ideas while keeping the structural pattern intact. The sax and piano solos are woven around the harmonic framework. Even when the chords fall silent during the piano solo, the harmonic pattern continues as it is outlined by the solo and bass lines.

Thelonious Monk

Thelonius Monk has been an innovative and highly influential jazz figure since the 1940s, when he first came to the attention of the musical world as a leading exponent of the "bop" idiom.

Sundance, like most of the music of Keith Jarrett (b. 1945), is eclectic in harmonic language. The performance begins with an introductory passage in which the progression IV–I is arpeggiated and insistently repeated in the piano bass. (The IV–I formula is often called an "amen" cadence, since it customarily occurs at the end of hymns. It underlies the harmonic motion of many gospel, soul, rock, and jazz tunes.) Against this static backdrop, pianist Jarrett overlays much more complex harmonic patterns in the right hand. As a result of numerous chromatic inflections and "blue" notes, these right-hand harmonies hover around a minor tonality. Immediate tonal tension is established between the foursquare background harmonies in major (bass) and impulsive foreground harmonies in minor (treble).

The theme of this work is presented not continuously, but in segments interspersed with brief piano and saxophone solos. The theme features two saxophones, outlining a chord progression that is embellished in the piano and guitar (the x's are nonfunctional chords):

$$\mathrm{I}-\mathrm{IV}-x-x-\mathrm{V}-\mathrm{I}$$

This harmonic pattern is repeated several times, both in fragments and in its entirety.

In contrast to *Hackensack,* the harmonic framework of *Sundance* is not retained in the solos that follow the theme. The solos are asymmetric in length, comprising "free form" excursions rather than "choruses." The piano and saxes drop out at the conclusion of the theme, leaving a solo guitar, bass line, and two percussionists. The lines are highly chromatic, developing melodic fragments without reference to the original harmonies. There is no tonal center. Tenor saxophonist Dewey Redman enters, incorporating expressive wails and "sheets of sound" (rapid melodic runs) into a rhapsodic line.

Near the end of the solo passages, the piano enters with a vamp—a repetitive harmonic figure that embellishes a single chord. By "sitting" on this chord (the second *x* of the theme), the piano reestablishes a tonal framework, preparing the return of the theme.

With its driving IV–I changes, *Sundance* reflects the earnestness and tonal simplicity of its soul, rock, and "funk" influences. The highly ornamental and chromatic treble piano riffs, and the enraptured solos that shatter the harmonic and pitch framework, are equally vital to the quality of expression in this performance, however.

While *Hackensack* features a secure harmonic framework and consistent tonal idiom, *Sundance* generates much greater tonal tension as it cuts across a wide stylistic spectrum. Both works turn simple changes into an expansive vehicle for group expression. Jazz is at bottom a performer's art; the harmonic thread is a point of departure, channeling the creative energies of each performer to personal invention.

Terms and Concepts For Review

harmony
chord
texture
- monophonic
- homophonic
- polyphonic

interval
consonance and dissonance
- resolution of dissonance

triad
- root, third, and fifth
- major and minor triads

arpeggio
tonic and dominant harmonies
cadences
- full stop
- half stop
- deceptive cadence

functional and non-functional chords
non-harmonic tones

Chapter 5
Instruments and Voices

The **orchestration,** or **scoring,** of a composition is the way it is arranged for instruments. In orchestrating a passage a composer determines which instruments will play the melody, which will perform the harmonic voices, and which will be used for added depth or punctuation. When combining instruments, the composer may seek to blend them into a homogeneous sound or to emphasize their separate tone colors. Composers tend to develop personal styles of orchestration—distinctive ways of treating and mixing instruments—in much the same way they evolve recognizable melodic and harmonic styles. Some composers, such as Debussy, have developed this skill to a special degree, so that brilliance of orchestration is one of the most notable features of their music. For the listener, familiarity with the basic characteristics of instruments can broaden one's appreciation of how the scoring of a work contributes to its structure and expression.

Properties of Instruments

The particular capabilities of an instrument depend largely on its construction and on the way in which it produces sound. The basic properties of any instrument or voice are its pitch range, dynamic range, timbre, and idiomatic characteristics.

Pitch Range

The **pitch range** is the number of tones, from lowest to highest, that can be produced on an instrument. The human voice has a range of about two octaves, the violin about three and a half octaves, and the piano over seven octaves (88 notes). A portion of an instrument's total range is called a **register** (for example, high, middle, or low register). Most composers make only occasional use of the very highest tones, since these are generally more tiring to produce and more difficult to play in tune. Many 20th-century composers, however, employ extreme ranges to create striking tone colors. The upper range of string and wind instruments has expanded steadily over the last 200 years.

Dynamic Range

The **dynamic** level of a sound is its loudness. Composers indicate how loudly or softly a passage should be played by means of **dynamic markings.** Like tempo markings, these abbreviations have traditionally been expressed in Italian. The common dynamic markings are listed in the following table.

Dynamic marking	*Italian term*	*Meaning*
pp	*pianissimo*	very soft
p	*piano*	soft
mp	*mezzo piano*	moderately soft
mf	*mezzo forte*	moderately loud
f	*forte*	loud
ff	*fortissimo*	very loud
sf	*sforzando*	suddenly loud and stressed
<, *cresc.,*	*crescendo*	gradually becoming louder
>, *dim., decr.*	*diminuendo, decrescendo*	gradually becoming softer

Music written before 1750 rarely includes dynamic markings. Dynamic levels were assumed to be self-evident, and contrasts between loud and soft resulted naturally from changes in orchestration. **Tutti** ("all") passages, in which all the performers play, alternate with lighter passages scored for small groups of instruments. Most 19th-century music, on the other hand, features frequent or even continuous changes in loudness. These dynamic nuances, notated in exacting detail by such composers as Wagner, underscore the more volatile expressive character of Romantic music. Here is a typical example:

Tristan and Isolde, *measures 24 – 29*

Since some instruments are naturally louder than others, dynamic markings are only a relative guide for performers and conductors. Many instruments have particular dynamic characteristics. The flute, for example, is capable of only limited volume in its bottom octave, but it can project a roaring torrent of sound in its highest register. Singers and brass players find it difficult to perform high notes softly.

Timbre

The unique sound of an instrument or voice is called its **timbre** (pronounced *tam*-ber). *Tone quality* and *color* are synonymous terms. If a clarinet and violin successively play the same pitch at the same dynamic level, we easily can distinguish the two instruments by their difference in timbre.

Tone color is a complex phenomenon determined by many acoustical factors. Specific timbres can be described only vaguely in words: "shrill," "dark," "rich," and so on. Instruments with a relatively neutral timbre, such as the flute and horn, blend easily; others, like the oboe, produce a more penetrating, complex timbre which tends to remain distinct even when combined with several other instruments.

Idiomatic Characteristics

The flute and violin are well suited to the performance of rapid, intricate passages. A similar passage attempted on the tuba would sound, at best, curious. Composers generally strive to write *idiomatically* (that is, effectively and appropriately) for each instrument by exploiting the instrument's unique technical and expressive capabilities and by avoiding impractical demands.

The technical standards of an age result from its expressive ideals. But they are also affected by changes in the construction of instruments and the influence of virtuoso performers who demonstrate the full technical capabilities of their instruments. Since the late 18th century, composers have demanded increasingly greater facility from performers. Several of Beethoven's symphonies were considered extraordinarily difficult in the early 1800s; today they frequently are peformed with minimal rehearsal by professional orchestras. Contemporary composers often write passages that would have been considered unidiomatic or even bizarre fifty years ago. Even in the most technically demanding music, however, musical intensity more often results from an inner tension between contrasting ideas or patterns than from an avalanche of notes.

The Human Voice

Human voices are divided into six ranges, as designated below. These pitch ranges are approximate, and most trained singers can exceed the given upper limits by several pitches. Most choral music is written in four parts: *soprano, alto, tenor,* and *bass.*

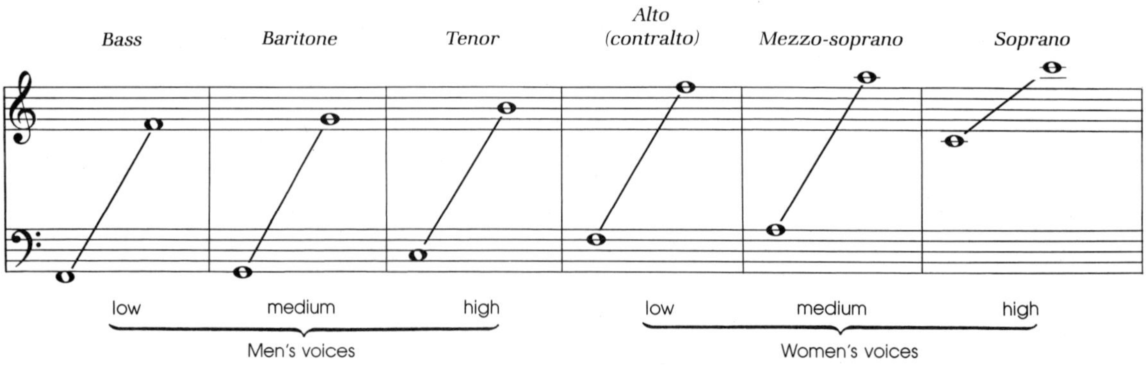

Human voices possess a greater and more distinctive range of timbres than any instrument. We can immediately recognize the voice of a well-known singer, but we tend to identify an instrumentalist less by tone quality than by his or her style of playing. Vocal music, too, encompasses a very wide range of styles, which require different tone qualities and singing techniques. For most songs and choral music a pure, unforced quality is appropriate. Music of a dramatic character, such as opera, generally demands more forceful delivery and a heavier, richer timbre, achieved by singing "from the chest" rather than "from the head." For increased brilliance, singers add **vibrato**—rapid, slight variations in pitch which give the tone a quavering quality. In some jazz, rock, and contemporary concert pieces, vivid emotive projection is more crucial to the musical expression than beauty of tone quality. We will survey these and other vocal styles in later chapters.

There is a uniquely human and personal quality to vocal music, which has been expressed eloquently by folk singer Joan Baez: "To sing is to love and affirm, to fly and to soar, to coast into the hearts of the people who listen, to tell them that life is to live, that love is there, that nothing is a promise, but that beauty exists, and must be hunted and found."

Instruments

Most modern instruments belong to one of four families: *strings, woodwinds, brass,* and *percussion.* A miscellaneous fifth category includes keyboard instruments, harp, guitar, and electronic instruments (discussed in Chapter 20). The instruments within each family are similar in construction and means of sound production. When several members of a family play together, they comprise a **choir,** a group of low-, medium-, and high-pitched instruments of similar timbre. The symphony orchestra, on which our examination of instruments will focus, includes choirs of string, woodwind, brass, and percussion instruments.

Strings

The four instruments of the string family are the violin, viola, cello, and double bass. Strings make up between half and two-thirds of a symphony orchestra and are its most important and versatile section. They are equally effective in performing expressive, slow melodies, rapid technical passages, and sharp rhythmic punctuations. Strings blend more readily into a homogeneous choir than any other family.

Stringed instruments are played by drawing a bow across the strings (called *arco*), or by plucking the strings with the fingers of the right hand (*pizzicato*). *Pizzicato* produces percussive attacks, in which the sound decays rapidly in volume and cannot be sustained.

Other special indiomatic resources of the strings include:

1. Muted passages: A mute is a small piece of wood placed in contact with the strings, which reduces volume and produces a mellower, darker timbre.

2. Tremolo: a trembling quality produced by very rapid alternation in bow direction. The effect is similar to rapidly moving one's jaw up and down while singing a pitch. String tremolos are frequently used to create tension or suspense.

3. Multiple stops: two, three, or four notes played simultaneously on different strings.

4. Harmonics: very high, pure, soft tones, produced by touching (rather than pressing) the strings at specific points.

5. *Sul ponticello*: bowing on or near the bridge. This creates a nasal timbre, like holding one's nose while singing.

Violin. The violin is the soprano voice of the string choir. It was the first orchestral instrument to reach its modern form, and the finest violins available today remain those made over 250 years ago by such Italian craftsmen as Antonio Stradivari (1644–1737). The unrivaled expressive and technical capabilities of the violin have made it the most important member of instrumental ensembles since the 17th century. The solo repertoire of violin works is more extensive than that of any other orchestral instrument. In the orchestra, the violins are usually divided into two groups; the first violins often carry the principal melody, while the seconds generally play a harmonic part.

A violinist produces specific pitches by "stopping" one of the four strings (that is, by pressing it against the fingerboard) with the fingers of his left hand. The higher up on the fingerboard a string is stopped, the shorter is the length of the vibrating portion of the string, and the higher its resulting pitch. The left hand also creates vibrato by means of a shaking motion of the wrist and fingers. Dynamics and tone color are affected by the amount of pressure applied with the bow. The bow is drawn alternately up and down over the strings. To produce a unified tone quality and phrasing, the members of a string section change bowing directions simultaneously. Orchestral bowings are determined by the concertmaster (the first violinist) or the conductor.

Viola. The viola looks and sounds very much like a violin, but is about one-seventh larger and has longer, thicker strings that produce a darker tone color. Its range is seven half-steps lower than that of the violin. The viola has traditionally been an ensemble, rather than a solo, instrument. While it often has been assigned rather pedestrian accompanimental parts, it is also an effective melodic instrument, particularly suited to lines in the alto register.

Cello. Although the cello (or *violoncello*) must be held vertically due to its larger size, it is played in the same manner as the violin and viola. Its expansive pitch range (encompassing bass, tenor, and alto vocal ranges), expressive tone quality, and remarkable technical capabilities make it one of the most versatile members of the orchestra. The cello section most often plays the orchestral bass line, but it also frequently carries the principal

String instruments. The violin (top left) is the soprano voice of the string choir. The viola (bottom left, here played by Marcus Thompson) is larger, lower in pitch, and darker in tone color. The cello (above) generally carries the bass line but is also an expressive melodic instrument.

melody in its tenor register. A significant body of solo literature exists for the instrument.

Double Bass. The largest and lowest-pitched stringed instrument, the double bass (or *contrabass*) almost always plays the bottom orchestral line, frequently doubling the cellos at the unison or an octave below. The terms "double" or "contra" indicate that the range of the instrument extends down about an octave below that of the human bass voice. Because of its very low range, which would be cumbersome to notate, double-bass parts are written an octave above the actual sounding pitches.

The double bass adds resonance and depth to the orchestra. Due to its prodigious size, it is capable of less technical agility than the higher strings. It is often played pizzicato, particularly in rapid and more delicate passages. The double bass is a staple of jazz and rock ensembles, though today often replaced by the more powerful and fluent, if less resonant, electric bass guitar.

The stringed instruments

Record Set Side 2, Band 8

Woodwinds

In the woodwind instruments, a column of air inside the instrument is set into vibration when the performer blows across a mouth hole (flute and piccolo), past a single reed (clarinet and saxophone), or between two narrow reeds (oboe, English horn, and bassoon). The length of the vibrating air column, and thus the resulting pitch, is varied as the performer opens and closes a series of holes and keys running along the length of the instrument. The fingering systems of all modern woodwinds are similar, having been standardized in the 19th century.

The various woodwind instruments produce remarkably different timbres. In addition, the tone quality of each instrument tends to vary noticeably between its low, middle, and high registers. Consequently, the instruments of the woodwind section do not blend as readily as the strings or brass; they tend to retain their individual identities, rather than merging into a homogeneous choir.

Flute. The flute is a high soprano instrument with extraordinary technical capacity. Its timbre is acoustically simpler than that of any other instrument. The somewhat breathy and ethereal lower register is beautifully exploited in Debussy's *Prelude to the Afternoon of a Faun.* The middle register has a birdlike quality, while the upper range is brighter and at times shrill. An extensive repertoire of solo music for the flute has been composed in the 20th century. These works often explore the many special timbral effects available on the instrument. The most common of these resources is "fluttertongue," a buzzing timbre similar to a string tremolo, produced by trilling the tongue.

The *piccolo* (from *flauto piccolo,* or "little flute," in Italian) is a small flute, often made of wood rather than metal. The third flutist in the orchestra customarily doubles on piccolo. Its range is basically an octave higher than that of the flute, extending up to the very top notes of the piano. The piercing timbre of the piccolo often provides a brilliant top to orchestral tutti passages. In the 20th century, alto and bass flutes, larger instruments with lower ranges, have also been introduced.

Oboe. The oboe is one of the most difficult instruments to play. Sound is produced by the vibration of air between two narrow reeds. The oboe "speaks" (produces tone) more slowly than the flute or single reed instruments, and is therefore less adept at rapid technical passages, particularly those involving repeated notes. Its timbre is acoustically complex—reedy and nasal, but delicate—and is ideally suited to expressive or poignant melodic lines. Since the pitch of the oboe can be "humored" (adjusted) less than that of other symphonic instruments, the orchestra customarily tunes to the oboe's concert pitch. The range of the oboe is roughly equivalent to that of the soprano voice.

The *English horn* (which is neither English nor a horn) is similar to the oboe, but larger, with a lower alto range and a more somber tone color. It is most often featured in slow, expressive melodic solos.

Bassoon. The bassoon is another double-reed instrument, but its tone is less penetrating than that of the oboe. Despite its cumbersome appearance, the instrument is capable of considerable facility. Its pitch compass extends through bass and tenor ranges. Until the 19th century, composers consistently employed the bassoon on the orchestral bass line, frequently doubling the cellos and double basses. Later composers have written many expressive solo lines for the instrument in its upper (tenor) register, where it has a haunting quality.

The *contrabassoon* is a ponderous giant that produces a very gruff, rather awesome tone quality. Its range, an octave below that of the bassoon, extends down to the lowest notes of the piano.

Clarinet. The clarinet is a single-reed instrument. It evolved more slowly than the flute, oboe, and bassoon, and joined the orchestra a few years later. Its extremely wide pitch, dynamic, and expressive ranges and technical facility (second only to the flute and piccolo among the winds) quickly made the clarinet an indispensible part of the woodwind choir. The clarinet's timbre varies considerably between its low, middle, and high registers.

The imposing but agile *bass clarinet* looks something like a wooden saxophone because of the curved bell at the bottom of the instrument. It sounds an octave below the clarinet, and produces a deep, rich bass timbre. A small *piccolo clarinet,* pitched five half steps above the standard instrument, has appeared from time to time in orchestral works of the last hundred years.

Saxophone. The saxophone is used infrequently in the symphony orchestra, but is increasingly common in contemporary chamber music and is a staple member of jazz and rock ensembles and the symphonic band. The instrument is named after its inventor, Adolphe Sax, who patented a model in 1846. Saxes come in five common sizes, from the soprano, with a range slightly below that of the oboe, to the elephantine bass sax, which gives the impression that it is about to swallow its performer. Alto and tenor sizes are most common. The saxophone is an instrument of hybrid construction whose timbre is midway between that of the woodwinds and brass. Jazz saxophonist Charlie Parker (1920–1955) was the first universally recognized virtuoso on the instrument; his celebrated improvisational style and technical facility exerted great influence on contemporary and later performers.

Woodwinds. The flute (top right) has a high soprano range and is capable of great technical agility. The clarinet (upper left) possesses a particularly wide range of pitch, dynamics, and tone colors. The oboe (bottom right) is nasal and expressive, while bassoons (bottom left) are deeper in pitch and less penetrating.

Listening

The major woodwind instruments

Record Set Side 2, Band 9

Brass

Brass instruments—the horn, trumpet, trombone, and tuba—are the most powerful section of the orchestra. (Mindful of this dynamic power, composer Richard Strauss advised conductors never to encourage the brass, "except by a curt glance.") A brass player's lips act as a double reed, directing a thin stream of air through a cup or funnel-shaped mouthpiece into the instrument. A single trumpet or trombone can hold its own easily against a sea of woodwinds and strings, but the brass can also create a luminous, solemn, or even delicate quality. Brass timbres can be modified by means of various types of mutes inserted into the bell of the instrument.

Trumpets and horns are among the most ancient musical instruments, but they were among the last members of the orchestra to evolve into their present form. Until the 19th century they were incapable of producing a complete chromatic scale, and they were limited in their lower registers to a few pitches. Performers could produce many chromatic pitches in the higher registers through slight changes in lip pressure. In the early 19th century the invention of valves controlled by three keys (four on the tuba) enabled these instruments to play the complete chromatic scale throughout their ranges.

Trumpet. The trumpet is the highest-pitched and loudest member of the brass family. The instrument first achieved orchestral prominence during the first half of the 18th century, when a virtuosic method of playing developed, featuring technically elaborate passages in an extremely high register. This art died out after 1750. During the later 18th and early 19th centuries trumpets were used sparingly, generally held in reserve for climaxes and solo passages of a fanfare character. In the 20th century the instrument has been put to more varied use, and many special techniques developed by jazz trumpeters have become common symphonic resources.

Horn. The modern horn (or *French horn*) evolved from a hunting horn with a hole in the middle so that the player could sling the instrument over his arm while on horseback. The horn is a somewhat softer member of the brass section which blends easily with woodwinds and strings. It is a difficult instrument to play, because the mouthpiece is so small it leaves little room for the player to adjust his lips to form different notes. As a solo instrument the horn can evoke a great variety of moods; it is equally effective in lyrical, martial, and intense passages. Due to its unique blending qualities, the horn is the most common choice of composers for sustained inner parts, and in general plays more continuously than the other members of the brass section. Horn players frequently alter timbre and pitch by *hand-muting,* inserting their right hand into the bell of the instrument.

The brass family. The trumpet (top right) is the highest brass instrument, with a brilliant, penetrating timbre. The horn (top left, played by Robert Routch) has a mellower, more rounded tone. The trombone (bottom left) is deep, rich, and solemn in timbre. The tuba (bottom right) is the bass instrument of the brass choir, lending weight and resonance to orchestral tuttis.

Trombone. The trombone was the first modern orchestral instrument to develop into its present form. It evolved from a large trumpet in the 15th century and is, in fact, a sort of bass trumpet. The tone color of the trombone is midway between that of a trumpet and a horn: deep, rich, and solemn. The instrument produces the full range of chromatic pitches by means of a movable slide that varies the length of tubing of the instrument. This mechanism makes the trombone less suited to rapid passages than the trumpet or horn, and it requires considerable skill for the performer to connect pitches smoothly.

The trombone did not become a regular member of the symphony orchestra until the 19th century and has always functioned more as an ensemble than solo instrument. Its sustained rich tone in bass and tenor registers adds brilliance to many orchestral tuttis.

Tuba. The tuba is the bass instrument of the brass section, adding depth and resonance to the orchestra. In tone color it more resenbles the horn than the trumpet. Modern tuba players have achieved a surprising degree of virtuosity on so massive an instrument, and tuba parts are no longer confined to grunts and whole notes.

Listening

The brass instruments

Record Set Side 2, Band 10

Percussion

The percussion section of the modern orchestra most often includes three to five performers, each of whom may play several different instruments during the course of a performance. Many of today's most common percussive instruments are of comparatively recent origin. Early symphonic composers made relatively little use of the percussion, and only the timpani were regular members of the orchestra until the 19th century. In the 20th century and is, in fact, a sort of bass trumpet. The tone color of the tance, not only as a source of rhythmic accentuation and added brilliance in orchestral tuttis, but also in the creation of evocative new color combinations. Increased use of percussion in the present day has coincided with the growing interest of many modern composers in exploiting tone color as a major source of musical interest. These instruments also figure prominently in contemporary chamber music, including pieces written entirely for percussion, as well as in symphonic bands, jazz, and rock.

Percussion instruments are commonly divided into two groups: those which produce tones of definite pitch, and those which produce complex timbres lacking a well-defined focal pitch.

The modern percussion battery includes a wide variety of instruments. (Top) tympani, snare drum, and orchestral chimes. (Bottom) xylophone, cymbals, and tam-tam. Part of the bass drum can be seen in the lower right.

Instruments of Definite Pitch. The *timpani* (also called *kettledrums*) are large copper drums that can be tuned to a specific pitch by means of hand-turned screws, which tighten or relax the tension of the drum head. On modern timpani, the tuning screws are replaced by a foot pedal that facilitates more rapid pitch changes. Early symphonies generally featured two timpani, but many modern scores call for three or four.

The *xylophone* and *marimba* consist of a series of tuned wooden bars laid out like a piano keyboard; the xylophone produces a very dry, incisive timbre, while the marimba is mellower and more resonant. *Orchestral bells* (*glockenspiel*) are smaller, made of metal bars, and have a bright, high-pitched ringing quality. The *vibraphone,* most common in jazz ensembles, produces a pure, flute-like sound. *Chimes* are sets of large metal tubes vertically suspended, producing a sound like church bells. The *celesta* looks like a miniature piano. It produces a light, soft tone color in the treble range. The celesta is most often played by a pianist rather than a percussionist.

Unpitched Percussion. The unpitched percussion instruments comprise a variety of drums and metallic instruments.

The *snaredrum* produces a raspy, high, but indefinitely pitched timbre. It is usually played with two wooden drumsticks, although wire brushes are also used, particularly by jazz drummers. Sustained sounds can be produced by rolls—very rapid, continuous alternation of the sticks. The much larger *bass drum,* usually played with a single large padded stick, has a heavy, low, resonant sound. The *tambourine* is a small drum with metal jingles attached. It is usually held in one hand and struck against the knuckles or palm of the other hand, or else shaken to create a sustained sound.

The most common unpitched metallic instruments are the cymbals, triangle, and tam tam. *Cymbals* are large brass plates that may be struck together or mounted and played with drumsticks. The *triangle* is a small three-sided metal bar struck with a metal beater, producing a resonant, high "pinging" timbre. The *tam tam* is a large, vertical metallic gong. Its complex and resonant timbre can sound mysterious when played softly, shattering when struck forcefully. Other orchestral performers tend to be nervous when seated close to the tam tam or cymbals.

Many other unpitched percussion instruments are common in modern music. Several are of Latin American origin, such as the bongos and maracas. Taken together, these instruments have immeasurably increased the range of sound colors available to the contemporary composer.

Listening

The major percussion instruments

Record Set Side 2, Band 11

Other Major Instruments

Harpsichord and Piano. The *harpsichord* was the principal solo and accompanimental keyboard instrument of secular music up until the later 18th century. Harpsichords produce sound by means of a mechanism that plucks the strings. The instrument is therefore less sensitive to variations in touch than the piano. Whether a key is delicately depressed or energetically whacked makes relatively little difference to the resulting timbre and volume. The harpsichord produces a crisp, incisive tone color, irreverently characterized by Sir Thomas Beecham as sounding like two skeletons making love on a tin roof; it has less sustaining power than most instruments and cannot produce smooth, continuous changes in dynamic level. In the Record Set, Bach's *Invention in F* is played on the harpsichord.

A two-manual French harpsichord from the 18th century. Different sets of strings can be coupled to each keyboard, or manual, making possible a variety of timbres, from brilliant and metallic to light and delicate.

The *piano* was invented around 1709 and underwent many alterations during the next century and a half. The piano is both a percussive and a stringed instrument; when the performer depresses a key, a felt-tipped hammer is activated to strike one, two, or three strings tuned to the same pitch. The dynamic level varies according to the force with which the performer depresses the keys. The resulting wide dynamic range was responsible for the instrument's original name, *pianoforte.* By the end of the 18th century the piano had replaced the harpsichord, which passed out of general use until its revival in the 20th century. There is a larger and more varied body of solo literature for the piano than for any other instrument.

Organ. The organ is a wind instrument consisting of a single or multiple set of pipes controlled by one or more keyboards (called *manuals*) and foot pedals. Each set of pipes, called a *stop,* produces a different timbre. Organs vary greatly in size, depending upon the number of stops available. Most early organs were relatively small, but in the 19th century the organ grew to massive proportions, capable of a brilliant tutti when all the stops were coupled. In recent years, electronic organs have become increasingly common because of their comparatively modest cost. These instruments produce pitches by means of tone generators, which vary the frequency of an alternating current, rather than by pipes.

Harp. Although dating back to antiquity, the harp did not achieve its present form until the early 1800s, and only became a regular member of the orchestra at the end of the last century. Basically a diatonic instrument, the harp can produce only seven of the chromatic pitches at any one time. By means of foot pedals, the harpist can alter the tuning of the strings in order to play the other five pitches.

The range of the harp is only slightly less than that of the piano. Its tone is light, best suited to thinly scored passages. A very common special effect is the *glissando,* a gushing sound produced by rapidly sweeping the fingers over several strings.

Guitar. The guitar is a six-stringed instrument that originated in Spain. Although often used today to provide chordal accompaniment, the guitar was a virtuoso solo instrument in the 18th and 19th centuries, and this tradition has been revived by Andrès Segovia and other modern performers. The electric guitar used in rock music is connected to an amplifier, which boosts and controls the volume and makes special tonal effects possible.

The Symphony Orchestra

The symphony orchestra has been the most important large instrumental ensemble for over two hundred years. The basic instrumentation of the modern orchestra was established during the latter half of the 18th century. During the 19th century each of the four sections of the orchestra doubled in size, and the standard ensemble came to number over 80 players (see the table on the next page). Many works written around 1900 call for orchestras of monumental size. Stylistic and economic considerations have prompted 20th-century composers to write for smaller forces. At the same time, however, composers' interest in novel sound colors has led to enlargement and greater use of the percussion section.

A large instrumental or vocal ensemble requires the leadership of a conductor, whose responsibilities include setting tempos, assuring rhythmic precision from the players, and balancing the relative loudness of the various parts. Most important, the conductor provides a unifying interpretation of the work as a whole. Conductors indicate pulse and meter by beating time with the right hand. The first beat of each measure is indicated by a downward motion; upward and sideward movements are used for other beats. The left hand is used to cue important entrances and depict nuances. Eye contact, facial expressions, and "body language" further suggest the precise musical quality the conductor wishes to achieve.

The role of the conductor as we know it is fairly recent, but it has grown in importance as large ensembles have been called upon to perform music of increasing rhythmic and textural complexity. In the 1600s most orchestras were led from the keyboard by an organist or harpsichordist. In the 18th century the musicians watched the first violinist. Only in the early 19th century did the conductor become a separate performer. The symphonic ideal of the Romantic era was an elevated but supple musical expression, in which a sea of musicians executed rubato rhythms and interpretive shadings with the clarity of a single performer. Such ensemble precision required firm direction. Thus the conductor's role gradually grew from one of "traffic cop" to that of *"maestro"*—the inspired master interpreter through whom the composer's ideas were communicated to musicians and audience. In its headiest form, this aggrandizement of the conductor led some impressionable audiences to an almost mystical awe of the wizard on the podium, who was seen as a towering virtuoso who "played" the orchestra.

	A TYPICAL ORCHESTRA ABOUT 1800	A TYPICAL ORCHESTRA ABOUT 1900
Woodwinds	(2 Flutes)	(3 Flutes, Piccolo)
	(2 Oboes)	(3 Oboes, English horn)
	(2 Bassoons)	(3 Bassoons, Contrabassoon)
	2 Clarinets (introduced around 1790)	(3 Clarinets, Bass clarinet)
Brass	(2 Horns)	(6 Horns)
	(2 Trumpets)	(4 Trumpets)
		(3 Trombones, Tuba)
Percussion	(2 Tympani)	(4 Tympani) (Snare drum, Bass drum, Cymbals, etc.)
Additional		(2 Harps)
Strings	(8 First violins) (6 Second violins)	(18 First violins) (16 Second violins)
	(4 Violas)	(14 Violas)
	(4 Cellos, Double bass)	(12 Cellos, 10 Double basses)

Conductor Zubin Mehta leading an orchestral rehearsal

The resulting star system, still very much a part of today's professional orchestral scene, is sometimes subject to abuse: empty theatrics, exaggeration of expressive nuances "for effect," and so on. (Oscar L'evant observed of one famous conductor, "He uses music as an accompaniment to his conducting.") The virtuosity of modern orchestras and conductors, however, also results in performances of a quality that most composers of earlier periods heard only in their imaginations.

Terms and Concepts for Review

orchestration (scoring)
register
dynamic level
dynamic markings
tutti
timbre (also tone quality, tone color)
idiomatic writing
soprano, alto, tenor, and bass voices
string, woodwind, brass, and percussion families
vibrato
pizzicato
mute

Unit 2
Musical Forms

Form is the architecture of music. The form of a composition is the way its musical ideas are shaped into a convincing whole. Because it is cumulative, formal design rarely arrests our attention at any single point. But when we can follow what is going on in the music and find the expression rewarding, we are responding in large part to this overall design.

Form begins with musical ideas: motives and themes. Like the major characters of a novel, these ideas draw us into a work and give focus to its expression. For this reason, they generally are introduced early in a work; we normally do not expect the appearance of important new motives or themes late in a composition any more than we anticipate the entrance of major new characters in the last chapter of a novel.

Once presented, ideas are normally developed. *Musical development is somewhat like the plot of a novel; it is what happens to the initial ideas, the process by which they are integrated into a larger statement. Many elements contribute to the way musical ideas are put together. Some are formal principles that a composer adopts from common practice. The shared musical language of any age includes not only characteristic types of harmonies and rhythms but also typical formal practices. These consist of both outlines and procedures. An* outline *is a general plan or sequence of events, such as:* this—that—then this again; *the outline is the broad profile of a work, establishing its boundaries and major points of arrival. A* procedure, *on the other hand, is a technique with which a composer creates formal patterns. It is a means of organization, a set of tools rather than a master plan. The design of almost any work consists of a series of events created by specific procedures. For the listener, musical form is not just a matter of "what's happening" (procedure) but also of "where we are going" (outline) and "how it feels" (overall formal shape).*

Although a composition may incorporate traditional outlines and procedures, its design *is unique, growing out of its particular musical ideas and pacing-out of events. Only the most unimaginative musical hack would grind out compositions according to stale formal recipes. To be vital, a piece of music must create its own sense of order, its own inevitabilities, and its own quality of spontaneity. In short, there are no absolute rules to musical form. To understand musical structure, and to feel the expressive design of the music, it is necessary to listen moment by moment to the ways in which the musical ideas are interrelated.*

In this unit we will examine common principles and types of forms that have proved adaptable to many styles of music. More important, we will consider how composers apply these resources in a highly selective and individual manner, tailoring them to the particular expressive qualities of a piece. The form of a work is much more than the arrangement of its melodies and harmonies; it is the way musical expression is being communicated. Formal procedures serve to create ideas, to develop them, and to supply a thread of continuity that binds them into one *work.*

Chapter 6
Sectional Forms

A formal design normally provides both *unity* and *contrast.* Contrast is the dynamic element of form, introducing a tension or complication that impels the music forward. Contrast may be centered within the ideas themselves. In Bach's *F Major Invention* two motives are set into opposition. During their subsequent development these motives are reconciled; by the end of the piece we hear them as the balanced halves of a single larger idea. Chopin's *Prelude in E Minor,* on the other hand, presents a single theme built around a single motive. Contrast comes later. The theme changes character as it undergoes alterations during the second half of the piece. In both works, integration of contrasting elements into a larger design serves to unify the music and to bring ideas to a logical conclusion. Should our attention wander midway through one of these pieces, we can pick up the melodic and harmonic thread again, but our perception of the unity of the work will remain incomplete. Some pieces of the puzzle will be missing.

"Becoming" Music and "Being" Music

Most of the music with which we are familiar, and which we will examine in this unit, is goal-oriented; that is, we feel it "going somewhere." The level of musical activity and pacing keeps changing. The music develops a sense of direction and shape as it moves toward points of maximum and minimum tension. Our interest is concentrated on what happens to the original ideas, on the process at work in the composition. The musical design is always *"becoming"* more complete.

Some types of music, however, are based upon a different approach to form. Many works contain neither contrast nor clear-cut goals. Such works might be termed *"being"* music, because the level of tension, whether high or low, remains constant. Nothing "happens" to the original ideas. Musical interest is concentrated instead on the particular color and quality of sound. Throughout most of the flute "Vocalise" from Crumb's *Vox Balaenae* a single thematic idea is hypnotically repeated. The theme is not developed (it undergoes no substantive change), but is merely restated several times with subtle alterations. The design of the music is simply the surface motion within the theme, rather than a broader pattern of accumulation and release of musical energy. The flute theme seems to exist outside of time. Its form does not "become" (it doesn't take shape gradually), but merely "is." This static, "being" quality characterizes much of the music of Asia, such as the gamelan performance of *Baris,* as well as many contemporary works.

A similar distinction can be found in the visual arts. In a painting such as *Violon et Guitare* by Juan Gris, various representational and abstract figures have been combined to create a strong overall design, sort of an inverted T. The picture seems to emanate from the center outward. The longer we look at it, the more complete its overall design "becomes" to us. Jackson Pollock's *Full Fathom Five,* on the other hand, is a more one-dimensional ("being") work. In this painting we grasp the total design almost immediately, and every portion—for example, the lower left corner—reflects this design in microcosm.

Curiously, works that consist *entirely* of contrasting fragments, such as Pauline Oliveros' *Sound Patterns,* also have a "being" quality. When there is

(Left) Violon et Guitare *by Juan Gris; (right)* Full Fathom Five *by Jackson Pollock (New York, Museum of Modern Art, Gift of Peggy Guggenheim)*

no integration of ideas, no primary themes or unifying thread, we again must focus on the quality of the moment, and the individual sounds must be sufficiently engaging or bewitching to sustain musical interest. In short, a work which is either "all unity," like the "Vocalise," or "all contrast," like *Sound Patterns,* will not develop ideas. The formal design will be confined to the *present* ("what's happening *now*"), without reference to past or future events.

Themes: The Melodic Basis of Form

A **theme** is a complete, memorable melody, usually several phrases in length and constructed around one or more motives. Themes present musical ideas in their original, most stable arrangement. These ideas serve both as unifying elements and as points of departure throughout the piece. After it has been presented, a theme may be treated in several ways during a composition:

1. The theme may be repeated exactly or with minor changes. "Scarborough Fair," like most popular songs, features several repetitions of the same melody. *Gymnopédie No. 1* includes a single restatement, with subtle changes in melodic contour and orchestration. When a complete theme recurs later in a work, after intervening passages, it is called a **return.** In Debussy's *Prelude to the Afternoon of a Faun,* an opening flute theme returns periodically throughout the work.

2. The theme may be repeated, but with significant alterations. The *varied repetition* introduces some element of contrast, such as the climactic build-up that occurs near the end of Chopin's *Prelude in E Minor.*

3. The theme may be *developed*—broken apart into motives which are treated separately or combined in new ways. The formal design of the Prelude to *Tristan and Isolde* is based on a process of continuous development.

Form in Tonal Music

In tonal music, unity and contrast result primarily from harmonic motion. Passages that remain in the tonic key normally are tonally stable and at rest. Passages that modulate into a new key create a feeling of "stepping up" or "down" and introduce a change in the musical landscape. The formal design of many works centers around the tonal contrast between two key centers.

The thematic outline of a piece—how many themes are presented, and when they are introduced—serves to clarify the harmonic motion. Major themes usually occur at tonally important points, coinciding with the establishment of the tonic and secondary keys and with the return of the tonic. We generally feel a shift in tonality more easily and strongly when it is accompanied by new melodic ideas.

The most common formal outline in music is a simple pattern of statement, contrast, and return. In the *statement,* the tonic key and basic character of the piece are established through presentation of an opening theme. *Contrast* generally results when the harmony moves into a new key

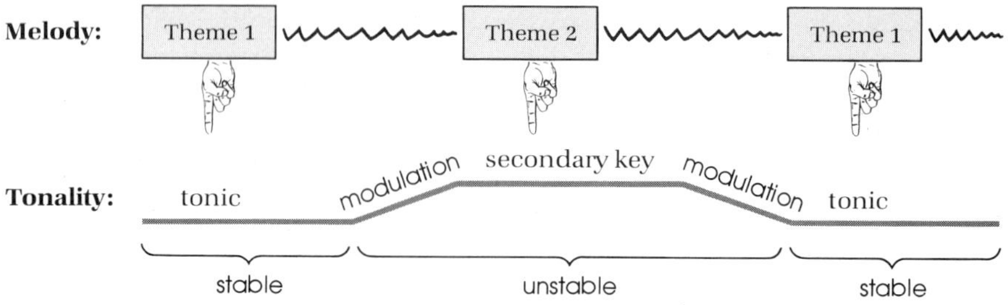

and something new happens in the melody to underscore this shift. A second theme may be introduced, or the first theme may be varied or developed. In the *return,* the original theme is recalled in the tonic key.

Connecting Passages

The design of a composition is determined not only by its musical goals—principal tonal centers, themes, and developments—but also by the way these goals are prepared and connected. **Connecting passages** shape the music around its major events, spacing them apart so that they stand out in relief, but also providing a coherent link that maintains continuity and enriches the structure. The most common types of connecting passages are:

Introductions: passages, generally at the beginning of a work, that lead the listener to anticipate a theme.

Transitions: passages that connect two themes, or link a theme with its development. Transitions usually include a modulation.

Episodes and Interludes: brief digressions, or "breathing" passages, of a fragmentary nature. Episodes and interludes function somewhat like literary subplots. They often mark a low point in musical tension somewhere in the middle of a work, a "valley between two peaks."

Closing Passages: passages at the end of a section of music that create a feeling of finality and closure. **Codas** are closing passages, sometimes of considerable length, at the very end of a composition. Short codas, lasting only a few measures, are termed *codettas.*

Sectional Construction

Most compositions can be divided into two or more *sections,* or parts. Each section ends with a full stop, grouping the events within the section into a unit and bringing them to completion. *Two-* and *three-part* formal outlines are particularly common, especially in tonal music. Most often, these outlines are based upon the principle of contrast and return.

It should be noted that the actual number of sections frequently is *not* one of the features we are most aware of while listening to a piece of music, and that many pieces do not fit neatly into one or the other of these general outlines. More important than the sectional construction of a work is the particular way in which unity and contrast are created. *This* is the design of the music, to which we respond, and it is what musical form is all about.

In the rest of this chapter we will look at several short tonal pieces in two or three sections, and at one song without clear sectional divisions. Musical interest in these works is concentrated in the statement of (or contrast between) themes. In Chapters 7 and 8 we will survey the more complex procedures of variation and development, on which most longer works are based.

Two-Part Forms

Compositions in **two-part form** present ideas in two groups. The song "America" is a simple example:

> *Part I:* "My country 'tis of thee, sweet land of liberty, of thee I *sing*." (*strong cadence*)
>
> *Part II:* "Land where my fathers died, land of the pilgrims' pride, from every mountainside, let freedom *ring*." (*stronger cadence*)

The first section may remain in the tonic key or cadence in a secondary key. The second section always cadences in the tonic. The two sections may be of any length and may include several weaker, interior cadences. Although the second part begins as a "fresh start," it also serves to bring the ideas of the opening section to a logical conclusion.

In *Gymnopédie No. 1* the two parts are based on the same melody, and the formal outline is labeled *A–A′* (the prime indicating a varied repetition). More often, as in "America," the second part introduces a new, "answering" melodic idea, and the outline is designated *A–B*. In some two-part pieces one or both of the sections is immediately repeated. This is indicated in the notation by **repeat signs** at the beginning and end of the section:

Since the repetition is exact, introducing no contrast or new formal elements, it does not alter the basic two-part feel of the music.

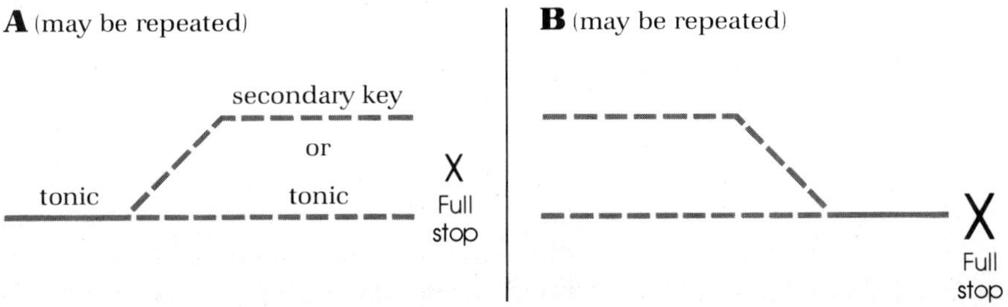

Lullaby *(Cradle Song),* Op. 49, No. 4, *by Johannes Brahms (1833–1897)*

Record Set Side 3, Band 2

Brahms' *Lullaby* is familiar to most of us as a nursery tune. We frequently hear it issuing from all manner of wind-up mobiles, teddy bears, and musical playthings. It is believed that Brahms wrote the song to commemorate the birth of a child to a woman he once loved. The song consists of a single theme divided into two parts. Each half of the theme, in turn, contains two phrases. The formal design of the song is:

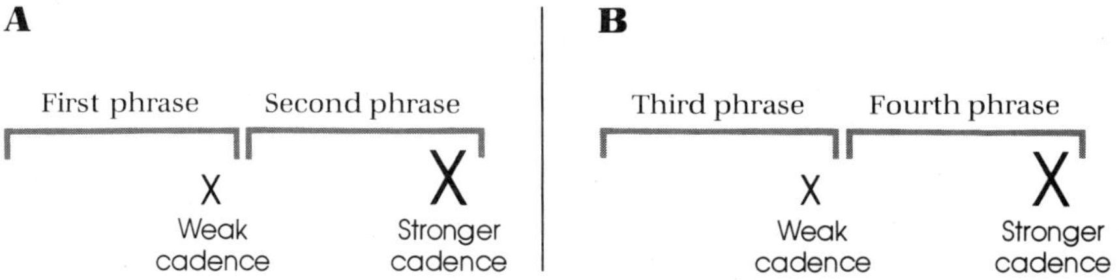

The harmonic motion of the song never strays far from the tonic. Every measure begins with the tonic note E♭ in the bass, and Brahms uses only three chords (I, IV, and V_7). The opening phrase introduces the recurrent motive ♫|♩. The melody encircles and cadences on the dominant note. The second phrase brings the thought to completion with a full stop.

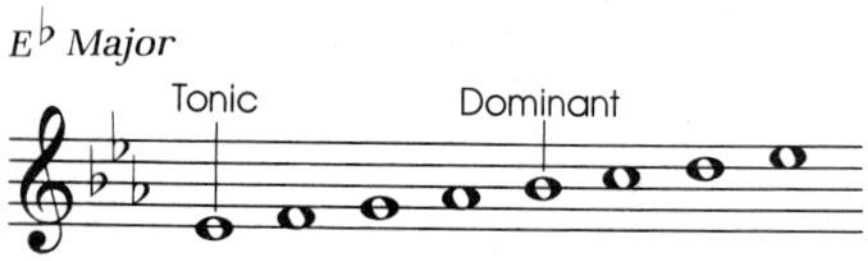

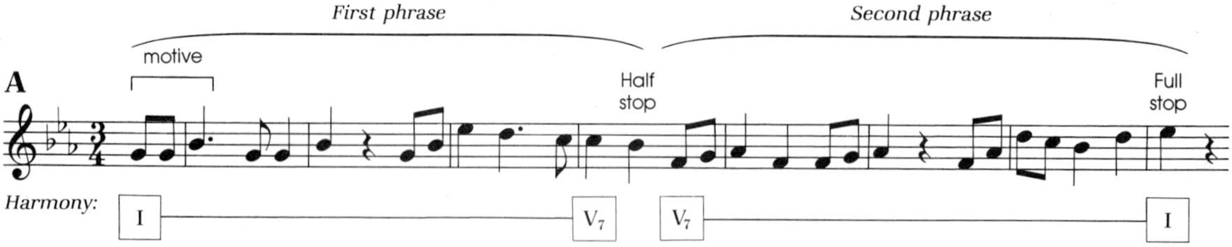

Continuing rhythmic motion in the harmonic accompaniment, however, leads us to expect a continuation.

In the second half of the theme the motive is altered slightly to ♫|𝅗𝅥 and intervalically expanded to an octave. The two phrases are similar, differing only at the cadences.

The two halves of the song are unified by the recurring motive and by similar cadence patterns (weak–strong). They contrast in melodic contour, which generally ascends in the first section and descends in the second, and in the use of larger melodic skips during the second half.

The Baroque Suite

A **suite** is a collection of short instrumental pieces. In the first half of the 18th century the suite was an important genre of solo and chamber music. Baroque suites consist of a series of brief, independent movements, each based on a traditional court dance.

The Baroque suite as a whole is unified in several ways. The movements are all in the same key. Each dance is in two-part form, with an immediate repetition of each half. The two sections may be of equal length, or the second may be longer; both sections often share the same motives, but the second half usually introduces melodic contrast. The tonal plan is symmetrical; the opening section modulates to, and cadences in, the dominant key; the second half begins in the dominant, often modulates further afield, then returns to the tonic. The formal structure of each dance is:

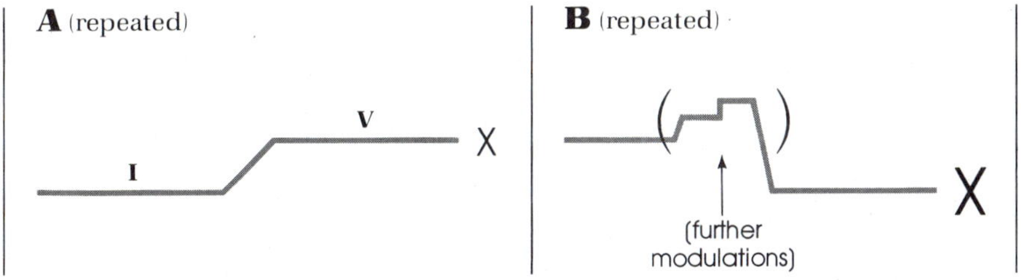

Listening

French Suite No. 6 in E Major *by Johann Sebastian Bach (1685 – 1750)*

Allemande: Record Set Side 3, Band 3

Bach's six *French Suites,* written between 1722 and 1725, typify the formal conventions of the Baroque suite. In Bach's day, keyboard suites always contained at least four movements: Allemande, Courante,

Sarabande, and a concluding Gigue (pronounced "zheeg"). Several optional dances could be inserted before the Gigue. The *French Suite No. 6* contains eight movements:

1. *Allemande.* Duple meter ($\frac{4}{4}$), moderate tempo, 2 voices (melodic lines).
2. *Courante.* Triple meter, moderately fast, 2 voices.
3. *Sarabande.* Stately triple meter, slow, 5 voices.
4. *Gavotte.* Duple meter, moderate tempo, 3 voices.
5. *Polonaise.* A Polish dance in moderately fast triple meter, 2 voices.
6. *Bourrée* ("bur-ay"). Duple meter, fast, 2 voices.
7. *Menuet.* Triple meter, moderately fast, 2–3 voices.
8. *Gigue.* $\frac{6}{8}$ meter, fast, 2 voices.

The tempo and meter of each dance was dictated by convention, but the number of melodic lines was up to the composer.

Allemande. The two-voiced Allemande features a bustling treble melody over a rhythmically more variable bass line.

Beginning of the first section (A)

At the beginning, the lower voice is a sort of "walking bass," providing a strong harmonic and rhythmic foundation as it trots up and down the scale in steady eighth-notes. Later, it joins in the development of rapid melodic figures introduced earlier in the top line. Midway through the opening section, the music modulates into the dominant key, where it cadences.

After the repeat of this opening half, the second section begins with an exact transposition of the first measure.

Beginning of the second section (B)

New ideas are then introduced. The motive ♫|♪, heard only in passing in the first section, is developed first in the bass, then in the upper voice. By means of *sequences* (motives repeated on different starting pitches) Bach moves briefly into minor, then returns to the tonic for the concluding full stop.

In listening to the other dances of this suite, try to observe the following characteristics within each movement:

1. Tempo, meter, and number of voices.
2. Important motives.
3. Tonal shifts to the dominant, through more distant keys, and back to the tonic.
4. The way in which Bach prepares and creates a full-stop at the end of each section.
5. Contrasts and unifying elements between the two sections. (In the Courante, Gavotte, and Bourrée, for example, the cadence at the end of the second section is brought about through a return of the melodic figures that closed the first section. The last few measures of the two sections contrast in key, and thus have a different quality, but they are melodically almost identical.)

Three-Part Forms

Compositions in three-part form contain three independent sections. The harmonic motion is usually based upon the principle of contrast and return. The opening section establishes the tonic; the middle section is in a secondary key; and the third section returns to the tonic. In most instances all three parts end with a full stop. Often, however, the cadence at the end of the middle section is weakened in order to provide a smoother link into the return of the tonic.

The melodic outline of most three-part pieces features a pattern of statement–contrast–return (*A–B–A*). The slow movements of many symphonies, sonatas, and chamber works follow this outline. The return may also be a varied repetition, incorporating changes within the harmony or melody. Occasionally, as in Schumann's *Papillons No. 3,* both of the later sections are varied repetitions of the original theme (*A–A′–A″*). In other works, each section presents a new theme (*A–B–C*).

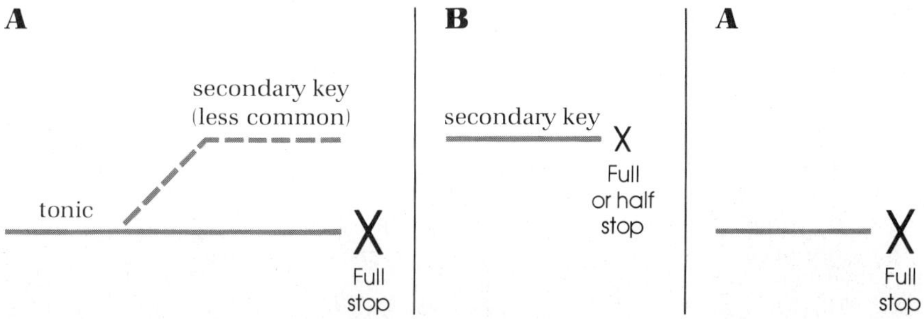

Three-part form is sometimes called "song form" because many songs follow this outline. In jazz and popular tunes, the music of the opening section is normally repeated (with different lyrics), leading to an *A–A–B–A* structure. Since the musical repetition is exact, however, introducing no contrast, it does not alter the underlying three-part form. A familiar, if inelegant, example of *A–A–B–A* structure is "Old MacDonald Had a Farm." The theme of Thelonius Monk's "Hackensack," discussed at the end of Chapter 4, is also an *A–A–B–A* design.

Listening

"The Linden Tree" (Der Lindenbaum) from* A Winter's Journey *(Die Winterreise) by Franz Schubert (1797–1828)

Record Set Side 3, Band 4

The **song cycle,** a form first developed by Beethoven, is an extended work made up of a series of songs. The songs present a continuous story line or depict various aspects of a character or situation. Schubert's *A Winter's Journey* (1827) is a cycle of 24 songs on a familiar Romantic theme. A young man, rejected by his lover, has become a wanderer. His life no longer has meaning, and he feels like an outsider wherever he goes. His changing moods range from melancholy and despair to bitterness, but center around his sense of loss. At times his depression lifts briefly and he finds momentary comfort in the tranquility of nature. Just as often, however, the sight of a particular tree or brook stirs painful memories and associations. There is no lasting peace; his opportunity has come and gone. Each song has a unique character and portrays a different frame of mind.

"The Linden Tree," the fifth song of the cycle, begins as one of the more contemplative settings, but it undergoes a brief, dramatic character change later. The song is in three-part form with a varied repetition of the opening section: *A–A′–B–A*.

	Text	Translation
	Piano introduction	
A	*Am Brunnen vor dem Tore,* *da steht ein Lindenbaum;* *ich träumt' in seinem Schatten* *so manchen süssen Traum.*	At the well before the gate there stands a linden tree; I have dreamed in its shade so many a sweet dream.
	Ich schnitt in sein Rinde *so manches liebe Wort;* *es zog in Freud' und Leide* *zu ihm mich immer fort*	I have carved into its bark so many words of love; in joy and sorrow I have been drawn to this place.
	Piano interlude	

A′	*Ich musst' auch heute wandern* *vorbei in tiefer Nacht,* *da hab ich noch im Dunkeln* *die Augen zugemacht.*	Today, also, I had to pass by in the deep of night; there, even in darkness, I had to close my eyes.
	Und seine Zweige rauschten, *als riefen sie mir zu:* *komm her zu mir, Geselle,* *hier findst du deine Ruh'!*	The branches rustled as though calling to me: "Come here to me, friend, here you will find peace."
	Short piano interlude	
B	*Die kalten Winde bliesen* *mir grad ins Angesicht,* *der Hut flog mir vom Köpfe,* *ich wendete mich night.*	Cold winds blew straight in my face; my hat flew from my head, but I did not turn.
	Piano transition	
A	*Nun bin ich manche Stunde* *entfernt von jenem Ort,* *und immer hör ich's rauschen:* *du fandest Ruhe dort!*	I am many hours distant from that place, and still I hear that rustling voice "You would find rest here."
	Piano postlude	

Piano introduction. Almost every song of *A Winter's Journey* begins with a short piano introduction that establishes the tonal center, mood, and one or two important motives of the song. This introduction features a rapid, rustling motive and abrupt pauses, suggesting the movement of leaves in the wind, the recurrent metaphor of the text.

A Section. The lyrical vocal melody has a folklike quality. It contains four phrases and ends with a full-stop in the tonic. The piano accompaniment is rhythmically placid and harmonically simple, never leaving the tonic triad for long.

Piano interlude. During a shortened variation of the introduction the tonality suddenly shifts to minor.

A′. The repetition of the vocal theme is exact, except for the significant shift to minor in the first two phrases, underscoring the darker character of the text (*"Ich musst' auch heute wandern vorbei in tiefer Nacht"*). The tonality then returns to major. The rhythmic pacing of the piano accompaniment is more active in this varied repetition.

B Section. The piano reintroduces the rustling motive, which continues throughout this section. The vocal melody becomes rhetorical, in marked contrast to the tranquil original theme. The tonality begins in minor, a further contrast to the prevailing major quality of the *A* section. Later the tonal center is obscured briefly by a chromatic flurry in the piano. Growing harmonic and rhythmic tension comes to a climax just before the vocal cadence. The *B* section concludes with a transitional piano passage featuring the rustling motive.

Return to A. The original vocal theme is repeated exactly. The piano, however, returns to the figuration of *A′*. The tonality is in major throughout. As a result of these minor variations, none of the three statements of *A* are identical.

Piano postlude. The rustling motive returns a final time, framing the song and providing a distillation of its central pictorial idea.

Listening

"My Love's Wedding Day" (Wenn mein Schatz Hochzeit macht) from* Songs of a Wayfarer (Lieder Eines Fahrenden Gesellen) *by Gustav Mahler (1860–1911)

Record Set Side 3, Band 5

Gustav Mahler in a caricature by Oscar Garvens

Works written near the end of the 19th century often have a formally loose or complex harmonic plan, modulating through distant tonal centers, sometimes beginning and ending in different keys. Composers of this period explored the *coloristic* possibilities of harmony, seeking expressive new types of sonorities and progressions; they were less concerned with *functional* harmonic motion, in which each chord is heard in relation to the tonic. In works no longer unified by a single reference pitch, tonal motion is a less decisive factor in formal structure. The original tonic may never return. To clarify the formal design of such compositions, composers tended to emphasize or even exaggerate *thematic* contrasts. The formal sections contrast strongly in melodic style, mood, texture and rhythm.

Mahler's *Songs of a Wayfarer* (1884) was the composer's first major work, written when he was 24. He would later incorporate portions of these songs in his *Symphony No. 1.* The story line of the cycle is similar to that of Schubert's *A Winter's Journey,* but the wanderer's tribulations are compressed here into only four songs.

The opening song, "My Love's Wedding Day" (Wenn Mein Schatz Hochzeit Macht) follows an *A–B–A* outline. The middle section forms a complete musical contrast to the outer parts.

A Section. A brief orchestral introduction presents the principal motive of the accompaniment, which will always recur in the woodwinds, and establishes the opening key of D minor. The vocal theme incorporates the woodwind motive:

The five phrases of the vocal melody are separated by brief orchestral connecting passages. The *A* theme itself is in two parts. After the third phrase *("hab' ich meinen traurigen Tag!")*, an orchestral closing passage brings the harmonic motion to a full stop in the original key. The second half of the theme modulates to the key of G minor, where it cadences. The mood becomes hushed; the vocal melody is accompanied by muted strings, with a single interjection of the woodwind motive just before the final phrase.

B Section. The middle section contrasts in every way with the preceding theme. The B theme establishes a much brighter color, introducing a harmonic shift to major, a faster tempo, a more animated $\frac{6}{8}$ meter, a higher vocal register, and a glistening orchestral texture. Mahler uses every musical resource to convey the wayfarer's temporary change of mood and exhilaration in the joys of nature. The words *"Vöglein süss"* ("sweet little bird") provoke a flurry of bird-call figures in the woodwinds and solo violin. The tonal motion is fluid, moving briefly into minor *("Du singst auf grüner Heide")* before coming to rest in another new major key *("Ach! Wie ist die Welt so schön!")*. The *B* section concludes with an orchestral passage that rounds out the section, leading to a weak cadence and momentary pause.

Return to A. The return of the *A* theme is shortened, containing a single orchestral interlude. The tonality again begins in D minor and ends in G minor, and the woodwind figure is recalled in an orchestral codetta. The three-part structure of this song, based upon the principle of contrast and return, mirrors the two moods of the text.

	Text	*Translation*
A	*Wenn mein Schatz Hochzeit macht,* *fröhliche Hochzeit macht,* *hab' ich meinen traurigen Tag!* *Geh' ich in mein Kämmerlein,* *dunkles Kämmerlein.* *Weine! wein'! um meinen Schatz,* *um meinen lieben Schatz!*	My love's wedding day, joyful wedding day, is a sad one for me. I go into my little room, dark little room, and weep. I weep for my love, for my dearest love.
B	*Blümlein blau! Blümlein blau!* *Verdorre nicht! Verdorre nicht!* *Vöglein süss! Vöglein süss!* *Du singst auf grüner Heide* *Ach! wie ist die Welt so schön!* *Ziküth! Ziküth! Ziküth!*	Little blue flower, little blue flower! Do not fade, do not fade! Sweet little bird, sweet little bird! You sing in the green meadow. Ah, the world is so beautiful! Chirrup, chirrup!
A	*Singet nicht! Blühet nicht!* *Lenz ist ja vorbei!* *Alles Singen ist nun aus!* *Des Abends, wenn ich schlafen geh'* *denk' ich an mein Leide!*	Sing no more! Bloom no more! Spring is gone! All singing is finished! At night, when I go to sleep, I think on my sorrow.

Through-Composed Forms

Through-composed is a cumbersome but common term applied to musical forms that lack well-defined sectional divisions and thematic return. Individual motives may recur throughout the work, but only in a varied or developmental way. Complete themes are never brought back, and the melody never lingers for long on a single idea. The tonal and thematic motion is continuous, lacking strong cadences or any feeling of completion until the end of the work. New ideas are continually introduced, but they often seem to grow out of earlier motives, so they still serve as unifying elements within the structure.

Vocal music in which the text presents a series of contrasting images naturally lends itself to through-composed structure. In an opera, for example, if two characters argue at the beginning of a number and one then kills the other, a return of the opening music would be dramatically ridiculous; the victim would need to exclaim, "Surprise! I'm not really dead!" in order to return to the *A* music. A more likely conclusion would be for the number to end with entirely new music expressing the aggressor's feelings of remorse or self-justification.

Listening

"I Have a Burning Dagger" (Ich Hab' ein glühend Messer) from* Songs of a Wayfarer *by Gustav Mahler

Record Set Side 3, Band 6

The tempestuous third song of the *Wayfarer* cycle is the climax of the work. The song begins with a blustering tutti introduction that sets the frenzied mood while establishing the original tonal center and drumming in a recurrent orchestral motive. The wayfarer has reached the breaking point. Mahler depicts his unrestrained outpouring of rage through the continuous introduction of new motivic ideas:

A	*Ich hab ein glühend Messer,* *ein Messer in meiner Brust,* *O weh! O weh!* *Das schneid't so tief* *in jede Freud' und jede Lust,* *so tief!*	I have a burning dagger, a dagger in my breast. Oh grief, oh grief! It cuts so deeply through every joy and happiness. So deeply!
B	*Ach, was ist das für ein böser Gast!* *Nimmer hält er Ruh', nimmer* *hält er Rast!*	Ah, what an evil guest! It never stops or rests!
C	*Nicht bei Tag, nicht bei Nacht,* *wenn ich schlief!* *O weh! O weh!*	Not by day, not even at night, when I sleep! Oh grief, oh grief!
D	*Wenn ich in den Himmel seh',* *seh' ich zwei blaue Augen steh'n!* *O weh! O weh!*	When I look into the sky I see those two blue eyes! Oh grief, oh grief!

Wenn ich im gelben Felde geh'
seh' ich von fern das blonde
Harr im Winde weh'h!
O weh! O weh!

When I walk through the golden fields,
I see her blond hair
blowing in the wind.
Oh grief! Oh grief!

E *Wenn ich aus dem Traum auffahr'*
Und höre Klingen ihrs bern Lachen,
O weh! O weh!

When I awake from a dream
I hear her silver laughter ringing.
Oh grief! Oh grief!

F *Ich wollt' ich läg auf dem*
schwartzen Bahr;
Konnt' nimmer, nimmer die
Augen aufmachen!

I wish I lay dead
on a black bier
never to open my eyes
again.

The structure of the song looks diffuse on paper, but it is unified by a continuous dramatic sweep in performance. The new ideas are run together and interrelated by the prevailing mood. Each idea colors this mood in a different way; each is a different reflection of the same anguish. The only ideas that recur are the orchestral motive and a descending motive in the vocal line on the repeated text *"O weh!"* None of the cadences—not even the last one—is strong; none interrupts the forward motion of the song. Tonal motion is also continuous, moving through a series of modulations and winding up in a key distant from the original tonic. The volatile rhythmic pacing ebbs and flows between the two climactic points *C* and *F*.

Although the through-composed musical structure has no clear sectional divisions or melodic returns, the song does have a three-part dramatic structure. After the first climax, at *C*, an orchestral transition dissipates much of the dramatic tension. Idea *D* is musically slower, almost whispered, and lightly scored. Passage *D* is the dramatic low point of the song, a quiet moment that contrasts in character with the beginning and ending. The original mood, though not the original tonality or theme, returns at *E*.

The ghostly orchestral postlude transforms the orchestral motive into an eerie, phantom-like figure. The postlude dissipates the tension of the song but does not resolve it, suggesting a mental collapse. The wayfarer has lost touch with reality and is at the point of suicide.

Listening

"My Love's Two Blue Eyes" ("Die Zwei Blauen Augen") from Songs of a Wayfarer *by Gustav Mahler*

Record Set Side 3, Band 7

It would be uncharitable to leave Mahler's wayfarer so distraught, without the solace the composer has provided. In the first three songs of the cycle the wanderer has experienced the various psychological stages of loss: denial, anger, grief, and withdrawal. In the final song, "My Love's Two Blue Eyes," he comes to the final stage, acceptance. The song is in three-part form, each section presenting a separate theme *(A–B–C)*. However, the song as a whole is unified by a single mood and the recurrent rhythmic motive :

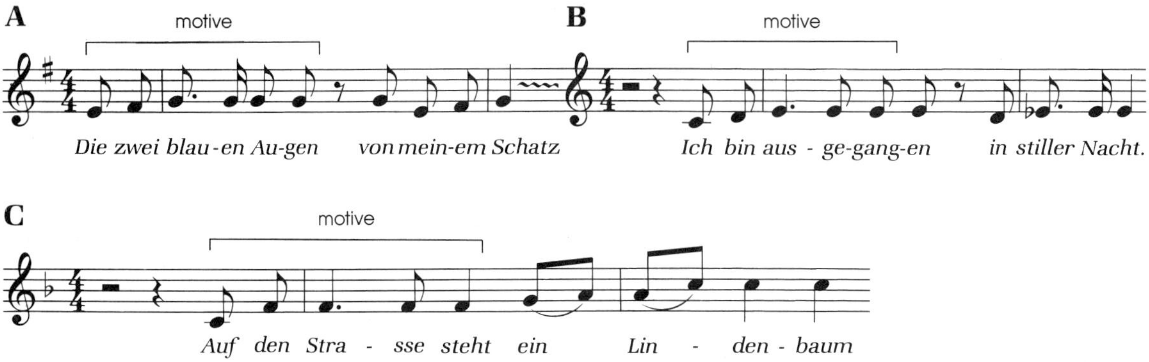

A	*Die zwei blauen Augen von meinem* *Schatz die haben mich* *in die weite Welt geschickt.* *Da musst ich Abschied nehmen* *vom allerliebsten Platz!* *O Augen blau, warum habt ihr* *mich angeblickt?* *Nun hab' ich ewig Leid und Gramen!*	My Love's two blue eyes have sent me out into the world. I have had to say goodbye to the place I loved most of all. Oh blue eyes, why did you ever look at me? Now I have constant sorrow and pain.
B	*Ich bin ausgegangen in stiller Nacht* *in stiller Nacht* *wohl über die dunkle Heide;* *hat mir niemand Ade gesagt.* *Ade! Ade! Ade!* *Mein Gesell' war Lieb' und Leide.*	I went out into the silent night, into the silent night over the dark heath. No one said goodbye to me. Farewell! My companions were love and sorrow.
C	*Auf der Strasse steht ein Lindenbaum* *da hab' ich zum ersten Mal* *im Schlaf geruht!* *Der hat seine Blüten* *über mich geschneit—* *da wusst' ich nicht, wie das Leben tut* *war alles, alles wieder gut!* *Alles, Lieb' und Leid,* *und Welt, und Traum!*	By the road stands a linden tree, where for the first time I found peace in sleep. Under its blossoms, which snowed on me, I knew not what life does— everything seemed good again. Everything! Love and sorrow, the world, and dreams.

Each section is in a different key. Each ends with a full stop, which serves to clarify the three–part form in the absence of tonal or thematic return. The song has three obvious beginning and ending points, but each section reflects a single idea, mood, and musical motive.

Schematic Diagram of "My Love's Two Blue Eyes"

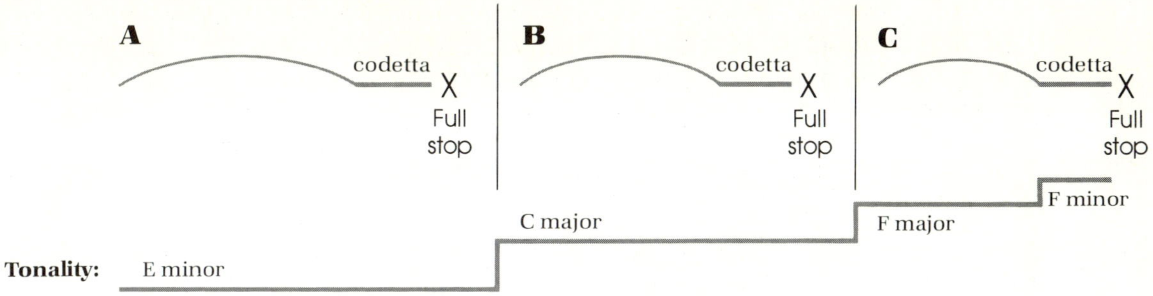

Minuet and Trio Form

The minuet was originally a two-part dance movement included somewhere in the middle of a suite. The seventh movement of Bach's *French Suite No. 6* is a representative example of this form. During the latter half of the 18th century the instrumental suite and most of its movements passed into history. The minuet, however, was expanded into a larger three-part outline, called **minuet and trio form,** that became the third movement of many symphonies and chamber works. This later minuet retained the moderately fast triple meter and elegant dancelike quality of its ancestor.

The minuet, still in two parts, comprises the first section within the expanded form. It is followed by the trio, also in two parts. A return of the minuet rounds out the movement. The movement as a whole thus has a three-part *A–B–A* outline; each of these sections, however, is itself composed of two parts.

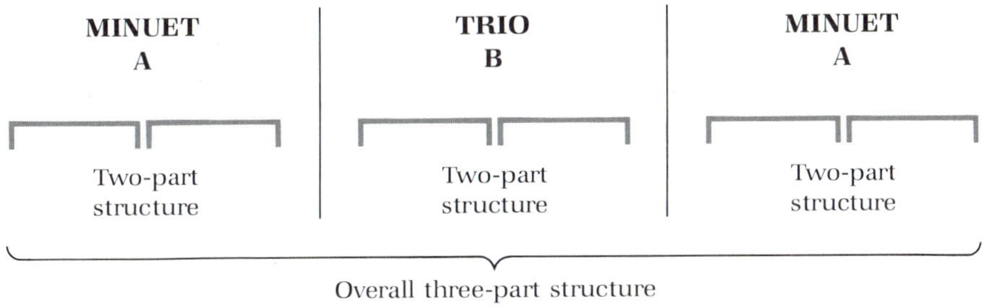

In the minuet section an opening theme leads to a full stop, and the entire passage is repeated. In the second half of the minuet an answering idea, concluding with a weak cadence, is followed by a shortened return of the original theme. This second half is also repeated.

The trio is similar in internal structure. It introduces contrasting ideas and establishes the secondary key of the movement. It also contrasts with the minuet section by its simpler rhythmic style and texture. Many trios feature a reduced texture of only three lines, the origin of the term "trio."

The return of the minuet section is an exact repetition, except that the two halves are not repeated. Minuet and trio form is highly symmetrical. Each of the three sections mirrors in microcosm the statement–contrast–shortened return outline of the movement as a whole.

Listening

Third Movement from the* Symphony No. 40 in G Minor *by Wolfgang Amadeus Mozart (1756–1791)

Record Set Side 7, Band 4

Minuet Section. The energetic opening theme features sequential repetition of a phrase built around a syncopated figure:

The second half of the minuet section begins in major with a two-voice contrapuntal texture. The original motive is sequentially repeated in the lower strings and woodwinds against a new countermelody in the violins. The two lines are rhythmically out of phase, producing a series of cross-accents (marked *) that give the passage a strong rhythmic drive:

The cadence at the end of this passage is weak; the idea has not been brought to completion. The rhythmic momentum continues through a varied return of the original theme, now treated contrapuntally between the first and second violins with a series of cross-accents that climb ever higher. The minuet section concludes with a woodwind codetta.

Trio. In addition to presenting a new theme, the trio section contrasts with the minuet in many ways. It is thinner in texture (generally in three voices). It is in G *major* rather than minor. And the rhythmic style consists of simple flowing quarter-notes without the cross accents of the minuet. The second half of the trio opens with a question-and-answer figure between the lower strings and woodwinds, followed by a brief return of the opening trio theme.

Minuet Return. The minuet return is an exact repetition of the minuet, except that the two halves of the section are not repeated.

The Scherzo

During the early 1800s symphonies and sonatas increased in length and emotional breadth. Composers sought greater weight and contrast within each movement, and the minuet gave way to the more robust scherzo (pronounced "*scare*-tso"). The early scherzo was identical to minuet and trio form in outline, but it differed in style and character. The scherzo is faster and more energetic, and it is often abrupt, boisterous, or whimsical in nature (*scherzo* means "joke" in Italian). Beethoven was the first composer to include scherzo movements consistently in his major instrumental works. In his later scherzos, such as the third movement of the *Symphony No. 7,* he expanded the form; and additional varied repetition of both the trio *(B)* and scherzo *(A)* sections results in an *A–B–A′–B′–A″* outline.

Suggested Listening

Third Movement from the* Symphony No. 7 *by Anton Bruckner (1824–1896)

The third movement of Bruckner's *Symphony No. 7* typifies the rhythmic vigor of the scherzo. The movement follows the outline given on page 123. The two halves of each section are considerably longer than in the older minuet, however, and therefore are not repeated. The sectional divisions are easy to hear, as each of the full stops is followed by a pause. The scherzo section is constructed around three motives announced at the beginning of the movement:

The lyrical trio stands in marked contrast to the bouncing rhythms and climactic buildups of the scherzo section. At the conclusion of the trio, the scherzo returns with full vigor.

Terms and Concepts for Review

- unity and contrast
- "becoming" music and "being" music
- theme
  - return
  - varied repetition
  - development
- statement–contrast–return
- connecting passages
  - introduction
  - transition
  - episodes and interludes
  - closing passages
  - coda
- two-part forms
- three-part forms
- through-composed forms
- minuet and trio form
- scherzo

Chapter 7
Rondo and Variation Forms

Musical forms based upon contrast and return are not limited to two or three sections. In this chapter we will examine multi-sectional designs featuring a recurring theme. Since the 18th century most such designs have been organized by means of rondo or variation procedures.

Refrain Forms

Many poems contain a *refrain,* one or two lines repeated at the end of each stanza. The refrain is sometimes stated as the beginning of the poem as well. When setting such a poem to music, composers naturally tend to use the same music for each appearance of the refrain. Often, a single musical setting is used for the stanzas as well. The resulting musical design consists of several alternations of two themes.

Listening

"Je Ne L'Ose Dire" (I Shouldn't Tell You) by Pierre Certon (c. 1510–1572)

Record Set Side 5, Band 3

A common genre of Renaissance vocal music was the *part-song,* a song arranged for four or five voices ("parts"). Many part-songs are built on a refrain structure; the sectional construction is made obvious by short phrases, animated rhythms, and strong cadences at the end of the refrains.

Pierre Certon was a singer at Notre Dame Cathedral in Paris and later at the royal chapel. His droll part-song "Je Ne L'Ose Dire" typifies the formal outline of the refrain song. Refrain sections with identical text and music *(A)* alternate with a second theme, creating a five-part overall design: *A–B–A–B–A*. The song "Je Ne L'Ose Dire" is urbane and mischievous in tone and masterful in its simplicity of expression. The seeming innocence of the music belies the ribald nature of its text. Witless husbands, whose total ignorance of their wives' love affairs merely added to the amusement of onlookers, were a favorite topic for song writers of the period.

A	*La, la, la, je ne l'o, je ne l'o* *je ne l'ose dire;* *La, la, la, je le vous dirais,* *et la, la, la, je le vous dirai.*	La, la, la, I shouldn't tell you, La, la, la, I will tell you anyway.
B	*Il est un homme en no ville,* *Qui de sa femme est jaloux.* *Il n'est pas jaloux sans cause,* *Mais il est cocu de tout.*	There is a man in our city who is jealous of his wife. He is not jealous without cause, but is cuckolded by every man.
A	*Et la, la, la, je ne l'o. . . (etc.)*	La, la, la. . .
B	*Il n'est pas jaloux sans cause,* *Mais il est cocu de tout.* *Il l'aprete, et s'il la mene* *Au marche, s'en va a tout.*	He is not jealous without cause, but is cuckolded by every man. He brings her to market, where everything goes against him.
A	*Et la, la, la, je ne l'o. . . (etc.)*	La, la, la. . .

Rondo Forms

Refrain-like structures are common in instrumental as well as vocal music. A rondo is an instrumental piece in which a principal theme returns several times in alternation with contrasting passages. The rondo is not a rigid structural outline with a specific number of sections; rather, it is a flexible, additive format. Any number of contrasting sections and returns may be incorporated within the design:

A (principal theme) – contrast – A – contrast . . . (additional returns and contrasting sections) . . . A

The principal theme usually returns in the tonic key at each appearance, while each contrasting section is in a different secondary key. The contrasting sections are excursions, presenting different responses to the same statement. Among the most common rondo schemes are the three diagramed on the next page.

Rondo structures most commonly are encountered as the final movement of sonatas, symphonies, chamber works, and concertos. Most rondos are simpler in structure and lighter in tone than the preceding movements. Although rondo designs look highly segmented when diagramed, the composer can play with the listener's expectations by delaying an anticipated return, interjecting brief episodes, or introducing false returns in which the

Common Rondo Designs

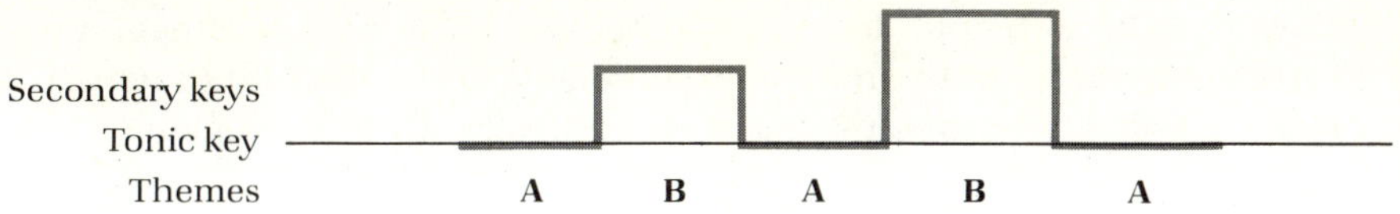

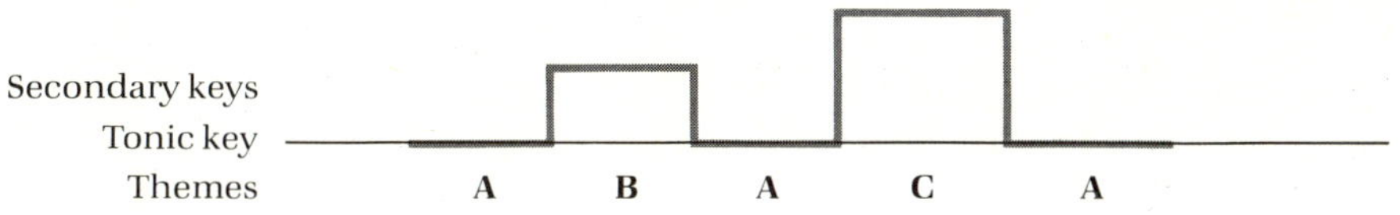

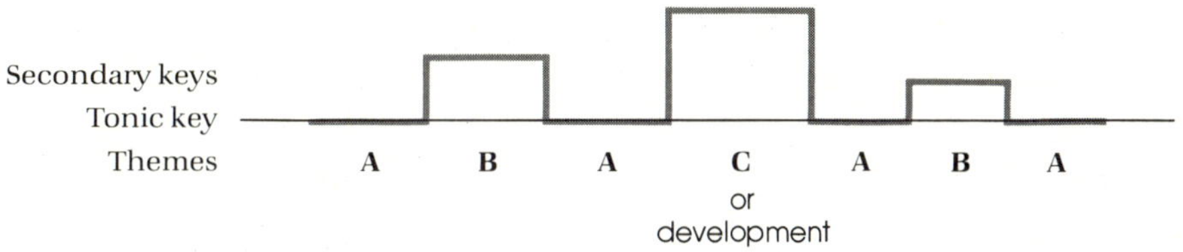

beginning of the theme appears but then collapses. Developmental passages are also common. Many movements labeled simply "rondo" actually are cast in a more complex format called sonata-rondo, featuring an extended developmental passage in the middle.

The rondo is a game, and the composer's ploys are effective precisely because the background structure is so simple and predictable. The listener knows that the rondo theme must eventually return but does not know when, how often, or how it will be led into each time. Sometimes the theme is anticipated, and we nod in acknowledgement at its reappearance; at other times, it comes in "through the back door," taking us by surprise.

Listening

Third Movement from the Piano Concerto No. 3 in C Minor *by Ludwig van Beethoven (1770–1827)*

Record Set Side 4, Band 1

Beethoven's rondos are prime examples of the sporting possibilities of rondo form. The composer whom Stravinsky called "the hammerer and thunderer" could also unbend in whimsical rondo finales which serve to counterbalance the earnest tone of earlier movements. In his concerto finales, the *formal* interplay between the rondo theme and the contrasting sections is matched by a *textural* give-and-take between the soloist and orchestra. The last movement of Beethoven's *Piano Concerto No. 3,* completed in 1800, follows a typical structural outline:

A–B–A-development–A′–B–Coda (A″). Before reading the summary below, it might be helpful to close the book and listen on a general level. Be aware of returns of the opening theme and of the manner in which themes are shared between soloist and orchestra.

Rondo theme: A. The genial rondo theme begins with a melodically concentrated phrase. Within this brief phrase Beethoven incorporates several motives that will recur throughout the movement:

First phrase (a) of the rondo theme

(brackets indicate individual motives developed later)

The theme itself has an *a-a-b-a′* structure, with further repetition within the longer, concluding portion *(a′)*:

				a′		
a –	*a* –	*b* –	*cadenza* –	*(a′* –	*b* –	*a)*
piano	orchestra	piano	(solo passage)	piano	orchestra	orchestra

The *b* idea begins as a variant of *a*: compare the first two measures below with the opening of the rondo theme above.

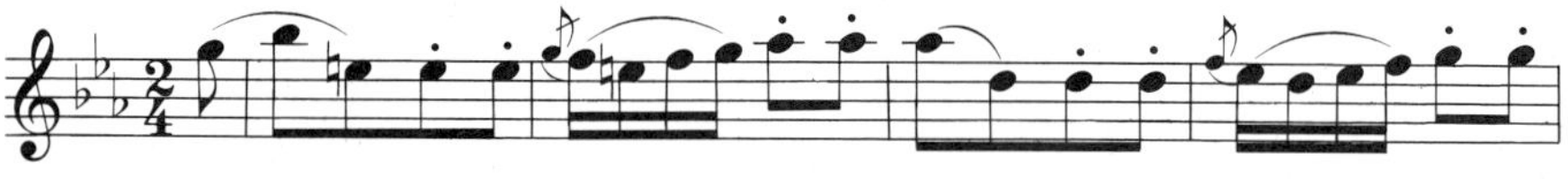

The *b* idea soon breaks apart, however, becoming stuck on a rhythmically spasmodic descending figure (*). The rondo theme seems to be winding down at a curious point, just where it was developing momentum. A brief *cadenza* (rapid solo run) in the piano jolts the theme back to life for the final, extended restatement of *a*. Abrupt or heavyhanded changes in pacing, during which the theme momentarily becomes hesitant or "lost" before reasserting itself, are common in Beethoven's rondos. The rondo theme ends with a full stop, both in this opening statement and in subsequent returns.

The B Section. The *B* section begins with an introductory fanfare figure in the winds, alternating with gruff responses in the piano. The *B* theme proper, heard first in the piano, then in the violins, is in E$^\flat$ major, the secondary key area. It is based on the rhythmically halting figure from the rondo theme (marked * above). The *B* theme incorporates several motives of the rondo theme and maintains the prevailing rhythmic and melodic character of the movement. It is followed by *passagework,* scalar and arpeggiated figures in the piano. A rapid descending and ascending sweep provides a transition into a return of the original rondo theme.

Return of A. The rondo theme returns with only minor alterations:

a –	a –	b	–*longer cadenza*–	a′
piano	orchestra	piano	piano	orchestra and piano

Development. The development section begins in a distant key (A major) with a new theme, which passes from the clarinet to the piano. Like the *B* theme, this new melody incorporates motives of the rondo theme. It is followed by passagework in the piano, then by three-voiced imitative treatment of the opening of the rondo theme in the strings. Fragments of the rondo theme are scattered through the orchestra, then reassembled briefly by the piano—but in the "wrong" key and with a more lyrical character. Beethoven resolutely avoids the original key of C minor throughout this tonally unstable development section. Then, in another cadenza, the piano gallumphs up, down, and back up the scale through several octaves. By now the listener has come to associate such sweeping runs with the imminent reappearance of the rondo theme and original tonality.

A′. A shortened return:

a –	a
piano	orchestra

B. The *B* theme returns in the tonic, though still in major, in contrast to the minor-key rondo theme. Beethoven is done with introducing new themes, and the music is moving in a smaller tonal orbit as it nears its conclusion. The *B* theme is followed by a mini-development, a pause on an unstable chord in the orchestra, and another sweeping cadenza.

Coda: A″. The rondo theme undergoes substantial changes in the coda. The tonality shifts to major, and the meter to $\frac{6}{8}$, the tempo is quicker, and the theme retains only the skeletal outline of the opening motive:

Coda theme

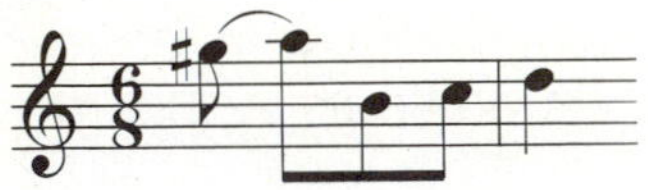

Original rondo theme

Any lingering tension is dispelled in this exuberant coda. The pacing increases and the texture swells to include full orchestra as the movement comes to a vigorous close.

For Further Listening

***"Turkish Rondo" from Mozart's* Piano Sonata in A Major, K.331.**

Record Set Side 7, Band 1

The rondo principle can be applied in many ways, and frequently leads to formal designs that bear little resemblance to the one heard in Beethoven's *Piano Concerto No. 3.* Mozart's celebrated "Turkish Rondo," for example, exhibits the following three-part outline:

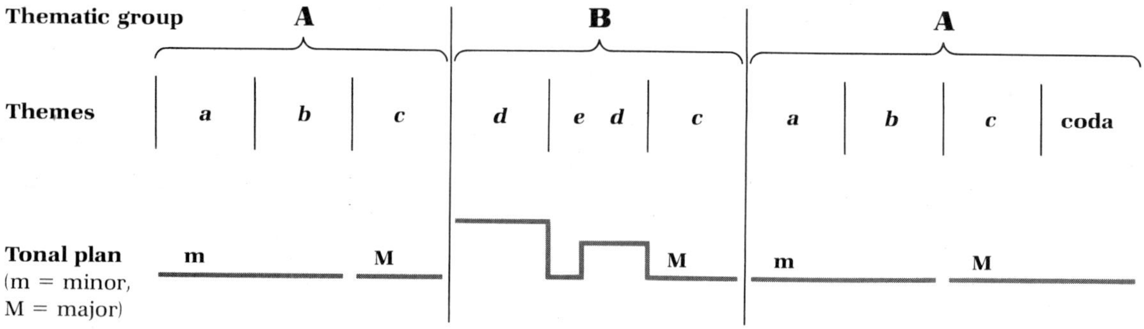

Each of the three large sections of the movement consists of a chain-like series of themes. The theme treated in rondo fashion turns out to be the third one we hear *(c)*. At each appearance, this theme pulls the music into its home key of A *Major*. The charm of the "Turkish Rondo" comes partly from its good-humored tone and pointed themes, but it also springs from the formal game in progress. The unexpected reappearance of *c* "too early" in the middle section turns this interior theme into the dominant idea of the movement.

Variation Forms

Variation is the most universal formal procedure in music: a theme is stated, then repeated with significant alterations and a new emphasis. As melodic, harmonic, rhythmic, and textural modifications are introduced, the theme undergoes changes in character. It may even become virtually unrecognizable for a while, though retaining its skeletal formal outline.

Variation is the simplest, most economical way for a composer to achieve both unity and contrast. Practically all formal procedures rely in part upon the principle of variation. In the rest of this chapter we will survey forms in which variation is the determining element of structure.

Theme and Variation

In **theme and variation** forms a theme is stated first in its simplest arrangement, then repeated several times with alterations. Theme and variation formats are common both within individual movements of large instrumental works (symphonies, sonatas, and so on), and as the basis of independent single-movement compositions. The theme may be an original one, or it may be borrowed from a folk tune, an aria from an opera, or some other source. Beethoven, for example, wrote a set of 33 variations on a waltz tune by Anton Diabelli, a publisher and minor composer of the day. Another set of Beethoven variations is based on "God Save the King" (our "America"), and a third features an aria from Mozart's opera *Don Giovanni.* While a series of four to twelve variations is most common, works such as the *Diabelli Variations* contain many more.

Listening

Second Movement from the* Symphony No. 94 *("Surprise Symphony") by Franz Josef Haydn (1732–1809)

Record Set Side 4, Band 2

At the end of his career, Franz Joseph Haydn wrote twelve symphonies for performance at a series of gala concerts in London. The *Symphony No. 94* was premiered in 1792 and, like others in the series, achieved immediate success. The source of the symphony's nickname is found in the second movement, where a crashing chord interrupts an otherwise tranquil theme. Such a "surprise" may seem rather tame to modern listeners, but to 18th-century ears the effect was startling. A number of apocryphal stories surrounds the origins of this chord. Most concern the supposed drowsiness or chattering of an audience sitting through a long after-dinner concert (which in Haydn's day could last four or five hours). The chord has been construed as Haydn's way of rousing listeners on the verge of a snooze, or of frightening the gabbers into respectful attention. A simpler explanation, attributed to Haydn himself, is that he merely wished to try something new; such a motivation, whether true or not, would have been in character.

Theme. On a first hearing, the theme already has a familiar ring, perhaps reminiscent of a folk tune or nursery rhyme. It is, however, original. The melody is simple and direct, outlining tonic and dominant harmonies:

The theme is in C major and in two parts, both repeated. An eight-measure phrase, idea *a*, ends with a half-stop. The repeat concludes on the "surprise" chord (still a half-stop). Idea *b*, an answering eight-measure phrase, completes the tonal motion, cadencing with a full-stop. In the repetition of *b*, winds are added for the first time, producing a fuller texture as the theme draws to a close.

Variation 1. The first variation opens with another resounding chord, for the benefit of those who enjoy a joke more the second time around. In the first variation the theme remains intact; the original melody and harmonic structure are repeated in the lower strings. Above the theme, the first violins enter with a rhythmically more animated countermelody, punctuated by accents *(sf)*:

The second half of the variation continues the interplay between the original theme and the new countermelody. The introduction of such countermelodies is a common variation technique.

Variation 2. The second variation moves farther afield. The tonality shifts to C minor. The first four measures of the theme are stated in stark unharmonized octaves. The character change seems to be a false alarm, however, when the strings conclude the *a* section softly in a new major key (A major). The first half of the theme has been broken apart into two strongly contrasting phrases: menacing bare octaves in minor, followed by a hushed echo in a distant major key:

In the second half of the variation Haydn jettisons the original *b* melody. In its place he introduces a developmental passage, featuring fragments of the *a* section (lower strings) against rapid scale runs in the violins. The dramatic force of this passage is strengthened by a series of modulatory shifts, a fuller texture, and a loud dynamic level. This passage is the climactic point in the movement, in which Haydn moves furthest away from the original theme and tonality. The variation concludes with vigorous scale sweeps, followed by a brief transitional solo in the violins.

Variation 3. In the third variation Haydn begins a process of reintegration, bringing the original character of the theme back into focus. The variation begins with a simple rhythmic variant of the theme in the oboe. The original tonality, harmonic structure, texture and (soft) dynamic level are also restored.

Original theme
(transposed an octave higher)

Violins

Variation 3

Oboe

Instead of repeating the first half of this variation, Haydn then states the theme in its original eighth-note rhythm in the violins and introduces a new countermelody in the flute and oboe. The decrease in rhythmic pacing produces a feeling of further relaxation. The countermelody continues over idea *b* during the second half of the variation.

Variation 4. Final variations usually present the theme in easily recognizable form and sum up the movement as it nears completion. The last variation of this movement opens with full orchestra and heightened rhythmic energy. The repeat of the *a* section, however, offers a marked contrast. The texture is reduced to strings and the dynamic level is soft. Section *b* continues in this hushed character, but the repeat returns to the rhythmically emphatic tutti scoring with which the variation began.

Coda. Codas are tonally stable passages that bring a movement to a close. Usually there is little harmonic motion; rather, a coda serves to zero in on the tonic, resolving any lingering tonal tension and confirming a feeling of tonality. In fast movements the coda is usually a rousing final flourish. In slow movements like this one, the coda is more often an epilogue or tapering-off. A simplified version of the theme returns in the oboe and bassoon, serving as a final reminiscence that brings the movement to a quiet conclusion.

Continuous Variation Forms

A different approach to the principle of variation is found in **continuous variation forms.** Here a bass line or chord progression is repeated over and over throughout a work. Above this unchanging foundation, one or more freer voices introduce a series of new melodic ideas. The variations follow one another without interruption, strong cadences, or sectional divisions.

Theme and Variation Form

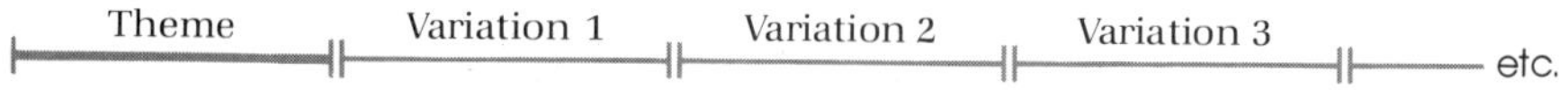

Continuous Variation Forms

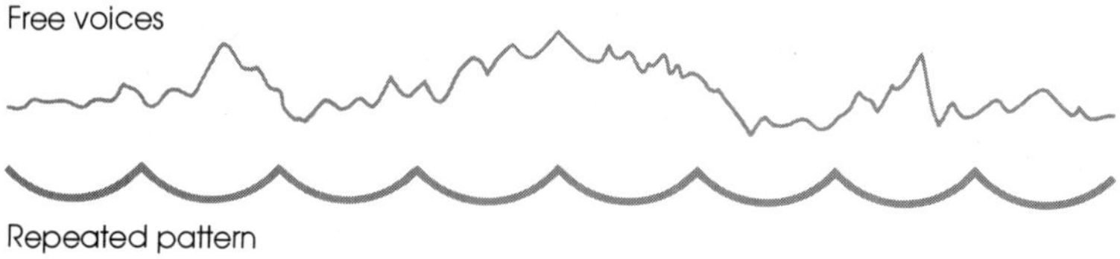

The three most important continuous variation forms are the **ground bass,** the **passacaglia,** and the **chaconne.** These forms are encountered most often in music of the Baroque period (1600–1750) and occasionally in 20th-century works.

Ground bass. The **ground bass,** or **basso ostinato,** is a pattern of bass notes, usually a few measures in length, continuously repeated in exactly the same form throughout a composition. The upper voices move freely, without internal repetition, against this unvarying bass theme. In works built on a ground bass, formal contrast and return occur simultaneously; the upper voices continuously develop new ideas, while the rigorous bass line repeats the same pattern without changes or additions. Although sometimes heard in instrumental works, ground basses are most common as an instrumental accompaniment to vocal works, particularly ones expressing grief or sadness.

Listening

"Dido's Lament," recitative and aria from Act III of* Dido and Aeneas *by Henry Purcell (1659–1695)

Record Set Side 6, Band 1

Henry Purcell was the most gifted English composer of the Baroque period. His opera *Dido and Aeneas* (1689), written for performance by the students at a girls' boarding school, contains three arias (songs) on ground basses. The opera lasts only an hour and is well suited to performance by amateur musicians, but it is also highly expressive. The second-last number is a recitative and aria sung by Dido, the Queen of Carthage, who has been abandoned by her lover, Aeneas. The recitative is a rhythmically free introduction to the aria; Dido is nearing death and asks her faithful servant Belinda to remain with her to hear her final thoughts. At the conclusion of the recitative ("Death is now a welcome guest"), the ground bass pattern of the aria begins:

Ground bass from "Dido's Lament"

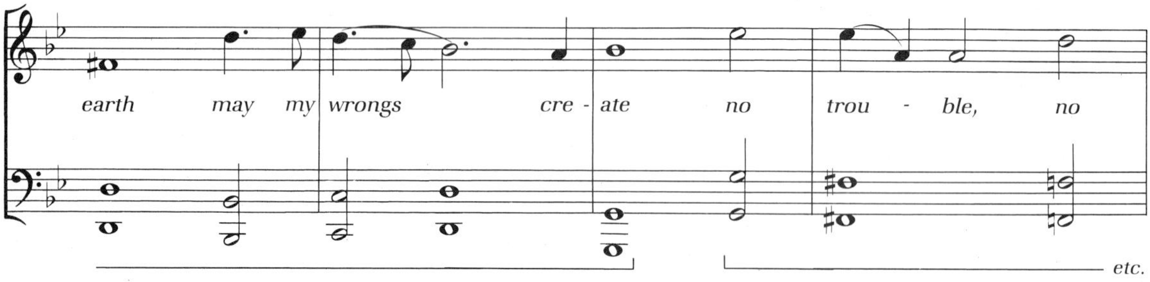

The ground bass pattern is repeated continuously, without breaks or alterations, eleven times. The vocal line is melodically free, introducing new motives ("Remember me," "But ah!") and cadencing at irregular intervals. Dido's lament is moving in its simple acceptance of unfulfilled love and death. Dido blames no one, expresses no bitterness or remorse, and asks to be remembered only for the quality of her love. Although the rigid ground bass holds the music firmly in the tonic key and provides an austere foundation to the song, the melodic variations have a sense of emotive freedom and carefully depict the individual lines of the text:

> When I am laid in earth, may my wrongs create
> No trouble in thy breast!
> Remember me! But ah! forget my fate.

Passacaglia and Chaconne. The passacaglia (pah-sah-*call*-ya) and chaconne (sha-*kone*) are two closely related variation forms, so closely related, in fact, that many composers have considered them identical. Each consists of a series of continuous variations over a repeated bass line or chord progression.[1] The theme is most often in slow triple meter and in minor, and is usually about eight measures in length. It remains recognizable during the first few variations but undergoes transformations later, appearing in upper voices with rhythmic and melodic alterations. As the variations roll by in unbroken succession, the theme comes in and out of focus—sometimes distinct, at other times subordinate to other voices.

Listening

Fourth Movement from the Symphony No. 4 in E Minor *by Johannes Brahms (1833–1897)*

Record Set Side 4, Band 3

The best known chaconne since the Baroque era is the final movement of Brahms' *Symphony No. 4* (1885). It is also the only movement of a major symphony in this form. Brahms borrowed the

[1] Some modern scholars, in attempting to clear up the longstanding confusion between these two terms, have proposed that *passacaglia* be reserved for works featuring a repeated bass line, and *chaconne* be applied to works based on a repeated chord progression.

theme from Bach's *Cantata No. 150, "Nach dir, Herr."* It is stated at the opening of the movement in the woodwinds and brass. The trombones, silent throughout the first three movements of the symphony, are prominent in the scoring of the theme. This powerful opening statement is stern, almost defiant, indelibly engraving the theme in the listener's memory.

The movement then presents thirty variations, each eight measures in length, and an extended coda, all based on the omnipresent theme. So rigid a structure, while assuring formal unity, presented Brahms with unique structural problems when applied to a symphonic movement. Foremost were the dangers that under such relentless repetition the theme could grow tiresome, the movement as a whole could lack direction or contrast, and the exaggerated tonal stability (the movement remains firmly rooted on the tonic note E throughout) could prove monotonous.

Brahms provided ingenious solutions to each of these potential structural pitfalls. The problem of tonal monotony was solved in part by his initial harmonization of the melody, which begins in minor but cadences in major, an unexpected twist. In the variations, this initial harmonization is continuously altered; only two variations (numbers 1 and 24) retain the original chord progression.

Brahms also subjects the theme to extensive melodic changes, transforming its character and emotional tone. In the twelfth variation, for example, the burly original tune is concealed in a delicate solo flute line:

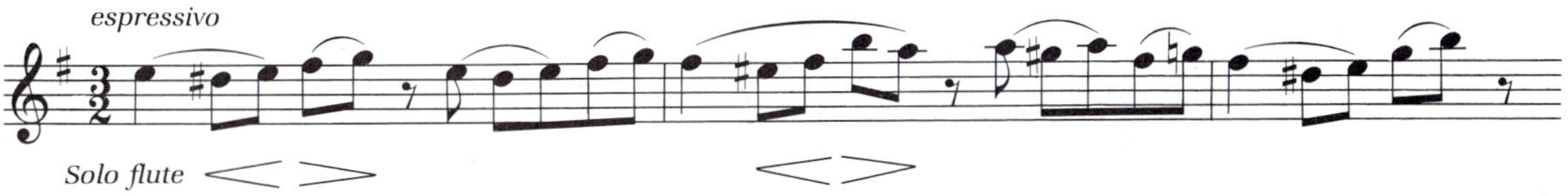

Brahms avoids the potential rhythmic squareness of the form by overlapping the phrases of the free voices with those of the theme. Many of the variations seem to build upon the ideas of preceding variations, producing larger patterns with a sense of ongoing direction and fusion of motives. The emotional tone of the movement is broad. Rhythmically forceful variations dissolve into tender answers, which in turn rebuild into climaxes. While the theme remains essentially intact, its context is changing constantly. Musical interest is sustained by the immense variety of moods and textures Brahms achieves within a very strict form.

Continuous Variation in the Music of India

As mentioned earlier, variation is the most universal formal procedure in music. Many musical cultures that have evolved along very different paths from Western traditions, employing tuning systems, textures, and rhythmic practices unfamiliar to Western audiences, have developed highly sophisticated formal procedures based upon continuous variation.

Within the past few decades, growing numbers of American and European listeners have become acquainted with, and warmly responded to, the classical traditions of Indian music. They have found the music of both northern and southern India—two very distinct traditions—to be compelling, eloquent, and emotionally involving. Through this broadening of musical experience these listeners have discovered a gateway to the understanding of other, previously alien, musical styles, and found that they listened to familiar music with fresh ears and new perspectives.

The theory and practice of Indian music is complex but flexible, demanding original invention from the performers within a tightly structured format. **Improvisation**—spontaneous variations on a theme—is fundamental to Indian music, as it is to jazz. In Indian music this free play of ideas is guided by a strict melodic and rhythmic framework.

Tuning. The first aspect of Indian music that strikes most Western listeners is its unique tuning system, noticeably different from our twelve-tone division of the octave. The Indian intonation system divides the octave into 22 pitches. These include ten **microtones,** intervals smaller than a half-step that lie "between the cracks" of the piano keyboard. Additional microtonal decorations are added by performers as they slide into and away from important notes. Of the 22 basic pitches, between five and seven serve as primary notes of a performance, functioning somewhat like our seven-tone scales. A composition usually contains a central tone and one or two prominent notes that function somewhat like a dominant, serving as upper or lower poles to which the melody frequently returns.

Texture. Melody and rhythm are the essential elements of Indian music. Harmony and counterpoint, as we know them, do not exist. Although there are *sonorities*—that is, groups of notes sounded together—there are no chord progressions. The sonorities result instead from **drones,** sustained or repeated notes sounded together with the melodic line. There is only one melodic line—no bass voice or inner lines—and in this sense there is no counterpoint. There is, however, a constant *rhythmic* interplay between the solo line and the accompaniment. Because Indian music is "pure melody and rhythm," without harmonic or contrapuntal enrichment, its melodic and rhythmic practice is highly sophisticated; in fact, it often far surpasses the pitch and rhythmic innovations of contemporary concert music and jazz in complexity and subtlety.

The resulting texture can be said to be "layered." Each instrument performs a specific melodic, rhythmic, or drone function, and each remains a distinct layer and color of sound with its own formal structure. There are three essential textural layers:

1. The solo melody, which may be performed by a singer or an instrumentalist
2. A rhythmic accompaniment, performed on percussive instruments (usually small drums)
3. The drone: sustained notes played on a stringed instrument

Instrumentation. Three of the most common Indian instruments are the sitar, tabla, and tamboura.

The **sitar** is a plucked string instrument with a four-octave range; it has existed in its present form for about 700 years and is the most popular solo instrument of Northern India. Its six or seven main strings are played with a wire plectrum, or pick, worn on the index finger of the right hand. Nineteen additional strings vibrate sympathetically (without being played) when the note to which they are tuned is sounded in the melody; they may also be plucked with the little finger, providing a drone accompaniment.

The **tabla** is a pair of small drums that produce a clear, dry sound; the closest Western counterpart would be bongo drums. The right-hand drum (the *actual tabla*) is tuned to the central tone; the left drum (called the *bayan*) produces lower, bass notes. The pitch of the bayan is varied by the performer

Sitarist Ravi Shankar in concert, flanked by tabla (left) and tamboura (right).

by changing the amount of pressure supplied by the palm of the left hand against the drum head.

The **tamboura** is an accompanimental drone instrument with four or five strings, tuned to specific notes and continuously plucked.

The Basis of Variation: Raga and Tala. Indian music consists of continuous improvisational variations on a skeletal pitch pattern (the **raga**) and a rhythmic structure (the **tala**). A raga is the melodic basis of a performance: the essential pitch structure, which remains constant. It is not a melody, motive, or scale, but rather a series of notes, with a separate ascending and descending pattern (usually of between five and seven notes each). These notes serve as the primary melodic tones and the pitches of the drone accompaniment. The raga of *Mar̄u Bihāg,* the Listening example, is comparatively long:

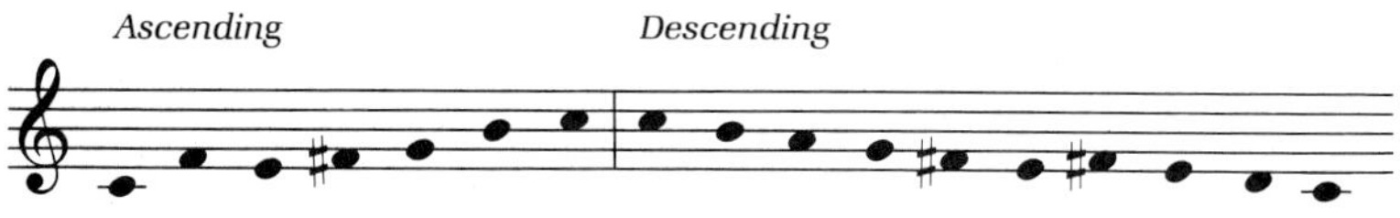

The raga forms the melodic theme of a performance, but not as a pre-composed melody; rather, it serves as an underlying pitch framework supplying characteristic intervals and melodic figures that are realized by the performer in improvisation. Microtonal ornamental notes must be used in specific ways in relation to the main melodic notes of the raga. The performer must stick to the notes of the raga and use these notes according to their original relationships. The performer also introduces specific ornamental notes and figures associated with the raga.

The raga establishes the mood, color, and pitch relationships of a performance. Each raga evokes a unique quality, such as happiness, sadness, or love, and is intended for performance at a particular time of day. Many are reserved for festive or ceremonial occasions and functions. The number of ragas in common use has been variously estimated at between 50 and 300 or more. These ragas are not notated; rather they are learned aurally through years of intensive study.

The tala is the rhythmic structure of a performance: a continuously repeated pattern of one accented beat followed by many unstressed beats. The tala establishes a fixed pulse, tempo, and "meter" (grouping of beats). The principal beat, called the *sum* (pronounced "soom"), is followed by many weaker beats grouped into units by secondary accents. Divisions of 6, 7, 10, 12, 14, and 16 beats are most common. The tala of *Mar̄u Bihāg* is a pattern of ten beats, grouped 2 + 3 + 2 + 3:

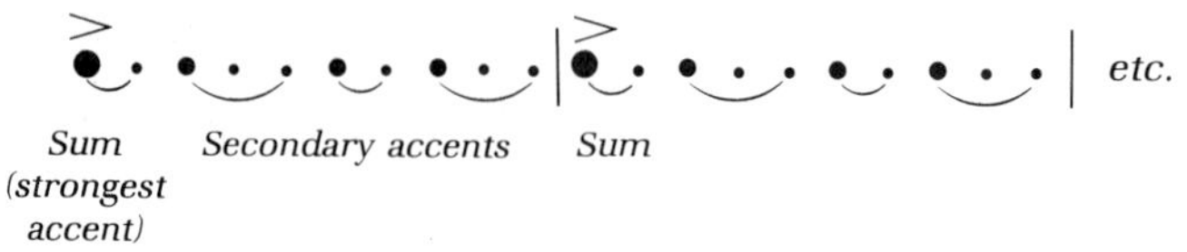

The tala is established by the percussion instrument and, like the raga, remains constant throughout a number. The pulse is strong and regular, never speeding up or slowing down. The drummer begins with simple statements of the tala, then begins to improvise increasingly complex cross-rhythms and rapid figures on top of it. The melodic instrument and drums begin a rhythmic interplay. Each performs complex rhythmic patterns on top of the unvarying structure of the tala. The two instruments pull apart rhythmically at the beginning of each "measure," coming back together with a strong accent on the sum:

When the tala conains many weak beats, the pattern of beats is partially obscured by cross-rhythms, and the strong accents are (by our standards) widely spaced. Western listeners often lose the sense of "metrical" divisions, but they can still distinguish the coming-together of instruments on the accented *sum.* The resulting rhythmic flow sounds to our ears intricate and structurally free, punctuated by accents at regular intervals. Indian listeners can follow a tala pattern throughout a performance, and they delight in the interplay and tension that result as the performers pull apart rhythmically at the beginning of each pattern, then come together again on the *sum.*

Listening

Marū Bihāg, *performed by Ravi Shankar*

Record Set Side 1, Band 6

Indian music is characterized by a feeling of highly ornamental surface motion over unchanging melodic and rhythmic patterns—a quality of freedom within a very tight structure. The formal structure of *Marū Bihāg* is typical of the performance of ragas. The performance begins with a slow invocation in a style called *alap.* Over a drone accompaniment in the tamboura, sitarist Shankar improvises a series of rhythmically free short phrases in a meditative style. The alap is somewhat like a theme or exposition. The pitch content and emotional tone of the raga are established as the performer presents scalar fragments of the raga and explores its characteristic decorative patterns. The raga of *Marū Bihāg* is a contemplation on the melancholy of separated lovers, and has a longing, introspective quality. Ornamentation is not a mere enrichment or complication, but a *fundamental* part of the music. The degree of elaboration a performer introduces will depend upon his technique, his interpretation of the raga, the occasion of the performance, the attitude of the performers, and the response of the listeners.

With the raga pattern well established, the melodic line becomes more expansive and rhythmic. The sitarist begins playing longer phrases, with rapid repeated notes and greater embellishment. The rhythmic structure is still free.

The tabla enters, marking the beginning of the main body of the performance, with a series of straightforward statements of the tala. This second section of the piece begins as an exposition of the *rhythmic structure:* several repetitions of its simplest form. During this rhythmic exposition, the sitarist continues a series of comparatively simple variations on the raga. The variations gradually become longer and melodically and rhythmically more complex. After the drummer has firmly established the tala, he, too, begins to overlay increasingly complex rhythmic variations upon it, and the pacing grows more animated. Much of the joy and excitement of a performance is centered around the dialogue between the melodic and percussive instrumentalists, as they pull apart and back together, play complex cross-rhythms, and sensitively respond to each other's nuances and ideas.

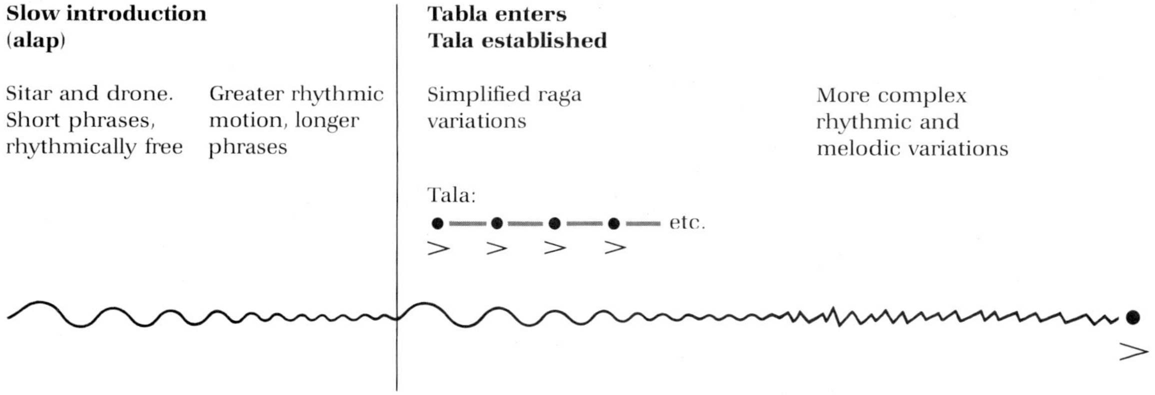

The improvisational variations that follow have a deliberate, inward-looking quality, a feeling that a moment of eternity has become "frozen" and can be experienced, understood, and considered without haste. The music often generates considerable rhythmic excitement, but the overall mood is serene and unhurried. The performers and listeners, each in their own way, reflect upon the limitless possibilities of the underlying patterns, upon the many levels of meaning of the raga. This is "being" music, without sectional divisions (which would interrupt the flow of contemplation), and without clearly defined, imposed musical goals or points of arrival beyond the recurrent *sum.* The performers attempt to evoke a particular emotional quality and sustain it at a high level, letting this quality speak individually to each listener, allowing each listener to respond in his own way.

For many Western listeners Indian music presents an unfamiliar conception and dimension of musical time. It is neither "clock" time nor "psychological" time; it is not measured by the passage of either seconds or events. The quality of time is not determined by how much happens during the performance, but by the quality of ideas and moods themselves.

For the listener unfamiliar with Indian music there are two ways to approach a performance. On preliminary hearings, it is often helpful to follow the formal structure as closely as possible, concentrating on the interplay of ideas and the ways in which they are structured into a unified whole. One can listen for the way in which the tones of the raga are always the same but heard in ever new combinations; for the subtleties and shadings of mood the performers introduce; for the interaction between melodic and rhythmic lines. On subsequent hearings, after one has gained familiarity with the style, it is often best to abandon all preconceptions, formal models and "analysis," and to immerse oneself totally in the cyclical flow of the music. To do this, it is necessary to concentrate on the *sounds themselves,* and on one's own response to them. This type of reflective listening is not passive daydreaming, but a total involvement in sound—*thinking sound,* rather than imagining how the sounds could be schematically diagramed. Such listening requires every bit as much concentration as more analytic perception.

These two types of aural perception—the structural (listening for design) and the sensual (immersion in the sounds themselves)—are essential to all music. Without a basic understanding of the musical structure of a work, the listener will grasp only fragmentary pieces of its design and never apprehend the full richness of musical meaning. Without the concurrent ability to "listen with open ears" and respond intuitively to a performance, however, the listener's enjoyment will be limited in an even more crippling way. Understanding the formal principles of work is of little value unless it encourages, informs, and even liberates the listener's intuitive response to the music.

Terms and Concepts for Review

refrain
chanson
part-song
rondo
variation
theme and variation form

continuous variation forms
  ground bass
  passacaglia and chaconne
Indian music
  raga
  tala

Chapter 8 Sonata Form

The term **sonata** is among the vaguest musical designations in origin and meaning. It originally meant nothing more than a piece to be played ("sounded") by instruments, as opposed to a "cantata," a piece to be sung. Since the mid-18th century, it has meant a large multi-movement work for piano or for a solo instrument (usually violin) with piano accompaniment.

In addition to the sonata, the major instrumental genres of the last 200 years include the string quartet (a work for two violins, viola, and cello), the symphony (a work for orchestra), and the concerto (a work for soloist and orchestra). These genres are similar in formal outline, and represent the application of the same basic organizing principles to solo, chamber, and orchestral mediums.

Structure of Multi-Movement Works

Most large-scale instrumental works contain three or four movements. Each movement has its own formal plan. There is also a design to the work as a whole, a pattern of greater or lesser tension between individual movements. The movements are interlocking units that together comprise a unified, though many-faceted, musical statement.

The first and last movements are the structural pillars of a work. These movements are generally both in the tonic key, and they largely determine the overall emotional tone of the composition. The first movement is the most dramatic in conception and the most complex in design. The inner movements are usually simpler in structure. The level of tension is generally lower, and contrasts are less extreme. The final movement is a conclusive summation to the work, often providing a reply, counterbalance, or more decisive resolution to the first movement.

The first movement, and frequently one or two of the other movements, is based upon a principle of organization that might best be termed *sonata procedure.* This procedure is the most important organizing device in music of the 18th and 19th centuries, and has exerted continuing influence into the present century. Though usually called *sonata form* for convenience, it is *not* a specific thematic outline. Rather, it is a highly adaptable *method* of organization, governed by a single broad pattern of tonal tension and resolution. Sonata form is applied to various movements of instrumental works as well as to independent compositions, and it can produce simple or complex designs. It assumes different emphasis and proportions when applied to first, second, and final movements, but the principle of organization remains intact.

It is apparent by now why considerable confusion surrounds the term "sonata." This term is used to designate both a genre and a formal principle. It is thus important to distinguish between

> **sonata:** a multi-movement solo work

and the more limited meaning of

> **sonata form:** an organizing procedure used in one or more movements of a sonata, chamber work, symphony or concerto.

This chapter concerns sonata form.

During the late 18th century, the movements of both symphonies and chamber works became standardized according to the following scheme:

Movement	*Tempo*	*Most common forms*
I	Fast	Sonata form
II	Slow	Three-part form, Theme and variations, or Sonata form
III	Moderately fast, triple meter	Minuet and trio or Scherzo
IV	Fast	Rondo, Sonata-rondo, Theme and variations, or Sonata form.

Most concertos and many sonatas are in only three movements, omitting the minuet or scherzo movement. Works of the Classical period (late 18th and early 19th centuries) generally adhere closely to this formal scheme. In later 19th- and 20th-century music, this broad outline has been treated with greater freedom, but remains the basic frame of reference.

Sonata Form Procedures

The basis of a sonata-form movement is a symmetrical pattern of tonal motion, similar in structure to (but much longer than) the two halves of a Baroque suite movement:

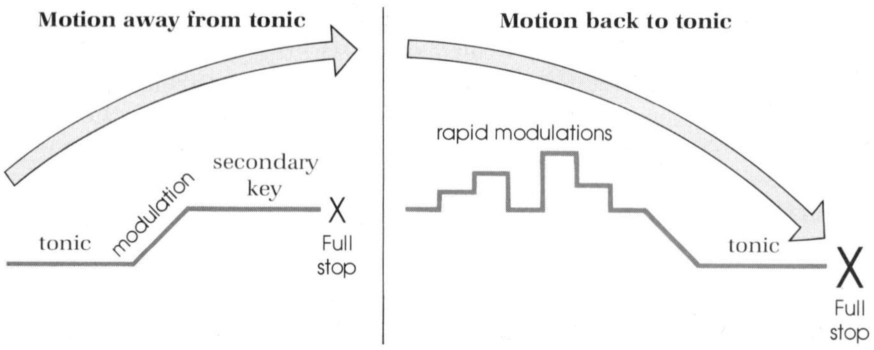

The movement begins with establishment of the tonic key. There follows a modulation into a secondary key, which produces tonal motion and tension.[1] This secondary key is prolonged throughout the rest of the opening half. Tonal motion in the first section is directed away from the original tonic and toward a concluding full stop in the secondary key.

The second half begins by building greater tonal tension by means of a series of modulations through more distant keys. Resolution occurs gradually, as the harmony pulls back into the original tonic key (absent since the opening of the movement), prolongs the tonic key, and finally cadences with a full stop. In 18th-century works, roughly half of the movement is tonally stable (in the tonic) and half unstable (in other keys). Later composers altered these balanced proportions, emphasizing tonal tension and instability. This is one reason why so many 19th-century works have a restless, searching quality.

This tonal scheme by itself is unexceptional. Departure from and return to the tonic key is the basic tonal pattern of most 18th-century music. However, in sonata form this tonal motion is carefully *articulated* (brought out) and *emphasized.* The process of modulation into the secondary key is more than a connecting link; it is an important *event* in its own right, something that must be attained over a period of time. The secondary key is then prolonged for a considerable duration, usually longer than the original tonic. The long-delayed return of the tonic is also strongly articulated. Just as we felt a deliberate step "up" into the secondary key, there is a corresponding sense of stepping "back down" into the home key. Articulation of the tonal scheme is achieved by means of themes, and through changes in rhythmic pacing, texture, and color.

There are three pivotal events in a sonata-form movement. The **exposition** establishes the thematic material of the movement and effects the initial motion away from the tonic to a full stop in the secondary key. The **development** is characterized by further harmonic motion into more distant keys, heightening tonal tension. The **recapitulation** returns to the original thematic material and reestablishes the tonic key.

[1] In 18th-century works this secondary key is usually the dominant (V). If the movement is in minor, the secondary key is generally the relative major (the major key having the same key signature).

Exposition

Some expositions are preceded by a slow **introduction,** thematically unrelated to the rest of the movement. When present, the introductory passage serves as a "curtain raiser" to the work and prepares the statement of the first theme.

The exposition itself begins with a **first tonal group:** one or more thematic ideas that affirm the tonic and provide initial character definition. This tonal group may consist of a single theme, a fragmentary idea that is extended, or a series of thematic ideas linked together. After the first tonal group, a **transitional passage,** either short or long, initiates tonal motion by pulling away from the tonic and preparing the establishment of the secondary key. In some works the transition begins with the presentation of a new theme or motive. More often it starts like a varied repetition of the first tonal group which then goes astray, becoming stuck on an isolated motive or breaking into scale-like runs. Rhythmic pacing almost always increases during the transition, coinciding with the breakdown of the original tonality and the loss of any sense of theme. There is usually a feeling of forward propulsion as the tonal motion approaches its new goal. The transition may end with a rhythmically strong cadence, or it may flow directly into the new key area.

The secondary key is confirmed and prolonged by additional thematic material: a **second tonal group** of one or more themes. The material in the second group often contrasts in character, texture, and rhythm with the material of the tonic group, but this is by no means always true. In any event, it is the *tonal shift,* not the number or character of the themes, that is the decisive event in the exposition. The second group ends with **closing material:** cadence patterns that prepare the full stop in the secondary key—the ultimate goal of the exposition.

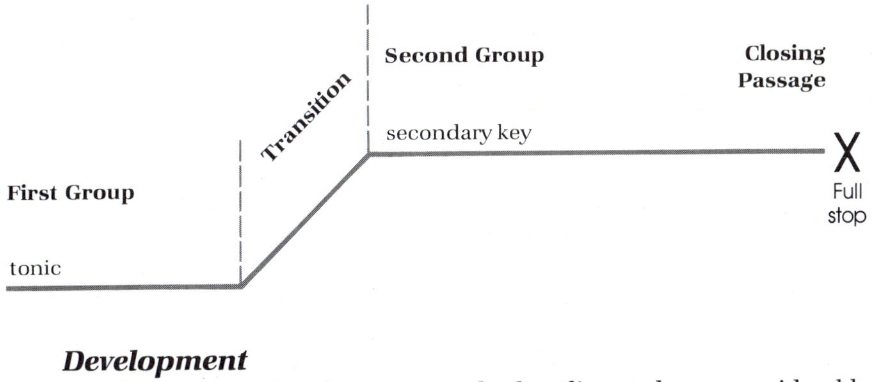

Development

Development sections have no standard outline and vary considerably in format. Various thematic fragments from the exposition are juxtaposed, repeated, and torn apart, often in argumentative fashion. The development is a sifting process in which motives are stripped away from their original thematic and tonal context. Some motives become ascendent while others fall by the wayside. The texture is generally more contrapuntal, with motives presented simultaneously or in rapid succession. Tension grows as the unstable harmonic motion veers through a rapid succession of distant keys, rarely cadencing. A point of maximum tension is reached, followed by a passage normally called the **retransition** ("transition back to. . .") in which the composer prepares the return of the tonic.

Recapitulation

The recapitulation is a varied repetition of the exposition, introducing some important alterations:

1. The entire recapitulation remains firmly rooted in the tonic key. The transition is recomposed so that it feints at modulation but then pulls back into the tonic key. The material originally heard in the secondary key is transposed into the tonic. The recapitulation is the most stable part of the movement; themes return in their complete form, and all of the material of the exposition now serves to confirm and prolong the tonic.
2. The texture, orchestration, and dynamic levels often are changed to provide a more forceful summing-up to the movement.
3. Any portion of the exposition may be condensed, especially if the material of that portion was featured prominently in the development section. The recapitulation often ends with a coda.

The overall structure of a sonata-form movement can be diagramed as follows:

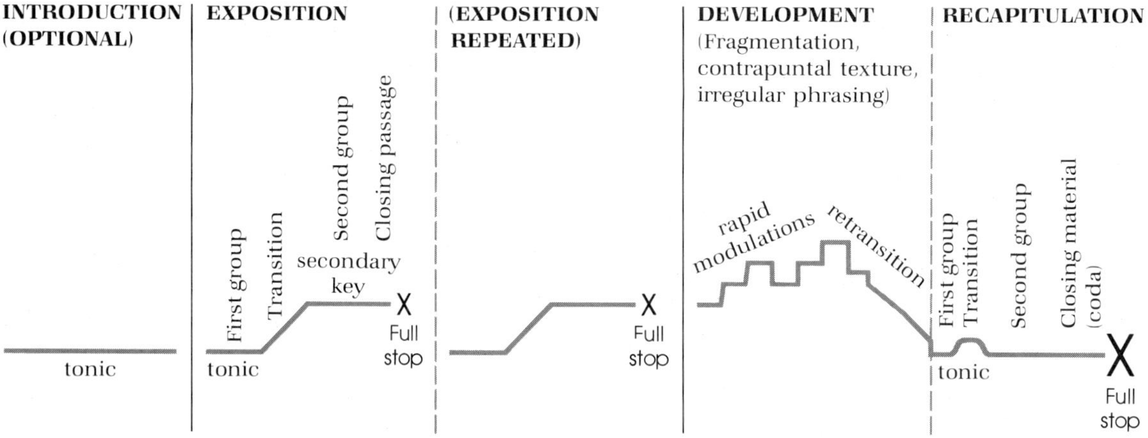

The exposition, development, and recapitulation are roughly equivalent in length. Classical composers generally specified that the exposition be repeated. Many performers today omit this repeat, feeling that is is redundant, but others believe that repetition of the exposition clarifies the two-part tonal plan and enables the listener to absorb the thematic relationships more fully. Sonata forms in later music are longer, featuring more complex tonal motion and a greater number of themes. Romantic composers rarely specified repetition of the exposition, because balanced formal proportions were not an essential (or even intended) feature of the music.

First Movement from the Symphony No. 40 in G Minor *by Wolfgang Amadeus Mozart (1756–1791)*

Record Set Side 7, Band 3

Mozart's last three symphonies (Nos. 39, 40, and 41) were composed in the astoundingly short period of about six weeks during the summer of 1788. Mozart's late works rarely reveal any trace of the increasingly desperate personal circumstances and despair that clouded the last decade of his short life.

The first movement of the Symphony No. 40 is an exemplary illustration of the Classically concise procedures of sonata form. Mozart's genius lay less in formal innovation than in his ability to infuse accepted Classical forms with a consummate personal expression and spontaneity. Music was a separate world to Mozart, one in which he possessed an almost magical facility and mastery. He was untroubled by questions of style and never seemed to struggle for ideas or labor over structure.

Exposition. The tonic key is established by a single theme, which features an insistent three-note motive (♫ ♩):

The theme is characterized by its formal balance. In the first phrase, for example, the melodic contour is static at first, then suddenly leaps up in the third measure—somewhat like a wind-up and a pitch. In exactly the same rhythm, the second half of the phrase balances the contour in descending motion, bringing the theme to its first breathing point:

The first theme is a tonally and melodically stable jumping-off point. Its simple underlying harmony firmly establishes the tonic G minor, concluding with a half-stop on the dominant; the carefully balanced melody produces a coherent, complete musical thought, presenting important motives in their simplest, most symmetrical arrangement.

The *transition* begins as though it were a restatement of the first time, stating the first few measures of the melody in original form. Melody and harmony then undergo alteration, pulling away from the tonic G minor. A loud, rhythmically emphatic tutti passage confirms the tonal shift out of the tonic G minor and into major. The modulation is made into a dramatic event by the sudden change in texture and dynamic level, more forceful rhythms in the violin melody, and a complete change in tone. The music grows more earnest and impetuous. Rhythmic pacing increases as the violins break into rapid ascending scalar runs over heavy accents in the rest of the orchestra. A strong cadence and a measure of silence signal the end of the transition. The modulation has been completed, the first theme is now only a memory, and Mozart is ready to state the next major idea of the movement.

The *second tonal group,* in B♭ major, contrasts with the first in rhythm and texture as well as in key. It begins with a graceful question-and-answer exchange between the violins and woodwinds, based on descending contours and long-short rhythmic motives:

The brief eight-bar melody is repeated, followed by a gradual swell into an animated tutti passage. The *closing material* features abrupt soft-loud contrasts and combines the principal motives of the first and second tonal groups:

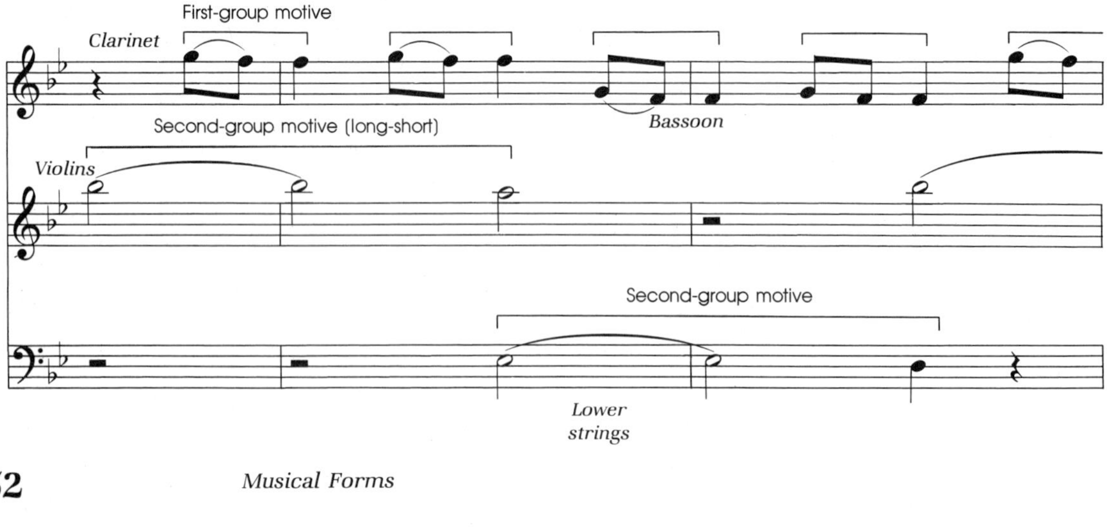

The closing material serves as an echo of the two major themes of the movement and builds to a vigorous tutti. Increased rhythmic pacing, textural depth, and dynamic level, and a simplification in the harmony, produce a growing sense of urgency, a rush to the ultimate tonal goal of the exposition: a full stop in the secondary key.

Exposition repeat. As was customary in the Classical period, Mozart specified that the exposition be repeated. Upon a second hearing, the tonal shift from minor to major and the structure of the themes and connecting passages are solidified in the listener's ear. These structural features will serve as a frame of reference during the more turbulent development section.

Development. In sonata-form movements one of the most important qualities of a theme is its potential for development. The development section of this movement is built almost entirely on fragments of the first-group theme, which thus becomes the dominant melodic idea of the movement. This thematic concentration is remarkable considering how many echoes of the first theme have already occurred in the closing material of the exposition. The motives of this theme retain their vitality because they are malleable, and can become both assertive and tender within new contexts.

The development begins with three tonally varied statements of the opening phrase of the movement. The phrase has been cut loose from its original secure harmonic framework and is no longer balanced by the original answering phrases. Chromatic alterations in the melody enforce a feeling of descent, but the music never quite "touches bottom." (This would require the establishment of a firm tonal center—something we will not hear again until the recapitulation.) The end of the third statement of the phrase is cut short as the strings break into a loud thematic crossfire. The original phrase is stated by the lower strings and bassoons; the violins respond with a strenuous new countermelody:

The fragmentary original theme and the new countermelody are exchanged several times by the upper and lower strings. With each textural swap the tonality changes and the woodwinds interject a brief figure.

The climax of the development section is a tutti passage featuring a descending sequence in the violins:

Sequences of this sort, involving the repetition of a thematic fragment at a higher or lower pitch level, are the most common af all developmental techniques. Sequential repetition enables the composer to move in any harmonic direction while drumming in a prominent melodic idea. This particular sequence, occurring about halfway through the development, marks the point of maximum tension in the development section. Rhythmic motion is rapid and continuous, and the tonality keeps shifting every few measures. The effect of this climactic passage is intense but unsettled.

The climactic passage comes to a forceful half-stop cadence, but the violins continue repeating the first-theme motive. This melodic fragment, which has been wandering through various keys and instruments, suddenly becomes absolutely stationary. The rest of the orchestra falls silent, but the violins continue echoing the motive; the effect is one in which the bottom drops out and the principal melodic idea of the movement stands out in relief.

End of climactic passage

One of the most prominent structural features of this development section is its increasing fragmentation of the theme. As the development proceeds, the initial theme is broken into ever smaller units. The section began with a four-measure quote of the theme, which was reduced to two measures at the end of the climactic passage. Now, during another loud sequential passage, the theme is further pared down to its smallest recognizable unit, the three-note motive :

This tutti passage is the second major structural goal of the development. While the strings wrestle for control of the motive, the horns remain planted on the note D, the dominant of the home key. The passage is at once a textural climax and a harmonic preparation for a return of the tonic key. The development then concludes with a lyrical retransition. The three-note rhythmic motive alternates between the flute and clarinets in a chromatically descending sequence, eventually melting into the return of the first theme. Development sections do not end with a cadence, but rather lead back into the tonic without a break.

Recapitulation. The simultaneous return of the tonic key and of the complete first-theme group at the beginning of the recapitulation reestablishes structural stability. Even the listener with no knowledge of sonata procedures easily senses a feeling of re-integration and tonal resolution at this point.

The first tonal group is repeated almost exactly. The transition, however, is altered so that, for all its commotion, it winds up back in the tonic key. Mozart expands the transition—the only unstable part of the recapitulation—so that it becomes similar in style to (and thus an echo of) the development section. The second tonal group, now in the tonic key of G minor rather than the original B♭ major, has a more haunting character and sounds more like a continuation of the first theme, due to the shift in mode. The closing material is followed by a coda, which ends with a resounding series of tonic and dominant chords.

Mozart's *Symphony No. 40* is unusual in that three of its four movements (all except the minuet movement) are in sonata form. In the slow second movement, Mozart specified that the second half be repeated as well as the exposition.

Sonata Form in the 19th Century

Sonata form remained the most important structural procedure in instrumental music for more than a hundred years after the death of Mozart. Its basic principles—strong articulation of tonal motion and extensive development of thematic material—were also applied to other forms, such as theme and variations, rondo, and *A–B–A* designs. As a result, the individual movements of most symphonies, sonatas, and chamber works, while different in outline, all reflect the influence of sonata procedure.

During the 19th century, composers expanded and altered the proportions of sonata form, adapting its already flexible format further to accomodate the specific expressive character of a work. Composers explored more distant key relationships between the tonic and secondary keys, and frequently incorporated several thematic ideas within both tonal groups. Strong contrasts within themes, as well as between tonal groups, are characteristic of 19th-century works. New thematic material is often introduced during the transitional and closing passages. The increased length and complexity of the exposition results in a corresponding expansion of the development section, recapitulation, and coda.

Listening

First Movement of the* Piano Quintet in F Minor, Op. 34, *by Johannes Brahms (1833–1897)

The first movement of Brahms' *F-Minor Piano Quintet* (string quartet plus piano) illustrates how sonata-form movements expanded in thematic material, emotional range, and length in the generations after Mozart. At the outset of the work, two contrasting thematic ideas are juxtaposed; a lyrical opening phrase is answered by rapid arpeggio figures in the piano:

Alternation of these contrasting ideas during the first tonal group sets the tone of struggle that pervades the movement.

The transitional passage is built around a new violin theme that begins as a gentle, imploring line, then swells to a forceful cadence. An extended second tonal group follows in the distant key of C♯ minor. The thematic material of this group, also, features the alternation and varied repetition of two distinct melodic ideas. In this passage, however, the ideas are complementary and incorporate similar triplet rhythms in the accompaniment:

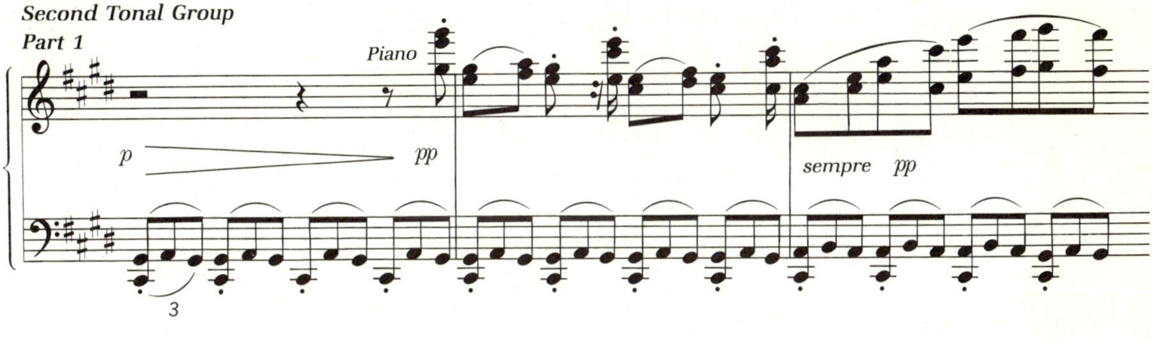

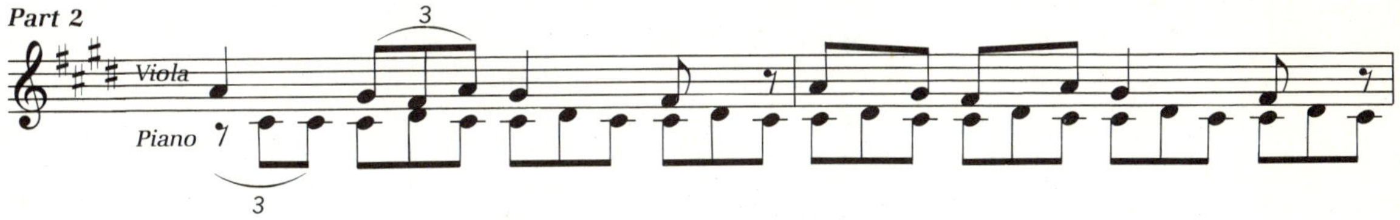

A lengthy closing theme in major rounds out the exposition. The theme presents three contrasting motives. As in the first group, energetic rhythmic figures serve as a reply to a lyrical opening idea:

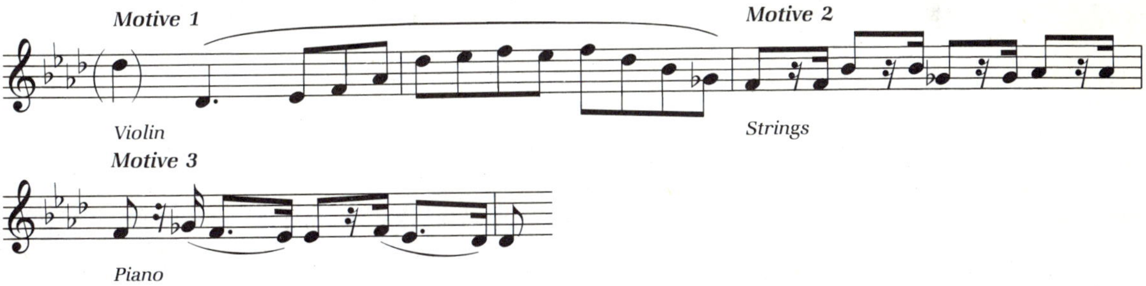

At the conclusion of this theme the music becomes subdued and almost motionless. The exposition is then repeated.

The beginning of the development section marks the structural lowpoint of the movement. An eerie calm unfolds around a three-note fragment of the first theme. The body of the development is based on fragments of the second tonal group. Agitated triplet rhythms in the accompaniment spur the music forward, attended by a gradual increase in rhythmic momentum, loudness, and textural density. A forceful climax is followed by a textural and dynamic relaxation, then a second energetic build-up that hurtles directly into the recapitulation.

The recapitulation begins with the second part of the first theme: the piano arpeggiation figure. The only other deviation from the standard recapitulation format occurs in the second tonal group, which begins in the key of F♯ minor rather than in the tonic. The movement concludes with a long coda based upon the arpeggio figure. In a final flourish, vigorous string arpeggios are pitted against thick piano chords that break with the force of crashing waves.

Sonata Form in the 20th Century

The first few decades of the 20th century witnessed a reaction to the profusion of themes and extended formal designs of late-19th century instrumental music. Such composers as Béla Bartók sought a return to concise expression, stripping away subordinate and connecting material and honing down thematic ideas to their most concise form. The process of thematic statement and development often takes precedence over clearly defined tonal motion. Some composers, in fact, have incorporated sonata procedure in works lacking any central tone. More often, however, sonata form has been employed by those composers still seeking broad tonal as well as thematic definition of ideas.

Listening

First Movement from the* String Quartet No. 4 *by Béla Bartók (1881–1945)

Record Set Side 12, Band 1

Béla Bartók

Béla Bartók ranks among the major composers of the 20th century. He was also an accomplished pianist and a leading authority on the folk music of his native Hungary and adjoining countries, which he collected and published over a period of ten years. Bartók's concert works reveal the influence of these folk traditions in their incisive rhythmic motives and asymmetric melodies, which often undergo extensive development and transformation. Like Mozart, Bartók achieved only limited renown and little financial reward during his lifetime. In 1940 he moved to the United States, where he spent his last five years in virtual obscurity, with little hint of the success his works would soon enjoy.

Bartók's six string quartets, written between 1908 and 1939, exemplify his striving for economy of design. Bartók himself observed, "In my string quartets, extreme concentration prevails." The process of motivic development, rather than the statement of complete themes, is the principal melodic event in the music. Development of these motives frequently begins immediately after (or even simultaneously with) their initial statement. As a result, the works tend to grow "organically" out of one or two ideas. In the absence of tonal harmonic motion, developmental procedures also provide the unifying thread that binds the work together.

Bartók's fourth quartet (1928) features this kind of musical compression. The first movement, a modified sonata design, grows out of a rudimentary idea: the interval of a half-step. The interval is used both melodically and "harmonically." It frequently takes the form of imitative statements that pile up on top of one another, as in the fifth measure:

The three-note cello motive (which begins with the half step E♭–D) is repeated sequentially, a half step higher each time, by the other strings. The resulting sonority at the end of the measure is a **tone cluster,** a group of half steps sounded together. (To "hear" the sound quality of a cluster, imagine dropping your fist on a piano keyboard.) The dense sound of tone clusters, which lack any root or harmonic focus, pervades the first movement, resulting in strongly dissonant pitch quality. Some early hearers of the work were discomfited by Bartók's use of strident clusters as the *basic sonority* of a work; one belligerent critic wondered whether such "repulsively ugly" sounds could possibly be "the legitimate heirs of the harmonies we have hitherto known."

Bartók, of course, had no intention of writing "pretty" music for easily pained ears. He conceived of the string quartet as a forceful medium, ideally suited to the projection of needle-sharp musical ideas. The stinging dissonances that resound throughout this movement spur the music forward and define its hard-edged, gritty character.

Formal Design. The movement follows the traditional sonata format in basic outline. An exposition (not repeated) presents two contrasting thematic ideas, which are fragmented in a development section and return in a recapitulation. A long coda based on the first idea features further development, then brings the movement to a vigorous close. Bartók's concern for structural concentration, however, results in several significant departures from traditional sonata-form procedure. The diagram on the next page summarizes the structure, and may help you follow the design of the music while listening. Be prepared, above all, for the movement's extreme structural economy. Its entire duration is less than six minutes, and the first minute alone sets forth not only an introduction, but also the initial statements of the two related motives that dominate the rest of the movement. This extreme compression presents a striking contrast to the expansiveness of the Brahms *Piano Quintet.*

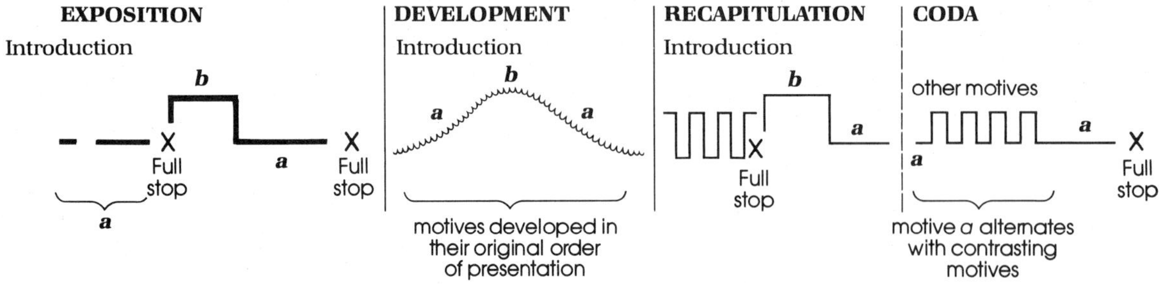

Exposition. A short introductory passage at the beginning of the exposition features imitative statements of two- and three-note figures. The passage instills the basic interval (half-step) and "harmonic" quality (tone clusters) of the work. Midway through the passage the cello interjects a motive that will dominate the work:

All five movements of the quartet are structured around the developmental expansion of this trenchant idea, which we will label motive *a*. The isolated cello statement of this motive flashes by in the blinking of an eye. The motive is built entirely of half steps, and thus is severely compressed in range as well as in length.

The introduction leads directly into a *first group,* during which motive *a* is heard simultaneously in original form and in contrary motion:

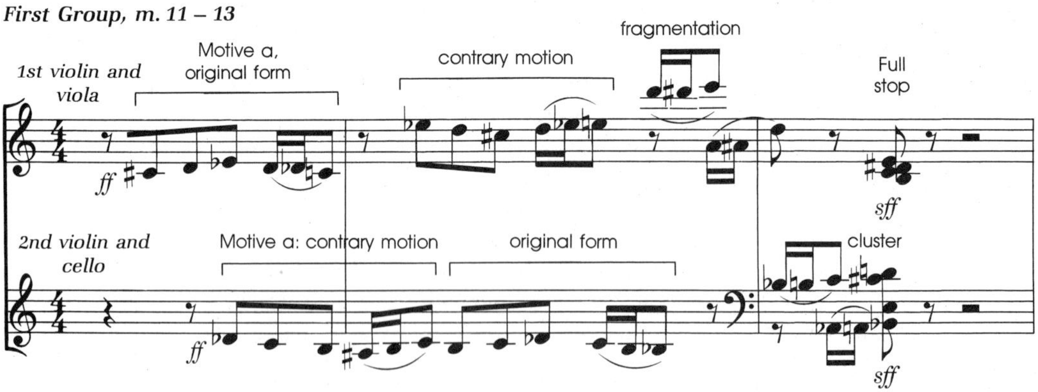

The very short "first group" initiates the process of developmental expansion of motive *a*, but this development is cut short by an abrupt full stop on a dense cluster.

In this movement there is no transitional passage between the two thematic groups: The second group begins immediately after the first, with a soft four-note figure in the viola. Around this repeated accompanimental figure the other strings weave a series of overlapping statements of a new idea, motive *b*. Like its predecessor, this idea is little more than a musical scrap:

Motive *b* is a derivative of *a*. Its six notes follow a similar ascending-descending contour, but the intervals and pitch range are slightly larger and the rhythm more relaxed. Motive *b* functions as a more lyrical ("singing") second thematic idea, but it also represents a further development of *a*. In this movement developmental procedures are not limited to the development section proper but permeate the entire musical fabric. All other melodic ideas heard in the movement are related in some way to *a* or *b*. The resulting design, in which every motive grows out of an earlier one, is a particularly rigorous application of the sonata principle.

In place of closing material, Bartók substitutes an additional passage based on motive *a*. This passage, which rounds out the exposition, serves as a more extended continuation or restatement of the interrupted first group. Simultaneous statements of the motive in original and contrary motion are interspersed with scale-like runs and hammered clusters.

Development. In the middle part of the movement the motives undergo more extensive transformation. They are treated in their original order of presentation: pyramiding half-step figures, *a*–*b*–*a*. Motivic fragments frequently collapse into *glissandos* (a sliding between pitches) and trills (rapid alternation between two notes).

Recapitulation. The beginning of the recapitulation is recomposed. The introductory passage and first group are combined in alternation, producing a feeling of even greater formal compression. Motive *b* returns, this time shorn of its original accompanimental figure. The restatement of *a* is abbreviated, leading directly (without a cadence) into a lengthy *coda*. In this developmental summation, motive *a* is juxtaposed in sharp alternation with several of its descendants. The motive becomes more insistent and continuous as the music pulls toward a cadence on its ultimate center tone, the note C.

The Mozart, Brahms, and Bartók movements, quite different in structural outline and tone, demonstrate the extraordinary richness of the sonata principle. In its Classical usage sonata procedure represented the full flowering of the principles of tonality. Thematic design served to clarify tonal motion. As the tonal harmonic language changed, so the emphasis in sonata procedure changed from a process of tonal definition to one of thematic contrast and elaboration. In 20th-century works featuring new types of harmonies and pitch structure, statement and development of thematic ideas have generally become more closely intertwined. In later chapters we will encounter a series of works that chart this evolution of sonata procedure.

Terms and Concepts for Review

sonata
sonata form (sonata procedure)
- exposition: tonal groups connected by a transitional passage
- development: fragmentation, rearrangement, and sequential repetition of ideas
- recapitulation: return of the tonic key and original thematic material
- coda: final summation

Chapter 9
Contrapuntal Forms

Most of the works we have looked at so far have been texturally **homophonic;** that is, they consist of a principal melody with harmonic accompaniment. Homophonic textures predominate in music written between 1750 and 1900, and also in popular and folk music. Most compositions written before 1750, however, as well as many 20th-century concert works, feature a greater textural equality of voices.

Contrapuntal, or **polyphonic,** textures contain two or more simultaneous melodies of roughly equal prominence. Melodic interest is distributed among all the parts rather than concentrated in a single voice. In this chapter we will survey formal procedures unique to counterpoint.

Contrapuntal Procedures

Most contrapuntal works contain a specific number of melodic lines, and this number remains constant throughout the piece. (Individual lines, however, may occasionally drop out for brief periods, so that a four-voice piece may contain passages with only two or three voices.) Each line is a complete, independent melody which we can follow throughout the work. Each line has its own contour, phrase structure, and musical goals. At the same time, these melodies are interrelated, so that they create a dialogue of ideas and common formal patterns. Melodic ideas are tossed back and forth between the voices, and this interplay serves as the basis of formal structure.

Unity, contrast, development, variation, and return are as important to contrapuntal designs as they are to homophonic forms. These principles, however, are usually realized in a different way in contrapuntal music. Many contrapuntal pieces follow a two-part outline (the movements of Bach's *French Suite No. 6,* for example), and others are structured into three sections. However, the design of most contrapuntal works is a continuous fabric without clear sectional divisions. Contrapuntal music is generally characterized by continuation—a perpetual foward motion only occasionally interrupted by cadences. Formal contrast occurs between the voices, rather than (as in homophonic music) between different sections of a work.

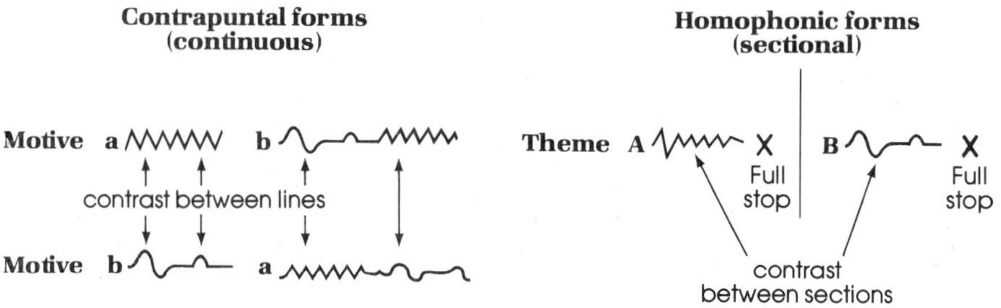

Independence of Voices

If contrapuntal melodies are to retain separate identities so that the listener can follow each line distinctly, they must contrast in some way. Composers frequently use *rhythmic differentiation* to keep the voices distinct, as when one line moves more rapidly than another. The primary rhythmic interest may shift from one voice to another several times during a composition. Bach's Inventions and Suites feature this type of rhythmic interplay. As the rhythmic drive is relaxed in one voice, it is transferred to another part.

Rhythmic differentiation of voices: opening measures of Bach's Two-Part Invention in F

Rhythmic contrast, however, is not indispensable to contrapuntal independence of voices. Even when the lines move in identical rhythm, they may develop a separate momentum and remain distinct if their *contours* are sufficiently different. Contrapuntal lines usually move in **contrary motion;** that is, instead of moving up and down together, they normally move in opposite directions:

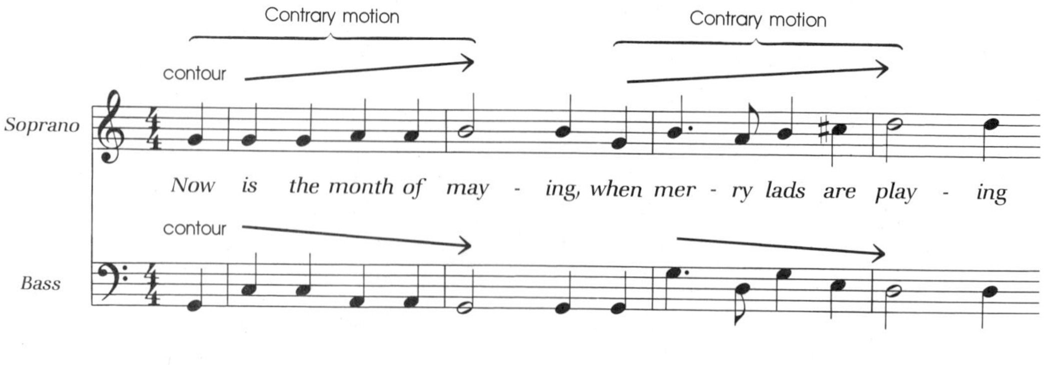

Imitation

The goal of the contrapuntal composer is to introduce enough contrast between voices to keep them distinct, but at the same time to interrelate these voices so that each reflects the same musical ideas. The most common procedure by which the voices are interrelated is **imitation:** a melodic idea, either short (a motive) or long (a complete theme), is stated in one voice and then repeated in one or more other lines. The repetition may be exact, like an echo, or it may be varied in some way, so that it is heard as a reply.

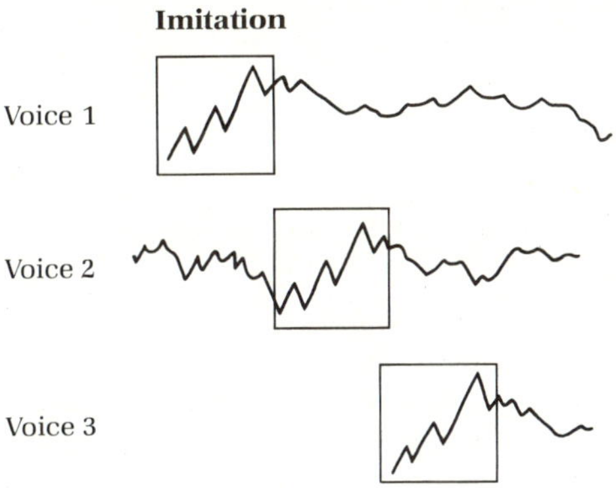

Imitation is the primary unifying device in Bach's *Two-Part Invention in F Major*. In the first seven measures of this piece the bass voice is an exact imitation of the upper line, playing the same pitches (an octave lower) in identical rhythm one measure later (see page 49). In the middle of the piece the imitation is reciprocal, featuring an exchange of motives between the two lines:

By means of imitation, a composer can juggle important motives back and forth among all the voices. The individual lines gain equality as each participates in the statement and development of an idea. Imitation enables the composer to obtain maximum mileage from a motive. By shifting the motive to a new voice, the composer may continue to exploit it with renewed freshness. For this reason, contrapuntal pieces are often more "economical" than homophonic works, stretching out a few initial ideas for long periods without the need for new themes or sectional divisions.

Listening

Third Piece from Papillons, Op. 2, *by Robert Schumann (1810–1856)*

Record Set Side 2, Band 3

Schumann's whimsical early work *Papillons (Butterflies)*, is a collection of miniature waltzes and polonaises for piano composed around 1830 and inspired by a ballroom scene from a novel by Jean Paul. The third piece of the cycle was associated in Schumann's mind with the bizarre image of "an enormous boot wearing itself and sliding about." The piece is in three sections and features a single theme. The second and third sections provide a simple illustration of contrapuntal procedures.

The opening section *(A)* states the gallumphing theme as a solo bass line. In the middle *(A′)* section the theme is shifted to the treble register against a slower-moving bass line. The two voices remain completely distinct. Each maintains its own characteristic melodic pattern, with no exchange of ideas. The lines contrast in rhythmic motion and contour:

Middle section (A′)

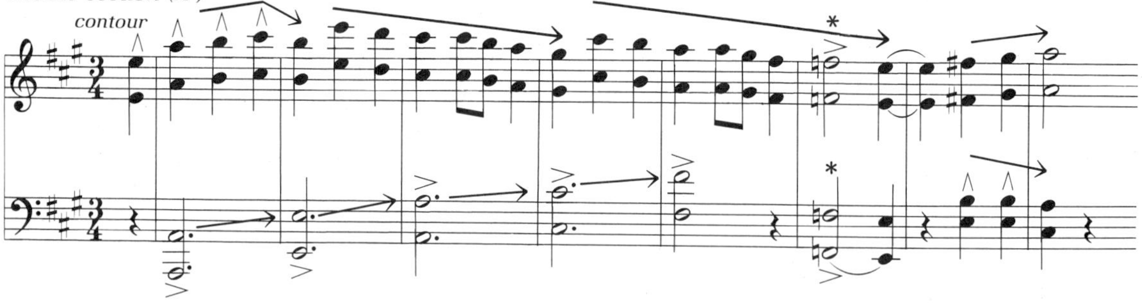

Schumann introduces a burlesque touch just before the cadence. The bristling independence of the voices is interrupted as they bluntly collide on a chromatically descending figure (marked * above)—a sort of musical guffaw. The parts then go their separate ways.

In this second section, contrapuntal independence was established by contour and rhythmic contrast. In the final section, independence results from imitation. The theme is stated in the original minor in the treble, and imitated with great self-importance, two octaves lower, by the bass.

Third section (A'')

This brief piece demonstrates how imitation, while unifying a work, can also provide just as great a feeling of independence of parts as can rhythmic and melodic contrast. Contrast between voices and imitation among voices are the two most common procedures employed by composers to structure contrapuntal pieces.

Strict Imitation: Canons and Rounds

The third section of Schumann's ungainly little waltz is an example of a canon. Canons and rounds are the strictest of all contrapuntal forms. In both, a complete melody is imitated for note, from beginning to end, by one or more answering voices.

Rounds are stylistically unpretentious vocal pieces often based on folk tunes. We are familiar with such simple rounds as "Row, Row, Row Your Boat" and "Frere Jacques." Due to their elementary tonal structure, such melodies may be imitated by almost any number of voices. The imitation is always exact (either at the same pitch level or at the octave). When the individual voices reach the end of the melody, they begin it again—hence the name "round." The piece continues indefinitely until the performers, nearing exhaustion or having had enough, drop out one by one.

Canons are usually more complex in organization. The original melody may be imitated at a new pitch level. An answering voice may perform the melody twice or half as fast, invert it (play it in contrary motion), or even perform it backward. Through such procedures, the melody may change character to such a degree that the listener is not even aware of the imitation. The rigid formal structure of the canon can become a dry or pedantic exercise, a sort of musical crossword puzzle. In the hands of inventive composers, however, this strict framework can be an added spur to the composer's imagination, resulting in eloquent, highly expressive works.

Canons have been written in all styles, but are most common in Renaissance vocal music and Baroque keyboard works. The canons in Bach's *Goldberg Variations, A Musical Offering,* and *Art of the Fugue* vary from simple two-part examples at the octave to ingenious multivoice canons employing all the techniques of canonic variation in the answering voices. The perfect symmetry of these works can produce a sense of awe similar to what one feels at the sight of a massive, perfectly proportioned Gothic cathedral.

Listening

Third Movement of the* String Quartet in D Minor, Op. 76, No. 2, *by Franz Joseph Haydn (1732–1809)

In 18th- and 19th-century music, canons are encountered less often as independent pieces than as one section of a larger work or movement. The third movement of Haydn's *String Quartet in D Minor,* Op. 76, No. 2, is an unusual formal hybrid, following minuet and trio form to the letter while maintaining a strict contrapuntal structure. The minuet is a two-voice canon at the octave. The trio is based on freer imitation; a repeated note figure rebounds back and forth between the violins and lower strings.

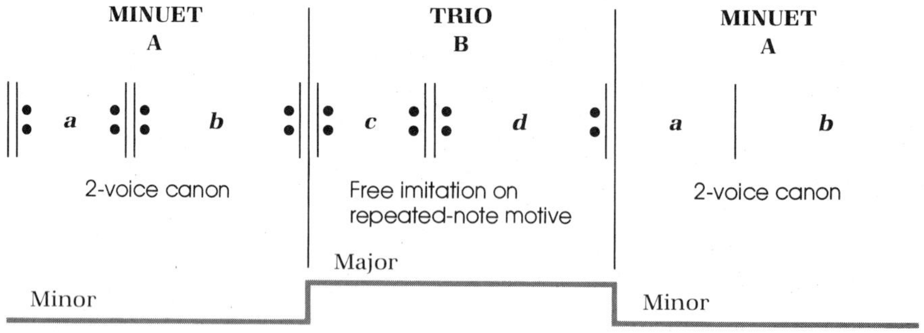

Freer Imitative Forms

Canonic imitation is continuous, presenting staggered statements of a single theme. Other contrapuntal genres feature several sections of music, each based on a different theme and particular imitative procedure. The Renaissance motet exemplifies this type of sectional construction and freer imitative treatment. During the Renaissance, the **motet** was a sacred, polyphonic choral composition for between two and six voices. Four- and five-voice ensembles were most common.

Listening

Motet: Ave Maria, Gratia Plena *by Josquin Des Prez (c. 1450–1521)*

Record Set Side 5, Band 2

Josquin Des Prez was the most renowned musician of his time. His music exerted a far-reaching influence on both contemporary composers and on those of following generations. Born near the present border of France and Belgium, Josquin spent most of his life in Milan and Rome, returning to France only near the end of his life. He held many court and church appointments, including several years service as a singer in the Papal choir, and he excelled equally in the composition of sacred and secular works.

Josquin des Prez in a contemporary woodcut

The structurally free form and expressive texts of the Renaissance motet were ideally suited to Josquin's musical style. His four-voice setting of the ancient text *Ave Maria* incorporates a variety of imitative procedures that serve to unify the voices thematically while keeping them distinct.

Each clause of the text is set to a separate, short melodic theme, generally begun by one voice and imitated successively by the other three voices. The four lines enter and drop out at different points, resulting in an overlapping of phrases. As one voice comes to a cadence, another may be in the middle of a phrase, and a third may have already begun the next phrase. Only at the ends of stanzas do the voices cadence together, and even at these spots there is occasional overlapping. The piece is thus highly sectional in melodic structure but continuous in its rhythmic motion.

In the first stanza the opening phrase "Ave Maria" begins with a simple motive in the soprano, imitated in succession by the alto, tenor, and bass. The second phrase, "Gratia plena," follows the same order of imitation:

The third phrase maintains the previous order of entrances, but the imitation becomes freer; in the answering voices the phrase is melodically altered and shortened. In the fourth phrase ("Virgo serena") the order of entry is alto–soprano–tenor–bass, and the imitation is freer still.

Text	*Translation*	*Musical Setting*
Ave Maria, Gratia plena,	Hail, Mary, full of grace,	Imitation
Dominus tecum, Virgo serena.	the Lord is with thee,	
	serene Virgin.	*(cadence)*
Ave cujus conceptio,	Hail, whose conception,	Imitation
Solemni plena gaudio	full of jubilation,	
Coelestia, terra restria,	fills heaven and earth	
Nova replet laetitia.	with new joy.	*(cadence)*
Ave cujus nativitas,	Hail, whose birth brought	Imitation
Nostra fuit solemnitas,	us joy,	
Ut lucifer lux oriens,	As Lucifer, the morning star,	
Verum solem praeveniens.	went before the sun.	*(cadence)*
Ave pia humilitas, Sine	Hail, pious humility,	Imitation
viro foecunditas,	fruitful without a man,	
Cujus annunciatio, Nostra	whose Annunciation	
fuit salvatio	brought us salvation.	*(cadence)*
Ave vera virginitas,	Hail, true virginity,	Chordal (voices
Immaculata castitas,	immaculate chastity,	move together
Cujus purificatio,	whose purification	rhythmically)
Nostra fuit purgatio.	brought our cleansing.	*(cadence)*
Ave praeclara omnibus,	Hail, glorious one,	Imitation
Angelicis virtutibus,	in all angelic virtue	
Cujus fuit assumptio,	whose Assumption	
Nostra glorificatio.	was our glory.	*(full stop)*
O Mater Dei,	O Mother of God,	Chordal
Memento mei, Amen.	remember me, Amen.	*(full stop)*

The overlapping of vocal phrases in this opening stanza produces an unbroken rhythmic flow in which the texture varies from between one to four voices:

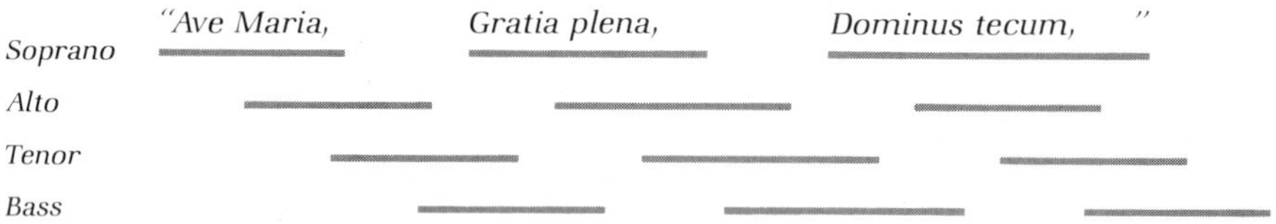

In the second stanza ("Ave cujus conceptio . . ."), Josquin treats the voices in pairs. Duets between the upper two voices are later imitated by the lower voices and vice versa. Josquin alternates between two-voice and four-voice textures throughout the motet. In the final stanza ("O Mater Dei . . .") rhythmic independence and imitation give way to a chordal texture, in which the voices move together rhythmically.

Ave Maria is a representative example of the imitative polyphonic style, occasionally interrupted by chordal passages, typical of much

Renaissance vocal music. The narrow pitch range of the melodies, equality of voices, more or less constant rhythmic pacing, and overlapping of phrases result in a continuous, serene textural flow, despite the highly sectional construction.

The Fugue

The **fugue** (pronounced "fewg") is the most complex form of imitative counterpoint. It was the culmination of a long tradition of imitative procedures in Renaissance and Baroque instrumental music. Although its primary development occurred during the 17th century and was brought to its highest level of artistry by Bach, the principes of fugal writing neither began nor ended during that period.

The fugue is not a specific tonal/thematic outline like minuet and trio form. Nor is it a general format like the rondo. Tonal motion and thematic design follow no prescribed model. It is more accurate to think of the fugue as a flexible set of procedures or as a style of contrapuntal writing, rather than as a specific formal plan.

Characteristics of Fugal Writing

Like the canon, the fugue is based upon the systematic imitation of a theme by answering voices. In a fugue, however, strict imitation does not continue throughout the piece, but alternates with other passages containing freer types of imitation and other contrapuntal procedures. Despite significant differences in length, structure, and complexity, all fugues share certain characteristics:

1. The fugue is a single-movement contrapuntal work for a specific number of melodic lines. Most fugues contain three or four voices.
2. The fugue is based on a short, memorable **subject** (theme), usually about four measures long, that incorporates several motives. The subject is open-ended, concluding with increasing rhythmic motion rather than with a cadence.
3. The opening passage, commonly called the **exposition,** begins with a statement of the subject by a single voice. Each voice enters in succession with a complete statement of the subject, while the others continue with new contrapuntal material.

After the exposition, the design of a fugue is almost completely free. The complete subject is recalled from time to time in one or more voices. Tonal motion is fluid, roaming through several keys before returning to the tonic near the end of the work. Almost always, the final statement or group of statements of the subject is in the home key. In between returns of the subject, the theme is fragmented and developed. In these episodic passages, motives are isolated, imitation is less strict, the texture may be thinned, and fragmentary new melodic ideas may be introduced. The fugue is a continuous fabric without strong interior cadences or sectional divisions. The term "fugue," derived from the Latin word *fuga* ("flight"), refers to the way in which various complete and partial statements of the theme chase each other throughout the piece.

Listening

"Little" Fugue in G Minor *by Johann Sebastian Bach (1685–1750)*

Record Set Side 6, Band 2

J. S. Bach's *"Little" Fugue in G Minor* is a short four-voice organ work composed about 1709, when Bach was organist at the Court of Weimar. It is designated "Little" to distinguish it from a longer fugue in the same key. The theme of this fugue, like many of Bach's fugal subjects, is made up of two parts, commonly called the "head" and "tail." The first two measures establish the G minor tonality by outlining tonic and dominant triads. The "tail" emphasizes the dominant note D as a repeated bottom note against which the melodic contour ascends.

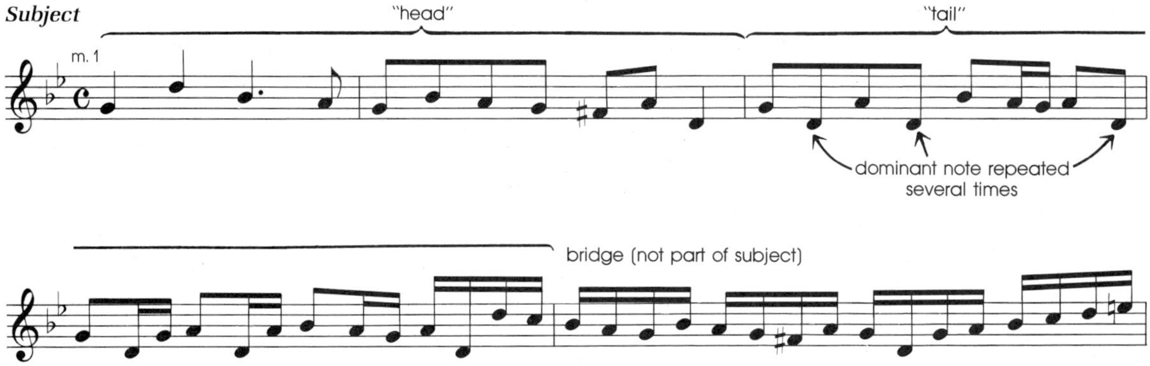

Rhythmic pacing increases throughout the subject, accelerating from quarter-note to eighth-note motion in the "head," and to sixteenth-note motion in the tail. This gives the theme a sense of forward propulsion that provides much of the rhythmic energy of the piece.

Exposition. At the beginning of a fugue the subject is stated in succession by all the voices. Each voice is prominently "dealt in" to the texture as it announces the subject. The number of statements of the subject is determined by the number of voices. (In some fugues, however, the first voice will take a second lick at the subject after the other voices have joined in.) In this exposition, each statement of the subject occurs at a successively lower pitch level. The order of voice entrances is soprano–alto–tenor–bass (played on the organ pedals).

The opening statement in the soprano voice is followed by a one-measure bridge passage that effects a modulation and frequently follows the theme throughout the piece. The subject is then stated by the alto, but transposed into the key of D minor. Because of the tonal shift, such transposed statements are called **answers.** Except for the key change, the answer is a note-for-note repetition of the subject, including the bridge measure.

During the answering statement, the soprano line continues, introducing new motives. If, as in this fugue, the countermelody recurs consistently throughout the fugue against statements and answers of the subject, so that it assumes thematic significance in its own right, it is called a **countersubject.**

Second statement of exposition

At the end of the answering statement the tonality threatens to drift further afield, menacing the tonal unity of the exposition. In an additional short bridge, Bach reins the two voices back into the tonic G minor.

The third statement of the subject—by the tenor in the original key—is escorted by the countersubject in the alto. The soprano voice takes a momentary breather, then continues in a low register with free contrapuntal material, incidental motives that will not return.

The fourth statement—in answer form, back in the key of D minor—is announced in the pedals (bass voice), and is slightly altered at the end to conclude the exposition with a strong harmonic cadence. Rapid rhythmic motion, however, continues unchecked through the cadence, avoiding a sectional division and linking the exposition to the following episode.

The structure of the first exposition can be diagramed:

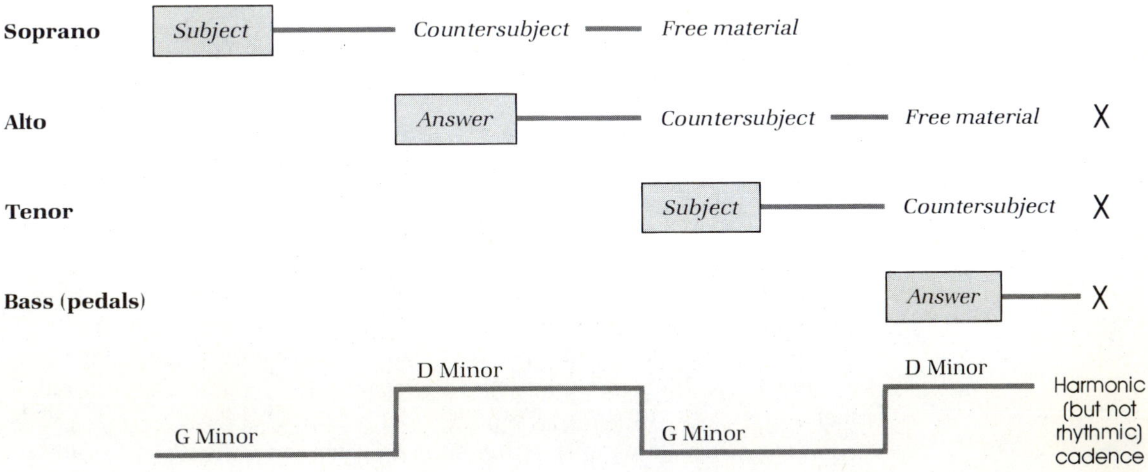

The exposition is followed by an episodic passage during which the pedals fall silent. A new motive is developed in imitation between the top two voices while the driving rhythmic motion is maintained by the more active tenor line:

At the end of the episode Bach introduces a standing joke of both the Baroque fugue and the Classic rondo—the **false entry.** The tenor line heralds the opening measure of the subject in the tonic key but then, in a burst of energy, abandons the theme in favor of the countersubject. False entries play with the listener's expectations of the return of the theme ("Now you hear it, now you don't"). The effect is like suddenly falling down a hole. False entries often immediately precede a real thematic return, and usually occur in a lower voice (often the horn or cellos in orchestral works)—the jest being that "the big fellow comes in too early."

At the point where the false entry in the tenor goes astray, the top voice begins a complete statement of the subject. The opening of this statement is partially concealed by a ruffle of sixteenth notes that ornament the first two notes of the theme (circled):

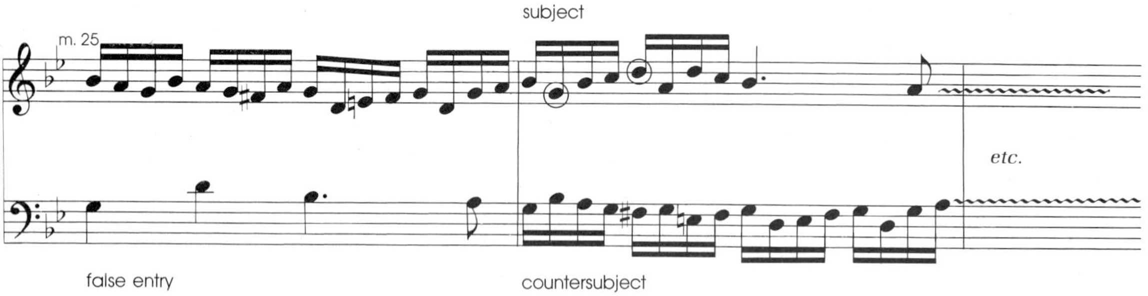

Toward the end of this statement the pedals come to rest on a sustained dominant note. (Sustained notes are often called **pedal notes** or **pedal points** because that is where they usually occur in organ music.) The held pedal tone produces growing tension. When at last the bass moves, ambling steadily down the scale, there is a feeling of tonal relief.

Four more statements of the subject, interspersed with episodic passages, occur during the rest of the fugue. The final statement, in the previously silent pedal voice, coincides with the return of the tonic key, signaling the impending conclusion of the piece. As is often the case in Baroque music, the final chord is the tonic major, rather than minor, producing a heightened feeling of resolution and finality.

Counterpoint in Later Music

Already during Bach's lifetime, the style of tonal music was evolving away from contrapuntal textures and forms and toward the homophonic practice of Haydn and Mozart. Classical composers continued to employ fugal procedures in sections of their choral works (especially Masses), string quartets, and symphonies. Fugal sections that occur in otherwise homophonic works are called **fugato** passages. An example occurs in the development section of the rondo of Beethoven's *Piano Concerto No. 3,* discussed in Chapter 7. During the Romantic period, contrapuntal procedures took a back seat as composers explored the coloristic possibilities of harmony. During the second half of the 19th century, however, the search for ever richer, more expressive harmonic textures led to renewed melodic interest in the inner voices.

As the principles of tonality were stretched to the breaking point at the beginning of the 20th century, homophonic forms based upon tonal motion lost their unifying force. In their search for alternative types of structural organization, many composers were drawn to the contrapuntal procedures of Bach and other Baroque masters. Whereas such Romantics as Chopin had thought in terms of sensuous vertical blocks of sound, composers like Bartók, Hindemith, and Webern strove for leaner horizontal textures in which each voice was melodically significant. In the years between the two world wars, the musical pendulum swung back to a revival of contrapuntal textures. Such traditional procedures as imitation, canon, and fugue, now applied within new styles of pitch organization, are vital to the structure of many 20th-century works.

After World War II, several leading composers began pursuing alternative, nontraditional types of contrapuntal organization based upon rigorous independence of lines. In such music, each voice presents its own melodic ideas, follows its own inner course of development, and is basically unaffected by what happens in the other parts. Each voice is highly charged and concentrated, expressing its own dynamic form. The resulting texture is an assemblage of highly distinct individual lines, fitted together to form mosaic-like patterns of changing color, rhythms, and densities. This new approach to counterpoint and structure, characteristic of much of the music written in the 1950s and 1960s by such composers as Elliott Carter, Karlheinz Stockhausen, and Pierre Boulez, was an attempt to find techniques and forms that grew naturally out of the new pitch language—to address in full the consequences of the loss of tonality and complete the "revolution" in music which these composers felt had begun at the beginning of the century.

Third Commentary on "Hangmen of the Solitude," from **Le Marteau Sans Maître (The Hammer Without a Master)** *by Pierre Boulez (b. 1925)*

Pierre Boulez is the most prominent French composer and musical essayist of the present generation. He is perhaps best known in the United States as the former conductor of the New York Philharmonic. Upon leaving that position in 1976 he became the director of a government-sponsored center for electronic and experimental music in Paris.

Boulez was a leader of the post-World War II avant-garde in Europe, organizing every element of his compositions—pitch, rhythm, dynamics, and so on—by means of pre-set patterns. However, the tight controls in his work are counterbalanced by electric, frequently atmospheric sound colors, reflecting Boulez' belief that "music should be a collective magic and hysteria."

These two elements—abstract precision coupled with a sense of "mystery"—coalesce with particular force in Boulez' most widely performed work, *Le Marteau sans Maître* (1953—54). The eighth moveent, the third "commentary" on the poem "Hangmen of the Solitude," is scored for four instruments: alto flute, xylorimba (which produces a timbre midway between the dry sound of a xylophone and the mellower quality of a marimba), vibraphone, and a battery of percussion including claves (two thick wooden sticks struck together), cowbells, bongoes, and maracas. The resulting sound quality, lacking any low-pitched instrument, is brilliant and transparent. The basic texture is four-part counterpoint.

The opening section features three layers of sound:

1. A peppery exchange between the vibraphone and xylorimba; the similar tone color, melodic style, and frequent pitch crossings of these two lines blur their contrapuntal distinction, and they generally blend together to form a single, rhythmically animated web of sound.
2. A dry, purely rhythmic impetus provided by the claves, sometimes cutting through the vibraphone – xylorimba tissue like a knife, at other times propelling the music forward with a softer undercurrent of rhythmic energy.
3. A more subdued, "distant" flute line that enters late and drops out when its thought is completed. After a long silence the flute reemerges on a single sustained note at the very end of the section.

Following a breath-pause, the second section begins in a slower tempo. The textural emphasis now shifts to the flute line, a highly ornamental but introspective flow of melodic ideas. The other voices punctuate this flute line with isolated attacks and brief figures. They have become discontinuous and are woven around the preeminent flute melody. The percussionist plays the more delicate cowbells. The giddy energy of the first section has evaporated and given way to a more contemplative quality.

After another breath-pause, a loud, accented low vibraphone note sets the third section into motion. The lines are now equally prominent, but the textural focus keeps shifting between the three melodic instruments. Bongos provide a backdrop of pointed accents to the contrapuntal motion.

Pierre Boulez

In the final section the instruments are treated more soloistically. The contrapuntal fabric is interrupted, first by a solo flute interlude, then by an agitated, highly ornamental gust of pitches that passes from the vibraphone to xylorimba. At the end of the movement the lines are gradually disentangled and notes are spaced ever further apart, as though a whirling roulette wheel were winding down until we can make out its individual numbers and colors. We hear isolated figures, then single notes, piercing through silences. The maracas, punctuated with strenuous bongo attacks, become most prominent, and the movement finally dissolves into an evanescent wisp of sound.

The frequent density of the texture and complexity of the individual lines often make it impossible to follow each voice distinctly. Even as seasoned a "listener" as Igor Stravinsky confessed that there were many passages of *Le Marteau* in which he consciously focused on a single line and was content to be merely "aware" of the others. Although there are no memorable motives or themes, and the individual lines go their separate ways with little melodic correspondence, the piece develops a sense of overall continuity through *vertical* sound patterns—fluctuating colors and densities, changing rhythmic and dynamic contours. Even in a style based on uncompromising independence of parts, the vertical dimension of counterpoint—sonorities and textural patterns that result from the superimposed lines—is an essential element of musical form and coherence.

Terms and Concepts for Review

- contrapuntal (polyphonic) textures
- independence of voices
  - rhythmic differentiation
  - contrary motion
  - imitation
- round
- canon
- motet
- fugue
  - exposition
  - subject
  - answer
  - countersubject
  - episodes
  - fugato

Unit 3
Musical Styles

As we listen to a piece of music, we respond both to its substance (musical ideas) and to its style. **Style** *consists of the particular musical language and manner in which a composer presents ideas. Most of our study so far has concerned substance: motives, themes, formal designs, and so on. The three chapters of this unit examine the evolution of musical styles.*

The style of a given work represents a synthesis of many qualities, reflecting broad musical trends as well as the particular concerns of the composer. As a result, when we attempt to understand why a piece of music sounds the way it does, we must take several factors into account. Most historical periods, for example, are distinguished by their own conventions, limitations, and characteristic attitudes toward the composition and performance of music. These features form the basis of a common musical practice, which we recognize as a specific historical style. *In listening to a work about which we know absolutely nothing—not even the title or composer—we can usually guess the approximate date of its composition by recognizing harmonic, rhythmic, or textural similarities with other pieces from the same era.*

For social, political, or purely musical reasons, most composers feel a special affinity for the music of their own country. Distinct national styles *develop as composers build upon native traditions and seek to express national ideals in their music. In addition,* regional *differences within a single country may become prominent, as in the characteristic "East Coast" and "West Coast" American jazz styles of the 1950s and 1960s.*

Taken together, composers' works not only reflect the general musical practice of their time and place, but also embody an individual style. *We can identify consistent procedures, personal conventions, and other characteristics that distinguish one composer's works from those of his contemporaries. Performers, too, develop individual styles. Two performers may emphasize different aspets of a composition because they work from different stylistic premises. One of the first decisions a performer will make in interpreting an 18th-century work, for example, is whether to strive for a historically accurate realization, attempting to recreate the way the music sounded as performed by 18th-century musicians on instruments of the period, or to incorporate more recent performance techniques. These two concerns are not mutually exclusive, but the emphasis will vary in different interpretations.*

Style, then, is a many-faceted aspect of music. It is the set of beliefs and working principles with which musicians approach their craft. To describe a piece of music by reference to its style is not only to place it in a historical context, but also to define its general characteristics. Specific methods of tonal organization, use of particular forms, and other aspects of structure and expression are associated with particular styles. Extramusical factors, such as where a composition was meant to be performed, for what purpose, by what vocal or instrumental medium, and before what kind of audience, are also involved. But although a musical style is influenced by all these considerations, it is recognized by the way it sounds. *Stylistic descriptions are valuable only to the degree that they contribute to our understanding of what composers and performers are trying to do.*

Every historical style reflects not only the distinct musical vocabulary of a particular age and society, but also a world view of that society, embodying a philosophy of life and the place that music occupies within it. As personal values and life styles change, so, too, do musical concerns. Changes in musical style, however, are not solely a consequence of what is "in season" at different times. On a deeper level, they result from the way in which musicians respond to the world around them and address the particular concerns of their age. In this sense, musical style is never fixed, but is always in a state of evolution. Franz Liszt characterized successive musical styles as temporary "resting places—like tents pitched and taken down again on the road to the Ideal."

Chapter 10
Medieval, Renaissance, and Baroque Styles

For centuries most musicians accepted without question the view that music, like science and medicine, was following a necessary course of evolution and was becoming "better" as increasingly sophisticated tonal resources enabled composers to write more expressively. Until comparatively recently the music that was widely performed was always the music of "today." Past musical styles were viewed as archaic forerunners of a richer, more mature art; they were assumed to be of interest only to scholars. Even Bach's music, though it was studied and revered by such later composers as Mozart and Beethoven, passed into near oblivion after his death. Writers of the following generation considered Bach's works long-winded, graceless, and, above all, "old-fashioned."

When earlier music *was* revived, it was generally subjected to "improvements" to make it seem less alien. Rhythms were altered; modern instruments were substituted for the "raucous" or "unplayable" originals; ornaments and dynamic contrasts were added in an attempt to make the music more amenable to current taste. This tinkering even extended to "corrections" in pitches. It was assumed either that earlier composers could not possibly have intended such "crude" dissonances—that they represented copyists mistakes—or that modern performers had the prerogative to correct the gaucheries of earlier periods. The notation of Medieval and Renaissance works in particular seemed curiously incomplete, lacking accidentals and tempo or dynamic indications, and not even specifying whether a given melody was to be sung or played. Rather than attempting to determine how the music had originally been performed, musicians preferred to adapt the scores to current practice.

As a result, the original performance styles of Medieval and Renaissance music were almost completely lost. Not even Gregorian chant was immune; by the 1800s, it was commonly performed in banal metered rhythms and made to conform to the major–minor tonal system. Baroque music, when performed at all, suffered similar (if less severe) adulteration.

A gradual change in attitude began first among English historians in the late 1700s. Through a more thorough and unbiased study of earlier music, these scholars came to the conclusion that something is lost as well as gained when musical styles change. Music, they felt, reflects the esthetic and philosophical values of its own age; these artistic values, unlike scientific formulations, are not invalidated by subsequent changes in perspective. In this view, the music of any period will speak most eloquently to later ages when heard as it was originally conceived.

In 1829 Mendelssohn directed a performance of Bach's *St. Matthew Passion,* the first performance of the work since the composer's death almost 80 years earlier. Renewed interest in Bach's music led to the formation of a society (the Bach Gesellschaft) dedicated to the publication of reliable editions and accurate performances of his music. Nineteenth- and twentieth-century musicologists directed their attention to other Baroque composers as well, unearthing and dating neglected works, publishing them in authoritative editions, restoring an understanding of Baroque performance practice, and prodding performers to play this repertoire. More recently, similar intensive scholarship has been directed at Medieval and Renaissance music. In the last two decades, attention has also turned to a period formerly assumed to be lacking in textural and performance problems—the 19th century.

Musicological research is often a tedious endeavor, a sifting of fragmentary, widely dispersed, and sometimes contradictory historical evidence in the attempt to reconstruct the musical values and practices of previous eras. To fill in the gaps in our understanding, the historian must rely not only on direct evidence—the music itself—but on indirect sources: contemporary writings and pictures about music, publishers' catalogues, and so on, and frequently on inspired guesswork supported only later, if at all, by documentation. The ultimate goal of this research is to enable the listener to hear authentic performances of the music of all periods.

The Medieval Period, 900–1450

In the Middle Ages, the Roman Catholic Church was the unifying intellectual, social and artistic force among the nations of Europe. Through the Church, Medieval society had a collective set of beliefs and rituals, a unifying religious language (Latin), and a common vocal repertoire: the music of the Mass and other church services. This body of liturgical music, which evolved over many centuries, is collectively called **Gregorian chant** (after Pope Gregory I, head of the church from 590 until 604), or **plainchant.** The liturgies of both the Western and non-Western branches of the church were descended from the monophonic music of the Jewish synagogue. These chants consisted of a single, unaccompanied melodic line sung by men's voices. Many chants were performed **antiphonally;** alternate verses would be intoned by a soloist (a priest) and a chorus, or by two halves of the chorus. Gregorian melodies were anonymous in origin, evolving over a period of twelve centuries from the early Christian era through the end of the Middle Ages. About 3000 of these melodies survive. They represent a special kind of folk music—sacred songs transmitted orally through many generations, undergoing inevitable changes and accretions, finally standardized, codified, and written down.

Plainchant never obscures the text, but is subservient to it, representing a heightened form of vocal inflection. Gregorian melodies are characterized by an eloquent simplicity of style and an objective "unemotional" (but highly expressive) tone. The simplest (and, usually, earliest) chants are often constructed around a repeated reciting tone:

Gregorian Notation

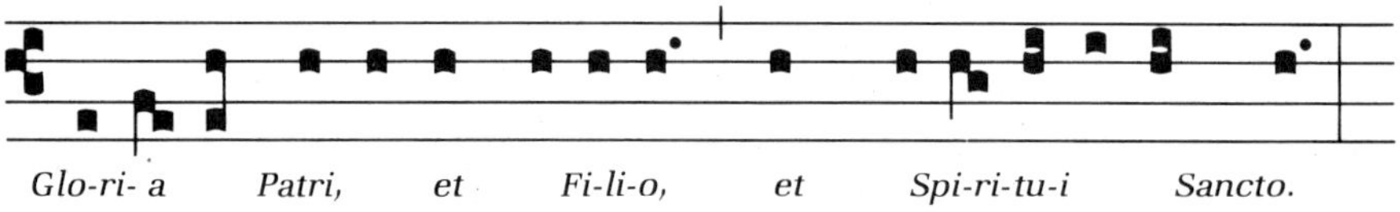

Modern Notation (rhythm approximate)

Chants with lengthy texts are generally *syllabic* in style, with a single note to each syllable. Those with shorter texts often incorporate three- and four-note figures on key syllables. More elaborate chants contain runs of ten to twenty notes, called **melismas.**

Chant melodies are modal in pitch organization[1] and usually have a modest range of about an octave. The rhythmic performance of chant has been a subject of considerable debate. The prevailing theory is that these unmetered melodies were performed with a flexible but fairly steady pulse, without accents but with *nuances* (subtle stresses, a slight leaning on certain notes) determined by the text and phrase structure. In temper, chant is dispassionate and serene, reflecting collective rather than personal beliefs, but it is compelling in its dignity, warmth, and sonorous quality (particularly when sung in a highly resonant stone-walled church).

Listening

Salve Regina *(Gregorian chant)*

Record Set Side 5, Band 1

Salve Regina is one of four hymns to the Virgin Mary, each of which is sung during a portion of the church year. It is a comparatively late and elaborate chant. The text and music were probably composed

[1] Modes were seven-tone scales which eventually evolved into the modern major and minor scales. (See pages 40–41).

in the first half of the 11th century. The text begins as a collective hymn of praise to the Virgin but ends with a very personal plea for intercession. Although formally through-composed (like most chants), the hymn features several subtly varied recurrences of the opening melodic phrase. The free-flowing rhythmic declamation and brief melismas (especially on the penultimate phrases, "O Clemens: O pia: O dulcis") grow effortlessly out of the text and intensify its mood of reverent exaltation.

Plainchant is historically important, not only as a highly expressive musical style which until very recently was the official music of the Roman Catholic Church, but also as a fertile resource for later composers. Chant melodies were borrowed by later composers as pre-existent, familiar melodies, to which new polyphonic voices could be added.

Secular Music

Our knowledge of secular (that is, non-Church) music before the 11th century is sketchy. Education and literacy in Medieval Europe were confined almost exclusively to the clergy. The earliest forms of music notation were developed in monasteries, and church scribes had little time or inclination to transcribe "frivolous" secular songs. The earliest surviving examples of courtly monophonic songs date from 12th-century France. Aristocratic amateur poet-musicians, called troubadors or *trouvères,* composed melodies and texts on amorous and philosophical subjects. The actual performance of the songs was left to groups of traveling minstrels who provided carnival-like exhibitions (dancing, juggling, magic tricks, displays of "exotic" animals, poetry readings) in addition to music. These secular songs were similar in pitch style to chant but, as far as we can tell, featured a more regular and marked rhythmic pulse, possibly with metric accents.

Polyphony

The most important musical development during the Medieval period was the rise of **polyphony:** the simultaneous performance of two or more *independent* melodic lines. A *rhythmic* interplay of parts is a feature of many musical cultures, and it is not uncommon to find a melody presented in several simultaneous embellished versions, as performers improvise variations upon the same tune. However, the concept of a musical texture made up of separate, equally prominent melodies has been unique to Western music. This concept ultimately led not only to the contrapuntal textures and forms of the Renaissance and Baroque periods, but also to the recognition of chords and the system of tonal harmony. In this sense, we can trace almost all subsequent styles and techniques of Western music—from a simple folk song to a Bach fugue or a contemporary orchestral score—back to their origins in early polyphony. Three- and four-voice textures, in which each line has a distinct contour and rhythmic structure, became the distinguishing vocal style of the later Middle Ages.

Most Medieval and Renaissance polyphonic music features a **cantus firmus** (or "fixed voice"): a melody borrowed from an earlier source, fitted with a new rhythm, and presented by the tenor (second-lowest) voice. Plainchant was the principal source of cantus firmus melodies, but composers were increasingly drawn to the use of well-known secular tunes, even when setting the Mass. The cantus firmus line usually moves more slowly than the other voices, in long, sustained tones, so that it often is barely recognizable. (In this way, composers often incorporated secular melodies associated with trifling or even bawdy texts without arousing the wrath of clerics. It is likely that most of the congregation never knew what was going on.)

The 14th century was a period of considerable innovation and technical development, and of a broadening of the emotional range of vocal polyphony. In a spirit of self-congratulation, musicians contrasted their expressive *Ars Nova* ("new art") with what they considered the severe, lackluster "older practice" (Ars Antiqua). Fourteenth-century polyphony, particularly in France, was characterized by greater independence of parts and increasing rhythmic complexity. The austere, controlled sound of early polyphony was replaced by a greater freedom of melodic invention, with each voice pursuing a separate course of development. Although the voices periodically cadenced on consonant sonorities, composers were less concerned with vertical (that is, harmonic) control in the middle of phrases, and there are long passages that bristle with continuous dissonance.

The forerunners of our modern strings, winds, and keyboard instruments were used with increasing frequency. French and Italian secular songs of the 14th century were performed with instrumental accompaniment on the lower parts. But there was no clear distinction between vocal and instrumental music or styles, and manuscripts did not specify any particular instrumentation. Realization of polyphonic works was left to the performers. It would vary depending upon what combination of singers and instruments was available.

Medieval and Renaissance Performance Practice

The notation of Medieval and Renaissance music, which indicates pitch and rhythmic durations but very little else, presents performers with fundamental questions of interpretation. At the outset, performers must determine what size and type of ensemble (vocal, instrumental, or some combination) is appropriate. The presence or absence of a text does not necessarily resolve the issue, since copyists often omitted well-known texts, and instrumentalists frequently doubled or replaced singers. Medieval ensembles varied in size and were usually heterogeneous in make-up, mixing string, wind, and percussion instruments. The prevailing vocal quality appears to have been a thin, "pure" falsetto-like timbre, without the vibrato (rapid minor fluctuation in pitch) added in the performance of most later music.

Further questions arise when the performers turn to the printed score. Medieval and Renaissance copyists frequently left out accidentals, assuming that the performers would know when notes were to be flatted or sharped. The omission of accidentals from the written score (called *musica ficta,*

Musical notation around 1600. This is the beginning of one voice of a part-song by Thomas Morley.

because the music was not meant to sound the way it looked) has led to vehement disputes among present scholars, who hold diverse opinions as to how "diatonic" or "chromatic" this repertoire actually was. We know that the original performers also introduced ornaments and improvisatory embellishments, but how often and of what kind is problematical. Further questions concern rhythm (strong or weak pulse), dynamics (how loud, and whether the dynamic level should be constant or varied) and articulation (whether notes should be detached or smoothly connected). Performers must even decide whether to transpose the music; the notation was often meant to indicate only pitch relationships rather than specific tones, and vocal lines sometimes appear to be written in a preposterously low range. In addition, the music was performed according to various tuning systems; our present tuning, which divides the octave into twelve equal steps, was not standardized until the early 1700s.

Because these questions of performance practice are so fundamental and wide-ranging, the performance of early music entails considerable study and preparation, far beyond merely "learning the notes." Today's performer, centuries removed from the "common sense" of earlier periods, must rely upon informed conjecture to determine how "reverently" to treat the score. Recent scholarship has provided coherent guidelines on which to base these interpretive decisions. Of necessity, most performers of Medieval and Renaissance music are specialists in this repertoire, teaching themselves to play archaic and sometimes recalcitrant instruments and keeping abreast of recent findings and opinions in the field.

The Mass

Practically every major composer up until the late 1500s composed settings of the Mass, the central act of worship and ritual of the Catholic church. The text of the Mass is divided into portions that are used on every day of the year, called the Ordinary, and other portions that change daily, referring in more specific detail to the Feast being celebrated. These changing texts are collectively called the Proper. The Ordinary contains five sections:

Kyrie Eleison ("Lord have mercy on us, Christ have mercy on us, Lord have mercy on us.")

Gloria ("Glory to God in the highest, and on earth goodwill to man . . .")

Credo ("I believe in one God, and in Jesus Christ his Son . . .")

Sanctus and *Benedictus* ("Holy, Holy, Holy, Lord God of hosts . . . Blessed is he that comes in the name of the Lord . . .")

Agnus Dei ("Lamb of God, who takes away the sins of the world, have mercy on us.")

The Kyrie and Agnus Dei are prayers, the Gloria a hymn of praise, the Credo a statement of belief, and the Sanctus–Benedictus an invocation that precedes the most solemn moment of the Mass, the Consecration (in which the wine and wafers become the body of Christ).

Listening

"Kyrie" and "Gloria" from the* Notre Dame Mass (Le Messe de Nostre Dame) *by Guillaume de Machaut (c. 1300–1377)

Guillaume de Machaut was one of the most highly regarded musicians and poets of the 14th century. He is one of the first composers about whom much beyond probable birth and death dates and locale is known. Born in northern France of a noble family, he was ordained in the priesthood but preferred to move in secular circles. Most of his literary and musical works are monophonic and polyphonic secular songs. At about the age of 20 he became secretary to the king of Bohemia and began traveling widely throughout Europe on military campaigns. He later served at the French court, and he spent his final years as a canon at Reims.

By the 14th century the Gregorian repertoire of melodies for the Mass was complete, and composers had begun writing polyphonic settings of individual portions of the Ordinary and Propers. Machaut's *Notre Dame Mass* is among the earliest surviving settings of the complete Ordinary. It also incorporates a sixth movement, the closing salutation "Ite missa est" ("the Mass is over"). The exact date and occasion for which this Mass was written are not known; it was probably composed sometime after 1337.

Machaut's Mass was conceived as a single, unified work rather than as a series of isolated movements. This unity, however, is more easily heard than described. While the individual movements are not interrelated by such later techniques as identical openings or recurrent motives, they do feature similar techniques and reflect a consistent stylistic approach.

The Mass is written in four voices. We do not know the original make-up of the performing ensemble, or even whether Machaut had a specific combination of voices and instruments in mind. The Gloria and Credo contain several brief interludes in the lower two parts that were almost certainly intended for instruments. Whether instruments doubled all the vocal parts or were used in place of voices on the lower two lines, whether the instruments played continuously or only in certain sections, exactly which instruments were used—these are questions to which modern scholars can give only educated guesses. Modern listeners sometimes find the nasal, penetrating tone quality of Medieval instruments initially jarring or "unrefined." Once we become accustomed to these deep-toned timbres, however, they seem well suited to the solemn character of the music.

Kyrie Eleison. The text of the Kyrie contains three short lines:

Kyrie Eleison ("Lord have mercy on us"). (Sung 3 times)
Christe Eleison ("Christ have mercy on us"). (Sung 3 times)
Kyrie Eleison ("Lord have mercy on us"). (Sung 3 times)

Because it has so few syllables, the Kyrie text receives comparatively elaborate treatment in most Masses, with long stretches of polyphony over each word. Machaut's Kyrie is usually performed with three statements of the identical music for each line; occasionally a Gregorian melody is substituted for the middle statements.

The basic texture throughout the *Notre Dame Mass* is a continuous four-part polyphony comprising two faster-moving upper parts, employing frequent rhythmic syncopation, over two slower-moving bottom voices. The rhythmic differentiation between the upper and lower parts is particularly pronounced in the Christe section. The music has a stark, abstract, but forceful quality. Rhythmic pacing, texture, and dynamic levels remain essentially constant for long periods. Melodies move within narrow pitch ranges. Phrases are long and continuous, cadencing only at the end of each section on hollow-sounding bare sonorities. Sharp dissonances and occasional triads occur during the middle of phrases. The music is heard in broad, unbroken arcs, rather than in the kind of shorter articulated segments typical of later periods. Machaut was less concerned with explicit word-by-word depiction of the text than with rendering its broader essence. Each moment seems to reflect the same emotional quality, and this lack of surface contrast serves to focus our attention on the larger, cumulative quality of the work. In this sense, Machaut's *Mass* exhibits certain parallels with the non-goal-oriented esthetic of Indian ragas and such contemporary works as Crumb's flute "Vocalise."

The cumulative breadth that gives the Kyrie an expansive, almost free-form quality belies the strict organizational patterns of the movement. The pitch content of the tenor voice is derived from a Gregorian melody. A short rhythmic pattern,  is superimposed on this cantus firmus and repeated over and over throughout the first Kyrie section. Application of a repetitive rhythmic pattern to a cantus firmus melody—a technique called *isorhythm*—was a common 14th-century device and occurs in four of the movements of the *Notre Dame Mass.*

Beginning of the Gregorian melody used as the cantus firmus

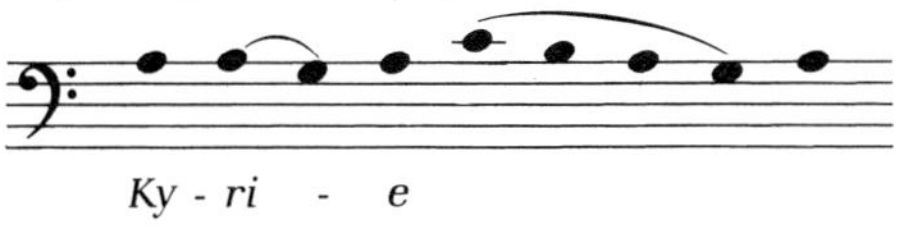

Tenor voice, opening of the Kyrie of Machaut's Mass

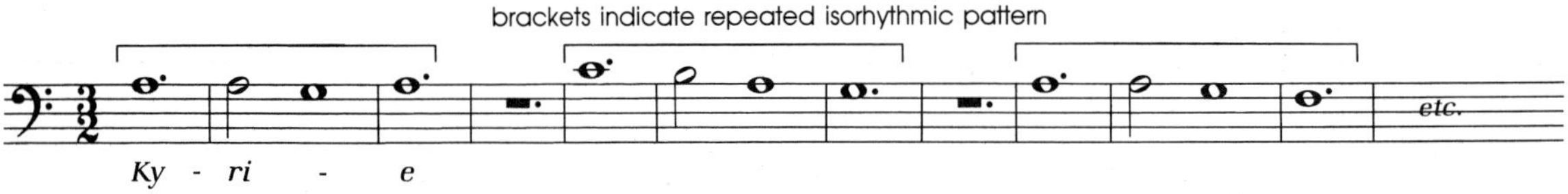

Gloria. The text of the Gloria is much longer and is therefore treated in a more syllabic style (more nearly one note per syllable). In polyphonic Mass settings, the opening phrase of the Gloria ("Gloria in excelsis Deo") has traditionally been intoned in plainchant.

To delineate the individual lines of the Gloria text, Machaut structures the music into shorter phrases with clear cadences. A recurrent short instrumental interlude, and a related vocal motive heard several times in the upper voices, serve to unify the movement. The melodic motive was first heard in the Christe Eleison and is incorporated into later movements as well, but is not systematically developed.

Instrumental interludes

Upper-voice melodic motive

Another notable feature of the Gloria, which became a tradition in later settings of the Mass, is careful treatment of those portions of the text featuring the name of Christ. Both times the words "Jesu Christe"

appear in Machaut's Gloria, rhythmic motion and polyphony are abruptly halted, and four sustained chords call attention to the focal point of the text.

The Renaissance, 1450–1600

The Renaissance (literally, "rebirth") was a time of increased commercial, social, and artistic interchange among the formerly fragmented societies of Europe. Cities grew into cultural centers, and many fundamental attitudes of the Medieval world, such as the supreme authority of the Church in human affairs, were called into question. Insight and broad experience came to be prized above abstract speculation, and there was increasing emphasis on individual achievement. The foundations of modern science were laid, and renewed interest in classical Greek culture led to intensive activity and new objectives in the arts, beginning in 14th-century Italian literature, architecture, and painting. By the middle of the 15th century, Renaissance values had spread throughout most of Europe and new musical styles and genres were taking hold.

The dominant intellectual movement of the Renaissance was *humanism,* a concern with the capabilities, achievements, and values of the human spirit. The educated Renaissance man was assumed to be conversant with every major area of human accomplishment—philosophy, science, the arts, history, politics, and so on—and to have attained a coherent practical wisdom and world view. Members of the aristocracy were expected to be proficient amateur musicians able to participate in the performance of polyphonic music. The Church remained an important patron, but the center of intellectual and artistic life shifted to the more relaxed atmosphere of the courts, which employed resident musicians, poets, and visual artists. The Protestant Reformation of the 16th century divided the Western church into warring factions, further weakening its authority in social and artistic matters. The development of music printing in the late 1400s facilitated the spread of new musical genres, stylistic changes, and the fame of major composers throughout Europe.

Polyphonic and Homophonic Textures

The terms *polyphony* (simultaneous melodic lines) and *homophony* (a principal melody with chordal support) are broad stylistic categories. There are many specific styles of each and many gradations between them. The most distinguishing feature of any polyphonic style is the relative importance of *linear independence*—equality and clear distinction between voices—and *vertical control,* the subordination of independent melodic development to harmonic considerations, so that the lines form a coherent series of chords.

The predominant musical medium of the Renaissance was vocal polyphony. Within this polyphonic framework, however, composers sought a smooth blending of voices, and harmony became an increasingly important dimension of the music. Triads replaced the hollow sonorities of the Middle

Ages. Whereas the strong linear independence of Medieval polyphony sometimes resulted in a series of consecutive dissonances within the middle of phrases, Renaissance composers employed dissonances sparingly and always resolved them to consonant intervals.

At the beginning of the Renaissance, four-part textures, with three or four singers on each part, were most common. The lower vocal parts were often doubled by an organ or by string or wind instruments. After 1450, *a capella* ("for voices alone") became the norm for sacred music and eventually for secular works as well.

Sacred and Secular Styles of Vocal Polyphony

By the early 1500s sacred and secular polyphony had diverged from a common practice into two distinct styles. Sacred music was generally performed by unaccompanied choirs of between 20 and 30 singers. The music is characterized by long, flowing melodies in all parts. The individual lines are similar in character. They share the same melodic ideas, often presenting rhythmically staggered statements of a theme. Musical interest is concentrated in the interweaving of voices—in the total sound quality that results as motives or entire themes pass in imitation through several voices. In listening to this music, we cannot latch onto a single melody to guide us through a piece, nor can we follow a give-and-take between contrasting voices as in Bach's fugues; it is necessary instead to take in the whole texture (rather than attempt to disentangle the lines) and to follow the group presentation of ideas.

The principal genres of Renaissance sacred music were the *Mass* and the *motet.* Most Renaissance Masses are unified by recurrent motives or cantus firmus melodies that are incorporated within several of the five movements. Cantus firmus melodies, either borrowed from a Gregorian Chant or secular song or else newly composed, usually occur in the tenor voice.

During its long, continuous evolution between about 1220 and 1750 the *motet* underwent many changes in format and style, and motets of different periods are often quite dissimilar in texture and form. Most motets are single-movement choral pieces on a Latin text, intended for performance during church services at points where there was not designated plainchant.[1] Renaissance motets generally feature imitative polyphonic textures of from two to six voices. The motet allowed the composer a free choice of texts and became the most progressive genre of sacred music.

Secular vocal music of the 16th century was usually performed with a solo singer on each part, and shows a growing tendency towards homophonic textures. The voices generally move in almost identical rhythm, producing a more homogeneous texture and easily heard chord progressions. The individual voices take on separate functions, with the soprano line following a well-defined contour, the inner voices flowing in stepwise motion, and the more active, harmonically-governed bass bounding about in

[1] There are abundant exceptions, however, including secular works with French texts, motets with separate texts for each voice (often in different languages), and, during the Baroque period, motets for vocal solists with orchestral accompaniment.

larger intervals. The top line becomes "first among equals"—a principal melody on which our attention naturally focuses, supported by inner melodies and a strong harmonic bass.

The principal genre of secular music in the 15th and early 16th centuries was the **chanson**, a French part-song for three or four voices. Most Renaissance chansons are light and fast, with animated rhythms and short phrases. During the 16th century the chanson was superseded by the **madrigal.** Originally performed at Italian courts, madrigals were settings of short, elegant poems for between four and six voices.

Listening

Motet,* Ave Maria, Gratia Plena, *by Josquin des Prez (c. 1450–1521); and the chanson,* Je Ne L'Ose Dire *("I Shouldn't Tell You") by Pierre Certon (c. 1510–1572)

Record Set Side 5, Bands 2 and 3

The distinction between the imitative polyphonic style of sacred music and the more homophonic textures of secular works of the late Renaissance is clearly evident in a comparison of Josquin's motet with Certon's chanson. *Ave Maria* features continuous imitation. Identical melodic ideas are presented with delayed entrances and overlapping phrases between the voices. The rhythmic structure features a steady but weak pulse, without accents, and long, continuous phrases. Cadences are infrequent. Rhythmic pacing and dynamics remain essentially constant. The resulting sound quality is characterized by restraint and inner tranquility, a seamless flow of related ideas without strong contrasts or divisions.

Certon's saucy part-song achieves much of its vitality through its more homophonic, note-against-note rhythmic and textural style. The pulse and duple meter are strong and regular, with occasional cross-accents between voices. Strong harmonic direction results in frequent cadences, short, epigrammatic phrases, and a statement–reply format. These traits relate this song to stylistic features of Baroque and Classical music and exemplify the forward-looking tendencies of Renaissance part-songs.

Instrumental Music

The late Renaissance marks the beginning of an independent tradition of instrumental music. Before 1500, instruments had been confined to supporting roles, accompanying songs for solo voice and doubling or replacing voices on the lower parts of polyphonic works. In the 16th century the organ and lute (a plucked string instrument similar to the guitar) became important solo instruments. Composers also began writing polyphonic works for groups of instruments. The exact make-up of these ensembles was not specified until the end of the century, but the instrumentation was more homogeneous than in earlier periods, often employing families of such instruments as the recorder (an early flute) and viol (forerunner of the modern strings). Renaissance instruments, which underwent gradual technical improvement, had a mellower, less penetrating timbre than their Medieval forebears. Keyboard instruments, the organ and harpsichord, became fully chromatic, though the tuning systems of the time restricted them to certain keys. Strictly instrumental forms such as variations, fantasia, and *ricercar* (essentially a "motet" for organ) developed, along with a tradition of music for dance. Ensemble instrumental music was chiefly associated with social occasions—court dances, town processions, and so on—but was also incorporated into church services.

Listening

Queen Elizabeth's Galliard *by John Dowland (1563–1626)*

Record Set Side 5, Band 4

John Dowland, an almost exact contemporary of Shakespeare, was the most renowned composer and performer of lute music at the end of the Renaissance. He was also an accomplished singer and is best known today for his solo and part-songs. Thanks largely to the efforts of lutenist Julian Bream, as well as renewed interest in the repertoire of "classical" guitar and related instruments, Dowland's compositions for solo lute have received widespread hearing again during the last 20 years.

The *galliard* was a court dance, usually paired with a more subdued dance, the *pavane.* Although Renaissance galliards sound stately

The lute

First phrase of the theme of Queen Elizabeth's Galliard

and rather genteel today, they were considered among the most "spirited" dances of the period. Elizabethan balls were hardly disco scenes; the aristocratic dancers, encumbered both by layers of apparel and by social conventions, generally remained almost stationary.

Queen Elizabeth's Galliard (1610) is a work tinged with irony. Dowland had sought appointment to the court of Elizabeth I (reigned 1558–1603), but was spurned by the proud monarch for his "obstinate" Catholicism. Forced into exile both by his religion and by his habit of running up immense debts, he traveled widely throughout Europe and attained the position of Musician for the Lutes to the English King only in 1612, nine years after Elizabeth's death.

The piece manifests the tendency of late Renaissance instrumental work away from polyphony and toward homophonic textures. The principal melody, in the top voice, incorporates many ornamental figures, principally chordal arpeggios and scalelike runs. The harmonically-governed bass line moves in larger intervals, while the slower-moving inner voices fill out the harmonies. This type of homophonic texture, in which musicial interest is concentrated in the outer parts, would become a distinguishing feature of Baroque music. The piece consists of an eight-measure theme followed by three variations based on the original chord progression. The strong triple meter, short, balanced phrases, and alternation between two-note and three-note division of the beat are typical features of Renaissance dance music.

Major Renaissance Composers[1]

Between 1400 and 1550, Flemish composers, hailing from the region that now includes northern France, Belgium, and the Netherlands, held most of the important musical positions in Europe. **Guillaume Dufay** *(c.*

[1] This list of major Renaissance composers, and subsequent lists at the end of later style periods, is intended as a general reference and overview of the period, and not as a table to be memorized. The roll calls are by no means complete, and the absence of a composer's name does not mean that his music is "unimportant." The composers mentioned are those whose works exerted significant historical influence and are most frequently performed today. When more detailed biographical information on a composer appears elsewhere in the text, this is noted in parentheses.

1400–1474), ***Johannes Ockeghem*** *(c. 1430–1495), and other composers from this area established the basic style of equal-voiced polyphony that dominated the period. The greatest of the Netherlanders was* ***Josquin des Prez*** *(c. 1440–1521), whose works include 18 surviving Masses, about 100 motets, and some 70 chansons. A cosmopolitan later figure was* ***Orlando di Lasso*** *(1532–1594). Born in the Netherlands, Lasso spent most of his career in Germany and achieved great fame for his chansons, madrigals, and German songs as well as for his sacred music.*

The latter half of the 16th century was dominated by Italian composers. The Masses and motets of ***Giovanni da Palestrina*** *(c. 1526–1594) exemplify the traditional style of imitative polyphony characteristic of late Renaissance sacred music (see Chapter 13).* ***Carlo Gesualdo*** *(c. 1560–1613) was an eccentric figure whose highly chromatic madrigals have fascinated modern audiences. In Venice, a new tradition of instrumental and vocal music, emphasizing brilliance of sound, culminated in the works of* ***Giovanni Gabrieli*** *(1557–1612) (see Chapter 15). The Elizabethan age was a fertile period in English music during which Italian influences were assimilated and distinct English traditions established.* ***William Byrd*** *(1543–1613) was the major figure of the time, composing prolifically in sacred, secular, and instrumental genres;* ***John Dowland*** *and* ***Thomas Morley*** *were others.*

Baroque Music, 1600–1750

The trend toward homophonic textures that characterized instrumental and secular vocal music of the late Renaissance culminated in a major style shift around 1600. The rise of opera was attended by a simplification in musical style. Believing that vocal music should enhance but never obscure the text, composers of early 17th-century operas repudiated polyphony, regarding it as an artificially elaborate and cluttered musical practice. The new operatic style, called **monody,** consisted of a bare-boned single vocal melody accompanied by sustained chords. This simple homophonic style was applied to the madrigal and other vocal genres as well. Composers soon chafed under the severe restrictions of monodic style and began reintroducing rhythmic, melodic, and harmonic "complexities." Nevertheless, the austere homophonic style of the early 1600s signaled a fundamental change in musical thinking: chords were now recognized as expressive musical elements that could exist apart from polyphony; harmony had become the basis of pitch combination and musical structure.

Ironically, the Baroque era, which began with this conscious simplification in musical style, ultimately became an age associated with dense contrapuntal textures, richness of sound, and elaborate ornamentation. "Baroque" was originally a derisive term applied by later generations to the ornate style of 17th-century architecture and painting. It meant "extravagant," "ostentatious," or "bizarre"—a fascination with decoration more than substance. Baroque art was rational (rather than subjective) but very much concerned with effect. Theorists codified emotions into categories called *affections.* Human feelings were not treated as complex and often ambivalent phenomena, but instead were reduced to distinct "affections": sorrow, joy, awe, and so on. Theorists believed that each of these discrete qualities had an ideal musical setting which could be realized through the application of a specific musical formula. Compositions were thought most effective when they represented a single affection. Thus, in the realm of dance music, the gigue was meant to arouse "heat and eagerness," and the courante, "sweet hope and courage." In practice, however, many composers had little use for such naïve theoretical abstractions, and their works often express complex psychological states or eschew any pictoral connotations. The wide currency of the doctrine of affections, however, exemplifies the pervasive influence of rational Enlightenment thought on Baroque music.

Musical style underwent several stages of transformation during the Baroque era. The period 1600–1640 was dominated by Italian composers and the new textural style of monody. Vocal music, and opera in particular, was the principal medium. Pitch treatment was in a state of transition, as the major and minor scales gradually superseded the many modal scales of Renaissance music. During the later 1600s the principles of tonality became firmly established and the older modes fell into disuse. The period of rapid stylistic change was followed by years of standardization and refinement of tonal forms. There was a surge of instrumental composition, first in Italy, then in Germany, and a great variety of new instrumental genres developed. Baroque *sonatas* featured one or two solo instruments (usually violins) with keyboard accompaniment; three or four movements, alternately fast and slow, became the standard format. A similar scheme of movements was applied to the *concerto,* a work in which one or more soloists performed in alternation with a larger group. Orchestras, then comparatively small ensembles of 20 or so players, became a fixture at most courts. There was no fixed instrumentation to these ensembles; they consisted mostly of strings, with keyboard accompaniment and a few winds. Instruments underwent alterations that increased their sounding power and technical capabilities. Whereas Renaissance polyphonic works had been adaptable to different combinations of voices and instruments, Baroque composers specified the exact make-up of an ensemble and attempted to write idiomatically for each instrument.

The first half of the 18th century, the late Baroque period, is the age most people think of as *the* Baroque, for it was during these years that Antonio Vivaldi, George Frideric Handel, and Johann Sebastian Bach fused diverse stylistic currents and national influences into highly expressive personal idioms. Late Baroque music was characterized less by innovation than by a summation of the vocal and instrumental traditions of the preceding century.

Stylistic Characteristics

The most important musical development of the Baroque period was the evolution of the major–minor tonal system, which would serve as the basis of pitch organization for all subsequent musical styles up until the early 20th century. Baroque music is generally diatonic. The harmony usually moves through a series of transitory modulations before returning to the tonic key, but it adheres closely to the scale tones of each successive key. There are, however, some striking exceptions, individual compositions written at the beginning and end of the era that feature continuous chromatic inflections.

The first half of the 18th century saw the widespread (though not yet universal) adoption of our present method of tuning. Called "equal temperament" because the octave is divided into twelve equal steps, this system enabled musicians to perform in any major or minor key and to modulate into any other key, neither of which was possible under older tunings. To demonstrate the advantages of the new tuning system, Bach wrote two sets of 24 preludes and fugues, one pair in each major and minor key, collectively published under the title *The Well-Tempered Clavier*.

Baroque melodies are often highly ornamental, incorporating rapid dissonant figures that embellish the basic contour. Bach carefully notated these ornaments, but many other composers notated only skeletal melodies, expecting soloists to enrich the music with improvisational flourishes. Musical interest is generally centered in the top and bottom voices. The basic texture of the period is a florid principal melody in the soprano line, a rhythmically active, harmonically-governed bass, and supporting chords in the inner voices. Bach and other late Baroque composers often included additional contrapuntal lines.

Composers rarely bothered to write out the chord progressions of the inner parts. Instead, the chords were suggested by a system of musical shorthand called **figured bass.** In figured bass notation, the composer wrote out the principal melody, the contrapuntal lines (if any), and the bass voice. The bass, called **basso continuo,** was performed by a keyboard instrument (usually a harpsichord or organ) doubled by a cello or bassoon. Above or below the continuo part, the composer included arabic numbers and accidentals that indicated which chords were to be added. Keyboard players translated these numbers into three- or four-voice chords played with the right hand. The continuo performer was expected to improvise such realizations at sight and to incorporate appropriate embellishments. Any player who merely plodded from chord to chord, without ornamentation or "style," was considered a rank amateur better suited to duties in the kitchen or stable.

The *basso continuo* sound is the most characteristic textural feature of Baroque music. Even contrapuntal works that included all the notes of the harmonies in the written voices were accompanied by continuo. The example on the next page is a typical specimen of figured bass notation, with one possible realization.

Rhythmic energy is one of the most important features of Baroque music. Strong pulsation and unvarying tempos create an insistent forward drive. The music is structured into long, continuous phrases. Rhythmic and harmonic patterns often develop the momentum of an onrushing locomotive; most cadences are merely "whistle stops" where the harmonic cycle begins over again, rather than points of structural arrival or relaxation.

Baroque textures frequently feature the division of an ensemble into two or more groups which perform *antiphonally* (in alternation) throughout

Recitative from "Dido's Lament" by Henry Purcell

a piece. The opposing groups usually contrast in tone color (chorus versus orchestra, for example) or in size. In instrumental music, this contrast often takes the form of a tug-of-war between a small group of soloists and a larger ensemble, a practice that culminated in the development of the concerto. The larger harpsichords and organs of the late Baroque were capable of similar patterned contrasts in color and volume as the performer alternated between different stops (tone colors) and manuals (keyboards).

Listening

Saul, Saul, *by Heinrich Schütz (1585–1672)*

Record Set Side 5, Band 7

Heinrich Schütz served for 55 years as music director at the court of Saxony in Germany. He adopted the innovations of early Baroque Italian composers, and his works in turn strongly influenced Bach's sacred choral compositions. *Saul, Saul* (published in 1650), one of Schütz' most dramatic and moving works, is one of 21 anthems published in his collection of Sacred Symphonies, Part III. (The term "symphony" here has no relation to the Classical–Romantic orchestral symphony). It features the kind of polychoral ("more than one chorus") antiphonal textures characteristic of much Baroque vocal music. Three groups of singers are contrasted: a solo sextet (two sopranos, two tenors, two basses) and two separate four-part choruses. They perform singly, in various combinations, and in massed tuttis. Two violins and continuo accompany the three choral groups. The text, taken from Acts 9:4 of the New Testament, depicts the conversion of Saul (St. Paul):

A	*Saul, Saul, Saul,* *was verfolgst du mich?*	Saul, Saul, Saul, why do you persecute me?
B	*Es wird dir schwer werden,* *wider den Stachel zu löcken.*	It will be difficult for you to kick against the thorns.[1]

The insistent call of Jesus to Saul, heard first as a stern, fathomless untterance in the solo basses, then imitated in succession by the tenors and sopranos, finally bursts into massed antiphonal exclamations in the full choral ensemble. The two lines of the text alternate in rondo-like fashion: *A–B–A–B–A.* By means of textural contrasts, Schütz underscores the dramatic contrast within the text. The *A* sections—an urgent appeal for repentence—feature the full ensemble, while the *B* sections—a solemn warning—employ only the solo voices. The second statement of *B* incorporates a typical example of Baroque word-painting on the text "kick *(löcken)* against the thorns." The total effect of the piece is one of grandeur, portraying an overwhelming spiritual encounter.

The Culmination of Baroque Practice: Johann Sebastian Bach

The Baroque ideal of richness of sound led to a reemergence of polyphonic textures by the beginning of the 18th century. In the music of Handel, this counterpoint often takes the form of comparatively brief stretches of imitation between voices, or of the interweaving of a counter-melody around a principal line. In the music of Johann Sebastian Bach (1685–1750), however, there is a more pronounced and continuous melodic independence between the voices. Simultaneous melodies pursue their own course of development, but at the same time are governed by firm harmonic

[1] An idiom meaning, "You're heading for trouble."

controls. Bach's music represents the culmination of many tendencies in Baroque music, and his greatest achievement is found in his synthesis of late Baroque contrapuntal and harmonic practices.

Johann Sebastian Bach

Born of a German family that produced noted composers and musicians for over two centuries, including four of his own sons, Bach was essentially self-taught. He attained a thorough knowledge of German, Italian, and French Baroque styles as a youth in a manner that few later composers have wished to emulate: by copying out his own library of scores in longhand. Bach's career was outwardly uneventful and rather sedentary. At 18 he became a church organist in Arnstadt, and at 23, court organist at Weimar. Between 1717 and 1723 he was music director for the Prince of Cöthen, directing a small orchestra. Most of his important instrumental works were composed during this period. From 1723 until his death Bach was the Cantor (music director) of St. Thomas Church in Leipzig. His duties included composing music for church services, rehearsing the choir and orchestra, teaching at the church school, and giving private organ and composition lessions. His catalogue of over 1000 works covers every major Baroque genre except opera. During his lifetime, however, Bach was known primarily as a virtuoso organ performer, esteemed for his improvisations, mastery of the fugue, and technical knowledge of the instrument. There were several other composers whose contemporary reputation eclipsed his own, and his music was little known outside of his native Germany.

Listening

Brandenburg Concerto No. 2 *by Johann Sebastian Bach (1685–1750)*

Record Set Side 6, Bands 3–5

Bach's six Brandenburg concertos, written between 1718 and 1721, are his most celebrated orchestral works. The second concerto features a small solo group consisting of trumpet, flute, oboe, and violin, performing in alternation and together with an orchestra of strings and continuo. The work is in three movements. Each movement is characterized by a uniformity of tone, growing out of a single opening theme in a seamless flow. The themes are at once incisive and richly ornamental, often outlining triads and passing through the ensemble in imitation. Dynamic levels remain essentially constant throughout each movement. Gradations in these levels result naturally from the tutti–solo contrasts.

The theme of the first movement is stated by the full ensemble at the outset and is recalled in varied form during the subsequent tutti passages. After each appearance it is answered by a different contrapuntal continuation in the solo group. Perpetual-motion melodic figures, riding on top of the strong pulsation, create a continuous rhythmic drive. Tonal motion is also continuous, cycling without break through a series of transitory new keys before returning to the tonic. The virtuosic trumpet part forms a brilliant top to the overall sound quality. Trumpet players sometimes claim they can develop lip blisters merely by looking at such Baroque parts, which were pitched mercilessly high because the Baroque trumpet, lacking valves, could produce complete scales only in its highest register.

The second movement is scored for three of the solo instruments —flute, oboe, and violin—with continuo accompaniment. A lyrical theme, profound in its simple eloquence, is imitated and then fragmented in the three lines.

Fresh from a stint of rest and recuperation during the slow movement, the trumpeter announces the theme of the fast third movement, a four-voice fugue. Exposition of the fugue subject, in the order trumpet–oboe–violin–flute, is followed by a series of episodes and subject returns, accompanied by the string orchestra. A movement such as this belies the corny old joke that "a fugue is a piece in which the voices enter one after another and the audience exits one after another." There is nothing labored or academic in this spirited fugue. While the structure is rigorous, the tone is jubilant, and there is a spontaneous quality to the interplay of the lines.

Principal Composers of the Baroque Era

Claudio Monteverdi *(1567–1643). Italian. A transitional figure between Renaissance and Baroque practices, Monteverdi was the first major composer of opera (see Chapter 19) and a master of the madrigal.*

Arcangelo Corelli *(1653–1713). Italian. Corelli's concertos and his violin and trio sonatas are well-crafted works that established the basic format of these genres.*

Antonio Vivaldi *(1678–1741). Italian. A prolific composer in all the major vocal instrumental genres of his time, Vivaldi is best known today for his concertos (see Chapter 17), some of which were adopted as models by Bach.*

Jean-Phillippe Rameau *(1683–1764). French. A noted opera composer, Rameau was also the most influential music theorist of his time, codifying the principles of tonal harmony in a series of lengthy treatises.*

Johann Sebastian Bach *(1685–1750). German. The pre-eminent Baroque composer, Bach is universally recognized as the supreme master of tonal counterpoint. His organ works, particularly the fugues, still comprise the basic repertoire of the instrument. Other major instrumental works include his keyboard and orchestral suites, concertos, and sonatas. Bach's cantatas, passions, and* Mass in B Minor *are a summation of the practices of late Baroque vocal polyphony (see Chapter 13). The only other composer to exert so continuous and far-reaching an influence on later generations has been Beethoven.*

George Frideric Handel *(1685–1759). German-English. A cosmopolitan figure born in Germany, Handel achieved international fame for his Italian operas (see Chapter 19), which he produced in his adopted home of London. He also composed a large number of masterful instrumental works. His best known compositions today, however, are his sacred oratorios (see Chapter 13).*

Domenico Scarlatti *(1685–1757). Italian. A transitional figure between Baroque and Classical styles, Scarlatti composed about 500 one-movement keyboard sonatas. Like his other works, these sonatas are distinguished by strongly articulated rhythmic and harmonic motion, and by dramatic formal conceptions.*

Terms and Concepts for Review

Middle Ages:
- Gregorian chant (plainchant)
- polyphony
- *cantus firmus*

Renaissance:
- imitative polyphony
- homophony
- sacred and secular vocal styles
- motet
- part-song (chanson and madrigal)
- instrumental music

Mass
- Ordinary
- Proper

Baroque:
- doctrine of "affections"
- homophonic textures
- basso continuo
- antiphonal textures

Chapter 11
Classical and Romantic Music

The terms "classical" and "romantic" are often used to designate two broad approaches to art. Works that are objective in structure and tone are said to represent a "classical" esthetic; works characterized by a free play of poetic imagination or the projection of subjective feelings are termed "romantic." In more specific musical usage, however, *Classical style* refers to the general qualities of late 18th- and early 19th-century music, while *Romantic style* encompasses the distinctive features we find in music of the middle and later 19th century.

Because these terms have general esthetic connotations, and because they are so often defined in distinction to one another, a too rigorous application of them to individual artists or works can result in distortion. The impression is sometimes conveyed that classical and romantic esthetics are mutually exclusive, or that the Romantic period began with an abrupt reversal in musical language and values, or that we can neatly pigeonhole composers into one camp or the other. In fact, no such hard-and-fast distinctions can be made. Classical and romantic elements, in the broadest meaning of the terms, exist in the music of every age. More to the point, Franz Joseph Haydn—the "father" of Classical style—composed many works that are highly romantic in tone, particularly during the middle of his career. Elements of Classical and Romantic styles coexist in near equal measure in many compositions by Beethoven, Schubert, and Mendelssohn. Finally, such Romantic figures as Brahms sought to continue the traditions of Classical style. For these reasons, it is difficult to choose any clear cut-off date between the two periods.

From our present perspective, the changes in musical style that occurred between the beginning of the Classical period and the end of the Romantic era seem no greater in degree than those which took place during the Baroque era. The forms, genres, and tonal principles systematized in the late 18th century remained the basis of musical construction throughout the 19th century. Because of this continuous evolution, many scholars prefer to think of Classical and Romantic styles as the two halves of a single historical epoch during which composers worked within a homophonic tonal language. To be sure, we will encounter very real differences in emphasis and materials between Classical and Romantic works, but these differences should be viewed against the broader historical continuity.

Classical Style 1770–1830

While Bach and Handel were at the height of their careers, many younger composers were growing dissatisfied with the rich polyphonic textures of their elders' music. Like composers at the beginning of the Baroque era, they sought a simpler, more direct musical language. The result was a lighter style, called *galant* or *rococo,* in which the ideals of elegance and grace were achieved through simple textures of accompanied melody. After 1750, a group of German composers led by one of Bach's sons, Carl Philipp Emanuel, took a different tack, emphasizing personal expression and strong contrasts in mood. This more dramatic style, sometimes called *Sturm und Drang* ("storm and stress"), featured rapid changes in texture, dynamics, and tonal center. Eventually, these two seemingly incongruous reactions to Baroque polyphony were absorbed into a unified new musical language, which has come to be called Classical style.

In common usage, the term "classical music" is often applied indiscriminantly to the entire sweep of Western "art" music from Machaut to the present, as distinguished from jazz, folk, and popular musical traditions.[1] The original, more limited meaning of "Classical," however, is a reference to Greco-Roman ("classical") philosophy, which saw formal beauty as deriving from clarity of outline and detail and a balance of parts within the whole. Late 18th-century composers sought to embody this classical ideal in musical form. Their chief concerns were concise expression and clear design. Emotion was important as well, but as an undercurrent that vitalized the musical structure without ever dominating or obscuring it.

Listening

"Turkish Rondo" from the* Piano Sonata in A Major, K. 331, *by Wolfgang Amadeus Mozart (1756–1791)

Record Set Side 7, Band 1

The finale of Mozart's A major sonata will serve as a brief introduction to the elements of Classical style in the discussion that follows. Listen to the movement first on a general level, comparing its musical qualities with those of late Baroque music as heard in Bach's *Brandenburg Concerto No. 2.* Notice, in particular, the harmonic orientation of the music, the clear differentiation of thematic ideas, and the way in which the piece progresses in distinct, balanced segments.

[1] The alternative terms "serious music" and "concert music" are, like "classical," too restrictive in scope. Much of this music is hardly "serious" in tone, and much of it was intended for performance in churches, living rooms, outdoors, and other places far removed from the concert hall. The loathesome terms "long-hair" and (shudder!) "high-brow" have mercifully passed into near oblivion.

Elements of Classical Style.

The most obvious feature that distinguishes Classical music from that of the late Baroque is the replacement of multi-voice polyphony with a lighter *accompanied melody texture.* Clear tonal motion and discrete, memorable themes are the essential elements of Classical style. The bass and inner parts are simplified into supporting voices that provide a harmonic framework for the melody.

The rate of chord change is generally slower and more variable than in Baroque music. The eight-measure opening theme of the "Turkish Rondo," for instance, is built on a single chord change. In the middle of the piece, a more rapid melodic line is accompanied by one chord per measure:

Middle section of the "Turkish Rondo"

The listener has time to hear each sonority distinctly, and to feel its pull away from or back toward the tonic. Such deliberate harmonic motion might sound sluggish if the lower voices merely perched on chord tones for several beats. To maintain rhythmic momentum, Classical composers usually combined the harmonic voices into a single, animated *figuration pattern,* rapidly repeating or alternating the notes of the harmony.

Classical works are structured in groups of short, related phrases. Frequent cadences mark off melodic ideas and produce a stop-and-go motion. Half stops are soon followed by full stops, balancing the harmonic motion and bringing a melodic idea to completion. Another idea is then presented in similarly concise fashion. Rhythmic emphasis is concentrated more on meter than on pulsation. Groups of notes are heard in relation to strong downbeats. Metric accents usually coincide with functional chord changes, strengthening the force and clarity of the harmonic progression.

The essential dynamics of Classical style are *contrast* and *reconciliation.* Where a Baroque work often maintains a single mood, and continuously develops the same thematic ideas from beginning to end, its Classical counterpart presents a more varied emotional and melodic spectrum. The structural contrast of separate themes in distinct key areas produces two or more moods. In the "Turkish Rondo," contrast takes the form of alternation between minor and major tonalities. In addition, the themes themselves are built up from distinct motives that are played off against each other to produce balance and completion.

Continuity of expression is one of the most important elements of Classical style. Contrasts between key centers, themes, and moods are clearly articulated and serve to differentiate principal musical ideas. However, these contrasts are rarely extreme. Thematic ideas are linked by harmonic transitions and by gradual changes in rhythmic pacing and dynamic level. The themes are not violently opposed, but usually represent different shadings of the same temper. We hear later themes as a reply to, or continuation of, the opening theme, rather than as totally new ideas. Opposition is not, as in many works of the Romantic period, the goal or most important quality of the music. In sum, Classical formal structures are based upon the *integration* of separate but complementary ideas into a consistent musical statement.

A characteristic of the Classical period as a whole was the growth of instrumental music as a medium of expression. Vocal output was hardly insignificant: Mozart's comic and serious operas are masterpieces of economy and vivid characterization; the concert Masses of Haydn, Mozart, and Beethoven reveal the composers' ability to incorporate Baroque contrapuntal procedures within Classical textures; and in their solo songs these composers achieved a warmth and directness of expression that laid the foundations for the development of the Romantic *Lied.* Classical composers poured most of their energies into instrumental works, however, and the most significant developments of the period occurred within the new homophonic instrumental forms.

The piano became the preeminent solo instrument. With its more lyrical tone color, greater dynamic range, and ability to sustain tones, the piano was better suited to the new homophonic style than the harpsichord, which passed out of use until its revival in the 20th century. Chamber music became a major genre; works for string quartet, and for various combinations of strings with piano, represent a significant portion of the instrumental music of the period. The symphony orchestra became the most prominent medium of concert music. The four-movement format of symphonic form was established, and the basic instrumentation of the modern orchestra was standardized. Finally, the form and style of the modern concerto were solidified in the works of Mozart and Beethoven.

Principal Composers

Three composers—Haydn, Mozart, and Beethoven—dominated the Classical period. All three were active in Vienna, which became the most important center of European musical life. The late 18th and early 19th centuries were a time of continuing social upheaval, as political revolutions and protracted wars threatened the old class system. The landed gentry and rising middle class coexisted uneasily, forming two distinct musical publics. The nobility, often amateur performers themselves, employed resident performers and composers to provide entertainment for social functions. Merchants and professionals spent much of their newly-gotten wealth and leisure time at public symphonic and chamber music concerts and at the opera. Amateur music-making spread to the growing middle class, which demanded a repertoire of "not too difficult" pieces for personal enjoyment. The general populace had access to free concerts of dance and festival music. Haydn, Mozart, and Beethoven each moved through these distinct musical worlds, with varying degrees of success.

Franz Joseph Haydn

Haydn. Franz Joseph Haydn (1732–1809) scratched out a precarious living as an itinerant musician and teacher during his teens and twenties. At 29 he entered the employment of an aristocratic Hungarian family, the Esterházys, as musical director at the family's country estate. During his 28 years of service, Haydn was responsible for supervising the preparation and performance of several concerts each week, composing new works for these concerts, and overseeing the personal as well as professional activities of resident instrumentalists and singers. Haydn was to be the last major composer to work under the patronage system. His younger contemporaries Mozart and Beethoven disdained the master–servant relationship as demeaning to the composer. Haydn, however, felt no such resentment. Although he occasionally chafed at the isolation and rusticity of country life, he was able to please his patrons without compromising his personal integrity. With little financial worry, and with an assured sympathetic audience at hand to hear his latest works, he was able to explore the new forms at his own pace.

Following the death of his longtime patron in 1791, Haydn went to London, where he composed and supervised the premières of his last twelve symphonies. These "London symphonies," which include the *Symphony No. 94* ("Surprise"), were an immediate triumph, and remain his most frequently performed works today.

Haydn's stylistic development was continuous. He was never content to repeat old formulas, even if they were his own formulas. Almost singlehandedly, he standardized many of the formal elements of the symphony, string quartet, and Classical sonata. At the same time, he kept abreast of other composers' works and learned from them. Mozart, in particular, although 24 years his junior, exerted a profound influence on Haydn's mature compositions. The mutual respect and personal warmth between these two composers of very different backgrounds and temperament is a moving footnote to the Classical period.

Haydn composed prolifically in every major Classical genre. As his fame spread, several publishers brought out pieces by obscure contemporaries under Haydn's name, hoping to boost the otherwise feeble sales potential of these works. This common 18th-century practice has provided gainful employment for generations of historians, who are still at the task of compiling an authentic catalogue of Haydn's music.

Wolfgang Amadeus Mozart, in a portrait from 1782

Mozart. Wolfgang Amadeus Mozart (1756–1791) was probably the most gifted child prodigy of all time. By the age of six, he was already an accomplished keyboard and violin performer noted for his improvisations, and he had begun composing. Mozart's father, a composer and performer of modest accomplishment, wasted no time in launching his son on a career as concert pianist. Aristocratic audiences were dazzled by the proficiency of the boy wonder, but, as has frequently been the unhappy lot of prodigies, they lost interest as the youth reached his teens and became less of a curiosity.

Mozart's overbearing father and sequestered childhood left him ill-prepared to manage his personal and professional affairs as an adult. A brief, disastrous stint in the service of an oppressive archbishop led him to renounce patronage and seek his fortune as a freelance musician in Vienna. He was unable to capitalize on the early success of his operas, however, and spent his final ten years in growing financial exigency and despair.

Mozart was more concerned with consolidation of the musical art of his time than with innovation. In an offhand remark to his father he declared, "I can more or less adopt or imitate any kind and style of composition." Such an assertion would sound presumptuous coming from most composers. In Mozart's case, however, it merely reflects self-recognition of his special gifts: facility and naturalness of expression. Working within a well-defined musical style, Mozart was able to conceptualize ("hear") the themes and formal design of a composition in his mind; actual notation of the music was a quick and sometimes almost mechanical process. But his reputation for "effortless" composition became a source of annoyance to the composer, who protested, "Those who believe my art comes easily are incorrect. No one gives more time and thought to composition. I have studied the works of every great composer time and again."

Listening

Haydn and Mozart

In addition to the "Turkish Rondo" movement, we have already examined several Classical-period works with respect to specific musical techniques and forms in earlier chapters. These works include:

Haydn: Second movement from the *Symphony No. 94* ("Surprise") (see pp. 133–136)
Third movement from the *String Quartet Op. 76, No. 2* (see p. 168)

Mozart: Second movement from the *Piano Concerto No. 21 in C Major, K. 467* (see pp. 76–79)
First movement from the *Symphony No. 40* (see pp. 151–155), and third movement (see pp. 124–125)

In a rehearing of one or more of these movements, or of other movements of these works, listen on a more general level for those stylistic features that distinguish the music from works of earlier and later periods. The checklist below can serve as a guide (admittedly oversimplified) to typical Classical practice, pointing out those stylistic features you are most likely to hear in the music. It should be noted, however, that no work of any imagination will wholly conform to such an after-the-fact inventory, nor will it use every convention in catalogue-like fashion. The enduring quality of most works results in large part from the interplay between the *expected*—the given elements of a style—and the *unexpected* or unique musical solution.

A Checklist of Classical Practice

Texture

Homophonic, with harmonic support of a principal melodic line

Harmony

1. *Functional harmonic progressions heard in relation to the tonic, resulting in frequent cadences and a clear definition of key areas*
2. *Rate of chord change is variable and comparatively slow*
3. *Harmonic voices are generally combined into figuration patterns*

Melody

1. *Sharply outlined diatonic themes are structured in short, balanced phases*
2. *Themes generally occur at points of tonal arrival, coinciding with the establishment of a new key area*

Rhythm

1. *Metric accentuation is generally strong*
2. *The pulse is more flexible than in Baroque music, occasionally speeding up* (accelerando) *and slowing down* (rallentando)
3. *There is greater variety and contrast between rhythmic figures and motives than in earlier styles*
4. *Rhythmic pacing is also more variable; changes in pacing produce a sense of direction toward structural goals*

Form

1. *Formal designs are based upon a series of articulated events, rather than on perpetual motion or continuous development; frequent starts and stops space ideas apart*
2. *Thematic ideas are carefully balanced; similar balance exists in overall formal proportions between unstable harmonic passages and tonally stable passages at the beginning and end of a work*
3. *Changing dynamic levels reinforce structural motion to musical goals*

Beethoven. Ludwig van Beethoven (1770–1827) began his career in Vienna during the last years of Mozart's life. Beethoven was an intense, self-directed man, driven by inner motivation and a lifelong struggle for freedom of expression and action. His youthful piano performances and improvisations were acclaimed by aristocratic audiences. Beethoven, however, had no intention of submitting to the sometimes fickle tastes and condescending treatment of high society. He believed that genius was the only legitimate "aristocracy" of mankind: "There are many princes, and will be many more, but there is only one Beethoven!" Convinced of the power of his artistic vision to ennoble humanity, he felt it his right and duty to manipulate sources of wealth and power to endure the widest possible hearing of his music. Despite his imperious, often choleric demeanor, and his steadfast refusal to compromise his visionary musical ideals to popular taste, Beethoven was able to gain financial security without loss of artistic independence. A group of patrons, believing in his genius, commissioned new works and paid him generously for private concerts and lessons. At the same time, publishers outbid each other for new compositions to satisfy the strong demand of middle-class audiences and amateur performers for his music.

Ludwig van Beethoven

In spite of this external success, Beethoven's life was marked by loneliness and turbulence. A restless, introspective perfectionist, seeking both structural purity and vivid personal expression in his music, he composed with difficulty. Composition was to Beethoven an act of intense personal will: "Stimulated by those moods which poets turn into words, I turn my ideas into tones which resound, roar and rage until at last they stand before me in the form of notes." In working out these musical ideas, he sought the unique rather than the conventional formal soultion, but at the same time applied a ruthless self-criticism to each departure from tradition. As a result, his musical style underwent prodigious development and change.

The most traumatic affliction Beethoven overcame was his loss of hearing, which began in 1798 and was nearly total by 1818. A moving testament written in 1802 reveals both his anguish and indomitable moral courage: ". . . what a humiliation for me when someone standing nearby heard a flute in the distance and *I heard nothing,* or someone heard a shepherd singing and again I heard nothing. Such incidents drove me almost to despair. A little more and I would have ended my life. Only my *art* held me back. Ah, it seemed to me impossible to leave the world until I had brought forth all that was within me."

Beethoven is a transitional figure between Classical and Romantic esthetics. The Classical forms and conventions he inherited from Haydn and Mozart were well established but still capable of enrichment and expansion. Most of his early works adhere closely to Classical formal proportions, but they also manifest a characteristic rhythmic energy and a breadth of imagination that is at once transcendent and intimate. From his third symphony (1803) on, Beethoven began systematically expanding the length and scope of Classical forms. His last works, completed only after exhaustive reflection and countless revisions, were performed only infrequently during his lifetime, and for many decades were received with "fingertip" applause by respectful but puzzled audiences. Beethoven accepted this situation, as he had his early successes, with full confidence in the ultimate vindication of his musical vision.

Although Beethoven sometimes stretched the boundaries of Classical procedures to their limits, his insistence upon architectural symmetry and coherence was unyielding. Although the individual sections of his works are generally longer and more complex than those of Haydn and Mozart, and there frequently is greater emphasis on tonal motion than on tonal definition, the ultimate structural goal remains the same: the integration of ideas into a balanced pattern. Passages of sustained tonal tension are eventually balanced by emphatic confirmation and prolongation of the tonic at the conclusion of a work.

Beethoven is most celebrated for music that challenges the heavens with personal assertion, but his works are also imbued with humor, eloquence, and moments of understated poignancy. This vast emotional range, which plumbs the heights, depths, and quiet moments of human experience, bewitched every major 19th-century composer.

Listening

First Movement from the **Piano Sonata No. 21 in C Major, Op. 53,** *the "Waldstein," by Ludwig van Beethoven (1770–1827)*

Record Set Side 8, Band 1

Beethoven's *"Waldstein"* (pronounced "*vahlt*-shtine") *Sonata,* written in 1804, exemplifies his ability to maintain the integrity of Classical forms while shaping them into expansive vehicles for the development of emotionally charged ideas. The first movement, in sonata form, is pervaded by stark contrasts in mood and abrupt tonal shifts between major and minor. Driving rhythms lead to a series of climactic peaks, interspersed with moments of complete tranquility. The volatile structural motion has a roller-coaster quality in the way it builds, dissipates, and rebuilds tension in roaring and plunging arcs.

The movement opens with a rumbling theme characterized by its dense, low spacing (with motivic interjections in higher registers) and "nervous" repeated-chord rhythms. There is little sense of melody or tonal definition. The theme hurdles through a series of transitory modulations before coming to a strong rhythmic cadence on the dominant. The *transition* begins as a varied repetition of this theme, shifted to a higher register. A climactic surge is followed by a relaxation in rhythmic pacing and a softer dynamic level.

The theme of the *second tonal group,* in the distant key of E major, is lyrical, almost hymn-like, standing in complete contrast to all that has come before. The theme is repeated with more rapid triplet rhythms in the melody. Gradually, this theme, too, unleashes a torrent of rhythmic energy that culminates in high-register trills (rapid alternation of notes). The *closing material* introduces a new thematic idea: a rapid, high melody over a chord progression that vacillates between major and minor. There is no full stop at the end of the exposition. The closing theme dissolves back into the opening theme, and the exposition is repeated.

The *development* section is characterized by a propulsive rhythmic motion that never slackens. At the outset, the first theme is fragmented into progressively smaller motives, resulting in extreme registral shifts and abrupt loud–soft contrasts. The middle of the development centers around the triplet rhythms of the second-group theme. A feverish build-up, from very soft to very loud, then propels the music into the recapitulation.

The *recapitulation* incorporates several minor alterations and additions within the material of the exposition, and introduces one major new twist in structure: the second-group theme returns in the key of A major rather than in the tonic, undermining the tonal unity of the recapitulation. The closing theme is also tonally unstable.

The most significant departure from Classical sonata procedure, however, occurs in the *coda,* which is expanded greatly in length and complexity. Most of the coda is, in reality, a second development; themes are fragmented and juxtaposed, and the tonality wanders far afield. At the end of the coda, fragments of the two principal themes return in the tonic C major. The coda functions somewhat like a shortened, varied repetition of the development and recapitulation sections.

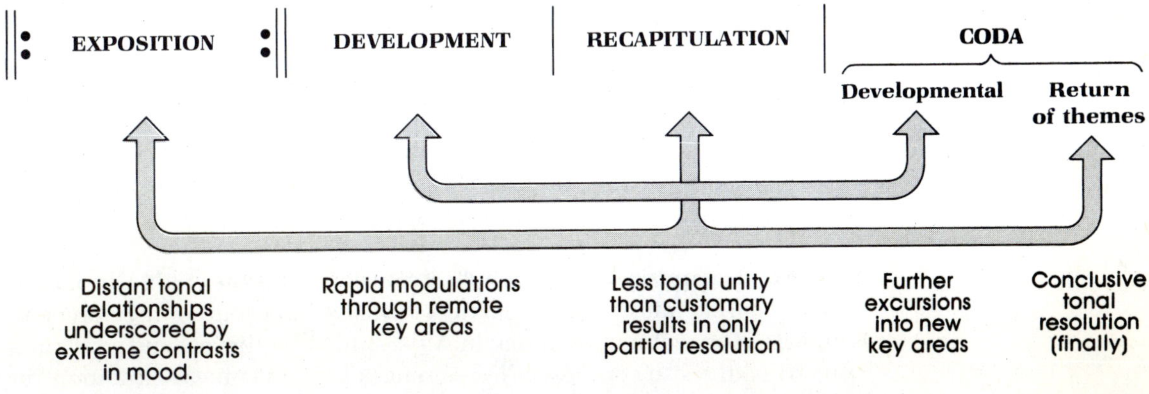

Anticipations of Romanticism. Like many of Beethoven's major works, the first movement of the "Waldstein" sonata is of heroic dimensions. The exposition sets two themes and moods into seemingly implacable opposition; the barricade-storming first theme and the introspective, almost devotional second theme are psychologically worlds apart. But contrast for its own sake is not Beethoven's intention. By themselves, the first theme and its related passages would be exuberant but too unbridled and diffuse to sustain interest, while the second theme would be an unexceptional little song tune. Held in tension by the formal structure, however, these themes become the two poles of a single, comprehensive musical statement.

The movement as a whole generates a feeling of *imposed* order. The principal themes have no "natural" affinity or connection; structural relationships and unity of expression must be *enforced* upon the antagonists. As the piece unfolds, an emotional continuum is built to bridge the vast gulf that separates them. The restless surge of the music between points of maximum and minimum tension is this bridge. Transitional and developmental passages are not merely connecting links, but the means of structural and emotional integration. The formal design has a quality of struggle, of gradually overcoming initially irreconcilable differences.

Live performances of the movement generate a sense of excitement somewhat like that aroused by a high-wire performer. By intentionally exaggerating contrasts, Beethoven runs the risk of a pretentious debacle. If the themes are not consolidated successfully into a larger, coherent statement, they can seem like the alternate mood-swings of a neurotic. The pianist must carefully shape and control changes in pacing to effectively communicate the sense of imposed structure. If the contrasts are too sharply etched, the indispensable thread of continuity that holds the movement together will be lost. On the other hand, if contrasts and transitions are handled in too glib or diffident a manner, the tension between ideas—an equally vital element of the structure—will lack necessary force. This is not the kind of movement that "plays itself," or about which one can feel (as in many Mozart works) that "although the performance was appalling, the quality of the musical ideas still comes through." Bad performances of the "Waldstein" sound very bad indeed, because the music is so dependent upon sensitive interpretation to achieve its clarity of design.

If we compare our intuitive responses to this movement with the "Checklist of Classical Practice" on page 210, many of the items seem not to apply, or to require qualification, or to be only abstractions that don't really get to the heart of Beethoven's musical style. Classical forms and stylistic conventions provide a superstructure and basis for coherence, but Beethoven's music transcends the Classical esthetic and anticipates the more volatile style of Romantic compositions.

Schubert. The music of Franz Schubert also illustrates the gradual evolution of the Romantic idiom within Classical forms. Schubert lived in Vienna and assimilated the techniques of Haydn, Mozart, and Beethoven, and so is often grouped with these composers in references to the Viennese "tradition" or "school." He composed in most of the major Classical genres but also explored new modes of expression that were to become staples of the Romantic era, notably the character piece for piano. His early instrumental works, such as the *Symphony No. 5 in B♭ Major,* exhibit Classical proportions and clarity. His last two symphonies (No. 8, the "Unfinished," and No. 9, the "Great C Major") and other late works reveal the influence of Beethoven in their breadth of conception. Schubert's songs, which we will examine in Chapter 13, established the basic style and formal conventions of the Romantic art song.

Suggested Listening

Second movement from the* Quartet No. 14 in D Minor, *"Death and the Maiden," by Franz Schubert (1797–1828)

Schubert's D Minor quartet, the best known of his 15 string quartets, was composed in 1826. The work derives its nickname from one of the composer's early songs, a fragment of which is incorporated within the theme of the second movement. The theme, presented in simple chordal style, is in two parts, both repeated, with the first in minor and the second in major. The theme is followed by six variations that adhere closely to the theme's original harmonic structure, while introducing a series of new figuration patterns that grow increasingly animated and impassioned. Schubert relaxes the rhythmic pacing and reharmonizes the opening phrase in major at the beginning of the fourth variation, then rebuilds rhythmic momentum and textural depth. At length the theme is brought back into focus, and the movement comes to a somber conclusion. The warmth and naturalness of expression, subtle harmonic nuances, and singing character of the music, even in rhythmically forceful passages, are hallmarks of Schubert's style that exerted continuous influence throughout the Romantic era.

Romantic Style, 1830–1900

Romanticism is less a specific style than an attitude, in which emotion and individual expression, rather than clarity of form, are seen as the essence of art. This attitude did not originate in the 19th century, but it did become, for the first time, the dominant musical influence of an age.

The Romantic movement began in late 18th-century German literature. Goethe, Schiller, and later lyric poets, disdaining what they considered the lifeless formalism of Enlightenment thought and Classical humanism, turned their attention inward. The Romantic poets extolled the simple, unaffected passions of human feelings. The movement quickly spread to England (Wordsworth, Byron, Shelley, Keats), France (Rousseau, Hugo), and all of Europe.

In an era when the authority of the state and church was in decline, art was seen by many as the greatest human achievement—an elevated means of expression which, by its urgency and beauty, could communicate truths far better than rational philosophy. For Romantic writers, human experience (and the artist's response to it) was the natural concern of art. The content of a poem was deemed more important than its structure. Artists believed that their fundamental purpose was to reveal a deeper vision of the sanctity and potential of human life, and to make this revelation as compelling as possible. Where reason failed to accomplish this, art would succeed, because it would speak to the heart as well as to the mind.

For the Romantics, truth was not simply something to be learned, but a quality present from birth, to be nurtured and enriched by personal experience. The artist was seen as a commanding figure, uniquely sensitive to feelings, able to communicate mankind's most elemental and exalted aspirations. At the same time, the artist retained a childlike sense of wonder. Free of inhibitions and presumptuous erudition, he could learn from nature, from children, or from any source of beauty or innocence. To the most fervent Romantics, "too much" knowledge or technical skill could be inimical to original creation, beclouding intuitive insight. Almost all of them believed that technique and structure should be at the service of emotional expression—not, as in Classical art, the other way around.

The Romantic movement was a fertile but comparatively brief period in literature. In music, however, it encompassed nearly a century. From Schubert's early songs (c. 1815) through Mahler's final symphonies (1910–11), composers strove for spontaneity of expression and vivid communication. They unabashedly considered music the "greatest" of the arts, because they believed that instrumental music, alone, could express passions that defy verbal description. The image of Beethoven, seen through a Romantic filter, became a paradigm for the age. The Beethoven that most Romantics wished to emulate, however, was not the master of Classical forms and architectural proportion but the uncompromising genius of poetic imagination, accountable only to his own ideals, who had set music on a new course.

During the 19th century the traditional patrons of art, the church and the aristocracy, declined as a source of support, and the rising middle class became the principal consumers of music. With rare exceptions, composers could no longer latch on to a single patron or small coterie for financial support, but had to appeal to a broader audience. Many found this difficult. While seeking personal expression, they also wished, in the manner of Beethoven, to make universal musical statements addressed to "all mankind." The mankind they envisioned was flush with Romantic ardor, inherently responsive to genius, and contemptuous of banality.

Such an idealized discriminating audience, however, was hard to come by. More often, Romantic composers were confronted with a less exalted and more mercurial public. Their writings often bristle with resentment and thwarted expectations; they make sardonic references to audiences of "philistines" and "dilettantes" who clamor for accessibility, superficial brilliance, and a good time—with, possibly a little spiritual enlightenment on the side. Many Romantics were disturbed by the discrepancy between their own view of art as an all-consuming, even moral, human endeavor, and the more prosaic desire of audiences for entertainment. Some, like Chopin, withdrew from public performance, confining their activities to a select inner circle. Others supported themselves as traveling virtuosos (Liszt) or as conductors (Mahler). Many (Schumann, Berlioz, Wagner) took to print, devoting much of their energy to explaining what they and their contemporaries were trying to accomplish. Composers who experienced difficulty receiving a sympathetic hearing often consoled themselves in the belief that genuine art is always ahead of its time.[1]

It is important, however, not to overdraw the disparity between the aspirations of Romantic composers and the reality of 19th-century concert life. In retrospect, the 19th century was a period of enormous dissemination of music to new listeners, who had previously been denied access by social position. In no other age was music so thoroughly discussed and debated by professional and layman alike. The spread of public opera houses and concert halls, and the founding of permanent symphony orchestras, enabled unprecedented numbers of people to hear concert music. The new audience was also eager to study and perform music, providing a greatly expanded market for piano pieces and songs. Most major composers received a widespread hearing, and many were lionized by partisans. Music was considered important. Nineteenth-century audiences were highly demonstrative, bellowing approval, booing with rage, sometimes even breaking into fistfights. The genteel atmosphere that pervades all too many modern concert halls was little known to the Romantics.

Musical Developments

The 19th century was a period of continuous enrichment of the tonal harmonic vocabulary. Harmonic progressions became more dissonant and chromatic, incorporating many tones outside of the prevailing key.[2] The harmonic emphasis gradually shifted from *functional* progression (chords heard in relation to the tonic) to *coloristic* exploration: chords defined by their special qualities and degree of dissonance. Frequent modulations, together with passages in which the tonic is temporarily obscured, give many Romantic pieces a restless, unsettled quality. The volatile harmonic motion is underscored by changes in dynamic level, texture, and tempo.

[1] This widespread assumption has been hotly debated since the early 19th century. For every Mozart, Schubert, Schönberg, or Ives, whose true achievement was never grasped by his contemporaries, one can cite a Josquin, Handel, Haydn, or Stravinsky, who enjoyed great renown during his lifetime. Composers such as Bach, whose music was esteemed by the limited audience who heard it, and Beethoven, who experienced acclaim and misunderstanding in equal measure, further complicate the issue. The question is ultimately unanswerable because it is oversimplified. Still, it has proven a provocative and seemingly irresistible source of speculation for generations, perhaps because it often helps one discover his own conception of the essence of artistic expression. Schönberg, Varèse, and other composers, as well as many general writers, have held that a piece of music is by its very nature a reflection of its time, but that *audiences* often lag behind in an understanding of their own age.

[2] See pages 78–80.

With respect to formal structure, Romantic composers can be roughly divided into two broad groups. Those composers who saw musical Romanticism as a direct outgrowth of Classical style, such as Mendelssohn, Brahms, and Dvořák, attempted to incorporate the expanded harmonic language of their time within traditional forms. Other composers, including Chopin, Berlioz, Liszt, and Wagner, believed that these forms had been exhausted by Beethoven, and that the new harmonic resources demanded new approaches to structure. These composers freely adapted the Classical forms, altering proportions, adding new sections or extra movements, sometimes connecting the movements with transitions; in Liszt's *Piano Sonata in B Minor,* for example, the separate "movements" are incorporated without pauses into a continuous design. Traditional forms and genres were often transformed beyond recognition or abandoned entirely in favor of more rhapsodic types of structure.

As both a source of initial inspiration and as an aid to the listener's comprehension of unorthodox musical structures, many Romantic composers made use of literary or pictorial associations. Such **program music** portrays a mood, story line, or some similar extra-musical quality. The program may be general in nature, as when a picturesque title is supplied as a vague frame of reference; it may also be very specific, following a story line in exacting detail and musically transliterating its events.

The two tendencies, the classically-oriented and the more revolutionary, that continued throughout the Romantic period in music can be heard in two orchestral works, both written around 1830, of Mendelssohn and Berlioz.

Listening

Hebrides Overture *by Felix Mendelssohn (1809–1847)*

Record Set Side 9, Band 1

Felix Mendelssohn

Felix Mendelssohn was a cosmopolitan figure who held various posts in Berlin and Leipzig and traveled widely. An independently wealthy, multi-talented man (composer, pianist, conductor, writer, administrator, amateur painter), he revered the music of Bach, Mozart, and other Baroque and Classical masters. Mendelssohn composed in every major genre except opera, with a facility reminiscent of Mozart's. Although he favored picturesque titles for his instrumental works and exploited novel harmonic progressions and orchestral colors, his music is, on the whole, more Classical in conception and structure than the works of his contemporaries. Personal expression is always subordinate to the formal design. Unique colors and structural contrasts (which are never extreme) are not ends in themselves, but a means to clarify this design. The most characteristic features of Mendelssohn's music are elegance, lightness, geniality, and Classically balanced proportions.

The *Hebrides Overture,* also called *Fingal's Cave,* was inspired by the composer's visit to a famous cave off the coast of Scotland. It is an example of the **concert overture,** a genre first explored by Beethoven and Schubert. Concert overtures are short, single-movement works designed as opening numbers on symphonic concerts.

The *Hebrides Overture* is programmatic only in the broadest sense. In the magical opening bars, sequential repetitions of a one-measure motive are molded into a wave-like theme, against a sustained harmonic accompaniment that suggests that reverberant hollowness of a spacious cave.

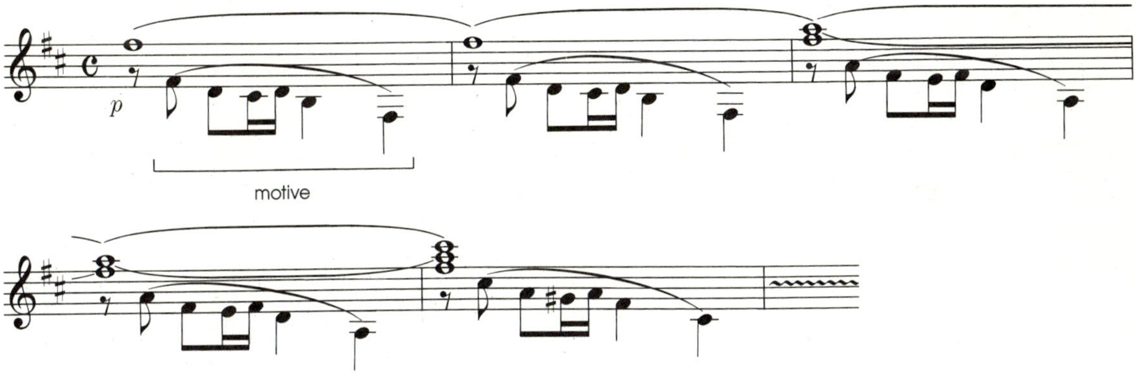

The eternal restless surge of the sea is similarly intimated in an agitated undercurrent in the lower strings, which accompanies immediate repetition of the theme. As the piece progresses, one may (or may not) "hear" the swirling of water into the cave, "sense" the vast expanse of the ocean, and "feel" its sudden or gradual changes in appearance and mood; the extended coda of the work may bring to mind a raging storm, which, in the final bars, subsides as quickly as it blew up. Mendelssohn's tone painting is always discreet, however, and is largely left to the listener's imagination. The overture "works" equally well if heard without reference to its programmatic allusions, and the listener who scrutinizes the piece too carefully for graphic depiction or hidden meaning (sea gulls? ships?) will likely be disappointed.

The formal design of the overture adheres to the key scheme, format, and proportions of Classical sonata form, with only minor alterations: the exposition is not repeated, the lyrical second group is abridged in the recapitulation, and the structural climax of the piece occurs in an elongated coda. The opening motive dominates the development section and the overture as a whole. Concentrated development and repetition of this motive results in a unity of tone despite surface contrasts. The *Hebrides Overture* evokes a sense of mystery and expansiveness, but it does so within a "nuts and bolts" structural framework. Descriptive images are never overt, but they color our perception of the musical ideas.

Fourth Movement ("March to the Scaffold") and Fifth Movement ("Dream of a Witches' Sabbath") from the Symphonie Fantastique ("Fantastic Symphony") by Hector Berlioz (1803–1869)

Record Set Side 9, Bands 2 and 3

Hector Berlioz

The French composer Hector Berlioz was among the most fiery Romantics in musical and personal temperament. Essentially self-taught, he had only a spotty knowledge of past musical styles—a condition he considered a virtue rather than a deficiency. Berlioz felt that music had begun "in earnest" with Beethoven (he considered Haydn a composer of children's music). There were, to him, two distinct kinds of art: that which was merely an attractive diversion; and that, like Beethoven's, which seized the imagination, drawing it into a special world of exalted meaning. For music to transcend the conventions of its time, he believed, it must be closely allied with poetic images: only as a dramatic art could music realize its full potential and become *more* itself. All of Berlioz' major works contain some form of pictorial or dramatic association.

Berlioz never mastered an instrument, and his lack of pianistic ability—unusual for a composer of the time—proved a unique spur to his musical imagination. Unable to work his ideas out at the piano, he conceived them directly for orchestra. In his study of scores and in his own early works, Berlioz focused on sound quality rather than on "correct" harmonic practice or formal niceties, and he became the first great master of orchestration. His textbook, *Treatise on Instrumentation,* (1844), which included detailed commentaries on each instrument, became the definitive work on the subject. Berlioz' arresting orchestral effects startled early listeners and have continued to influence composers down to the present day. Wagner, never one to toss bouquets lightly to other composers, was spellbound when he first heard Berlioz' music: "This was a wholly new world to me. . . . I was stunned by a force of orchestral virtuosity of which I had yet no idea. At that time I truly felt like a student in front of him."

Berlioz' unorthodox musical style was influenced by his ability to conceptualize directly for orchestra. He delighted in audacious harmonic progressions and formal designs that flouted traditional practice. Academics upbraided him for clumsy bass lines, inept chord connections, and other harmonic felonies. His rambling tonal schemes, ironic use of bathetic themes and subject matter, and fascination with the bizarre rankled more fastidious composers. Berlioz, however, was little troubled by their reproaches, considering them the squeamish qualms of small minds. "The prevailing characteristics of my music," he wrote, "are passionate expression, intense ardor, rhythmic force, and unexpected turns."

The *Fantastic Symphony* was Berlioz' first major work, written when he was 26. The Romantic esthetic burst into full flower in this venturesome composition, resulting in several bold departures from traditional symphonic format. The symphony is in five movements rather than the customary four. Several of the movements bear little resemblance to Classical models. "The design of the symphony is free," Berlioz stated, "just as the composer's thought is free." For the Paris première, Berlioz included a detailed, fantastical program. A sensitive young musician, despairing of unrequited love, attempts suicide with an overdose of opium. The narcotic is too weak to kill him but produces a series of delirious visions, which comprise the five movements of the work:

I. *Reveries and Passions.* The artist's thoughts are engrossed in conflicting images of his beloved.

II. *A Ball.* His enjoyment of a ball is interrupted by a vision of his love.

III. *Scene in the Fields.* Two shepherds pipe to each other on a summer night. The artist is buoyed by the scene of pastoral tranquility, until his love suddenly appears, casting him into even deeper torment. One shepherd begins playing again. As the sun sets, distant thunder is heard—then only silence, and solitude.

IV. *March to the Scaffold.* He has killed his love and been condemned to death. As he is led to execution, the processional march grows alternately grave and boisterous. A final fleeting image of his beloved, then—slam!—off with his head.

V. *Dream of a Witches' Sabbath.* A ghastly rabble of witches, demons and monsters has assembled to celebrate his funeral. Diabolic groans, shrieks of hideous laughter, and other unearthly sounds are heard. A specter of the beloved, now debased and unworthy, joins the revel. Church bells toll the death knell. The fiends dance with furious abandon.

The program was, in Berlioz' own words, "entirely autobiographical in intention." Three years earlier, the composer had fallen madly in love with a Shakespearean actress. Frightened by the vehemence of his suit, and fearing that he was deranged, she refused to have anything to do with him. Berlioz channeled his fervor into the symphony, seeking to fashion a work of unprecedented emotional concentration and impact. The work was intended not to imitate his experience but to transcend it, by driving to the very core of human passion and revealing the vital emotional bond between art and life.

The image of the unobtainable loved one is associated throughout the symphony with a recurrent theme, which Berlioz called the *idée fixe* ("ee-day feex") or "fixed idea." The theme, which comes to symbolize the artist's obsessive passion, is introduced as the principal theme of the first movement and recalled in various transformations during each of the following movements:

Idée Fixe theme from First Movement
Violins

End of Fourth Movement
Clarinet

Fifth Movement
E♭ Clarinet

The cyclical reappearance of a theme in altered form became a common structural procedure in 19th-century instrumental music, called **thematic transformation.** The *idée fixe* theme assumes a different character, tempo, rhythm, and harmonization in each movement, but remains melodically recognizable. Through manipulation of this melody, Berlioz attempted to unify the symphony around a single musical–dramatic thread.

The last two movements of the *Fantastic Symphony* comprise a double finale, opening a Pandora's box of extravagant musical gestures and dramatic allusions. Formal balance, restraint—indeed, everything prized by the Classical mind—are swept away in a consuming billow of Romantic imagery. Not surprisingly, Mendelssohn was aghast at such excess, describing it as "mere grunting, shouting, screaming back and forth." This is not music to be admired through a jeweler's eyepiece, but music to be experienced with psychological abandon, like a bewitching horror story.

Fourth Movement: "March to the Scaffold". The fourth movement opens with an atmospheric introduction that is pure tone painting. Melody, harmony, and rhythm are atomized. All interest is concentrated on the extraordinarily dark sound quality: portentous, icy, funereal. It is an unnatural calm, disturbed only by distant drum strokes, which finally erupt in a thunderous roar. A forceful opening theme, beginning with a two-octave stepwise descent down the minor scale, is stated by the lower strings, then repeated in shifting registers against various countermelodies. The full brass section enters (for the first time in the symphony) on the second theme of the movement, an initially jaunty march tune featuring syncopated rhythms. The march becomes increasingly ominous and threatening through incessant repetition, building to a frenzied climax. The *idée fixe* theme is recalled in the solo clarinet for a suspended instant (the second example on the previous page), then the guillotine crashes with graphic force. The patently obvious and unflinching portrayal of decapitation struck some 19th century listeners as "monstrous bad taste." Berlioz made no apologies, flourishing his brazen vision as just another slice (sorry) of life. Further horrors await.

Fifth Movement: "Dream of a Witches' Sabbath". The frantic concluding movement demonstrates Berlioz' mastery of vivid orchestral colors. In form, the movement is an aberrant cross between variation and rondo procedures, but it is heard as a continuous dramatic sweep. The movement begins, like its predecessor, with an assemblage of inscrutable musical fragments. Eerie and macabre, this introduction sets the tone of the movement; anything can happen as the forces of hell erupt. A grotesque travesty of the *idée fixe* theme, now in dance rhythm with mocking trills, is sounded by a shrill piccolo clarinet (the third example on the previous page); nothing is sacred. Two statements of the theme alternate with rampaging tuttis, followed by an ill-boding melodic transition in the lower strings.

Church bells, tolling implacably on the same two notes, signal the beginning of a blasphemous ritual. A parody of the Gregorian Chant melody *Dies Irae* ("Day of Wrath") from the Mass for the Dead is intoned by a tuba and four bassoons. The tune passes to the trombones and horns in quicker rhythm, then to the woodwinds in an ironic dance rhythm similar to that of the parodied *idée fixe* theme. The insistent bell strokes and three variants of the *Dies Irae* are cyclically repeated to form an unholy incantation.

Dies Irae Theme

A tonal shift to major signals the beginning of a witches' round dance, based upon fugal treatment of a mock-heroic theme in the strings with syncopated accents in the brass. The dance builds to a furor, collapses in an interlude during which fragments of themes intermingle, then rebuilds. The witches' dance (strings) and *Dies Irae* are finally combined, leading to a harrowing concluding fanfare.

For its time, this music was a striking depiction of the hidden, terrible side of nature and the human mind. The 18th century had disdained superstition as an embarrassing anachronism, but many Romantics were fascinated by it, believing that ancient tales of witchcraft and sorcery revealed secret truths. The element of mystery—of a clandestine but very real underworld just below the surface of daily life, capable of erupting at any time—held particular allure for Berlioz and was an undercurrent throughout much Romantic art. Later fanned by dissemination of Freud's theories, it exploded into the expressionist and surrealist movements of the early 20th century.

Virtuosity and Lyricism

Two contrary tendencies—one toward increasing power and brilliance, the other a striving for intimacy of expression—persisted throughout the 19th century. Symphonic music was dominated by the former trend. The increased length and complexity of symphonic forms was accompanied by an expansion in the size of the orchestra, as composers sought greater tonal weight and unique colors to accentuate structural contrasts. The symphonic ideal became one of rich, full textures, with occasional solo passages in which a theme assumes a particular coloristic shading. Many Romantic piano compositions reflect a similar striving for richness of sound. Such composers as Liszt exploited the recently expanded pitch and dynamic ranges of the instrument in passages of overwhelming technical and sonic brilliance.

The Romantic esthetic encouraged interpretive leeway by the performer, not only in such obvious matters as tempo variations and dynamic nuances, but in the overall conception of a composition. The performer was expected not merely to play a work but to breathe fire into it through brilliance of execution. The growing level of technical accomplishment among musicians resulted in the rise of **virtuoso performers**—highly gifted, charismatic pianists, violinists, and singers who became cultural heroes. Virtuoso performers were sometimes esteemed more for their showmanship than their musical sensitivity, and the more self-serving of them subordinated musical considerations to ostentatious display. Such virtuosos as Franz Liszt, however, while hardly self-effacing, strove for a balance between exhibitionism and clarity of structure and exerted a far-reaching influence on musical life.

At a time when the price of opera productions and symphonic concerts was prohibitive to much of the middle class, Liszt's solo piano transcriptions of symphonies and operatic excerpts afforded listeners their only opportunity to hear this music. Public glorification of the virtuosos resulted in the composition of works of unprecedented difficulty. At their worst, these virtuoso pieces were musically empty "lollipops," tiresomely parading bravura flourishes. In the piano works of Chopin, Liszt, and Brahms, however, technical brilliance was made to serve and heighten musical expression, becoming but one element of the total musical experience.

Listening

Feux-follets ("Will-o'-the-wisp"), *Transcendental Etude No. 5 by Franz Liszt (1811–1886)*

Record Set Side 10, Band 1

Franz Liszt

Franz Liszt was the most prodigious and celebrated pianist of the 19th century, mesmerizing audiences on a series of concert tours between 1839 and 1847. Liszt always denigrated mere bravura, however, as much as he did classical formal structures, believing that music was lifeless unless it was "poetic." His compositions are rhapsodic in structure and tone. The twelve *Transcendental Etudes,* begun in 1826 when the composer was only fifteen, contained such inordinate technical demands that no one but Liszt himself could perform them. In a revised edition published in 1852, Liszt reworked many passages and simplified the more impenetrable difficulties.

Most *etudes* are instructional pieces designed to help the student master a specific technical skill (scales, arpeggios, crossing of the hands, and so on) through dogged reiteration of a figuration pattern. Purely utilitarian etudes are little more than didactic "finger busters" for private study. The etudes of Liszt, Chopin, and Debussy, on the other hand, are concert works aimed at giving some aspect of technique its ultimate musical expression.

"Feux-follets" is a composition of great delicacy, requiring fluent dexterity in the right hand and the ability to make rapid registral shifts in the left hand:

Cascading runs in both hands encompass the full range of the instrument and give the score an awesome visual appearance—black with notes like a swarm of bugs on the page. When played, however, the music has a blithe, whimsical quality. Technical fireworks have been made to serve a poetic musical end.

Concurrent with the trend toward expanded forms and technical demands was a movement toward more intimate and lyrical expression. **Character pieces,** musical miniatures lasting only a few minutes and depicting one or two moods or ideas, replaced the sonata as the most common genre of piano music. These works—variously titled preludes, impromptus, etudes, intermezzos, and so on—have a poetic quality derived from lyrical themes and coloristic harmonic motion. Technical demands were usually modest, since these pieces were often intended for amateur performers. Chopin's *Prelude in E Minor,* discussed in Unit 1, is a representative example.

In vocal music, we find a similar divergence between long, complex works—notably in French and Italian grand opera and Wagner's music dramas—and the rise of the Romantic *lied* ("leed"), a song for voice and piano. Schubert's "Der Lindenbaum," discussed in Chapter 6, typifies the eloquent but natural expression and simple formal structure of most lieder. Like character pieces, lieder were generally performed before a small gathering, often by amateur musicians.

The trends toward very large ensembles on the one hand and solo performing media on the other resulted in a comparative dearth of chamber music during the Romantic era. Only those composers strongly influenced by Classical procedures, such as Schubert, Mendelssohn, and Brahms, wrote a significant number of chamber works.

Growing Diversity in Idiom

The Romantic emphasis on originality in statement and idiom led to a growing diversity in musical styles and the gradual loss of a common practice. The mutual antipathy between classically-oriented late Romantics (for whom Brahms was the paragon) and those seeking a "new art" (in emulation of Wagner) was symptomatic of this increasing split.

For many late 19th-century composers, particularly those in Germany and Austria, Richard Wagner (1813–1883) was a pivotal figure in the history of music. Much as Beethoven's formal and harmonic innovations had been a jumping-off point for the early Romantics, Wagner's operas (which he termed *music dramas*) seemed to many composers of the next generation to have irrevocably altered the materials and syntax of music. In such works as *Tristan and Isolde,* Wagner stretched the principles of tonality to their furthermost limits. The *Tristan* prelude also exemplifies Wagner's style of "endless melody," in which thematic ideas undergo continuous development, resulting in long, through-composed designs without clear sectional divisions. Above all, Wagner's music dramas seemed to many to be the definitive realization of the essence of Romanticism: that music must spring from, and vividly portray, human emotion.

Johannes Brahms (1833–1897) and his followers, however, were having none of this. Brahms found Wagner's music dramas overblown and diffuse, bombastic tokens of a stylistic wrong turn and musical dead-end. In his own major instrumental works, such as the *Piano Quintet in F Minor,* Brahms sought to demonstrate that Classical formal procedures remained the consummate vehicle for Romantic expression, providing a common bond between composer and listener and giving the artist a firm basis for musical judgment. To Brahms, true originality resided in the quality of a statement, rather than in the materials with which it was made. He believed emotional expression to be more moving when felt as the moving force behind a work, rather than as its ultimate goal. Peter Ilyich Tchaikovsky (1840–1893), on the other hand, felt no such constraint. Tchaikovsky's instrumental works generally conform to the outward superstructure of Classical forms but are animated more by vivid contrasts in mood, brilliance of orchestration, and—above all—a very "up-front" emotional tone.

Nationalism

The latter half of the 19th century marked the beginning of many distinct new national styles of concert music. **Nationalism**—the belief that music should reflect the character and aspirations of the composer's country—began as a reaction to the long dominance of German (and, to a lesser degree, French and Italian) influence on European musical life. It flowered first in Russia, fanned out to the other nations of eastern and northern Europe, and eventually spread to Spain, England, and the Americas. While these countries generally lacked a strong independent tradition of concert music, they were rich in folk traditions. Nationalistic composers sometimes incorporated folk tunes directly into their works. More often, they sought to capture the distinct rhythmic, melodic, and harmonic flavor of these native influences, and to write music that would have special meaning for their countrymen. The nationalist movement led to further diversity in stylistic idiom—a process that continues today—and to further enrichment in the musical materials available to composers of all countries.

Suggested Listening

Russian Easter Overture ***by Nikolai Rimsky-Korsakov (1844–1908)***

Rimsky-Korsakov was one of a group of composers, collectively known as "The Five," who sought to create a uniquely Russian idiom. The most gifted of the group, Modest Mussorgsky (1839–1881), composed the masterpiece of Russian opera, *Boris Godunov.* Mussorgsky's bold harmonic language, however, bewildered most of his contemporaries, and it was Rimsky-Korsakov who became the leader of the Russian nationalist movement. Although his early musical education was meager, Rimsky-Korsakov undertook a thorough study of technique after his appointment to the St. Petersburg Conservatory in 1871 and became the most polished, as well as financially successful, of "The Five."

About the *Russian Easter Overture,* which he composed in 1888, Rimsky-Korsakov later wrote that it could be appreciated fully only by those who had attended an Easter Eucharist in a large cathedral crowded with people from all social classes. He attempted to depict the sense of mystery surrounding the Easter ceremony, but also the secular festivities associated with the feast and the ancient pagan rituals of spring, all of which he believed to be vital elements of the Russian spirit. Asymmetric rhythms and harmonic passages based on Medieval Russian scales, as well as melodic borrowings from the Orthodox liturgy, give the work an unmistakably Russian character. The masterful tone colors and brilliance of sound Rimsky-Korsakov has drawn from the orchestra, however, reflect his careful study of German and French symphonic music.

The overture has a fantasy-like structure loosely based on sonata form. It begins with a lengthy slow introduction in which Rimsky-Korsakov sought to convey the somber atmosphere of the Holy Week rituals. Two themes, both based on liturgical chants, alternate with cadenza-like solo passages in the violin and flute. The shift to a rapid tempo signals the beginning of the main body of the overture. The music builds to the statement of a stirring new theme based on the alternation of two minor chords followed by sweeping runs in the strings. The second introductory theme is recalled in the new tempo. After a lugubrious trombone solo reminiscent of the introductory mood, the rapid tempo is resumed and the three themes undergo development and varied repetition.

End of an Age

By the turn of the century the Romantic movement had essentially run its course, and its major stylistic breakthroughs were being assimilated into, or superseded by, various national idioms. In Germany and Austria, the countries with the richest Romantic legacy, however, the movement blossomed a final time in the music of Gustav Mahler (1860–1911), Hugo Wolf (1860–1903), and Richard Strauss (1864–1949). Keenly aware of their historical position, these composers sensed that they were living at the end of a golden age, suspended between a receding world of familiar values and an unknown new order about to take its place. Music, too, seemed to have passed from youthful vigor (the early Romantics) through maturity (Wagner and Brahms) to what French composer Erik Satie called "a very old age." Mahler, Wolf, and (during the first half of his long career) Strauss saw their principal role as one of extending the tonal and expressive resources of Wagner's operas to new genres, notably to symphonic music and song. While seeking to make a final contribution to and summation of their Romantic heritage, these composers also paved the way for important new developments in 20th-century music.

Mahler and Strauss employed enormous instrumental resources in their symphonic music. The orchestral brilliance of these works, however, includes not only thunderous tuttis, but also passages in which the outsized ensemble is treated as a warehouse for new coloristic combinations in soloistic and chamber textures. The tonal language covers a very broad spectrum, from almost naïvely simple themes of a folk-like character to long, complex chromatic passages in which all feeling of tonal center is suspended. The homophonic textures of most Classical and Romantic music are often replaced by a dense, contrapuntal web of sound that reflects the influence of Wagner. Wolf specialized in the composition of songs, in which he attempted to mirror every detail of the text. His complex harmonic progressions frequently result in a borderline tonal practice in which various key centers come in and out of focus.

"Drinking Song of Earth's Sorrows" from Das Lied von der Erde *("Song of the Earth") by Gustav Mahler (1860–1911)*

Gustav Mahler is in many ways the most complex of the late Romantics. Mahler was among the most celebrated conductors of his age, holding a variety of positions from the age of 20 until his death. Possessed of a phenomenal ear (he would interrupt tutti passages in rehearsal to reprove individual string players for faulty intonation) and a fanatical zeal for the music he believed in, he produced legendary performances of Wagner, Mozart, and Beethoven during his ten years as director of the Vienna Opera. From 1908 until his death in 1911, he was conductor of the New York Philharmonic. Rigorous rehearsal schedules during the concert season left him only the summer months for composition.

Mahler's stormy, heavy-laden music reflects the composer's anguished temperament. His symphonies and song cycles are all vaguely autobiographical, revolving around the central image of a sensitive, inquiring mind coming to grips with life's paradoxes. Mahler sought an art that was at once direct and transcendent. "For me, to write a symphony is to build a world," he declared. His "worlds" are a personal commentary upon the entire spectrum of 19th-century music. They encompass the evolution of ever more complex symphonic forms, but also folk songs, the tawdry march and waltz tunes of village bands, and brash rhetorical flourishes. Through such associations Mahler sought to convey the richness of meaning he believed inherent even in the commonplace and banal.

Mahler's unabashed striving for the "Big Statement," made with sweeping gestures and tinged with both irony and naïveté, seems to strike a particularly responsive chord in the present age; perhaps this is because his music anticipates many of the concerns of our own time but also represents, in the words of Henry James, "the still visitable past"—an era just now disappearing over the horizon.

Song of Earth (1908), written 24 years after the *Wayfarer* songs discussed in Chapter 6, illustrates the complex musical style that attended the twilight of Romanticism and tonality. The year before its completion, Mahler had been traumatized by the death of his eldest daughter and by the discovery that a heart defect gave him, at most, a few more years to live. Mahler's irascible temper mellowed, but his constitutional melancholy deepened. Writing to his protégé, the conductor Bruno Walter, he declared, "At the end of my life I must go back to living like a beginner . . . to find my way again and overcome the terrors of loneliness." During this period of introspection, he became captivated by an anthology of classic Chinese poems in German translation. The pensive verses seemed to distill his own bittersweet sentiments: each person must search in solitude for inner peace; the world offers no solace, only temporary escape and vanity; youthful enthusiasm inevitably turns to disillusionment; life must be cherished, but surrendered without bitterness.

The opening song, "Drinking Song of Earth's Sorrows," encapsulates the two conflicting moods of the entire cycle—a fierce will to live versus a quiet resignation. Intoxication, in life as well as wine, is glorified as a liberating, if temporary, escape from the terrible, unanswerable questions of existence. In Mahler's adaptation of the text there are three verses, each ending with the stinging refrain, *"Dunkel ist das Leben, ist der Tod!"* ("Dark is life, dark is death"). The verses are separated by orchestral interludes. The third is by far the longest. An abridged translation of the text reads:

> "This is a song of life's sorrows.
> Joy must wither and pass.
> Life is dark, and so is death.
>
> *(orchestral interlude)*
>
> Wine and music were made for each other.
> A full glass of wine is worth more than all the riches on earth.
> Life is dark, and so is death.
>
> *(orchestral interlude)*
>
> Earth will remain, and bloom each spring until eternity.
> But you, man, how long do you have?
> In the graveyard, the cry of a wild phantom—
> an ape—shrieks through earth's sweet air.
> Take your wine glasses, friends, and drink to the fullest.
> Life is dark, and so is death."

The song opens with a coloristically brilliant fanfare introduction. The ensuring vocal melody features rhapsodic development of motives, constantly transformed to suit the changing nuances of the text. Despite its division into three stanzas framed by a refrain, the song is through-composed. Juxtaposition of contrasting moods—by turn expansive, tormented, swaggering, and contemplative—is vital to the dramatic impact of the song. The vocal line makes exorbitant demands upon the performer. The tenor must soar in a mercilessly high range above raging orchestral tuttis. The tenor's arduous struggle is itself an element of word painting, metaphorically portraying the exhausting struggle of life that wears man down and leaves him ultimately submissive to death.

The unsettled harmonic motion of the music constantly pulls to new keys, never settling for long in any tonal area. Tonality has become an elusive, distant frame of reference, rather than a fixed structural center. At points where the vocal line cadences, the orchestra begins a new phrase, binding the music into a single, unbroken thread. The music is always "becoming," but never quite "arrives." Even the final chord—an unceremonious grunt in the low brass—sounds more like an exclamation, or even interruption, than a conclusion. Throughout long passages, the music drifts or reels through a sea of changing colors and tonalities. While this, too, is partially attributable to word painting (the vocal melody and harmonic motion often seem to totter precariously, in the manner of an inebriated carouser), it also reflects the continuing search for ever more expressive chromatic inflections. This search would soon lead many composers to abandon tonality entirely.

Principal Composers of the Romantic Period

The list of major 19th century composers is a lengthy one, for no other musical period produced so many composers who have become household names. The following list is a selective reference. German and Austrian composers, who dominated 19th century musical life, have been grouped together, followed by composers of other countries. More complete biographical information on several of these composers follows in Unit Four, as indicated in parentheses.

German and Austrian Composers.

Franz Schubert (1797–1828). Austrian. Sometimes considered a Romantic, though his style is generally closer to that of Viennese Classicism, Schubert is best known for his last two symphonies and over 600 lieder (see Chapter 13).

Felix Mendelssohn (1809–1847). German. The most Classically-oriented early Romantic, and among the most versatile and prolific.

Robert Schumann (1810–1856). German. An important composer of lieder, symphonies, and sonatas, Schumann also composed many sets of piano character pieces in a warm, lyrical style (see Chapter 14).

Richard Wagner (1813–1883). German. A controversial figure who created his own type of opera, Wagner exploited densely chromatic harmonies and formal procedures based on continuous development of motives (see Chapter 19).

Anton Bruckner (1824–1896). Austrian. Known for his nine symphonies and church music, Bruckner applied Wagner's harmonic innovations to symphonic forms.

Johannes Brahms (1833–1897). German. Brahms sought to reconcile Romantic expression and chromatic harmonic resources with Classical formal principles. His symphonies, sonatas, and chamber music feature balanced formal proportions and traditional key schemes (see Chapter 15). His songs and piano character pieces are more overtly Romantic in tone.

Gustav Mahler (1860–1911). Austrian. Mahler's nine symphonies represent the end of the long line of Austro-German symphonic development stretching back to Haydn. His songs, generally with orchestral rather than piano accompaniment, alternate between lyrical and dramatic expression.

Richard Strauss (1864–1949). German. Although his style underwent radical change later in his career, Strauss is best known for the lush harmonic style and orchestral brilliance of his early operas and symphonic poems (see Chapter 16).

Composers of Other Countries.

Gioacchino Rossini *(1792–1868). Italian. Rossini was the major Italian composer of the first half of the 19th century. His masterpiece,* The Barber of Seville, *1816, exemplifies his mastery of Italian comic opera traditions.*

Hector Berlioz *(1802–1869). French. Berlioz is most celebrated for the striking orchestral colors and vividly programmatic nature of his symphonies.*

Frédéric Chopin *(1810–1849). Polish. An exile who spent most of his career in Paris, Chopin composed almost exclusively for the piano (see Chapter 14).*

Franz Liszt *(1811–1886). Hungarian. The most famous piano virtuoso of the 19th century, Liszt composed solo works demanding extraordinary technical facility. In his orchestral works he pursued new types of through-composed structure.*

Giuseppi Verdi *(1813–1908). Italian. Verdi dominated Italian musical life throughout most of his career, and remains among the greatest (and most frequently performed) composers of opera (see Chapter 19).*

Modest Mussorgsky *(1835–1881). A bold innovator who produced the greatest works of the Russian nationalist movement, Mussorgsky is most celebrated for his opera* Boris Godunov *and the suite* Pictures at an Exhibition, *which can be heard both in its original piano version and in an orchestral transcription by Maurice Ravel.*

Peter Ilyich Tchaikovsky *(1840–1893). Russian. While clearly Russian in character, Tchaikovsky's symphonies, ballets, and concert overtures reflect more a cosmopolitan than a nationalist approach to music (see Chapter 16).*

Antonín Dvořák *(1841–1904). Czech. A symphonic composer who admired Brahms' music, Dvořák was also strongly influenced by the folk music of his native Bohemia (see Chapter 16).*

Terms and Concepts for Review

Classical period:
- accompanied-melody textures
- figuration pattern
- integration and reconciliation of ideas
- balanced proportions

Romantic period:
- individual expression
- coloristic harmonic motion
- new formal procedures
- program music
- thematic transformation
- virtuosity
- lyricism and intimacy of expression
- diversity of styles
- nationalism

Chapter 12
An Age of Stylistic Diversity, 1900–1945

The early years of the 20th century marked a turning point in the evolution of musical styles. The rise of various national styles after 1860 had already led growing numbers of composers to define their art as distinct from the German Romantic tradition. By 1900 Romanticism no longer seemed capable of renewal. The collapse of the Romantic esthetic had far-reaching consequences. Many basic resources of music—tonality, homophonic textures and forms, the ideals of lyrical melody and rich harmonies—had been exploited so extensively and successfully during the 19th century that they had become thoroughly associated with the Romantic esthetic. To many early 20th-century composers, it seemed that the Romantic movement had not only exhausted itself, but had also cashed in these basic resources, carrying them as far as they could go. Feeling the need for a fresh approach to their art, many believed it necessary to begin with new materials.

Usually, periods of rapid stylistic change have been precipitated by a coherent new set of musical values and goals. No such consensus existed early in the present century, however. Composers instead found themselves confronted with many alternatives. Elements of musical practice formerly determined by convention now became matters for conscious decision. While sharing Igor Stravinsky's assessment of this situation as an "abyss of freedom," most composers also shared his conviction that "art is the opposite of chaos." For most composers, then, the overriding esthetic question was no longer how to expand inherited musical resources further, but how to fashion a consistent musical language in which to work.

From our present vantage point, the many individual solutions to this question seem to fall into three broad categories. Such composers as Claude

Debussy and, early in his career, Stravinsky wished to begin anew, with a different concept of musical expression. These composers were attracted to musical resources that had been neglected during the 19th century; they sought to mold new and often eclectic materials into a personal idiom. Other composers, such as Arnold Schönberg, attempted to discover new possibilities inherent in, or suggested by, the language of late Romantic music. A third solution, embraced by Béla Bartók, Sergei Prokofiev, and a majority of composers during the second quarter of the century, was to adopt some other tradition—usually the music of some earlier style period or national idiom—as a working model.

Style, then, was no longer a given element of music after the turn of the century. Instead, it had become a matter of preference or choice from among many possibilities. Composers consciously selected frameworks and procedures to channel their energies. Such figures as Stravinsky adopted widely different stylistic principles at various points in their careers, sometimes abruptly changing course. This functional view of style was poles apart from the Romantic composers' passionate sense of commitment to a musical language they considered historically inevitable and "more expressive" than all others.

The result was a pluralism of styles: the coexistence and simultaneous development of many types and languages of musical expression. The *rate* of stylistic change also accelerated. New types of pitch organization, formal devices, and esthetic attitudes were explored by composers of diverse nationality and interests, sometimes to be discarded or transformed within a few years. The major new currents that dominated musical style during the first half of the 20th century, however, were on the table by the mid 1920s; during the next two decades they were systematized and consolidated. In this chapter we will focus on these dominant influences, as heard in the music of the composers who pursued them first or with most telling effect.

Impressionism: Claude Debussy

The French composer Claude Debussy (1862–1918) sought a clear break with the German Romantic tradition. Debussy ("De-byou-*see*") was a *bon vivant* more comfortable in cafés than in academic surroundings, preferring the company of writers, painters, and "night people" to that of musicians. A witty, widely read connoisseur, he prized discretion in life and art, and found the bravado of many Romantic works overweening and distasteful. His music reflects the influence of the symbolist poets and impressionist painters, for whom the immediate sensuous quality of a work—the actual sounds of words or the shadings of tints and images—was more important than either formal structure or personal sentiment.

Claude Debussy

A similar sensuous quality pervades Debussy's music. At the very outset of one of his works the music creates its own environment of sound. This distinguishing quality, which Debussy called *ton juste* ("precise sound"), is the essence of the musical statement. Often defined by a particular combination of colors or the spacing of a chord, the "precise sound" establishes the framework of a composition. Most of his music evokes a distinct atmosphere that is at once vivid and somewhat hazy. His formal designs are subtle and his ideas are usually understated. Images are often suggested or merely hinted at, rather than stated and contrasted. The picturesque titles of his works generally convey a concern with life's little pleasures and quiet moments: a girl with golden hair, clouds, a festival day, the games of young lovers in a park. The artist is a sensitive but dispassionate observer, taking a fresh look at the commonplace, recording unique perspectives, but reserving final judgment, never imposing opinions or proselytizing.

Debussy's music has a surface amiability and polish that belies its unconventional approach to form. He disavowed systematic methods of composition, preferring to trust his ear, in the belief that "it is instinct alone—as old as the world—that can save you." He attempted to fashion formal patterns that would unfold naturally out of opening ideas, rather than to mold these ideas into an imposed design. In many of his works, there is no driving force, no urgency, no struggle of conflicting elements, but rather an inner repose. His music is more often "being" than "becoming." Sounds are meant to be savored for their own quality. With characteristic trenchancy he declared, "I am ever more convinced that music is not something that can be cast into a traditional or fixed form. Music consists of colors and rhythms. The rest is a lot of balderdash. . . ."

Debussy's music incorporates a broad range of tonal resources. Diatonic and chromatic passages intermingle and flow effortlessly into other passages employing five-tone or whole-tone scales, Medieval modes, and other types of pitch structures:

Various types of pitch selection in Debussy's Prelude to the Afternoon of a Faun

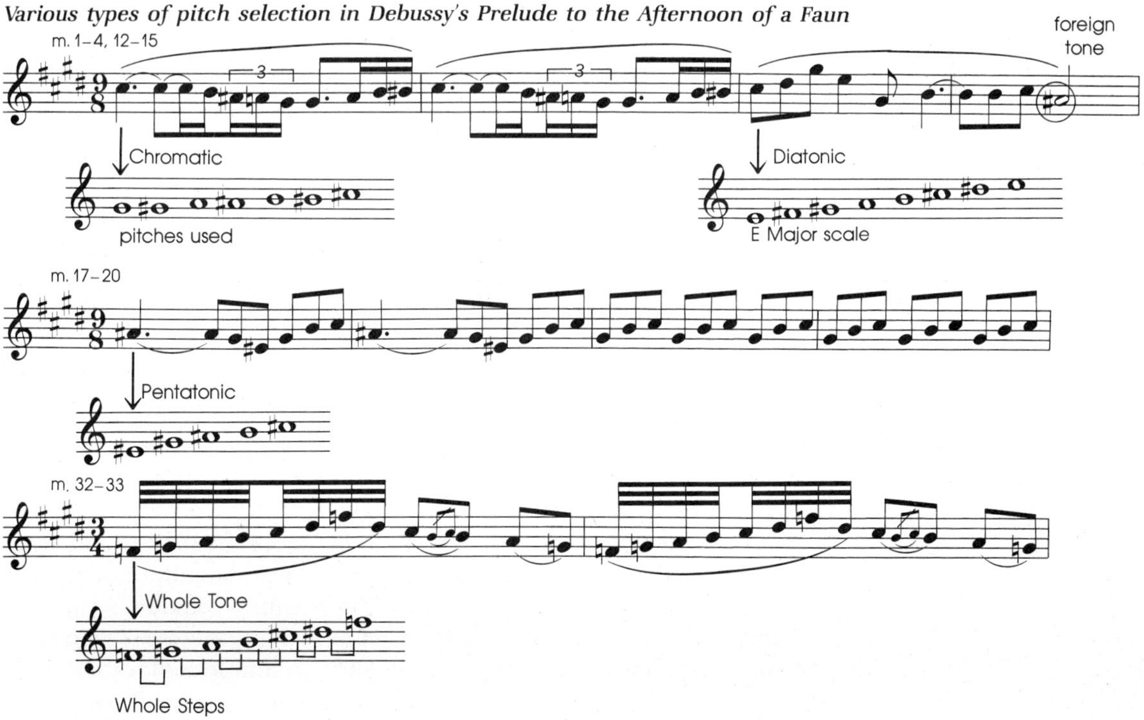

Triads and seventh chords, richer sonorities, and complex chords built up in intervals of seconds, fourths, or fifths (rather than thirds) are used in combination, often within the same phrase. Chords and dissonances are employed for their intrinsic sound color, rather than to create patterns of tension and resolution. In fact, the sense of dissonance begins to disappear, because the harmonic motion is generally non-functional. Chords are often heard in relation to each other as various shadings of the "precise sound" of the piece, rather than with respect to a fixed tonic.

Debussy's melodies often are based upon a continuous linking of motives and fragments into long, asymmetric chains that rarely cadence. Development is not a distinct reworking of these ideas but a process of continuous extension of them. Statement and development are intertwined and often take place simultaneously; one idea flows into, or is overtaken by, another.

Listening

Prelude to the Afternoon of a Faun (Prélude à l'après-midi d'un faune) *by Claude Debussy (1862–1918)*

Record Set Side 11, Band 1

Debussy's tone poem *Prelude to the Afternoon of a Faun,* completed in 1894, was inspired by a poem of Stephane Mallarmé. A fabled forest creature, half-man, half-goat, awakens and idly muses about a magical encounter with lovely nymphs. Upon further reflection, he begins to wonder whether the incident really took place or whether it was merely a dream. The warm summer air is soporific, and the listless faun, unable to sort things out, sinks back into slumber.

To the late German Romantics, such subject matter would have seemed frivolous—a pointless bubble of nothing, and hardly the stuff to ennoble mankind. Debussy, however, was attracted by the languorous, dreamlike quality of the verse and its portrayal of a fleeting moment that could be crystallized in music. The overall flavor of Mallarmé's verse—delicate, misty, elusive, as though the scene were witnessed from a distance of time or space—takes the musical form of a "precise sound": a solo flute in its "breathy" lower register, accompanied by muted strings and harp. This combination of colors opens the piece and recurs periodically. It is varied, reshaped, and developed as other instruments enter and drop out, and thus functions much like a melodic theme.

The basic musical gesture of the piece is one of breath-like patterns that swell and ebb. In the opening measures, for example, the flute "exhales," the harp run "inhales," and the horn figure "exhales." The overall design of the piece is similarly balanced, rising to a peak midway through and tapering to a murmur at the end. Rhythmic motion is fluid, connecting ideas in a seamless flow. Pulse and meter are weak, and there is little feeling of accent as individual motives and colors melt into new ideas.

The tonality of the opening flute line is ambiguous, and the melody dissipates on a rising inflection rather than coming to a cadence. The flute theme recurs ten times, usually in slightly altered form, but is never systematically developed or extended; it is a static, "frozen" element of structure. The harmonic accompaniment, however, changes at each reappearance of the theme. Thus musical interest is concentrated on the changing relationships between a fixed melodic idea and the continuously evolving harmonies and colors of its accompaniment.

The formal design features variation procedures within an overall three-part structure. The first third of the piece presents five statements of the fragmentary flute theme. Each statement presents the theme in a new context and is followed by a different continuation. A more animated oboe melody then begins a transitional passage in which the music pulls away from its original theme, colors, and mood. The middle *(B)* section is more lushly scored, more urgent and "Romantic" in tone. It features a soaring melody, heard first in the woodwinds, then in the strings, and finally in a solo violin:

B Theme

This melody, too, is followed by a new answering passage at each appearance.

In the concluding section the flute theme recurs five more times, answered by a new series of continuations. The E major tonality is gradually clarified and the "precise sound" with which the piece began refocuses, then is blurred again. Two small cymbals present a final shimmering answer to the theme. In a whisper, Debussy had announced the dawn of a new musical age. Individual sounds and colors could be treated not merely as the raw materials of melody and harmony, or as decoration; they could become formal elements in their own right, and the substance of a musical statement.

Maurice Ravel

Maurice Ravel (1875–1937) is often linked with Debussy and musical impressionism, since his music evinces a similar concern with evocative colors and harmonies. In fact, however, impressionism was more an influence than a coherent movement in music, and the art of Ravel, like that of Debussy, was an eclectic but highly personal achievement. Ravel's works are generally more harmonic in conception and more traditional with respect to tonal logic and form. While Debussy's style, for all his protestations to the contrary, can be seen as a descendant of the poetic art of Chopin and other Romantics, Ravel's music hearkens back to Classical style.

Suggested Listening

"Le Tombeau de Couperin" by Maurice Ravel (1875–1937)

Le Tombeau de Couperin, or "Tribute to Couperin," was intended more as a salute to 18th-century French music in general than as a specific homage to François Couperin (1668–1733), a Baroque composer best known for his keyboard suites. Ravel began work on the piece in 1914 but was forced to lay it aside during a period of military service. He completed the original version, a six-movement piano suite, in 1917, and orchestrated four of the movements two years later. Although emotionally dazed and physically debilitated by the effects of World War I, Ravel created music of disarming ease and wit. By turn stately, wistful, and vivacious, the music of *Le Tombeau de Couperin* is perhaps Ravel's most convincing fusion of the traditional dance rhythms and vibrant new colors that spark many of his works. The piano and orchestral versions provide equally good introductions to Ravel's style, but his mastery of orchestral color can be best appreciated if the orchestral transcription is heard after the piano suite.

Free Atonality: Arnold Schönberg

A quite different approach to the question of how to create anew grew directly out of the late Romantic tradition. Arnold Schönberg (1874–1951) was born in Vienna, the city where Mozart, Beethoven, Schubert, Brahms, Mahler, and Wolf spent much of their careers. Schönberg ("Shurn-bairg") was acutely conscious of this august musical hertiage, and this awareness would color his historical perspective and sense of personal destiny. A self-taught composer, he immersed himself in the study of scores during his twenties while supporting himself as a bank clerk, conductor of amateur choruses, and orchestrator of popular music. His growing reputation began to attract promising young composers for private study. Between 1910 and 1944 he held a series of academic appointments. Fleeing from the Nazis in 1933, he eventually settled in Los Angeles and joined the faculty of the University of California at Los Angeles. In fact, Schönberg was among the first of an eventual flood of composers who would seek their livelihood in academia. In previous centuries, universities had been notorious strongholds of musical pedantry, regarded by most composers as an enemy camp. In the present era, the university has become the principal patron for composers of concert music, and for contemporary arts in general. This is particularly true in the

United States, which lacks the extensive European tradition of direct governmental and institutional support of artists.

Schönberg's Esthetic

For a composer who remains the most controversial musical figure of the 20th century, Schönberg was a man of essentially conservative principles, seeking to continue a tradition he revered. His early compositions were firmly in the late Romantic tradition. *Verklärte Nacht (Transfigured Night)*, a tone poem for strings written in 1899, is reminiscent of Wagner's *Tristan* prelude in its intense emotional tone and continuous chromaticism. His adoption of traditional forms and methodical structural procedures in other early works reflects the influence of Brahms. Throughout his career, Schönberg felt the need for clear working principles and a specific sense of direction to guide his creative faculties and provide objective criteria for self-criticism. Schönberg was, in short, the kind of composer who spends considerable time thinking about music as well as writing it, clarifying his procedures until he has total confidence in their validity.

Unlike Debussy, Stravinsky, and a majority of later composers, Schönberg did not believe that the growing diversity of stylistic choices required a more broad-minded or expedient esthetic outlook. He adhered staunchly to a more traditional view: that the language of music had followed, and should follow, a more or less logical course of evolution. For Schönberg, excellence in art required a legacy, a language that could be expanded from the inside out. It could not be attained, he felt, by repudiating the past and groping in the dark for "modern" alternatives. Schönberg believed the Austro-German tradition to be the supreme achievement of Western music. If this tradition had brought music to its present stylistic impasse, he reasoned, it would inevitably be the same tradition that would provide a solution.

By 1908, the year Mahler completed his *Song of the Earth*, Schönberg had become convinced that the major–minor tonal system must be superseded by new means of structure. His own previous music had contained long passages of "harmonies in search of a tonic," that slipped into a specific key only at the very end of a work. The concluding tonic had not been intimated throughout the work, as in Debussy's *Prelude to the Afternoon of a Faun*, but was more a case of "any port in a storm." Such endings now came to seem like tacked-on appendages extraneous to the true structure of the music, which consisted of the moment-by-moment growth of melodies and harmonies from opening motives. Schönberg felt the time had come for the ultimate evolution of tonality: its abandonment. He saw this step, however, *not* as a repudiation of the expressive Romantic tradition, but rather as a way of enabling it to continue.

Arnold Schönberg, in a self-portrait painted in 1918

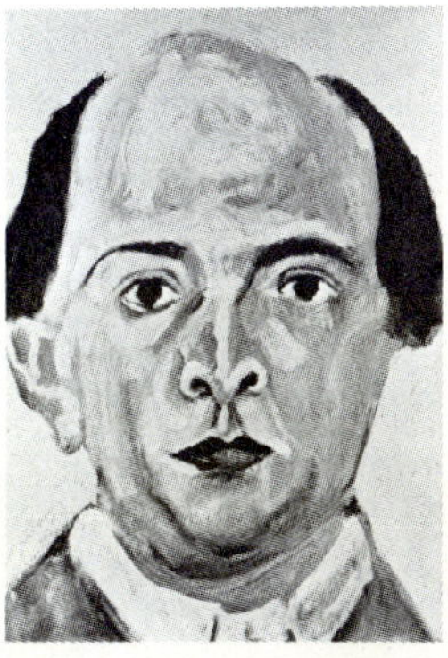

In Schönberg's new works, oblique tonal references disappeared from the body of the compositions, and the obligatory tonal clarification was jettisoned. Schönberg no longer wanted his music to be heard in terms of these distantly spaced points of tonal articulation, but rather in terms of the *intervallic consistency* of the specific work. Intervallic patterns—particular combinations of intervals recurring throughout the melodies and harmonies of a work—replaced a fixed reference pitch as the basis of form. All notes of the chromatic scale were treated as equal, but were usually combined in such a way that certain intervals would predominate.

Schönberg took pains to eliminate any tonal implications in these new works. He avoided major and minor triads and made certain that no pitch received special emphasis. He reasoned that such traditional elements would create false expectations, leading the listener to search for a tonic that would never materialize. One result of this new type of pitch organization was what Schönberg called the "emancipation of dissonance." Any pitch could be followed by any other. Dissonances did not have to resolve into consonances. Indeed, they *should* not resolve, since this could establish a functional (tonal) relationship.

Schönberg's new pitch style was dubbed *atonal* ("without tonal center"), though Schönberg himself resented the word's negative connotations. He believed he had taken an inevitable but admittedly a giant step. He saw his atonal works as different in conception, rather than in style, from his earlier compositions. He had no illusions, however, that the musical establishment would esteem or even understand his aims; he feared that his esthetic would be spurned as overly cerebral or nihilistic. He felt very much like the messenger who brings the bad news, and was particularly anguished because he saw his achievement as good news, opening up new channels for expression: "Now that I have set upon a new path, I am conscious of breaking through the boundaries of traditional esthetics. I advance toward my new goal with confidence, but am aware of the resistance I will have to overcome. I sense the emotional intensity with which my work will be rejected, and fear that even those who have believed in my art until now will not realize the necessity of this new development."

His words were prophetic. Mahler and Strauss, for example, were mystified. Mahler continued to encourage him, sensing that Schönberg's music heralded a new age that he (Mahler) would only dimly comprehend. Strauss was more acerbic, remarking that Schönberg "would do better to shovel snow than scribble on music paper." To listeners who had come to think of tonality as a natural, inherent law of music—like the force of gravity in the physical world—Schönberg's esthetic seemed an invitation to anarchy, destroying the lifeblood of music while offering nothing in its place. Schönberg countered that, "Tonality is not a universal law of music, but simply a means of achieving musical form." Other means were possible, he felt, and were now necessary if music was to remain a dynamic, growing art.

Schönberg was keenly, even nostalgically, aware of all that he was giving up in abandoning tonality. "Like every innovation, it destroys while it creates. Colorful new harmony was offered, but much was lost." What was lost was not merely traditional harmonies and formal schemes, but the basic principle of musical organization. For the rest of his career, Schönberg would be obsessed with the hunt for alternative structural principles, but would also seek links with the past.

"Free atonality" is a style with no givens. The composer establishes his own working principles and boundaries, his own unifying devices, and works within this private world to achieve meaningful integration.

Atonal melodies generally feature large skips, since stepwise motion tends to imply a scale pattern. Harmonies do not so much accompany a melody as provide a separate thread, or backdrop, against which it is heard. Textures are frequently contrapuntal, due to a *compression of musical thought,* an attempt to make every note count. Schonberg's atonal pieces are short and intensely concentrated. Nothing is extraneous; every note fits into a mosaic-like pattern. Repetitions, even in varied form, are rare; events tend to occur only once. The overall character of the music is usually static, because of the lack of tonal direction, but it is often filled with striking internal contrasts.

Listening

First Piece from Three Piano Pieces, Op. 11, *by Arnold Schönberg (1874–1951)*

Record Set Side 11, Band 2

Schönberg's *Three Piano Pieces,* Op. 11 (1908), are among his first atonal works. The first piece of the set is somewhat unusual in its traditional three-part design. Brief pauses separate the sections:

Exposition	*Development*	*Recapitulation*
Statement and initial development of ideas	More extended, rhapsodic development of ideas, incorporating new but related motives	Varied restatement and final development of ideas

The piece begins with a fragmentary, lyrical theme, accompanied by two intervallically similar chords. The entire piece grows out of the intervals of thirds and half-steps that dominate the theme. These intervals constitute the essential pitch language of the piece.

Theme

The rest of the "exposition" presents a continuous development of these intervals. There are rapid changes in texture, gesture, and mood. The development of ideas in all three sections is highly fragmented, broken into bits and pieces that seem to end in mid-air in such a way as to suggest a stream-of-consciousness quality. Ideas are constantly transformed, in a technique which Schönberg called "perpetual variation," evolving into unexpected new forms in dizzying succession. Some moments echo Schönberg's Romantic origins; others are dispassionate, and a few are jarringly intense. The ideas are so compressed that they seem at times almost simultaneous.[1] The music often bursts into several different directions within a matter of seconds. The ever-changing emotional tone suggests a frenzied release of pent-up moods and gestures.

Perspective on Atonality

Upon initial exposure to atonality, many listeners experience uneasiness. It is common to hear sentiments like: "I can intellectually understand what the composer is trying to do, but I don't *feel* it. Is it *my* fault? What is the music actually expressing—if anything?"

The language of atonal music is at first foreign to almost every listener, for obvious reasons. We have grown up surrounded by tonal music, from folk songs to commercial jingles to symphonies, so when we hear an unfamiliar tonal piece for the first time we already have some idea of what to expect. Atonal music requires an initially different orientation: an ability to listen without preconceptions, without expecting to hear certain things and waiting to see if the music fulfills these expectations. It won't; the music will instead supply its own frame of reference. In this sense, atonal music requires us to set aside learned or accustomed aural habits and focus directly upon the play of sounds. When we do this, it quickly becomes apparent that atonality is not a single style, but an *approach* to style, in which less is taken for granted and the framework becomes clear only gradually. Individual atonal pieces do not "all sound alike" any more than tonal pieces do. Each has its own character. Some are lyrical, some intense; some express a single mood, others a variety of moods; still others express nothing but their own internal structure, in the same manner as a Bach fugue.

Schönberg's music is imbued with his own restless, serious-minded personality, but these traits are by no means common to all atonal music. The Italian composer Luigi Dallapiccola, for example, adopted many of Schönberg's techniques, but did so in the desire to write "music that could smile again." Schönberg himself always emphasized the distinction between style and idea. The style of a work—its means of organization—is merely the vehicle for the expression of unique musical thought. It is the musical idea—*what* is being expressed through the language—to which the listener responds.

[1] A similar technique is found in certain cubist paintings of the period. To convey the many qualities of an object, Picasso and Braque sometimes superimposed various images of it alongside of or on top of one another. Juan Gris' *Violon et Guitare*, reproduced on page 108, is a good example.

Schönberg's period of free atonal composition was prolific, but it lasted barely five years. Between 1913 and 1921 he wrote very little music. This was partially due to the disruption of European music life by World War I and Schönberg's own conscription into the military. There was also, however, a more personal reason. Schönberg had grown increasingly dissatisfied with the heavy burden that free atonality placed upon the composer: the need to begin each piece from scratch, erecting a fresh set of structural principles each time. Much of the composer's energy was absorbed in laying out the ground rules for each new work. Schönberg's attempt to give his musical imagination free rein, while at the same time assuring structural coherence, had become a precarious juggling act, because he lacked a consistent method or framework. Each new work was like a child's first step. Schönberg thus began searching for a more systematic, general procedure of atonal composition—for some kind of "given" that would enable him to devote less attention to style, more to ideas. This search culminated in his development of the **twelve-tone method.**

The basis of the twelve-tone method is a principal called **serialism:** the use of a predetermined pattern, or *series,* of pitches that recurs in varied form throughout a work. The pitch pattern is called a **set** (sometimes also called *tone row* or *series*). It consists of a specific arrangement of the twelve notes of the chromatic scale, each appearing once. The set provides a network of pitch relationships that is heard over and over again, in ever new arrangements, during a composition. The twelve-tone method is, in Schönberg's words, "a *conscious* unifying procedure," replacing intuition with a rational basis of structure. "It grew out of necessity," he claimed, ". . . to replace those differentiations formerly provided by tonal harmonies." If free atonality can be considered an *approach* to style, the twelve-tone method is a *principle* of pitch organization, like tonality; it is an organized method of atonal composition.

The set is neither a theme, a motive, nor a scale. Conceptually, it is more similar to an Indian raga. Like a raga, the set is a predetermined pitch pattern whose musical quality is defined by its collection of intervals. This collection serves as the basis of continuous variations. The set, however, is more rigorous in both content and application. It contains all twelve chromatic pitches, so that no single note will be heard more prominently than any other. And the set is treated as a single element, always used in its entirety rather than in fragments. It may be employed melodically (the notes are used in succession), harmonically (adjacent notes are combined into chords) or contrapuntally (different portions of the set are heard in separate voices). Every note of the composition springs from the set. Horizontal and vertical pitch dimensions are related to a single source, the set, just as they are related to a tonic in tonal music.

Since it is the specific collection of intervals, rather than the resulting notes, that defines the quality of a set, the set may take many varied forms and still maintain its identity. It may be presented in its original (or prime) form.

The following set is the basis of Schönberg's *Suite* for Piano. The twelve notes are numbered from zero (original, starting pitch) through 11:

Basic set of Schönberg's Suite for Piano

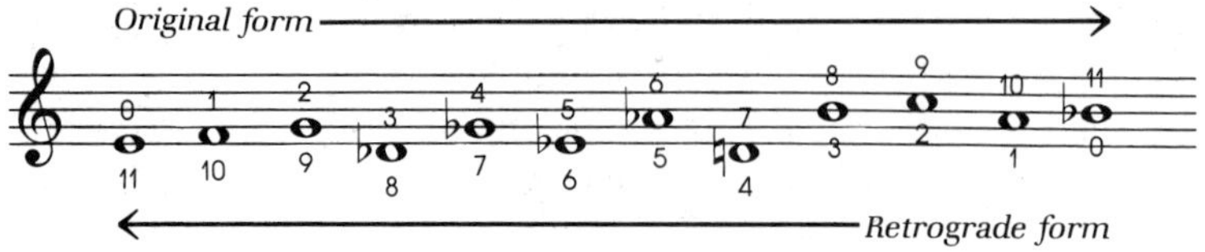

The set may also be used in reverse order: the intervals remain the same but are heard in opposite order. This set form is called the **retrograde.** The set may also appear in **inversion:** the intervals of the original set remain intact, but they now occur in the opposite direction; a half-step up becomes a half-step down, and so on:

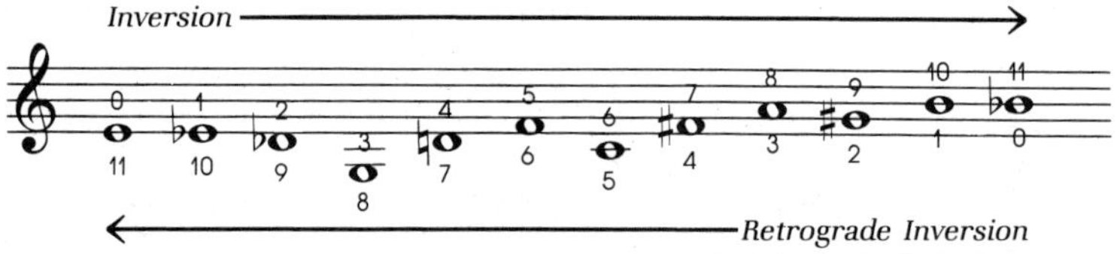

Finally, the inverted form of the set may also be used in reverse order, so that the original set is now backward and upside down. This set form is called **retrograde inversion.** These four set forms may be transposed to any new starting pitch during the course of a piece. The notes of a set form may also occur in any octave.

Listening

Suite for Piano, Op. 25, *by Arnold Schönberg (1874–1951)*

Prelude: Record Set Side 11, Band 3

Schönberg's *Suite* was the first composition written entirely within the twelve-tone method. In his early serial works, Schönberg frequently adopted traditional formal schemes, possibly to simplify structural questions while he concentrated upon his new technique, and perhaps also to demonstrate that the twelve-tone method was not a rejection of the past. Thus he based his *Suite* for piano upon the model of the Baroque keyboard suite, discussed in Chapter 6. Each movement adheres to the structural outline and general character of its Baroque ancestor.

The opening movement is marked *Prelude.* Preludes were the most rhapsodic movements of Baroque suites, improvisatory in tone and free in form. Schönberg's through-composed prelude carries this impulsive character much further; it is the most volatile and complex movement of the *Suite.* The prelude begins contrapuntally. Two versions of the original set form are stated simultaneously, one at the initial pitch level (right hand), the other transposed to a new starting pitch:

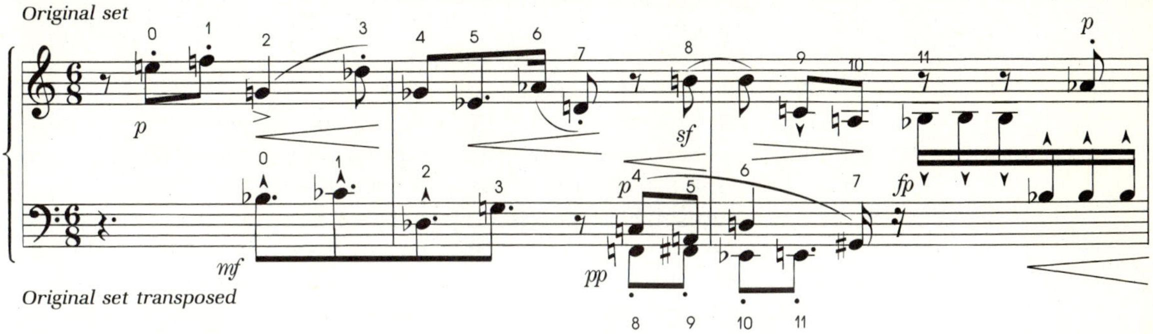

The opening of the movement features a strong rhythmic drive propelled by rapid repeated notes (as at the end of the third measure above). As the piece continues, the pacing begins to undergo abrupt shifts, slowing down and speeding up in irregular thrusts. Schönberg uses his serial technique as a basis for commentary upon his musical heritage. The tone vacillates between "Baroque" objectivity and rhythmic drive and "Romantic" contrasts, nuances, and subjectivity. The movement is a collage of contrasting elements—some new, some familiar, some twisted into new shapes—and all compressed into a teeming microcosm.

The second movement *(Gavotte and Musette)* is more delicate and transparent in quality, and follows the traditional *A–B–A* design. The third movement *(Intermezzo)* begins with an aimless, floating quality, which gradually transforms into a highly-charged emotional tone similar to that of the Prelude. The following *Minuet and Trio* (also *A–B–A*) is, like the Gavotte and Musette, quieter and more uniform in tone. The *Suite* concludes with a spirited *Gigue,* a virtuoso movement exploiting abrupt changes in tempo, texture, and character.

Some listeners find Schönberg's music difficult to grasp not so much for its atonal pitch language as for its relentless concentration of material. His textures are thick and saturated with musical ideas. The amount of material that might comprise a ten-minute composition in a more relaxed idiom is often condensed into three or four minutes. The result, at times, can border on "information overload" unless we can attune ourselves to Schönberg's compressed style of musical development. Otherwise the listener may feel under siege by music that seems convulsive, constantly on edge, or simply incoherent. Schönberg's music rarely makes a single statement that can be grasped instantaneously. The melodies, harmonies, and gestures are fragmentary because they are part of a continuous chain of ideas. It is this chain—the structure—that comprises the heart of the musical statement. If we approach Schönberg's music as an intellectual puzzle, like a code to be broken, the game soon grows tiresome, for Schönberg wished his structures to be felt rather than figured out. Rather, it is necessary to absorb the music as one takes in the conversation of someone who talks very rapidly over a wide range of topics.

Perspective on Serialism

The twelve-tone method is, like sonata form, a procedure of composition rather than a specific musical style; the set is a basis for structure, not the structure itself. Actual use of the set is left to the composer's imagination. Serial procedures may be applied rigorously or freely. In many works, both Schönberg and his pupil Alban Berg employed sets containing scale fragments, triads, or other tonal implications, thereby attempting a rapprochement between tonality and serialism. Many composers have combined serial procedures with other techniques, or have applied the method in highly individual fashion. On the other hand, Anton Webern, another of Schönberg's students, employed the twelve-tone method in exacting fashion, seeking a stylistically consistent approach to serial logic. Building on Webern's techniques, later composers applied serial procedures to other elements in addition to pitch: rhythm, dynamics, and so on—so that every aspect of the music springs from the same organizing principle. Boulez' *Le Marteau Sans Maître,* discussed in Chapter 9, employs extensive serial procedures.

Appreciation of serial music obviously does not require that the listener be able to recognize and follow transformations of the set throughout a piece, or even that the listener be aware that he is listening to a serially organized composition. As in any other kind of music, the listener's attention should naturally gravitate to wherever musical interest is concentrated. Serialism is not the basis of all, or even most, modern music. It is one alternative—and one of the most provocative—to the question of how music can be structured in a post-tonal age. There are several other alternatives, including tonality itself.

The Emancipation of Rhythm: Igor Stravinsky

The music of Igor Stravinsky (1882–1971), a Russian composer living in Paris, came to public awareness shortly before World War I. For many listeners of the time, Stravinsky's works seemed not only to epitomize the collapse of the Romantic esthetic, but also to represent a furious onslaught on traditional musical practices and values. Stravinsky had rethought melody, harmony, orchestration, and—above all—rhythm, and put them at the service of a pointed new esthetic. Brilliance of sound and rhythmic fire were the driving forces of his "brave new music."

Like Schönberg, Stravinksy sought new organizing procedures around which to build his art. Stravinsky's search, however, was less concentrated on the question of pitch relationships, and he formulated no general theory or rigorous method of composition. He approached the "crisis" in early 20th-century music as one who, by choice as well as birth, stood outside of the

German Romantic tradition. He felt a greater affinity for the music of his native Russia, for French music (especially that of his friend Debussy), and for works from the Baroque and Classical periods. Stravinsky observed the decline of Romanticism with satisfaction rather than a sense of loss. He believed that the efforts of Schönberg and others to continue this tradition were futile. Stravinsky was at ease in a world of artistic preferences rather than imperatives. He approached stylistic questions with detachment, investigating a given compositional procedure from the viewpoint of what it could do for him.

Stravinsky's approach to music was essentially one of problem solving: "To proceed by elimination—to know what to *discard* . . . that is the great technique of selection . . . [it is] the search for the *One* out of the *Many*." As noted earlier, Stravinsky adopted widely varying stylistic frameworks at different points in his career. In his early works, the framework was largely intuitive; later, it became increasingly a matter of rational procedures. To have a viable framework was, for Stravinsky, more important than the specific characteristics of the chosen procedures. He believed enduring art was possible in many styles, as long as the stylistic procedures of a work were clear.

Although Stravinsky always considered himself a Russian, the Bolshevik revolution of 1917 was little to his taste, and he spent the last 57 years of his life as an expatriate living in Switzerland (1913–20), Paris (1920–39) and the United States (1939–71). (His eventual residence in Los Angeles was only a few blocks from Schönberg's home, but the two composers, separated by profound esthetic and personal differences, had little contact.) Stravinsky had no use for the popular image of the composer as a starving genius; he was a shrewd businessman who saw no reason why his music should not pay. He parlayed his early celebrity into lucrative, lifelong compensation,

Igor Stravinsky (right) and Pablo Picasso, in a caricature by Jean Cocteau

touring extensively as pianist, conductor, and lecturer. He enjoyed the company of luminaries from the visual arts and literature. In a series of essays, articles, and memoirs, he held court on variegated artistic and social matters with penetrating insight and dry wit. Free of teaching obligations and financial worry, Stravinsky composed daily ("like a man with banking hours," he said), and amassed an impressive body of works in every major genre.

The catalyst for Stravinsky's rapid rise to fame was his association with the impressario Serge Diaghilev. Diaghilev was artistic director of the Russian Ballet, a company of enormous influence centered in Paris which commissioned music, librettos, and stage sets from leading European artists. Collaboration between the two men resulted in three ballets, *The Firebird* (1909), *Petrushka* (1911), and *The Rite of Spring* (1913). These ballets, each based on a Russian mythic subject, established Stravinsky's reputation as one of the most innovative and exciting composers of the time.

The most striking feature of these ballets is their explosive rhythmic energy. The rhythms are often abrupt, centering around incisive motives repeated over and over in various asymmetric arrangements. Powerful, shifting accents are superimposed on an absolutely rigid pulse. As the harmonies of Schönberg never settle into a secure tonal framework, so many of Stravinsky's rhythms never settle into a predictable metrical framework. This freeing of rhythm from traditional metric patterns has been called the "emancipation of *rhythmic* dissonance," since the pulse no longer "resolves" to a regular downbeat. The result is a feeling of elemental, unrestrained rhythmic force.

Similarly, the melodies of Stravinsky's ballets are constructed not in long, soaring arcs, but in brusque fragments. Needle-sharp motives and gruff, folk-like tunes are etched into themes that undergo varied repetition rather than development. Harmonies seethe with internal dissonance, but at the same time are static, going nowhere; dissonant sonorities are relentlessly repeated until tension nears the breaking point. The formal structure of these ballets is highly sectional. Each section creates a characteristic atmosphere. Many build to a riveting climax, then are abruptly cut off. Formal structure is additive both within sections and in the ballet as a whole; static blocks of sound are piled up to form sections, which in turn are piled up to form an overall design. The whole structure is held together by an inner tension and contrast of motivic ideas, and by what Stravinsky called the "polar attraction" of sounds toward a center pitch, which emerges at the end of the work. This pitch is not a tonic, but is more like the center of a wheel, around which individual melodies and harmonies (the "spokes") gradually converge. This additive approach to structure was another alternative to the question of how music could be organized apart from the traditional resources of tonal harmony.

Listening

"Fertility of the Earth," Part I from The Rite of Spring *(Le Sacre du Printemps) by Igor Stravinsky (1882–1971)*

Record Set Side 12, Band 2

The subject of The Rite of Spring is a pagan fertility ritual. The work is divided into two parts.

I. Fertility of the Earth: At the coming of spring, the elemental forces of life erupt.

II. The Sacrifice: A young girl is offered in sacrifice to propitiate these forces. Wise elders, seated in a circle, watch as the girl dances herself to death.

Although the major sections of the work carry picturesque designations, these are of a general nature, referring to the dance libretto rather than to specific events. Stravinsky denied the existence of any programmatic associations in the music. The impersonal, primordial tone of the libretto is matched by an even more impersonal, "barbarous" musical tone: the dancers are not human figures but prehistoric archetypes compulsively fulfilling a pagan ritual.

The ballet is a chilling spectacle that stood far outside the traditions of the genre. The première of the work in Paris (May 29, 1913) resulted in a legendary mêlée. The audience booed, hissed, stomped, and made animal noises. Infuriated, Stravinsky stood up and excoriated his outraged listeners; the pandemonium intensified and the performance was abruptly halted. A year later the work was presented in concert form and was hailed as a masterpiece.

Listening Outline to Part I

Introduction. A bassoon solo in an exceptionally high register opens the work. This theme exemplifies the intentionally "primitive," fragmentary, and repetitive melodic structure of *The Rite.* It is largely based upon a pentatonic (five-tone) scale, and features a series of arabesque but static variations on a descending three-note motive:

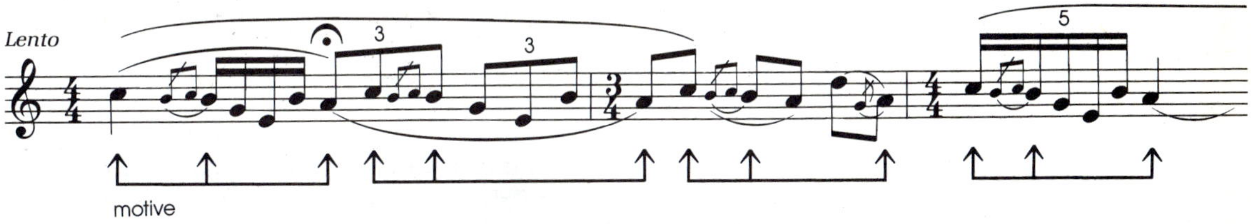

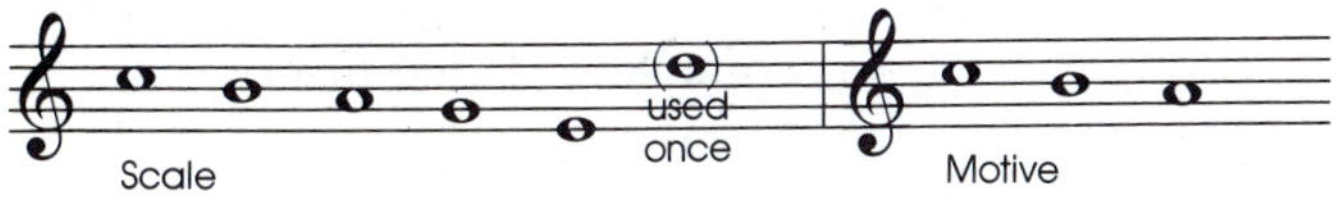

The bassoon theme is an incantation, charged with intensity by its rarified but penetrating tone color. (At a rehearsal in which a bassoonist effortlessly negotiated the difficult passage, Stravinsky wryly observed, "If I'd known it could be played that easily I would have written it *higher.*") Other woodwinds enter on various murmuring figures, suggesting the awakening of the earth. These motives, too, are fragmentary and repetitive. The texture is not contrapuntal, but rather consists of distinct *layers* of sound. The section builds to a strenuous climax as more and more independent motives pile up.

Transition. The woodwind tutti is abruptly broken off. The solo bassoon theme returns briefly, followed by a hesitant, then insistent, statement of a four-note figure in the violins. This figure establishes the basic sonority and thumping rhythmic energy of the following section.

Dance of the Adolescents. This section features two of the most celebrated techniques of *The Rite.* It is based upon a single complex sonority: an E♭ major triad with added seventh in the upper strings, superimposed on top of an E-*natural* major triad in the lower strings. The result is a stridently dissonant composite sonority. The simultaneous use of chords or melodies from two different keys is called *bitonality.* The listener rarely "hears" two simultaneous keys, however; as here, the sounds usually fuse into a single complex sonority that is in no key. This sonority is incessantly repeated, an example of the work's celebrated "pounding rhythms," with irregular sharp accents punctuated in the horns:

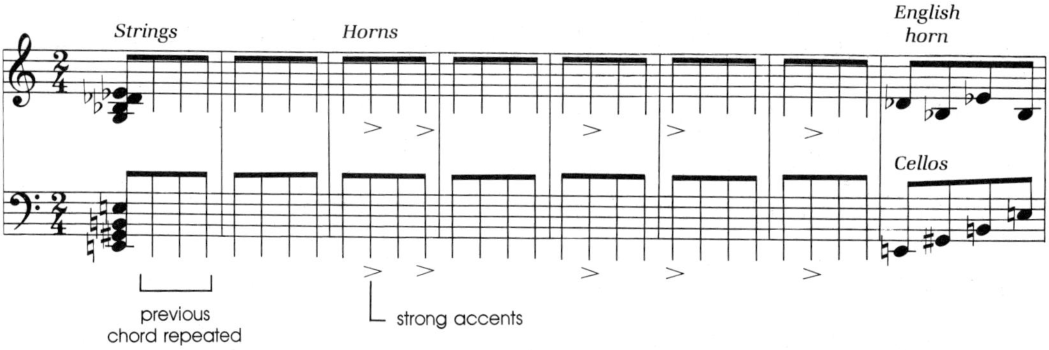

The pungent sonority serves as the basis for continuous variations, sounded alternately in hammered rhythms by the strings and broken into figuration patterns, as in the final measure of the excerpt above. New melodic ideas are interspersed on top of this primary textural layer. The gradual accumulation of motives, eventually sounded together, leads to another vehement climax.

Ritual of Abduction. A sustained brass chord under a rapid string figure initiates the third section. Fanfare figures in the woodwinds and brass build to a furious exchange between the winds and timpani. The urgent rhythmic pulse remains absolutely regular, but metric accents keep shifting. As in so many passages of *The Rite,* these measures generate tremendous internal tension between the "simplicity" of the melody—a repetitive figure using only five notes—and the complexity of its rhythmic development.

Spring Rounds. The pervasive frenzy of *The Rite* is periodically relieved by brief respites. *Spring Rounds* begins and ends on a moment of calm. A delicate flute trill accompanies a subdued melody, played two octaves apart by a piccolo clarinet and the large bass clarinet. A lugubrious, syncopated accompaniment figure in the cellos pulls the tonal structure into minor. A new theme, pensive at first, builds to a crunching climax, followed by a brief but furious episode. The flute trills and the clarinet theme then return.

Ritual of the Rival Tribes. An ominous rumble in the low brass and percussion unleashes another section of rhythmic and coloristic frenzy. At the "Procession of the Sage," tubas relentlessly reiterate a short ponderous motive against coloristic fireworks in the winds and strings. Further piling up of motives results in another climactic stampede. The revel is interrupted by a moment of stunned silence. In a mysterious interlude, the sage blesses the earth. A "distant," icy chord is whispered. Then—BANG!—the "Dance of the Earth" erupts in percussive fury, builds to another climactic sweep, and is cut off in mid-air, concluding Part I of the ballet.

The *Rite of Spring* was a unique answer to the question of artistic freedom. Stravinsky himself declared, "I was guided by no system whatever. . . . Very little immediate tradition lies behind it. I had only my ear to guide me." What was missed amid the tumult of the première, but quickly grasped in subsequent performances, was Stravinsky's re-integration of musical structure. The "explosion" of *The Rite* was carefully calculated to liberate new means of organizing sound. Stravinsky had reshuffled the deck, rearranging musical elements and giving them new structural priorities. In many passages, rhythm, color, and density of sound became the shaping elements of form, while melody and harmony became static points of reference.

In retrospect, *The Rite* appears less "revolutionary" than it did to stunned early listeners. (Stravinsky observed, "I was made a revolutionary in spite of myself.") It was a logical outgrowth of his earlier ballets, but also, like Wagner's *Tristan,* the endpoint of a musical style. It was not a work that could be easily built upon, because (like *Tristan*) it carried certain techniques to their esthetic limit. Listeners expecting more works in the vein of *The Rite of Spring,* or wondering, "Can he top that?", were in for a surprise.

Neoclassicism

World War I severely disrupted European musical life. Concerts were sporadic. It was difficult or impossible to produce new works requiring large performing ensembles. Several leading composers were cut off from royalties and other sources of income, and some were uprooted from their homelands. This enforced silence, together with the changed economic and social climate after the war, caused many composers to rethink their art. To a generation traumatized by the World War, Romantic beliefs in the essential goodness of man, "necessary" human progress, and art as an ennobling activity took on a very hollow ring—especially since the countries with the most illustrious Romantic heritage had been among the principals in the wholesale destruction. Many artists perceived an "abyss" within the human personality as well as in art—a dark underside, now grimly apparent, that made Romantic convictions seem hopelessly naïve. Art came to be seen in less grandiose terms—not as the savior of humanity, but as an engrossing diversion, an ordered activity apart from the chaotic "real" world.

During the years in which Schönberg formulated his serial procedures, most other composers were engaged in a process of redefining the nature and limits of their art. Many leading figures were disturbed by the growing distance that seemed to separate composer and listener. Traditional elements of form (melody, harmony, and counterpoint) had grown increasingly complex and diversified, and other resources (color and asymmetric rhythms) had gained new structural importance. Various alternative ways of organizing music apart from a fixed tonal center had been explored. The years when composers could write some of their most compelling music while still in their teens, as Schubert and Mendelssohn had done, seemed long gone. Composers now needed a longer period of apprenticeship to investigate stylistic alternatives, to gain a feel for the specific resources and limitations of each, to define their esthetic preferences, and to forge a personal style. (Stravinsky had been considered a comparative prodigy while in his late twenties.) The major achievements of early 20th-century music had been highly individual accomplishments, rather than generally applicable solutions to "the abyss." Many listeners felt unable to keep pace with the profusion of new resources, new choices, and new artistic voices.

Stravinsky, Paul Hindemith, and other major composers sought to redress this situation by restoring a more universal, less "personal" basis for musical communication. But this common basis would not be resuscitation of Romanticism, an esthetic that had become alien. Where, then, to turn for such a framework? One answer was to look back, beyond the 19th century, to Baroque and Classical music—to use these earlier styles as models for musical practice and esthetic orientation. Baroque and Classical esthetics provided general but flexible structural guidelines: an emphasis on clarity of design and solid craftsmanship rather than emotion; the use of well-defined structural frameworks for ideas; objectivity and restraint; and employment of modest performing resources.

The new movement came to be called *neoclassicism.* The term "classical" was used here in the general sense of "structure over emotion," rather than in the more limited sense of "Haydn, Mozart, and Beethoven"; Baroque principles were adopted in equal measure. Neoclassical composers did not attempt to write either "Classical" or "Baroque" music, or to confine themselves to the musical resources of these periods. Rather, they consciously adopted specific forms and procedures from these periods and reworked them. Neoclassicism was based upon the acceptance of conventions that provided a framework for new (hence *"neo-"*) ideas and resources.

Stylistic Characteristics

Neoclassical composers consciously limited the complexity of their works. Traditional genres (symphony, sonata, concerto) and forms (sonata form, fugue) were favored because they provided a framework for the integration of traditional and fresh procedures. Melodies and harmonic progressions were influenced by 18th-century practice; rhythms featured a strong, regular pulse (no rubato); phrases were short and cadences clearly marked; textures were transparent. Ensembles were reduced in size. Chamber music once again became an important medium.

The pitch language of most neoclassic works revolves around a central tone. This tone is established either thorugh repetition or through a characteristic cadential progression that develops its own logic in a given work. The simplified pitch language of neoclassicism is often diatonic, employing traditional major and minor scales, with the periodic introduction of chromatic inflections.

The underlying dynamic of the style is the contrast between the listener's expectations and what actually takes place in the music—in effect, a pouring of new wine into old bottles. Traditional sonorities and techniques are transformed or reinterpreted. With detachment, the composer comments upon these materials, twisting them into unorthodox shape and breaking their regular patterns. Since the model is clear, even subtle deviations are conspicuous and become an element of expression.

Listening

The Soldier's Tale *(L'Histoire du Soldat) by Igor Stravinsky (1882–1971)*

The Soldier's Tale was Stravinsky's first neoclassic work, completed in 1918. It was conceived as a compact stage work for narrator, dancers, and small instrumental ensemble, designed to be produced with the reduced performing resources available during wartime. The work is now often performed as a concert suite, without the narration and dance.

The story line is a droll parody of the Faust legend. A soldier is accosted by the devil in disguise, and is inveigled into exchanging his fiddle (his "innocence" or, perhaps, "talent") for a magic book that will assure riches. The soldier attains wealth but little happiness, and attempts to call off the bargain. During a card game with his adversary the soldier plies the devil with wine and purposely loses the remainder of his fortune. When the besotted demon collapses in a stupor, the soldier retrieves his fiddle. Good fortune follows. A king has promised his daughter's hand in marriage to anyone who can cure her of a mysterious illness. The soldier serenades the princess with his fiddle. She rises and dances a tango, waltz, and ragtime; they embrace and are married. The wily devil fumes, awaiting an opportunity to regain the upper hand and drag this upstart down to hell. During a trip, the soldier becomes careless, enabling the devil to seize the fiddle again and lead the soldier to his doom. The devil dances in triumph.

Stravinsky's score is a suite of fifteen brief numbers (eleven in the concert version) including four marches, four dances, two chorales, and five incidental pieces. The music is taut, bristling with rhythmic energy and ironic wit. There is a continual interplay between regular, predictable elements—the references or models—and unexpected twists. The make-up of the chamber ensemble is heterogeneous: clarinet, basson, cornet, trombone, violin, double bass, and a percussion battery performed by one player. Stravinsky chose a treble and bass instrument from each orchestral family—woodwind, brass, and strings—and exploited their timbral differences. The bright individual colors stand out in sharp relief rather than blending into a unified sound quality. Stravinsky's textures are either layered (the instruments performing separate functions) or contrapuntal.

Several diverse models and influences are explicit in the work. The strong rhythmic pulse, contrapuntal textures, and two chorales are a nod to Baroque music. There are obvious allusions to the traditions of band music (prominent use of the brass, especially in the marches) and chamber music (equal-voiced textures, especially in the number entitled "The Little Concert"). Viennese waltzes and jazz elements are also in evidence. "A good composer never imitates," Stravinsky noted wryly, "he steals."

L'Histoire is far more than a grab-bag of stylistic pickings, however. The separate numbers are unified by a consistent musical language and tone and by common structural procedures. Stravinsky bends the various models to his own purposes, extracting only what he wants and molding the materials into new shapes. New and old, sophisticated and banal, predictable and anomalous elements are fused into a lucid, consistent musical style. Much is borrowed, but the musical statement is new.

The opening number, "The Soldier's March," sets the ironic but genial tone of the entire work and establishes its basic dynamic: the musical materials are generally simple, but the way they are fitted together is highly sophisticated. "The Soldier's March" revolves around the pitch G. The double bass performs a repetitive, march-like accompanimental figure throughout much of the number, drumming in the center pitch and duple $\frac{2}{4}$ meter. This figure is the primary sound layer. On top of it, Stravinsky imposes various melodic, rhythmic, and contrapuntal patterns which often run counter to the bass figure. The melodic phrases are generally short and of unpredictable length.

Cadences often come as a surprise, and do not resolve tension or produce a sense of completion. Forward impetus is continuous (as in Baroque music), and cadences serve merely to separate ideas.

The different layers of the piece often clash in pitch structure and in rhythmic construction. The third phrase is typical. The double bass reiterates its two-note figure centered on the pitch G; despite the written changes of meter, the duple pattern ♪ 𝄾 ♪ 𝄾 is invariable. The second layer, duet for cornet and trombone, employs a D major scale but is centered around the pitches A (trombone) and E (cornet). The phrase begins in duple rhythm, but the meter then becomes irregular as the duet layer is torn free of the march-like framework of the bass. Rhythmic correspondence between layers has been broken, and they go their separate ways, cadencing on different beats.

Various echoes of march-like clichés are interjected between phrases and incorporated within the rhythmically chanted narration. Many of the instrumental lines are rhythmically out of step with the duple bass figure. The separate layers remain totally distinct; each has its own rhythmic structure and pitch organization. When the lines do come together on simple march rhythms, the sudden uniformity often comes as a surprise in this peculiar march. Irregular patterns develop their own off-beat logic and begin to sound "right" until they, too, are broken.

Much of the vitality of "The Soldier's March" comes from the barbed interaction between separate layers of sound. The technique is a reduced version of the piling-up of sounds that characterized *The Rite of Spring.* The difference is in the restraint with which the procedure is applied in *A Soldier's Tale.* The piling-up never gets out of hand; there are fewer layers, and each layer can be clearly heard at all times. This is in line with Stravinsky's neoclassic esthetic: "The more art is controlled, limited, worked over, the more it is free."

The ironic tone and obvious use of eclectic stylistic references heard in *A Soldier's Tale* are not common to all neoclassic music. Stravinsky's *Symphony of Psalms* (1930), for example, is a solemn sacred work that subtly incorporates chant-like melodies. Paul Hindemith's *Ludus Tonalis* (1942) is an homage to Bach, a collection of twelve preludes inspired by Bach's *Well-*

Tempered Clavier. Because neoclassicism was a principle of organization, rather than a specific technique or style, it was flexible and could be applied to a wide range of pitch styles.

National Influences and Idioms

Whereas Stravinsky stood outside the idioms with which he worked, chiseling them into a personal but "international" musical style, many other 20th-century composers have sought to explore national idioms from within. The nationalist movement of the later 19th century burgeoned in many new countries, and took many new forms, during the first few decades of the 20th century. Turning their gaze to the everyday world around them, composers discovered a fertile source of melodic, harmonic, and rhythmic materials, and a means to bridge the gap between folk music and concert music. Béla Bartók's incorporation of the asymmetric rhythmic and melodic idioms of Hungarian peasant music in many of his works was noted in Chapter 8; the melodic style of Leos Janáček (1854–1928) shows a similar debt to the Moravian folk music and spoken rhythms of present-day Czechoslovakia. National themes and influences, as heard in the music of Ralph Vaughan Williams (1872–1958) and Gustav Holst (1874–1934) led to a renewal of English musical life. Spanish dance rhythms pervade the music of Manuel de Falla (1876–1946), and similar influences pervade the music of such Latin American composers as the Brazilian Heitor Villa-Lobos.[1]

Nationalist tendencies have frequently coalesced with neoclassic formal procedures, since the materials and esthetic aims of these two influences are usually similar: the search for directness of expression and accessibility; the attempt to write "natural," effective instrumental parts that rarely make virtuosic demands; and the use of traditional scales and harmonies with a gravitational pull toward a central tone. Many American composers, including Roy Harris (b. 1898), Samuel Barber (b. 1910), and Aaron Copland have commingled American idioms derived from jazz, folk music, and popular music within traditional forms.

Listening

Appalachian Spring *by Aaron Copland (b. 1900)*

The music of Aaron Copland reflects many of the major stylistic currents of the last 50 years. His early compositions represent conscious attempts to write music in a uniquely American idiom. During the early 1930s he pursued more rigorous dissonant types of pitch organization. Worried by the widening chasm he perceived between composers and the ordinary concert-goer, he then endeavored "to see if I couldn't say

[1] In the Soviet Union, the government attempted to impose a national "proletarian" style in line with its doctrine of "socialist realism." Such composers as Serge Prokofiev (1891–1952) and Dmitri Shostakovich (1906–1975) frequently chafed under these stylistic restrictions, but assimilated them in many works.

what I had to say in the simplest possible terms." The resulting works of the late 1930s and 1940s established him as one of America's most widely performed composers.

Copland's *Appalachian Spring* (1943–44) was originally written as a ballet, scored for a chamber orchestra of 13 instruments. Set in the Pennsylvania hills in the early 1800's, it centered around the courtship and wedding of a young farm couple. In 1945 Copland arranged excerpts from the ballet as a concert suite for moderate-sized orchestra; the eight sections of the suite are linked by transitions and are played without pause.

During a slow introductory section, a recurrent sonority—a major triad with two added tones (a ninth chord)—unfolds several times in sustained arpeggiations in the strings, while melodic fragments are introduced in the woodwinds. Much of the score features such soloistic textures. Melodies are generally introduced by a single instrument and supported by transparent harmonies. In the ballet, this introduction accompanies the progressive appearance of each of the major characters.

The main body of the work features an assortment of country dances. The seventh and longest section begins with a theme, introduced by solo clarinet, based upon the Shaker tune, "The Gift to be Simple." The theme is followed by five variations, culminating in a resounding final tutti statement. In a hymn-like concluding section, a chordal string passage leads to a return of the woodwind motives of the introductory section. The bride and groom "are left quiet and strong in their new house."

There is considerable evocation of Americana in Copland's score, despite the fact that the Shaker tune is his only direct quotation. The pioneering spirit, tranquility, and piety of frontier life receive a correspondingly plainspoken orchestral expression, Copland's musical embodiment of the "gift to be simple."

Neoclassical procedures and national idioms were among the most widely adopted compositional frameworks during the second quarter of the 20th century. It is inaccurate, however, to label a composer a "neoclassicist" or a "nationalist" on the basis of a few works. Some composers, such as Bartók, were influenced by these resources but adopted them selectively, employing them only in certain works and combining them with more rigorous structural techniques. Stravinsky eventually abandoned the neoclassic esthetic, not because he believed it had been a "mistake," but because he characteristically wished to explore other possibilities. Many listeners were startled when Stravinsky and, soon thereafter, Copland turned to serialism. To some, this shift appeared to be an unprovoked turnabout, as though an atheist had suddenly embraced religion (or vice versa). In reality, however, Stravinsky was not striving for something "completely different"; rather, he was intrigued by the possibility of applying his learned craft to procedures that, in their objectivity, now seemed to offer a logical avenue for the further development of his classical esthetic.

For years many critics and listeners viewed the increasing pluralism of early 20th-century styles as an unnatural, temporary phenomenon. They anticipated that this "transitional" period would lead to the emergence of a new synthesis or dominant style. This did not happen, however. Musical styles had become too diffuse, and were being developed and refined along separate paths. Most composers saw no reason why there should be a single mainstream, rather than a wealth of choices.

The major new currents that opened up shortly before and after World War I were independently systematized and consolidated during the next two decades. There was considerable cross-fertilization, and sometimes the emergence of surprising parallels between styles, but there was no broad fusion. In fact, the years after World War II witnessed another "explosion" in musical practice, which is the subject of Chapter 20.

Principal Composers of the Early 20th Century

Claude Debussy *(1862–1918). French. Generally identified with impressionist tendencies in music, Debussy explored subtle new types of sound colors, harmonies, and formal designs in his search for an art free of Romantic "excess."*

Jean Sibelius *(1867–1957). Finnish. Sibelius is best known for his seven symphonies, which are characterized by a brooding tone. While his earlier works display a striving for national identification, his later compositions are broader and more philosophical in scope.*

Sergei Rachmaninoff *(1873–1943). Russian. Probably the most traditional as well as one of the most widely performed early 20th-century composers. Rachmaninoff continued the late Romantic traditions of Tchaikovksy in such works as his four piano concertos.*

Arnold Schönberg *(1874–1951). Austrian. A seminal figure in 20th-century music, Schönberg was the first composer to explore the resources of free atonality and serialism.*

Charles Ives *(1874–1954). American. Ives forged a unique personal idiom that stands outside all of the traditions and major currents of his time. His music, which achieved widespread recognition only near the end of his life, has exerted considerable influence in recent decades, and he is seen by many as America's greatest composer. (See Chapter 16.)*

Maurice Ravel *(1875–1937). French. In Ravel's finely crafted music, impressionist elements are generally structured by means of classically-oriented forms and procedures.*

Béla Bartók *(1881–1945). Hungarian. A composer of broad stylistic range and musical interests, Bartók shared Stravinsky's predilection for driving rhythmic energy, rapid metrical shifts, and the reinterpretation of traditional forms; he also, however, incorporated national elements within his works. Probably more than any other composer of the period, Bartók sought to fuse the diverse new resources at his* *disposal into a "universal" (but still highly personal) musical style. (See Chapter 8.)*

Igor Stravinsky *(1882–1971). Russian. Although he remains most celebrated for the rhythmic innovations of his early ballets, Stravinsky went through continuous stylistic evolution and sought classical ideals of form and content with increasing rigor during his later years.*

Edgard Varèse *(1883–1965). American, born in France. An individualist who sought the "liberation of sound" from traditional forms and conventions, Varèse formulated his own structural procedures and has been a major influence on the present generation of composers. (See Chapter 15.)*

Anton von Webern *(1883–1945). Austrian. A student of Schönberg, Webern employed his teacher's serial procedures with exactitude and clarity. His works pointed the way toward the comprehensive application of serial techniques to several dimensions of music. (See Chapter 16.)*

Alban Berg *(1885–1935). Austrian. Schönberg's other leading pupil, Berg sought to reconcile atonal and serial procedures with traditional forms and Romantic expression. (See Chapter 19.)*

Serge Prokofiev *(1891–1952). Russian. Generally identified with the neoclassical movement (as exemplified by his* Classical Symphony*), Prokofiev is the major 20th-century composer of Russian operas and ballets. (See Chapter 14.)*

Paul Hindemith *(1895–1963). German. Primarily a neoclassic composer, Hindemith sought to formulate general theories of composition and musical practice. He eventually settled in the United States, and from 1940 to 1953 taught at Yale University. His masterpieces include the opera* Mathis der Maler *(1935) and a symphony fashioned from its materials.*

Terms and Concepts for Review

style as a matter of choice
pluralism of styles
impressionism
- tone color
- non-functional harmonies (chords defined by their color rather than their relation to a tonic)
- simultaneous statement and development of ideas

free atonality
- intervallic consistency
- "emancipation of dissonance"
- compression of musical thought

serialism
- 12-tone method
- set, row, or series
  - original
  - retrograde
  - inversion
  - retrograde-inversion

"emancipation of rhythmic dissonance"
neoclassicism
nationalism

Unit 4
Musical Genres

As we listen to a composition for the first time, we gradually gain a feel for its musical language, for its organizing principles and design (form), and for the means and focus of its expression (style). We also come to understand how the composer exploits the idiomatic resources of an ensemble: how the piece is uniquely suited to its **genre**, *or performing medium. The genre of a composition influences the other features; certain types of textures and modes of expression, for example, are better suited to a work for solo piano than to one for orchestra.*

The most basic genres are vocal music and instrumental music. These, in turn, may be divided into works for soloist, for small ensemble (between two and about ten performers), and for large ensemble. A work is usually considered vocal even if it includes instruments as well as voices, since our attention tends to center primarily on the sung parts. Occasionally, however, the vocal parts are clearly secondary, comprising additional tone colors within an essentially instrumental texture.

Genres are further defined by their length, tone, and formal outline. The sonata and character piece are both solo piano genres, but there the similarity ends. The character piece is a short, lyrical work featuring one or two themes and moods; the sonata is a long multi-movement work covering a broad range of expression, in which formal contrasts precede final integration.

Common practices develop with respect to how various combinations of voices or instruments are treated. These conventions of individual genres often cut across historical style periods. In this unit, the works examined will be considered in relation to others of the same type drawn from many periods. In this way, the basic resources of a medium, and the development of conventions for handling these resources, will be brought into focus. As in every other aspect of music, however, the ultimate importance of these general characteristics is as a frame of reference against which we hear the unique qualities of each individual work.

Chapter 13
Vocal Music

The human voice is the original medium of musical performance and the only one common to all cultures. It is also the one medium in which all of us participate, whether in a formal or informal way. As a heightened form of speech, vocal music is the most explicit form of musical expression. The text tells us what is being expressed, but it is usually the music, with its particular range of tonal nuances, that determines the precise quality of the thought. Sometimes, in fact, a vocal melody will transcend or transform a text, conveying its point with greater immediacy or force than the words alone. Sentiments that might sound trifling, pontifical, or maudlin if spoken may seem highly affecting and completely natural in a musical setting. Often the music is able to communicate the conviction behind a thought, and to give it more concrete gesture.

Vocal Genres

Vocal music can be divided into three basic genres: **solo song,** with or without instrumental accompaniment; music for **small groups** of singers, in which each vocal line is sung by a single performer; and **choral music,** with several singers on each part. (**Opera,** which brings together all these vocal resources as well as aspects of orchestral music and drama, is the subject of the last two chapters of this unit.) All three of these vocal mediums cover a broad range of expression, but a few general observations can be made about the most common qualities of each. Choral music is often associated with ceremonial or festive occasions. The very presence of a large group performing together to common purpose constitutes a type of social event. Choral music forms a vital part of many civic functions and of most religious services, where it makes ritual observances more meaningful to the individual and aids in the handing down of traditions from one generation to the next. Whether one participates as a performer or a listener, group singing involves the individual in the life and beliefs of a community and creates a sense of sharing in a common experience. Choral music generally transcends personal feelings and offers instead a collective musical statement. Music for small vocal groups, on the other hand, is often "conversational" in tone. With a sole performer, and therefore a particular tone color, to each part, the separate lines tend to retain distinct identities; they usually create a dialogue of ideas rather than a homogeneous blend.

Solo song is among the most elemental and powerful vehicles for individual expression—a way to articulate, "This is what *I* feel and believe." Text and music tend to have the closest correspondence in solo song, partly because words are most clearly understood when sung by a single performer, but also because the musical nuances surrounding the text are concentrated in a single melody. Furthermore, the performer has greater interpretive freedom in its delivery. While choral music often conveys a composer's interpretation of or commentary upon a text, solo song is usually intended as an ideal musical realization of the verse.

In sum, then, the repertoire and styles of vocal music embody to a unique degree two of the most vital dimensions of musical performance—shared experience and personal expression.

Thoughts on the Shared and Personal Qualities of Music

There is sometimes strong peer pressure upon an individual to share in a particular type of music—be it "classical" ballet, the songs of an ethnic culture, Muzak, hard or soft rock, or whatever—as a sign of group association. The implication is, "*This* is *our* music; it expresses our values in our way. *That* is *their* music." There is often the further implication that one is expected to choose either "ours" or "theirs." In fact, all of us feel a particular affinity for certain kinds of music, and the reasons for these preferences are both internal and external to the actual qualities of the music. At times the process of group identification can take precedence over the musical experience itself, and the feeling of sharing becomes more important than what is being shared. When this happens, an individual's musical horizons can begin shrinking to conformity with whatever is socially acceptable. "Our" music becomes a badge of fellowship; "their" music seems alien, and holds little interest, if we believe it has nothing to say to us.

Such a rigid division of musical styles into categories of "friendly" and "that other stuff" is hardly necessary, and those more interested in the nature and possibilities of art than in its "uses" rarely feel obliged to choose up sides. There are many worlds of music, and a listener can make many choices. These preferences need not be esthetically consistent ("ours" versus "theirs"). In fact, they will often be more satisfying when *not* neatly compatible. The unique qualities of individual works and styles are all the more apparent against a broad backdrop.

A piece of music is meant to be enjoyed for its own sake and on its own terms. As a form of communication music is by definition a *shared* experience; otherwise nothing is being communicated. The listener's actual perception of a work, however, is very *personal;* otherwise he or she is being commanded to respond in a prescribed manner. If either dimension—the shared or personal—takes undue priority, the total experience can be diminished. We understand music best neither in isolation nor as part of a herd, but as individuals in concert with others.

Text and Music

A basic feature of any vocal piece is the relationship between the music and its text. Three types of correlation are most common:

(1) The music may be *subordinate.* Some melodies and choral settings are a form of musical recitation, enhancing the emotional tone of the verse, carefully molded to its natural spoken inflections, but never obscuring the words with purely musical invention.

(2) Music may be the *dominant* element. The text is treated freely, as a vehicle that provides an initial mood, a dramatic situation, or merely syllables to be sung. Interest is concentrated on the development of musical ideas and design.

(3) Interest may be *evenly divided* between text and music. The two elements blend into a single means of expression and seem inseparable.

Texts are most easily understood when there is one melodic note for each syllable of the verse. Such *syllabic* settings are characteristic of folk tunes and other simple songs, but are also common when the text is long or subtle in meaning or presents a story line. At the opposite extreme is a *melismatic* style, in which long runs of many notes occur on some syllables. The text may be partially or almost completely obscured, as though it were being spoken extremely slowly. Often, however, melismatic runs occur on words such as "amen," which can be understood even when the syllables are widely separated, as in the Bach example on the next page.

Sometimes a composer will set most of the words in syllabic style, but will draw out certain syllables with short melodic flourishes. In the following two phrases from "Dido's Lament" by Henry Purcell, the short melismas on "ah" provide variations in the pacing-out of the text and underscore its tone of resignation:

Idiomatic Characteristics of the Voice

The human voice, like any instrument, has particular technical capabilities and limitations. Some types of melodic lines are well suited to the voice and sound effortless in performance. Other melodic styles are difficult but effective if the singer can surmount their technical challenges. Occasionally we hear a passage that sounds unwieldy, or at best struggling, even in a virtuoso performance, because the music makes awkward demands upon the voice. Suitability and resourcefulness—and not the level of technical difficulty—are the measure of any work's idiomatic quality.

Singers obviously must interrupt the flow of sound periodically in order to breathe. Vocal melodies, therefore, are generally constructed in relatively short phrases, as in the Purcell excerpt, or else incorporate brief rests or long notes where the singer can steal a quick breath. Some composers, however, make little concession to this elemental idiomatic demand. Bach sometimes treats the voice like an indefatigable wind machine, constructing long, serpentine passages like the following:

Tenor line from the "Cum Sancto Spiritu" section of Bach's B Minor Mass

In choral music such unrelenting lines can be mastered through staggered breathing; the tenors would breathe individually at separate points in the phrase. In solo vocal music, however, such passages are a test of endurance.

Compared to most instruments, the human voice has a relatively small range: a little more than two octaves. Performing in tune is more difficult for singers than for instrumentalists. The vocalist cannot merely strike the appropriate key but must prepare each note mentally. Chromatic passages, particularly in atonal styles where there is no scale to serve as a pitch framework, require a keen ear and careful preparation. Large leaps are also comparatively difficult for the voice, requiring a different "placement" for each note. For these reasons, vocal melodies have traditionally featured smaller intervals and have been confined to a narrower pitch range than instrumental themes. Many contemporary composers, however, commonly employ wide leaps and continuous chromatic inflections in their vocal music. The relatively few singers blessed with "absolute pitch" (or "perfect pitch"), who can listen to the whine of a vacuum cleaner and observe, "It's C♯ but a little flat," obviously have an advantage in such music. However, it is possible for singers with good "relative pitch," who can complete a melody if given a reference pitch, to perform demanding music with equal success.

"Good vocal quality" is expected of singers, but this attribute varies widely in different styles and periods. Most songs require a lyrical quality—light, clear, unforced. Dramatic pieces demand a heavier, darker timbre and greater projection. Romantic music usually is sung with vibrato (rapid minor variations in pitch that produce a richer sound) and, frequently, with a rapid glide between some pitches (called *portamento*). The same techniques would sound "soupy" in Renaissance music, because they run counter to the vocal property most prized during the Renaissance era: purity of sound.

The Renaissance: Mass and Madrigal

Settings of the Ordinary of the Mass (the unchanging portions) comprised the single most important genre of Renaissance music. Many 15th- and 16th-century composers completed two dozen or more Mass settings, much as later composers concentrated their energies on such genres as the song or symphony. Most Renaissance Masses are unified by a *cantus firmus,* or given melody, which appears in several of the five movements. The cantus firmus might be drawn from any number of sacred or secular sources, or it might be newly composed for the work. Occasionally, composers would borrow several polyphonic voices from a popular song.

Between 1400 and the middle 1500s, Mass settings grew progressively more complex in style and technique. The Mass became a showcase for composers' polyphonic ingenuity. Intricate contrapuntal procedures—such as canons in which the voices move at different speeds, or the melody of one voice is performed backward in another voice, or elaborate melismas are incorporated within all the parts—were standard features of the Renaissance Mass. The liturgical text was sometimes casually grafted on to a composition that was, in essence, a purely musical invention. The words were frequently buried in a sea of notes and were often only dimly recognizable.

In response to growing secular influences within the church as well as to the Protestant Reformation, the Roman Catholic Church convened a synod of ecclesiastical authorities to clarify questions of doctrine and worship. This assembly, which met intermittently between 1545 and 1563 in Trent, Italy, condemned various abuses, and looked with particular disapproval upon the current state of liturgical music. Composers were censured for their melodic quotations from secular songs and for elaborate note-spinnings that obscured the text. Some members of the council wished to outlaw all polyphonic settings of the Mass and enforce the uniform use of plainchant. A majority, however, preferred less severe measures. The Council of Trent established guidelines for a reformed liturgical style; it was to be reverential in tone and purged of secular influence and technical exhibitionism, and music was again to be put at the service of the text.

Listening

Kyrie from the Missa Papae Marcelli (Pope Marcellus Mass) *by Giovanni da Palestrina (c. 1524–1594)*

Record Set Side 5, Band 5

Giovanni Pierluigi, called Palestrina after the town of his birth, became the figurehead of the reformed Catholic liturgical style. Palestrina spent much of his career as organist, choir director, and composer at St. Peter's in Rome. His works include over 100 Masses and some 450 motets, which became models of the purified sacred style of the Counter-Reformation. His *Pope Marcellus Mass* was dedicated to

Giovanni Pierluigi da Palestrina

Marcellus II, who had taken particular interest in the Papal choir during his tragically brief three-week Pontificate. The work is *a cappella* (for voices alone), written for a six-part chorus of about 25 singers. It is one of comparatively few Renaissance Masses not based on any known cantus firmus.

The *Pope Marcellus Mass* is written in an imitative polyphonic style roughly similar to that of Josquin's motet, *Ave Maria,* discussed in Chapter 10. Palestrina's Kyrie, however, is more continuous in design, less segmented into discrete phrases. The movement is divided into three large sections, corresponding to the three lines of the text:

Kyrie eleison	Lord have mercy
Christe eleison	Christ have mercy
Kyrie eleison	Lord have mercy

Each section ends with a full stop. These are the only points in the movement where the contrapuntal motion is broken and the voices come together rhythmically; otherwise, every element of the music is subordinate to an overriding sense of continuity and transcendence. The two words of each section are incessantly repeated in staggered rhythms through the ensemble, but are always clearly audible. Melismas are short, limited to occasional five- or six-note runs during which other voices reiterate the text. The call for mercy is intoned again and again, both in the individual voices and in the ensemble as a whole. Personal and collective belief merge into a single persistent but composed plea, eloquent in its restraint.

The individual voices are similar in melodic style, sharing the same motives and moving almost entirely in consonant intervals. No single voice is ever more prominent than the others. The voices frequently cross in pitch range and overlap in phrasing, blending into a single indivisible web of sound. The number of voices singing at any one time keeps changing, but the tone of the music remains constant. Rhythmic pacing is also uniform, lacking accents or embellishment. Nothing disturbs the flow of the music or interrupts its continuous development of motives.

Palestrina's Masses are supra-personal, catholic (as well as Catholic) expressions of faith. The individual lines are important for their contribution to the overall expression. Each voice mirrors the same thought and tone. The effect is like a "polyphonic chant"—sounding somewhat as though different portions of a single long melody were sounded simultaneously by many voices.

Madrigal

The Italian **madrigal** was the principal secular vocal genre of the late Renaissance. Madrigals were entertainment pieces often conceived for impromptu performance by aristocratic amateurs. They were written for small *a cappella* ensembles of between four and six voices, with a single singer on each part. The medium was flexible, however. Instruments occasionally doubled or replaced singers, and well-known madrigals were transcribed for solo and chamber instrumental performance. Madrigal texts cover a broad range of subjects. Many recount the delights and pangs of love. Others are satiric, humorous, or concerned with mundane matters of daily life.

Madrigals of the early 1500s were generally written for the enjoyment of the performers rather than for formal presentation before an audience. They featured a simple homophonic style and could be read at sight by accomplished amateurs seated around a table. By the middle of the 16th century the madrigal had evolved into a more complex polyphonic style, with continuous imitation between voices and a broader expressive range. During its final stage of evolution (c. 1580–1620), the madrigal assumed several new forms, reflecting the stylistic tendencies of the early Baroque. Madrigals of this period are often theatrical in conception, exploiting vivid contrasts and word painting within chordal homophonic textures. Many of the later madrigals of Claudio Monteverdi (1567–1643) are virtuosic solo songs with instrumental accompaniment.

During the late 1500s the simpler types of Italian madrigals were widely favored among English aristocrats, and an independent school of English madrigal composers developed. English madrigals are generally light and humorous in tone, homophonic in texture, and highly sectional in construction. Thomas Morley was among the most prolific and celebrated of the Elizabethan madrigalists.

"The Singers," a 16th-century woodcut

"Now is the Month of Maying" by Thomas Morley (1557–1602)

Record Set Side 2, Band 4

Various aspects of the rhythmic, melodic, and textural construction of this madrigal were discussed in Unit 1. The piece, like Palestrina's *Pope Marcellus Mass,* illustrates the Renaissance vocal ideals of a smooth blending of voices and collective presentation of thematic ideas. Here, however, the blend is harmonic rather than contrapuntal. A principal melody in the top voice and a harmonically-governed bass line outline a chord progression that is completed in the three inner parts. None of the voices is accompanimental in character, however; each follows a distinct melodic contour and comprises an important thread in the development of ideas, particularly during the *"fa la la"* passages.

The voices generally move in identical rhythms, declaiming the text in unison. The musical rhythms, although they sound "natural" or "effortless," have been carefully molded to the inflections of the text. Accents and melodic stresses always fall on important syllables. Harmonic motion is rapid, with a separate chord on nearly every syllable, resulting in short phrases and frequent cadences.

The text contains three stanzas, all sung to the same music. Each stanza comprises a two-part design, and the two sections are immediately repeated *(A–A–B–B).* The sections, in turn, each contain a verse and refrain. Formal continuity results from the structural balance between the motives of the verses and those of the refrains, rather than from continuous development of initial motives, as in Palestrina's Mass.

Section:	**A**		**B**	
Texture:	*Homophonic*		*Imitative polyphony*	
Stanza:	1. *Now is the month of maying . . .*	*fa la la . . .*	*Each with his bonny lass . . .*	*fa la la . . .*
	2. *The spring clad . . .*	*fa la la . . .*	*And to the bagpipes . . .*	*fa la la . . .*
	3. *Fie then why sit we . . .*	*fa la la . . .*	*Say dainty nymphs . . .*	*fa la la . . .*
Form:	*Verse*	*Refrain*	*Verse*	*Refrain*
	half stop	full stop	half stop	full stop

The individual parts are easy to sing. The piece can be given a polished performance with minimal rehearsal. Like most madrigals, it is meant to charm rather than to inspire or overwhelm. Rhythmic verve (strong pulse and metric accentuation) and simplicity of expression are among the most winning features of the music.

The Baroque Period: Handel and Bach

The many stylistic innovations and changes that occurred during the Baroque period led to new approaches to vocal writing. Techniques first developed in 17th-century operas were eventually applied to the other major vocal genres. The emphasis in opera is on the portrayal of sharply drawn emotions through solo singing. Most operas contain two types of solo numbers, distinguished by their very different approaches to text setting. In **recitatives** the text is delivered rapidly, in a style that is often midway between speech and melody; there is a separate note for each syllable, and the melodic contour imitates natural speech inflections. **Arias,** by contrast, are songs with a clear formal outline and, usually, a lyrical character. Large-scale Baroque vocal works, such as cantatas and oratorios, consist of a series of recitatives and arias and occasional ensembles. **Ensembles** are numbers for two or more soloists or for chorus. They are often similar to arias in form but are usually more dramatic in tone.

Baroque vocal music is almost always supported by *basso continuo,* as discussed in Chapter 10.[1] The *a cappella* ideal of the late Renaissance sounded pallid and austere to 18th-century ears. In the Baroque, it was replaced by a striving for full sonorities and rich textures, particularly in ensemble numbers. There was relatively little distinction between vocal and instrumental melodic styles. Baroque vocal melodies frequently contain long ornamental passages that reflect the influence of instrumental music. These melodies require more forceful projection and a heavier timbre than the light, pure vocal quality favored during the Renaissance. Sacred and secular music of the period is generally indistinguishable in style. Bach frequently incorporated pieces from his secular compositions into later sacred works, changing only the text.

The Oratorio: Handel

Although often considered "the greatest English composer," George Frideric Handel was in reality an international figure, and his later works represent a fusion of the Baroque resources of German instrumental music, Italian opera, and English choral traditions. Born in northern Germany in 1685, he spent his early twenties in Italy, where his operas were widely acclaimed. After a brief return to Germany, he settled in London in 1712 and remained in this adopted city until his death in 1759.

A worldly and sophisticated man, Handel openly desired fame and carefully tailored his works to the musical preferences of his audience. When he arrived in London, Italian opera was the favored form of musical entertainment among the aristocracy, and Handel established his reputation as the preeminent composer in this medium. During the late 1720s, however, his success began to wane. In 1728, John Gay's *The Beggar's Opera,* an unassuming production with simple arias and an English text, captivated London audiences, signaling a shift in public taste. To his dismay, Handel found his lavish serious operas becoming commercial white elephants. By

[1] Basso continuo was the practice in which keyboard players improvised harmonies over a bass line according to chord abbreviations supplied by the composer.

George Frideric Handel

1737 his operatic company was near bankruptcy and the composer was physically exhausted by the effects of a stroke. In attempting to reach a broader public, Handel began writing oratorios. In 1741, when the dismal failure of his final opera had left him despondent and financially near ruin, he composed *Messiah,* the fifth of his Biblical oratorios. In the years that followed he produced a series of superbly crafted oratorios, and through these works he gradually regained his position as England's leading composer.

The **oratorio** originated in Italy as a music drama depicting the lives of Biblical characters and saints. By the late 17th century it had become a widespread form of aristocratic entertainment in Italy and Germany, performed privately for the nobility as a spiritually edifying substitute for opera during Lent. Oratorios are not church music, but rather concert works on a sacred subject for vocal soloists, chorus, and orchestra. They are performed without stage action, costumes, or sets, making them considerably cheaper to produce than opera.

The English oratorio tradition begins (and, for most non-English listeners, ends) with Handel. The familiar subject matter and English texts of Handel's oratorios made them attractive to middle-class audiences. Most of his 26 oratorios are based upon stories from the Old Testament. Even *Messiah* contains more quotations from the Old Testament than from the New. The solo arias of Handel's oratorios are similar in form and style to his operatic arias. Most are preceded by a recitative. The chorus, however, assumes much greater prominence in Handel's oratorios, and choral numbers frequently take the place of solo arias. Handel was a master of effective choral writing, creating rich textures that exemplify the Baroque love for brilliance of sound. Most of his choral numbers feature a driving rhythmic momentum and a dramatic interplay between chorus and orchestra.

Handel's music is less rigorously contrapuntal than Bach's and employs dissonance more sparingly. The texture of his choruses usually alternates between polyphonic and chordal passages. Imitative polyphonic passages are frequently a "wind-up" to brilliant homophonic tuttis. Handel's arias and choruses are generally sectional in construction, based upon contrast and balance of ideas rather than continuous development. Periodic strong cadences separate the principal ideas of a number.

Messiah. Composed in the amazingly brief period of 24 days, *Messiah* is in many ways unique among Handel's oratorios. It is a reflective work with no story line, based entirely on scriptural texts rather than on poetic paraphrase. The text was compiled from various books of the Bible by Charles Jenner, a minor writer who collaborated with Handel on several oratorios. Unlike the Passion, a related Baroque genre which depicts specific events of Christ's life by setting selected passages from one of the gospels, *Messiah* is a broader dramatic commentary upon the prophecy and fulfillment of man's redemption. The work is divided into three parts:

I. The prophecy and coming of the Messiah
II. The salvation of mankind through the sacrifice of Christ
III. Thanksgiving for the ultimate victory over death through faith

After the London premiere of the work, Handel was quoted as saying that he would be disappointed if he had only entertained his audience, for he had hoped to inspire them to be better people as well.

Listening

"For Unto Us a Child is Born" from Messiah *by George Frideric Handel (1685–1759)*

Record Set Side 6, Band 6

One of the most brilliant choruses of *Messiah* is the twelfth number of Part I, "For unto us a child is born." The four-voice chorus is preceded by a recitative ("For behold, darkness shall cover the earth") and an aria for bass voice ("The People that walked in darkness") that somberly depict humanity's longing for deliverance. The chorus, which announces the arrival of the promised Messiah, projects a complete contrast in mood, one joyous and full of hope:

Musical sections	*Text*
A	"For unto us a Child is born, unto us a Son is given,
B	and the government shall be upon his shoulder; and His Name shall be called
C	Wonderful, Counsellor, the Mighty God, the Everlasting Father, the Prince of Peace

The formal outline of the number centers around the varied repetition of three themes:

Introduction *(orchestra)* –*A*–*B*–*C*–*A*–*B*–*C*–*A*–*B*–*C*–*A*–*B*–*C*– *Postlude* *(orchestra)*

varied repetitions

Introduction. The orchestral introduction establishes the jubilant tone of the piece and introduces two motives. The first will be developed by the chorus into the theme of the *A* sections. The second, a driving rhythmic figure in continuous sixteenth notes, will return in the strings during the climactic tutti passages of the *C* sections.

A. "For unto us . . .". The principal theme is stated by the sopranos, then successively imitated with variations by the tenors, sopranos, altos, and basses. The second soprano statement and the final statement in the basses contain an elaborate melisma on the word "born" that contrasts with the straightforward syllabic setting of the rest of the section:

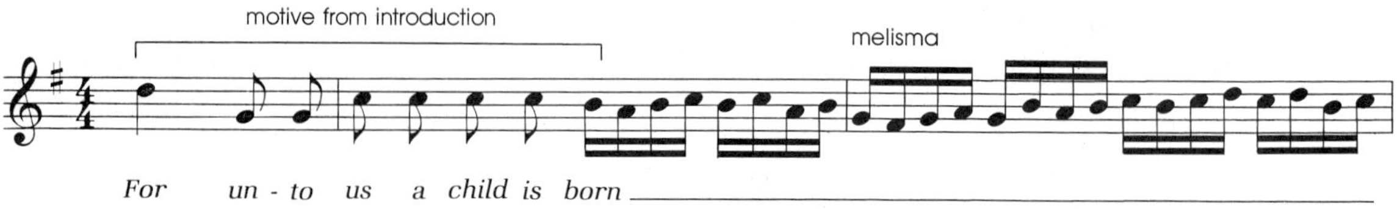

The alternation of syllabic and melismatic passages, frequent repetition of the text, and intermittent (rather than continuous) use of imitation are typical features of Handel's choral style. Despite the strong rhythmic drive of this section it evokes a mood of restraint. The dynamic level remains soft, and the imitations of the theme are widely spaced so that no more than two vocal lines are ever heard at once. The music frequently seems ready to break into a full tutti, but Handel delays fulfillment of this expectation. By storing up energy he builds a mood of growing anticipation.

B. "And the government . . .". The shorter *B* section is built around repetition of a new phrase in dotted (long–short) rhythm. Imitation is widely spaced at first, then comes at increasingly shorter intervals until all four vocal parts come together. The entire passage is a textural and dynamic swell, building tension to a point where it must be released.

C. "Wonderful, Counselor . . .". The brilliant texture of this climactic passage illustrates Handel's distinctive style of choral–orchestral tutti writing. The words are set syllabically. The voices sing in identical rhythm, with strong punctuations. Rhythmic momentum is maintained by a sixteenth-note figuration pattern in the violins. The entire passage is firmly rooted around repetition of the tonic chord.

The rest of the movement consists of the cyclical recurrence of these three sections, during which variation procedures and key changes are introduced. Despite the simplicity of the unchanging motivic material and the considerable textual and musical repetition, there is great variety to the presentation. The individual sections retain freshness because of the incisive quality of the original ideas, the smooth transitional links that connect contrasting passages, and the varied forms of their presentation. As in almost all of the choruses of *Messiah,* Handel achieves both brilliance and directness of expression.

The next number ("Pastoral Symphony") is a quiet, delicate orchestral piece. Coming after the triumphant proclamation of the chorus, it creates a very different aura—one of mystery and awe—to depict the actual humble circumstances of Christ's birth. Handel was a master of timing and dramatic contrast. The powerful expression of "For unto us a Child is born" is particularly striking when heard in its context within the oratorio, framed by the two sombre bass solos that precede it and the hushed orchestral interlude that follows.

Bach's Vocal Music

Bach's vocal works are less specifically tailored to the idiomatic qualities of the voice than those of Handel. Although his music contains occasional examples of word painting, Bach was generally less concerned with word-by-word declamation of the verse than with rendering its overall tone and meaning. His settings are generally melismatic, and the emphasis is on the continuous development of ideas into a rich musical fabric and expansive design. We are sometimes less aware of listening to music that is specifically "vocal" in character than of hearing a musical statement, perfect in every detail, that takes on added meaning because we are hearing it *through* the human voice.

The major genres of Bach's vocal works include:

Cantatas. Generally lasting twenty to thirty minutes, the cantata resembles an operatic scene in format, containing a series of recitatives, arias, duets, and choruses. It may be on either a sacred or a secular text, and features one or more vocal soloists, small orchestra, and often a chorus. The subject matter is usually serious in nature, but there are numerous exceptions. The *Coffee Cantata,* for example, concerns a headstrong girl's intemperate love of coffee. In desperation, her irascible father promises to find her a husband if she will curb her indulgence. Undaunted, she resolves to love husband and coffee equally. Bach is thought to have composed over 300 cantatas, of which about 200 survive. His church cantatas, originally performed on Sundays and Feast Days at St. Thomas Church, are better known today.

Passions. Bach's two surviving Passions, the *St. Matthew* and *St. John,* are much longer works for narrator, soloists, chorus, and orchestra. Gospel passages are set in recitative. The arias and choruses are generally set to contemporary poetic texts.

Chorales. Chorales are Protestant hymn tunes dating from the 16th and 17th centuries intended for congregational singing. Bach composed over 300 harmonized settings of these traditional melodies, incorporating them into his cantatas and Passions and using them as the basis for organ works.

The Mass in B Minor. The *Mass in B Minor,* one of Bach's most monumental works, was composed intermittently during his years at Leipzig. In 1733 Bach aspired to be appointed composer to the (Roman Catholic) court of Dresden, and he submitted the Kyrie and Gloria as evidence of his compositional skill. The Credo, Sanctus, and Agnus Dei movements were added in later years. The *Mass* was completed no sooner than 1747 and, to our knowledge, was never performed in its entirety during Bach's lifetime. It is a concert work, far too long to be used in a Eucharistic service, and Bach had neither the facilities nor the financial resources to produce a concert performance. The work was a labor of love, the product of a transcendent musical and spiritual vision heard only in his mind.

The five movements of the *Mass* are divided into independent sections of choruses, arias, and duets. Several of these sections were reworkings of pieces from his earlier cantatas. Such borrowings by composers from their own and others' works were common during the Baroque era. Originality *per se* was less prized than in later periods, and copyright laws were unknown. Composers faced strict deadlines, and major works often gathered dust after their initial performances, leaving the composer to wonder, "And now what am I supposed to do with all this music that took so long to write?" Handel's "For unto us a Child is born" was such an adaptation, based upon a duet from one of his early operas.

As in *Messiah*, it is the chorus that dominates the *B Minor Mass*. Unlike Handel's oratorio, however, Bach's *Mass* contains no recitatives or purely instrumental movements, and the texture remains contrapuntal throughout. The polyphonic lines are longer and more continuous than in Handel's music, resulting in a denser, more uniform musical fabric. Rhythmic momentum is continuous, and cadences are widely separated.

Listening

"Kyrie" from the Mass in B Minor *by Johann Sebastian Bach (1685–1750)*

The Kyrie movement of the *Mass* contains three separate numbers:

(1) *Kyrie eleison.* A choral fugue with orchestral accompaniment.
(2) *Christe eleison.* A duet for two sopranos with violins and continuo.
(3) *Kyrie eleison.* Another fugue for chorus with orchestral accompaniment.

Kyrie eleison. The opening number, a five-voice choral fugue (the sopranos are divided into two groups), instills the mood of profound yearning after the eternal that pervades the entire *Mass.* A four-measure homophonic tutti proclaims the text in a series of resounding chords that rise slowly from the tonic to the dominant. A long, serene orchestral introduction follows. The theme that will serve as the subject for the choral fugue is stated twice in the woodwinds, then in the basso continuo, against free contrapuntal lines in the strings.

Having stated the text and the theme in a double introduction, Bach then combines these two elements in the choral fugue. The exposition presents six statements of the theme in the voice order T–A–S1–S2–B–S1:

The exposition leads without break to a long passage of freer imitation among the five vocal lines. This passage is similar to a normal fugal episode in its imitative style and fragmentation of the theme, but it is unusual in its considerable length and maintenance of the full tutti texture. Bach interprets the Kyrie as an eternal prayer without beginning or end, uninterrupted in thought. By the continuous use of imitative tutti textures he welds the exposition and episode into a seamless, homogeneous entity. The choral parts eventually come to a full-stop in the minor dominant key, but rhythmic motion and imitative fragmentation of the theme continue in an orchestral interlude.

In a second complete six-voice statement, the subject is heard at ever higher pitch levels. The order of entrances is B–T–A–S1–S2–S1. This series of statements is followed by another extended continuation during which the imitation and five-voice texture are maintained. A final statement of the subject in the basses and a brief codetta bring the fugue to a resounding cadence on a tonic major triad.

Christe eleison. The *Christe* section provides textural relief from the massive choral textures of the surrounding fugues. It opens with a gentle, winding violin melody that will recur several times as a contrapuntal accompaniment to the vocal lines. The two soprano lines alternate between a contrapuntal interplay and passages in which the voices move in parallel motion, blending into a single textural thread. Phrases are shorter than in the Kyrie (though still long by common standards) and cadences are more frequent. The prayer to Christ, man's intermediary, is more tender, less solemn and awestruck, than the preceding supplication to God the Father.

Kyrie eleison. The third number of the movement is a four-voice choral fugue built around a subject that is highly compressed in both pitch range and length:

The five vocal entrances of the exposition occur in the order B–T–A–S–(interlude)–B. Imitation continues, with the same order of voice entry, in an episodic passage based on the following phrase:

A four-voice return of the subject features a common fugal device, called *stretto,* in which the second statement begins almost immediately after the first. The time distance between imitations has been condensed. Alto–tenor and soprano–bass statements are paired in stretto, producing a sense of further compression within an already succinct theme:

Another episodic continuation featuring imitation of this motive follows, leading to a final statement of the subject by the sopranos and a concluding codetta.

The vocal style of this fugue is at once soaring and uncompromising in contrapuntal rigor, bringing to mind Stravinsky's observation that "the more art is controlled, limited, worked over, the more it is free." The six words of the text are spun into a movement of vast scope, but one in which every note is structurally controlled and contributes to a clear formal design. There is an unfathomable quality to the music that seems to encompass the countless meanings and nuances inherent in the simple text. Listeners can respond deeply to the music in very different ways. Some find it a glorious affirmation, others feel an unutterable sadness in the music, and still others are most struck by a feeling of reverence or transcendence.

Solo Song: The German Lied

Although solo song is common to all periods and societies, it has not always been a major genre of public performance. Our knowledge of the songs of antiquity is sketchy, since this music was rarely notated and only a few fragments (mostly texts) survive. The 12th and 13th centuries marked a period of intensive song composition and performance in France and Germany, and several hundred of these songs, mostly concerned with courtly love, have come down to us. By 1300, solo songs were normally accompanied by instruments. During the latter half of the 15th century, however, the accompanied solo song was superseded by the part-song for three or more voices, a genre that culminated in the vast repertoire of Renaissance chansons and madrigals. Solo singing rose to prominence again during the Baroque era, but it generally took the form of arias and recitatives incorporated within operas and other large-scale works.

Renewed interest in accompanied solo songs began in Germany during the second half of the 18th century. In contrast to most arias, these *lieder* (pronounced "*leed*-er"; German for "songs") are characterized by a simplicity and directness of expression. The vocal melodies often have a folklike quality, and the piano accompaniments are unpretentious. Haydn, Mozart, and Beethoven composed many lyrical songs in this vein, but it was Franz Schubert who devoted a major portion of his creative energy to the genre and established the basic format and style of the Romantic lied.

The 19th century was a period of unprecedented song production in Austria and Germany. The lied became a major genre—an alternative to opera for several leading composers—and many of its features were carried over into instrumental music. The lieder of Schubert, Schumann, Brahms, Wolf, and others are character pieces for voice and piano, generally sustaining one or two moods and cast in simple formal outlines. The lyrical texts, emphasis on personal expression, and modest technical demands of these songs made them ideally suited to professional or amateur performance before a small audience. Lieder were performed more often in the home than in the concert hall.

The Lieder of Schubert

Franz Schubert

With the exception of a brief, dismal tenure as a schoolteacher (1814–17) Schubert held no job, but devoted himself exclusively to composition. Unlike Beethoven, whose financial and artistic independence he wished to emulate, Schubert achieved relatively little public recognition. He taught piano, realized a small income from the sale of his works, and received support from a small circle of friends. All the while he composed prolifically, writing 144 songs in 1815 alone. "When I have finished one piece, I begin another," he remarked.

Although Schubert excelled in orchestral, chamber, and piano genres, his unique achievement is found in his more than 630 lieder. He ranged freely among lyric German poets in his search for texts, producing songs of surpassing beauty on both sublime and undistinguished poetry. (Hugo Wolf believed that some of Schubert's most moving songs were written to verse of the quality of a cheese label.) Three Romantic poets who inspired many of his greatest efforts were Johann Wolfgang von Goethe (1749–1832), Johann von Schiller (1759–1805), and Heinrich Heine (1797–1856). Schubert's settings are distinguished by a masterful balance between poetry and music, voice and piano, spontaneous expression and formal clarity. His songs are concentrated in gesture and often seem to distill perfectly, or even sharpen, the qualities of the verse. Liszt observed that Schubert was, simply, "the most poetic musician who ever lived."

In the lieder of Schubert's predecessors the piano generally played a secondary role, outlining harmonies with minimal embellishment. In his own songs the piano became an equal partner to the voice, with its own motives and development of ideas. Schubert's lieder generally begin with a short piano introduction that sets the poetic mood of the song and establishes a figuration pattern that will run throughout the accompaniment as a unifying idea. The introduction is balanced by a piano postlude at the end of the song that brings the figuration pattern to conclusion and summarizes the emotional quality of the piece.

The body of the song may be cast in any of a number of common formal outlines. In many lieder, each stanza of the text is set to the same music, so that the identical (or nearly identical) vocal melody is repeated three or more times. Commonly called **strophic form,** this is the simplest type of song structure, characteristic of hymns, popular and folk songs, and lieder in which a single mood is sustained. In some strophic lieder, the music undergoes significant alteration during one or more stanzas, such as a shift from minor to major, creating a changed expressive tone. *Three-part(A–B–A)* forms, as in "Der Lindenbaum" from *Die Winterreise* (see pages 116–118), are common when the text features a dramatic contrast between two moods. *Through-composed* designs contain a different musical setting for each stanza; the musical structure evolves continuously, introducing new ideas from beginning to end.

Within these basic outlines Schubert achieved an immense variety of formal designs, shaping the development of each song according to his dramatic conception of the text. Many of his songs are formal hybrids, incorporating, for example, elements of both strophic and through-composed organization.

Listening

"Gretchen am Spinnrade" ("Gretchen at the Spinning Wheel") by Franz Schubert (1797–1828)

"Gretchen at the Spinning Wheel," composed to a text from Goethe's drama *Faust* in 1814, when Schubert was 17, concerns the musings of a lonely girl who dreams of her absent lover as she spins thread. There are eleven stanzas in the text, divided into three musical groups. The opening stanza serves as a refrain, beginning each group and returning at the end of the song:

Refrain

"Meine Ruh ist hin,	"My peace is gone,
Mein Herz ist schwer,	My heart is heavy,
Ich finde sie nimmer	Never again will I find peace,
Und nimmermehr."	Never again."

Summary of the Text

Refrain, Stanzas 2 and 3. The girl pours out her sense of isolation and longing.

Refrain, Stanzas 5, 6, and 7. Her thoughts turn to her lover's physical characteristics and gestures—his walk, smile, eyes, touch, and kiss.

Refrain, Stanzas 9 and 10. She aches to hold and kiss him again.

Refrain

Schubert achieves unity of mood through continuous repetition of a one-measure figuration pattern introduced in a brief piano introduction:

The pattern is broken only at the dramatic climax of the song: *"und ach, sein Küss!"* ("and oh, his kiss!"). Like many of Schubert's accompanimental motives it has a double programmatic significance, portraying both the hypnotic hum of the spinning wheel and Gretchen's agitation.

The refrain verse is another unifying feature, always set to the same music, and framed by piano interludes before and after each appearance. The other verses receive freer musical treatment, introducing new motives to portray the changing tone of the text. The song contains elements of both strophic and through-composed organization: exact repetition of the refrains but new musical settings for the other verses. In this way, Schubert tailors the music to the inflections of each line but also relates the various images back to the central thought of the text. The song is an interior drama. No one watching the girl quietly spinning would suspect the inner ferment of her thoughts, or realize that her heart is breaking.

Listening

"Der Erlkönig" ("The Erlking") by Franz Schubert (1797–1828)

"The Erlking," one of Schubert's most dramatic songs, was written a year after "Gretchen at the Spinning Wheel." Goethe's text is an interpretation of an old legend that tells of a father riding home on horseback through a stormy winter's night, carrying his son in his arms. The boy hears the voice of the mysterious forest king calling to him. His father, who hears nothing but the horse's galloping hoofs, vainly tries to calm the child's fear. As the Erlking persists in his seductive entreaties, the boy's terror intensifies and his father spurs the horse on ever faster. The story is told through four distinct voices: narrator, father, boy, and the Erlking.

Schubert's setting of this ballad is a through-composed design that grows in tension until the final climax. It is unified by an urgent piano figuration pattern, relentlessly drummed in, beginning in the piano introduction. Driving triplet rhythms in the right hand over an ominous bass motive portray the galloping of the horse and the Gothic frenzy of this wild ride into the night:

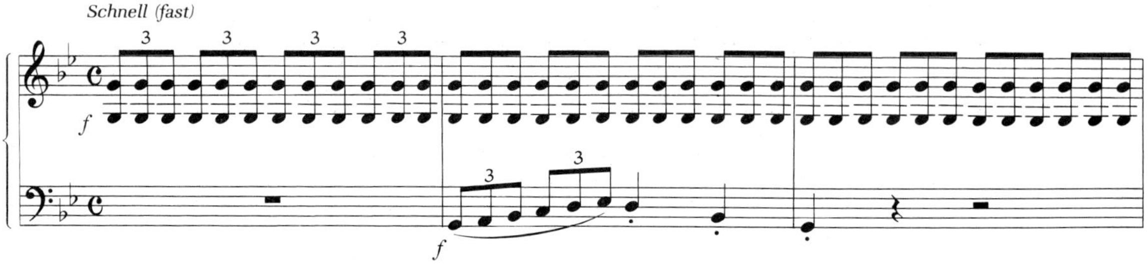

If the piano motive sounds familiar, it is with good reason. It was widely employed by commercial musicians earlier in this century and still pops up from time to time in unlikely surroundings. Silent-movie organists twisted it into a hackneyed motif to announce the appearance of the villains (the chaps with the curled mustaches), inciting high-spirited boos and chuckles. Heard out of context, it now has a rather musty, overly familiar quality. In Schubert's original setting, however, the much-abused motive retains remarkable freshness. There is nothing sleazy, melodramatic, or humorously ironic in its usage here. The motive is incisive, setting and maintaining a mood of chilling terror. The Erlking is no farcical "heavy," but a spiritual evil: the force of death.

Schubert exploits differences in vocal range, harmonic and textural accompaniment, and melodic style to keep the four characters distinct. The father's part is set in a low range, and the child's in a high register that keeps rising throughout the song as his panic increases. In addition, the harmonic sonorities are more dissonant during the boy's passages:

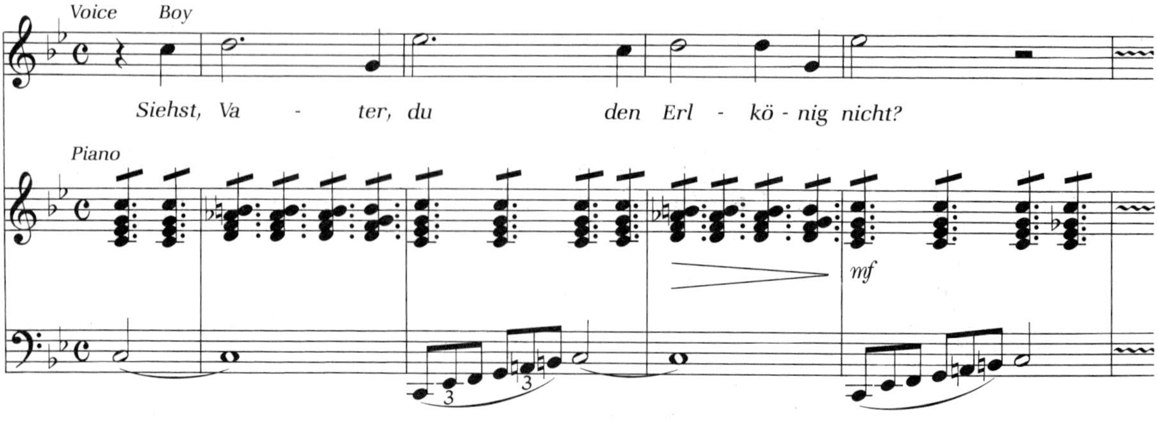

At the entrance of the wily Erlking the tonality shifts to major. The vocal line grows lyrical, and the rhythmic accompaniment becomes lilting. The Erlking's mock assurances are musically depicted by similar means throughout the song.

Toward the end of the piece the pacing accelerates, and pitch and dynamic levels continue to rise, conveying the father's increasingly frantic efforts to reach home. The narrator's final, inevitable pronouncement is declaimed in a barren recitative, accompanied by stark chords: "In his arms, the child was dead."

Vocal Music in the 20th Century

Twentieth-century innovations in vocal music have occurred primarily in the areas of technique and style rather than genre. Solo songs, part songs, cantatas, Masses, oratorios, and other traditional genres have retained continuing vitality and have been adapted to new types of pitch organization and melodic construction. Our present survey of vocal practices concludes with a work based upon traditional frameworks, Britten's *War Requiem*. In Unit Five we will examine vocal techniques and genres developed since World War II that depart more radically from previous practice.

Benjamin Britten, the most widely acclaimed and performed English composer of recent times, is best known for his vocal works. Preferring such familiar genres as opera, song cycle, and cantata, he composed in an eclectic style, incorporating new and old resources within a personal idiom. Traditional scales and harmonies commingle with passages of concentrated chromatic motion, frequent use of ancient or specially constructed scales, and, occasionally, serial procedures. Britten usually began with a dramatic conception of his chosen text, then selected those pitch materials and structural techniques best suited to its realization.

The *War Requiem* (1962) was commissioned to celebrate restoration of St. Michael's Cathedral in Coventry, England, which had been virtually destroyed during World War II. The text is drawn from two sources: the Latin Requiem Mass (Mass for the Dead), and selected poems of Wilfred Owen, a British soldier killed shortly before the 1918 Armistice. The tone of the Owen poems is by turn sorrowful, indignant, and desolate. "My subject is War," Owen wrote, "and the pity of War. The poetry is in the pity. All a poet can do today is warn." Embittered by the endless slaughter of a stalemated conflict, Owen saw war as an abomination that destroyed moral values as well as innocent lives. He spoke for the victims of war who maintained a courage and dignity in the face of devastation in the only way possible, by acting with compassion.

The texts of the Requiem and of Owen's poems both deal with death, grief, and judgment, but from quite different perspectives. The *War Requiem* is infused with a dramatic tension between the hope of atonement (the Mass) and a despair that makes belief in reconciliation appear a pipe dream (the poems). The large performing ensemble is divided into three groups, which generally perform separately but are combined in major numbers:

1. Most of the *Mass text* is set for soprano soloist, chorus, and large orchestra. In these passages, the dead are mourned, God is beseeched to have mercy, and trust in the ultimate triumph over death is affirmed.

2. The *poems* are performed by tenor and bass soloists, respectively representing English and German soldiers, accompanied by a separate chamber orchestra. In these numbers, individuals are seen as powerless to alter the horrors of war, though they are able to salvage a remnant of mankind's divinity by remaining true to their moral convictions.

3. Certain portions of the *Requiem* text, particularly the prayers for peace, are set for boys' choir with organ accompaniment. The quiet strength of these texts and the purity of sound of boys' voices is psychologically far removed from the horrors of the battlefield. These passages are open to different interpretations. They may be heard as the "still small voice" of faith that cannot be extinguished or, more pessimistically, as the innocent trust of children that inevitably will be brutalized by future wars.

Listening

Concluding numbers of the "Dies Irae" from the* War Requiem *by Benjamin Britten (1913–1976)

The long second movement of the work contains several numbers centered around the Requiem text *Dies Irae* ("Day of Wrath"). In its stirring depiction of Judgment Day, this verse is the most dramatic portion of the Requiem Mass. In setting it, composers have customarily let loose with fiery rhythms, programmatic trumpet calls, and emphatic choral declamation. Britten's setting acknowledges these conventions, but it also brings the conflict between atonement and damnation (in both spiritual and worldly spheres) to a head. The movement opens with four numbers in which the Requiem text and Owen's poems are paired in contrasting statements. The second half of the Dies Irae movement, on which we will concentrate, begins after a brief pause.[1]

"Recordare Jesu pie." *Text:* Requiem—Jesus is implored to have mercy. *Ensemble:* four-part women's chorus. *Tempo and musical character:* slow, flowing, ethereal.

After a brief introduction for trumpets and strings, the women's chorus enters in fugal style, presenting four statements of a placid theme at progressively higher pitch levels. The theme is then fragmented

[1] In the recording of the work conducted by the composer (London OSA-1255), the "Recordare Jesu pie" begins Side 2.

and the vocal texture becomes homophonic. The tone is serene and timeless.

"Confutatis maledictus." *Text:* Requiem—"When the wicked are confounded" (basses); "I will kneel in contrition" (tenors). *Ensemble:* four-part men's chorus. *Tempo and character:* rapid, agitated.

A rhythmically animated bass line, accompanied by an interjectory two-note motive in the low brass, is answered by a more lyrical motive developed by the tenors. The two vocal figures are then contrapuntally combined.

"Be slowly lifted up." *Text:* Poem—God is implored to strike down the blasphemous gun of war, "before its sins grow worse." *Ensemble:* baritone solo, with interspersed timpani and brass figures. *Tempo and character:* slow, histrionic, inflamed with anger.

The baritone solo is highly rhetorical, midway between melody and recitation. The vocal line centers around a series of grimly declamatory reciting tones, and grows progressively more frenzied in each of the four phrases. Programmatic timpani and trumpet figures (the drums and trumpets of war, and of Judgment Day) contribute to the ruthless quality of this theatrically conceived number.

"Dies Irae." *Text:* Requiem—All creatures will be summoned to judgment. *Ensemble:* chorus. *Tempo and character:* fast, intense.

The Dies Irae theme, solemn in its original appearance at the beginning of the movement, now returns with vehement force. The text is segmented into one- and two-syllable exclamations, with cross-accents between chorus and orchestra. Fanfare figures in the brass peal through the tutti ensemble. This is the stern answer of the Old-Testament God to the baritone's call for vengeance. A transitional passage at the end of the number is built on a soft echo of the theme; the tempo gradually slows down, becoming halting and finally motionless.

"Lacrimosa." *Text:* Requiem—"Spare me, oh God, on that day of mourning and tears." *Ensemble:* soprano and chorus. *Tempo and character:* slow, imploring.

The chorus declaims the text softly, in the rhythm of the "Dies Irae" theme. Simultaneously, the soprano sings the same words in lyrical but sweeping phrases that grow increasingly effusive and impassioned. The contrast between the sober choral setting and rapturous soprano solo make this one of the most dramatic and moving numbers of the work.

"Move him into the sun." *Text:* Poem—A soldier stands by his dead comrade, shaken with grief at his futile death. *Ensemble:* tenor solo.

In this interjectory recitative, the "pity of war" and its corrosive desolation of the human spirit are laid bare in a melodic style that resembles pure recitation.

The "Lacrimosa" and tenor recitative alternate four times, interrupting and commenting upon each other. Both settings are tender expressions of grief. Together they form a quiet moment of meditation after the fury of "Be slowly lifted up" and "Dies Irae," and present a double mirror through which images of death and sorrow are reflected. The "Lacrimosa" holds out the hope of reconciliation: grief, and the worst horrors man can contrive, can be overcome through faith. The tenor recitative, by contrast, is inconsolable in tone; faith is something for children (boys' choir), not for men in battle.

"Pie Jesu." *Text:* Requiem—"Lord Jesus, grant them rest, Amen."

In a codetta to the movement, the chorus whispers a prayer for peace. The first two phrases cadence on a dissonant interval (C–F♯) that recurs in several numbers of the work to depict lack of reconciliation. The final phrase resolves to a major triad. The resolution, dramatic in its simplicity, underscores the tone that eventually emerges in the work, the belief that human faith ultimately runs deeper than despair. The identical phrase returns at the very end of the *War Requiem.*

Terms and Concepts for Review

relation of text and music
syllabic settings
melismatic settings
idiomatic characteristics of the voice
Mass
a cappella
madrigal
recitative
aria
ensemble
oratorio
lied
strophic form

Chapter 14
Piano Music

The repertoire of solo piano music begins with the Classical sonatas of Haydn and Mozart. Although Baroque keyboard works such as Bach's *Two-Part Inventions* are often performed by pianists, they were conceived for harpsichord or clavichord and are generally most effective when heard in their original medium. The piano was invented shortly after 1700 by an Italian instrument maker named Cristofori, but its primary development during the rest of the century occurred in Germany. The 18th-century piano was smaller than the modern instrument, with more limited pitch and dynamic ranges and a tone color more similar to that of its predecessors, the clavichord and harpsichord. During the 19th century the piano underwent many physical alterations that greatly expanded its technical capabilities. The modern piano has a pitch range exceeding that of the symphony orchestra. Unlike other keyboard instruments, it is highly responsive to variations in touch. On modern instruments, dynamic levels, articulation, tone color, and accents are controlled by the amount of finger, wrist, and arm pressure applied to the keys, and by the use of three foot pedals. Grand pianos are large concert instruments, usually between five and nine feet long, in which the strings are laid out horizontally behind the keys. In the smaller and less expensive upright piano, the strings are stretched vertically.

The increasingly broad technical range of the piano made possible many compositional approaches to the instrument and performance styles. Such composers as Mozart, Mendelssohn, and Schumann were most attracted to the piano's *lyrical* properties. Their melodies are often vocal in conception, necessitating *legato* articulation (smooth connection of notes) and a light but resonant tone quality. To convey the intimacy and finesse of this music requires precision of touch and a relaxed, well-modulated fluency. Beethoven frequently concentrated upon the commanding *power* of which the piano is capable. His denser textures often demand a more forceful, ringing projection. Liszt's virtuosic works, though also forceful, achieve their primary expression through exploitation of *technical facility*. Brilliant runs and highly ornamental textures often create a sense of vast spatial depth in which the listener feels "surrounded" by sounds—all produced by a solitary performer. Impressionist composers explored the *coloristic* potential of the piano, its ability to create "precise sounds" and subtle timbral nuances. Such 20th-century composers as Bartók and Stravinsky frequently concentrated on the inherent *percussive* qualities of the piano that 18th- and 19th-century musicians had sought to suppress.

Clangorous timbres and bruising rhythms of a kind that would have been considered uncouth or abusive of the instrument in former times became new expressive resources. This survey of the piano literature will focus upon the ways in which composers have employed these various idioms within major genres.

The Sonata

The most important genre of piano music is the **sonata,** an extended three- or four-movement work in which a broad range of themes, textures, and moods is interrelated to form a single expansive design. The basic scheme of movements consists of a fast opening movement in sonata form, a slow second movement, an optional minuet or scherzo movement, and a rapid finale.[1] The individual movements are self-contained in form, but are also links within a continuous expressive pattern that determines the overall tone of the work. Sonatas generally present a broad spectrum of pianistic resources, and contrasts in idiom are often as vital to the design and expressive quality of the work as are tonal and thematic contrasts.

Listening

Piano Sonata No. 21 in C Major, Op. 53, ***the "Waldstein," by Ludwig van Beethoven (1770–1827)***

Record Set Side 8

Beethoven, a pianist of great technical prowess, composed 32 sonatas for piano. Many are highly dramatic in conception, featuring vivid contrasts, both within and between movements, that are eventually reconciled into a unified (though many-faceted) musical statement. The *"Waldstein" Sonata* was conceived on a particularly large scale. Published under the title *Grande Sonata,* it demonstrates the extent to which Beethoven enlarged the emotional, harmonic, and idiomatic scope of Classical genres. The long, virtuosic first and third movements tax the full technical resources of performer and instrument. The short second movement is a complete contrast, restrained in tone, sustaining a single eloquent mood.

The first movement, discussed in Chapter 11, is permeated by a sense of struggle, mirrored in the Herculean technical demands upon the performer as well as in the force of structural contrasts. The piano almost seems pitted against itself, as Beethoven draws from it an extraordinary range of themes, textures, colors, densities, and moods. The striking contrasts and vehement energy of the movement are brought to a vigorous final flourish, but not to convincing resolution. At the end of the coda, the placid second theme and hammering first

[1] For more detailed information on the most common formal outlines of the individual movements, see page 147.

theme are juxtaposed in stark contrast a final time. The movement would make a curious statement if played by itself, gyrating between tempestuous and serene ideas, holding them in balance, but providing no emotional release. The movement is brought to formal completion, but the gesture remains incomplete. Continuation—the second and third movements—is necessary to create larger patterns and clarify the dominant tone of the work.

Beethoven originally planned a second movement of equal proportion, but eventually decided that this would stretch the sonata to excessive dimensions. He scrapped his first draft, publishing it separately, and substituted an epigrammatic slow movement based upon a single thematic idea. This *Introduzione* (introduction) functions as a transition to the third movement, ending with an inconclusive half-stop that serves as an upbeat into the following Rondo.

The slow movement contrasts strikingly in tone and style with the outer movements. The opening theme, played very slowly in halting rhythms, lingers on each note. The accompaniment is barren. Registral placement is unusually low and dark. The theme is based on sequential repetition of a three-note motive, drifting through a series of modulations before pulling back to a cadence on the tonic. The same motive is then developed into a more continuous melody with flowing harmonic accompaniment, followed by a varied return of the original deliberate figure. This time the motive grows intense, reaching ever higher over an insistent bass figuration, almost—but not quite—coming to a climax, then gradually dissipating this energy. The gesture is similar to slowly letting the air out of a balloon that was about to burst. The slow movement, like its predecessor, ends with a surplus of unresolved tension.

The rondo finale serves as an extended resolution of the accumulated tension of the first two movements. The formal outline of the movement is *A–B–A–C–A–coda.* The emphatic principal theme is riveted solidly on tonic and dominant harmonies:

Rondo theme

Allegro moderato

Harmony: I V I

Melodically and harmonically direct, formally simple but sharply etched, the rondo theme dominates the movement, providing a decisive answer to the abrupt upheavals of the first movement. For delayed resolution to be effective, it must rebuild earlier tension, this time channeling it to clear structural goals. The rondo theme generates tension through rhythmic and textural means. Rapid figuration patterns, encompassing the full range of the instrument, run throughout the movement. The left-hand part frequently crosses back and forth over the right hand, playing both the bass line and melody. This produces textural depth and brilliance, and sounds almost as though three hands were playing. The *B* and *C* sections, generally in minor, maintain the expansive, positive tone of the principal theme. The extended coda is a summation of the movement, alternating brilliant passagework with restatements of the rondo theme, now heard at double the original tempo. As in the first movement, the pianist must contend with prodigious technical demands, but the struggle now has a heroic rather than a desperate quality.

Character Pieces

Modifications in the construction of the piano during the 19th century extended its pitch and dynamic ranges, increased its sustaining power, and made the instrument more sensitive to variations in touch. As composers explored these new resources, their interests tended to shift away from the procedures of tonal and thematic contrast and integration that were the heart of the sonata, and toward the creation of distinct idiomatic frameworks for the presentation of musical ideas and moods. As a result, the **character piece,** a brief, lyrical work with a simple formal outline and poetic quality, became the most common genre of piano music. Concentration in thematic material and mood is generally underscored by the use of a single pianistic idiom. The simple format of the character piece enabled composers and performers to concentrate more fully upon the creation of finely drawn tone colors and coloristic harmonies, and these two aspects of the music are often closely linked. In the following pages we will look at representative examples of the character piece by Chopin, Schumann, and Debussy. Other masters of the genre include Beethoven, who first explored it, as well as Schubert, Mendelssohn, and Brahms.

Frédéric Chopin

Frédéric Chopin (1810–1849) was born in Poland, but settled permanently in Paris at age 21, living in exile during Russian occupation of his native land. He established early renown as a brilliant concert pianist and composer, but was temperamentally unsuited to a virtuoso's career and retired to a quieter life, composing, performing occasionally for small audiences, and teaching. (Several of his students were English aristocrats whose technique lagged far behind their earnest ambitions. Chopin lamented, "They watch their hands while playing, and play wrong notes with great feeling. Eccentric people, God help them.") Unlike Schumann and Liszt, who wrote first for the piano, then branched out into other genres, Chopin composed almost exclusively for the piano. His major works include three sonatas and two piano concertos, but he is best known for his etudes, preludes, scherzos, ballades, nocturnes, and other masterful sets of character pieces.

Frédéric Chopin

Listening

Nocturne in B♭ Minor, *Op. 79, No. 1, by Frédéric Chopin (1810–1849)*

Chopin's 19 nocturnes are among his most intimate and lyrical works. Most are relatively slow in tempo, reflective, often wistful or melancholy in character—in short, music suited to the quiet of night. Most sustain a single poetic mood and feature a strong textural differentiation between melody (right hand) and harmonic accompaniment (left hand). Harmonic progressions take the form of broken-chord figurations, arpeggiations of widely spaced chords.

The character of *Nocturne in B♭ Minor* is calm and introspective. A single homophonic texture is maintained from beginning to end, and the left hand plays 82 consecutive measures of a broken-chord figuration pattern. The formal outline, like that of most Chopin nocturnes, is *A–B–A'-codetta.* The lyrical *A* theme is simple in outline but embellished with graceful ornamental runs, a characteristic feature of Chopin's music:

The theme is stated twice. The ending of the second statement is recomposed, growing in intensity as the melody climbs higher and the dynamic level swells.

The longer and more repetitive *B* section, in major, is based upon a more rhythmically subdued, deliberate theme. The opening motive of this theme is stated six times, with different continuations at each appearance. A harmonically static transitional passage prepares the return of the *A* theme, which is shortened to a single statement. The work concludes with a brief codetta, ending on a major tonic triad.

The understated eloquence of the *Nocturne in B♭ Minor* is far removed from the commanding power of the *"Waldstein" Sonata.* Working within tight expressive, textural and formal limitations, Chopin concentrates upon subtle inflections: the unique quality of each ornamental run, nuances in the basic mood that result from varied repetitions, and gradations in the pacing-out of a continuous melody, which occasionally pauses on a fragmentary idea. The music is not static—it has its own momentum and points of arrival, but the range of expression is deliberately restricted so that each nuance becomes significant. "Beethoven embraced the universe with the power of his spirit," Chopin observed; "I do not climb so high. A long time ago I decided that my universe would be the heart and soul of man."

Robert Schumann

Chopin's nocturnes and other character pieces are independent numbers which may be performed separately or in groups. Robert Schumann (1810–1856) approached the genre from a different tack, composing sets of character pieces, related by a general poetic idea, intended for complete performance as a cycle.

Schumann's life and music embody all the distinguishing features of early German Romanticism. His original intention to become a piano virtuoso was dashed when his experiments with a mechanical contrivance designed to strengthen digital independence backfired, leaving one of his fingers permanently disabled. Undaunted, he transferred his impulsive energies to composition, writing at first almost exclusively for the piano, and producing groups of character pieces in feverish creative spurts. Schumann was bursting with musical ideas, sketching several works simultaneously, completing only a fraction of them, and including only a portion of these in his published cycles. He exulted in spontaneous lyric expression, avowing that he was "neither a connoisseur of academic harmony nor of counterpoint, but purely and simply guided by nature."

While still a youth Schumann fell in love with Clara Wieck, a gifted pianist and composer and the daughter of his piano teacher. Over the vehement objections of her imperious father, the two were married in 1840, bringing Schumann his greatest happiness. In that year alone he composed

Robert Schumann

over 100 songs. The influence of Clara, and of Schumann's study of Bach and other past masters, broadened the scope of his musical ambitions. He began working in larger forms, contributing major works to the symphonic and chamber repertoires. Schumann was a talented writer and critic as well, editing an influential music journal, championing the works of contemporaries and younger composers, and excoriating sham and philistinism with messianic zeal. Schumann was subject to fits of melancholy and despair throughout his life, and his mental health deteriorated rapidly after 1850. Following a suicide attempt in 1854 he was committed to an asylum, where he died two years later.

Listening

Kinderszenen (Scenes From Childhood), Op. 15, *by Robert Schumann (1810–1856)*

Schumann's character pieces are charming miniature fantasies, simple in structure, whimsical in tone. Simple themes are stated and brought to closure without development or complication. Schumann had a particular affinity for childhood, and for the child's view of the world, which he saw as the essence of Romanticism—wondrous, uninhibited, openhearted. Clara remarked that he often seemed like a child to her (meaning this as a compliment, not a rebuke), and several writers have marveled at Schumann's unique ability to communicate a child's sensations to adults. *Scenes From Childhood,* a cycle of 13 character pieces composed in 1838, is one of his most winning collections. The titles of the individual numbers are merely suggestive, and the music is not explicitly programmatic. The relationship between the poetic images and music is a subtle one. Schumann declared that "the titles were of course added afterward," but also called the cycle "a grown man's reminiscences of childhood." For Schumann, the music and pictorial images were not separate elements, but simultaneous expressions of a single creative idea; "Without our conscious awareness a (poetic) idea often develops along with a musical conception; the eye is busy as well as the ear. . . ."

The pieces are self-contained vignettes, each based on a seemingly independent musical idea and associated with a specific event in a child's day. All sustain a single mood. Most are in two- or three-part form. The outline of the first three numbers is the most common structure:

‖: ***A*** :‖: ***B A*** :‖

Many of the pieces maintain a single figuration pattern; in others, textural contrast is introduced in the *B* section. Although separate numbers, the 13 pieces also comprise a unified cycle. Closer examination of the work as a whole reveals an unsuspected organic conception. A recurrent motive, sometimes obvious, often partially hidden, appears in many of the numbers—an example of the common 19th-century technique of thematic transformation:

1. *"Of foreign lands"*

2. *"A curious story"*

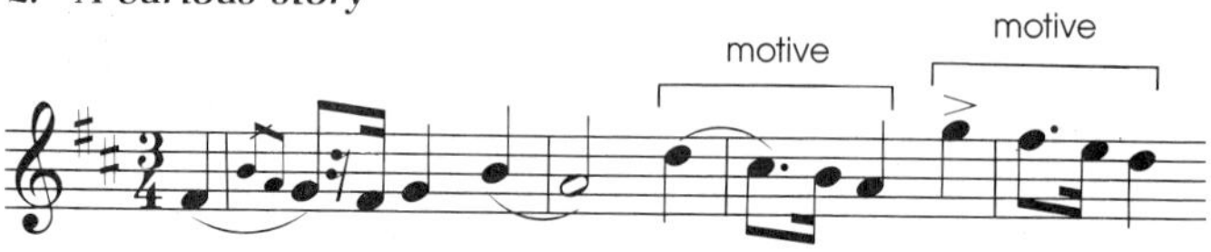

3. *"Blind man's buff"*

4. *"Pleading child"*

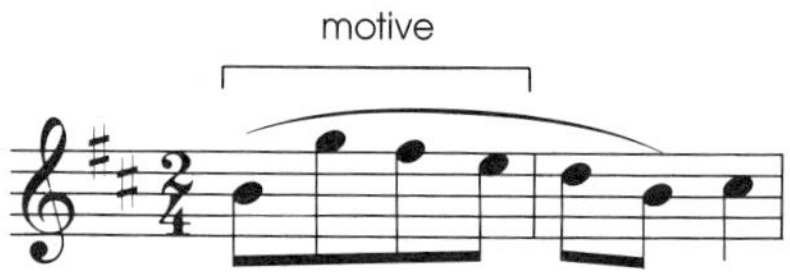

6. *"An important event"*

8. *"Dreaming"*

The eighth number, "Träumerei" ("Dreaming"), is the most celebrated piece of the cycle. It features varied restatements of a particularly touching theme. The cycle as a whole encompasses a considerable range of moods—thoughtful, impetuous, playful, and so on, but with a pervasive gentleness and amiability. The work looks and sounds deceptively simple in technical demands, but requires considerable finesse in execution for the performer to achieve the all-important lyrical tone quality. To hear a sensitive performance of the work, one would never suspect that the piano is an instrument that produces sound by means of hammers thwacking against strings.

Claude Debussy

Debussy's piano preludes, like those of Chopin, are individual character pieces, usually presented in groups of three or four on recitals or played separately as encores. Most carry a picturesque title (added after the composition was completed) and are evocative in character, creating a specific mood through finely etched colors and sonorities. Debussy preferred formally free, through-composed types of structure, and many of his preludes have an improvisational quality.

"La cathédrale engloutie" ("The Sunken Cathedral") from **Preludes, Book I**, *by Claude DeBussy (1862—1918)*

"The Sunken Cathedral," one of a collection of preludes for piano published in 1910, was inspired by an old French legend of a massive cathedral that periodically rises from the ocean floor to the surface. Tone color and careful spacing of sonorities are the most prominent musical elements. Melodic and harmonic ideas are often fragmentary, becoming submerged in the pervading sound quality. At the outset of the piece, Debussy establishes a feeling of vast expanse through three textural ideas: (1) widely spaced sonorities that move at a glacial pace; (2) an ascending five-note motive, thickened by harmonically neutral added tones, which rises—to nowhere; and (3) an ambiguous three-note bass motive, possibly suggesting distorted echoes of ancient chimes. All three ideas are constructed in hollow-sounding intervals of fourths and fifths:

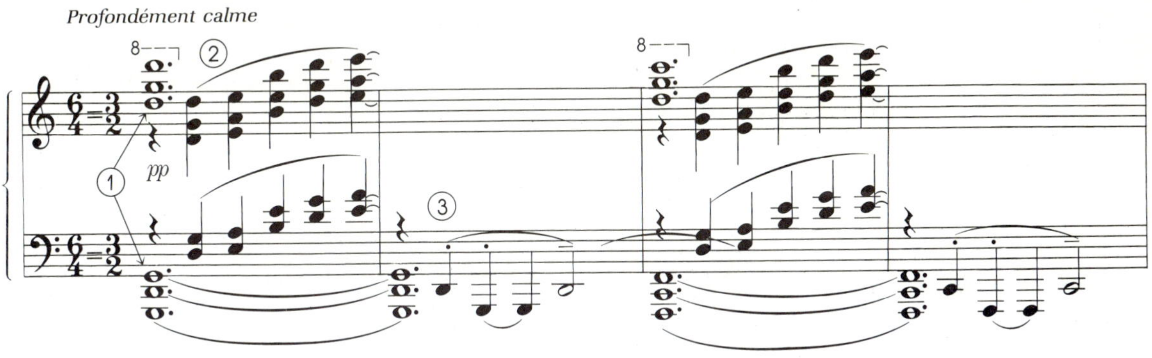

The three ideas blur into a single "precise sound" that sets the initial tone of the music—remote and impersonal. The chords (1) have no functional relationship to each other but are similar in intervallic construction, sustaining a single sound quality. The pitch context is vaguely reminiscent of Medieval modal scales, conveying a distant or perhaps ageless quality. The ascending five-note motive (2), with its archaic parallel motion in all voices, sounds like a fragment of Medieval organum, the earliest form of polyphony. This motive is stated three times, coming to rest on a high tone that is insistently repeated against a new fragmentary melody. The passage lacks any rhythmic or tonal direction. Like an ancient tolling of bells it stands outside of time.

During a varied return of the opening measures the rhythmic pacing and dynamic level increase. Growing momentum crests in the ringing statement of a hymn in massive parallel triads over a booming pedal note in the piano's lowest register:

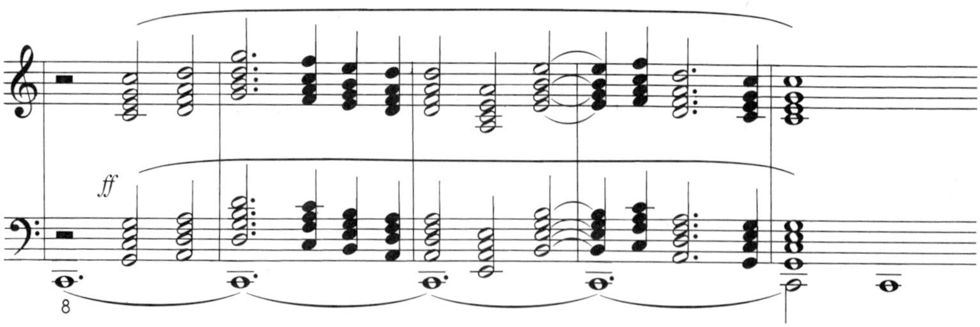

This is not a chord progression (the sonorities are not functionally related, and their connection violates every "rule" of harmony); it is a thickened single line, similar to the five-note ascending motive from which it is derived. The sonorities function texturally rather than harmonically, producing an organ-like richness and grandeur. The immense cathedral rises to full view, reverberating with echoes of ancient rituals.

Textural density gradually subsides as the cathedral slowly submerges again. Earlier motives are recalled, including a muted version of the climactic hymn heard over a hypnotically running bass. The theme grows faint, blurring into indistinct bell-like clusters, and is ultimately absorbed into a prolonged concluding triad. A profound calm unfolds. The cathedral has once again performed its primordial function, restoring peace. Although this cathedral is only a poetic vision, the sense of peace is very real.

Piano Idioms in the 20th Century

The multiplicity of styles that has characterized 20th-century concert music has resulted in a corresponding diversity of piano idioms. One of the most conspicuous features of contemporary piano music is the relish with which many composers have exploited the instrument's percussive qualities. Bartók's *Allegro Barbaro* (1911) was the opening salvo in a movement to wrest the piano from its Romantic pedestal. The work features motoristic rhythms and crunching accents of similar ferocity to those in Stravinsky's *Rite of Spring.* Later composers, seeking to coax new, mostly percussive, timbres from the instrument, have required the performer to reach inside the piano and pluck the strings or to strike them with various types of beaters. Pianists initially resisted such unorthodox techniques, considering them theatrical hocus-pocus, but during the past few decades these devices have passed out of the realm of "special effects" and have become common timbral resources. The piano part of Crumb's *Vox Balaenae* incorporates many such coloristic procedures. John Cage (b. 1912) has experimented further, writing works for "prepared piano" in which various wooden, metallic, and felt objects are placed in contact with the strings to alter their tone quality and articulation.[1]

[1] The evocative percussive colors Cage has created by means of prepared pianos can be heard on Columbia recording M2S-819: *John Cage: Music for Keyboard 1935–1948.*

Other composers have used simpler means to achieve new colors, frequently concentrating upon extreme high and low registers. Like any instrument, the piano responds differently in various registers. In performing Classical and Romantic works, pianists try to minimize these discrepancies and achieve a well-modulated quality throughout the piano's range; 20th-century composers deliberately exploit the timbral contrasts between brittle high registers and the gruff rattle of the piano's bottom register.

Sergei Prokofiev

The early career and works of Sergei Prokofiev bear certain parallels to those of his Russian countryman Stravinsky. Born in 1891, Prokofiev gained early renown for his pianistic brilliance and for the incisive rhythms, pungent harmonies, and ironic wit of his compositions. At the age of 26 he composed his celebrated *Classical Symphony,* a work in which he reinterpreted Classical formal procedures in light of contemporary harmonic and rhythmic idioms. In the same year he embarked upon an extensive concert tour of the United States. Two years later (1920) he settled in Paris, where he collaborated with Diaghilev in the production of several successful ballets. Never fully at home in the West, however, he returned to Moscow in 1933, during a period in which the Soviet government was taking a heavy hand in Russian artistic life. Although Prokofiev was held in high regard, his music was censured for its supposed "abstractness," "complexity," and "Western decadence," and his new compositions were at first poorly received. During his final 20 years, Prokofiev gradually came to grips with the repressive artistic atmosphere of Stalinist Russia, and in such works as his *Symphony No. 5* and the opera *War and Peace* he produced richly communicative music imbued with a distinctly Russian flavor.

Prokofiev's piano compositions include nine sonatas written between 1909 and 1947 as well as five concertos and various incidental pieces. All are highly idiomatic works. Most feature a characteristic mixture of crisp melodic and rhythmic ideas with a lyricism that echoes the 19th century but also has a steeled edge. The sixth, seventh, and eighth sonatas were begun almost simultaneously in 1939. The works contain no programmatic allusions but are often called the "war sonatas," a reference both to the time of their composition and to the sense of contention that pervades all three works. Forced to flee the advance of the German army on Moscow in 1941, Prokofiev took refuge in the Caucasus mountains and completed the three sonatas respectively in 1941, 1942, and 1943. The *Seventh Sonata* is the most strenuous of the three and is one of Prokofiev's most frequently performed works.

Listening

Third Movement from the* Piano Sonata No. 7, Op. 83, *by Sergei Prokofiev (1891–1953)

The *Sonata No. 7* reflects Prokofiev's thorough assimilation of Classical and Romantic traditions as well as his highly individual application of 20th-century resources. The work is unusually concentrated in dramatic form. Whereas most sonatas present a wide range of themes and moods, this one features the cyclical alternation of two pianistic idioms and resulting moods.

Suggested Listening: First and Second Movements. The churning first movement is a modified sonata form design. A jittery opening theme builds to a percussive climax in which a two-note treble motive descends over densely-spaced "drumbeats" in the bass. During an extended transition the texture thins and the rhythmic energy gradually evaporates. The slow, introspective second thematic group begins with a repeated-note figure. Repetition of the theme is followed by another lengthy transitional passage in which the rhythms and dynamic level grow more intense and the texture thickens. The bruising development section is based almost entirely on fragments of the opening thematic group. Propulsive melodic runs, sharp accents, and dense chords are interspersed, and the opening of the second theme is transformed into a booming bass line. In the recapitulation the themes are recalled in reverse order and the rhythmic energy of the abbreviated first group is dissipated.

The second movement, an *A–B–A* design, is serene in overall tone. During varied repetition and development of the *B* theme the music grows heavier and more animated in rhythm, but an underlying restraint and somewhat distant quality remain.

Third Movement. The finale is a *toccata,* a genre characterized by impetuous rhythmic motion and a free formal outline that dates back to the late 16th century. Prokofiev adopted this model in several works, and he employed it here as a means of redirecting the rhythmic energy of the first movement into a more positive statement. In fact, the second and third movements of the sonata represent an expansive continuation of the cyclical structure begun in the opening movement.

Cyclical Design of the Seventh Sonata
R = *driving rhythmic passage*
L = *lyrical thematic passage*

First movement					*Second movement*			*Third movement*
Exposition		*Development*	*Recapitulation*		A	B	A	
1st group	2nd group		2nd group	1st group				
R	L	R	L	R	L	(R)	L	R
Dominant idiom:		R				L		R

The movement begins with an impulsive theme, asymmetric in gesture but rigorous in internal construction; a stream of chords rises slowly over an ostinato bass figure:

Since the bass never plays on the downbeat, the seven-beat metrical pattern is only dimly felt, and the two hands create a continuous series of cross-accents. Driving pulsation is the basis of structure, and the movement lacks any internal rhythmic cadences or points of arrival. The right- and left-hand layers form solid blocks of sound that grind against each other and pull in opposite directions, occasionally crashing together on strident sonorities. Icy melodic fragments in higher registers and thick chords punctuate the rhythmic fabric from time to time, but the recurrent theme is anchored in the lower half of the instrument's range and keeps pulling back to the original bottom-heavy texture.

The middle of the movement maintains the precipitous rhythmic drive but is lighter in texture and higher in registral placement. Return of the opening theme leads to a massive concluding build-up in which the pianist must grab fistfuls of notes in both hands. Rapid chordal alternation between high and low registers and a thundering bass descent prepare the decisive final affirmation of the central tone B♭.

The technical virtuosity demanded in this movement is of quite a different kind from that heard in many Romantic works. While the music is highly percussive, Prokofiev was not seeking to write "machine music," but rather to create a sense of elemental force that, in his words, "comes from the ground." To project the sheer force of this movement, without exaggeration into empty banging, requires as keen a musical sensitivity as that needed to convey Liszt's rhapsodic textures, Debussy's subtle colors, or the poetic lyricism of Chopin and Schumann.

For Further Listening

"I Know That You Know," performed by Art Tatum[1]

Art Tatum (1910–1956) ranks among the major figures in the history of jazz. Through his dazzling technical command and fluid imagination, the nearly blind pianist opened up new avenues of jazz exploration and transcended the stylistic conventions of his time. Tatum concentrated

[1] Available on Columbia recording CS-9655, *Piano Starts Here*.

mostly on the performance of commercial "standards" rather than on original material or contemporary jazz numbers, but he breathed new life into many tattered old tunes with his matchless lyric flair. His improvisational rendition of a number usually consisted of a series of highly ornamental variations around the harmonic structure. These excursions rarely strayed very far from the outline of the tune; Tatum's art was primarily a poetic rather than a developmental one, and the musical substance of his performances generally lies more in the style and idiom in which he presented ideas than in the ideas themselves.

Tatum takes "I Know That You Know" at a flying tempo, first presenting a fairly straight version of the theme, then incorporating increasingly elaborate flourishes within the "windows" of the tune. By the third chorus the emphasis has shifted: the embellishments now become the primary thread of continuity, and bits of the original melody are fitted into the prevailing web of sound almost in the manner of quotations.

In the middle of the number Tatum takes a couple of choruses at half tempo, playing block chords in the accompaniment and ornaments of a more casual nature in the right hand, as though demonstrating, "This is how *other* people play this tune." After this interlude he resumes the original breakneck tempo. Although the rapid scale runs in the right hand are perhaps the most immediately striking feature of the final choruses, the most virtuosic element of Tatum's playing occurs in the cleanly articulated wide leaps and rich harmonies he weaves within the accompaniment. Tatum's virtuosity was never frantic but always relaxed, carefully controlled, and handled with finesse and humor.

Terms and Concepts for Review

piano idioms
- lyrical
- powerful
- virtuosic
- coloristic
- percussive

sonata
character piece
broken-chord figuration

Chapter 15 Chamber Music

Chamber music features a single instrumental performer on each part and is generally performed without conductor. As such, most chamber works share certain characteristics of the vocal part song; both emphasize group presentation of ideas and strive for balanced textures in which each line forms an important, continuous thread within the musical fabric. In fact, the origins of chamber music are closely linked to vocal genres, and can be traced back to the late Medieval period, when motets were sometimes performed by groups of instruments.

Independent traditions of instrumental music developed during the late Renaissance. One of the most important was the performance of dance movements, usually by string ensembles; another was a textural style that developed in Venice, Italy, in which distinct groups of instruments performed in alternation. Several new genres evolved out of these antecedents during the Baroque era. A favored Baroque medium was the **trio sonata,** a work that actually called for four performers, including two treble instruments, a bass instrument, and keyboard continuo. Trio sonatas and similar works for small groups of instruments provided social entertainment in the music rooms of the aristocracy and were often performed by amateurs.

Growing diversity in instrumental practice culminated, at the beginning of the Classical period, in the establishment of distinct genres and styles of chamber and orchestral music. Chamber music of the 18th and 19th centuries consists mostly of works for strings, sometimes with piano, and was generally intended for performance in a room (chamber) before a small audience. These works are similar in format to the sonata and symphony but generally more "economical" in texture, with a more equal division of musical interest among the parts. Expression and structure result largely from an interplay of the lines, and gestures are necessarily smaller and more subtle than in orchestral music.

For the symphonic musician who spends considerable time counting rests (". . . 47, 48, 49, *ta-dah,* 1, 2 . . .") or negotiating harmonic "filler" parts, chamber music can be a welcome change of pace. Chamber works require a sense of teamwork, an understanding of the total musical texture by each player, and a sensitivity to the other parts. They offer the performer a rewarding feeling of complete involvement in the music. Questions of style and interpretation are decided jointly by the performers rather than dictated from the conductor's podium. Players often feel that their total musicianship and training are more fully exercised. Many chamber groups develop a unique rapport and retain the same personnel over many years. Under optimum conditions, the intimacy of the chamber medium is communicated by the players and experienced by the listener as well. This occurs most often when the performance is given in close physical surroundings. A string quartet performed in a cavernous concert hall (or, for that matter, heard over headphones that padlock the listener's head in a vise-like grip) cannot create the same sense of warmth it might achieve in a small hall. Chamber music is a medium to be closely shared—musically and visually—by players and audience.

Composers have taken two distinct approaches to the chamber medium, depending upon the players and the performance situation for which they are writing. Works written for amateur performers usually make modest technical demands. In pieces conceived for professionals, on the other hand, composers have often explored innovative instrumental techniques and means of structure. The composer of symphonic music must allow for the technical limitations of weaker players (though with major orchestras this is much less true today than formerly), and must take into account the many ensemble problems that result when sixteen or more first violinists attempt to play a difficult passage in unison. With a single player on each part, however, rhythmic and pitch discrepancies are less problematic; the composer is less restricted by questions of immediate practicality and may choose to treat the ensemble as a group of soloists. In addition, it has often

been possible for composers, especially those just beginning a career, to receive a quicker and more sympathetic hearing of their music in the chamber medium. The concert manager of an orchestra is apt to look with suspicion upon a new work by a little-known composer. ("We have a lot of people out there, you know. Now are you *sure* this is a masterpiece?") Chamber music performers and audiences are often more open to departures from tradition, perhaps because the concept of group exploration is fundamental to the medium.

Early Instrumental Music

Prior to the late 1500s the music performed by instrumental ensembles consisted largely of adaptations of vocal music. In the 16th century, the favorite vehicle for transcription was the French chanson. The spirited rhythms, lighthearted tone, and comparatively simple textures of these polyphonic songs made them well-suited to arrangement for lute or keyboard solo, and (somewhat later) for groups of wind and string instruments. In the second half of the 16th century, Italian composers carried this practice a step further, composing new works conceived directly for instruments, in the style of the vocal chanson. Called *canzonas* (an Italianization of "chanson"), these unpretentious pieces were similar to their vocal prototypes in their sectional construction and alternation between homophonic and polyphonic textures.

By 1570 Venice had become the leading center of instrumental music. Giovanni Gabrieli (1557–1612), the organist of St. Mark's Cathedral from 1586 until his death, was the outstanding Venetian composer. He wrote an impressive body of both vocal and instrumental works and often combined voices and instruments in his major compositions. Civic ceremonies as well as religious services were held at St. Mark's, and Gabrieli's output was divided evenly between secular and sacred works. The distinctive textural style of his music was influenced by the symmetrical architectural plan of the Cathedral, which was built in the shape of a cross with four wings of equal length. Choirs and instrumental ensembles were divided into two groups placed in lofts on opposite sides of the church. This arrangement made **antiphonal** effects—alternation between opposing groups—a natural resource, one which Gabrieli in particular exploited to great effect.

The Venetian composers were the first to employ spatial separation of parts and contrast between opposing forces as structural techniques. The division of an ensemble into distinct groups, which perform both separately and together, became a distinguishing feature of Baroque music and led to development of the concerto. However, the spatial placement of sound—the structural emphasis on the location of the performers—would remain an isolated technique until well into the 20th century, when many composers began experimenting with unique seating arrangements and wide separation of performers. In recent years, spatial placement has become a vital feature of electronic music.

Gabrieli was an innovative composer. His *Sonata pian' e forte* (1597) was one of the first compositions to specify exact instrumentation and dynamic levels and to feature contrasts of soft and loud dynamic levels. His canzonas were freer in formal outline than those of his predecessors, often consisting of a series of short, self-contained sections each based upon a different melodic idea. Gabrieli's canzonas generally are performed today by brass instruments; in his day, cornettos (wooden instruments with a timbre midway between oboe and trumpet) and sackbuts (forerunners of the trombone) were used, and the ensemble sound was mellower and less brilliant.

Listening

Canzon Septimi Toni No. 2 ***by Giovanni Gabrieli (1557–1612)***

Record Set Side 5, Band 6

This lively canzona, one of many individual numbers from Gabrieli's *Symphoniae Sacrae I (Sacred Symphonies)* of 1597, is one of his most attractive short instrumental works. Written for two five-part ensembles, without indication of instrumentation, the work is often played today by ten brass instruments, with two trumpets, horn, and two trombones in each group. The title translates as "second canzona in the seventh mode," a reference to the modal scale used throughout the piece (the white keys from G to G on the piano keyboard).

Like most of Gabrieli's instrumental works, this canzona is highly sectional in form, and is essentially a through-composed design. However, the opening section returns for an isolated restatement near the end of the piece. (The sectional outline might be graphed—somewhat pedantically—*A–B–C–D–E–F–G–H–I–A–J.*) Each section is based upon a separate idea that is developed briefly, then brought to a cadence. Most of the piece is in duple meter, with marked rhythms and a strong pulse. Two contrasting sections, *legato* (smooth) and lyrical in style, are in slower triple meter. The sporting tone of the work results from the unpretentious verve of its motives and the antiphonal repartee between evenly matched ensembles, comprising a musical tug-of-war. The two groups play separately at the beginning of most sections, then together at the end. Textural alternation, rather than thematic development, is the basis of structure. Contrasting instrumental groups, textures, motives, and (in most performances) dynamics see-saw back and forth in statement-and-response fashion, then are combined in a tutti summation at the end of each section. There is no overall pattern to the work—no single climax or integration of ideas—but rather an engaging series of exchanges between friendly adversaries.

The Classical String Quartet

The modern era of chamber music begins with the Classical period. Works of the late Renaissance, and to a lesser degree Baroque suites and trio sonatas, were often performed by various combinations of instruments; the individual parts generally were not tailored to the particular idiomatic qualities of a fixed ensemble. Classical composers, by contrast, wrote for specific combinations of instruments and sought to gain maximum mileage from the idiomatic capabilities of each. The major genres established in the late 18th century have remained the primary mediums of chamber music down to the present day. These genres include:

Duos: works for string or wind instrument with piano accompaniment. The *violin sonata* is the most common example.

Trios: works for violin, cello, and piano (called *piano trio*), or for violin, viola, and cello *(string trio)*

Quartets: compositions for two violins, viola, and cello *(string quartet)*, or, less commonly, for violin, viola, cello, and piano *(piano quartet)*

Quintets: usually a string quartet augmented by piano *(piano quintet)*, by an additional viola or cello *(string quintet)* or by a woodwind instrument; a less common genre is the *woodwind quintet*, consisting of flute, oboe, clarinet, bassoon, and horn.

The central genre is the string quartet, which has inspired a vast repertoire of masterworks. Quartets of the Classical period are characterized by smooth integration of the four parts into unified, homogeneous textures. Haydn, who composed dozens of quartets over a period of almost forty years, established the basic style and format of the genre. However, his initial interest in the medium was the result more of necessity than of a flash of inspiration. In the summer of 1757 Haydn, a violinist, had only three other string players available with whom to provide musical entertainment for his employers. His earliest quartets are rather lightweight pieces dominated by the first violin, similar in this respect to the textures of his early symphonies. As he continued to explore the new genre, however, Haydn strove for greater equality between the parts. His middle quartets are more serious and substantial in character, and the lower parts participate more expressively in the statement and development of ideas. Haydn's late quartets were influenced by those of Mozart. The four parts became equal in importance (although the first violin still carries the tune most often and is first among equals), and the texture is frequently contrapuntal. Over his long career, Haydn developed the string quartet from a casual pick-up group—one of any number of instrumental combinations of the time that provided background music over the chatter of assembled guests—into a major musical genre. His later works, such as the six quartets of Op. 76, are as broad in scope and emotional tone as his late symphonies.

Listening

First Movement from the* String Quartet in B♭ Major, Op. 76, No. 4, *by Franz Joseph Haydn (1732–1809)

The sonata-form first movement of Haydn's quartet Op. 76, No. 4 (1797), typifies the close-knit textural style and rhythmic energy of the

Classical string quartet. Much of the charm of this and similar Classical chamber works results from the idiomatic string writing, which often makes it seem as though there were more than four performers, and from the constantly changing interplay between the instruments. Haydn combines and recombines the instruments into a great variety of textures. The following are most typical: melody with sustained chordal accompaniment; imitative counterpoint; a pairing of instruments into two alternating groups; passages in which three parts gang up on the fourth (usually the cello); and passages in which the four strings chug along in vigorous unison rhythms, fusing into a single thread.

Exposition. The opening theme begins with a lyrical phrase in the first violin accompanied by a sustained tonic triad in the lower strings:

Texture and rhythm change dramatically at the beginning of the transition. A driving sixteenth-note figure introduced by the first violin turns into a horse race as it passes rapidly back and forth among the three upper strings. The cello provides a harmonically forceful bass to the chase, which ends with a rhythmically forceful full stop.

The beginning of the principal theme of the second key area is similar in texture to the opening theme: a lyrical, sequentially repeated melodic idea, this time in the cello, supported by sustained chords. In the third phrase of the theme, however, the four parts become equally prominent and the pacing accelerates into another animated sixteenth-note passage. A brief closing theme features a pairing of instruments in rhythmic alternation:

Rhythmic pacing increases in a final rush to the full-stop cadence at the end of the exposition. The exposition is then repeated.

Development and recapitulation. The development begins with two tonally varied statements of the opening phrase of the first theme, followed by a longer passage based upon the energetic sixteenth-note figure. The texture keeps changing as the figure ricochets through various registers, instruments, and key centers. The final portion of the development is more subdued, based upon a reworking of the closing theme.

The recapitulation follows the standard Classical format. The end of the closing theme is altered, pausing on a loud, dissonant sonority. A coda, beginning on a fragment of the first theme, builds to a final flourish on the sixteenth-note figure, bringing the movement to a strong rhythmic close.

Expansion of the Classical Genres

Building upon the achievements of Haydn and Mozart, Beethoven expanded the emotional and structural range of the Classical chamber genres to profound new dimensions. Concentrating upon the string quartet at the end of his life, he produced five-, six-, and seven-movement works that are at once intimate in tone and fathomless in their psychological, almost mystical, expressive depth. To most 19th-century listeners these late quartets (Op. 127 through 135) were something of a puzzle, representing a rarified, "private" musical world far removed from the sweeping gestures of the *"Waldstein" Sonata*, the *Fifth Symphony*, and other earlier works. Today, they form a cornerstone of the quartet repertoire, and for many listeners represent a moving final distillation of Beethoven's musical vision.

Within two decades after Beethoven's death interest in chamber music had receded to a low ebb. The Romantic esthetic favored either very large performing ensembles, such as the symphony and opera, or very small ones, such as the lied and piano character piece. Composers tended to specialize in one or more of these genres, and their production of chamber music, which many considered "neither fish nor fowl," dwindled accordingly. Schubert, and such early Romantics as Schumann and Mendelssohn, wrote trios, quartets, and other chamber works of enduring quality based upon the Classical models, but it was Brahms, writing in the latter half of the century, who breathed new life into the chamber music tradition.

Johannes Brahms

Born in Hamburg, the son of a bass player, Johannes Brahms studied piano as a youth. In his teens he supported himself by playing the piano in seamy dance halls and bordellos while studying composition by day. In 1853 he met Schumann and Liszt while on tour as an accompanist. Liszt and Brahms were temperamental and musical opposites and had no further contact; Brahms' association with Schumann and his wife Clara, however, was to affect his life profoundly. In a magazine article, Schumann hailed the 20-year old Brahms in rhapsodic terms. When Schumann was committed to an asylum the following year, Brahms befriended Clara and lived in the Schumann house for two years. He came to love this woman, fourteen years his senior, but after her husband's death the two parted. Brahms' later life was uneventful and lonely. An introspective but crusty bachelor, feared for his caustic wit, he spent his last 35 years in Vienna; a modest income as pianist and conductor was supplemented by royalties from his compositions. A brooding melancholy and, at times, almost unutterable sadness pervade many of Brahms' works, but these qualities are tempered by an inner

Johannes Brahms

strength and reticence of expression. Brahms abhorred sentimentality and programmatic heroics. His slow movements are pensive, with a searing emotional undercurrent just below the surface of clear formal designs. These movements are counterbalanced, however, by passages of robust rhythmic and melodic energy in the outer movements, and the overall tone of his music is positive, never despairing.

Brahms saw himself as the heir of the Classical tradition of Haydn, Mozart, and, in particular, Beethoven. The Beethoven he admired, however, bore little resemblance to the revolutionary figure perceived by Berlioz, Liszt, and Wagner. To Brahms, Beethoven's music had achieved unprecedented expressive power because his innovations enriched, but never overwhelmed, Classical formal procedures. Brahms' own works are cast in traditional instrumental genres: piano sonatas, symphonies, and chamber works in four Classically-structured movements. Brahms' formal designs differ in many particulars from his Classical models, for he sought to extend, and not merely repeat, the traditions he admired. Although his harmonies are chromatic and frequently modulate into distant keys, they are always functional and clearly rooted around a tonal center. His movements are often long, incorporating groups of themes within the major key areas, but the thematic ideas are ultimately integrated into balanced designs. Like Beethoven, Brahms composed laboriously, continually revising his works and subjecting them to rigorous criticism.

Brahms' 24 chamber works were written for a variety of ensembles. In addition to three string quartets, three piano quartets, and three piano trios, he explored the dark, rich timbres of the lower strings in two sextets for pairs of violins, violas, and cellos, and he combined a solo clarinet or horn with strings in other works. The chamber work of largest scope, however, and one of the most Romantic in its emphatic gestures and richness of expression, is his *Piano Quintet*.

Listening

Piano Quintet in F Minor, Op. 34, *by Johannes Brahms (1833–1897)*

Like several of Brahms' major works, the *Piano Quintet* was composed with difficulty and underwent significant changes in format during a series of revisions. The first draft (1862) was scored for string quintet, with added cello. Brahms later rearranged the work as a sonata for two pianos. The final piano quintet version was completed in 1864. The powerful work is characterized by a breadth of conception and an insistent rhythmic drive. Even in the more lyrical sections there is an undercurrent of restless motion that contributes to the strenuous character of the work.

First movement. The sonata-form outline of the first movement was discussed in Chapter 8 (pages 156–158). The expansive formal proportions of the movement are matched by a corresponding expansion in idiomatic resources. Brahms' textures are frequently almost "symphonic" in density and are sometimes virtuosic in technical demands. Textural contrast is an important dynamic element of structure: passages in which the instruments fuse into a homogeneous ensemble, in the manner of Haydn's quartet, alternate with more extended passages in which they pull apart into two or more distinct textural threads. The first theme creates a sense of growing divergence between the piano and the strings. The opening phrase is stated in unison, comprising a point of textural correspondence that articulates the tonal center and principal thematic idea of the movement. In an answering phrase, the piano is set into strong opposition against the strings. This opposition is maintained during a varied repetition of the two phrases, and the piano and strings develop separate facets of the theme. Rapid arpeggios and massive block chords unfold in the piano, while the strings present lyrical melodic phrases and sharp rhythmic punctuations. The concerto-like interplay that develops between the soloistic piano part and the full-bodied string "tutti" dominates much of the movement.

The second tonal area is characterized by a textural dispersion of thematic ideas as the previously homogeneous string choir breaks apart into separate threads. Over tenacious triplet rhythms in the accompaniment, melodic figures pass in imitation and in question-and-answer fashion between the violins, lower strings, and piano. The instruments change function every few measures, rotating thematic fragments and accompanimental patterns. Whereas the opening theme consisted of the concentrated exposition of a few ideas, the themes of the second group have more of a variation quality; they intermingle and evolve together in changing textural relationships. In a closing theme at the end of the exposition, however, the concerto-like quality is reestablished as the strings unite and perform in alternation with the piano.

The development section features a similar branching out in texture; a quiet, homogeneous beginning gives way to passages in which the piano and strings are polarized. The same pattern occurs in the coda that follows the recapitulation. At the end of the coda the opening theme returns and is brought to resolution as the strings and piano, while maintaining their separate functions, build together in a final surge. The effect is somewhat like that of separate parties scaling a mountain from opposite sides and meeting at the top.

Second movement. The slow second movement is warm and lyrical throughout. The piano and strings are integrated into a composite melody-with-accompaniment texture, rather than pitted against each other in the concerto-like fashion of the first movement. This expressive movement in three-part form presents a self-contained tranquil contrast to the stormy rhythmic energy of the other three movements.

Third movement: Scherzo and Trio. The high-strung scherzo is rhythmically the most urgent and incisive movement of the quintet. It is constructed around the continuous alternation of three thematic ideas: *A*, a lyrical syncopated rising line; *B*, a percolating rhythmic motive that dominates the middle of the scherzo section; and *C*, a tutti theme that moves in dense chordal blocks:

A

B

C

The entire movement, including the trio, is built from these three opening ideas. The thematic outline of the movement is:

Scherzo	*Trio*	*Scherzo*
A–B–C–A–B–B (fugal)–*C–A–B* (climax)	*C′*	(repeat)

The scherzo section culminates in a relentless reiteration of motive *B*, with continuous cross-accents between piano and strings. Coy in its original appearance, the motive is here developed into a ruthless climactic passage of jabbing rhythms and headlong propulsion. The convulsive passage is one of immense ensemble difficulty, not recommended for players with high blood pressure.

Fourth movement. The finale of the work begins with a sustained slow introduction in which highly chromatic lines are presented in imitation. After a pause, a faster tempo is established and the cello introduces the principal theme. The movement is a rondo, with alternate appearances of the blithe cello theme and a more lyrical, chromatic *B* theme. The formal outline can be diagrammed:

Rondo (over *A–B–A–B*) *Coda*

slow introduction—*A–B–A–B*—*A′* (faster, $\frac{6}{8}$)–*B′*–codetta

The movement is characterized by a quality of impetuous forward motion that culminates in insistent triplet figurations during the long coda. The coda is a summation of the rhythmic energy that has dominated the work, this time channeling the energy to convincing resolution. Throughout most of the movement the string and piano parts are closely interwoven. The piano often provides harmonic accompaniment to the cello and violin themes and frequently doubles the string parts in climactic passages. The overall textural pattern of the work thus consists of the opposition between piano and strings in the first and third movement, and their coming together in the second and fourth movements.

Texture and Form

Gabrieli's canzona, Haydn's string quartet, and Brahms' piano quintet represent three different textural approaches to the chamber medium. Gabrieli treated his ensemble in conversational fashion, balancing antiphonal statements and replies between matched groups. Haydn integrated the instruments into a cohesive ensemble. A continuous melodic thread, relayed between the first violin and lower strings and supported by harmonic figuration patterns, runs throughout his quartet movement. Brahms chose to emphasize the timbral contrast within the piano quintet. The piano and strings often function as two separate textural layers that develop ideas in adversary fashion. When this process of counterstatement and rebuttal finally gives way to textural integration, the changed idiom heightens the feeling of structural resolution.

The *idiomatic style* of a composition is often a vital part of its formal organization—a feature easily overlooked if we reduce musical form to alphabet soup. The way a composer elects to combine instruments will frequently influence the choice of thematic plans and developmental techniques. Form is, after all, the relation of the parts of a work to the whole, and these parts include instruments and colors as well as themes and tonal centers. Gabrieli's antiphonal textures lend themselves naturally to a sectional formal design, because ideas are quickly brought to completion. Haydn's emphasis on textural integration and continuity enhances our awareness of the balanced proportions of his themes and tonal schemes. The textural opposition between instruments in Brahms' quintet leads to a work of much greater structural tension. It also requires the introduction of more motives, and a more extensive developmental working-out of ideas, to bring this opposition to resolution.

20th-Century Chamber Idioms

Chamber music has achieved unprecedented prominence in the 20th century concert repertoire, particularly during the last thirty years. The instrumental output of many contemporary composers has been concentrated in the chamber medium. The economics of American symphony orchestras, with their severely limited rehearsal time and subscription audiences of generally conservative taste, have led some recent composers to forswear symphonic writing. Many other composers, while not feeling locked out of Symphony Hall, have chosen to devote their energies to chamber works for esthetic reasons. They have found the chamber medium particularly well suited to their concerns for clarity and economy of expression, subtlety of nuance, and idiomatic writing.

The string quartet has remained the most important chamber medium. The quartets of Debussy, Ravel, Schönberg, Berg, Webern, Britten, Ruth Crawford, Elliott Carter, and others have explored the textural and coloristic potential of the quartet in various contemporary pitch idioms. The six quartets of Béla Bartók are modern classics, teeming with imaginative coloristic resources and driving rhythms within lucid, often traditional, structural frameworks.

Suggested Listening

String Quartet No. 4 by Béla Bartók (1881–1945)

First Movement: Record Set Side 12, Band 1

Bartók's fourth quartet (1928) illustrates his adroit blend of old and new techniques. The fiery sonata-form first movement, discussed in Chapter 8, and a companion fifth movement employing related themes and textures frame three interior movements in which the structure grows out of the unique coloristic resources of stringed instruments. The second movement is a coloristic study in which the strings are muted, reducing volume and creating a veiled, ghostly quality. There is little trace of melody or harmony. In their place Bartók presents an interplay of trembling, buzzing, and sliding sounds periodically punctuated by strong pizzicato accents. The strings create a bustling but shadowy undertone of sounds, perhaps reminiscent of the frenetic activity of a beehive. The instruments blend into a single, constantly changing textural web, humming with surface motion.

The slow third movement, in *A–B–A* form, opens with a long, rhapsodic cello solo under immobile sustained chords. The texture is static and distant in tone. The highly ornamental cello line has an incantational quality, rapidly repeating brief figures, stabbing at certain notes, growing alternately intense and icy. The *B* section is more rhythmically animated, with birdcall-like fluttering figures in all parts and a glistening sound quality. The return of *A* is a varied repetition in which mutations of the original theme pass between the cello and violin.

The entire fourth movement is performed *pizzicato.* Several contrasting types of pizzicato attacks are employed, including strumming figures, hard, thumping knocks, and scale-like runs that rebound up and down in imitation. Strong tutti accents flare up at irregular intervals. The dry, percussive tone of the movement has many shadings, ranging from delicate to violent.

In these three movements, Bartók exploits the special timbral capabilities of string instruments. The work could not possibly be performed in transcription by piano, winds, or any other group of instruments, because the musical ideas are indelibly linked to their performance medium.

New Combinations of Instruments

Two works discussed in previous chapters, Boulez' *Le Marteau sans Maître* and Stravinsky's *L'Histoire du Soldat,* illustrate several features that have become characteristic of 20th-century chamber music. Composers increasingly have preferred to write for **mixed ensembles**—heterogeneous combinations of winds, strings, and percussion—rather than for such homogeneous families as the string quartet. Mixed ensembles increase the coloristic possibilities and enable separate lines to stand out clearly in relief so that the listener can more easily follow concentrated contrapuntal or layered textures. Larger ensembles of six or more players have become common, and these ensembles often incorporate many instruments not traditionally associated with chamber music. Many permanent mixed chamber groups now specialize in the performance of contemporary music. Percussion instruments have become staple members of these ensembles. They are valued not only for their obvious coloristic and rhythmic resources, but for their melodic potential as well. Formerly considered severely limited in gesture ("crash," "thud," or "tinkle"), and used only to punctuate climaxes or introduce an element of exotica, the percussion have been freed from such prosaic supporting roles and are now treated as equal members of the ensemble. The composer who was most instrumental in this emancipation was Edgard Varèse (1883–1965).

Edgard Varèse

Edgard Varèse

Born in Paris in 1883, Varèse moved to New York in 1915 and remained in the United States until his death in 1965. Most of his works are for mixed ensembles of between five and thirteen players. A majority were written during the 1920s. Varèse's music was a highly individual achievement, revealing little external influence. He pursued an uncompromising new esthetic, purged of all Romantic "stardust," and sought to capture the rhythmic energy, pace, and temper of 20th-century urban life. He believed that, "Music, which should pulsate with life, needs new means of expression, and science alone can infuse it with youthful vigor."

Varèse strove for what he called the "liberation of sound." In his music, sound quality is the primary focus of expression and structure. "Don't call me a composer," he declared, "call me an engineer of rhythms, resonances and timbres." He preferred the bright, often piercing colors of winds and percussion to the mellower timbre of strings. His music is spatial in conception and generally more "being" than "becoming" in quality. Motives and sonorities are treated as fixed objects, and are often repeated throughout a section with subtle variations or expansion. Each sound has a characteristic registral placement (high, middle, or low) and its own color and inner density. The sounds are not meant to blend but to stand apart, with individual projection and articulation. Varèse's layered textures may be likened to the mobiles of abstract sculpture; each element is distinct, has its own shape, occupies a particular spatial area, and forms one part of a fixed pattern. Bristling with internal energy, the separate elements magnetically attract and repel each other. While pitched instruments remain fixed in content—frozen into immovable blocks of sound—the percussion becomes the free element, developing ideas in almost improvisatory fashion.

Listening

Ionisation *by Edgard Varèse (1883–1965)*

Record Set Side 12, Band 3

Varèse's exploration of the melodic, timbral, and rhythmic potential of percussion was realized in most concentrated form in *Ionisation* (1931), a chamber work for 13 performers who play a total of 35 percussion instruments. *Ionisation* was the first major work conceived for percussion ensemble. Varèse explained his lifelong fascination with percussion as "perhaps a desire to focus interest on harmonies of sound-quality alone—without the distraction of harmonies of pitch."

The instruments are treated in groups, almost in the manner of choirs of related timbres. The ensemble includes instruments of definite pitch (chimes, bells, piano), indefinite pitch (sirens, cymbals, gongs) and without pitch (drums, maracas, castanets, and so on). Varèse exploits the timbral differentiation between sustained metallic sounds (cymbals and triangles) and dry, wooden sounds (drums); he also exploits the relative high-low pitch distinctions between cymbals, gongs, and drums of different sizes. The work is through-composed, consisting of a series of brief sections strung together. Some sections feature a single metallic or wooden timbre; in other passages these contrasting timbres are combined into separate layers of sound.

The work opens with a brief introduction in which sustained, low metallic sounds are most prominent. The basic gestural idea is a swell—a sound that grows louder, then softer. Swells are heard in rapid, overlapping succession in the snaredrum, sirens, and cymbals against punctuated interjections from the drums and maracas. The introduction ends with a sudden surge of metallic sound.

The main body of the piece begins with the statement of a principal theme, a crisp, pulsating, unpitched "melody" for military drum (similar in quality to a snare-drum). A countertheme is presented simultaneously in the bongos. Punctuations in the maracas and cymbals provide a third layer. The dry timbre of drums dominates this section.

A condensed return of the metallic introduction leads to a series of developmental variations on these two rhythmic themes. Echoes of the themes pass through the ensemble, as Varèse gradually introduces new instruments and timbres. The pacing increases and the textures become more dense, but musical interest remains concentrated upon individual pulsating sounds.

Suddenly an abrupt, loud tutti figure for drums leads to the emphatic presentation and development of a new five-note motive—the first time the instruments have come together on a single idea. The drums perform mostly in unison. The texture remains dense, and the dynamic level loud, throughout this forceful passage. A brief varied return of the introductory metallic figures leads to further exploration of the principal motives, during which drum and metallic sounds are combined. The instruments generally pursue ideas independently, forming separate layers of sound; occasionally they come together on sharp metallic crashes and unison drum figures.

The coda begins with the entrance of piano, bells, and chimes on thick clusters. Reverberant pitched and metallic sounds fuse into a dense timbral web, pierced by fragments of the principal theme in the drums. Taken as a whole, the coda is an extended tapering-off. Pacing and dynamics decrease gradually until all sound disappears in a murmur. The coda completes the swell begun in the introduction, framing the main body of the piece.

Varèse's music has an electric, boldly assertive character. In *Ionisation,* he created an almost orchestral depth and variety of sound. But *Ionisation* is still a chamber work in conception and execution, stating ideas in individual voices and transparent textures and getting maximum mileage from each player.

For Further Listening

"Silver," ***performed by the Modern Jazz Quartet with Laurindo Almeida***[1]

The performances of small jazz ensembles comprise a major genre of 20th-century chamber music. In jazz idioms, each instrument performs a specific function, and the players develop ideas within a

[1]Available on Atlantic record SD-1429, *Collaboration.*

framework that provides ample opportunity for both individual and group expression. A theme is stated by one or more soloists, followed by a series of improvisational variations. The bass player outlines a harmonic structure, often a standard blues pattern, that is embellished by a pianist, while a drummer provides rhythmic impetus and elaboration. Fusion of these separate threads into a tightly-knit ensemble is achieved through the performers' sensitivity to the other parts, as they pick up, extend, and comment on each others' ideas.

Many contemporary jazz combos strive for a careful integration between written passages (or at least passages worked out in advance) and improvisational variations. The traditional format, in which statements of a tune at the beginning and end of a number frame a series of solos, remains the basis of most performances, but many groups also incorporate changes in tempo, texture, and character in an attempt to give the number a more expansive emotional and stylistic range. The Modern Jazz Quartet, one of the most influential recent groups, pursued chamber idioms of subtle lyric nuance and warm expression. Formed in 1952, the quartet consisted of John Lewis, piano; Milt Jackson, vibraphone; Percy Heath, bass; and, beginning in 1955, Connie Kay on drums. The group disbanded in 1974, and the four musicians have since pursued separate careers.

In the spring of 1964, the Brazilian guitarist Laurindo Almeida, previously best known for his performances of Spanish concert works, joined the quartet on a highly successful European tour. Studio recordings of several of the numbers performed on tour resulted in one of the MJQ's most acclaimed albums, *Collaboration.* The album opens with John Lewis' tune "Silver," a number cast in a symmetrical formal design:

(vamp)
solo melodic bridge
theme (a 12-measure piano chorus answered by a 12-measure vibraphone chorus)
vibraphone solo
piano solo
rapid blues passage followed by a gradual slowing down
solo melodic bridge
(vamp)

The introductory vamp passage, played four times, features a piano trill and a repeated guitar chord over an ascending bass line. The crisp rhythmic precision and the smooth blending of parts into a homogeneous ensemble sound were characteristic features of MJQ performances. A brief melodic bridge, in which the guitar plays in unison first with the bass, then with the vibes, leads to the main body of the performance. A theme based on a blues progression passes from the piano to the vibraphone. Vibist Jackson then develops motives from the theme into a flowing improvisatory line. Notice how the guitar and piano fuse together during the vibes solo to create a rich but transparent harmonic accompaniment. The vibraphone line is gradually overtaken by a piano solo—one of many smooth links in the performance—as Lewis picks up the melodic thread and carries it in new directions. The vibraphone rejoins the ensemble near the end of the piano solo, beginning a transition to the return of written material. A rapid blues passage, reminiscent of the theme, is followed by a harmonic passage in which the tempo slows down. A mirror-like return of the bridge passage and opening vamp, and a final blues tag, round out the number.

The decade of the 1960s saw the emergence of several "third stream" idioms, in which traditions of concert music and jazz were combined. The Modern Jazz Quartet created some of the most convincing music in this vein, always with naturalness of expression and an assured musicianship. The group never emphasized stylistic fusion as an end in itself, and thus avoided the sometimes labored or pretentious "experimental" quality of third-stream music, but rather sought to expand the horizons of jazz performance and to assimilate musical materials from many sources within their own idiom. To hear how thin the dividing line between jazz and "classical" music can be, listen to the group's performance of the slow movement of *Concierto de Aranjuez,* a guitar concerto by the Spanish composer Joaquin Rodrigo (b. 1902), on the same album. Almeida's evocative performance of the guitar solo, and the sensitive rendition of the "orchestral" parts by the members of the MJQ, transcend stylistic and genre distinctions and create absorbing musical textures of great eloquence.

Terms and Concepts for Review

canzona
string quartet
chamber textures
- antiphony
- integration of instruments
- opposition of instruments
- layered textures

mixed ensembles

Chapter 16

Orchestral Music

For many people the orchestral repertoire is the gateway to the understanding and enjoyment of concert music. Since its inception in the middle 1700s, the public orchestral concert has provided a forum through which composers have communicated their ideas to large, diversified audiences. While many chamber and solo instrumental works have been conceived primarily for the enjoyment of performers and their friends, orchestral music has always been addressed directly to the listener.

Prior to the 18th century, instrumental music was performed almost exclusively by chamber groups, and large ensembles were assembled only for special occasions. Monteverdi, for example, employed a group of over forty players in his opera *Orfeo* (1607). However, this orchestra was considered extraordinarily large and remained secondary in importance to the vocal soloists. During the 17th and early 18th centuries, instrumental ensembles at major European courts grew in size until they comprised small orchestras of twenty or more players. The instrumentation and size of these orchestras varied widely, however, and there was no large-scale genre in which the orchestra functioned as a unified ensemble. Baroque suites were relatively lightweight collections of individual dance movements. Concertos of the period, such as Bach's *Brandenburg Concerto No. 2,* generally divided the ensemble into solo and tutti groups. Musical interest in Baroque orchestral music was concentrated in contrapuntal textures—the interweaving or alternation of distinct lines—rather than on a dramatic overall formal design.

During the 18th century, popular taste increasingly came to favor instrumental over vocal music. As public concert halls opened throughout Europe, music moved out of the courts and churches and became accessible to a wider audience. Public concerts were festive social occasions, in contrast to the chummy aristocratic soirées that had been the rule at courts and country estates. Permanent civic orchestras were established, and several became renowned for their ensemble precision and brilliance of sound. The increasing importance of orchestral music led to the creation of a new genre, the **symphony**, through which most modern orchestral practices have developed.

Origins of the Symphony

The term "symphonia" originally meant nothing more than "playing together," and was applied loosely during the Baroque era to a variety of short instrumental works following no common formal plan. For example, the "Pastoral Symphony" that follows "For unto us a child is born" in Handel's *Messiah* is an orchestral interlude—a relatively minor number within the oratorio—and Bach called his three-part keyboard inventions *Sinfonien.* "Sinfonia" was also a catchall term bestowed on orchestral introductions to operas, cantatas, and suites.

In modern usage the term "symphony" has two meanings. Like "philharmonic," which originally denoted a group of patrons who supported an orchestra, it is frequently used as a synonym for "orchestra." In more specific use, however, **symphony** refers to the principal genre of orchestral music: a large-scale, multi-movement composition in which diverse themes, moods, and developmental techniques are integrated into a unified statement.

The symphony evolved out of several Baroque sources, including the operatic overture, the dance suite, and the Baroque concerto. Initial development of symphonic style and form was centered in Mannheim, Germany, and in Vienna and Bohemia, between 1740 and 1770. These early symphonies were three- or four-movement works lasting less than twenty minutes. Most were written in an elegant, graceful style based upon simple homophonic textures. Replacement of Baroque contrapuntal textures with a simpler accompanied-melody style enabled composers to treat the orchestra as a cohesive ensemble. The make-up of the orchestra and function of the instruments became fairly standard. Strings formed the heart of the ensemble, playing almost continuously. The first violins generally carried the tune, supported by a harmonic figuration pattern in the lower strings. Four to ten winds, often augmented by timpani, performed a subordinate role, playing together rather than individually and adding increased weight to tutti passages.

The pre-Classical symphony represented a new approach to instrumental composition. The symphonic ideal became not merely a "playing together," but rather the creation of a unified orchestral sound in which the players performed "as one." By such means as frequent dynamic variations, including long, continuous swells and sudden, loud interjections, early symphonists began to exploit the *medium* of orchestral performance. The most important step in the evolution of the symphony, however, was the development of a standard formal plan.

The Classical Symphony

Around the beginning of the classical era, Haydn, followed by Mozart and other composers, standardized the format of the symphony into a predictable sequence of movements each cast in a common formal outline. Within this framework Classical composers sought greater emotional breadth, a clearer distinction in tone between the individual movements, and a more concentrated and dramatic unity to the works as a whole. Standardization of

Formal Outline of the Classical Symphony

The Classical format of the symphony is similar to that of the string quartet. Sonatas and concertos follow the same general scheme but usually omit the minuet or scherzo movement.

First movement

Tempo: fast (with optional slow introduction)
Key: tonic
Form: sonata form

Second movement

Tempo: slow
Key: closely related key, usually the dominant or relative major or minor
Form: A–B–A, theme and variations, or shortened sonata form

Third movement (Always in triple meter)

Tempo: relatively fast
Key: tonic
Form: minuet and trio, or, later, scherzo and trio

Fourth movement

Tempo: fast (usually the fastest movement of the work)
Key: tonic
Form: rondo, sonata–rondo, sonata, theme and variations

the movements came to function somewhat in the manner of the text in vocal music: it supplied the listener with a frame of reference against which to follow the development of musical ideas. Much of the eloquence and wit of Haydn's and Mozart's symphonies consists in the way these composers were able to achieve highly personal expression, and to fashion a unifying tone to individual symphonies, while working within a conventional structural framework.

Private orchestras of the 18th century, such as the one Haydn wrote for at Esterhazy, generally contained only twenty or so players, offering the composer a limited choice of colors and a relatively small range of dynamic contrasts. Most Classical symphonies, however, including all of Mozart's mature works and Haydn's later symphonies, were written for larger civic orchestras of around forty players. By 1790, the expanded wind section of the orchestra generally included pairs of flutes, oboes, clarinets, bassoons, and horns and, usually, two trumpets and timpani. The winds occasionally functioned in a solo capacity but were used more often for textural reinforcement.

Listening

First Movement from the Symphony No. 94 *("Surprise"), by Franz Joseph Haydn (1732–1809)*

Record Set Side 7, Band 2

The opening movement of Haydn's *"Surprise" Symphony* (1791) typifies the verve and humor of the Classical symphony. Humor in Classical style, as in most music, only occasionally takes the form of outright "jokes" such as the ponderous "surprise" in the second movement of this symphony. It more often results from general *esprit:* the enjoyment one takes in listening to a pro at work as he paces his troops through a spirited romp.

The first movement of the *"Surprise" Symphony* is in sonata form, beginning with a slow introduction. The introductory theme is stated in question-and-answer alternation between winds and strings. The rest of the movement, however, is dominated by the strings. The two major thematic ideas of the exposition are presented by the first violins. The winds are treated as a choir, bolstering the weight of tutti passages and occasionally answering or continuing a figure begun in the strings. There are many tutti passages in the movement; portions of both principal themes, and most of the transition, codetta, and development section, are played by the full ensemble. The texture alternates between phrases for string choir and for full orchestra, and the frequent tuttis are for the most part textural swells rather than climactic points of arrival.

The themes of the two key areas are similar in tone, rhythmic structure, and contour, both featuring an underlying three-note descending figure (circled):

Rhythmic pacing is characterized by a sense of continuity, alternating between eighth-note and sixteenth-note motion (respectively a "brisk walk" and a "medium jog"). There are no tempo changes (except for the slow introduction) and no rubato passages or sustained holds.

Haydn treated the orchestra as a tightly-knit ensemble, and there is a transparency to many of his textures similar to that of chamber music. In fact, Classical symphonies were frequently performed without conductor. The players took their tempo and cues from the concertmaster (the first violinist), and it was assumed that all would go well if the musicians played in tune at the proper dynamic level and phrased together. Beethoven was the first composer to devote considerable rehearsal time to discussions of correct interpretation, and many of his players were annoyed at such unwonted "lecturing."

None of this should imply, however, that Haydn's symphonies are mechanical in construction or can be performed in a perfunctory manner. The spirited energy of this movement is lost in an indifferent performance or a casual listening, because much of the music lies "between the notes," in the way they are connected and shaped into expressive designs.

Beethoven's Symphonies

The late symphonies of Haydn and Mozart brought the symphony to its first pinnacle of achievement, establishing a formal model and revealing the expressive potential of a unified large-scale orchestral work. Within a few years after the composition of these definitive Classical works, Beethoven undertook new directions in symphonic writing, laying the foundations for further development of the genre during the 19th century. Beethoven's approach to symphonic composition was intensely serious, coupling powerful concentration of musical invention with fervent emotional expression. In his hands the symphony became the weightiest instrumental genre, a vehicle for exalted musical statements at once universal and deeply personal in tone.

Beethoven expanded the scope of the symphony from the inside out, stretching its formal proportions, substituting the more forceful scherzo for the traditional minuet movement, and introducing a rhythmic urgency that propels the music forward. The basic sound quality of Beethoven's orchestral writing is generally heavier than that of Haydn's or Mozart's, resulting from denser textures and greater use of winds and percussion (sometimes including instruments new to the symphony). The process of musical development, in which initial motives grow into ever larger patterns while retaining their unifying identity, was for Beethoven the fundamental working principle of composition. He applied it to each movement of the symphony, often constructing works of vast scope from simple beginnings, with all elements related to a central core. Beethoven also heightened the dramatic element of symphonic form, intensifying structural contrasts to emphasize points of tonal motion and arrival. Striving for greater expressive and thematic unity within the symphony as a whole, he often incorporated similar motives within the separate movements and created a progression of moods that evolve according to a single master plan. Occasionally he incorporated programmatic ideas, as in his portrayal of scenes from country life in his *Symphony No. 6* (the *"Pastoral" Symphony*), but these allusions are of a general nature and are not a determining element of structure.

Beethoven wrote only nine symphonies, compared to Mozart's 41 and

Haydn's more than 100. His symphonies are longer and more complex than those of his predecessors, and each represents a unique approach to the genre. In general, the odd-numbered symphonies are momentous in tone, while the even-numbered works adhere more closely to Classical proportions. The *Symphony No. 5,* though relatively short in duration, is in many ways a compendium of Beethoven's symphonic technique. It is both densely compressed in material and broad in emotional range. The work was composed between 1804 and 1808, during the most desperate period of Beethoven's life, when he was forced to come to grips with his increasing deafness and isolation. The tone of the work reflects both this inner struggle and Beethoven's indomitable will to prevail.

Listening

Symphony No. 5 in C Minor, Op. 67, *by Ludwig van Beethoven (1770–1827)*

First movement. The sonata-form first movement demonstrates motivic development in its most concentrated form. A brusque introduction heralds the four-note motive that dominates the movement and forms the seed of the entire symphony. The motive is often summarized as "three shorts and a long" (• • • —) and has been likened to "fate knocking at the door," an analogy attributed to Beethoven himself. Compressed into a few sharp impulses, it is at once fragmentary in design and complete in thought. Introductory presentation of the motive is stern, almost defiant.

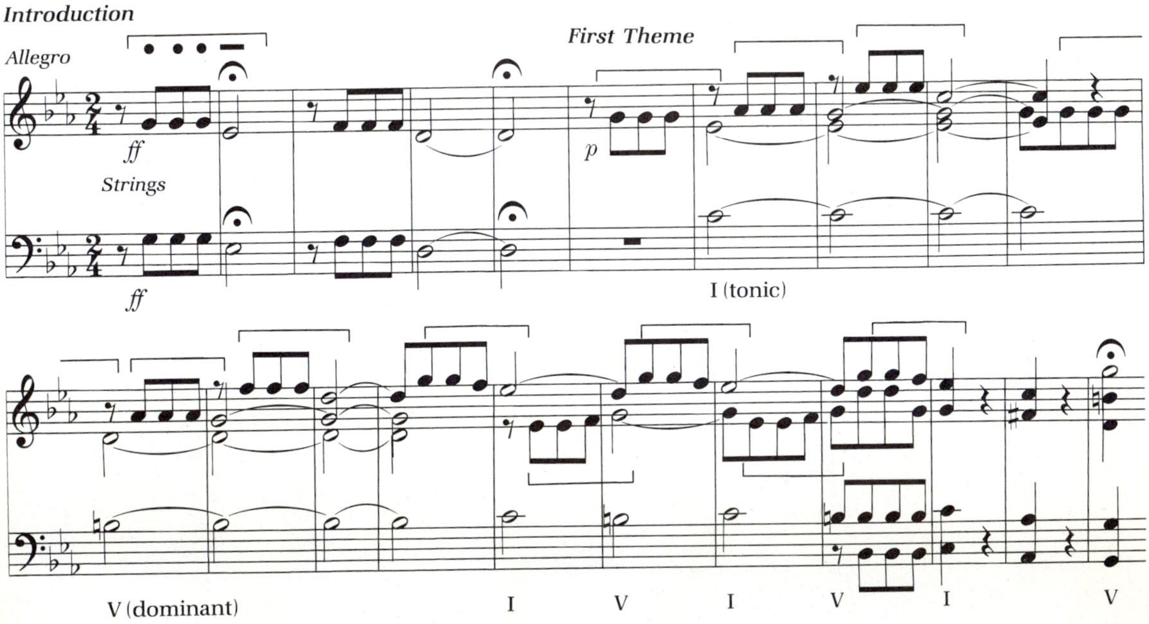

Developmental expansion of this gruff, energetic motive begins immediately in the *opening theme.* The essence of the theme is not a melody—no one leaves a performance whistling this passage—but rather a driving series of rhythmic imitations, bracketed in the figure above, around the four-note motive. The imitative fragments pile up to produce an alternating series of tonic and dominant harmonies, establishing the C minor key center, and setting the tone of the movement: restless and grimly earnest.

The short first theme lurches to a half stop on a held note. The following *transition* passage begins with a tutti interjection of the opening figure, then continues the development of the motive. Growing rhythmic and dynamic urgency accentuate the impending tonal shift, but at the actual point of modulation the music grinds to another sudden halt on two isolated chords. Abrupt changes in pacing pervade the exposition. The introduction, tonic theme, transition, and second theme are separated by holds or pauses. In contrast to the smooth continuity of the opening movement of Haydn's *"Surprise" Symphony,* Beethoven states his ideas in impulsive thrusts.

The *second tonal group,* in major, begins with a horn call in which the basic motive is intervallically expanded and stretched into three shorts and three longs. This call is answered by a lyrical violin melody based on the same four notes as the horn call (B♭–E♭–F–B♭). The original motive still lurks in the background, however, periodically interjected by the lower strings.

The *closing passage* is similar in style to the transition. The original rhythmic motive is stated in descending arpeggios by the winds, then in isolated exclamations by the full orchestra. Every thematic idea in the exposition has been derived from the original motive, creating an extraordinary concentration of energy and material:

Original motive

• • • —

↙ ↘

First group → *Transition* → *Closing material*

Horn motive → *Violin melody* } *Second group*

The *development* section is structured into two large units, based on just two ideas: respectively, the original motive and the horn-call figure derived from it. This leads to even greater concentration of material—the unyielding reiteration of a fixed idea that won't go away. In the first half of the development, rhythmic pacing and dynamics gradually increase, and the texture builds to a climactic peak. The second half of the development presents an opposite process—one of dissolution. The horn motive first is stated with resolute authority by the violins, then is broken apart into halting, fragmented rhythms. The three-short, three-long motive is reduced to two longs, then pared down to a series of isolated single notes that alternate between winds and strings. Dynamics decrease to a whisper, and the motive almost disappears entirely. This passage is the structural low point of the entire symphony. All semblance of melody, harmonic direction, and rhythmic energy have evaporated; very little remains—only a series of detached chords, going nowhere in particular.

At the end of the transition the original motive comes charging back and builds to a roaring culmination at the beginning of the *recapitulation.* The recapitulation follows the standard format, with one notable interpolation: the first theme and transition are now separated by a brief but plaintive oboe solo. This solo seems to contain the seeds of an expressive theme that might have softened the ruthless tone of the movement—but it remains a solitary murmur, never heard again. The *coda* is long and stormy, like a second development section, thundering the original motive with relentless urgency.

The first movement as a whole generates a sense of grim, almost fatalistic inevitability. Though the formal proportions are neatly balanced, the emotional tone is lopsided. A challenge has been hurled into space, and has not yet received an answer. That answer will come in the fourth movement.

Second Movement. The slow second movement, in A♭ major, is reflective but resolute in tone. This movement combines rondo and variation procedures, resulting in the alternation and varied repetition of two themes:

$$A–B–A_1–B_1–A_2–A_3–B_2–A_4$$

The *A* theme, introduced by the violas and cellos, is a broad phrase featuring dotted rhythms and continuous changes in contour direction. In its first two variations it is embellished by more rapid rhythmic motion.

In the third variation the theme is parceled out among the woodwinds, and in the fourth it is shifted into minor.

The *B* theme subtly incorporates the • • • – motive of the first movement:

Second theme (B)

Begun gently by the clarinets and bassoons, it quickly undergoes a change in character, becoming almost martial as the full orchestra piles in. A similar passage occurs at the end of the coda, bringing the movement to a forceful close.

Third Movement. The *Fifth Symphony* exemplifies the structural reasons that led Beethoven to abandon the traditional minuet in favor of the more robust and powerful scherzo. A simple dance movement would have been incongruous in this symphony, interrupting the earnest tone and sense of emotional struggle that pervade the work. This scherzo features two themes: a ghostly arpeggiation in the lower strings, and an ebullient repeated-note horn theme based upon the • • • – motive. The two themes are developed in alternation.

First theme

Second Theme

The trio is a fugue-like excursion on a blustery theme. After a brusque opening pronouncement by the low strings, the theme works its way upward through the string choir. In the second half of the trio, the lower strings assume control of the theme but do not seem to know what to do with it. After two false starts the cellos and basses initiate another fugato episode. The process is repeated, and the basses predictably fumble the theme again before recovering. A shortened return of the scherzo, this time played pizzicato, leads to an extended transition to the fourth movement, which follows without a pause. The transition begins very softly, with the timpani beating out the · · · – motive, then builds a throbbing tension that must be resolved.

Fourth movement. The final movement bursts forth with electrifying force on a tutti theme that jubilantly affirms the key of C major.

The shift to major is only partially responsible for the stirring power that Beethoven achieves at the start of the movement. Three instruments new to the symphony orchestra—piccolo, contrabassoon, and three trombones—are introduced for added brilliance and sonority. The ceaseless rhythmic drive and broad continuity of the movement, which unfurls in long, unbroken arcs, form a striking contrast to the jagged stop-and-go motion of the first movement.

The finale is an expansive sonata-form design with independent transitional and closing themes and a sweeping second theme that incorporates, yet again, the · · · – motive:

This triplet figure dominates the development section. Toward the end of the development, the mood shifts and Beethoven recalls the pizzicato scherzo section. By bringing back an entire passage from an earlier movement, Beethoven emphasizes the organic growth and interrelation of ideas and moods within this symphony. The recapitulation is followed by an extended coda in which the principal themes of the movement intermingle, reinforcing their uniformity of purpose and tone. Several times the coda seems about to end but takes off again with renewed force. Out of context this elongated coda might sound redundant, belaboring the tonic triad in an overly exuberant "summation to a summation to a summation." What Beethoven is actually doing, however, is balancing the symphony as a whole—vanquishing the black clouds of the first movement and supplying a triumphant answer every bit as insistent as the original motive.

Romantic Orchestral Music

The orchestra was the preeminent medium of instrumental music throughout the 19th century, and a majority of Romantic composers are best known today for their symphonic works. Romantic composers generally strove for powerful orchestral statements in which continuous subtle nuances are incorporated within broad overall gestures. Many of them saw the integration of vivid structural contrasts and mood changes into an emotionally meaningful whole as the crowning achievement of symphonic statement. Composers sought ever greater textural weight and tonal brilliance, and the orchestra gradually expanded to include 80 or more players. The winds assumed greater prominence, in both a solo and an ensemble capacity, and the brass section grew into a complete, independent choir.

Two distinct strands of symphonic expression evolved during the 19th century. Continued development of the symphony was centered in Germany and Austria. Composers from these countries, and other composers strongly influenced by the Viennese tradition, generally adhered to the broad outline of the Classical symphony while expanding the formal proportions of each movement. Most later 19th-century symphonies last 40 or 50 minutes, comprising an entire half of an average symphonic concert, and some works are considerably longer.

The second major current consisted of more radical departures from the Classical symphonic model. Such composers as Berlioz and Liszt concentrated more on the *medium* of orchestral performance than on traditional symphonic format. This shift in emphasis led to the evolution of new orchestral genres: single-movement works loosely based upon some aspects of the symphony, but cast in freer formal designs.

The German Symphonic Tradition

Whereas Beethoven concentrated on the dramatic formal potential of the symphony, his younger contemporary Schubert excelled at lyric expression, a quality that generally takes precedence over rigorous development or architectural symmetry in his symphonies. Lyricism is also the most persuasive feature of the symphonies of Felix Mendelssohn and Robert Schumann. The themes of all three composers are often long, flowing lines that create a precise emotional quality and therefore resist extensive developmental manipulation or transformation. The development sections of Schubert's and Schumann's symphonies are occasionally diffuse in structural logic, but they are compelling in emotional urgency. Mendelssohn's symphonies are more Classical in conception, less imperative in emotional tone.

For many listeners the four symphonies of Johannes Brahms, written between 1876 and 1885, represent the consummation of the Romantic symphonic tradition, combining the lyricism of the early German Romantic movement with the concentrated development and formal solidity of Beethoven's symphonic style. Brahms' veneration of Beethoven's achievement deterred him from undertaking the composition of symphonies until he had gained total confidence in his technique, and he did not complete his first symphony until the age of 43. Brahms' symphonies are finely crafted and follow the four-movement Classical format. They also exhibit a warmth of expression and a deep, if restrained, inner passion. Like most later Romantics, Brahms favored rich, dark, full textures. A distinguishing heaviness of sound, as well as of spirit, pervades his orchestral works, but the musical structure is always crystal clear. The finale of Brahms' *Symphony No. 4,* discussed in Chapter 7, exemplifies his fusion of traditional formal procedures and Romantic expression.

National Currents

The superstructure of the German Romantic symphony was adopted by many composers of other countries. Later 19th-century symphonists from eastern Europe frequently sought to integrate national elements, which would give the music a special meaning to their countrymen, within traditional forms and procedures that assured international comprehensibility.

Antonín Dvořák

The Czech composer Antonín Dvořák (*Dvor*-zhak) shared many of Brahms' esthetic predilections but was also strongly influenced by the nationalist movement. Dvořák came from a peasant background and spent most of his career in Prague. He was a relatively obscure composer until his mid-thirties, when Brahms became acquainted with his music and encouraged its publication. From that time on, the hearty spirit of Dvořák's music won him growing international renown. Dvořák's works are direct in form and expression, reflecting the straightforward rhythms and melodic contours of the Bohemian folk music he revered. Though Dvořák did not directly quote folk songs, he internalized their spirit within incisive themes well suited to symphonic development.

In 1892 Dvořák became the founding director of an ill-fated music conservatory in New York. His three-year stay in the United States was marked by homesickness, but also by a growing interest in American music, particularly the music of black, Indian, and rural southern cultures. The candid expression and deep sense of community he sensed in black spirituals and work songs greatly impressed him: "These beautiful and varied themes are the product of the soil. They are American. They are the folk songs of America, and our composers must turn to them . . . to express the true sentiment of the people." He believed black music, which he found "pathetic, tender, passionate, melancholy, solemn, religious, merry, gay, gracious . . ." could provide inspiration for a uniquely American style of concert music, much as the peasant folk songs of Bohemia had infused his own works.

First Movement from the* Symphony No. 9 in E Minor *("From the New World") by Antonín Dvořák (1841–1904)

Record Set Side 10, Band 3

During his American stay Dvořák composed his most celebrated work, the Symphony *"From the New World."* Acknowledging the profound influence of his impressions of the United States and its music on the work, he declared, "Anyone who has a nose must smell America in the symphony." In style and structure the work was similar to his earlier symphonies, however, and Dvořák made no pretentions of writing specifically "American" music.[1]

The sonata-form first movement opens with a slow introduction in which several fragmentary ideas are presented. A short, meditative theme is followed by sharp rhythmic punctuations that foreshadow the rhythmic energy of the main body of the movement; an agitated figure in the horns and low strings is later transformed into the first theme of the exposition. The introduction accumulates a growing momentum that culminates in a sharp timpani roll.

Exposition. The *tonic theme* consists of triadic arpeggiations in the horns answered by a more rapid figure, also in dotted rhythms, in the woodwinds:

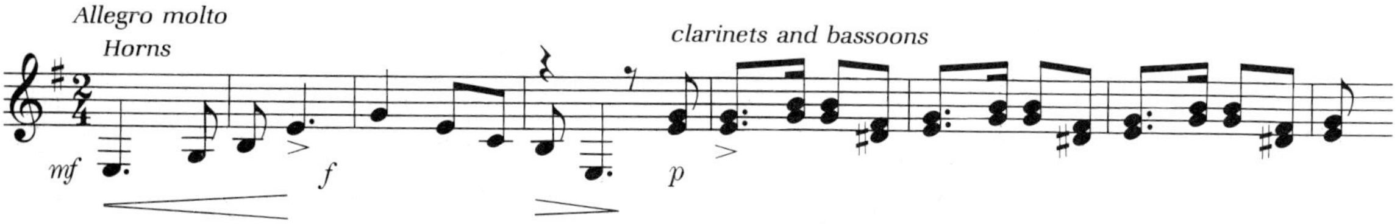

Several writers have heard echoes of either the enterprising spirit of 19th-century industrial America or European peasant tunes in this sharply-drawn theme. At any rate, the forthright character of the theme is a musical rather than a pictorial quality, and results largely from the symmetrical balance within both ideas, as indicated in brackets. The theme retains its original "up-front" character during subsequent development, and even when recalled in altered form during the second and third movements. In this opening statement it builds to a vigorous tutti, followed by a brief developmental excursion. Most of the themes in the symphony are stated first by a solo instrument, deriving much of

[1] The *New World Symphony* has been a natural source of background music to films and documentaries that attempt to portray the character of American life, and its themes have often been lifted out of context to accompany travelogue footage of blast furnaces, the Statue of Liberty or Grand Canyon, the vast wheat fields of the plains blowing in the wind, and so on. There is nothing wrong in this, to be sure, but it should not be confused with the substance of the work, which is its symphonic design.

their character from this initial tone color, and then are immediately restated by full orchestra.

The extended *transition* is typical of late 19th-century practice. It begins not as a "bridge," but as a well-defined, independent section, with its own theme, tonal center, and character. A lilting figure in the woodwinds creates a wistful mood:

Flute and oboe

The actual transitional link to the second key is based on a rhythmic motive drawn from the second measure of this theme.

The principal theme of the second key area is reminiscent of a portion of the spiritual "Swing Low, Sweet Chariot" (leading some writers to wonder, "Did he or didn't he . . . ?"), while the dotted rhythms of the first two measures parallel those of the earlier horn figure:

Theme

The theme passes from solo flute to strings, then to the brass in a full tutti, bringing the exposition to a forceful close. Dvořák specified a repeat of the exposition, but this is often not observed. (One prosaic but common reason that conductors often ignore repeat signs in Romantic symphonies is to squeeze the first two movements onto a single side of an LP record, which is limited to about 25 minutes.)

Development and Recapitulation. Dvořák's development sections, like those of Tchaikovsky and many other late Romantic composers, usually preserve a recognizable identity of themes and motives. Fragments of themes are tossed around through the orchestra, but are not broken down into tiny scraps or subjected to rigorous working-out as in the symphonies of Beethoven and Brahms. Ideas generally retain their original character and shape but are heard in new contexts. There is less contrast between the exposition and development of themes than in Classical works, because the emphasis of the music is centered more on the character and various shadings of the ideas than on their transformation into new relationships. Most of the development section of this movement is based upon the second ("Sweet Chariot") theme. Toward the end, two false recapitulations of the first theme are stated by full orchestra, followed by several partial statements of the theme in the woodwinds. A more Classically oriented composer would have held the first theme in reserve until the recapitulation, restoring tonal and thematic stability simultaneously. Dvořák instead plays with the listener's expectations, volunteering the theme "too soon" but withholding tonal stability and original instrumentation (horn) until the recapitulation, so that the theme becomes a transition into itself. The recapitulation retains the original instrumentation of the themes and is followed by an energetic coda that combines the two principal themes of the movement.

Contrast is not a conspicuous feature of the movement, nor, indeed, of the symphony as a whole. The thematic ideas are complementary and are smoothly interwoven, comprising different facets of an expansive, affirmative statement. The *"New World" Symphony* is neither a searching personal disclosure nor an innovative formal design. It is what it was meant to be: a heartfelt expression of musical ideas imbued with the special character of two national cultures.

Freer Symphonic Forms

The symphonies of Anton Bruckner and Gustav Mahler represent an end point in the evolution of the Viennese symphonic tradition. Bruckner, a contemporary of Brahms, followed the general four-movement profile of the Classical symphony. His nine symphonies are solemn, inward-looking works that mirror the composer's deep religious convictions in their cumulative breadth and sometimes mystical tone. The basic quality of motion and structure is one of very gradual accumulation of energy. Elemental motives slowly evolve into complete themes, and extensive repetition of ideas—a process of "three steps forward and two steps back"—creates a growing momentum that often culminates in majestic hymn-like finales. In the slow second movement of his *Symphony No. 7,* for example, the music seems static at any given point but creates a searing overall design of great power. The third movement of the same symphony, discussed briefly at the end of Chapter 6, is typical of Bruckner's scherzos in its use of dance rhythms that build to energetic climaxes.

Mahler's nine symphonies, on the other hand, are commanding works that cover a vast expressive range and exemplify the loosening of symphonic format that accelerated around 1900. Mahler viewed the symphony as an all-embracing framework for the communication of an exalted world view. Several of his symphonies are in five or more movements, and several include prominent vocal parts. The individual movements incorporate only the general principles, rather than the specific outline, of Classical forms. The relaxation of symphonic format is also evident in the brooding symphonies of Finland's Jean Sibelius (1865–1957) and in most other symphonic works of the early 20th century.

Alternative Genres

As the Romantic symphony evolved into ever larger, more complex, and freer types of designs, new orchestral genres grew up alongside it and underwent similar expansion. The *concert overture,* a single-movement work similar in form to the first movement of a symphony but with less extensive development, was explored first by German composers. Mendelssohn's *Hebrides Overture,* discussed in Chapter 11, is a representative early example of the genre, and Brahms' sonorous *Academic Festival Overture* and *Tragic Overture* typify its later development. Outside of Germany the concert overture became increasingly programmatic in conception and freer in form.

The novel formal procedures, brilliant colors, and audacious programmatic elements of Hector Berlioz' 1830 *Symphonie Fantastique* fascinated most later Romantic composers. Seeking to carry Berlioz' poetic ideal further, Franz Liszt frequently abandoned the symphonic model altogether in favor of the **symphonic poem,** or *tone poem,* a long, rhapsodic single-movement work loosely based on a poem, painting, myth, or story line. The symphonic poem is a uniquely Romantic genre, "symphonic" more in breadth than in structure. It embodies the programmatic ideal of the fusion of music with other arts in its most concentrated form. Although the symphonic poems of Liszt and later composers contain elements of development and repetition of thematic material, they follow no common formal outline.

The Programmatic Overture: Tchaikovsky. In the popular mind Peter Ilyich Tchaikovsky epitomizes musical Romanticism. His music is unashamedly emotional in tone and immediate in its impact. Although he was influenced by the rising tide of nationalist sentiment, Tchaikovsky believed that Russian composers needed to assimilate the technical mastery of western European composers before they could write enduring works. His six symphonies are patterned on the German Romantic model, but formal structure is secondary to the delineation of fervent moods and epic contasts. Tchaikovsky's developmental technique is based on varied repetition of themes rather than on a scrupulous working-out of motivic relationships. His vivid, often pictorial thematic ideas retain separate identities, and there is an impulsive, highly sectional quality to his formal designs. For these reasons, Tchaikovsky has always been a controversial composer and his music has undergone wide fluctuations in critical opinion. His late works are enthusiastically received by audiences, but are disdained by some critics for their alleged "cheap thrills" and unimaginative, if solid, formal structure. In the first half of the 20th century his symphonies were performed more frequently than those of any other composer except Beethoven. Since 1950, renewed interest in the symphonies of his formerly neglected contemporaries—notably Bruckner and Mahler—has come partly at Tchaikovsky's expense. While Tchaikovsky's works no longer dominate the orchestral repertoire to their former degree, they are still widely performed and admired as outstanding examples of the emotive power of late Romantic symphonic music.

Peter Ilyich Tchaikovsky in 1879

Tchaikovsky's personal life was marked by melancholy and self-doubt. Tortured by his repressed homosexuality, fearing that his music was facile in appeal and deficient in structure (especially when compared with that of his favorite composer, Mozart), Tchaikovsky was subject to periods of deep depression. This dark side of his personality is evident in his music and has been pilloried by those who claim his symphonic works encompass only three emotions: sad, very sad, and utterly without hope. Such a lugubrious mix, however, would hardly account for the stirring appeal many listeners find in Tchaikovsky's music. Grace, a sense of drama, and fiery tutti passages give his scores an uncommon rhythmic force and emotional breadth.

Listening

Romeo and Juliet: Overture–Fantasy ***by Peter Ilyich Tchaikovksy (1840–1893)***

Romeo and Juliet was composed in 1869 and thoroughly revised in 1881. It is a lengthy concert overture in sonata form, framed by a slow introduction and an epilogue. The subtitle of the work, "Overture–Fantasy," attests to the rhapsodic tone and relatively free structure of the work. Shakespeare's play was the inspiration for the overture, but Tchaikovsky attempted to capture only the feverish emotions that arise in the story, not to distill its involved plot.

The grave introduction, associated with the gentle Friar Laurence who forsees impending tragedy in the feud between the Montague and Capulet families, is remote in tone, setting the mood for a long-ago but still compelling human drama. The main body of the work is based upon the extreme contrast between two themes. The first depicts the violent contention between the warring families and illustrates Tchaikovsky's ability to create rousing tutti passages driven by urgent rhythmic motion and sharp accents. The lyrical second theme, introduced by English horn and violas, portrays the love of Romeo and Juliet. Like many of Tchaikovsky's expressive themes, it has been exploited commercially and regularly shows up in collections of "50 of the World's Most Beautiful Melodies." The two contrasting themes form the two poles of the musical drama.

The development section centers around the "battle" theme. In the recapitulation, the love theme becomes more prominent. Rescored for full orchestra and extended by additional phrases in which the melodic contour soars ever higher in the strings, it is transformed into an impassioned climax. Inevitably, the conflict erupts again, as the battle theme returns and the star-crossed lovers are driven to suicide. In the concluding epilogue, a funereal timpani figure accompanies fragments of the love theme. The introduction is recalled, and a fragment of the battle theme brings the work to a grim conclusion.

Development of ideas plays only a minor part in the strong impact of the work. Unity of expression is achieved not through a reconciliation of ideas, but by dramatic means: a decisive concluding mood is established that overwhelms earlier contrasts and brings the piece to its emotionally definitive end.

The Symphonic Poem: Richard Strauss. Richard Strauss, the unrivaled master of the symphonic poem, carried the Romantic penchants for programmatic associations, rhapsodic formal structures, and large performing ensembles to new heights. Like Bruckner and Mahler he adopted the chromatic pitch language of Richard Wagner. In temperament, however, he was a post-Romantic. An ironic, sophisticated composer, he preferred impersonal narrative structures and coloristic brilliance to subjective expression. Mahler remarked, "His manner of thinking and feeling is worlds apart from mine. I wonder if we two will ever meet on the same planet." An eminent conductor with an encyclopedic knowledge of instruments, Strauss made full use of the expanded coloristic and textural resources of the late 19th-century orchestra.

Listening

Till Eulenspiegel's Merry Pranks *by Richard Strauss (1864–1949)*

Strauss's tone poem *Till Eulenspiegel's Merry Pranks* (1895) is scored for an outsized orchestra of 27 winds, a large percussion battery, and about 64 strings. The inspiration for the work was the legend of a Robin Hood-like 14th-century vagabond who traveled through Europe in search of adventure. A self-appointed champion of the little man and gadfly of the establishment, Till pursued his fancies and practical jokes with a dauntless energy free of ill-will.

The work is episodic in structure, portraying several of Till's brash escapades. Strauss refused to publish a detailed program with the work, however, hoping that (German) listeners familiar with the legend would grasp the substance of his narrative through their own imaginations. Though probably the most graphically pictorial composer of his time, Strauss was chary of explicit extra-musical scenarios, declaring that, "Even in program music, the first and most important question is always one of the quality and strength of the musical idea."

While free in structural outline, the work employs a rondo-like recurrence of two themes associated with the irreverent hero. The opening section sets a fairy-tale mood. The strings introduce a wistful, fragmentary first theme:

The second theme, a syncopated melody in the horn, follows immediately.

The extraordinarily wide range and rapid attacks of this theme make it a formidable virtuosic challenge, and it is frequently divvied up between two players. The horn theme builds to a climax and is answered by a mocking variant of the opening string theme, now whistled tartly by the clarinet:

Strauss's transformation of the naïve string theme into a shrill, nose-thumbing clarinet motive is typical of the metamorphoses both ideas undergo throughout the work.

In the first episode Till bumptiously rides his horse through a crowded marketplace, upsetting carts and enraging the merchants. The second episode begins with a lilting folklike tune in the bassoons and violas; thinly disguised as a priest, Till preaches a nonsensical sermon to perplexed onlookers. Suspecting that they are being duped, the people nevertheless listen attentively on the off chance that the twaddle they are enduring is an inspired prophecy. During the third episode Till falls madly in love, then rails furiously when the lady scorns his affections. In the fourth episode, he chances upon an assemblage of pompous scholars and taunts them with unanswerable trick questions. And so it goes. At length Till is hauled before a court of justice and condemned to death. In a passage that owes an obvious debt to the concluding bars of Berlioz' "March to the Scaffold," the brass intone a ponderous death knell. Impenitent to the end, Till replies contemptuously with the clarinet motive. He is put to death, but, as in all good fairy tales, his spirit lives on. A brief epilogue begins nostalgically but ends with a characteristically tumultuous final flourish.

It is not necessary to follow a blow-by-blow synopsis of the program to understand the music or appreciate Strauss's orchestral mastery; indeed, too close an attention to the program can distract one from the quality of Strauss's musical inventions. The formal structure is a pastiche of attractive, dissociated ideas, with smooth transitional links and the unifying presence of two ideas that keep popping up in new guises. The expression of the work lies primarily in its ingenious exploitation of orchestral colors and textures.

Orchestral Music in the 20th Century

The 20th-century orchestral literature reflects the diversity of idioms and practices that have characterized the present epoch. Many composers have continued to treat the symphony as a grand design, employing large ensembles and drawing freely upon both traditional and less conventional formal structures and developmental procedures. The nine symphonies of Ralph Vaughan Williams (1872–1958), for example, are skillfully crafted works, quite different in individual format and tone, but all imbued with a distinctly English character. National elements, in fact, have been a major element in much 20th-century symphonic music, particularly in Russian works.

The most pervasive trends of the last 60 years, however, have been a paring down in the length and scope of the symphony, a corresponding reduction in instrumentation, and greater interest in alternative genres. For both esthetic and economic reasons, most major composers of the period between the two World Wars chose to write for orchestras of modest size, eschewing the sweeping gestures and extra-musical associations of late Romantic idioms and instead seeking clarity of texture and design. The classically-oriented symphonies of Stravinsky (*Symphony in C*, 1940, and *Symphony in Three Movements*, 1943) and Paul Hindemith (*Mathis der Maler Symphony*, 1934), and such works as Prokofiev's *Classical Symphony* (1917), follow 18th-century formal models while incorporating 20th-century melodic, rhythmic, and harmonic resources. Neoclassical composers, finding inherited formal procedures a spur rather than impediment to original creation, were the last major group of composers to devote much of their energies to the composition of symphonies. Bartók excelled in the orchestral medium, but preferred freer genres and composed no symphonies.

The years since World War II have witnessed a continuing decline in the output of symphonies as composers have explored alternative types of orchestral writing in single-movement works and suites. The symphony *per se* is no longer the definitive genre of contemporary orchestral music, and has been largely superseded by shorter, more concentrated types of structural design. Furthermore, today's composer is more likely to fashion a major instrumental work for chamber ensemble than for orchestra, finding this a much easier way to achieve a widespread hearing. Many observers, whether viewing this trend with alarm or equanimity, have questioned the future of the symphony orchestra, speculating that it might soon become dedicated almost exclusively to the preservation of a historically completed repertoire. Others, however, believe that the quality, if not quantity, of contemporary orchestral music equals that of any earlier period and assures a living symphonic tradition into the foreseeable future. Our brief survey of the 20th-century orchestral literature focuses on two divergent "historic" symphonies that have exerted a wide-ranging influence upon the present generation of composers. More recent orchestral techniques will be examined in Chapter 20.

Charles Ives

Charles Ives (1874–1954), one of the most fascinating figures in 20th century music, composed strikingly original works in almost total obscurity and did not hear most of his pieces performed until decades after their composition. While growing up in Danbury, Connecticut, he absorbed the experimental musical inclinations of his father, a band leader, organist, pianist, arranger, and all-around town musician. Ives credited his father with

Charles Ives

teaching him to use "ears and mind to think for themselves and be more independent—in other words, to be less dependent on customs and habits." To the young Ives, the combined sound of two marching bands playing different tunes from distant points in a parade was an entrancing musical experience.

Ives studied music at Yale, where his unorthodox compositions mystified and affronted his conservative teachers. Convinced that "a man can keep his musical interest stronger, cleaner, bigger, and freer if he doesn't try to make a living at it," he took up a career in the insurance business while composing nights and weekends. (The precarious sociological position—or non-position—of American composers who have sought freedom from both commercial and academic constraints is far removed from the European patronage system: can anyone imagine Beethoven selling life insurance?) Cut off from the musical establishment, Ives pursued his own uncompromising musical vision, making little concession to "accessibility" or "idiomatic suitability." A heart attack in 1918 curtailed his activities, and he composed very little after 1921. His music gradually came to the attention of performers and listeners during the 1940s and 1950s. In more recent years the extraordinary power of his musical imagination has gained widespread recognition throughout the world, and Ives has become a pivotal figure in any study of American music.

Esteeming "substance" over "manner," Ives held a down-to-earth and yet almost mystical view of music as something that revealed and strengthened a person's character. He disdained all methods and systems of composition. "Stylistic consistency," "architectural symmetry," and "purity of . . .(whatever)" seemed to him textbook concepts that sapped music of its vigor. Discussions of the relative merits of tonality and atonality were equally irksome: "Why tonality as such should be thrown out for good I can't see. Why it should always be present, I can't see."

The energy of Ives' music is derived less from the originality of his themes than from the relationships and commentaries he created with them. Addicted to quoting marching tunes, hymns, and similar material in his music, Ives was seeking neither local color nor incongruous humor. Rather, his goal was to reveal the "substance" he perceived in such everyday music. He preferred the amateur renditions of volunteer choirs and bands, replete with wrong notes and faulty intonation, to the polished but often perfunctory performances of the concert hall, because such home-grown music was not a business but a spontaneous expression of individual and community spirit. Technical flaws were, in fact, an element of expression in Ives' view, proceeding more often from exuberance than from ineptitude. Ives delighted in writing his own "wrong notes," "late entrances," and unexpected twists into his music.

Ives spurned traditional formal principles. Repetitions are rare in his music, and many of his pieces are developmental from beginning to end, without a clear initial statement of ideas. Diverse themes are presented and developed simultaneously in thick, layered textures. Musical ideas are presented as a totality, abounding with internal contradiction, rather than laid out in "logical" succession. Ives left it to the listener to focus on specific strands in his swarming textures or, conversely, to take in the overall sweep without attempting to follow the individual ideas. He expected the listener to ferret out his own sense of meaning and, above all, to "use your ears like a man!"

Listening

Second Movement from the Symphony No. 4 *by Charles Ives (1874–1954)*

Record Set Side 11, Band 4

Ives' *Fourth Symphony,* completed in 1916, is scored for an enormous ensemble and anticipates techniques that did not become common until 50 years later. The orchestra is frequently divided into groups that play in unrelated tempos and meters, necessitating the use of two or three conductors in several passages. The four movements were conceived independently over a 15-year period as separate pieces, then reworked and compiled to form the symphony.

Ives was intensely proud of the diversity and vitality he discerned within the United States, and he believed these qualities should be reflected in its music. He distinguished two antagonistic streams running through American history. One was the frugal spiritual character of the Pilgrims, Transcendentalists, religious fundamentalists, and rural and small-town communities. The other was the bustling energy, technological ingenuity, and outright hucksterism of the cities and country fairs. Ives esteemed these "two Americas" equally and rejoiced in the tension between them, believing it to be the greatest source of the nation's vitality. In the second movement of his *Fourth Symphony* he sought to portray this dichotomy, pitting "the quiet contemplation of the spirit vs. the raucous, boisterous world" by juxtaposing serene passages against raging tuttis. Ives envisioned the movement as "a comedy—in which an exciting, easy and worldly progress through life is contrasted with the trials of the Pilgrims."

As the movement unfolds, the exuberant tutti passages grow ever more complex and insistent, overflowing with a maze of ideas. The instruments go their separate ways, producing a torrent of sound without any specific focus or goal. "Clarity of design" is completely beside the point in this movement. The listener cannot possibly follow everything that is going on. Snippets of many familiar tunes, including "Turkey in the Straw," "Yankee Doodle," and "Camptown Races," are vaguely heard amid the din. Toward the end of the movement the clamor intensifies to a circus-like pandemonium, then suddenly collapses, as the music vanishes into thin air within a few seconds. Needless to say, the tension has not been resolved, and Ives has made no attempt to tie up the loose ends of the music into a neat package.

Ives's image of America is the view of an insider who finds strength in the contention and apparent disorder of a vast, heterogeneous society. As such, it contrasts markedly with the carefully sifted and structured impressions heard in Dvořák's *"New World" Symphony.* For Ives, individual currents were less significant than the resulting mix. Although his *Fourth Symphony* does not contain a single memorable original melodic theme, it is an arresting statement—both memorable and original—of musical *ideas.* Schönberg grasped this unique quality of Ives' music when he wrote in 1945, "There is a Man living in this Country—a composer. He has solved the problem of how to preserve one's self and learn. . . . His name is Ives."

Anton Webern

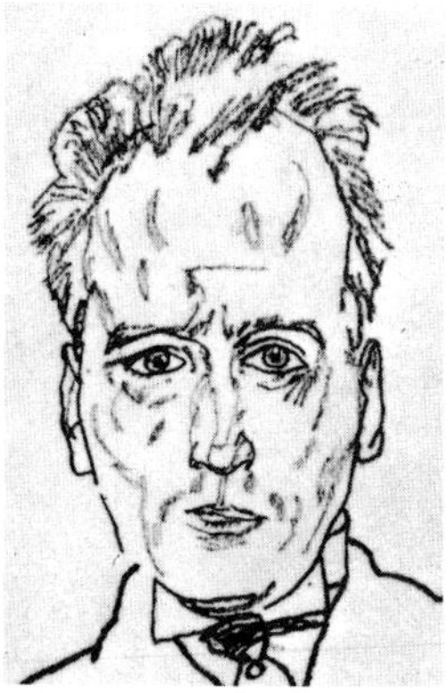

Anton Webern in a portrait by Egon Schiele

A more extreme contrast to Ives' "comedy" movement could hardly be found than the *Symphony* of Anton Webern (1883–1945). Throughout his career Webern strove for the utmost clarity and succinctness in musical design; although it runs only about ten minutes, the *Symphony* is one of his longest works.

Webern sought to work out the esthetic implications of Schönberg's serial procedures. Concentrating upon the rigorous pitch and formal designs, chiseled out with exacting care, he stripped his music of all embellishment, rhythmic and textural complexity, and overt emotional connotations. In his epigrammatic works every note is heard clearly, contributes to a network of pitch relationships, and becomes a small but important part of an intricate structural mosaic. Webern's scoring is soloistic, and the resulting delicate tissue of sound is subtle in nuance and color. The expressive range is small and dispassionate, comprising a transparent statement of serene musical logic.

Listening

Second Movement from the Symphony, Op. 21, *by Anton Webern (1883–1945)*

Webern's *Symphony* (1928) is a two-movement work for a chamber orchestra of nine instruments: clarinet, bass clarinet, two horns, harp, and string quartet. The second movement consists of a theme, seven variations, and coda, and is rigidly organized according to serial procedures. The brief theme is stated (one is tempted to say "understated") by the clarinet against a rarified accompaniment in the harp and horns. The clarinet melody is not particularly arresting. It is, indeed, extremely simple in rhythm and almost neutral in emotional tone, and it is not recalled in anything like its original form in any of the variations. Pitch relationships, rather than a melodic theme, form the basis of Webern's variation technique, and the function of the clarinet is to introduce the characteristic intervals that will be heard throughout the movement.

Each of the seven variations establishes and maintains a single textural, coloristic, and rhythmic focus. The first, for strings, is rhythmically animated. Skittish two- and four-note fragments, alternately bowed and plucked, overlap in rapid succession. The variation might at first seem to have little to do with the theme. It is quite different in nearly every respect, and the original melody has been fractured into scattered motivic remnants. The variation is a new musical fabric, but it is constructed from the same pitch relationships. The second variation features a bustling horn solo that threatens to run over anything that gets in its way. The accompanimental parts keep a respectful distance. The remaining variations feature a similar concentration of tone and gesture.

Webern's process of variation can perhaps be grasped most easily through a visual analogy. If we walk around a piece of abstract sculpture, the work can take on various apparent outward forms, and can seem to change in quality or emphasis, while still retaining a characteristic identity, or inner form. The inner form Webern is working with is a pitch framework, which remains constant while assuming a series of new articulations.

In certain respects, a work such as Webern's *Symphony* represents the coming to full cycle of symphonic format. Webern's stylistic framework is, of course, far removed from the tonal syntax of a Haydn or Mozart symphony. Nevertheless, its formal controls, economy, and overriding concern for structural clarity and articulation have many parallels with the Classical symphonic model and reflect its continuing influence. In more recent years, several leading composers have instead taken the late Romantic idiom as a point of departure and transformation. In sum, the history of symphonic music—or of any other genre—is not merely a succession of style changes, but rather a process of constant evolution and periodic renewal of basic expressive resources. For most composers, in fact, the principal source of inspiration is not a tune sent from heaven, but a knowledge and love of the unique achievements and musical traditions of their predecessors, which fire the imagination and lead to new creation.

Terms and Concepts for Review

- the Classical symphony
  - balanced formal design
  - reconciliation of ideas
  - standard sequence of movements
- Beethoven
  - expansion of formal and dramatic scope
- the Romantic symphony
  - increase in size, length, and emotional weight
  - lyric expression
  - freer types of structure
- concert overture
- symphonic poem (tone poem)

Chapter 17
The Concerto

A **concerto** is a large-scale composition, usually in three movements, for one or more soloists and orchestra. The origin of the term was probably the Latin *concertare,* which meant to "contend" or "strive together." Usually the soloist(s) and orchestra are treated as equal protagonists, playing in alternation and together in a continuous dialogue. Whereas symphonic and chamber works generally feature an integration and blending of instruments into unified textures, the solo and orchestral parts of most concertos form two distinct textural layers, with musical interest bouncing back and forth in ping-pong fashion between the "one" and the "many." The soloist's part is generally virtuosic and the orchestral textures are full and rich; in this way, technical brilliance (the solo) is set against textural depth (the tutti).

Within this basic framework, the actual division of labor and the relationship between the two parts varies considerably among individual works and historical periods. In 18th-century concertos the solo and orchestral parts are generally complementary, exchanging ideas in question-and-answer format and often picking up each others' phrases in the manner of a relay race. Later concertos generally feature greater musical and dramatic contrast between the participants and a stronger sense of rivalry.

The Baroque Concerto

Like "sonata," "cantata," and "symphony," the term "concerto" was originally vague in meaning and indicated a performing medium rather than a specific genre of composition. It was applied during the late Renaissance to choral pieces with instrumental accompaniment, as distinguished from *a cappella* vocal works. This original usage continued, somewhat anachronistically, until the time of Bach. The Baroque *instrumental concerto,* however, evolved independently during the 17th century. Its earliest ancestor was the canzona, a short chamber work such as the Gabrieli *Canzon Septimi Toni,* discussed in Chapter 15, in which instrumental groups played in alternation. Gradual expansion of this structural principle into a three- or four-movement work, and of the ensemble into a small orchestra, led to the establishment of the concerto format. Concertos were at first performed both in church and at court, but since the early 18th century the genre has been a completely secular one.

The most common type of Baroque concerto was the **concerto grosso,** which pitted a small group of instruments (often two violins and continuo) against a string orchestra, sometimes augmented by winds. The concerto grosso was the most important genre of orchestral music until superseded by the symphony. It exemplifies the division of ensembles into contrasting groups that characterizes much Baroque music. In early concerti grossi there is little stylistic differentiation between the small and large groups, which take turns at the same thematic material. However, by 1700 the solo parts had grown technically more brilliant and demanding. Professional musicians normally were hired only for the more exacting solo parts, however; the orchestra was populated largely by the servants at court, enabling the nobles to save some coin. The format of the concerto grosso was standardized into three movements, successively fast–slow–fast, a scheme that has characterized the concerto ever since. Bach's *Brandenburg Concertos* represent the artistic culmination of the Baroque concerto grosso.

The Baroque **solo concerto,** in which a single soloist takes on the orchestra, developed somewhat later. The soloist was almost always a violinist, playing rapid *passagework* (arpeggios and scale-like runs) in alternation with thematic statements in the orchestra. In Baroque concertos, the soloist continued playing during the orchestral passages, doubling the first violin part, but was absorbed into the tutti sound. Bach was the first composer to write concertos for keyboard (harpsichord) soloists. The majority of these works were transcriptions of violin concertos by Vivaldi, other composers, and Bach himself.

The rhythmically spirited music of Antonio Vivaldi (1678–1741) enjoyed great fame during his lifetime and significantly influenced the music of his contemporaries and such later composers as Bach. Renewed interest in Baroque music, which began in the 19th century but accelerated around 1950, has restored his music to widespread public recognition, and today he ranks immediately behind Bach and Handel as the most frequently performed Baroque composer.

Antonio Vivaldi

For many years Vivaldi was director of music at the Pietà Conservatory, a girls' orphanage in Venice, and he composed prolifically for the excellent student orchestra at his disposal. Vivaldi possessed a mind-boggling facility. In addition to nearly 50 operas and another 50 major vocal works, he wrote about 450 concertos, 300 of which are for violin solo. Obviously these works are not all stunningly individual achievements; like most Baroque composers, Vivaldi wrote according to well-established structural formulas. His works are of uniformly high quality, however, and never give the impression that they were hastily whipped off before breakfast.

Most of Vivaldi's concertos follow the standard fast–slow–fast sequence of movements. The first movement customarily features an emphatic opening theme. In many works, this theme recurs several times in the movement, somewhat in the manner of a tutti refrain, and is called a **ritornello.** The solo violin provides a series of rejoinders and continuations. The second movement usually consists of a lyrical theme in the solo violin accompanied by a simple figuration pattern. The third movement is a vivacious rhythmic finale, commonly alternating a ritornello tutti theme against animated solo passagework. Vivaldi did not originate this format, but he perfected it, broadening the scope of each movement and expanding the role of the soloist. He infused his works with a rhythmic drive and an exhilarating spirit of interchange between soloist and tutti that came to typify the late Baroque concerto.

Listening

"Summer" from* The Four Seasons (Le Quattro Stagioni) *by Antonio Vivaldi (1678–1741)

Typical of Vivaldi's instrumental technique and among his most engaging solo concertos are the first four works of his Opus 8 collection, which are named after the four seasons. Each of these concertos was printed with a sonnet describing the sights, sounds, and temper of the season. The lines of the sonnet are included in the score, along with additional annotations indicating particular images expressed in the music. Certain passages, for example, are identified with the chirping of birds or the rustling of leaves. *The Four Seasons* is thus an early example of program music; as is usually the case, however, it can also be enjoyed without reference to the specific pictorial associations. Published in 1724, these four short works, lasting about ten minutes each, became immensely popular in the musical capitals of Europe. "Summer" *("L'Estate"),* the second concerto of the cycle, centers around the image of a thunderstorm, which threatens in the first two movements and breaks in full fury in the finale. The orchestra is composed of strings and harpsichord continuo.

First Movement. The outer movements of Vivaldi's concertos are highly sectional in outline, consisting of alternations between thematic ideas in the strings and solo passagework. The first movement of "Summer" contains seven sections:

(1) *Tutti introduction:* The ritornello theme occurs at the end of the introduction and is based upon a repeated rhythmic motive:

The section depicts the summer doldrums of a shepherd and his flock, "scorched by the sun in this harsh season."

(2) *Solo:* At a faster tempo, the soloist launches into perpetual-motion passagework featuring rapid repeated notes that depict the call of the cuckoo:

(3) *Tutti:* The strings pick up the violin figure, then recall a shortened version of the ritornello theme.

(4) *Solo:* The violin presents more birdcall figures, this time of a gentle, pastoral nature.

(5) *Tutti:* The text depicts summer winds, which blow softly at first but suddenly become gusty. The passage begins as a variation on the ritornello theme, then bursts into an impetuous dash, portending the coming storm.

(6) *Solo:* The shepherd is uneasy, fearing for his flock. The violin melody is lyrical and plaintive, and is the only chromatic passage in the movement.

(7) *Tutti:* Storm motives of the third movement are foreshadowed, bringing the first movement to a vigorous close.

Like most of Vivaldi's music, this movement is characterized by incisive rhythms and simple, diatonic harmonic motion. The texture is homophonic rather than contrapuntal—a "progressive" trait in Vivaldi's music—and the movement remains riveted in the tonic G minor most of the time. Orchestra and soloist generally present separate ideas. Alternation of solo and ensemble—the primary means of structure and expression—is underscored by the highly sectional construction and by dynamic contrasts (loud in the tutti, soft in the solo passages).

Second Movement. The short second movement presents a single, continuous theme in the solo violin. The string accompaniment features two contrasting motives: a dotted (long–short) rhythm, and a loud, rumbling storm motive. The eloquent violin line incorporates many chromatic inflections. Alarmed by distant thunder and by a swarm of flies and hornets stirred up by the charged atmosphere, the shepherd is unable to rest.

Third Movement. Many composers have taken pleasure in reeling off a good storm movement: Beethoven in the fourth movement of his *"Pastoral" Symphony,* and Rossini in his *William Tell Overture,* to name but two. Vivaldi was among the first to have a go at it. In this finale, the strings and soloist play eleven times in alternation, but the orchestra dominates. Three motives unleash a torrent of energy: the agitated repeated-note figure from the previous movement; rapid descending scale lines in imitation between the two violin sections; and a series of lightning-like ascending sweeps. Perpetual-motion rhythmic drive is broken at only a few spots. The pivotal image of a storm that occurs in all three movements of this concerto, anticipates the cyclical structures of Berlioz, Liszt, Strauss, and other Romantic composers. It is an unusual example of musical–dramatic unity of conception in a multi-movement Baroque work.

The Classical Concerto

The style and structural outline of the Classical concerto were established by Mozart, whose achievement in the genre roughly parallels that of Haydn in the symphony and string quartet. In revamping the format of the concerto, Mozart provided a model for generations of later composers.

The Baroque concerto was segmented in form, a quilt-like design of tutti and solo passages. The soloist, or small group of soloists, were a part of the orchestra and continued playing when the rest of the ensemble took a breather. Mozart's concertos, by contrast, are broad designs that incorporate extensive development of ideas. His greatest achievement in the genre is seen in his piano concertos, which represent a synthesis of his solo piano and orchestral techniques. Most were written expressly for Mozart's own performance, and they blend technical fluency with a musical expression that is both dramatic and lucid. The soloist and orchestra are equal participants, so that, in the Classical spirit, there is a textural as well as a formal balance of parts in the music. Mozart himself characterized his piano concertos as "a happy medium between too easy and overly difficult; they are brilliant, agreeable, and natural without being insipid." The solo parts are technically demanding, but virtuosity *per se* is a less important quality of the music than continuity of expression.

The formal outline of the Classical concerto is similar to that of the sonata, symphony, and string quartet, with a few significant departures. The three-movement scheme is:

(1) *Fast,* in sonata form
(2) *Slow,* in three-part, variation, or sonata form
(3) *Fast,* in rondo or sonata-rondo form, and usually lighter in tone than the concluding movement of a symphony.

In the first movement, the customary statement and exact repetition of the exposition are replaced by a double exposition, in which the thematic material is recomposed the second time through. The first exposition is played by orchestra alone, remains in the tonic key, and is usually abbreviated. A certain tension is built as the audience observes the soloist, center stage, doing nothing. At the conclusion of the orchestral statement the soloist enters, usually with introductory passagework that announces, "Here I am!," and then launches into the opening theme. The soloist dominates the second exposition and introduces new thematic material to create a fuller statement of ideas. The second exposition follows the usual tonal scheme, modulating to the dominant or relative key. Soloist and orchestra engage in a more disputatious repartee during the development section. The recapitulation is a reworking of the second exposition. It remains in the tonic and leads to a solo cadenza and a tutti coda.

Toward the end of the first movement, and usually of the third movement as well, Classical and Romantic concertos come to a dead stop on a sustained orchestral chord, followed by a **cadenza** by the solo instrument. The cadenza functions either as an interlude or, more often, as a climax, and affords the soloist an opportunity to demonstrate his or her virtuosic skill. Usually free in tempo and rhythm, it is a rhapsodic passage that combines thematic quotes from the movement with brilliant passagework. In the Classical period, the soloist (who was often also a composer) was expected to improvise a stirring cadenza that would manifest his creative as well as interpretive skill.

Mozart was an inspired improviser, even in his youth, but not all performers were so gifted. Some used the cadenza as a pretext for ostentatious display, interjecting assorted scales, warm-up exercises, and other musical "weeds" devoid of expressive content; others turned the cadenza into a laborious second development section, seeking to distil ideas that had already been thoroughly worked out, while the orchestra waited impatiently for its cue and distracted listeners noticed that they were becoming thirsty. The art of improvisation waned at the end of the Classical period. Beginning with Beethoven (himself an unrivaled improviser), composers began writing out their own cadenzas, seeking to protect their works from empty theatrics and to integrate the cadenza more organically into the musical structure. Mozart supplied cadenzas for some of his concertos, but they were optional and were generally intended for student performers.

Listening

Piano Concerto No. 21 ***in C Major, K. 467, by Wolfgang Amadeus Mozart (1756–1791)***

First Movement. The *Piano Concerto No. 21* illustrates the very free thematic designs that Classical composers sometimes created within sonata form. The opening theme is a soft but resolute march-like idea, stated by the strings:

The two expositions of this movement contrast to an unusual degree. In the first, the winds and strings present a series of thematic ideas, most of which will be recalled only in passing later in the work. The beginning of the original theme pops up here and there, indicating that everything we are hearing is part of the first tonal group. The same motive forms the basis for the closing passage.

The piano enters without fanfare, slipping rather than splashing into the orchestral texture. After a pause, the second exposition begins with a piano trill against the opening theme in the strings. The piano assumes control of the theme, presenting it in highly embellished form, and dominates the rest of the second exposition. A transitional passage ends with an ascending scalar run in the orchestra that seems to confirm a tonal shift to the dominant key, G major. What follows, however, is a surprise shift to minor as the unaccompanied soloist interjects a fragmentary theme. The theme dissolves back into passagework, briefly accompanied by strings. When the strings drop out again, the piano at last effects the tonal shift to G major, the secondary tonal area, and leads by chromatic ascent into a more extended theme that confirms the new key:

The piano part becomes increasingly brilliant during a recomposed closing passage. With the exception of the first-group theme, the orchestra and soloist have shared little material in the double exposition. The piano has followed an unusually independent track for a Classical concerto, presenting its own ideas rather than commandeering the orchestral themes. The result, however, is not a struggle for dominance but a skillful amalgam of tutti and solo ideas, perhaps with a touch of, "I can do it differently as well as better" in the piano.

The development begins with a forceful tutti in which the martial first-group motive is heard in the bass. The orchestra generally plays in broad, lyrical phrases, recalling those ideas from the first exposition that the piano ignored; the pianist parries with yet another new theme, then with rapid passagework. Piano and orchestra pursue separate paths, but with little rancor. The musical drama lies in the textural alternation and thematic fragmentation rather than in hostile confrontation. The orchestra is ascendant at the beginning of the development section, the piano at the end, mirroring the sequence of the double exposition.

The recapitulation is abridged, with the second group following closely upon the heels of the first. In the coda several of the neglected ideas of the first exposition are recalled, and this time shared, by pianist and orchestra. Mozart did not write out the cadenza that occurs near the end of the coda. The soloist is free to select from among several that have been supplied by later composers and pianists.

Second Movement. The second movement presents a series of variations on a lyrical theme which we examined in Chapters 3 and 4. Technical virtuosity is held in abeyance during this movement. The technical demands of the solo part, in fact, would not intimidate a pianist of modest attainment—but to play the part with the simultaneous precision and expressive subtlety it requires taxes the interpretive prowess of the most sensitive artist, and brings to mind an observation by the Romantic French composer Gabriel Fauré: "Mozart's music is particularly difficult to perform. His astonishing clarity demands absolute cleanness; the most trifling inaccuracy stands out like black on white. Essentially simple and natural, it requires a simple and natural expression as well."

Third Movement. The sonata-rondo finale is lighthearted in tone. The brisk rondo theme is stated by the strings, then repeated by the piano:

Such exchange of material ("What's yours is mine") is more typical of the Classical concerto than the rigorous separation of ideas that characterized the first movement. The strong articulation of tonal motion and extensive development of thematic ideas in this movement are characteristic of sonata-rondo (as opposed to rondo) designs.

Expansion in the 19th Century

Beethoven's concertos, particularly his *Piano Concerto No. 5* (The "Emperor"), are similar to his symphonies in their forceful tone and dramatic conception. Marked contrasts between themes and between soloist and orchestra pervade the first movements. The solo part counters the increased weight of the Beethoven orchestra with a corresponding increase in technical brilliance. Rigorous working-out of thematic ideas is often accomplished through a process of almost ritual combat. By contrast, Beethoven's slow movements are often touching in their simplicity of expression and design. The concluding rondos, such as the third movement of his *Piano Concerto No. 3,* discussed in Chapter 7, are among his most winning music.

Early Romantic concertos, such as Mendelssohn's for violin and Schumann's for piano, are essentially lyric works. However, as the 19th century wore on and public fascination with virtuosi grew, the soloist generally gained the upper hand. The concertos of Chopin and Liszt feature bravura solo parts, while the orchestra sometimes sounds as though it were playing in another room. In the concertos of Johannes Brahms, on the other hand, a Classical balance is restored. Brahms' solo parts are technically brilliant and immensely challenging, but virtuosity always serves an expressive and structural end. As in his symphonies, Brahms took Beethoven's works as his model, adding a Romantic warmth and lyricism. His concertos, while often stormy encounters, are clear in design, and collectively represent the highest achievement within the genre during the Romantic period.

First movement from the* Violin Concerto in D, Op. 77, *by Johannes Brahms (1833–1897)

Brahms' *Violin Concerto* was composed in 1878 for performance by his longtime friend, the violinist Joseph Joachim. The solo part features wide leaps, multiple stops (two to four notes played simultaneously), and involved passagework, frequently at rapid tempos. Initial reception of the work was lukewarm. The solo part was considered knotty and graceless, and the work was stigmatized as a concerto *against* the violin (a quip, never much of a knee-slapper to begin with, that critics have applied with tiresome regularity to later works as well). This opinion was soon reversed, however, and today the work comprises, with the violin concertos of Beethoven and Mendelssohn, the backbone of the instrument's concerto repertoire.

The orchestral exposition begins with a first thematic group of three ideas:

A: Bassoons and low strings

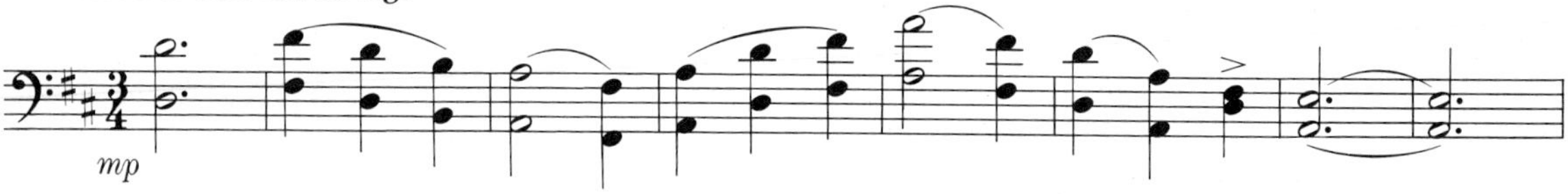

B: Oboe

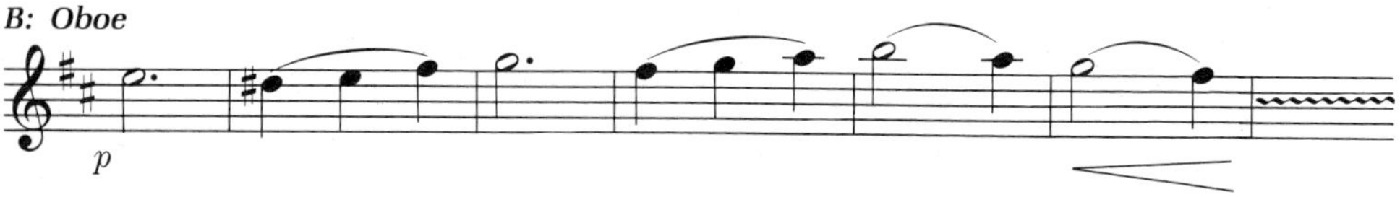

C: Tutti

The *opening group* immediately establishes the broad emotional range of the concerto as well as its basic structural dynamic—the contrast between lyrical ideas in major and rhythmically forceful ideas in minor. Idea *A* is a placid unison line that sets the D-major tonal center. Idea *B*, a lyrical, stepwise oboe melody, begins with an expressive tonal shift before pulling back into the tonic. Idea *C* is an energetic rhythmic tutti, featuring large leaps and a more extended tonal shift, this time into minor.

The *transition* begins like a tutti repetition of the first theme, heard in imitation between the basses and violins. Rhythmic pacing increases, leading to a strong cadence that coincides with the beginning of the second tonal group in the oboe and horn. The *second group* is abbreviated in this exposition. The thematic material is fragmentary in character (something is obviously missing) and dissipates into a static "waiting" passage. In place of a simple closing passage, Brahms presents an extended new theme—another typical feature that stretched the length of Romantic works. This *closing theme* is rhythmically forceful and back in minor, building to a climax in preparation for the arrival of the soloist.

The violinist enters dramatically with an extended introductory flourish. Comparison of this long, rhetorical entrance with the unobtrusive entry of the piano in the first movement of Mozart's concerto illustrates the greater emphasis on virtuosic brilliance in Romantic works. The introductory solo also incorporates the major–minor and lyrical–rhythmic contrasts that permeate the movement. It concludes with a long scalar run and a trill.

The *second exposition* contains considerable new material in the solo part. The *A* and *B* ideas of the first thematic group are separated by solo passagework. The violin presents an ornamented version of idea *B* and provides a new, syncopated countermelody in multiple stops against idea *C*. The original transition is jettisoned, and the second thematic group is extended and "completed" by the addition of its missing link—a lyrical melody and answering developmental passage, in the solo:

The closing theme is played by the soloist. Gruff, multiple-stop barks in long–short rhythms lead to a perpetual-motion run and, at length, to a climactic solo sweep. The sense of struggle that emerges with particular clarity and force at the end of the second exposition exemplifies virtuosity put to structural purpose.

In the *development section,* motives from the exposition are jumbled in rapid succession and the soloist stands apart from the orchestra. After an opening flare-up between the strings and winds the music becomes lyrical at the introduction of the "missing link" theme and then pensive at the reappearance of the violin. The process of character change is then reversed, as a series of flustered trills in the solo leads to agitated rhythmic motion that culminates in a sweeping violin run.

Brahms achieves a reconciliation of the thematic ideas in the *recapitulation and coda* by means of a smoother linking of material. The solo and orchestral parts retain individual characters and still seem to be standing on separate mountain tops, but they no longer face in opposite directions. By the end of the movement, the earlier sense of strife has been superseded by a quality of joint statement, which continues during the exquisite slow movement and jubilant rondo finale. Brahms left the cadenza for the soloist to improvise or compose, an unusual practice in so late a work, but a sign of his respect for Joachim. Joachim's original cadenza is usually performed, but several others have also been supplied.

20th-Century Practices

Most major concertos written in the first half of the 20th century feature either neoclassical or serial procedures and employ an orchestra of modest size, reflecting the general stylistic tendencies of the period. Stripped of its 19th-century textural bulk, the orchestra often assumes some of the virtuosity of the solo, and the two parts generally contrast less in function and style than they do in Romantic works. Virtuosic demands usually take the form of motoristic melodic lines and rigorous developmental expansion of motives, rather than of rhetorical flourishes. Neoclassicists generally downplayed technical brilliance in favor of a balanced solo–tutti statement of ideas and sharp rhythmic impetus. Several composers have revived and extended the concerto grosso concept, writing "concertos for orchestra" that spotlight various instruments and small groups within the orchestra in a succession of solo passages alternating with tutti. Bartók's *Concerto for Orchestra* (1944) is the most widely performed example of this type.

The concerto has thus far proven to be the most durable of the traditional instrumental genres, probably because its underlying dynamic is a flexible textural concept (the joint statement of ideas) that is adaptable to changing stylistic frameworks, rather than a specific formal design. While the sonata and symphony have generally fallen by the wayside in the last quarter century, being succeeded by freer types of structure, the concerto has been able to absorb many recent formal innovations. The Classical formal scheme has been abandoned or transformed, and the Romantic emphasis on emotional expression and textural confrontation has given way to a concentrated working-out of structural relationships; but the broad multi-movement (or multi-sectional) Big Statement of the traditional concerto remains an essential feature of recent works.

Double Concerto for Harpsichord, Piano, and Two Chamber Orchestras, *by Elliott Carter (b. 1908)*

Eliott Carter

Elliott Carter is among the most prominent American composers of the present era. Carter began as a neoclassicist, but in the years around 1950 his style evolved into a more rigorous and personal musical language. His style can be characterized as a linear form of chromatic atonality, in which individual lines and rhythms are less arresting than the ways in which they interact to form structural patterns. Carter's output is relatively small. He composes with painstaking care, producing a major work every three or four years.

Carter's *Double Concerto* (1961) is written for 18 players divided into two balanced groups, and thus straddles the border between orchestral and chamber music. Each group features a soloist and chamber orchestra of eight players—four winds, two strings, and two percussionists who play a wide array of instruments of indefinite pitch. Carter asks that the two ensembles be as widely separated on stage as possible, so that the individual lines will stand out in relief and antiphonal interplay between the groups will be emphasized.

One problem Carter faced at the outset was how to reconcile the very different idiomatic characteristics of the two solo instruments. Although both are keyboard instruments, they respond to the touch in dissimilar ways, and the harpsichord has considerably less dynamic range and sustaining power. In a no-holds-barred contest the piano could easily bully and overwhelm its overmatched cousin. Carter's solution was to write for the two instruments in an essentially similar style—one of propulsive melodic runs—while gradually differentiating their separate thematic material. The soloists function as leaders and focal points of their respective ensembles. The orchestral instruments generally play independent lines, often in concert with their soloist. The resulting linear textures are centered around the development of characteristic figures in the solo instruments, enriched by the simultaneous statement of other ideas within the orchestras. The two groups often perform antiphonally, and at times pitches and motives can be heard to travel (spatially as well as texturally) between the ensembles. Often, however, various instruments from the two orchestras perform together, producing a more homogeneous texture. Differentiation is less pronounced between orchestras than between soloists.

The basic dynamic of the *Double Concerto* is a process of gradual differentiation of musical ideas and character between the soloists. The harpsichord and piano parts come to function somewhat like the "right and left hands" of a single keyboard player, performing separate materials but in a similar idiom. To realize this conception, Carter establishes a continuum of sound treatment between *percussive* gestures (the natural habitat of the harpsichord) and *lyrical* ideas (the traditional preserve of the piano).

The two soloists act as intermediaries between the percussive and linear layers of the texture. At the beginning and end of the work, the soloists play undifferentiated riffs—short, repetitive figures, with little sense of line or direction, that mirror the percussive gestures. Throughout the main body of the work, the soloists develop long declamatory lines that serve as the center of musical interest, but also interject occasional percussive jabs. The soloists thus serve as advocates and umpires between the two textural layers, forming a double nucleus from which ideas are spun out.

The work is in seven interconnected sections: (1) introduction; (2) cadenza for harpsichord; (3) allegro scherzando; (4) adagio; (5) presto; (6) two piano cadenzas; and (7) coda. The third, fourth, and fifth sections function somewhat in the manner of the three movements of a Classical concerto. The music generally flows continuously between sections, but pauses precede numbers three and seven. Our study will focus on the first two sections, which establish the basic dynamic of the concerto.

Introduction. The work begins with nebulous wave-like incitements—rolls and brief figures—in the four percussion parts. There are no pitched sounds, no memorable motives, merely a potential impetus for musical ideas. Winds and strings enter imperceptibly, mimicking the percussive figures, and the piano joins in similar fashion with a growling roll-like figure. The harpsichord enters in short gasps, and for the first time a sense of pitch direction—the seed of a line—is felt. Throughout the rest of the section, musical ideas take increasingly definitive shape, like a dancer who gradually arises from a collapsed position and projects ever more precise and detailed gestures.

The structural emphasis centers on process rather than on specific themes or motives. Harpsichord and piano generally play in alternation. They begin with short, ejaculatory figures, with much internal repetition, that convey little feeling of breadth or shape. Gradually these figures become more extended, assuming a sense of line and character. A similar transformation occurs in the orchestras, which begin to forge sonorities and melodic contours out of indistinct earlier figures. The texture slowly evolves from coloristic to linear. The two orchestras come together on a tutti build-up, followed by a long, arabesque harpsichord line. The harpsichord increasingly dominates the rest of the section, becoming a single focal point of musical interest. (The piano will become dominant later in the work.) At length the two orchestras build to another tutti climax, with strong accents, out of which the harpsichord cadenza emerges.

Cadenza for Harpsichord. In the preceding section, Carter has established the style of solo writing in the work: long, propulsive lines that unravel to form solid blocks of sound. The harpsichord cadenza is a concentrated exposition of this solo style, distilling ideas heard in fragmentary form in the introduction. The cadenza thus functions in reverse manner from Classical practice; it is here a clarification and statement of musical ideas, rather than a free embellishment or breaking-down of earlier themes.

The cadenza also illustrates Carter's technique of "metric modulation"—the smooth connection of different tempos. The apparent tempo seems to shift several times during the cadenza, but these internal variations are actually different subdivisions of one underlying tempo. Near the end of the cadenza the orchestral instruments enter on sustained sonorities, and the section dissolves quietly back into indistinct percussive figures. (In the coda a similar dissolution takes place. After a tumultuous opening tutti, solo and orchestral lines become fragmented and are eventually absorbed into percussive figures, reversing the structural process of the introduction and producing a mirror-like symmetry to the piece as a whole.)

If one were to stand at a busy city intersection and attempt to make sense of the activity going on, it would at first seem aimless and chaotic. But gradually, patterns would begin to emerge: these guys go *this* way, those guys go *that* way. At times, the pattern might become so complex, with U-turns, jaywalkers, and so forth, that it would be temporarily lost. But it would ultimately re-emerge and be seen in a larger light (these guys *usually* go this way). The "traffic patterns" in the *Double Concerto* are similarly complex, and must be grasped over a period of time. Individual lines are driven by separate internal dynamics and are separate textural units. The overall expressive dynamic of the piece is its cyclical patterned motion, as ideas take shape and dissipate, going from dust to dust.

Terms and Concepts for Review

- technical brilliance (solo) vs. textural brilliance (tutti)
- passagework
- Baroque concerto
  - concerto grosso
  - solo concerto
  - ritornello
  - sectional structure
- Classical concerto
  - double exposition
  - cadenza
- Romantic concerto
  - increased emphasis on solo virtuosity
- 20th-century concerto
  - rigorous development generally replaces rhetorical virtuosity
  - concerto for orchestra

Chapter 18
Introduction to Opera

Opera is drama set to music. It is the most complex theatrical genre, combining several independent art forms: music (both vocal and instrumental), dramatic action, poetry, and often dance. Stage design, lighting, and costumes also contribute significantly to the dramatic impact.

To musical and dramatic purists, opera has often seemed a diffuse artistic hybrid whose commingling of so many elements inevitably leads to clutter and confusion. A widely quoted, if facetiously overdrawn (and very French), example of such criticism is the following definition of opera: "a bizarre affair made up of poetry and music, in which the poet and musician, each equally obstructed by the other, give themselves no end of trouble to produce a wretched result."[1] In fact opera is neither a concert nor a play. The music is not a mere accompaniment, and the poetry and stage action are not simply vehicles or excuses for song. Music and drama are united into a multidimensional expression of human feelings.

Spectacle and illusion are essential to operatic production. What happens on stage is in most cases not even a rough approximation of realistic events: in everyday life people do not spontaneously burst into song when emotionally aroused. Most operas are closer to the realm of myth, seeking to portray inner realities and passions. The outward events require a certain suspension of belief. We are not asked to ponder the logic of the narrative, but to open ourselves fully to its quality of expression. In mediocre operas or poor productions, music, poetry, and action may coexist awkwardly or unconvincingly, so that the actions seem remote and our involvement remains superficial. In successful productions of great operas, however, these elements fuse together and speak directly to our emotions; the music seems to spring naturally from the dramatic situation, to intensify it, and to make it more compelling. When this happens, opera attains its full potential.

[1] Saint Évremond, *Oeuvres*, iii, 248, quoted in the Harvard Dictionary of Music, second edition, Willi Apel, editor, Belknap Press of Harvard University, Cambridge, Massachusetts, 1970, p. 592.

The Libretto

The **libretto** is the text of an opera. It is usually written by a poet or playwright and occasionally by the composer. Many composers have collaborated closely with librettists, helping map out the scenario, suggesting that a particular character needs another solo number or a breather, and so on. The actual story line may be either borrowed or original. Well-known plots are often chosen, and certain tales have been used again and again. Novels, plays, ancient myths, national or folk legends, and fairy tales are common sources which, by their familiarity, immediately involve the listener in the drama.

The requirements of a good libretto differ from those of a stage play. *Hamlet,* or any other play, could not be set directly to music; it would be too long and verbose in a musical setting (we sing more slowly than we speak) and too complicated by subplots and subtleties. Because the poetry is but one element of opera, rather than the major focus of our attention, it must be simplified in order to be successfully set to music. Highly sophisticated poetry often sounds like babble when sung; it does not meet the musical demand for clear, uncomplicated expression of feeling.

The world created by opera librettos is usually an elemental one. Traditional conventions include faraway settings and archetypal characters who act on impulse rather than consider their options. To draw us into a realm where feelings reign supreme, librettists frequently appeal to our need for escape, enabling listeners to empathize with larger-than-life figures who act decisively, without the ambivalence or fear of consequences that temper our own actions. The operatic stage has historically been a high-crime district, where mistaken identity, disguise, murder, and retribution are commonplace events. Georges Bizet, the composer of *Carmen,* believed that, "If one were to suppress adultery, fanaticism, crime, evil, and the supernatural, there would no longer be the means for writing one note." As in Greek tragedy, operatic characters often fulfill foreordained ritual actions, and the dramatic emphasis centers less on the actual events than on what they mean and how they are experienced. Simplification of character motivation and plot allows for exalted states of emotion: those simple but powerful feelings that can almost seem to demand musical realization to relieve dramatic tension. It should be noted, however, that not all operas conform to these conventions. Many composers, especially in the last 100 years, have sought not to create a fantasy world, but to express a national or ethnic heritage, to present social commentary or satire, or merely to provide an absorbing diversion. A certain heroic dimension, however, is common to nearly all operas, even those with a comic plot.

The stage action of most operas is not continuous, but is rather a stop-and-go sequence in which the primary focus of interest alternates between the drama and the music. While a dramatic situation is developing, the music is often simple and delivered rapidly. As events come to a head the action stops and the emphasis shifts to the music; one or more of the protagonists reflect upon affairs, revealing their feelings in song. Character development takes place primarily in solo songs. In a spoken play such frequent interruptions would soon become tedious; in opera they are generally essential to the dramatic impact, since our attention can only rarely center equally on the music and drama at any given point.

Librettos sometimes appear ridiculous when read apart from their musical settings. The actions may seem grotesque or silly, the poetry repetitive, pompous, or sentimental. This is because the libretto is not meant to stand by itself. It is the music that breathes life into these elemental actions by sharpening the depiction of mood and character. The otherwise blunt dialogue and quixotic exploits of the characters become meaningful, touching, even cathartic, through the power of musical expression.

Operas are usually peformed in their original language—especially for some reason, in the United States; performances in translation are more common in Europe. This means that most productions are in a language unfamiliar to a majority of American listeners: usually either Italian, German, or French. Performers and audiences have long debated the relative merits of producing operas in their original language or in that "of the people." H. L. Mencken, for one, believed opera in English to be "about as sensible as baseball in Italian." For the listener thoroughly familiar with the plot the choice of language makes relatively little difference; to the fellow in the next seat with no knowledge of the story, however, the language barrier can be very real, particularly in the case of comic operas based on complicated intrigues and deception. In tragic operas, periodic deaths and arguments, and—more important—the emotional intensity of the music can provide a thread of continuity even for those who have only the vaguest idea of what is being sung. One reason producers have been reluctant to stage operas in English has been the legendary poor quality of many traditional translations, which sometimes provoke unintended laughter through maladroit paraphrases, anachronisms, or obviously desperate rhymes. Such gaucheries detract from the strength of the opera and destroy its quality of illusion. More recent translations are generally of much higher quality, so these traditional issues no longer weigh as heavily.

While making an opera accessible to a wider audience, however, translations create other problems. The translator must strive to preserve the original meaning of the verse while simultaneously assuring that the vowel sounds of important notes are singable. (Some vowels, like *"ee"*, cannot be gracefully sustained on high notes.) The translator must also decide whether to attempt to reproduce the original rhyme scheme. Italian and French have a different accentual rhythm from English; there are fewer accents and they are given less stress. Translations into English can sound clumsy, lacking the even flow of the original declamation, particularly in rapid passages. Most importantly, no translation can convey the precise nuances and flavor of the original text. Listeners should always take the time to acquaint themselves with the plot and characterization *before* hearing an opera, so that they can concentrate on the dramatic power of a performance rather than on trying to figure out what is going on. There are distinct advantages to productions in both English and the original language, and both types should be enjoyed for their particular qualities.

Staging

Staging, which includes the physical movement of characters, scenery, and lighting, strengthens the import of an opera, visually reinforcing what we hear. Without good staging, opera is little more than an elaborate concert.

Scenery and lighting subliminally establish mood and setting. The lighting is most often focused on whoever is singing, but is also used to create special effects—storms, fires, and so on—that significantly contribute to the dramatic illusion. The stage designer strives to make effective use of a limited amount of space, creating sets that are both imaginative and functional; the singers should be able to move through (and not merely in front of) the scenic backdrop. Stagehands must be able to break down and change sets quickly between scenes, before a restive audience begins kibitzing and loses the continuity of the drama.

A stage director plans the general placement, movement, and actions of the characters. He or she is responsible for the overall dramatic interpretation of the work. Unless completely autocratic, the stage director will discuss with the singers the way in which each character should contribute to this interpretation and will elicit their suggestions. In blocking out the actions during rehearsals, the stage director will try to incorporate the singers' own insights into the motivations of their characters and will attempt to utilize

Alfredo confronts Violetta at a party, in Act III of Verdi's La Traviata. *Opera requires the coordination of acting and singing, orchestral playing and stage direction, scenic design, costuming, and lighting into a unified and emotionally convincing whole.*

the unique acting strengths of the major performers. Most operatic performers are trained primarily as singers rather than actors, although the best master both skills; without clear stage direction the action may be leaden, the timing poor, and the gestures of the characters poorly synchronized.

Dance has usually been incidental to opera, often comprising part of a setting, such as a ball or march. In some operatic styles, ballets became an obligatory interjection, extraneous to the dramatic action and used solely for diversion and spectacle. More recently, dance sequences have been given greater attention and vitality in opera, possibly through the healthy influence of Broadway musicals, where major dance numbers help carry the action and form an integral part of the production.

When we listen to a recording of an opera we are experiencing only a portion of the impact of a live production. Situations that might seem far-fetched in the abstract can be vitalized through dynamic acting, set designs, lighting, and movement. Opera, more than any other traditional musical genre, must be experienced *live* if it is to be experienced fully.

Singers

Opera singing is a specialized and highly demanding career. Most singers concentrate either on opera or on the concert and song repertoire. Opera requires special natural abilities and training. The singer's natural voice must not only be beautiful, it must be large. He or she must develop the ability to project effectively through halls that are often too large or acoustically dead. While singing, the performer must move about the stage and occasionally assume positions detrimental to good vocal production. All the while, the singer must appear spontaneous and genuine, while surreptitiously watching a distant conductor out of the corner of one eye. Opera singers begin their careers only after years of study; they must not only develop their natural voices but also learn roles (they must sing from memory) from both musical and dramatic standpoints.

The customary vocal ranges given in Chapter 5 are further qualified in opera by the "weight," character, and facility necessary for the performance of certain roles. This is particularly true of higher voices (sopranos and tenors), which are usually given the leading vocal parts. The *dramatic* soprano or tenor needs a powerful, projecting voice, capable of carrying over a full orchestral tutti. *Lyric* singers excel at expressive, tender melodic lines, and have a lighter timbre. Roles for *coloratura* soprano demand a very high range and technical virtuosity: the ability to perform instrumental-like scale passages, trills, and rapid runs. While some soprano roles are tailored to one of these qualities, others demand that the singer master all three.

Singers are often aided by prompters, who sit in a small box at center stage unseen by the audience. Prompters cue entrances, supply words (and sometimes starting pitches), and indicate stage actions. Many singers learn 30 or more roles, and memory slips are inevitable. The function of prompters is to help avert such lapses, or enable singers to recover quickly before a slip becomes a catastrophe.

Conductor, Orchestra, and Chorus

Opera orchestras are generally of symphonic proportions but with fewer strings. The orchestra is seated in a pit below the front of the stage, and the conductor is elevated in order to be seen by the singers. The conductor is responsible for the overall musical interpretation of the work, as the stage director is for the action. While holding the music together, the conductor must allow the singers some interpretive leeway and rhythmic flexibility and, in certain passages, even be able to follow or anticipate the singer's phrasing. In Europe, many symphonic conductors begin their careers in an apprenticeship as opera coaches, accompanying singers at the piano during rehearsals.

The orchestra accompanies the singers but also has its own independent numbers that establish mood and underscore stage action. Most operas begin with a five- to ten-minute orchestral number, called an **overture** or **prelude.** The themes of the overture are often drawn from memorable vocal passages of the opera. Overtures serve to establish the overall tone and emotional quality of an opera at the outset. Many are cast in a traditional form, usually a simplified sonata-form design, and are frequently played as independent compositions on symphonic concerts. Preludes are generally shorter and freer in form.

The chorus performs a limited function in most operas. Like the chorus in a Greek tragedy, it comments occasionally on the action. The members of the chorus often form groups or crowds (soldiers, nobles, patrons of a tavern, and so on) and appear in the more festive scenes.

The Formal Structure of Opera

Operas, like plays, consist of from one to five acts (major divisions), each of which is further divided into several scenes. A scene contains a series of musical numbers, some self-contained (ending with a full-stop), others run together. Most of the numbers are recitatives, arias, or ensembles.

Recitatives (from the Italian for "recite") generally follow the natural rhythms and inflections of speech. They are usually performed by a solo singer but may also take the form of a brisk dialogue. Recitatives serve to disclose information, push the action along, or reveal character motivation. Words are delivered rapidly, and musical interest is sometimes minimal. The simplified vocal line, often only a skeletal melody, contains many repeated notes; the pulse is free and the mood generally hurried.

An **aria** is a complete solo song, with metrical rhythms and a more structured design. The text is delivered less rapidly than in recitatives. Many famous arias were written by composers with specific performers in mind. Mozart once remarked, "I like an aria to fit a singer as perfectly as a well-tailored suit of clothes."

Duets are numbers for two singers, often resembling arias in format. **Ensembles** feature three or more singers, who project a variety of contrasting emotions simultaneously. The independent vocal lines often contrast markedly in melodic and rhythmic style. The different characters are typically self-absorbed, unaware of or indifferent to their companions. In a famous quartet from Verdi's *Rigoletto,* the following actions are sung simultaneously: the Duke is seducing Maddalena, a barmaid, inside a tavern; Maddalena flirts with him. Outside, spying through the window, Rigoletto demonstrates to his daughter that the Duke was only dallying with her feelings. Rigoletto cries for vengeance, while his daughter, seduced and abandoned by the Duke, sobs with despair.

In a play, so much action, with the characters all speaking at once, would be incomprehensible. In opera, the separate music of each character makes such concentrated action not only possible but dramatically powerful. Many acts conclude with a vigorous ensemble.

Serious and Comic Opera

"Serious" and "comic" opera traditionally have been distinguished not only by differences in tone and subject matter but also by formal and stylistic distinctions. Serious opera, the older genre, is sung throughout. "Serious" does not necessarily imply "grim," and these operas often contain lighter moments. The emotional range runs the gamut from joy to desolation, and the characters are involved in matters of consequence. Serious operas are most often in three acts, with each act running close to an hour.

Comic opera developed in the 18th century and appealed to a broader middle-class audience. Early examples were breezy in tone, built on a farcical or satiric plot, and much lighter in musical character. Most importantly, recitatives were replaced (in all countries except Italy) by spoken dialogue in order to move the action more quickly. Comic operas are generally shorter, usually in two acts.

By 1800 many comic operas had become weightier in both musical and dramatic style. Recitatives were introduced, and the traditional formal distinctions between serious and comic operas became less pronounced. A concurrent offshoot was the apperance of **operetta**—a short theatrical production with arias, ensembles, and orchestral numbers (frequently dances) in a popular style. Operetta is the antecedent of American musical comedies.

Terms and Concepts for Review

libretto
staging
dramatic, lyric, and
  coloratura vocal qualities
overture
prelude
recitative
aria
ensemble
serious and comic opera

Chapter 19
Opera

The Origins of Opera

Although the use of music in combination with drama can be traced back to the choral songs and dances of ancient Greek theater, opera as we know it originated in Florence, Italy, around 1600. There were several musical antecedents for the new genre, but the primary impetus came from theoretical speculation. A group of Florentine intellectuals and musicians, who collectively called themselves the *Camerata*, objected to the dense style of Renaissance vocal polyphony. Believing that vocal music should portray a single emotion, heightening the dramatic impact of the text, they felt that this ideal was impossible when contrasting vocal lines (and often different words) were sung simultaneously. The Camerata found in ancient Greek drama a model for what they hoped would be a more coherent vocal art. They imagined Greek drama to have been a uniquely powerful and pure form of expression, in which music of a simple character underscored the qualities of the verse. Their efforts to emulate this ancient practice were hardly authentic, since they had only the vaguest notion of how Greek drama actually sounded. The stylistic principles they formulated, however, led to the composition of the first operas by Jacopo Peri and Giulio Caccini, and soon exerted a far-reaching influence on musical practice.

The first operas were performed at court before gatherings of nobles. Not surprisingly, the librettos were based on classical Greek myths. The music consisted largely of **monodies,** declamatory melodies that adhered closely to natural speech inflections. Monodies were supported by a bare-boned harmonic accompaniment performed by lutes and strings. Purely musical interest was limited, so as not to detract from the centrality of the text. To modern ears this succession of carefully calculated speech-songs can sound austere, but to the original audiences the effect was striking. Much of this impact was probably due to the directness and novelty of the new style. The historical significance of these early operas is considerable. The preeminence of solo song, which has characterized opera ever since, was established, and the simplified accompanied melody textures signalled the beginning of a harmonically-governed practice that culminated in the system of tonal harmony.

Claudio Monteverdi

Claudio Monteverdi (1567–1643) was the most versatile and gifted composer of his age. His early years were spent as a musician and music

Claudio Monteverdi

director at the court of Mantua. In 1613 he was appointed choir master of St. Mark's Cathedral in Venice. Monteverdi was a master at both sacred and secular forms and is best known today for his many madrigals, which encompass a broad range of styles, forms, and expression. His greatest achievement, however, was the unprecedented musical vitality and emotional power he brought to opera. He fused Florentine monody with the rich traditions of 16th-century polyphony and made the music a fully equal partner with the drama.

Although his first opera, *Orfeo* (1607), was written only a few years after the early works of Peri and Caccini, it was quite different in tone, displaying Monteverdi's characteristic emphasis on dramatic intensity. His characters were not impersonal stereotypes; they were flesh-and-blood protagonists with human passions, weaknesses, and cunning. They are characters with whom we can identify. Monteverdi was able to transform the academic doctrines of the Camerata into dynamic musical and dramatic forms. He accepted their basic premise that "the text should be the master of music, not the servant," but was too much a composer to let his vivid musical imagination be constrained by doctrinaire theories.

Monteverdi was a highly innovative craftsman. His recitatives are melodically arresting and are supported by rich, forceful harmonies. He introduced arias, duets, choruses, and dances into opera, not as diversions, but to heighten dramatic impact. In *Orfeo,* he expanded the orchestra to an ensemble of over 40 instruments. Even in his later operas, where the orchestra is reduced to strings and harpsichord, it is given independent numbers. Several instrumental effects that later became commonplace, such as string pizzicatos and tremolos, appeared first in his operas.

Listening

Act I, Scenes 1-3,[1] *from* The Coronation of Poppea *by Claudio Monteverdi (1567–1643)*

The Coronation of Poppea was written in Venice in 1642 when the composer was 75. The plot, unusual for its time in depth of character development, remains one of the more brazen in the annals of opera. It is a story of ambition, lust, perfidy, and murder, made dramatically powerful through the force of the music. The action is set in Rome in 65 A.D., and takes place in a single day.

Scene 1. The opera opens with a brief sinfonia, a forerunner of the later overture. The orchestra consists mostly of strings and continuo instruments (harpsichords and lutes). The sinfonia is in *A–B–A* form and is homophonic in texture. Musical interest is concentrated in the

[1] The opera is often abridged in modern performances and the first three scenes have occasionally been combined into a single opening scene.

harmonic progressions, particularly in the frequent alternation between major and minor. The melody is simply the top harmonic voice, played by the violins.

The action begins at daybreak outside Poppea's house. Ottone, who still thinks himself Poppea's lover, returns home after foreign travels. In a series of brief arias he expresses his desire to see Poppea again. The arias are framed by short orchestral interludes called **ritornelli.** Ottone's buoyant mood quickly evaporates when he discovers two of Nero's soldiers sleeping in front of the house. As his anxiety grows, Ottone's melody becomes continuous and alternates between passages in recitative and aria style. These two vocal styles are much less distinct here than in later operas, and Monteverdi smoothly interweaves them into an unbroken thread. Ottone's rapid changes of mood—from one of anticipation, to surprise, to the grim realization that Nero is sleeping inside with Poppea—are articulated by changes in tempo, rhythm, melodic style, and harmony. The role of Ottone was originally sung by a male soprano, but in modern revivals it is usually performed by a baritone.

Scene 2. The two soldiers awaken and complain of their tedious duty (soldiers rarely fight in opera, but frequently complain), then gossip about life and intrigues at the palace. Solo song dominates the opera, and ensembles are limited to a few brief duets. Even within the duets, as in the soldiers' exchange here, the singers generally perform in alternation rather than together. The vocal lines fluctuate rapidly between recitatives and arias. Nothing of consequence happens. The banter of the soldiers serves to establish the corrupt and cynical mood of the Roman palace, where everyone is pursuing his or her own "hustle" and duplicity is rampant.

Scene 3. Poppea and Nero enter. Poppea, anxious to marry Nero and be placed on the throne, schemes to persuade him to renounce his present wife, Ottavia. Nero, though madly in love with Poppea, is at first noncommittal to her appeals. The wily Poppea avoids confrontation. When Nero expresses hesitation, she assures him of her love; when he returns her expressions of desire, she presses him to act. The soldiers' sarcastic dialogue already has alerted the listener to view Poppea's words and actions with skepticism. Monteverdi's charming musical setting of her lines, however, temporarily allays this suspicion. Her expressions of love are poignant and appear genuine. Were Poppea depicted as a grasping shrew throughout the opera we would soon lose interest in her intrigues. Instead, Monteverdi is able to arouse our dramatic sympathies through musical means (the greatest achievement of any operatic composer). Poppea's recitatives contain several striking chromatic inflections, particularly when she professes to be on the verge of tears or fainting.

The lovers become resolute, swear fidelity, and in two memorable short arias prepare to part:

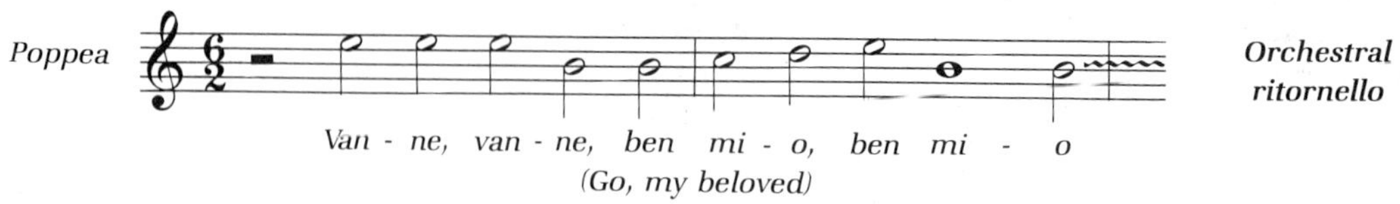

Before she will let Nero go, however, Poppea seeks more concrete assurances of his intentions. Nero is brusque at first, but slowly melts at her importuning. In one of the most celebrated passages of the opera, Poppea asks, "Will you return?" *("Tornerai?").* Nero briefly assures her of his love. Hardly satisfied with this perfunctory answer, she repeats the question. In a brief aria, Nero attempts to mollify her at greater length. This is still not the answer she is looking for, and she presses the question a third time, more intensely, in a higher register. When he promises to return, she urgently demands, "When?" *("Quando?")*; "Right away" *("Ben tosto")* he answers.

The lovers part in a simple, moving final recitative *("Addio").* The singers were expected to draw out this passage with improvisatory vocal embellishments to heighten its dramatic force. A later composer would likely have set much of this scene (particularly the *"Addio"*) as an impassioned duet, sacrificing some clarity in the poetry for the added musical and visual impact gained by having the lovers sing together. Poppea and Nero, however, never sing simultaneously. It is a mark of Monteverdi's musical and dramatic skill that he is able to heighten emotional tension and bring it to a convincing resolution through a simple alternation between the two singers. The strength of the music lies in the way the composer has carefully set every word with attention to meaning and feeling; dramatic expression has determined the musical form.

As the plot unravels, Seneca, a wise man who has resisted Nero's plan to marry Poppea, commits suicide at Nero's orders. Ottavia is exiled and Poppea attains her throne. Evil triumphs over good, lust and ambition overcome genuine love. By itself, the libretto would arouse little sympathy or interest in the cabal of such scruffy characters. It is Monteverdi's music, consistently engaging, always theatrically apposite, that infuses human feeling into the drama and creates an absorbing stage work.

Later Baroque Opera

In 1637 the first public opera house opened in Venice. Opera was no longer exclusively a private entertainment for the rich, but became accessible to a broader audience. Italy—particularly Venice—remained the center of opera throughout the Baroque period. The gradual spread of opera houses throughout the major cities of Europe, however, enabled audiences in other countries to attend productions of Italian operas, and eventually led to the development of distinct national operatic styles based on the Italian model in Germany, England, and France.

As the form and conventions of serious opera developed, they became far removed from the original sober ideals of the Camerata. Operas became longer and more elaborate. The emphasis shifted from the drama and poetry to visual and musical display. Staging featured opulent sets and costumes and frequently incorporated such grandiose effects as battles, shipwrecks, and gods descending from the heavens. The number of major characters increased by leaps and bounds; plots became highly involved, sometimes bewilderingly complex. Most important, recitative and aria became totally distinct vocal styles, and arias became the principal attraction of the production.

Late-17th and early-18th-century operas were dominated by virtuoso singers. Leading singers were expected to add elaborate improvisatory embellishments to arias. The written melody sometimes provided little more than a skeletal framework for exhibition of a singer's technique, as in the following illustration:[1]

Serse, *Act I, Scene 1, by Handel*

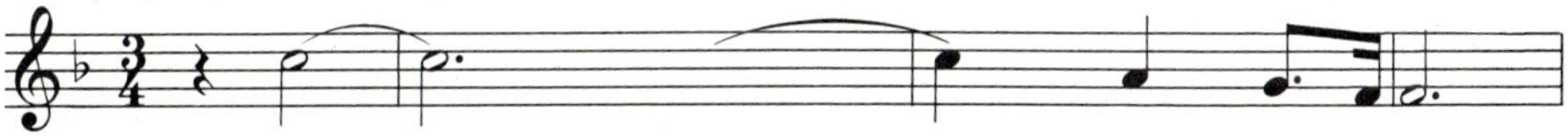

The most celebrated virtuosi of Baroque Italian opera were *castrati,* who performed many leading roles, both male and female. The barbarous custom of castrating promising boy singers to keep their voices from changing was widespread in Italy. Castrati had a high (boy's or woman's) vocal range, a nasal timbre that fascinated audiences, and great powers of projection. They were celebrated for their technical facility.

By the early 18th century, opera had become a highly conventionalized form of theater and was the dominant musical genre in Italy. Singers, rather than the drama, were the drawing cards. *Bel canto* vocal technique, which emphasized beauty of sound and technical prowess rather than dramatic power, became the vocal ideal. The greatest composer of late Baroque Italian opera was, paradoxically, a German who produced his operas in London—George Frideric Handel. Handel's arias cover a wide range of expression, from simple folklike melodies to virtuosic coloratura writing. The

[1] Quoted in Donald J. Grout, *A Short History of Opera,* Columbia University Press, New York, 1947, page 194.

principal numbers of his operas are ***da capo* arias,** *A–B–A* designs in which the middle section contrasts in mood, tonality, and melodic style with the opening theme. Baroque composers did not write out the return of the *A* theme, but merely indicated it by the words *da capo* ("from the beginning") at the end of the *B* section. Singers customarily introduced more elaborate ornaments during the return, and the three sections often served to spotlight different aspects of the singer's craft: lyricism and purity of sound *(A)*; forceful projection *(B)*; and technical virtuosity *(A')*. Most of Handel's da capo arias are preceded by a *secco* ("dry") recitative, which sets up the aria and is accompanied only by continuo (harpsichord and bass instrument).

Suggested Listening

***Recitative, "E pur cosi in un giorno," and Aria, "Piangerò la sorte mia," from Act IV of* Giulio Cesare *by George Frideric Handel (1685–1759)*[1]**

Handel's *Giulio Cesare* (1724) is his best-known opera today. The libretto concerns the love between Caesar and Cleopatra, and Cleopatra's contention with her brother Ptolemy for the Egyptian throne. In the third act Cleopatra is imprisoned, and expresses her fear of death in this secco recitative and da capo aria. The *A* sections of the aria typify the *bel canto* vocal style that dominated 18th and 19th century Italian opera. In the contrasting *B* section (*"Ma poi morta d' ogn' intorno . . ."*—"but from the grave I will haunt the tyrant day and night") Cleopatra vents her fury at her brother.

Opera in the Classical Period: Mozart

Despite the rise of symphonic and chamber music during the late 18th century, opera remained the musical genre with the widest public following. In Vienna, where Mozart spent the last ten years of his life and wrote his greatest works, the musical life of the city revolved around its opera houses, and leading singers were idolized by the populace.

Mozart was heir to a number of operatic traditions. By the late 18th century, the long hegemony of ***opera seria*** (serious opera), with its plots from Greco-Roman history and mythology, rigid conventions, and total lack of dramatic realism was coming to an end. Mozart's *Idomeneo* (first performed in 1781) is one of the last, as well as greatest, works in this tradition. The Italian ***opera buffa*** (comic opera) was a more flexible form, peopled by such stock characters as star-crossed young lovers, the honorable father, and an array of crafty, foolish, and obtuse servants. The sometimes threadbare plots

[1]This recitative and aria are available on a single-band excerpt in performance by Elly Ameling on Philips record 6570-113. In the abridged recording of the opera by Beverly Sills and the New York City Opera (RCA LSC-6182) the aria is shifted to Act I two-thirds of the way through side 1, and the recitative is omitted.

were based on mistaken identity and bedroom farce. Within the tradition of *opera buffa*, however, there was also room for more serious characterization. Most of Mozart's operas are comedies, written either in German (with spoken dialogue) or Italian (with recitatives). His *Così fan tutte, Marriage of Figaro,* and *Don Giovanni* are three of the greatest masterpieces of Italian comic opera.

Listening

Excerpts from* Don Giovanni *by Wolfgang Amadeus Mozart (1756–1791): Overture; Act I, Scenes 1 and 2; Act II, Scene 5.

The tale of Don Juan, a libertine who devotes all his energies to the pursuit of women, first appeared in Spanish literature in the 17th century. It has been a source of continuing fascination for generations of writers and composers, including Cervantes, Molière, Purcell, Gluck, Byron, Shaw, and Richard Strauss. Don Juan (or, in the Italian, Don Giovanni) is an existential character of heroic proportions who disdains traditional moral and religious codes. Guilt-free and unaffected by the human suffering he causes, he is able to follow any whim or desire without regard to consequences. Ultimately, however, he must pay the penalty for setting himself outside the rules of human conduct; either he will be driven to self-destruction, or divine forces will intervene to strike him down.

Attracted by the operatic potential of the myth, Mozart engaged Lorenzo Da Ponte, who also wrote the texts for *The Marriage of Figaro* and *Così fan tutte,* to prepare a libretto on the subject. Both the libretto and the music accentuate the dramatic aspects of the story. Comic episodes are secondary to the increasing isolation of the Don. At the start of the opera he is at the height of his power and notoriety, but his customary good luck soon deserts him. By killing a nobleman, he goes too far, inviting divine retribution. His three attempted seductions in the opera are all unsuccessful, each ending in ignominious retreat, and his growing circle of victims swears revenge. Their efforts are unavailing, but this only serves to make supernatural intervention all the more inevitable. We await his certain downfall to see if it will provoke repentence or further defiance. The end comes swiftly and with great dramatic power. The opera transcends the conventions of *opera buffa* and is ultimately serious in tone. The première of the work took place in 1787 in Prague, where *The Marriage of Figaro* had achieved great success the preceding year.

Overture. The overture is in two parts. An introductory passage is slow and ominous, presenting thematic material that will be recalled at the climax of the opera. The following allegro incorporates several brief themes within a sonata-form outline, and typifies the verve of the *buffa* overture.

Act 1, Scene 1. Leporello, Don Giovanni's servant, stands outside the palace of the Commendatore (commanding officer).

Aria: Leporello. Paraphrase of the text:

> I slave night and day for an ungrateful master. I would like to be a gentleman, and don't want to serve any longer. No, no, no, no . . . I don't want to be a servant. My master dallies inside with a pretty lady, while I stand tedious watch. Someone is coming . . .

Leporello is a fretful, reluctant servant, weary of his master's contemptuous treatment. His opening aria is a type of patter-song, a common convention of opera buffa.

Trio: Donna Anna, Don Giovanni, Leporello. Giovanni, masked to conceal his identity, enters in flight. He is pursued by Donna Anna, the haughty daughter of the Commendatore, whom he has unsuccessfully tried to seduce. Paraphrase:

> *Anna:* "Do not think you can escape before I discover who you are."
> *Giovanni:* "You'll never find out, silly woman!"
> *Leporello:* "What commotion! My master is in trouble again."
> *Anna:* "People, servants, come help me!"
> *Giovanni:* "Impetuous woman!"
> *Anna:* "Scoundrel!"

This trio exemplifies Mozart's skill in depicting the individual disposition of each character within ensemble numbers. The outraged Anna and mocking Giovanni hurl insults at each other in breathless gasps. Leporello's nervous apprehension takes the musical form of jittery rhythmic motion with rapid repeated notes. The three voices overlap in phrasing, rarely cadencing together, giving the number an unbroken rhythmic and dramatic sweep.

Trio: Commendatore, Giovanni, Leporello. The Commendatore appears and draws his sword. Anna flees. Paraphrase:

> *Commendatore:* "Get away from her! I challenge you to duel!"
> *Giovanni:* "I won't fight an old man!"
> *Leporello:* "I want to get out of here!"
> *Commendatore:* "Defend yourself, villain!"
> *Giovanni:* "If you're determined to die, so be it."

Overlapping of the vocal phrases heightens the dramatic urgency as the action and music approach a climax.

During a stormy orchestral passage the Commendatore and Giovanni duel. The aging Commendatore is no match for his powerful adversary. As Giovanni strikes a fatal blow, the orchestral passage ends abruptly on a dissonant sonority.

Trio: Commendatore, Giovanni, Leporello. Paraphrase:

> *Commendatore:* "Help! The murderer has slain me!"
> *Leporello:* "This is terrible!"
> *Giovanni:* "He falls in agony, his soul is departing . . ."

This slow andante trio forms an anguished contrast to the energetic music of the opera so far. The dark mood is intensified by the low range of all three men's voices. As the Commendatore dies, Giovanni and Leporello exit hastily.

Recitative: Giovanni and Leporello. In this furtive secco recitative, master and servant attempt to regain their composure. The dazed Leporello asks who has died. Exasperated at the inane question, the Don retorts, "The old man, of course! He asked for it." *Leporello:* "Bravo. Two good deeds. You ravish the daughter and kill the father!" The brief number establishes the essential cynicism of the two characters, their mutual distrust, and their shaken self-confidence at the unexpected swift events of the night.

Recitative and duet: Donna Anna and Don Ottavio. Donna Anna returns with her earnest but ineffectual suitor, Don Ottavio. The opening dialogue is set in a common 18th-century style known as **accompanied recitative,** in which the singers are supported by full orchestra rather than by continuo. The style was normally reserved for the more important or dramatic recitative numbers. In most cases, as here, the orchestra does not so much "accompany" the singers as alternate with them, underscoring emotional conflicts with abrupt changes in mood and tempo. Mozart employs this style to portray the characters' initial shock and growing horror at the sight of the dead Commendatore. In the allegro duet that follows, Anna and Ottavio swear to avenge the murder.

Scene Two. At dawn, on a street outside the city.

Recitative: Giovanni and Leporello. In this rapid secco recitative, Leporello musters his courage and haltingly tries to reprove his master's profligate ways. Giovanni curtly dismisses this impertinence. While plotting a new assignation for that evening, he is distracted, then aroused, by the sight of an approaching woman. "What an eye!" Leporello marvels, "He's on fire again!"

Aria: Donna Elvira. Donna Elvira enters during an orchestral introduction. A former conquest of the Don's, she boils with rage in a fiery aria: "If I ever encounter that vile monster again, and he doesn't make amends, I'll tear his heart out!"

Trio: Giovanni, Leporello, Elvira. Giovanni is both amused and inflamed by what he hears:

> *Giovanni:* "Listen. A poor girl abandoned by her lover. I will console her."
> *Leporello:* "He's already consoled 1800 others in the same way."
> *Elvira:* "I'll tear his heart out!"

Secco recitative: Giovanni, Elvira, Leporello. As he begins to introduce himself, Giovanni suddenly recoils, realizing that the "poor girl" is Elvira and that her imprecations are directed at him. She excoriates him further ("Faithless man! Monster!"). Giovanni nervously tries to placate her, Elvira seethes, and Leporello enjoys the uproar. Hoping to extricate himself from the embarrassing situation, Giovanni commands Leporello to "explain the misunderstanding." Elvira's wrath is deflected to the hapless, stammering servant, and the Don seizes the opportunity to escape. With his master gone, Leporello speaks more freely: "Take heart, lady. You are neither the first nor the last. This book I carry is full with the names of his victims."

"Catalogue aria": Leporello. In what is probably the most famous aria of the opera, Leporello invites Elvira to read with him a list of the Don's conquests: in Italy, 640; Germany, 231; France, 100; Turkey, 91; but in Spain—ah!—1003:

As he sings of Spain, the tempo slows and Leporello caresses each note. The music is charming and seductive.

The second half of the aria is a stately minuet, detailing the physical types the Don favors: dark and light, heavy and slender, tall and tiny; he is, in short, a man of the most catholic taste. For the Don's "favorite form of sinning, with one who's just beginning," Leporello's song grows tender. The aria is a musical depiction of the Don's gifts of persuasion, and Mozart here portrays Leporello as identifying strongly with his master.

After several adventures and narrow escapes through the rest of Act One and the first scene of Act Two, the Don senses a tightening net and takes refuge in a cemetery. There he is confronted by a statue of the Commendatore. For laughs, the Don bids Leporello to invite it home for dinner. To their amazement, the statue accepts.

Don Giovanni, *Act II. The sinister statue of the Commendatore accepts Leporello's invitation to dinner, and the net tightens around the Don (right).*

Act Two, Scene Five (Finale): The dining hall at Giovanni's palace.

As Giovanni dines, his private orchestra (a wind ensemble onstage) serenades him with three arias from popular operas. Unable to resist a little self-promotion, Mozart quotes a melody from his own *Figaro* as the third number. Leporello drolly comments, "I know this one very well."

The repartee between Giovanni and Leporello is interrupted by the sudden appearance of Elvira, still hopelessly in love with the Don and hoping to soften his heart. In an animated trio, Giovanni scorns her, Elvira curses him, and Leporello bewails his master's pitiless indifference. Elvira departs, but immediately returns, shrieking in terror ("Ah!"). Leporello goes to discover what is the matter, then cries out in similar alarm. He returns, shaken by a vison of the statue tapping *("Ta, ta, ta, ta")* at the door.

Trio: Commendatore, Giovanni, Leporello. A repeated orchestral chord—the same harmony that signaled the death blow to the Commendatore—announces the appearance of the stone statue. In rigid, uncompromising phrases the statue condemns Giovanni. The grim orchestral accompaniment, which features the brass for the first and only time in the opera, is drawn from the beginning of the overture. Within the harmonic context of Classical style, it has an awesome, other-worldly quality, and is, in fact, a sort of grotesque requiem for the Don. As Leporello trembles, muttering in rapid but aimless and repetitive melodic sequences, Giovanni stands his ground, disdaining a last minute conversion. Even as he feels the statue's ice-cold hand and realizes that supernatural forces are aligned against him, he makes no apologies and asks for no mercy. The orchestral accompaniment grows more dissonant and the vocal lines keep ascending as rising dramatic tension prepares the climax of the opera. Again and again, the statue demands penitence; again and again, Giovanni scornfully refuses:

Flames erupt, slowly transporting Giovanni down to hell. Voices of the spirits (a male chorus) welcome him to his appointed fate in a soulless monotone. Giovanni and Leporello cry out in terror.

In a final ensemble that serves as an epilogue to the drama, Giovanni's victims assemble and listen with delight as Leporello recounts their tormentor's demise. Each then speculates on what he or she will do, now free from the specter of the Don. This vivacious ensemble—a typical *buffa* finale—offers a total dramatic and musical contrast to the preceding cataclysmic events. Moral order has been reaffirmed, and yet most listeners feel an ambivalence towards the celebrants. Of all the characters in the opera, only Don Giovanni has commanded our respect. He was an arrogant and callous philanderer, but ultimately courageous in the face of death and willing to accept the consequences of his life without flinching. The audience, if not the characters on stage, keenly feels his loss.

Romantic Opera: Wagner and Verdi

Any assessment of 19th-century opera must inevitably focus on two composers, Wagner in Germany and Verdi in Italy. Despite vast differences in personal temperament and musical style, and totally different conceptions of what opera should be, each exemplified the Romantic conviction that above all else music must vividly portray human emotions. Each believed that opera (rather than concert music) was the genre with the greatest expressive potential and devoted his energies almost exclusively to works for the stage.

Richard Wagner

Richard Wagner

Richard Wagner (1813–1883) remains one of the most controversial figures in the history of music. In the latter half of the 19th century, the German musical public was bitterly divided into two factions. Pro-Wagnerians were convinced that the composer had revolutionized the harmonic and formal structure of music and, by revealing the full expressive potential of opera, had set music on a new course of development. Anti-Wagnerians believed with equal fervor that his complex musical style and theories were chaotic, bombastic, and contrary to essential principles of musical coherence. Imperious and often profligate in both public and private life, Wagner believed in the myth of the artist as superman, whose actions were justified by his personal genius and were beyond the understanding of petty censure of society.

Born in Leipzig to a family of actors, Wagner grew up around the stage but was virtually self-taught as a composer. In his twenties he became a chorus master at a provincial opera house and composed his first operas. The enthusiastic reception of his first mature work, *Rienzi,* established his reputation, and he received the prestigious position of conductor of the Dresden opera.

Due to the absence of strict copyright laws in Germany, Wagner received piddling financial reward for operas that cost him years of work, a situation that exacerbated his disdain for the musical establishment. Constantly in debt (with no intention of repaying) and scoffing at critics, Wagner provoked many enemies as well as an ardent coterie of disciples. Many of his operas were poorly received. Confident of his destiny to transform opera from a "frivolous" social entertainment to an almost mystical art form, he attributed this indifference to the narrow-mindedness of a corrupt society. In the political turmoil of 1848 he foresaw a potential revolution that could lead to a new social order more sympathetic to his dramas. When this uprising was crushed, Wagner fled to Switzerland. His career seemed at an end. In exile for ten years, with no financial or political resources, he could not hope to see his operas produced. In this period, Wagner concentrated much of his energy on a series of essays, attempting to clarify—both in his own mind and for an indifferent public—his theories of drama.

Wagner's Theory of Drama: The Total Art-Work. Wagner's fundamental criticism of traditional opera was that music had come to dominate the drama. Poetry and stage action were mere excuses for a series of isolated musical numbers; plots were either stilted (in serious opera) or nonsensical (in comic opera), and it was impossible to build upon this sorry tradition. Instead, Wagner proposed a new form of theater that he called **music drama.** This new form would be serious in tone, speaking to the deepest truths of human experience. For Wagner truth was instinctual—something already present within the hearts of the (German) people, fathomless but indispensible to meaningful existence. Truth was elemental, and as such could only be disclosed and experienced through art, the purest form of expression.

Wagner's librettos are based on medieval myths, which he believed contained poetic truths of collective human experience in symbolic form. For Wagner, drama and symbolism were inseparable; he was concerned not with outer events, but with inner meanings. To bring the expressive, almost religious power of these myths to fulfillment, Wagner conceived of a union of the arts—poetry, drama, music, staging, and scenery—all articulating the same message. In this concept of a **total art-work** *(Gesamtkunstwerk),* the separate arts, united in unprecedented harmony and concentration, would become one. Each element of the total art-work would intensify the same dramatic idea. To achieve such a union, there would have to be a single mind behind a music drama. Wagner not only wrote both the texts and music to his dramas but also supervised their production.

In reality, music remains the dominant and most convincing element in Wagner's dramas. His librettos frequently are grammatically convoluted, and such works as *Tristan and Isolde* have only minimal stage action. Wagner was, fortunately, more an artist than a dogmatic theorist. The ultimate importance of his theories was as a catalyst to his musical imagination.

Wagner reasoned that if music was to serve (not dominate) the drama, it must be continuous rather than broken into separate numbers. The artificial distinction between recitative and aria must also disappear. Wagner's vocal melodies lie somewhere in between these traditional two operatic styles. They resemble recitatives in their careful rhythmic adherence to natural speech accents, but also have the broad pitch contours, repeated motives, and greater music interest of arias. Like the Camerata, Wagner believed that solo singing was the highest form of musical expression; he wrote few duets, ensembles, or choruses, in which the text could easily be obscured.

The orchestra, which Wagner expanded in both size and importance, assumed a vital new function. Wagner conceived of drama as having a two-fold meaning: outer events and passions, which would be realized in the poetry, stage action, and vocal lines, and inner feelings and truths, too profound to be expressed in words. The function of the orchestra was to convey this inner meaning, disclosing the true significance of the actions. Wagner's orchestration is full and rich and his operas have been called "symphonic dramas." The vocal lines often become a part of the contrapuntal orchestral texture, and were intended, in his own analogy, to "float" over the dense orchestral texture "as a ship floats on the sea." The orchestra is an equal participant, just as the poetry and music were meant to be equal. Wagnerian singers are often specialists, requiring great powers of projection (to be heard above massive orchestral textures) and physical stamina.

Wagner's harmonic language is often highly chromatic. His works are ultimately tonal and are frequently structured into simple underlying formal schemes *(A–A–B, A–B–A).* These forms are subliminally perceived but are not obvious, due to the enormous length of each section.

To clarify the elaborate symbolism and recurring dramatic "truths" of his dramas, Wagner made extensive use of a compositional device called *Leitmotif* ("leading motive"). A leitmotif is a short thematic idea always associated with a particular character, action or object. It is usually a melodic motive, but also can be a chord progression or even a rhythmic pattern. Leitmotifs recur throughout the drama and can be varied, developed, and combined with others to suggest complex new relationships. The understanding of Wagner's music, however, does not require that a listener be able to identify or recognize the countless leitmotifs in his music, since they are often buried in the orchestral texture and were usually meant to function on a subconscious level. It was not Wagner, but his later admirers who exhausted themselves cataloguing, naming, and tracking down each reappearance of these themes. This kind of detective work, too earnestly pursued, can turn Wagner's highly expressive music into an abstract jigsaw puzzle.

Listening

"Prelude" and "Love-Death" from Tristan and Isolde *by Richard Wagner (1813–1883)*

Prelude: Record Set Side 10, Band 2

Tristan and Isolde, one of Wagner's most commanding music dramas, was based on a Medieval Celtic legend about a guilty and fatal love affair. Isolde, an Irish princess, is captured by the young knight Tristan, who takes her to Cornwall to be the wife of his uncle, King Mark. Tristan has killed Isolde's fiancé and has cruelly tricked her in the process of capturing her. Before they reach Cornwall she talks Tristan into drinking a death potion with her to end his shame and her despair. When Isolde's maid substitutes a love potion for the death potion, they become both blessed and cursed by unending love. When Mark discovers that they are in love, he berates Tristan for his treachery and unfaithfulness. One of Mark's eager knights, thinking to avenge his king, wounds Tristan seriously. Tristan withdraws to Brittany to recuperate and to wait for Isolde, who promises to join him. When she does, he is so overwrought that his wound ruptures and he dies. Mark appears, ready to forgive all, but arrives too late, and Isolde soon joins her lover in death.

The score of *Tristan and Isolde* was completed in Switzerland in 1859. The whole work was not produced until 1865, when Ludwig II, the 18-year-old King of Bavaria, became the composer's patron. In lieu of a complete performance of the work during his exile, Wagner mounted a concert of excerpts from the drama in Paris in 1860. One of these excerpts consisted of the juxtaposition of the very beginning and very end of the opera—the orchestral Prelude to Act I, and the finale of the third act, known as the "Love-Death and Transfiguration" *("Liebestod").* According to Wagner's own explanation, the Prelude expresses all the force and tenderness of the hopeless love of Tristan and Isolde during their brief life together; the finale, with Isolde's dying words over the lifeless body of her lover, expresses the ideal of an indissoluble union in death. Together, the two passages constitute about fifteen minutes of supremely powerful music.

Prelude. The melodic structure and harmonic style of the Prelude have already been discussed in Chapters 3 and 4. Wagner called the orchestral introduction to the drama a "prelude" rather than "overture" because of its free, rhapsodic form. It is a piece of great musical and emotional concentration. There is no distinction between thematic statement and later development, no structural contrast between themes or tonal centers. Rather, a group of related motives is interwoven and subjected to continuous development and varied repetition. The Prelude is a microcosm of the entire drama. Like the opera as a whole, it sustains a single mood—the struggle of the lovers, totally absorbed in each other, to find a way in which their passion can survive in an unsympathetic world. The yearning, unfulfilled quality of this love is associated with the principal leitmotif of the opera, which is introduced at the very beginning of the Prelude and recurs throughout the drama:

The formal design of the Prelude is a single continuous swell, from a hushed beginning to an overwhelming climax, then back down to a whisper.

Love-Death (Finale). The finale features a similar upward surge and emotional intensity. It is, in fact, the fulfillment of the Prelude. Tristan is dead. Isolde studies his face, unable at first to believe that he no longer can see her. The music alternately builds and subsides, as her spirit rises to acceptance but her own physical strength falters. Isolde's melody features a recurrent motive that is sequentially repeated:

Voice and Bass clarinet

Both the vocal line and the contrapuntal orchestral texture incorporate several leitmotifs heard earlier in the drama. The orchestra develops independent musical ideas in a rich symphonic texture. The complex inner emotions of Isolde are represented in the orchestra, while her "endless melody" is their conscious expression. The vocal line is sometimes song-like, sometimes in a style approaching recitative. The chromatic harmonic progressions modulate in kaleidoscopic fashion, frequently adrift from any secure tonal base or point of arrival; like the lovers' passion, the harmony seemingly has no beginning or end. As Isolde's melody rises to its final resting point ("I know the greatest ecstasy!"), she falls upon Tristan's body, and the lovers are finally united completely in death. The leitmotif that opened the Prelude returns in the orchestra for the last time, and now, finally, undergoes tonal resolution.

Giuseppe Verdi

While Wagner glorified instinct as an abstract ideal, Giuseppe Verdi (1813–1901) trusted it as the basis of his art. Verdi had little use for elaborate theories, labyrinthine mythical plots, symbolism, or complex symphonic textures. What he wanted was rapid and bold dramatic action, involving "real" (rather than archetypal) characters and human passions—"Passions above all!"

Giuseppe Verdi

Opera was the principal form of theater and social entertainment in 19th-century Italy and was patronized by all social classes. Verdi was able to build upon the tradition of lyric opera established by his predecessors, Gioacchino Rossini, Vincenzo Bellini, and Gaetano Donizetti. Preferring immediate popular acclaim to the veneration of a small circle of enthusiasts or the considered approval of posterity, he strove for commercial as well as artistic success, and his works were carefully tailored to the taste of his audience. His 26 operas, written over a period of 54 years, dominated the Italian stage during his lifetime, and remain among the most frequently performed staples of the operatic repertoire.

Declaring that "in the theater, the public will stand for anything except boredom," Verdi demanded librettos with swift action and vivid emotional encounters. The plots of his operas are serious, melodramatic, often grim and violent—an unblinking study of infatuation, seduction, murder, and ruthless ambition. Verdi possessed an unerring instinct for the stage. His works are characterized by an abundance of energy, a direct and natural expression, and emotional intensity. They are, in the Italian tradition, singers' operas. Supreme at writing for the voice, Verdi excelled at composing simple but moving vocal lines. His melodies often appear trifling on the page, but seem spontaneous and ideally suited to the dramatic situation in performance. This vocal mastery is equally apparent in his duets and ensembles, which carry the action and reveal characterization with depth and precision. The action often climaxes in festive or tempestuous crowd scenes. Although his orchestral writing is inventive and often brilliant, it never overpowers the singers. In disparaging Wagner's dense orchestral textures, Verdi observed, "Opera is opera and symphony is symphony." Verdi's final operas, written in his seventies, bear some superficial similarities to Wagner's music dramas; the music is more continuous, with fewer separate numbers and less distinction between recitative and aria. These stylistic features, however, were the result of Verdi's own independent musical development, and not an influence of the "German" music he scorned.

Act I from La Traviata *by Giuseppe Verdi (1813–1901)*

La Traviata (1853), one of Verdi's best-known operas, was written immediately after the equally celebrated *Il Trovatore.* The libretto, by Francesco Piave, was based on the play *La Dame aux Camélias* ("The Lady of the Camellias") by Alexandre Dumas. The opera's early popularity was due in part to the scandalous nature of the plot. The story concerns an illicit affair between Violetta, a notorious lady of pleasure, and Alfredo, the son of a prominent family. The heroine, dying of tuberculosis, is touched by Alfredo's love. Their passion and hopes for a new life grow until his father, a symbol of conventional morality, intervenes. The play was perceived by many as an assault on marriage. Others regarded it as an attack against the oppressive sexual mores of the age. Verdi was living with a mistress (who would later become his second wife) at the time he wrote *La Traviata,* and relished the controversy his work caused, noting that few, if any, other composers would have dared take on so risqué a subject.

The première in Venice was disappointing. In a break with tradition, the opera was staged in a modern (1850) setting and dress. The contemporary trappings dismayed a tradition-bound audience that preferred escape into distant historical settings. The role of Violetta was sung by a grossly overweight woman. When, in the final scene, the Doctor announced that she was wasting away to nothing, the audience roared with laughter. Undeterred, Verdi mounted a second Venetian production 14 months later, with a historical setting (and, presumably, a more svelte heroine), that achieved great success.

La Traviata is a prima donna's opera. The demanding role of Violetta requires a tireless dramatic soprano, but also features intricate coloratura passages and *bel canto* arias. Violetta not only sings most of the major arias, but is also in the thick of the action throughout the opera.

Act I. Prelude. The short orchestral prelude that opens the opera presents three themes. A haunting slow introduction for high strings instils the mood of tragedy that pervades the drama. The main body of the prelude introduces a lyrical theme that is associated with the love of Violetta and Alfredo throughout the opera. As this theme is repeated in the cellos, the violins play a more animated, rather flippant countermelody, probably meant to convey Violetta's free spirit.

Opening ensemble. Verdi's operas customarily begin with a vigorous ensemble. Violetta is throwing a party. An ebullient orchestral introduction establishes the general merriment of the evening and leads to a model Verdian crowd scene in which the chorus takes prominent part. As the guests exchange pleasantries, Violetta plays the social butterfly, declaring that pleasure is the only goal of life. Her amused guests are delighted by the thought and repeat it. Violetta is introduced to Alfredo Germont, and is told that he has been her secret admirer. Not believing the report, she asks him if it is true, and is surprised by his forthright answer, "Yes!"

Drinking song. Violetta calls upon Alfredo to sing a drinking song, a common operatic convention of the period. Although initially reluctant, he obliges after she tells him how much it would please her:

The spirited, repetitive tune receives typical Verdian ensemble treatment. It is passed around to Violetta, the chorus, and back to the future lovers in a duet, and finally concludes with a flourish in the chorus.

Waltz. As the guests repair to the dining room, Violetta suddenly grows faint, the first sign that she is ill. She asks to be left alone to recover her strength, but Alfredo remains.

Duet: Alfredo and Violetta. In the love theme first heard in the prelude, Alfredo expresses his passion:

Significantly different from a leitmotif, this *bel canto* melody recurs as a continuing reference to the love that grows from hesitant beginnings in this duet to a consuming fire in the second and third acts. Verdi frequently uses themes in this manner, but seldom so insistently as in *La Traviata.*

Violetta answers that she can only return friendship, not love, and asks him to forget her. The dramatic contrast between Alfredo's passionate suit and Violetta's coy demurrer is depicted in the contrasting nature of their melodic lines. She answers his entreaties with a whimsical coloratura passage, a virtuoso display of scales, arpeggios, and rapid runs. In the hands of lesser composers, such passages can be musically vapid, an empty technical exhibition extraneous to the characterization and action. Here, it complements the dramatic situation and sharpens the depiction of Violetta's capricious nature. The duet ends with a cadenza for the two voices.

Waltz. The brisk waltz theme returns. After a brief intrusion by a snooping guest, Alfredo persists in his suit. Moved by his ardor, Violetta asks him to return tomorrow, and they part *("Addio")*.

Ensemble. As dawn approaches, the guests return and the party breaks up in another spirited chorus.

Finale: Recitative and Aria. Violetta, alone and confused, reflects on the events of the evening in a troubled recitative. The aria that follows begins pensively, then incorporates the love theme. Her mood changes abruptly in an interjectory recitative. Believing her dreams are futile (*"Follie! Follie! deliro vano è questo!"*—"Folly! This is madness!"), she resolves to live for the pleasure of the moment and give no thought to her clouded future. Her rapid coloratura aria, *"Sempre libera,"* grows more abandoned and desperate. This aria, the climax to the first act, contains abundant technical flourishes. Alfredo is heard in the distance singing the love theme; Violetta repeats her intention to be free of all entanglements.

Synopsis of Acts II and III. At the beginning of the second act we learn that Alfredo and Violetta have been living an idyllic country life together for three months. Alfredo's father confronts Violetta and tells her that because of her disreputable past he can never sanction a relationship between her and his son. In addition, their flagrant liason is bringing disgrace to the family, jeopardizing the hopes of Alfredo's sister for an advantageous marriage. The elder Germont is impressed by Violetta's sincerity but remains adamant, demanding that she leave Alfredo. Suspecting that she is going to die, and knowing that she cannot realistically expect to marry Alfredo, she reluctantly agrees to make this sacrifice. Unaware of what his father has done, Alfredo learns only that she has left him. He pursues her to a party where he publicly shames her, to the outrage of the guests (see the photo on page 359).

The curtain to the third act rises during a hushed prelude, similar in character to the opening of the prelude to Act I. Violetta's condition has worsened, and the doctor assures her maid that death is inevitable. Her only solace is a letter from Alfredo's father, which she reads while the love theme is murmured in the orchestra. The elder Germont explains that he has told his son everything, and that Alfredo will beg her forgiveness. But she despairs that she will die before he arrives, and sings the opera's most plaintive aria, *"Addio del passato."*

Alfredo does arrive, and Violetta is momentarily revived by his appearance. In the duet *"Parigi, o cara,"* they express the desperate hope that she can recover. She rallies briefly ("I feel life returning, my strength is renewed. Oh joy!"), but this is an act of pure will, a final defiance of her unhappy destiny. As her grieving lover and friends stand helplessly by, she falls onto the bed and dies.

The musical–dramatic idioms of Verdi and Wagner were distinctive personal achievements, very different in conception:

VERDI	WAGNER
Vocal melodies preeminent	Voice and orchestra equal; orchestra has its own important motives and dramatic function
Homophonic textures; orchestra accompanies the singers	Contrapuntal textures; vocal lines are sometimes submerged in thick orchestral textures
Human dramas, rapid action	Mythical, symbolic subjects; stage actions secondary to the many levels of "inner meaning"
Simple and direct expression	Complex, "elevated" expression

While these two operatic styles could not be successfully imitated, each exerted a profound influence on the next generation of composers. Verdi's theatrical flair influenced Italian and French composers who sought greater dramatic realism and musical accessibility. Bizet's *Carmen* (1875) is an early example of the movement toward believability on stage. The operas of Giacomo Puccini, notably *La Bohème* (1896) and *Madame Butterfly* (1906), are musically direct, with characters and situations drawn from everyday life.

Richard Strauss combined the Wagnerian harmonic idiom, which he sometimes carried to the brink of atonality, with a graphic dramatic realism. His *Salome* (1905) and *Elektra* (1909) feature massive orchestral textures, continuous music within each act, and leitmotifs. A stridently dissonant, tonally ambiguous harmonic language underscores the macabre horrors of the plots: lurid, ritualistic murders of vengeance. *Der Rosenkavalier* (1911), on the other hand, is written in a more diatonic tonal idiom, befitting its 18th-century setting and comic libretto.

Opera in the 20th Century

A majority of the leading composers of the first half of the 20th century wrote one or more important operas. A representative list of major works includes Debussy's *Pelléas et Mélisande* (1902), Bartók's *Bluebeard's Castle* (1911), Prokofiev's *Love for Three Oranges* (1921), Schönberg's unfinished *Moses und Aron* (1932), Hindemith's *Mathis der Maler* (1938), and Britten's *Peter Grimes* (1945). Various new pitch languages have been employed, but many composers and performers have felt that greater restraint and "respect for tradition" is necessary in opera than in concert works, owing to the physical distance between singers and orchestra, the demands of stage action, and the sheer economics of operatic productions. (Nothing "bombs" with a heavier thud than an unsuccessful opera.) In the United States, such composers as Gian Carlo Menotti, Douglas Moore, and Samuel Barber have achieved notable triumphs within traditional formats.

The general tendency in opera, as in symphonic music, has been away from the lengthy, elaborate traditions of the 19th century and toward more concise, dramatically concentrated productions. The neoclassical movement led to a revival of late-18th-century comic opera traditions in such works as *The Rake's Progress* (1951) by Stravinsky. National subject matter and musical influences, important operatic resources ever since Mussorgsky's *Boris Godonov,* form the basis of many works, including Copland's *The Tender Land* (1954). Folk operas incorporating popular musical idioms sometimes straddle the distinction between opera and operetta or (in the United States) musical comedy. This survey of opera concludes with examination of a dramatically explosive work by Alban Berg and a folk opera by George Gershwin.

Expressionist Opera: Alban Berg

Several 20th-century composers, influenced by such writers as Ibsen, Chekhov, and Kafka and by the theories of Freud, have written stage works that are psychological studies, probing the primal emotions of the subconscious. *Expressionism,* an outgrowth of the more subjective currents within Romanticism and of the late 19th century realist movement, was an attempt to transcend literal meanings and expose the inner, "ultimate" reality of naked human needs and fears. In the visual arts this took the form of purposeful distortion and exaggeration—images seen through a cracked glass, revealing a frightening but dynamic instinctual energy. Expressionist dramas were concentrated studies of neurotic characters driven by psychic torment to the edge of insanity. Musical expressionism is generally associated with the stage works of Schönberg and Alban Berg written between about 1909 and 1935.

Alban Berg began the study of composition with Arnold Schönberg when he was 19. His formal study lasted six years, but he remained a close friend and apologist for his teacher throughout his life. Berg's early works were written in the densely chromatic idiom of free atonality. Later, he adopted Schönberg's twelve-tone technique, applying this pitch system in a more relaxed and flexible manner than his mentor. Berg was the first composer who consciously attempted to bridge the stylistic gulf that many listeners perceived between serial procedures and traditional tonal resources. The comparative accessibility of his music—particularly its lyricism—made him the first atonal composer to receive a widespread hearing. Many of his works are stylistically eclectic, combining different types of pitch and melodic treatment, but they are unified by a clear overall design and keen sense of pacing.

Listening

Act III from Wozzeck *by Alban Berg (1885–1935)*

Wozzeck is one of the most original and dramatically powerful stage works of the 20th century. Berg first conceived the opera in 1914 after seeing a production of the play *Woyzeck* by Georg Büchner (1813–1837). Büchner's drama, although written in the 1830s foreshadowed many expressionist themes. The principal character of the play is a hapless, highly repressed figure, described as "moving through the world like an open razor," who murders his unfaithful mistress and then destroys himself. Berg arranged the original 27 scenes of the play into a libretto of three acts, each with five scenes, which he completed in 1917. He then composed the music between 1917 and 1921.

The Berlin premiere in 1925 provoked an uproar that catapulted the composer from obscurity to notoriety. Some believed that Berg had achieved a unique synthesis, creating a work contemporary in every respect and proving that the supposed stylistic limitations of opera were attributable merely to the conservatism of performers and audiences. Others found the musical style raucous and the stage action depraved. A newspaper critic felt he had been "not in a public theater, but in an insane asylum." During the next ten years the work was performed over 1200 times in 28 European cities, enabling musicians and listeners to gain familiarity with the atonal idiom which they had read about but rarely been able to hear.

In the bleak expressionist world of Berg's opera there are no heroes, only impassive characters sapped of humanity by a brutal social order, a psychotic Captain and Doctor, and Wozzeck, an unsophisticated army private who is victimized at every turn. In the first two acts, Wozzeck is pushed toward the breaking point by a succession of abuses and defeats, culminating in the infidelity of his mistress, Marie, the mother of his illegitimate child.

Wozzeck, driven to rage, strikes his defiant mistress, Marie.

Berg conveys the anguish of the drama through a complex atonal pitch style. (The work makes only minimal use of serial techniques.) He also interweaves tonal passages, sometimes in a style reminiscent of the late German Romantics, but also grotesque parodies of waltzes, polkas, and marches. At other times, tonality provides a poignant simplification of the musical style, as in Marie's lullaby in Act I, Scene 3. The wide spectrum of atonal and tonal pitch treatment is one of the most remarkable features of the opera. The music is continuous within each act, and recognizable leitmotifs recur. The most prominent motive is associated with Wozzeck, the principal representative of "we poor people":

In the third act, the motive is heard immediately preceding Wozzeck's death:

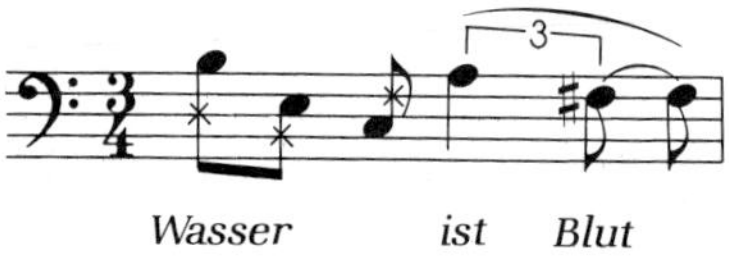

In addition to singing, the vocalists also speak and perform in *Sprechstimme* (literally, "speech-voice"), a rhetorical style introduced by Schönberg. Sprechstimme is notated with an X through the note stems, as in the figure above, and is half spoken, half sung. The written notes indicate general contour rather than exact pitches. The vocal parts are difficult (the premiere required 137 rehearsals!) but this is due more to the general density of musical style and ideas than to virtuosic solo demands.

The orchestra rarely "accompanies" the singers, but rather, in the manner of *Tristan and Isolde*, creates a throbbing undercurrent meant to depict inner emotions. The orchestral music is loosely based on traditional instrumental forms. The five scenes of Act I, for example, present a suite, a rhapsody and hunting song, and march and lullaby, a set of passacaglia variations, and a rondo. These forms are not obvious, however, and were not meant to be. In a lecture discussing the opera, Berg asked his listeners to forget all theories and formal devices, allow these techniques to operate on a subliminal level, and direct their conscious attention to the dramatic and musical expression.

Each scene creates a particular mood and projects a single point of view. The scenes within each act are connected by orchestral interludes that maintain a continuous sense of musical direction during scene changes and offer a commentary on the dramatic action, in the manner of a Greek chorus. The overall pacing is swift and vivid; vocal lines are short and disjointed, heightening the nightmarish rush of the action to catastrophe.

Act III. *Scene 1.* Marie reads from the Bible the story of Mary Magdalene, a sinner who repents and finds redemption. Her reading, in Sprechstimme, is interspersed with sung passages in which she comforts her child and cries out to God for mercy. An orchestral postlude concludes with two ethereal arpeggiated runs under which a low tone is introduced. This tone, the pitch B, is sustained throughout the entire next scene.

Scene 2. Marie and Wozzeck are walking through the forest. Their conversation is stiff and remote, revealing the emotional distance that now separates them. Wozzeck kisses her, then stares at the rising moon, which has a blood-red hue. The pitch B, which began in the orchestra as a barely perceptible whisper, grows ever more insistent, culminating in a relentless series of timpani strokes that depict Wozzeck's obsession with Marie's infidelity. As Wozzeck runs his knife into her throat, Marie shrieks and falls. The timpani strokes subside. Wozzeck, insensible, utters the single word, *"Tot!"* ("Dead!").

The orchestral postlude to the scene is a musical distillation of the dramatic action. The instruments enter one by one on the pitch B, producing a ferocious crescendo that is cut off by a shattering dissonance. Hammer-blows in the timpani introduce a rhythmic motive that will be grotesquely parodied in the next scene. Another deafening crescendo on the pitch B further drives home the savage horror of the murder:

Scene 3. At a tavern, an out-of-tune piano plays a bizarre polka. The rhythm of the "melody" reiterates the preceding timpani motive:

The crazed Wozzeck prattles incoherently, exhorting the bewildered patrons to dance, then cursing them. When he makes a boorish pass at Margaret, she recoils at the sight of his blood-stained hands and arms. As the stupefied onlookers chant, "Blood, blood . . . ," Wozzeck rushes back into the forest. In the orchestral postlude, several echoes of the timpani-polka motive resound, gradually fading into the quiet of the night.

Scene 4. Wozzeck returns to the scene of the murder to find his incriminating knife, which he throws into a deep pool of water. The rarified orchestral texture has an unearthly, vaporous quality, aimlessly ascending and descending in thin clusters. Wozzeck's vocal line is set almost entirely in Sprechstimme, hovering between music and speech as Wozzeck himself hovers between consciousness and total delirium, life and death. Wozzeck wades into the water to cleanse himself, but in his demented state "the water becomes blood," and he must wade ever deeper in search of peace. The murmuring orchestral texture dissolves into rising, overlapping ripples of sound. Wozzeck drowns, without a whimper of protest, without awareness. He simply disappears from a life without hope or meaning. The Captain and Doctor appear. They realize what has happened but, having no wish to involve themselves in a distasteful matter, hurry off.

The *adagio* orchestral postlude is a moving commentary upon the futility of Wozzeck's life and actions, a requiem for the luckless victims of oppression. Personal (but not sentimental) in tone, strongly tonal at beginning and end, it is stylistically reminiscent of the soaring slow movements of Mahler. Berg has juxtaposed contradictory dramatic moods throughout the opera. The emotional character of this postlude provides a quality of human concern that stands in relief to the callous indifference of the Captain and Doctor.

Scene 5. In the understated, ironic, but touching final scene, a group of children play ring-around-the-rosey. Marie's son is riding his hobby horse. In the strangely cruel fashion of some children, one boy blithely calls out, "Hey you! Your mother is dead!" The curious children run off to see the body. Marie's son, very young, innocent, and engrossed in play, does not comprehend what they are saying, and continues to ride his favorite toy—*"Hop, hop! Hop, hop! Hop, hop!"* Not wishing to miss out on the fun, he then dashes to catch up with his friends, to see what new discovery they have made. The orchestral texture swells, then slowly dissipates in a swirling trill-like figure.

American Folk Opera: George Gershwin

The dissemination of jazz from New Orleans to the major cities of America and eventually to Europe during the first quarter of the 20th century aroused the interest of many European composers. Some viewed the styles of ragtime, blues, and dixieland as curios—trifling but agreeable diversions, and a welcome antidote to the self-conscious earnestness of late Romanticism. Others took this new musical language more seriously, discovering in it novel rhythmic, harmonic, and timbral resources that they could incorporate into their own music. Such composers as Erik Satie, Igor Stravinsky, and Paul Hindemith wrote works that embody superficial stylistic features of early jazz. Most of their counterparts in the United States, suffering from a collective inferiority complex and still emulating 19th-century European styles, did not know what to make of this new musical language which had developed on their own soil, independent of both the academic and commercial musical establishments. Most composers, musicians, and listeners blandly accepted the dichotomy between "high art" and "pop culture" as a necessary and even desirable result of a pluralistic society.

George Gershwin did not accept this distinction. He was among the first of many American composers to take genuine pride in native American musical idioms. Gershwin, like Charles Ives, resolved to write recognizably American music, but his career could hardly have been more dissimilar to that of Ives. Born in New York in 1898 of Russian immigrant parents, Gershwin established early renown as a composer of popular songs and, somewhat later, of Broadway shows and film scores. His ambitions, however, extended beyond popular acclaim and musical comedies. Believing that "Music lives only when it is serious in form," he hoped to bring to concert music the rhythmic vitality and melodic freshness he admired in jazz and popular music. His first symphonic work, *Rhapsody in Blue* (1924) is a quasi-concerto for piano and instrumental ensemble (later rescored for a larger orchestra), that incorporated the syncopated rhythms and coloristic resources of early jazz.

Gershwin's use of jazz materials was neither ironical nor detached. Believing that "American music should be based on American material," he endeavored to fuse the European, jazz, and pop traditions he admired into a single, vital musical language. Although he saw himself first and foremost as a song composer, he desired to make expansive statements in larger genres. Acutely aware of his technical limitations, he undertook further study while at the height of his fame in order to overcome these deficiencies.

One evening in 1926, Gershwin read the acclaimed novel *Porgy*. Captivated by the story, he immediately wrote to the white South Carolinian author, DuBose Heyward, to see if he had any interest in turning *Porgy* into an opera. Heyward answered affirmatively, but was dismayed when Gershwin told him that it would be several years before he would be technically prepared to undertake the work. Gershwin had only a casual knowledge of opera and felt distant from the southern black culture in which the novel was set. It was six years before the two men, along with Gershwin's librettist brother, Ira, began collaboration on the opera. In the interim the novel was produced as a highly successful play.

In preparation for the composition of what would be his last work and only opera, Gershwin spent the summer of 1934 with Heyward on a small island ten miles off the coast of Charleston. He immersed himself in the cultural life of the Gullahs, a remote community still close to its African roots. In this society, he found an ideal model for an American folk opera, observing that the Gullahs "express themselves not only by the spoken word, but quite naturally by song and dance." Gershwin was fascinated by "the drama, the humor, the superstition, the religious fervor, the dancing, the irrepressible high spirits" of this isolated subculture. *Porgy and Bess* reflects not only the street cries, gospel shouts, and spirituals of this society, but also its close-knit social order.

Act I from **Porgy and Bess** *by George Gershwin (1898–1937)*

Porgy and Bess was addressed to a mass audience and, although an opera rather than a musical comedy, is more often performed by commercial producers than by "classical" operatic companies. Believing that "opera should be entertaining," Gershwin "hoped to have developed something in American music that would appeal to the many rather than to the cultured few." The work was also a social commentary, portraying a world in which white and black live apart in conflict and misunderstanding. The element of humor was particularly important to Gershwin. It arises not from gags or satire, but springs from the inherent wit and energy of the characters. Although bawdy, it is also generous, and this humor is the greatest resource of the characters—their key to survival.

Many of the numbers have a simple charm and folklike character, but the music was all original. The composer explained that he "decided against the use of original folk material because I wanted the music to be all of one piece." In the recitatives, he attempted to faithfully reproduce the natural vocal inflections of southern blacks.

Gershwin was not trying to write "black music," however, any more than Stravinsky was trying to write "jazz" in *L'Histoire du Soldat;* rather, he sought to reflect faithfully the musical and emotional vitality of a society that had deeply impressed him. Although the original production featured black singers and the score was strongly influenced by authentic black folk music, the composer, librettists, stage director, conductor, orchestra, and most of the audience were white. The opera was written 20 years before the civil rights movement. The pidgin English and occasional "Uncle Tomisms" of the characters ("I don't know nuttin' 'bout it, Boss") discomfit some listeners and are often altered in modern performances. Even in 1935 the singers stumbled uneasily through much of the dialect. Like most operas, *Porgy and Bess* is a period piece, set in the Charleston ghetto at the turn of the century. The setting, parlance, and concerns of the characters are no more contemporary than those of *Don Giovanni* or *La Traviata.* If we identify with the characters—which is essential if we are to experience the power of the music and drama—it is with their qualities of strength, wit, and charity, and not according to how closely their political awareness reflects current sensibilities.

The unabridged original version of the opera runs about four and a half hours. In a normal production schedule of eight performances a week, such length would quickly reduce the cast to a hoarse whisper. Gershwin eliminated several minor numbers, and further cuts are customarily made in modern performances and recordings.

Act I. Scene 1. The residents of Catfish Row, a slum tenement, are returning home from their labors, and gradually assemble in the courtyard for some conversation and recreation. Clara sings her baby to sleep in the haunting song, "Summertime," a lullaby with blues shadings. Performance of this and several other songs in the opera requires the inflection of "blue notes," pitches sung slightly flat in terms of concert tuning. "Blue notes" are a characteristic expressive feature of black music, a survival of African intonations; they are naturally inflected by performers and are not notated in the score.

Ensemble. The men begin playing craps. Fearing trouble, Serena begs her husband, Robbins, not to play. Robbins is eager for diversion, however, and scoffs at her apprehension. For the amusement of Clara's still fretful baby and his peers, Jake taunts the ladies in a droll ballad, "A Woman is a Sometimes Thing."

Ensemble. An orchestral introduction accompanies the appearance of Porgy, a crippled beggar. Crown, a ruffian feared by all, and his woman Bess, regarded as a shameless hussy by the women, approach from a distance. The crap shooters harass Porgy for his obvious interest in Bess, which he denies, declaring, "When Gawd make a cripple, he mean him to be lonely."

Catfish Row—the crap game, from the original production of Porgy and Bess.

Ensemble. Crown belligerently joins the game while Bess delights in scandalizing the "good women." The game grows more serious as Crown, drunk and high on dope, becomes increasingly abusive. When Robbins wins all the money, Crown attacks him. As the two men scuffle, the music erupts into a furious ensemble that features nine independent vocal parts. The voices enter and drop out at irregular intervals, never singing all at once, producing a hubbub in which no single part is distinctly heard. The fight continues during a frenetic orchestral passage. Robbins falls dead. Fearing the inevitable arrival of the hated white police, the people make themselves scarce. Crown flees, but tells Bess he'll be back "when the hell dies down." Sportin' Life, a flamboyant street hustler, invites the abandoned Bess to come with him to New York, but she spurns his offer ("I ain't come to that yet"). The self-righteous people turn a deaf ear to her cries for help; only Porgy offers her sanctuary.

Scene 2. *Chorus: "Gone, Gone, Gone."* A wake for Robbins is in progress. Gershwin had been particularly moved by the gospel chants of the Gullahs. In this number he portrays the empathy and commiseration of the community. The people rally to support each other in times of adversity, collectively sharing the widow Serena's grief and financial burden.

"Overflow." During a spirited ensemble the mourners drop coins in a saucer to collect money for Robbins' funeral. Joy and sorrow are intertwined in this number and throughout the scene. Robbins' life is celebrated as his death is mourned, and the community gathers renewed strength in this ritual. In a fervent recitative influenced by the gospel "shouts" of southern blacks, Porgy exhorts the people to fill the saucer until it overflows. When the original tune returns it is treated polyphonically. Such ensemble passages demonstrate the greatly increased technical resources and assurance Gershwin attained shortly before his untimely death.

Recitative. In a largely spoken recitative, a contemptuous white detective questions the people about the murder of Crown and arrests the innocent Peter as a material witness. Porgy laments this injustice.

"My Man's Gone Now." Serena bewails her loss in a moving lament. Several interjectory wailing passages culminate in a chilling finale, in which Serena, and then the chorus, glide from a low to a very high register.

Recitative. The local undertaker quibbles briefly over the price of the funeral before reluctantly agreeing to bury Robbins for fifteen dollars.

"Leavin' For The Promise' Lan'." With a Christian burial assured, Bess leads the mourners in an exultant spiritual that expresses not only the community's religious faith, but also their hopes for a better life.

Synopsis of Acts II and III. Bess finds unexpected happiness with Porgy and is warily accepted by the community. Porgy's new-found joy is expressed in his song "I Got Plenty o' Nuttin'" and in the duet "Bess,

You is my Woman Now." During a picnic on Kittiwah Island, Sportin' Life beguiles the people with his religious non-credo, "It Ain't Necessarily So." Crown, who has been hiding on the island, entices Bess to remain with him. She returns to Porgy several days later, delirious with fever. Serena's faith-healing and Porgy's loving care restore her to health, and their love is renewed ("I Loves You, Porgy"). The people gather to wait out a hurricane. Crown joins them briefly and laughs at their fear. The second act ends with a six-voice communal prayer.

In the third act, Crown returns to reclaim Bess. In a fierce struggle Porgy kills Crown and is arrested by the police. The people fear that he will inevitably break down under ruthless interrogation. Sportin' Life, ever the opportunist, induces the despairing Bess to accompany him to New York. To everyone's amazement, Porgy is released, and he searches desperately for Bess ("Oh Bess, Oh Where's My Bess"). When he learns that she is still alive and has run off to New York, he sets out after her in his goat-drawn wagon. Admiring Porgy's dauntless courage, if not his prudence in the face of impossible odds, the people see him off ("Oh Lawd, I'm on My Way").

Porgy and Bess is unquestionably Gershwin's finest achievement, both in its quality of musical expression and in its convincing assimilation of American folk idioms into operatic format. Arnold Schönberg, a composer stylistically poles apart from Gershwin, asserted his admiration for Gershwin's music, declaring, "He expressed musical ideas, and they were new—as is the way in which he expressed them."

Terms and Concepts for Review

- Baroque period:
  - Camerata
  - monody
  - bel canto
  - da capo aria
  - secco recitative
- Classical period:
  - opera seria
  - opera buffa (comic opera)
  - accompanied recitative
- Romantic period:
  - Wagner:
    - music drama
    - total-art work
    - leitmotif
  - Verdi:
    - singers' opera
- 20th Century:
  - expressionism
  - *Sprechstimme*

Unit 5
The Music of Today

Chapter 20
New Materials, Forms, and Genres

From our present vantage point, the course of 20th-century music appears to consist of two periods of intensive stylistic innovation, each followed by a period of consolidation and synthesis. The first cycle, which we examined in Chapter 12, began with the bold rhythmic and pitch departures of such composers as Stravinsky and Schönberg. During the second quarter of the century these new resources were systematized, and many composers sought to integrate them within traditional structural formats. The second "explosion" occurred between about 1950 and 1965. It encompassed not only renewed stylistic innovation, but also fundamental questions concerning the nature of art and music, the relationship between composer and listener, and whether it was desirable—or even possible—to make "enduring" musical statements.

As a result, the age in which we live is one of unprecedented multiplicity and contrast, not just between shadings of three or four basic idioms, but of a broad continuum of musical practice. In such works as Boulez' *Structures* (1955) or Milton Babbitt's *Composition for Four Instruments* (1949), every pitch, duration, and dynamic mark—indeed, every facet of the music down to the smallest detail—has been worked out according to rigorous formulas; at another extreme stand composers who leave practically everything to chance. A proponent of "antimusic" might require a cellist to slide into a bucket of water (one way to make a musical splash). Other composers prefer simple tonal styles, and believe that the lyrical traditions of 18th- and 19th-century music provide an inexhaustible legacy on which to build.

The great majority of composers, of course, have positioned themselves somewhere between these poles. Most try not so much to absorb everything they can from the passing parade as to discover their own musical instincts and to forge an individual style specifically tailored to the kind of expression they are seeking. Composers and listeners have become increasingly familiar with non-Western musical cultures, and have realized that a pluralism of musical practices has always existed—we just weren't aware of it from our corner of the globe. As this awareness has grown, the present "disarray" has come to seem less burdensome and unnatural. For a growing number of people, in fact, it seems a necessary and exhilarating feature of the current age, giving the listener access to many types of musical expression that appeal in different ways and speak to different needs.

This final chapter surveys works that represent several of the leading currents in recent musical thought. The works diverge, not just in pitch practice, but in their basic esthetic orientation. Some are highly organized, others relaxed in tone and design. Some attempt to continue a tradition, others stake out new ground. None fits within the familiar genre categories of the previous chapters.

New Coloristic Resources

The exploration of new tone colors is the primary concern of many of today's composers. Timbre is hardly a new resource, of course; Debussy's creation of "precise sounds," and the striking orchestral effects of such composers as Berlioz, Strauss, and Stravinsky, have demonstrated how sharply-drawn colors can contribute vitally to the shape and definition of musical ideas. For many contemporary composers, however, tone color has taken on an unprecedented expressive and structural importance, so that it often serves not merely to convey ideas, but as the *principal* idea and substance of a musical statement. As Hans Hofmann and other modern painters have used solid blocks of colors rather than individual lines to create formal designs, so many of today's composers fashion blocks of sound colors (rather than melodies) into textural and formal patterns.

The use of solid blocks of tone colors as the basic building materials of music finds its parallel in the visual arts in paintings such as Hans Hofmann's To Miz-Pax Vobiscum *(1964).*

The search for new tone colors has taken several forms. Some composers have supplemented ensembles with non-Western or folk instruments or created new instruments of their own design. Many have turned to the electronic medium. The greatest number, however, have sought to coax new sounds from traditional instruments.

Another major current in recent music has been the exploitation of the dramatic, ritualistic, or even theatrical aspects of musical performance. This emphasis, too, has antecedents, notably in opera and in the symphonic poems of the late 19th century. Several contemporary composers have sought to infuse their chamber and orchestral works with a powerful visual as well as musical projection, so that even a performance by a trio becomes a type of stage work. One result of this tendency has been the rise of mixed-media presentations in which music is combined with light shows, poetry readings, film, slides, drama, and dance. The various elements are usually loosely synchronized, remaining separate dimensions of a "total experience."

"Getting into Sound": Harry Partch and Others

The music of Harry Partch (1901–1974) stands outside any tradition, except perhaps the "go it alone" tradition of Charles Ives, Carl Ruggles, and a handful of other hardy American individualists who have created their own musical worlds with little outside influence. A self-taught visionary who formulated his esthetic beliefs in his twenties, Partch had little contact with established musical institutions. He lived as a hobo for eight years during the Depression, supported himself at odd jobs later, and eventually settled in southern California, where he single-handedly created his own musical workshop and environment.

Partch held a broad view of music, similar to that of the ancient Greeks, and had little interest in concert genres. Believing that music should be a form of theater and closely allied with the other arts, he sought to unite aural and visual expression. Music was to be but one element of a total sensuous experience that would be realized through a synthesis of "sound-magic, visual beauty, and experience-ritual." In some respects, Partch anticipated the multimedia performances of the 1960s. In his conception, however, the various elements were more closely related, springing from a common source.

Partch discarded the equal-tempered tuning system and in its place devised a tuning with 43 tones to the octave, based upon a mathematically "purer" arrangement of intervals common in Renaissance vocal music and in the present-day music of Asia. Partch invented and hand-made his own collection of instruments and used them exclusively in his compositions. Some were adaptations of familiar string (viola, guitar), percussion (marimba), or keyboard instruments (reed organ). Most, however, were new creations, constructed from liquor bottles, hubcaps, artillery shell casings, and other unlikely sources. Many are arresting to look at, in line with Partch's concern for "visual beauty," and they often form a part of the dramatic sets against which is works are played and acted out. Of necessity, Partch developed his own notational system, and in later years he gathered a group of young disciples around him, teaching them how to play his "orchestra."

Harry Partch playing one of his instruments, the boo, a marimba-like construction of bamboo segments.

Partch's works were conceived for performance in an informal setting. Virtuosity was foreign to his thinking, and his performers were usually musical amateurs rather than conservatory-trained musicians. He termed his esthetic approach to art "corporeal," and there is indeed a "bodily" or "physical" quality to his works that has attracted listeners of diverse musical interests.

Listening

Daphne of the Dunes *by Harry Partch (1901–1974)*

Daphne of the Dunes was composed as the sound track for a motion picture and is one of comparatively few of Partch's works with no vocal part. In the original recording the composer played the entire piece by himself, recording each part individually on a separate track of tape. In the more recent Columbia recording eleven performers took part. The texture is thin, however, with no more than four instruments playing at any one time, and many passages are duets.

The most characteristic and winning features of the music are its resonant percussive colors and motoristic rhythms. The underlying rhythms are simple, usually perpetual-motion divisions of the beat into groups of five, seven, or nine. Pulsation is strong and regular, and simple motives are repeated over and over. At the beginning of the piece, for example, the marimba part presents a steady stream of quintuplet (five-note) figures. The formal design consists of the juxtaposition of short, independent sections. Each section features distinct rhythmic patterns and a particular combination of instruments and barrels along with few, if any, cadences. There is no cumulative sense of direction, no point of arrival or thematic return. The music hints at no profundities, and contains no pictorial overtones. Although it originally accompanied nature images in the film, it is in no sense a commentary. It is, rather, "being" music, whose meaning lies on its surface in the impulsive rhythmic energy and unique colors Partch projects.

Several younger composers have shared Partch's interest in non-Western music and his desire to bring music "out of the concert hall and into the streets." Terry Riley (b. 1935) and Steve Reich (b. 1936) have pursued non-virtuosic types of performance based upon a hypnotic flow of sound. Their works reflect a desire to simplify musical expression down to a single process, such as a thickening in texture (Riley's *In C*) or the transformation of rudimentary rhythmic figures into more complex ones (Reich's *Drumming*).[1] The process evolves very slowly, often taking 40 minutes or more, and it is continuous, without any element of contrast or digression. The result is an attempt to encourage everyone involved to "get into sound" by focusing on the exact qualities of repetitive patterns and to feel their progressive maturation into a full design. For many listeners the extremely slow developmental thread creates a meditative quality, as though one's full powers of concentration were directed to the opening of a flower petal.

Electronic Music

The rapid growth of electronic music from makeshift beginnings to a highly sophisticated and versatile medium has been one of the major musical developments since World War II. By opening up new worlds of sound it has hastened a reexamination of the nature of musical expression and perception, and in so doing has influenced many composers who have never written a note of electronic music. Most of the music we hear today is, in the broadest sense, electronic. As Milton Babbitt, one of today's leading serial composers, has observed, even a recorded version of a Tchaikovsky symphony is an "electronic" rather than a "live" performance. The sound is produced by loudspeakers, and what we are hearing is most likely not a single continuous reading of the work but an assemblage of various "takes" spliced together. Similarly, most recorded rock tunes are dub-downs (final mixes) of several takes. Vocal, instrumental, and rhythmic layers are frequently recorded separately, sometimes weeks apart; reverberation is added, and exact balance levels are determined in the recording booth, not on stage.

Electronic music is not a single school or style of composition, and it is tied to no particular esthetic. It is, rather, a *medium* of music, like the orchestra, in which the fundamental technique is the manipulation and transformation of sound patterns while they are in an electronic state. The

[1] Riley's *In C* is available on Columbia MS-7178; Reich's *Drumming* can be heard on Deutsche Grammophon 2740106.

original sound sources may be either acoustic (something that actually sounds) or electronic in origin. In addition to voices and traditional instruments, acoustic sources often include *concrete sounds*—everyday sounds not normally associated with music, such as a door slam or the ring of an alarm clock. Purely electronic sounds are created by means of oscillators, circuits that produce an alternating current that is ultimately converted into sound by a loud speaker. In recent years, computer operations have often replaced oscillators and other electronic circuits.

Whatever the source of a signal (an electronic pattern), it is shaped and combined with other sources before being sent to a speaker. Step by step, the composer determines each musical characteristic of a sound—its pitch, color, length, and articulation—and builds up layers of sounds into a complete composition.

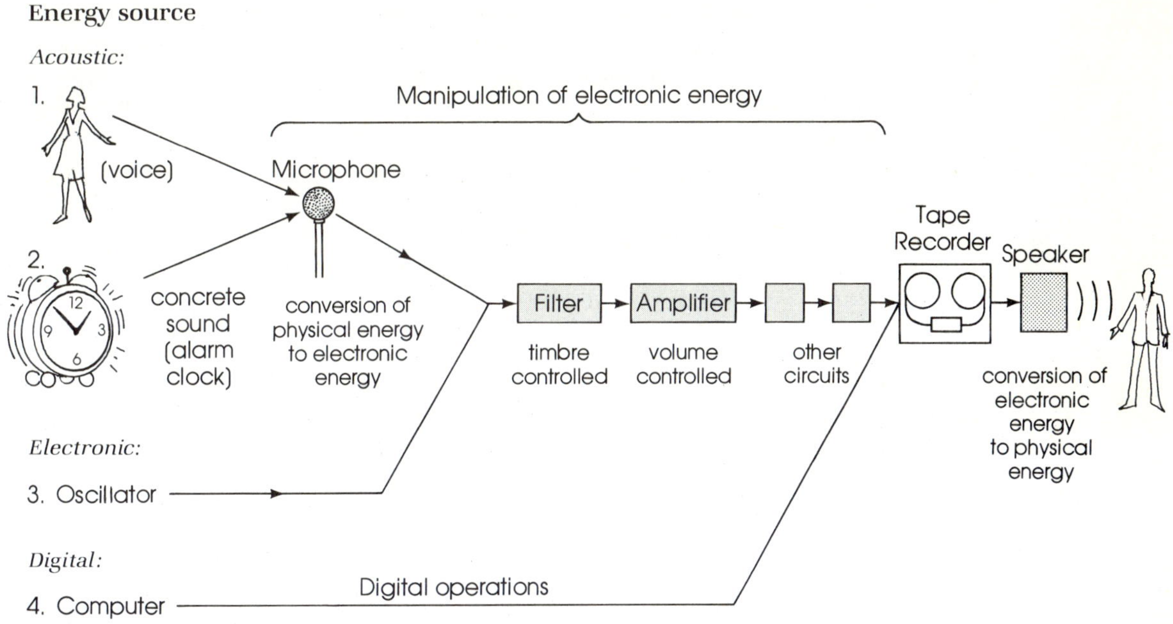

The variety of "electronic" music encompasses everything from recordings of "live" performances through computer-synthesized music. In each case a sound wave-form is generated, manipulated in some manner, and recorded and reproduced electronically.

Musique Concrète. Isolated experimentation with electronic instruments began early in the century. In the late 1940s a group of engineers and composers working at the government radio studio in Paris began recording concrete sounds, then arranging and combining them into compositions. Their works were called *musique concrète* ("moo-*zeek* kon-*kret*), or "concrete music," because of the nature of the sounds and because the act of composition was essentially a technological process. The composition required no score, performers, or interpretation. The composer worked directly with sounds (rather than with their notational representation) and communicated ideas directly to the listener without the intermediary of a performer. The work existed in a single, unalterable form on a disc recording.

Musique concrète was an extension of the search by Edgard Varèse, John Cage, and others for the "liberation of sound." As composers had explored new coloristic resources from percussion instruments during the first half of the century, seeking to use these "noise" sounds in a musical way, so many composers of the past thirty years have sought to incorporate a broader spectrum of "noises" within both electronic and nonelectronic works. Many composers have come to view *all* sounds as part of a continuum of sound colors, and believe that music is inherent, or at least potential, in "noise." The important qualities of a sound are its "feel" and how it is used, they argue, and not how it is produced.

The invention of the tape recorder shortly after 1950 spurred the development of electronic music by opening up a greatly expanded range of technical resources. Magnetic tape is a much more flexible medium than disc recording. For one thing, tape can be spliced. This enables composers to record successive sounds independently, then join them together, like beads on a necklace, into a continuous piece of tape. In addition, sounds to be heard simultaneously can be recorded one at a time on separate tracks. Tape can be played backward or at various speeds and can produce single or multiple echoes and reverberation. In these and other ways, composers manipulate sounds while recording, altering and superimposing them to create complex colors and textures. Spatial placement of sound is an important dimension of most electronic works. Sounds are positioned at various points along a continuum from left to right, or, if four or more speakers are used, at precise three-dimensional spots. Sounds are often moved between different "locations" or bounced between speakers.

During the 1950s the emphasis shifted from tape manipulation of concrete sounds to the use of purely electronic signals and controls. Electronic oscillators became the most common sound source. Depending upon its design, an oscillator can produce a single, steady frequency (heard as a single tone) or rapid, complex frequency alternations that produce a solid band of noise-like sound similar to radio static. They can create mellow or shrill timbres in any register within the human range of hearing, and they are not limited to the twelve-tone division of the octave. Filters, circuits that modify a timbre by simplifying it, can convert a trumpet-like timbre into something sounding more like a flute. With filters and other modification circuits, a composer can add to and subtract from an original sound source and mold it into a precise timbre unlike that of any traditional instrument.

Four-track Magnetic Tape

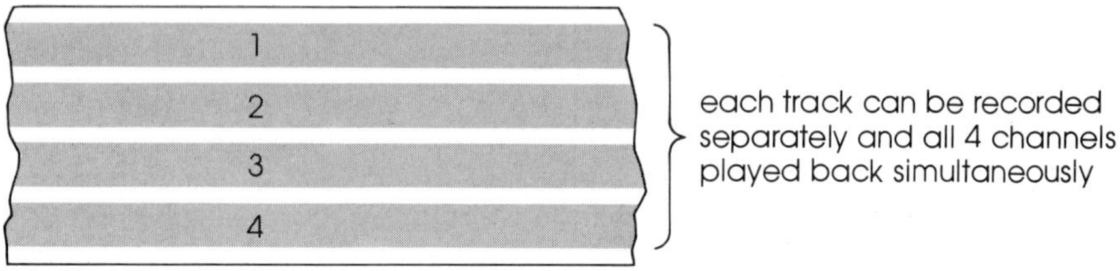

Listening

Poème Électronique *by Edgard Varèse (1883–1965)*

Varèse's *Poème Électronique* is an eloquent eight-minute tape piece composed for presentation at the Philips Radio Corporation's pavilion during the 1958 Brussels World's Fair. The piece was played continuously on over 400 loudspeakers while a series of slides chosen by the architect of the building, Le Corbusier, was projected. There was no sit-down audience. Visitors (16,000 a day) walked through the hall and were free to come and go as they pleased. The work contains an eclectic mix of acoustic and electronic sound sources including traditional instruments (voices, organ, percussion), concrete sources (church bells, sirens), and purely electronic signals. Some of the sounds are readily identifiable; others have been highly processed, and their source is uncertain. Varèse attempted to integrate these diverse sounds so that acoustic and electronic sources would not stand apart but rather merge into a broad spectrum of colors and rhythmic gestures. Some of the sounds are used motivically and recur. The opening church bells, and the sirens, voices, and a slyly ascending three-note "trombone" figure in the main body of the work are the most conspicuous examples. However, most of the sounds occur only once. Much of the piece is texturally monophonic, focusing on a single sound at a time. Considerable use is made of reverberation and spatial motion to add depth and definition.

Poème Électronique is among the best-known examples of *musique concrète.* (Varèse disliked the term, however, feeling that it smacked of dilettantism, and preferred to call his electronic works "organized sounds.") What distinguishes the composition from many tape pieces of the 1950s is its clear sense of progression and pacing, and an underlying quality of drama. Most of the sounds seem to issue "naturally" out of the preceding ideas, but there are also unexpected jolts that energize the music like a tensing of muscles. The work is both serene and charged with energy, and speaks to listeners in quite different ways.

Synthesizers and Computers. In 1959 the RCA Mark II synthesizer was put into operation at the Columbia–Princeton Electronic Music Center in New York, under the direction of Milton Babbitt. This immense instrument contained 36 oscillators and a vast array of modifying circuits, giving the composer access to all of the equipment that might be needed in one integrated unit. The early 1960s witnessed the rapid dissemination of much smaller (often portable) *voltage-controlled synthesizers,* also made up of oscillators and modifying circuits. The energy signal from an oscillator is sent along a path through the instrument, and its pitch, timbre, duration, and articulation are determined by the (voltage) control settings of individual circuits. These settings are established by a keyboard mechanism and/or

A voltage-controlled synthesizer in use in an electronic music studio.

other control circuits. The synthesizer is not intended to imitate the timbres of traditional instruments—it does this very poorly—but rather to create new timbres through a process of "synthesis" (an adding-together of the various components of a sound).

Synthesizers are designed either for *real-time* (live performance) or studio use. Real-time instruments contain a limited number of common circuit connections. They can be played like traditional instruments, and are staple members of many rock ensembles. Many are capable of producing only a single independently controllable tone at one time, and are often used for solo lines and special effects. Synthesizers intended for studio use are generally more complex and versatile in design and can create a much broader range of sounds. They are rarely performed "live." Instead, the various sounds of a piece are recorded individually, then mixed together. As in the traditional tape studio, it may take the composer weeks to produce a few seconds of music. Because of their flexibility, ease of understanding and operation, and relatively low cost, synthesizers quickly became the heart of most electronic studios and allowed many more institutions and individuals to gain access to the medium.

In the last decade, computer-generated music has emerged as the most sophisticated type of electronic music production. Instead of working with individual circuits, the composer specifies each characteristic of a sound numerically. This digital information is processed by the computer and is eventually converted to an electronic signal that can be recorded on tape. There is no splicing, mixing, or editing involved. The composer is usually able to hear the music only at the end of this chain, and must repeat the entire process to make alterations.[1]

Lacking any visual interest, prerecorded tape pieces are poorly suited to concert presentation. Audiences frequently feel awkward at the end of a performance, uncertain whether or not to clap (for the speakers?), and many composers feel that a living room or outdoor setting is a better environment for the reception of electronic works. Others have addressed the visual vacuum head-on, collaborating with other artists in mixed-media presentations. An increasingly common solution is to combine prerecorded tape segments with live performances.

Some listeners are disturbed by what they feel is an "impersonal" element in electronic music, a qualm reminiscent of Stravinsky's remark about the organ: "The monster never breathes." For those who feel that art is one of the last preserves of fully human activity in a world increasingly dominated by soulless machines, the hardware of electronic music may at first appear alien or intimidating. What should always be remembered, however, is that behind all those dials, knobs, or computer printouts stands a composer. Electronic music is an attempt to put technology at the artistic service of the human imagination, and to enable the composer to achieve sounds and sound patterns that could not be realized in any other way. The composer does not simply turn a synthesizer or computer on and retrieve the music sometime later, like a Pepsi from a vending machine. Electronic music production requires the same kinds of decisions necessary to the composition and performance of an instrumental work. By means of synthesizers and computers it is possible for composers to create sounds of such rapidity or complexity that they exceed the limits of human perception. It is these perceptual limits, and the composer's own sensitivity to musical gesture and expression, that provide the esthetic boundaries of today's electronic music.

Listening

Synchronisms No. 1 *by Mario Davidovsky (b. 1934)*

Mario Davidovsky, an Argentinian-born composer who has worked in and around New York since 1958, has written a series of works entitled "Synchronisms" that blend prerecorded electronic sounds with live performances by solo instrumentalists. His *Synchronisms No. 1* (1962), the first of these works, features a solo flute, and is characteristic of Davidovsky's attempt to integrate live and taped synthesizer sounds into coherent textures while exploiting the unique capacities of each.

The texture of the piece is transparent, and the tape part consists

[1] Dexter Morrill's *Studies for Trumpet and Computer,* available on Golden Crest 7068, is a good introduction to the resources of computer synthesis. For a relatively nontechnical overview of the subject, see the article "How Does a Computer Make Music?" by James Moorer in *Computer Music Journal,* Vol. II, No. 1 (Box E, Menlo Park, Ca 94025).

mostly of single, though rapidly changing, sound sources. Arabesque tape figures, sometimes approaching the limits of human perception in speed and extreme high–low registral shifts, are woven around the flute line. An underlying pattern of motion recurs several times: a sustained pitch is followed by lyrical or delicate figures, which grow more animated and culminate in a rapid burst of energy:

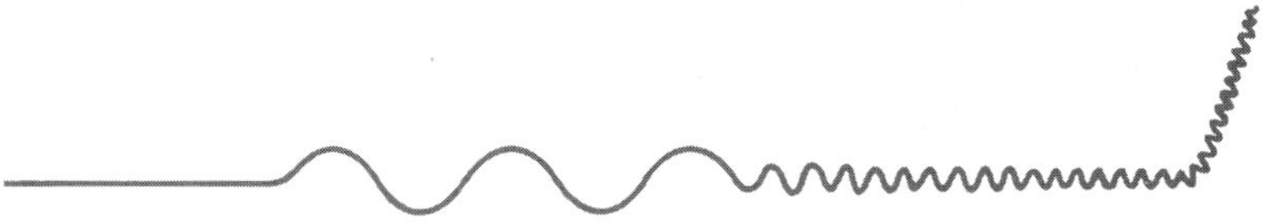

The piece opens with a "thematic" statement of this fundamental gesture, and ends with a condensed version of the same pattern. Throughout the body of the work the pattern is stretched and twisted into new shapes, somewhat in the manner of variation procedures, and different portions of the pattern are isolated and emphasized. The flute and tape parts usually pull apart into separate layers during the lyrical passages, then coalesce into a single textural thread on the agitated flurries. The synthesizer sounds do not conform to our traditional tuning system and frequently sound like rhapsodic echoes or transformations of the more focused solo line. The expressive tone is wide-ranging, often changing in the blinking of an eye from a whimsical interplay to a reflective calm.

New Sounds from Traditional Instruments

The search for new coloristic resources, which include "noise" and concrete sounds as part of the expanded continuum of musically usable material, has extended beyond the invention of novel instruments and electronic music to include exploration of unusual techniques with voices and traditional instruments. Seeking to arrest the listener's attention directly on sound quality as the *principal* element of expression, some composers have deemphasized or entirely eliminated the traditional bases of musical structure: melody, harmony, and rhythmic pulse. In their place, changing densities (thick–thin), registers (high–low), timbres (shrill–delicate), and articulations (rough–smooth) are juxtaposed or smoothly connected into expressive patterns. Oliveros' *Sound Patterns,* discussed in the Introduction, is an example of such techniques in the vocal medium. Krzysztof Penderecki is among the vanguard of those composers who have created new instrumental timbres with telling effect.

Listening

Threnody for the Victims of Hiroshima *by Krzysztof Penderecki (b. 1933)*

Constrained by government decrees that art reflect an egalitarian spirit and be readily comprehensible to all on first hearing, composers of Eastern Europe were cut off from the major new currents in music that developed after World War II. In 1956, however, the Polish government relaxed these restrictions and a vigorous new stream of composition burgeoned. Krzysztof ("*Kzish*-toff") Penderecki ("Pen-der-*et*-skee") has emerged as the most influential member of the new Polish school. In recent years he has toured, lectured, and taught extensively in Western Europe and the United States.

Penderecki incorporates concrete sounds into some of his works (for example, a typewriter and sawing of wood in his orchestral piece *Fluorescences,* 1961), and frequently calls for wind players to produce the highest possible sound on their instruments, which he notates ↑. His major innovations, however, have been with the strings. Performers are often instructed to tap various parts of the instrument with their fingertips, to bow behind the bridge, or to employ similar unorthodox techniques. Most of the resulting sounds are percussive, sometimes approximating electronically produced colors, and lack clear pitch definition. Discrete pitch, in fact, has almost disappeared from many of Penderecki's orchestral works, and been replaced by thick bands of sound. Penderecki makes considerable use of quarter-tone *clusters*—solid masses of sound in which the strings play not only all twelve chromatic pitches, but also pitches midway between the keys of a piano, so that 24 separate tones are sounded simultaneously within an octave. Such clusters are much too dense to be heard as "chords"; rather, they comprise highly charged "sheets" of sound that are combined into spatial patterns. Structural tension is determined by the relative density and stridency of adjacent sound masses.

Threnody for the Victims of Hiroshima, a "lamentation" composed in 1960, is the first and most celebrated of Penderecki's coloristic studies. Considered avant-garde when first performed, the piece sounds somewhat less revolutionary today, as many of its special effects have become common timbral resources. *Threnody* has lost none of its shattering dramatic impact, however. It is an agonized outcry, with an underlying fury that never lets up. It is not pretty—nor is its subject matter.

The work is scored for 52 strings. Like most of Penderecki's music, it is sectional in design. Each section is based upon a characteristic sound quality. In the first section, which lasts about 49 seconds, the strings enter loudly in groups, sustaining the highest possible tone they can produce. The resulting quality is a wrenching series of shrieks, punctuated by the successive entrances. The high cluster grows softer

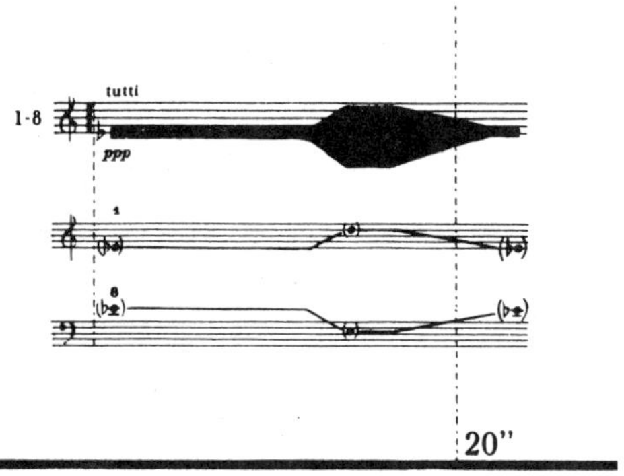

The bass lines from the beginning of the third section of Penderecki's Threnody. *Elapsed time is marked in seconds, and the notation graphically depicts swelling and diminishing "sheets" of sound.*

and fades into the second section, a kaleidoscopic series of percussive sounds. The strings again enter in groups, and there is much internal rhythmic motion, but no sense of direction or development. The third section features sustained sounds again. Single pitches diverge into clusters, which collapse back into single notes. Clusters are then superimposed to form a massive wall of sound that grows very loud before dissipating. The beginning of the third section is reproduced above. Penderecki uses a graphic form of notation, attempting to convey the shape of the music visually in the score. The opening three sections create a sense of foreboding—the specter of an accumulating horror. With the title of the work in mind, one may hear the sound of bombers, human screams, or other images, but the music is programmatic only in a general sense and does not attempt to translate specific incidents or symbols into musical terms.

The rest of the piece is similarly organized into discrete sections made up of static but intense blocks of sound. There is only one musical event going on at a time, and in this sense the piece is monophonic in conception, but each event is reduplicated and imitated in several layers, as though taking place in a hall of mirrors. The textures grow denser and louder toward the end of the piece, and finally detonate in a ferocious cluster that seems to absorb everything that has come before.

Music Without Structure

As Schönberg pursued the "emancipation of dissonance," much of Penderecki's music represents a trend toward what might be called the emancipation of *sound* from notes and rhythms. Penderecki manipulates colors into formal designs. Thus, for all the novelty of his coloristic textures, his esthetic orientation is traditional. Individual elements, now colors rather than melodies or chords, become meaningful as they are combined into patterns.

A more radical approach to "the emancipation of sound" has been taken by American composer John Cage (b. 1912) who has sought to free sound from context, and, by extension, from "music." Persuaded that no sound is inherently better than another, Cage believes that sound should be experienced for its own sake rather than manipulated or controlled. In his works, Cage has attempted to let sound "be itself," denying its traditional musical role as a vehicle for communication. Cage has removed himself from the control of sound by employing *chance* procedures, determining pitches, durations, and dynamic levels by rolling dice, tossing coins, and similar operations. The performer is often left to determine tempo, dynamics, and the order in which passages are to be played (or not played) through spontaneous impulse. Cage's most famous work, *4′ 33″*, carries his esthetic theories to an extreme. A pianist or other performer sits before the instrument for 4 minutes and 33 seconds, producing no sound. But sounds *are* present, both in reality (traffic noise, a cough, and so on), and in potential (what the performer *might* have played), and this is the whole point of the piece. Cage wants the listener to become more sensitive to those sounds that are present, and to mentally supply others he might wish to hear.

Listening

Aventures *by György Ligeti (b. 1923)*

During the 1960s, György Ligeti ("*Lig*-et-ee") and other avant-garde composers influenced by Cage undertook a kindred attempt to free sound from context by relating it to theatrical rather than "musical" gestures. *Aventures* (1962), for three singers and seven instrumentalists, is a disjointed series of histrionic gestures meant to be received as sound, not structured music. There is no "meaning" to the work beyond the sounds themselves. The singers chant intricate but meaningless phonetic syllables. The piece is devoid of any subject matter. It is "about" nothing in particular. Concrete, noise, and musical sounds intermingle. The singers pant, moan, clear their throats, laugh, perform rapid but directionless rhythms, and sing lines that are either disconnected or highly repetitive. The vocal parts are virtuosic in technical demands, but the virtuosity is, by design, idle, serving no structural end.

In this work, music is reduced to pure gesture, with a localized focus on whatever is taking place at the moment. The gestures are erratic and frequently exaggerated, verging on hysteria. At other times they are minimal—isolated puffs that light up and vanish. The instrumental parts have, in the words of one reviewer, "a sense of irrelevance and triviality." They present isolated fragments and neutral clusters and create no sense of continuity.

What, then, is going on? Theater of the absurd? Group therapy? An exhibitionist put-on? The tone of *Aventures* is ambiguous. It can be heard as a caricature, a serious statement of depersonalization in mass society against which isolated protests are heard, or in many other ways. There is a game-like quality to *Aventures* in its unpredictable sequence of events and frenzied actions that serve no ulterior purpose beyond the release of energy. Whether the game is a lark or deadly earnest, however, what the rules are, and whether it makes any difference if one figures them out, are questions that are left for the listener to decide. The work is more of a philosophical than musical statement. It has been intricately constructed and notated to produce a random sequence with no explicit meaning other than total involvement in sound.

Movements Toward Musical Synthesis

Many observers of the musical scene have predicted that the recent explosion in techniques and styles would be followed by a period of consolidation, during which composers would be less interested in the pursuit of still more possibilities than in a more thorough use and combination of the new resources already opened up. There are signs that this process is now taking place. Many of today's leading composers are seeking to make original musical statements through *re*-interpretation and integration of available musical resources. With the twentieth century now more than four-fifths over, composers no longer feel as strong a need to distance themselves from the Romantic legacy or tonal tradition, and many "progressive" composers have taken a backward look at tonal practice, finding it an unexpected "new" source of expression. This has not been a matter of mere retrenchment, but rather reflects a broader realization that musical originality lies more in the statement that is expressed than in the materials with which it is made.

Several composers are not only adopting tonal syntaxes, but are also incorporating actual quotations from other composers' works in their scores. This disturbs some audiences, who fear that their leg is being pulled, or that such quotations are a sign of despair (reflecting such dearth of original ideas that the composer is reduced to mimicking the works of his predecessors). However, *parody technique*—the incorporation of pre-existent music into a new work—was common throughout the Renaissance and Baroque periods. Its recent revival reflects a belief by a growing number of composers that the actual music (as well as techniques) of earlier periods can be incorporated into original statements.

Listening

Vox Balaenae (Voice of the Whales) ***by George Crumb (b. 1929)***

The compositions of George Crumb reflect many of the recent currents in contemporary music: economy of material and gesture; emphasis on striking colors as a primary element of expression; simplification of pitch style; parody quotes and stylistic references to tonal works; and a broad view of music as an essentially dramatic art.

Such a laundry list, however, conveys little of the unique flavor of Crumb's music. He seeks to project a quality of intuitive insight in his works, and his subject matter is primal human experience and emotions: life, death, the passing of time, the search for meaning. The tone of his music transcends the personal and attempts to embody collective insight as revealed in ceremonial acts. Crumb begins with a dramatic conception, then selects and molds his musical materials to suit the essential mood or gesture. His music is evocative rather than developmental, and his formal designs are like prisms: a central image or feeling is dispersed into individual colors and motives, which recur in varied form.

Vox Balaenae (1971), a trio for flute, cello, and piano, was inspired by the haunting sounds of humpback whales. The instruments are electronically amplified with contact microphones, enabling Crumb to exploit several special effects that would otherwise be too soft or indistinct for clear delivery. Nature imagery pervades the work. Crumb directs that the stage be bathed in blue light. The players wear masks. "By effacing a sense of human projection," he explains, the masks "are intended to give a symbolic representation of the powerful, impersonal forces of nature." Elemental two- and three-note motives recur throughout the piece, a characteristic feature of Crumb's music that reflects his striving for a direct, emotive type of expression.

First movement, "Vocalise (. . . for the beginning of time)." The opening movement, discussed in Chapter 3, consists mostly of a solo flute line. The performer sings into the instrument while playing, producing an eerie, highly emotive tone quality that seems slightly out of focus, as though heard from a great distance. Midway through this rhapsodic solo, Crumb interjects a transformed quotation of the principal motive from Strauss' tone poem, *Thus Spake Zarathustra.* The quote has become a musical symbol for "dawn of a new age" since its popularization by the film *2001: A Space Odyssey,* appearing like clockwork in numerous television commercials to cue the "dawn" of a new brand of deodorant or diapers. Here the motive is parodied in a musical sense. It is begun by the flutist, who sings three sustained notes while playing ornamental embellishments on the instrument, and is continued by the dramatic entrance of the piano. The gesture is theatrical, perhaps heralding the emergence of life in the sea, but it is carefully woven into the musical fabric. The movement concludes with murmuring two- and three-note figures—simple patterns that seem to echo through time and contrast with the rapturous arabesque figures of the beginning of the movement.

Second movement, "Variations on Sea-Time." The second movement consists of a theme and five variations. The theme, presented by the cello in harmonics (high, pure tones) revolves around a three-note motive. The theme is diatonic, establishing a seven-tone scale that forms the pitch basis of the second and third movements. It is accompanied by glissandos strummed over the lowest piano strings, comprising a distant drone in timeless rhythm.

The five brief sections that follow are not "variations" in the

Classical sense. Each evokes a different mood and projects a particular quality of color and rhythmic motion. The emphasis gradually shifts from pure coloristic evocation to rhythmic energy, then to a fiery chantlike melody played by the flute and cello. In the final variation, frenzied individual outbursts in the three instruments dissolve into echoes of the first movement.

Third movement, "Sea Nocturne (. . . for the end of time)." The third movement begins with a whistled version of the cello theme of the preceding movement. Cyclical recurrences of themes and motives between the three movements, like the frequent dronelike repetitive figures that run throughout the work, reflect Crumb's attempt to depict "a larger rhythm of nature." The first six notes of the theme are then played by the cellist on antique cymbals (small brass cymbals of definite pitch). A new but intervallically related theme emerges in imitation between the cello and flute, while the pianist plays a series of figuration patterns over an unchanging bass tone. What we are hearing—a lyrical accompanied-melody texture firmly rooted around a central tone—is a sort of musical flashback to Romantic syntax. The music is not tonal in the traditional sense—there are no functional harmonic progressions or points of cadential arrival—but it does represent a reemergence of basic tonal principles. The pitch language is simplified to a more or less traditional diatonic scale, and a central tone is established through repetition. The movement has a songlike quality reminiscent of certain passages in Mahler's slow movements.

The third movement distills in fullest form the "timeless" quality of the work, ending with a series of echoes of the whistled theme and piano figuration pattern. (The last figuration is played in pantomime. No sound is produced, but the figuration *is* heard, in the listener's imagination.) The movement is full of *stylistic* echoes as well: of tonality, Romanticism, lyrical song, and Mahler in particular. These echoes are also a musical reflection of the "larger rhythm of nature," the central image of the work. They reflect Crumb's belief that Romantic syntax and gesture are no longer forbidden territory for "progressive" composers. Put more positively, the third movement reveals Crumb's conviction that the musical language of the past is still a living, *usable* language, available today as an expressive resource ideally suited to certain musical and dramatic conceptions.

Listening

Third Section from* Sinfonia *by Luciano Berio (b. 1925)

Luciano Berio, the most prominent Italian composer of the present day, has composed in a variety of styles and media. Between 1955 and 1961 he produced an impressive series of tape pieces at the electronic studio of the Italian radio in Milan, which he helped found. During these years he also composed serial instrumental works and vocal and instrumental pieces employing chance and improvisational techniques. In the early 1960s his style evolved into a more eclectic and sensuous language. Dramatic concentration, always a distinguishing feature of his music, increasingly took the form of theatrical conception, manifesting Berio's belief that "music and theater are the most valuable tools today to help people transform themselves and things." In 1965 Berio joined the faculty of the Julliard School in New York, and since the mid-1970s has been the director of electronic music at IRCAM, a government-sponsored center for new music in Paris.

Sinfonia (1968) is a work in four large sections for eight singers and orchestra. The vocal parts were written expressly for the Swingle Singers, a virtuosic Paris-based ensemble led by American Ward Swingle, best known for their jazz interpretations of Bach. The work is not a symphony; the title refers to the 17th century meaning of *sinfonia,* a "sounding together" (in this case of voices and orchestra).

To understand what is taking place in the third section of the work, it is necessary to listen first to at least a portion of the third movement of Mahler's *Symphony No. 2* (the "Resurrection Symphony"). Mahler's scherzo movement is quoted, not just in bits and pieces, but in nearly original form throughout most of the third section of *Sinfonia.* On top of it Berio overlays a collage of additional musical and literary quotations. The vocal texts center around excerpts from *The Unnamable* by Samuel Beckett, with its insistent but cryptic cry to "keep going." Spinning off from the Beckett text is a profusion of seemingly unrelated quotations from the writings of James Joyce, undergraduate slogans, graffiti from the 1968 student uprisings in Paris, and conversations between Berio and his friends. In similar fashion, the Mahler movement provokes an eruption of musical associations from the works of 20 or so composers ranging from Bach, Beethoven, Debussy, and Ives down to Berio himself. These parodies are usually incorporated into the flow of the Mahler, but at times are superimposed as separate layers; sometimes they overwhelm the scherzo, which momentarily disappears, only to reemerge again downstream. The result is, in Berio's words, "a voyage . . . made on board" the Mahler movement, during which a potpourri of musical and verbal extracts surface and disappear in continuous succession.

The section was inspired by a performance of the Mahler symphony by Leonard Bernstein and the New York Philharmonic that deeply moved Berio. He attempted an homage to Mahler, "whose work seems to bear the weight of the entire history of music." Struck by the "stream-of-consciousness-like flowing that is the most immediate expressive character" of the scherzo, Berio set out to make explicit the many musical and philosophical associations, influences, allusions, and seeming contradictions that he felt were implicit in the music. He also sought to demonstrate that these associations continue, and are in fact expanded for modern listeners by additional relationships that have developed during the 20th century. In his homage, which he considers

Luciano Berio

"the most experimental music I have written to date," subjective associations are given free rein. They are no longer "just below" the surface of the music, but are now *on* the surface, in concrete form. Berio's collage is a piece *about* music. The stylistic juxtapositions can be likened to the many conscious and subconscious thoughts and feelings that might dart through a listener's mind during a performance of the Mahler movement. As the listener follows the development of musical ideas, a hundred associations might flash by—other compositions, conversations from earlier in the day, someone in the audience who looks like a former lover, lonliness, childhood study of music *("do re mi"),* religious feelings, a sinking feeling of despair ("All this can't stop the wars, can't make the young older or lower the price of bread")—and all the while the music surges forward, totally absorbing, setting off new sparks, touching raw nerves and healing at the same time.

The most obvious precedent for Berio's technique is the music of Ives, particularly the second movement of his *Fourth Symphony.* As in that movement, there is a crush of musical images and quotations, an interplay of foreground and background events, a feeling of coexistence and compression of "unrelated" ideas, and a definitive quality to the music that can only be called spiritual. Like the Ives movement, Berio's section cannot be fully grasped on any single hearing and may sound quite different is heard a few days later. Neither piece arranges ideas in "logical" succession. The perception of both works is left to the individual, who must draw upon his total (not just musical) experience to sort things out and grasp its expressive qualities. And this, it would seem, is the heart of the "meaning" of *Sinfonia*—that music cannot be "explained," and a listener cannot be told "what to listen for." A composition may have a lucid formal design, or, as in the music of Mahler, Ives, and the third section of *Sinfonia,* may hurl a barrage of ideas at the listener. The musical meaning of a work, however, is not something to be *received,* like a baseball, but *perceived,* as we come to understand the responses it evokes within us.

Listening

Rituals *by Ralph Shapey (b. 1921)*

Not all contemporary composers employ eclectic procedures or periodically shed stylistic idioms. Some follow a gradual course of stylistic evolution. A few hold a very rigorous esthetic outlook, believing that the framework in which they write is not a matter of choice but a personal imperative, which may change in externals but never in substance. In this view, style is not merely a vehicle through which musical statements are made, but a statement in its own right, which springs from a consistent musical vision; the only choices are how best to discover and develop this "inner voice" and how to give it fullest expression. One composer whose music embodies this uncompromising view of art with particular force is Ralph Shapey.

Shapey's music externally reflects few of the cross-currents of the present musical age. He has pursued a single-minded musical vision, grounded on a very physical view of music, which he sees as "an object in Time and Space." His works feature incisive, densely compressed thematic ideas which, like the three-shorts-and-a-long motive of Beethoven's *Fifth Symphony,* are fragmentary in design but complete in thought from the very outset. These ideas are not developed, undergo no character change and do not become part of larger patterns. Instead, they are stated and reiterated in new orders and combinations. Their context changes, but never their design or totality.

Rituals (1959) is a two-movement work for a modest-sized orchestra augmented by three saxophones and piano. Like much of Shapey's music, the piece is exactingly worked out but fiery in emotional intensity. "The piece deals," he writes, "with man's desire to create, to hold, to understand, to capture the unknown through the force, power and inflexibility of ritual, thus achieving states of ecstasy beyond imagination."

First Movement. In a terse exposition lasting only a few seconds, Shapey juxtaposes the three motives that dominate the work: (1) a fanfare-like horn call; (2) a rapid repeated-note figure in the trumpet; and (3) three brass chords.

Principal Motives Stated Together

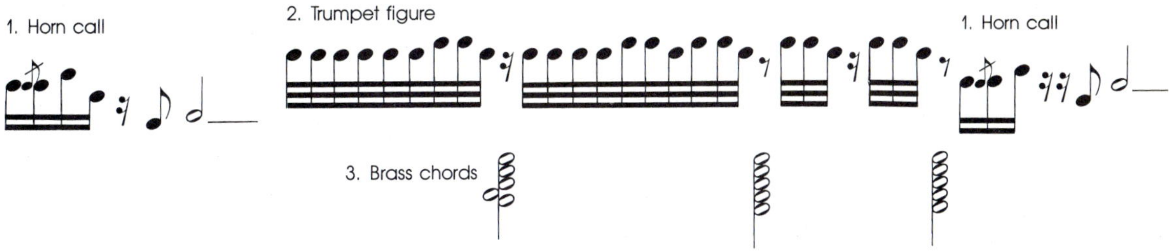

These motives are repeated at their original pitch level throughout the piece, and each is associated with a specific group of tone colors. Motive 1 "belongs" to the horns and saxes, and motive 3 is always played by the brass. The second motive covers a broader range of colors, including trumpet, percussion (especially woodblocks), flute, piano, and strings. It is often reduced to a three-note figure played by the timpani. While the motives remain essentially fixed in individual content, they are continually presented in new contexts and arrangements. The opening symmetrical arrangement is a source design, but never returns. The deck is continually reshuffled, resulting in various reorderings.

The movement has a rondo-like outline: *A–B–A′* (short) *–C–A.* The

A sections are based upon the three primary motives. The tone of these sections reflects, in Shapey's words, "imposed discipline by ritualistic reiteration." As in any ceremonial act, it is the act of repetition itself that creates meaning.

The *B* and *C* sections are each based on their own theme—a long, continuous melody that also is "ritualistically" repeated. *B*, scored for woodwinds, is contemplative, like a supplication, evoking a quality of mystery of the unknown. In *C*, a searing theme is treated in imitation by the strings. The final *A* section begins with a new ordering of the original motives: 2 (flute) – 1 (horn) – 2 (strings) – 3 (brass) – 2 (timpani). Further presentations of the motives overlap, and the texture grows in density as the movement builds to a climax on a strident final sonority.

Second Movement. The second movement picks up where the first left off. In Shapey's conception, ritualistic acts are life-giving as they create meaning, but they can also be limiting, even imprisoning, unless they ultimately free the individual from both emptiness and meaningless repetition. In the second movement, four soloists—three saxophonists and a pianist—"transcend" the rigid repetition of motives. Each is given thematic material around which to improvise; the piano, for example, "transcends" motive 2.

The movement begins with the same jarring sonority with which the first movement ended. The sonority "resolves" to a unison note. This same progression will recur at the end of the movement with the force of a crashing wall. The percussion begin an ostinato (repeated) pattern. Alto sax, baritone sax, piano, and tenor sax soloists enter in succession. As fragments from the first movement are reiterated in the orchestra, the soloists pull further and further away from the original material into rapturous outbursts. Shapey is attempting to express the same musical gestures simultaneously in their most rigorous and rhapsodic forms. The baritone and tenor sax solos transcend not only the original motives, but all pitch framework as well, transported into a world of purely emotive sounds in a manic outcry of human terror and joy.

For all their stylistic and esthetic differences, the compositions we have examined in this chapter reflect a common view of art as a purposeful, important human activity. For the composers we have surveyed, music represents a powerful means of discovering and expressing who we are and how we feel, both as members of a society and as individuals. To take the time and effort to seek a similar understanding on our own terms as listeners enables us to participate fully in this expression. Communication is a two-way street, and the composer and performer have much to learn from the listener. The most fertile periods in music generally have been those in which composers have drawn continuing insight from the responses of their listeners. We all know how a responsive audience can draw forth the greatest efforts of performers, but we sometimes forget that this is also true of composers. To be fully accurate, the diagram of musical communication on page 5 might be redrawn to reflect the circular nature of this process:

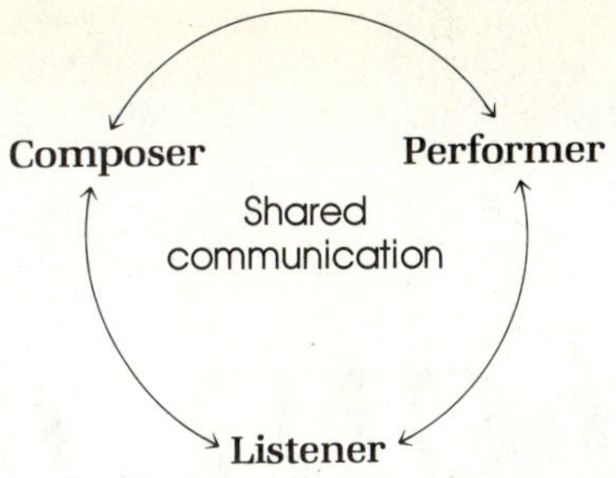

To help encourage and further this process in our time is the principal goal of this book.

Terms and Concepts for Review

new coloristic resources
dramatic, ritualistic, and theatrical aspects of musical performance
mixed-media
electronic music
- concrete sounds
- *musique concrete* (concrete music)
- musical use of "noise"
- spatial placement of sounds
- voltage-controlled synthesizer
- computer synthesis

new sounds from traditional instruments
tone color as a primary means of expression
music without structure
parody technique
tonality as a "new" resource

Appendix

Italian Tempo Markings

Tempo Marking	Speed	Literal Meaning
Slow		
grave	extremely slow	heavy, weighty, serious
largo	very slow	broad, large
lento	slow	tenacious
adagio	very slow, with motion	at ease
Moderate		
andante	slow but moving	walking
andantino	slow, but not too slow	(diminutive of *andante*)
moderato	moderate	moderate
allegretto	moderately fast	(diminutive of *allegro*)
Fast		
allegro	fast	happy, cheerful
vivace	lively, faster	with life, spirit
presto	very fast	at once
prestissimo	as fast as possible	(superlative of *presto*)

These markings are often modified by additional terms that define more precisely the exact tempo desired by the composer:

più	more	(*più allegro:* faster)
meno	less	(*meno allegro:* less fast)
non troppo	not too much	(*allegro ma non troppo:* fast but not too fast)
poco	a little	(*poco allegro:* somewhat fast)
molto	very	(*molto allegro:* very fast)

Glossary

a cappella: performed by voices alone, without instruments

accent: greater emphasis, resulting from a sharper or louder attack, given certain beats or notes in relation to other notes

accelerando: gradually becoming faster

accidentals: symbols that modify a written pitch. The sharp sign (♯) raises a written pitch by one half step, the flat (♭) lowers it by one half step, and the natural (♮) cancels a previous accidental.

aria: a solo song from an opera, oratorio, or other large scale vocal work

arpeggio: the melodic use of a chord; the chord tones are played successively rather than all at once.

atonality: music without a tonal center, with the twelve chromatic pitches treated as equals

basso continuo: in Baroque music, the bass line and improvised chords added by the keyboard player according to figured bass symbols

basso ostinato: see *ground bass*

"being" music: music without a strong sense of direction or (usually) contrasting elements

bel canto: an operatic vocal style emphasizing beauty of sound

cadence: a relaxation at the end of a phrase. *Full stop* cadences fully resolve musical tension and motion and bring a piece to a point of rest. *Half stop* cadences are inconclusive.

cadenza: a rhapsodic solo passage performed by a concerto soloist

canon: a piece in which the melody of one voice is imitated, exactly and continuously, in one or more other parts

cantata: a vocal genre for one or more soloists, often with chorus, and orchestra. The subject may be either sacred or secular. Most cantatas consist of a series of arias, recitatives, duets, and choruses.

cantus firmus: a "given" melody, borrowed from some earlier source (often Gregorian chant) and incorporated as one line of a polyphonic piece

canzona: a late Renaissance instrumental genre, usually sectional in outline and often performed by groups of wind and string instruments

chaconne: see *passacaglia*

chamber music: music for small groups of instruments, with a single performer on each part

chance procedures (indeterminacy): music in which the composer leaves some aspects of the composition to chance, either determining them in an arbitrary way or trying to involve the performer in compositional decisions

chanson: French for "song"; most often applied to the principal genre of 15th-century secular vocal music, a part song for three or four voices

character piece: a brief, lyrical work for piano, generally from the Romantic period, that depicts one or two moods

chorale: a hymn tune, generally harmonized in four parts

chord: a group of three or more tones sounded together. Harmonic progressions are made up of a series of chords. See *functional chord.*

chromatic scale: all twelve of the pitches available within equal-tempered tuning arranged in ascending or descending order.

clef: symbols at the left edge of the staff that indicate the general high or low range of tones and exact pitch relationships.

closing material: in a sonata-form movement, a passage at the end of the exposition that leads to a full stop in the secondary key

cluster (tone cluster): a group of half steps sounded together to form a dense sonority with no tonal focus

coda: a closing passage at the end of a work or movement that creates a feeling of finality and closure

concert overture: a short, single-movement orchestral work, often loosely based on sonata form

consonance: an interval or chord that is acoustically simple and sounds "at rest"

continuo: see *basso continuo*

contour: the curve, or profile, of a melody that results from the upward and downward motion of pitches

contrary motion: motion of two melodic lines in opposite directions simultaneously

cross accent: see *accent*

da capo aria: an aria in *A—B—A* outline; the return of *A* is often ornamented by the singer.

deceptive cadence: a harmonic progression in which the listener is led to expect a return to the tonic, but some other chord is substituted in its place

development: the formal process by which initial themes or ideas are expanded and integrated into a larger statement. This often begins with the breaking apart of themes into motives that are treated separately or combined in new ways.

development section: occurs after the exposition (or exposition repeat) in sonata-form movements. Thematic material from the exposition is fragmented and combined in new ways.

diatonicism: the use of one or more seven-tone scales in a work

dissonance: an interval or chord that produces an unstable harmonic quality, usually causing an increase in tension.

dominant: the fifth tone of a major or minor scale. *Dominant chords* built on this tone provide the strongest harmonic motion back to the tonic

downbeat: the first beat of a measure

dynamic level: loudness

dynamic markings: Italian abbreviations that indicate how loudly a passage is to be performed

duration: the length of a note

episode: a fragmentary passage; in fugues, a passage in which the complete subject is not present

electronic music: a medium in which the fundamental technique is the manipulation of sound patterns while they are in an electronic state

ensemble: in opera, a number for two or more vocal soloists with orchestral accompaniment

exposition: (1) the opening section of sonata-form movements, during which thematic material is stated (2) in fugues, the opening group of statements of the subject.

figuration pattern: a repeated rhythmic pattern superimposed on a chord progression

figured bass: a form of musical shorthand used by Baroque composers to indicate when chords should be filled in by the keyboard player

flat: see *accidental*

form: the architecture of music; the way in which the ideas of a composition are developed and shaped into a whole. The formal *outline* is the general sequence of events in a work, such as *A—B—A*

fugato: a fugal passage in an otherwise homophonic work

fugue: the most complex form of imitative counterpoint, in which passages in strict imitation alternate with other passages featuring freer contrapuntal motion

full stop: see *cadence*

functional chord: in tonal music, a chord that creates a feeling of change with respect to the tonic, producing greater tension or resolution.

genre: the general category and medium of a composition, such as a symphony (large-scale orchestral work) or character piece (brief piano work)

Gloria: a hymn of praise that comprises the second movement of most Mass settings

grand staff: a staff in treble clef over a staff in bass clef; used for instruments with a wide range of pitches, such as the piano

Gregorian chant: monophonic songs sung by male voices during the Mass and other services of the Roman Catholic church

ground bass (basso ostinato): a pattern of bass notes repeated over and over

half step (semitone): in standard Western tuning, the smallest interval between two tones.

half stop: see *cadence*

harmony: the overall sound that results when different pitches are played or sung together

homophony: a texture consisting of a principal melody with harmonic support

idiomatic: effectively written for a given medium

imitation: the repetition of a melodic idea in a new voice

improvisation: spontaneous performance, without written music

interval: the distance between two pitches

key: the tonal center and major or minor scale of a passage

key signature: accidentals placed at the beginning of a staff to indicate which major or minor scale is being used

Kyrie Eleison: a short prayer ("Lord have mercy on us") that begins the Ordinary of the Mass and comprises the first movement of most Mass settings

layered textures: textures in which each instrument or instrumental group performs a separate function, so that the resulting sound quality is an assemblage of highly distinct threads fitted together

leading tone: the seventh tone of a major or (often) minor scale, which is a half step below the tonic

legato: smooth connection of notes

leitmotif (leading motive): in Wagner's operas, a short thematic idea that recurs several times and is associated with a specific character or concept

libretto: the text of an opera or oratorio

lied: German for "song"; most often applied to lyrical Romantic-period songs with piano

line: a complete melody, whether primary or secondary in importance. In polyphonic textures, two or more lines are performed simultaneously.

lyricism: an unforced, "singing" quality that emphasizes beauty of sound

madrigal: the principal secular vocal genre of the late Renaissance; most often, a part song for between four and six singers

major interval: the larger form of many intervals, a half step larger than the minor interval

major key: a tonal center based on the use of a major scale. A piece "in G major" uses the seven notes of the G major scale.

major scale: a seven-tone scale with half steps between scale tones 3 and 4, and between tones 7 and 8

Mass: the central act of worship of the Roman Catholic church. Musical settings of the Mass generally are in five movements and present the text of the *Ordinary*, the unchanging portions of the Mass used every day.

measure: a group of accented and unaccented beats

melisma: in vocal music, an ornamental group of many notes sung to a single syllable of the text

melody: a series of tones in rhythm that create a sense of line and completeness

meter: the grouping of a pulse into patterns of strong and weak beats. The most common meters contain two, three, or four beats per measure.

metric accent: the accented first beat of a measure, which is followed by one or more unaccented beats

minor interval: the smaller form of many intervals, a half step smaller than the major interval

minor key: a tonal center based on the use of a minor scale

minor scale: a seven-tone scale characterized by the interval of a minor third between the tonic and the third note of the scale

minuet and trio form: a three-part outline in triple meter that forms the third movement of most Classical symphonies and chamber works

mixed media: music combined with various other art forms to produce a "total experience"

modes: seven-tone scales commonly used in music before 1600 and in folk music

modulation: a harmonic shift from one key to another

monody: the textural style of the earliest operas, consisting of a simple vocal line over a few chords

monophony: a single, unaccompanied melodic line. See *texture*

motet: most often, a single-movement sacred choral piece on a Latin text

motive: a brief rhythmic or melodic idea that recurs many times in original or altered form

musique concrète (Concrete Music): the earliest form of electronic music, in which natural sounds are recorded, altered, and combined

mute: a piece of wood placed over the strings of a violin, viola, or cello, or a device inserted into the bell of a brass instrument, to reduce volume and alter tone color

non-functional chord: a chord used to prolong or connect the functional chords of a progression. See *functional chords.*

non-harmonic tone: a tone in a melody or harmonic line that is not a member of any chord and that usually creates a dissonance

octave: two notes with the same letter name, twelve half-steps apart

opera: drama set to music; the largest and most elaborate musical genre, featuring vocal soloist, chorus, and orchestra

opera buffa: a comic opera in Italian

opera seria (serious opera): long, elaborate opera on a serious subject

opus (abbreviated Op.): Italian for "work." The term indicates the chronological order in which a composer's works were published.

oratorio: a large scale concert work on a sacred subject for vocal soloists, chorus, and orchestra

orchestration: the way a composition is arranged for instruments

ornamentation: embellishments added to a melody by a composer or performer

oscillator: an electronic circuit that produces a frequency (pitch)

overture: a brief orchestral number at the beginning of an opera. See also *concert overture*

pacing: the changing level of musical activity in a piece, which creates a sense of direction toward musical goals

parody technique: the incorporation of pre-existent music into a new composition, such as the use of a borrowed theme

part: (1) a melodic line (see *voice*); (2) a section of music (see *section*)

part song: a polyphonic song, such as a chanson or madrigal, usually intended for performance with a single singer on each part

passacaglia: a work based on continuous variations over a repeated bass line or chord progression

passagework: non-thematic material, often consisting of arpeggios and scale-like runs, performed by a concerto soloist *pedal point (pedal tone):* a long sustained note in one contrapuntal voice

phrase: a group of measures that ends with a cadence. Phrases are the basic units of musical form, and might be likened to the clauses of English sentences.

pitch: the exact high or low placement of a sound

pizzicato: plucking the strings of a stringed instrument to produce a percussive attack

polyphony: a texture in which two or more melodic lines are performed simultaneously, see *texture.*

program music: music that portrays a specific story line, mood, or other extra-musical quality

pulse: the basic unit of rhythmic motion, or "heartbeat," of a composition.

raga: in the music of India, a skeletal pitch pattern that forms the framework for improvised melodic variations

recapitulation: an extended passage at or near the end of a sonata-form movement in which the thematic material of the exposition is recalled

recitative: a vocal style in which the text is delivered rapidly, often in a manner midway between melody and speech

refrain: one or two lines of text that recur throughout a poem and are normally set to the same music

register: a portion of an instument's total pitch range, such as the "high register" of the bassoon

relative keys: a major and minor key that contain the same seven tones, but different tonic notes and scale patterns.

resolution: the motion of a dissonance into a consonance

rest: a silence

return: the recurrence of a theme later in a composition

rhythm: the way a piece of music organizes the time it fills, based on the relative length of each note

ritard (ritardando, rallentando): gradually slowing down

ritornello: in Baroque concertos, a recurrent tutti theme

rondo: a formal outline based on the alternation between a principal theme and contrasting passages. *Sonata–rondo* outlines include a development section and a return of the *B* theme.

root: the note on which a triad is built

rubato: a style of performance featuring almost continuous variations in the pulse

scherzo: a movement in triple meter, similar in outline to minuet and trio form but more robust

scoring: see *orchestration*

secco recitative: a Baroque recitative accompanied only by harpsichord.

section (part): a major division within a piece, such as the exposition in sonata form movements. Sections usually end with a full stop.

semitone: a half-step; in Western tuning, the smallest interval between two tones

sequence: a repeated melodic or harmonic fragment that is shifted to new pitch levels

serialism: the use of a predetermined pattern of pitches or other elements in varied form throughout a work.

series or *set:* see *twelve-tone method*

seventh chord: a four-note chord consisting of a triad with an added, dissonant note that forms the interval of a seventh with the root

sharp: see *accidental*

scale: a catalogue of the pitches most commonly used in a piece of music, arranged in ascending or descending order

sonata: since the mid-18th century, a large scale work in three or four movements, for piano or for a solo instrument with piano accompaniment

sonata form: the most important formal procedure in Classical and Romantic instrumental music, based on strong articulation of tonal motion and extensive development of thematic material.

sonata–rondo form: see *rondo*

song cycle: a concert work made up of a series of related songs

Sprechstimme ("speech-voice"): a vocal style first employed by Schönberg that is midway between spoken and sung delivery

staff: a group of five horizontal lines on and around which notes are written to indicate pitch

strophic: the formal outline of many songs, in which the same music is sung to each stanza of the text

structure: see *form*

style: the particular musical language and manner in which a composer presents ideas

subject: the theme of a fugue

suite: (1) in the Baroque era, a collection of short instrumental movements each based on a traditional dance; (2) later, a concert work made up of excerpts from a larger work, such as a ballet

symphony: the principal genre of orchestral music: a large-scale, multi-movement work

symphonic poem: a long, rhapsodic, single-movement orchestral work, generally from the 19th century

syncopation: the rhythmic effect created when accents are placed on normally weak beats of a measure, or between beats

synthesizer: an electronic musical instrument made up of various individual circuits, each of which controls one aspect of the resulting sound

tala: the rhythmic framework in Indian music, consisting of an accented beat followed by several unaccented beats

tempo: the speed of a piece of music

tempo marking: a brief description, usually in Italian, at the beginning of a score that indicates the appropriate tempo of the work. See Appendix for a list of common tempo markings

texture: the way the various elements of music (melodies, harmonies, rhythms, and tone colors) are combined and given focus in a work. *Monophonic* textures, the oldest type, consist of a single unaccompanied melody. In *polyphony,* two or more melodies are performed simultaneously. In *homophonic* textures, a principal melody is supported by a chord progression. Other types of textures, based on rhythm or color, are also common.

thematic transformation: the cyclical return of a theme in altered form. Thematic transformation is a common unifying device in 19th-century instrumental music.

theme: a complete melody that serves as the basis for part or all of a longer composition

theme and variations: a formal outline consisting of a theme followed by a series of variations on it

three-part forms: formal outlines consisting of three independent sections

through-composed forms: formal designs that lack clearly defined sectional divisions or complete thematic returns.

timbre (tone color, tone quality): the unique sound of an instrument or voice

tonal group: in sonata form, one or more themes that establish the principal keys of the exposition

tonality: a system of pitch organization in which the tones of major and minor scales function with respect to a central tone, the *tonic.* This system was used almost exclusively during the *tonal period* (c. 1650–c. 1900) and is the basis of most popular music.

tone color: see *timbre*

tone poem: see *symphonic poem*

tone row: see *twelve-tone method*

tonic: the center pitch of a tonal work, to which all other pitches are functionally related

transition: (1) a connecting link between two themes or key areas; (2) in the exposition of sonata-form movements, the passage linking the two tonal groups

transposition: the raising or lowering of a scale, melody, or chord to a new pitch level

tremolo: a special effect on stringed instruments created by very rapid changes in bow direction to produce a "trembling" quality

triad: the simplest type of chord, consisting of three tones. *Major triads* consist of the interval of a major third between the bottom two tones and a minor third between the top two tones. In *minor triads,* these intervals are reversed.

trill: the rapid alternation of two adjoining notes

triplet: a rhythmic figure that divides the pulse into three notes of equal length

tuning system: the number of pitches available within a musical culture, and the exact distances between these pitches. In most Western music the octave is divided into twelve tones each an equal distance apart.

tutti: a passage performed by all the instruments of an ensemble

twelve-tone method: a systematic approach to atonal composition, based upon the continuous varied repetition of a pitch pattern. This pattern, called the *set, tone row,* or *series,* contains all twelve chromatic tones in a specific arrangement.

two-part forms: formal outlines consisting of two sections

upbeat: a preparatory unaccented pulse

variation: the repetition of a theme with significant alternations or additions

vibrato: rapid, slight variations in pitch; often used by performers to add brilliance or richness to musical tone

virtuoso: a performer who possesses extraordinary technical skill

voice: (1) the human voice; (2) a term which, like "line" and "part," is often used to identify a particular melodic line, especially in polyphonic textures

whole step: an interval equal to two half steps

whole-tone scale: a six-tone scale made up entirely of whole steps (for example, C–D–E–F♯–G♯–A♯)

word painting: graphic music depiction of a text, often though the imitation of "natural" sounds

Credits

Photo Credits

Associated Music Publishers, Inc.: p. 413. Copyright © Beth Bergmann: pp. 359, 372, and 385. The Bettmann Archive: pp. 6, 14–15, 118, 187, 201, 208 (top and bottom), 211, 225, 234, 239, 247, 268, 269, 272, 279, 290, 292, 313, 329, 333, and 375. Brown Brothers: p. 379. Jim Cummins, Camera 5: p. 141. Collection of Mr. & Mrs. Ralph F. Colin, New York: p. 108 (left). Columbia Records: p. 399. Culver Pictures: pp. 154, 218, 220, 338, and 391. André Emmerich Gallery, Inc.: p. 397. Meryl Joseph: pp. 94 (top left), 96 (bottom left), and 99. Eve Arnold, Magnum Photos: p. 194. Jack Mitchell: p. 302. Mimi Forsyth, Monkmeyer: pp. 91 (top left, right), 94 (bottom right). Hugh Rogers, Monkmeyer: p. 94 (top right). Collection, The Museum of Modern Art, New York: p. 108 (right). Courtesy of the New York Philharmonic: pp. 101, 177. New York Public Library Picture Collection: pp. 169, 307, 340, 343, and 364. Louis Ouzer, Rochester, NY: pp. 394–395, 404. Louis Hood, The Philadelphia Orchestra: p. 98 (bottom). George Holton, Photo Researchers: p. 23. Judy Gurovitz, Photo Researchers: p. 96 (bottom right). F.B. Grunzweig, Photo Researchers: pp. 104–105, 178–179. John Veltri, Photo Researchers: p. 261. Christian Steiner: p. 96 (top left). James R. Holland, Stock Boston: pp. 7, 94 (bottom left). Martha Swope: pp. 96 (top right), 98 (top). Christian Steiner, Young Concert Artists: p. 91 (bottom left). UPI: pp. 31, 353. Wide World Photos: p. 84.

Music Credits

Stravinsky: *Le Sacre du printemps.* Copyright 1921 by Edition Russe de Musique. Copyright assigned 1947 to Boosey & Hawkes for all countries of the world. Reprinted by permission.

"All You Need Is Love" by Lennon/McCartney. Copyright © 1967 Northern Songs Ltd. All rights for the USA, Canada, Mexico & The Philippines controlled by Maclen Music, Inc. c/o ATV Music Group. Used by permission. All rights reserved. International copyright secured.

Joplin: *Gladiolus Rag.* © Copyright Edward B. Marks Music Corporation. Used by permission.

Foss: Time Cycle. Copyright © Carl Fischer, Inc. All rights reserved. Text © 1937–38 by Lawrence Houseman. By permission of Charles Scribner's Sons.

Crumb: *Vox Balaenae.* Copyright © 1972 by C.F. Peters Corporation, 373 Park Avenue South, New York, NY 10016. Reprint permission granted by the publisher.

Bartók: *String Quartet No. 4.* © Copyright 1929 by Universal Edition. Renewed 1956. Copyright and Renewal assigned to Boosey & Hawkes, Inc. (for the U.S.A.). Reprinted by permission of Boosey & Hawkes, Inc.

Debussy, *Prélude à l'après-midi d'un faune,* reprint permission granted by C.F. Peters Corporation, sole selling agents for Edition Eulenberg in U.S.A.

Schönberg: *Three Piano Pieces, Op. 11.* Used by permission of Belmont Music Publishers, Los Angeles, Ca 90049.

Schönberg: *Suite for Piano, Op. 25.* Used by permission of Belmont Music Publishers, Los Angeles, Ca 90049. © 1925 by Universal Edition. © Renewed 1952 by Gertrud Schönberg.

Debussy, *La cathédrale engloutie.* Copyright 1910 Durand et Cie. Used by permission of the publisher. Theodore Presser Company, Sole Representative U.S.A.

Prokofiev: *Piano Sonata No. 7.* Edited by Isador Philipp. Edition published by International Music Co., 545 Fifth Ave., New York, NY. Used by permission.

Varese: *Ionisation.* © 1934 and 1967 by Colfrane Music Publishing Corp., New York. By courtesy.

Strauss: *Till Eulenspiegel.* Copyright © 1904 by Aibel, renewed 1932 by C.F. Peters. Reprint permission granted by the copyright owner.

Berg: *Wozzeck.* Copyright 1931 by Universal Edition A. G. Copyright renewed. All rights for the U.S.A. and Mexico controlled exclusively by European American Music Distributors Corporation. Used by permission.

Penderecki: *Threnody.* Copyright © by Deshon Music, Inc. and PWM Editions. Used with permission. All rights reserved.

Index

A cappella music, 192
a tempo, definition of, 19
accelerando, definition of, 19
accidentals in pitch notation, 39
accompanied melody texture in classical style, 206
adagio, definition of, 19
affections and Baroque music, 196–197
Agnus Dei in Mass, 188
alap in Indian music, 143
allegro, definition of, 19
Almeida, Laurindo, 315–317
alto voice, 38, 88
andante, definition of, 19
antiphony and Gregorian chants, 183
arco and stringed instruments, 89
aria
    definition of, 271
    in opera, 361
arpeggio, 72
atonal, definition of, 240
atonality
    cubist paintings and, 242
    free, 238–242
    listener and, 242
aural perception, types of, 145

Babbitt, Milton, 400, 403
    Composition for Four Instruments, 396
Bach, Carl Philipp Emanuel, 205
Bach, Johann Sebastian, 200–202
    Brandenburg Concerto No. 2, 201–202, 318
    Brandenburg Concertos, 343
    Cantata No. 150: "Nach dir, Herr," 139
    cantatas of, 275
    chorales of, 275
    Coffee Cantata, 275
    concertos of, 343
    French Suite No. 6, 163
    Invention in F, 18, 30, 33, 48–51, 57, 69, 107, 164, 165
    "Little" Fugue in G Minor, 172–175
    Mass in B Minor, 275–276; *"Kyrie,"* 276–278
    Passions of, 275
    renewed interest in, 183
    vocal music of, 275–278
    Well-Tempered Clavier, 198
Baez, Joan, 89
Barber, Samuel, 256, 383
Baris, 22–24
baritone voice, 88
"Baroque" as musical term, 196
Baroque concerto, 342–345
    concerto grosso as type of, 343
    solo concerto as type of, 343
Baroque era
    composers of, 202–203
    improvisation in, 198
    melody in, 198
    orchestras in, 197
    sonatas in, 197
    vocal music in, 271–278
Baroque music, 196–203
    affections and, 196–197
    basso continuo in, 198
    figured bass notation in, 198
    gigue and, 197
    harmony and, 197–198
    monody in, 196
    Passion as genre of, 272
    rhythmic energy in, 198
    style in, 197–199
    texture in, 198–199
Baroque suite, 113–115
Bartók, Béla, 257, 258–259, 287
    Allegro Barbaro, 296
    Bluebeard's Castle, 383
    Concerto for Orchestra, 352
    String Quartet No. 4, 312; First Movement, 158–161
bass clarinet, 93
bass drum, 99
bass voice, 38, 88
basso continuo in Baroque music, 198
basso ostinato pattern, 137
bassoon, 93
bayan in Indian music, 141
beat, 17–19
Beatles
    "All You Need is Love," 24
Beethoven, Ludwig van, 133, 210–212, 287
    Brahms and, 308
    composing method of, 4
    concertos of, 349
    Fifth Symphony, 30
    performers and, 322
    Piano Concerto No. 3: Third movement, 129–131
    Piano Sonata No. 21, "Waldstein," 288–290; First Movement, 212–214
    string quartet and, 307
    symphonies of, 322–328
    Symphony No. 5, 323–328
    Symphony No. 6, 322
    Symphony No. 7, 125
"being" music, 107–109
    Indian music as, 144
    music of Harry Partch as, 400
bel canto vocal technique, 367
Bellini, Vincenzo, 379
Berg, Alban, 259, 384
    Wozzeck: Act III, 384–388
Berio, Luciano, 412–414
    Sinfonia, 412–414
Berlioz, Hector, 220, 232
    Symphonie Fantastique, 333; Fourth and Fifth Movements, 220–224
Bernstein, Leonard, 413
bitonality, definition of, 250
Bizet, George
    Carmen, 383
    on opera, 357
Boulez, Pierre, 176
    Le Marteau sans Maître, 313; *"Hangmen of the Solitude,"* 176–177
    Structures, 396
Brahms, Johannes, 226, 231, 307–311, 329
    Academic Festival Overture, 333
    Beethoven and, 308
    chamber works of, 308
    Clara Schumann and, 307
    concertos of, 349
    Liszt and, 307
    "Lullaby," 112–113
    Piano Quintet in F Minor, 156–158, 308–311
    Schumann and, 307
    Symphony No. 4: Fourth Movement, 138–140
    Tragic Overture, 333
    Violin Concerto in D: First Movement, 350–352
brass instruments
    horn or French horn, 95
    trombone, 95–97
    tuba, 97
Britten, Benjamin, 283
    Peter Grimes, 383
    vocal works of, 283
    War Requiem: "Dies Irae," 283–286

Brubeck, Dave
"Blue Rondo a la Turk," 22
Bruckner, Anton, 231, 232
Symphony No. 7, 332; Third Movement, 125–126
Büchner, Georg, 384
Byrd, William, 196

Caccini, Giulio, 363
cadences, 25–27
triads and, 73–74
cadenza
in classical and Romantic concertos, 346–347
definition of, 130
Cage, John, 296, 402, 408–409
4′ 33″, 409
Camerata and opera, 363
canons as contrapuntal music, 167–168
cantata as musical term, 146
cantatas of Bach, 275
cantus firmus
in Mass, 267
in polyphonic music, 186
in Renaissance music, 192
canzonas, 303
Carter, Elliott, 353
Double Concerto for Harpsichord, Piano, and Two Chamber Orchestras, 353–355
"metric modulation" technique of, 355
Casals, Pablo, 53
Castrati in Baroque Italian opera, 367
Catholic Church, liturgical music and, 267
celesta, 98
cello, 90–91
Certon, Pierre, 127
"Je Ne L'Ose Dire," 127–128
chaconne, 138
chamber music, 301–317
Classical string quartet as, 304–307
composer and, 302–303
definition of, 310
mixed ensembles in, 313
performer and, 301–302
20th-century, 311–317
chanson, 193, 303
character pieces, 225–226
definition of, 290
as piano music, 290–296
chimes as percussion instrument, 98
Chopin, Fredéric, 232, 290
concertos of, 349
Nocturne in B♭ Minor, 291–292
Prelude No. 4 in E Minor, 18–19, 30, 33, 48–51, 58, 69, 79–80, 107
choral music as vocal genre, 263
chorales of Bach, 275
chord motion, functional, 79
chord progressions, simple, 74
chords
chromatic, 79
definition of, 36
functional and non-functional, 75
intervals as basis of, 69–71
jazz and functional, 82–85
seventh, 75
chorus, opera and, 361
chromatic styles, 47
clarinet, 93
Classical concerto, 346–349
cadenza in, 346–349
Classical ideal, 205
Classical music as common term, 205
Classical string quartet, 304–307
Beethoven and, 307
Haydn and, 305
Classical style
accompanied melody texture in, 206
composers of, 207–215
contrast in, 206–207
definition of, 204
elements of, 206–207, 210
figuration pattern in, 206
opera in, 368–374
reconciliation in, 206
Romantic style, coexistence with, 204
Classical symphony, 319–320
formal outline of, 320
humor in, 321
performer and, 321–322
clefs in pitch notation, 37
closing material in sonata form, 149
closing passages in form, 110
codas, 110, 136
coloratura soprano, 360
coloristic exploration in Romantic period, 217
composer
chamber music and, 302–303
craft of, 9
idiomatic style of, 311
listener and, 416–417
performer and, 416–417
role of, 4–6
"concert music" as term, 205
concert overture, 332–333
concerto grosso, 343
concertos, 342–355
of Bach, 343
in Baroque era, 197, 342–345
of Beethoven, 349
of Brahms, 349
of Chopin, 349
Classical, 346–349
definition of, 342
of Liszt, 349
of Mendelssohn, 349
in 20th century, 352–355
concrete sounds in electronic music, 401
conductor
opera and, 361
role of, 101–103
consonance, 70–71
continuous variation, in Indian music, 140–145
continuous variation form contrasted with theme and variation form, 136
contour in melody, 56–57
contrabass, 91
contrabassoon, 93
contralto voice, 88
contrapuntal form, 163–177
canons as, 167–168
characteristics of, 163
fugue as, 171–175
homophonic form and, 164
imitation in, 165–166
independence of voices in, 164
motet as, 168–171
rhythmic differentiation in, 164
rounds as, 167
contrapuntal procedures, 163–167
in Mass, 267
in Romantic period, 175
in 20th century, 175–177
contrapuntal textures, 163
contrast
in Classical style, 206–207
in form, 107, 109–110
Copland, Aaron, 256
Appalachian Spring, 256–257
The Tender Land, 384
Corelli, Arcangelo, 202
cornettos, 304
counterpoint, *see* contrapuntal
Couperin, François, 238
Credo in Mass, 188
crescendo as dynamic marking, 87
cross accents, 31
Crumb, George
Vox Balaenae, 64–65, 107, 296, 410–412
cymbals, 99

Da capo arias in opera, 368
Da Ponte, Lorenzo, 369
Dallapiccola, Luigi, 242
Davidovsky, Mario
Synchronisms, 405–406
Debussy, Claude, 52, 234–236, 258
"La cathédrale engloutie," 295–296
character pieces of, 294–296
Pelléas et Mélisande, 383
Prelude to the Afternoon of a Faun, 19, 30, 57, 109
decrescendo as dynamic marking, 87
des Prez, Josquin, *see* Josquin des Prez
Desmond, Paul
"Take Five," 22
Diabelli, Anton, 133
Diaghilev, Serge, 248, 249
diatonic styles, 47
diminuendo as dynamic marking, 87
dissonance, 70–71

and tonality in 20th century, 80–85
dominant note, definition of, 47
Donizetti, Gaetano, 379
dorian mode, 41
double bass, 91
Dowland, John, 194, 196
"Queen Elizabeth's Galliard," 194–195
downbeats, definition of, 20
dramatic soprano or tenor, 360
drones in Indian music, 140–141
duets in opera, 361
duo as genre, 305
durational symbols, 27–28
Dvořák, Antonín, 232, 329–330
Symphony No. 9: First Movement, 330–332
dynamic markings, 87
dynamic range of instruments, 87

Electronic music, 400–406
concrete sounds in, 401
as medium of music, 400–401
musique concrète as, 401–403
synthesizers and computers and, 403–406
tape recorders and, 402
electronic oscillators, 402
english horn, 93
ensembles
definition of, 271
in opera, 361
episode as connecting passage, 110
exposition
repetition of, 150
in sonata-form movement, 148
expressionism, definition of, 384

Falla, Manuel de, 256
false entry, 174
fantasia as musical form, 194
Fauré, Gabriel, 348–349
fifth in triad, definition of, 71
figuration pattern, 206
figured bass notation, 198
flat, definition of, 39
flute, 92
"fluttertongue" on flute, 92
form(s)
chaconne, 138
closing passages in, 110
codas in, 110
connecting passages in, 110
continuous variation, 136–145
contrapuntal, 163–177
contrast in, 109–110, 197
episodes in, 110
fantasia as, 194
interludes in, 110
introductions in, 110
minuet and trio, 123–125
passacaglia, 138
refrain, 127–128
ricercar as, 194
rondo and variation, 127–145
scherzo, 125–126
sectional, 107–126
sectional construction in, 110–111
sonata, 146–162
statement in, 109
theme and variation, 133, 136
theme as melodic basis of, 109
three-part, 115–119
through-composed, 120–123
in tonal music, 109–111
transitions in, 110
two-part, 111–115
unity in, 107
variation, 132–145
forte as dynamic marking, 87
fortissimo as dynamic marking, 87
Foss, Lukas
Time Cycle: "When the Bells Justle," 55–56
free atonality, 238–242
french horn, 95
fugato passages, 175
fugue
characteristics of, 171–172
as contrapuntal form, 171–175
derivation of term, 172
false entry in, 174
functional progression during Romantic period, 217

Gabrieli, Giovanni, 196, 303–304, 311
Canzon Septimi Toni No. 2, 304
Sonata pian' e forte, 303–304
galant style, 205
galliard, definition of, 194
gamelan, 22–24
Gay, John
The Beggar's Opera, 271
Gershwin, George, 388–389, 393
Porgy and Bess: Act I, 390–393
Rhapsody in Blue, 389
Gesamtkunstwerk theory of Wagner, 375–377
Gesualdo, Carlo, 196
gigue in Baroque music, 197
glissando, 100
glockenspiel, 98
Gloria in Mass, 188
Goethe, Johann Wolfgang von, 279, 280
grand staff in pitch notation, 38
Gregorian chant, 41, 183–185
antiphony and, 183
melismas in, 184
Salve Regina as, 184–185
Gris, Juan, 108
ground bass pattern, 137
guitar, 100

Half step in pitch notation, 39
Handel, George Frideric, 200, 203
and Baroque Italian opera, 367–368
Giulio Cesare: Act IV, aria and recitative, 368
Messiah: "For Unto Us a Child is Born," 273–274
oratorios of, 271–274
hand-muting in playing horns, 95
harmony, 66–85
in Baroque era, 197–198
complex styles of tonal, 78–80
definition of, 68
18th-century shift in, 78
homophonic textures and, 68–69
intervals and, 69–71
jazz and, 82–85
monophonic texture and, 67
origins of, 66–71
polyphonic texture and, 67–68
polyphony compared with, 69
triads and, 71–80
harp, 100
harpsichord, 99–100
Harris, Roy, 256
Haydn, Franz Joseph, 208, 320
"London Symphonies" of, 208
and string quartet, 305
String Quartet in B♭ Major First Movement, 305–307, 311
String Quartet in D Minor: Third Movement, 168
Symphony No. 94: First Movement, 321–322; Second Movement, 133–136
Heath, Percy, 316
Heine, Heinrich, 279
Heyward, DuBose, 389
Hindemith, Paul, 259, 388
Ludus Tonalis, 255–256
Mathis der Maler, 337, 383
Hofmann, Hans, 397
Holst, Gustav, 256
homophonic forms, 164
homophonic textures, 68–69, 163
horn as brass instrument, 95
humanism in Renaissance, 191
Hyman, Dick, 8

Idée fixe, 221
Impressionism in music, 234–238
improvisation
in Baroque era, 198
cadenzas and, 347
in Indian music, 140, 143–144
jazz and, 316
opera and, 367
Indian music, 140–145
alap and, 143
bayan and, 141
as "being" music, 144
drones in, 140–141
improvisation and, 140, 143–144
listener and, 145
microtones in, 140
raga and, 142–144
sitar and, 141

Indian music (*cont.*)
tabla and, 141–142
tala and, 142–144
tamboura and, 142
texture in, 140–141
time in, 145
tuning system of, 140
instrumental music, early, 303–304
instruments, musical, *see also* specific instrument entries
brass, 95–97; *see also* brass instruments
choir of, 89
cornetto, 304
dynamic range of, 87
harp, 100
harpsichord, 99–100
idiomatic characteristics of, 88
Indian, *see* Indian music
lute, 193
organ, 193
percussion, 97–99; *see also* percussion instruments
piano, 99–100
pitch range in, 86
properties of, 86–88
recorder, 194
sackbut, 304
stringed, 89–91; *see also* stringed instruments
timbre of, 87–88
types of, 89–100, 102
viol, 194
woodwind, 92–94; *see also* woodwind instruments
interludes, 110
intervallic patterns, 239–240
intervals
as basis of chords, 69–71
consonant, 70–71
definition of, 69
dissonant, 70–71
Ives, Charles, 13, 258, 337–340, 398
Schönberg on, 340
Symphony No. 4, 414; Second Movement, 339–340

Jackson, Milt, 316
Janáček, Leoš, 256
Jarrett, Keith
"Sundance," 33–35, 82–85
jazz
European composers and, 388
functional chords and, 82–85
Gershwin and, 388–389
harmony and, 82–85
improvisation and, 316
rhythm and, 33–35
Jenner, Charles, 272
Joachim, Joseph, 350
Joplin, Scott
"Gladiolus Rag," 8, 30, 31–32
Josquin des Prez, 169, 196
Ave Maria, Gratia Plena, 169–171, 193

Kay, Connie, 316
kettledrums, 97
key signatures, 43
Kyrie Eleison in Mass, 188

Lasso, Orlando di, 196
Le Corbusier, 403
leading tone and tonic, 46
ledger lines in pitch notation, 37
legato articulation, 287
Leitmotif, definition of, 376–377
Levant, Oscar, 103
Lewis, John, 316
libretto of opera, 357–359
Lieder
characteristics of, 278
development of, 207
of Schubert, 279–283
solo song as, 278–283
through-composed designs in, 280
Ligeti, György
Aventures, 409–410
line in melody, 56–57, 64
linear independence and polyphony, 191
listener
atonality and, 242
aural perception and, 145
composer and, 416–417
Indian music and, 145
performer and, 416–417
role of, 9, 12–13
serialism and, 245–246
listening, casual versus active, 2–4, 10
Liszt, Franz, 232, 287
Brahms and, 307
concertos of, 349
and symphonic poem or tone poem, 33
Transcendental Etude No. 5: Feux-follets, 225
liturgical music
Council of Trent and, 267
in Medieval period, 183–185
live performances and recordings compared, 12
"London symphonies" of Haydn, 208
lute, 193
lydian mode, 41
lyric singers, 360

Machaut, Guillaume de
Notre Dame Mass: "Kyrie" and Gloria," 188–191
Madrigal, 193, 268–270
Mahler, Gustav, 229, 231, 232
Das Lied von der Erde: "Drinking Song of Earth's Sorrows," 229–231
Songs of a Wayfarer: "I Have a Burning Dagger," 120–121; *"My Love's Two Blue Eyes,"* 121–123; *"My Love's Wedding Day,"* 118–119
on Strauss, 335
marimba, 97
Mass
cantus firmus in, 267
contrapuntal procedures in, 267
in Medieval period, 188
in Renaissance, 192, 267–268
Medieval period, 183–191
Catholic Church role in, 183
Mass in, 188
performance practice in, 186–188
polyphony in, 185–186
secular music in, 185
melismas, 184, 265
melody, 53–65
in Baroque era, 198
continuity in, 57–62
contour in, 56–57
definition of, 53
line in, 56–57, 64, 140
motive in, 57
themes in, 62–65
Mencken, H. L., 358
Mendelssohn, Felix, 218, 287, 307, 328
concertos of, 349
Hebrides Overture, 218–219, 333
Menotti, Gian Carlo, 383
meter, 20–25
asymmetric, 22
mixed, 24
"metric modulation," 355
metronome, 20
mezzo forte as dynamic marking, 87
mezzo piano as dynamic marking, 87
mezzo-soprano voice, 88
microtones, 140
moderato, definition of, 19
Modern Jazz Quartet
"Silver," 315–317
modes, 41
modulation, definition of, 47
Monk, Thelonius
"Hackensack," 82–85
monody
in Baroque music, 196
in opera, 363
monophonic texture, 67
Monteverdi, Claudio, 202, 269
The Coronation of Poppea: Act I, Scenes 1–3, 364–366
Orfeo, 318–364
Moore, Douglas, 383
Morley, Thomas, 196
"Now Is the Month of Maying," 26, 69, 270
Morrill, Dexter
Studies for Trumpet and Computer, 405
motet

as contrapuntal form, 168–171
in Renaissance, 192–193
motive in melody, 57
Mozart, Wolfgang Amadeus, 208–209, 287, 320
on aria in opera, 361
composing method of, 4–6
Cosí fan tutte, 369
Don Giovanni: Overture; Act I, Scenes 1 and 2; Act II, Scene 5, 369–374
Fauré on, 348–349
Marriage of Figaro, 369
opera and, 368–374
Piano Concerto No. 21, 347–349
Piano Concerto No. 21 in C Major, 62–63, 76–78
Piano Sonata in A Major: "Turkish Rondo," 132, 205
Symphony No. 40: First Movement, 151–155; Third Movement, 124–125
music
shared and personal qualities of, 264
study of, 9–12
utilitarian, 1–2
music dramas of Richard Wagner, 226
musica ficta, definition of, 186–187
musical style
during Baroque era, 197–199
historical views on, 182
musical synthesis in 20th century, 410–417
musique concrète, 401–403
Mussorgsky, Modest, 227, 232
Boris Godunov, 384
mixolydian mode, 41

Nationalism
in 19th-century music, 227
in symphonic music, 329–332
in 20th-century music, 256–258
natural, definition of, 39
neoclassicism, 252–256
definition of, 252–253
stylistic characteristics of, 253
19th century
nationalism in music of, 227
sonata form in, 156–158
notation
definition of, 27
figured bass, 198
pitch, 36–45
rhythmic, 27–35

Oboe, 92–93
octave in pitch notation, 38
Oliveros, Pauline
Sound Patterns, 10–12, 406
opera, 356–393
aria in, 361
bel canto vocal technique
Bizet on, 357
Camerata and, 363
castrati in Baroque Italian, 367
chorus and, 361
in Classical period, 368–374
comic, 362
conductor and, 361
da capo arias in, 368
duets in, 361
ensembles in, 361
expressionist, 384
Gershwin and, 388–393
Handel and, 367–368
H. L. Mencken on, 358
improvisation and, 367
introduction to, 356–362
libretto of, 357–359
monody in, 363
Mozart and, 368–374
orchestra and, 361
original-language performance of, 358
origins of, 363
recitatives in, 361, 362
ritornelli in, 365
Romantic, 374–383
serious, 362
singers, 360
staging of, 359–360
structure of, 361–362
in 20th century, 383–393
opera buffa, 368–369
opera houses, 366–367
opera seria, 368
operetta, 362
oratorio
definition of, 272
of Handel, 271–274
Messiah as, 272–273
orchestra
in Baroque era, 197
opera and, 361
orchestral bells, 97–98
orchestral concert, inception of, 318
orchestral music, 318–341
in Romantic period, 328–336
in 20th century, 336–341
orchestration, definition of, 86
organ
in Renaissance, 193
as wind instrument, 100
Owen, Wilfred, 283

Pacing in rhythm, 32–33
Palestrina, Giovanni da, 196
Missa Papae Marcelli: Kyrie, 267–268
parody technique, 410
part-song, 127
Partch, Harry, 398–399
Daphne of the Dunes, 399–400
passacaglia, 138
passions, 272, 275
patronage system, 208, 216
pavan, definition of, 194
Penderecki, Krzystof, 407
Fluorescences, 407
Threnody for the Victims of Hiroshima, 407–408
percussion instruments, 97–99
bass drum, 99
celesta, 98
chimes, 98
cymbals, 99
of definite pitch, 97–98
Edgard Varèse and, 313
glockenspiel, 98
kettledrums, 97
marimba, 97
orchestral bells as, 97–98
snaredrum, 98–99
tam tam, 99
tambourine, 99
timpani, 97
triangle, 99
unpitched, 98–99
vibraphone, 98
xylophone, 97
performance styles, historical views on, 182–183
performer
Beethoven and, 322
chamber music and, 301–302
Classical symphony and, 321–322
role of, 7–9
in Romantic period, 224
virtuoso, 224
Peri, Jacopo, 363
"perpetual variation" of Schönberg, 242
phrases, musical, 25–27
phrygian mode, 41
pianissimo as dynamic marking, 87
piano
coloristic potential of, 287
compositional approaches to, 287
as instrument, 99–100, 287
invention of, 287
piano as dynamic marking, 87
piano music, 287–300
character music as, 290–296
idioms in 20th century, 296–300
sonata as genre of, 288–900
Piave, Francesco, 380
piccolo, 92
piccolo clarinet, 93
pitch, definition of, 36
pitch notation
accidentals in, 39
clefs in, 37
grand staff in, 38
half step in, 39
ledger lines in, 37
note-heads in, 36
octave in, 38
staff in, 36
tuning systems in, 39
pitch range in instruments, 86
pizzicato, definition of, 89

plainchant, 183–185; *see also* Gregorian chant
Pollock, Jackson, 108
polyphonic music, *cantus firmus* in, 186
polyphonic texture, 67–68, 163
polyphony
  14th century, 186
  harmony and, 69
  linear independence and, 191
  in Medieval period, 185–186
  vertical control and, 191
  vocal, 191–192, 192–193
Portamento, definition of, 266
prelude, definition of, 244
"prepared piano," 296
presto, definition of, 19
program music, 218
programmatic overture, 333–334
Prokofiev, Serge, 256, 259, 297
  Classical Symphony, 297, 337
  Diaghilev and, 297
  Love for Three Oranges, 383
  Piano Sonata No. 7: Third Movement, 297–299
  Symphony No. 5, 297
  War and Peace, 297
  "war sonatas" of, 297
Puccini, Giacomo
  La B⌒hème, 383
  Madame Butterfly, 383
Purcell, Henry, 137
  Dido and Aeneas: "Dido's Lament," 137–138

Quartet and quintet as genres, 305

Rachmaninoff, Sergei, 258
raga, 142–144
ragtime, 31
rallentando, definition of, 19
Rameau, Jean-Phillippe, 202
Ravel, Maurice, 258, 237–238
  Bolero, 33
  Le Tombeau de Couperin, 238
recapitulation in sonata-form movement, 148, 150
recitative
  definition of, 271
  in opera, 361, 362
reconciliation in Classical style, 206
recorder in Renaissance music, 194
refrain forms, 127–128
Reich, Steve
  Drumming, 400
Renaissance, 191–196
  cantus firmus in music of, 192
  composers in, 195–196
  humanism in, 191
  instrumental music of, 193–195
  Mass in, 192
  motet in, 192
  performance practice in, 186–188
  vocal music in, 267–270
  vocal quality in, 266
repeat signs, 111
retrograde inversion in serialism, 244
rhythm
  jazz and, 33–35
  meter in, 20–25
  pacing in, 32–33
  pulse in, 17–19
  tempo and, 19–20
rhythmic differentiation in contrapuntal melodies, 164
rhythmic energy in Baroque music, 198
rhythmic notation
  rhythmic motives in, 30
  syncopation in, 31
  time signatures in, 29
  triplets in, 28
rhythmic patterns, 17–27
ricercar as musical form, 194
Rifkin, Joshua, 8
Riley, Terry
  In C, 400
Rimsky-Korsakov, Nikolai, 227
  Russian Easter Overture, 227–228
ritardando, definition of, 19
ritornelli in opera, 365
Rococo style, 205
Rodrigo, Joaquin
  Concierto de Aranjuez, 317
Romantic concertos, 349
  cadenzas in, 346–347
Romantic period
  audiences during, 216–217
  character pieces in, 225–226
  composers in, 231–232
  contrapuntal procedures in, 175
  functional progression in, 217
  orchestral music in, 328–336
  performer role in, 224
  program music in, 218
  vocal quality in, 266
Romantic style, 215–232
  Classical style coexistence with, 204
  definition of, 204
  literature in, 215–216
rondo
  false entry in, 174
  and variation forms, 127–145
root, in triad, 71
Rossini, Gioacchino, 232, 379
rounds as contrapuntal music, 167
Ruggles, Carl, 398

Sackbut, 304
Salve Regina (Gregorian chant), 184
Sanctus in Mass, 188
Satie, Erik
  Gymnopédie No. 1, 3–4, 26, 54, 109, 111
saxophone, 93
scale(s), 39–45
  C major, 43
  central tone in, 40
  chromatic, 40
  E major, 43
  key signatures and, 43
  major, 42–43
  minor, 44
  modes in, 41
  relative keys in, 44
  transposition and, 42
Scarlatti, Domenico, 203
scherzo, 125–126
Schiller, Johann von, 279
Schönberg, Arnold, 238–242, 258
  dissonance and, 240
  intervallic patterns and, 239–240
  on Ives, 340
  Moses und Aron, 383
  "perpetual variation" of, 242
  serialism and, 243
  Suite for Piano, 244–245
  Three Piano Pieces: First piece, 241–242
  twelve-tone method and, 243
  Verklärte Nacht, 239
Schubert, Franz, 214–215, 231, 307, 328
  "The Erlking," 28, 281–282
  "Gretchen am Spinnrade," 280–281
  lieder of, 279–283
  Quartet No. 14 in D Minor: "Death and the Maiden," 215
  A Winter's Journey: "The Linden Tree," 116–118
Schumann, Clara Wieck, 292–293, 307
Schumann, Robert, 231, 287, 292–294, 307, 328
  Brahms and, 307
  character pieces of, 292–294
  on composing, 6
  Kinderszenen, 293–294
  Papillons No. 3, 3, 21, 29, 44–45, 166–167
Schütz, Heinrich, 199
  Saul, Saul, 199–200
scoring, definition of, 86
sectional forms, 107–126
secular music
  in medieval period, 185
  of 16th century, 192–193
Segovia, Andrès, 100
serialism, 243–246
  listener and, 245–246
  retrograde inversion in, 244
  set in, 243–244
serious music
  definition of, 2–3
  as musical term, 205
sforzando as dynamic marking, 87
Shankar, Ravi
  Maru Bihag, 142, 143–144
Shapey, Ralph
  Rituals, 414–416
sharp, definition of, 39
Shostakovich, Dmitri, 256
Sibelius, Jean, 258

Simon and Garfunkel
"Scarborough Fair/Canticles," 61–62
sinfonia, definition of, 413
sitar, 141
snaredrum, 98–99
solo concerto, 343
solo song
German lied as, 278–283
in history, 278
as vocal music, 264
sonata
in Baroque era, 197
as formal principle, 147
as genre, 147, 288–290
as musical term, 146
sonata form, 146–162
in 19th century, 156
in 20th century, 158–162
sonata-form movement, 148–150
closing material in, 149
diagram of, 150
tonal groups in, 149
tonic key in, 148, 150
transitional passages in, 149
sonata-form procedures, 146–155
song structure, strophic form as, 279–280
sonorities, 140
soprano voice, 38, 88
Sprechstimme, definition of, 386
statement, musical, 109
Strauss, Richard, 95, 231
Elektra, 383
Mahler on, 335
on melody, 53
Der Rosenkavalier, 383
Salome, 383
on Schönberg, 240
symphonic poem and, 334–336
Thus Spake Zarathustra, 411
Till Eulenspiegel's Merry Pranks, 335–336
Stravinsky, Igor, 246–251, 257–258, 259, 287, 388, 405
Diaghilev and, 248
L'Histoire du Soldat, see The Soldier's Tale
on melody, 53
The Rake's Progress, 383
The Rite of Spring (Le Sacre du printemps): "Cercles mystérieux des adolescents," 24; *"Fertility of the Earth,"* 248–251
The Soldier's Tale (L'Histoire du Soldat), 253–255, 313
Symphony in C, 337
Symphony in Three Movements, 337
Symphony of Psalms, 255
stringed instruments
arco and, 89
cello, 90–91
contrabass, 91
double bass, 91
guitar, 99
harmonics in, 90
multiple stops in, 90
pizzicato and, 89
sitar, 141
sul ponticello and, 90
tremolo and, 90
viola, 90
violin, 90
strophic form as song structure, 279–280
structural patterns in music, 9
Sturm und Drang style, 205
stylistic change in 20th century, 223–224
suite
Baroque, 115
definition of, 113
sul ponticello, 90
syllabic settings in vocal music, 265
syllabic style and Gregorian chants, 184
symphonic music, nationalistic influences on, 329–332
symphonic poems
Franz Liszt and, 333
Richard Strauss and, 334–336
symphonic tradition, German, 328–329
symphony
Classical, 319–320
meanings of, 319
origins of, 319
symphony orchestra, 101–103
syncopation, 31
synthesizers, 403–406
real-time, 404

Tabla and Indian music, 141–142
tala and Indian music, 142–144
tam tam, 99
tamboura, 142
tambourine, 99
tape recorders and electronic music, 402
Tatum, Art
"I Know That You Know," 299–300
Tchaikovsky, Peter Ilyich, 226–227, 232
programmatic overture and, 333–334
Romeo and Juliet: Overture—Fantasy, 334
tempo, 19–20
tenor voice, 38, 88
thematic transformation, 222
theme and variation forms, 133, 136
themes
definition of, 62
as melodic basis of form, 109
in melody, 62–65
return in, 109, 110
third in triad, definition of, 71
through-composed designs in lieder, 280
timbre, 87–88
time
in Indian music, 145
musical, 17–35
time signatures, 29
timpani, 97
toccata, definition of, 298
ton juste as musical term, 234
tonal groups in sonata form, 149
tonal music, form in, 109–111
tonal organization, 36–52; *see also* Pitch *entries*
in 20th century, 51–52
tonal shift in sonata form, 149
tonality
basic principle of, 45–51
chromatic styles and, 47
diatonic styles and, 47
and dissonance in 20th century, 80–85
modulation and, 47–48
tone cluster, definition of, 159
tone color
definition of, 88
as principle idea in music, 397
tonic triads, 45, 73
leading tone and, 46
in sonata form, 148, 150
total art-work theory *(Gesamtkunstwerk)* of Wagner, 375–377
transitional passages in sonata form, 149
transitions
in form, 110
scales and, 42
tremolo and stringed instruments, 90
triads, 71–80
arpeggio in, 72
cadences and, 73–74
definition of, 71
dominant, 73
doublings in, 71
major, 72
minor, 72
seventh chords and, 75
simple chord progressions and, 74
tonic, 73
triangle as percussion instrument, 99
trio as genre, 305
triplets in notation, 28
trombone, 95–97
tuba, 97
tuning system
current, 187
"equal temperament" and, 198
of Harry Partch, 398–399
in Indian music, 140
Medieval, 187
in pitch notation, 39
twelve-tone method, 243
20th-Century music
chamber idioms in, 311–317
concertos and, 352–355
contrapuntal procedures in, 175–177

20th Century Music (*cont.*)
national influences on, 256–258
opera and, 383–393
orchestral music and, 336–341
piano idioms and, 296–300
sonata form and, 158–162
stylistic change in, 223–224
vocal music and, 283–286

Unity in form, 107
upbeat, definition of, 20

Varèse, Edgard, 259, 313–314, 402
Ionisation, 314–315
percussion instruments and, 313
Poème Électronique, 403
variation forms, 132–145
Vaughan Williams, Ralph, 256, 337
Verdi, Giuseppi, 232, 379–380
La Traviata: Act I, 380–382
vertical control and polyphony, 191
vibraphone, 98
vibrato in voice, 89, 266
Villa-Lobos, Heitor, 256
viol, 194
viola, 90
violin, 90
Vivaldi, Antonio, 202, 343–344
The Four Seasons: "Summer," 344–345
vocal music, 263–286
of Bach, 275–278
of Baroque period, 271–278
choral, 263
genres of, 263–266
madrigal as, 268–270
Mass as, 267–268
melismas in, 184, 265
music and text relationship in, 265
oratorios of Handel as, 271–274
in Renaissance, 267–270
16th-century secular, 192–193
solo song as, 264
syllabic settings in, 265
text and music relationship in, 265
in 20th century, 283–286
vocal polyphony, 191–195
voice
idiomatic characteristics of, 265–266
vibrato in, 89, 266

Wagner, Richard, 231, 375–377, 382–383
on Berlioz, 220
music dramas of, 226
total art-work theory of, 375–377
Tristan and Isolde: "Love-Death," 377–379; *"Prelude,"* 59–60, 78, 377–379
Webern, Anton, 259, 340
Symphony: Second Movement, 340–341
Wieck, Clara, *see* Schumann, Clara Wieck
Wolf, Hugo, 279
woodwind instruments
bass clarinet, 93
bassoon, 93
clarinet, 93
contrabassoon, 93
English horn, 93
flute, 92
oboe, 92–93
organ, 100
piccolo, 92
piccolo clarinet, 93
saxophone, 93
World War I, effect on European music, 252

xylophone, 97